the Write Stuff

Evaluations of Graphology—
The Study of Handwriting Analysis

O O O

Edited by

Barry L. Beyerstein & Dale F. Beyerstein

Prometheus Books • Buffalo, New York

Published 1992 by Prometheus Books

The Write Stuff: Evaluations of Graphology, the Study of Handwriting Analysis. Copyright © 1992 by Barry L. Beyerstein and Dale F. Beyerstein.

96 95 94 93 92   5 4 3 2 1

Library of Congress Cataloging-in-Publication Data

The Write Stuff: evaluations of graphology, the study of handwriting analysis / edited by Barry L.Beyerstein and Dale F. Beyerstein.
    p.   cm.
    Includes bibliographical references.
    ISBN 0-87975-612-8—ISBN 0-87975-613-6 (pbk.)
    1. Graphology. I. Beyerstein, Barry L., 1949–   II. Beyerstein, Dale F., 1952–
BF891.W75 19991
155.2'82—dc20   91-21698
          CIP

Printed in the United States of America on acid-free paper.

This volume is lovingly dedicated to the memory of
Hilliard Harris William Beyerstein(1907–1990)
who taught us it is most important to think for ourselves
when the majority perceives something as obvious.

Contents

Acknowledgments

The editors of this volume would like to express their appreciation to their fellow contributors for the cooperation, good humor, careful thought, and hard work they have so generously lent to this project. The friendly help of Doris Doyle and Mark Hall at Prometheus Books has been instrumental at every stage, both in completing the volume and improving it. The excellent editorial and substantive suggestions of Dr. Lillian Leiber have added significantly to the quality of the chapters with which she assisted. Our profound thanks to them all. The assistance of Elliott Marchant and Deborah Nijdam is also gratefully acknowledged. Finally, we would like to express our love and thanks to Susie, Elsie, Lindsay, and Loren for their support and encouragement and for the many weekend and evening activities with BLB and DFB that they gave up so this book could be produced.

Section One

Introduction and History

1

General Introduction

Dale F. Beyerstein and Barry L. Beyerstein

The editors' interest in graphology (handwriting analysis) was piqued a couple of years ago when one of us (BLB) was phoned by the *Vancouver (Canada) Sun* to comment on the results of a piece of investigative journalism that would prove to be very embarrassing to local politicians. Apparently a local graphologist had approached employees of the Vancouver School Board with a solution to a serious problem. In the past few years, in schools across North America, there have been several cases of teachers who have been charged with sexual offenses against their students. School administrators are concerned with the welfare of their students, and rightly wish to prevent teachers from harming innocent children. One feels powerless to think that the many tests, evaluations, and checks that are given to applicants for teaching positions, and those already employed in the system, do not detect those people with sexual tendencies that could do so much damage to innocent lives. So, if one is offered a foolproof method that will detect these malefactors prior to their causing this harm, it would be a dereliction of duty to turn it down, would it not?

That was the gist of the offer made by a local graphologist to a harried and scientifically ill-informed school board official: the graphologist claimed to be able to detect pedophiles with unfailing accuracy, and offered a "scientific test" to prove it! Give him (without the writers' knowledge) some samples of handwriting, and he would find the pedophile! The story gets a bit murky at this point, since the Vancouver School Board, and the bureaucrat responsible, understandably do not like to talk about it. The

13

graphologist, on the other hand, does, and tells several *conflicting* stories about it. But the kernel of the story appears to be this: the graphologist was presented with ten (or, on other accounts, nine) handwriting samples —the school board doesn't, for obvious reasons, like to say *whose*, or how they got them—and he did his analyses. Much to his surprise, he found that nine (or was it eight?) of the samples were written by pedophiles *or potential pedophiles!* The graphologist was very proud of himself, having seen through the little twist in the experiment that might have caught him off his guard! He thought that he would be given one pedophile in the sample; but by his reckoning, there were more, and he caught them all! It was at this point that the local media thought this little backroom experiment was worthy of the public's attention.

Fortunately, BLB was not totally unprepared to comment when the reporter called. As a twelve-year-old, he was introduced to graphology in the way a great number of "professional" graphologists were: by buying a book from the occult section (now it would be the New Age section) of the local bookshop, and immediately began analyzing his friends.

The editors of this volume found that most of the graphologists they have debated over the years were introduced to the subject through short, non-credit night school courses offered by a local school board, community college, or university continuing education division. Some had taken a home study course through the International Graphoanalysis Society of Chicago, while many, including the graphologist who approached the Vancouver School Board, had made up their own system which they declined to divulge to anyone (and which, of course, had never undergone scientific evaluations). Several who were charging corporations for their services admitted having read only one popular book on the subject before "going into business."[1] In addition to the graphologists' lack of professional accreditation and scanty background in relevant academic specialties, the authors also typically found them eager to join the skeptics in condemning competing analysts' brands of graphology as "unscientific." Nonetheless, they remained steadfast in asserting their own scientific legitimacy. We have always asked in such encounters for published evidence that we might have overlooked that would substantiate their claims. Most promised but sent nothing, a few sent us self-published tracts, one sent us an uncritical article from *Playboy*; the few items received from practicing graphologists that were more substantial, we have reviewed in our contributions to other sections of this book. The obvious isolation of these graphologists from relevant fields of research and their lack of agreement on key issues within the discipline were disconcerting, to say the least.

In response to media queries about the school board case, BLB, having grown up and become a psychophysiologist instead of a graphologist, first searched for his boyhood text on graphology. It was hard to locate, but one does not part readily with something that cost that many weeks' allowance. Rereading it after all those years, he was astonished to find there was virtually no difference between its claims and procedures and those touted by the very latest graphology books. BLB next decided to run a computer database search to see if there was any independent support for graphological claims in the scientific literature. The results of the survey showed the scientific case for graphology to be exceedingly weak. Furthermore, polling university colleagues who specialize in psychological measurement and the psychology of individual differences produced a mere handful of reputable psychology texts in English that even mentioned graphology, and they did so only to dismiss it as a pseudoscience. Believers in graphology are virtually non-existent in North American psychology departments but some can be found in Europe and Israel. In preparing his chapters for this volume, BLB was forced to rely on garage sales, New Age booksellers, self-published tracts by graphologists themselves, and the occult sections of the local libraries to find the majority of the pro-graphology works he reviewed.

Returning to the saga that drew the editors into the graphology debate—the chairman of the Vancouver School Board was a thoughtful man as well as an astute politician. He was well aware of the damage that can be done to an individual's reputation by calling him a potential pedophile, and of the damage that can be done to the school board's budget if such a charge could not be substantiated. As soon as the story broke on the local Canadian Broadcasting Corporation (CBC) TV station, he immediately put a stop to use of graphology in the Vancouver school system, blaming their flirtation with it as the work of an overzealous underling. The media were understandably very sensitive to the issue of fairness in hiring and promotion in the workplace, and editorialized sternly about use of graphology in personnel matters. The *Vancouver Sun* even published its first ever handwritten editorial (see Fig. 1)! Not only that, reporters began to dig around, and discovered that seven municipalities surrounding Vancouver were using graphology, or, as some of their mayors would have it when cornered, "experimenting with" or "considering" it. As well, several private companies, including banks, credit unions, and construction companies, were discovered to be using it.

At this point, the junior editor of this volume (DFB) got involved. The British Columbia Civil Liberties Association (BCCLA), of which he is a director, has had a long history of dealing with questions of fairness in employee relations, including privacy considerations. They immediately jumped into the conflict, in cooperation with the Society of British Columbia Skeptics, an organization that supports the goals of the Committee for

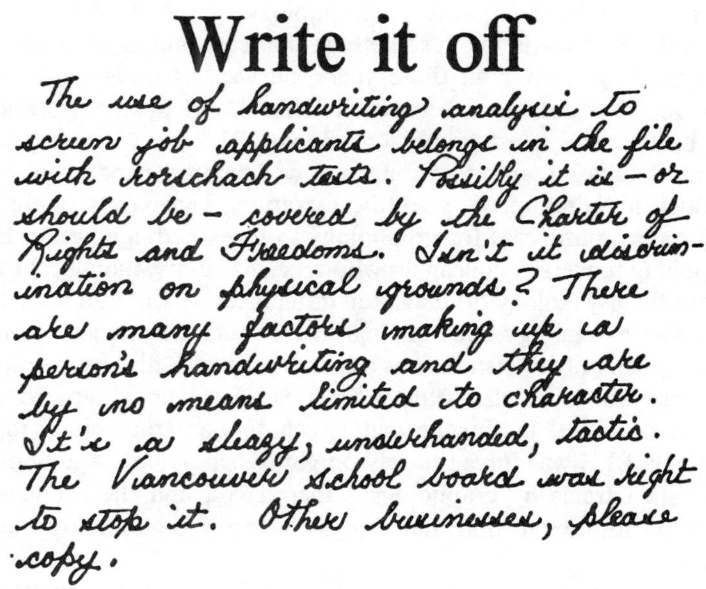

Write it off

The use of handwriting analysis to screen job applicants belongs in the file with rorschach tests. Possibly it is – or should be – covered by the Charter of Rights and Freedoms. Isn't it discrimination on physical grounds? There are many factors making up a person's handwriting and they are by no means limited to character. It's a sleazy, underhanded, tactic. The Vancouver school board was right to stop it. Other businesses, please copy.

Figure 1.

the Scientific Investigation of Claims of the Paranormal (CSICOP): education in scientific and critical thinking, and investigation of occult paranormal or pseudoscientific claims. The BCCLA's position on testing of employees in the workplace, whether for drugs, dishonesty, or general competence, is that testing must, first of all, be for attributes that are relevant to the job, and second, be the least onerous method of getting this required information—for example, the testing must not be unduly invasive of privacy. Third, the results of these tests must be kept confidential. But fourth, and most important for our present purposes, the test must be able to accurately detect the traits it promises to detect, and not lead to serious accusations—such as pederasty, dishonesty, or incompetence—that could ruin a person's career despite being unfounded.

The two editors of this volume provided the BCCLA with a brief on graphology, which provided our answer to the fourth question posed above: whether graphology's claims to accuracy in determining these traits could be justified. The BCCLA and the Skeptics provided arguments to the local municipalities and businesses using graphology, based on the available scientific information, which showed conclusively that the use of graphology as a personnel selection tool was unfair, given its demonstrated poor accuracy in scientific tests. The upshot of this campaign was that six of the seven municipalities, and most of the private companies, gave up on graphology. But the most interesting finding from this process was not about graphologists, but personnel managers. It became clear to us very quickly that they had chosen graphology on the basis of testimonials of fellow personnel managers and from the sales pitches of the graphologists. None of them had checked out the scientific literature on graphology until we presented it to them; and very few of them were conversant with the scientific literature on personnel selection and testing presented in chapter 11. Thus we saw the need for a collection such as this that would provide the necessary readings on the subject in one book. This also leaves us with the question of why graphology *seems* to work when it cannot pass careful scientific tests. This issue is dealt with in several places in this volume, notably chapters 13 and 16.

The B.C. Skeptics wanted to do more than refer to already published studies of graphology. They wanted to do replications of these studies, as well as new research. They offered to do studies of local graphologists, and contacted the professional associations of graphologists to engage their cooperation in these tests. But to no avail—most graphologists just are not very interested in scientific tests of their claims, it would seem. The closest the Skeptics got to a test was when a Toronto graphologist agreed to be tested, and after getting quite a bit of media attention, stopped off in Vancouver on a cross-country media and speaking tour to meet with them. Following the advice of James Randi, the Skeptics produced a written protocol for the test. The graphologist, confident that she would pass the test with flying colors, initialed the protocol and returned to Toronto. All that was necessary for the signature on the final protocol was for her to name an agent to oversee BCS operations in Vancouver (choosing subjects, observing to ensure that the protocols in Vancouver were followed properly, etc.), and for the graphologist to choose the passage from a book that the subjects who were to be tested would copy out. But, after having got all the media attention, she then backed out! After several attempts at telephone conversations to determine why she was stalling at her end, which were terminated by the graphologist hanging up, it became clear to us that this graphologist was far more interested in the publicity she derived from promising to do the test than in actually doing the test. The working graphologists that we have interviewed and/or debated on TV and radio have turned out to be an unimpressive lot. Most were sincere, but ill informed, even about their own field, let alone the scientific method and scientific principles of personnel selection. We began to wonder whether we were for some reason getting a biased sample, or whether Canadian graphologists and those from the northwest corner of the United States really were representative of graphologists in general.

We had an opportunity to answer this question in November of 1988.

This collection of papers grew out of a session on graphology at the 1988 CSICOP meeting in Chicago. BLB planned and chaired that session, and Edward Karnes and Richard Klimoski presented papers there. Their contributions in this volume are revised and expanded versions of their papers in that session. As is the case with many of the sessions at CSICOP conferences, the aim was to invite the leading practitioners and defenders of the field undergoing scrutiny to present the best evidence they have for their discipline—i.e., whatever they think should convince open-minded skeptics. Skeptics (in this case, Klimoski, Karnes, and B. Beyerstein) then offered their reasons for thinking that the evidence for the claims made by defenders is deficient. Rose Matousek, president of the American Association of Handwriting Analysts, and Felix Klein, vice-president of the Council of Graphological Societies, presented papers at this session, but they did not accept an offer to write up their talks for this volume. In any case, we do not feel the loss, since they chose not to present the material we requested when we invited them to participate in the Chicago panel, viz., scientifically acceptable data from research, by themselves or anyone else, attesting to the accuracy of graphology as a personality test or personnel selection device. The talks by these official representatives of two of the largest graphological associations in the U.S. concentrated instead on descriptions of their methods and numerous testimonials from satisfied customers. We had specifically recommended that they do not include the latter, because they cannot count as scientific evidence. Every astrologer, palm reader, tea leaf reader, and medium we have ever met has had his or her legion of clients who attest to the seeming accuracy of the reader's wares—why this is so, despite lack of scientific credibility of these character reading techniques, is explained by several authors in this book, e.g., Dean et al. (chapter 13). Matousek also chose to spend much of her time in the session attacking (on irrelevant grounds) fellow panelist Richard Klimoski for publishing the results of a carefully controlled study of graphologists he had conducted. Matousek's organization had originally approved the methodology, in addition to funding and participating in the study, but had tried, unsuccessfully, to suppress its publication when the results failed to substantiate the graphologists' claims.

The two graphologists on the CSICOP panel also unwittingly provided a demonstration of their penchant for post hoc reasoning when they showed slides of sample analyses they had done. They pointed out "obvious" signs of writers' characteristics exemplifed in the writing samples. The problem was that they admitted knowing in advance of doing the analyses what the writers were like!

The aim of this collection is the same as the CSICOP session: to present to the open-minded reader an overview of the best evidence available on both sides of the dispute about graphology. With this in mind, we invited papers from the leading critics of graphology, and specialists in personality, cognitive psychology, and psychological testing who were willing to assess graphologists' claims against the standards that are used in their fields. The response from this group was most encouraging. All the people we asked graciously agreed to write original essays for this volume. On the other hand, the response from the graphological community was less heartening. Perhaps because we are not graphologists ourselves, or known supporters of it, most graphologists did not think that our project deserved their support. Whatever the reason, we could not get from graphologists original essays defending graphology. So, we did the next best thing: we went to the published literature.

Our criteria for selection of pro-graphology chapters were the following: first, we wanted papers from practicing graphologists who were respected by their peers—those who, despite the wide disagreement to be found in the graphological community, would be recognized by graphologists as competent spokespersons for graphology. Second, we wanted representatives of a cross-section of the various schools of graphology. Third, we wanted those who had done original research themselves, and who were familiar with the best research of others in the field; i.e., we asked for papers that referred to what the proponents considered to be the best empirical research, so the open-minded reader would have a good bibliography to follow up. And fourth, we wanted papers that were originally published in respectable places. Most of the works on graphology are popular books, where references to empirical studies are not given (despite the fact that many graphologists who charge fees receive much of their training from such books), or self-published pamphlets or monographs. Interested readers can examine these popular books in the New Age section of their nearest bookshop, so there is no point in including excerpts from that material here. The self-published items from individual graphologists or societies are more difficult to obtain, but we decided against including any of the manuscripts we have in our possession on grounds of fairness. It would be too easy to make graphology look simply foolish by including a representative sample of this "pop-psychology" material. So we have included instead material that was addressed to a scientific or scholarly audience. Fifth, a point related to the fourth: we wanted graphologists who were respected by the scientific community; who would know the language of the sciences and be able to speak to those people who were interested in the evidence that graphologists had to offer. And last, we thought it was important to include material from foreign graphologists. North American graphologists often defend themselves against the charge that very little serious scholarly work is available to defend graphology by saying that all the good work is done in Europe.

We are pleased that one of Europe's most prominent graphologists, Oskar Lockowandt, responded to our request to summarize the scientific support for graphology as he sees it. We are also pleased that James Crumbaugh, the graphologist whom fellow handwriting analysts cited to us most frequently as their preferred spokesperson, agreed to contribute his statement in favor of the Graphoanalytic approach.[2] (Dr. Crumbaugh was invited to participate in the 1988 CSICOP panel on graphology, but other commitments prevented him from appearing. Unfortunately, the International Graphoanalysis Society declined repeated requests to send a representative in his stead.) We also thank Patricia Wellingham-Jones for permission to reprint one of her recently published graphological studies which we include as a representative example of current research being done by graphologists.

This book is divided into six sections. The first, which includes the present introduction, deals primarily with historical, cross-cultural, and definitional issues. It also includes a chapter by Joe Nickell that distinguishes his profession—that of a questioned document examiner—from the practice of graphology. The two are quite distinct in aims, philosophy, and practice, but are often confused in the public mind.

The second section presents the case for graphology as stated by two of the world's most respected and widely published graphologists, James Crumbaugh and Oskar Lockowandt.

Section Three weighs the scientific status of graphology according to the criteria of the philosophy of science (D. Beyerstein) and examines the underlying rationale for believing that particular characteristics of people are related to the configuration of their script (B. Beyerstein).

In Section Four, critics of graphology present their objections from the standpoints of personality assessment (Bowman), organizational psychology and personnel selection (Klimoski), psychological measurement theory (Dean), cognitive psychology (Dean et al.), and neurophysiology (B. Beyerstein).

Section Five presents representative empirical studies by a graphologist (Wellingham-Jones) and by psychologists skeptical of its utility (Karnes and Leonard). The results of these studies are interesting in their own right but are also included in order that the reader might compare the methodologies, experimental controls, statistical procedures, etc., used in studies that do and do not find support for graphology.

Given the possible consequences for one's professional advancement and reputation raised by use of a debatable assessment tool such as graphology, it is only a matter of time until parties who feel aggrieved by its use will seek redress in the courts, as they rightly did with regard to polygraph testing in the workplace. Thus in the final section of this book, we have asked two lawyers to address the practice of graphology in light of relevant statutes and precedents in the U.S. (Reagh) and Canada (Carswell). Recent legal restrictions on use of polygraphs have created a vacuum that graphologists have been eager to fill. Employers' desperate desire for a quick fix for problems of employee honesty and productivity has made them vulnerable to certain graphologists' hard-sell tactics and inflated, unsubstantiated claims. One particularly disturbing aspect of some of the advertising we have been seeing recently is that it informs prospective clients that one of graphology's great advantages is that it can be used without applicants or employees even being aware they are being evaluated! This was one of the selling points allegedly made by the graphologist who approached the Vancouver School Board, offering to identify sexual deviants in the teaching ranks.

The editors of this book would be remiss if they did not admit at the outset their strong skepticism about the value of graphology. Their dubiousness is based, however, on graphology's violation of well supported principles within areas of the editors' own professional expertise and a careful reading of both the pro- and anti-graphology literature. The editors have attempted to give the proponents of graphology in this volume ample opportunity to include any scientific evidence for its utility they wish, and to refute the skeptics as they see fit. The proponents were chosen for their prominence in the published literature and on the strong recommendation of numerous practicing graphologists.

Herbert Spencer (1829–1903) wisely wrote:

> There is a principle which is a bar against all information, which is proof against all argument and which cannot fail to keep a man in everlasting ignorance. That principle is, "Condemnation before investigation."

We invite the reader to enter into an open-minded investigation of the evidence for and against the practice of graphology.

NOTES

1. It is an especially worrying sign when the majority of popular books on a subject and the instructional "texts" most "professionals" in a supposedly technical field learn from and consult regularly are one and the same. This we have found to be the case repeatedly in our interactions with practicing graphologists.

2. In this volume, "graphology" and "handwriting analysis" will be used interchangeably to refer to any system that claims to discern personality, aptitudes, attitudes, proclivities, or medical data from the configuration of written letters, words, or sentences, or their distribution on the page. "Graphoanalysis" is a regis-

tered trademark that refers exclusively to the copyrighted system of handwriting analysis taught by the International Graphoanalysis Society (see chapters 2, 7, and 9, this volume).

2

A Brief History of Graphology

Joe Nickell

This historical overview should provide the reader with some background to the graphology debate. Dr. Nickell emphasizes the historic and present connection of graphology with mystical and occult doctrines, a point taken up again in chapters 3 and 9. This does not, by itself, refute graphology. After all, medicine and astronomy had some of their origins in doctrines that we know today—or even were known at the time—to be pseudoscientific, as graphologists like to point out. So the reader should look at Dr. Nickell's other contribution in chapter 4, as well as Oskar Lockowandt's review of the modern literature in chapter 5, and Barry Beyerstein's chapter 9, as well as both chapters in Section Five, before deciding what to conclude from this.

Graphology—the alleged science of divining personality from handwriting —is a branch of that large, amorphous field known as "character reading," and its roots are ancient.[1]

One of graphology's antecedents is physiognomy. In Old Testament times, when few could write, character was thought to be revealed in the face. And so it was said that "the shew of their countenance doth witness against them" (Isaiah 3.9).[2] A treatise attributed (falsely) to Aristotle compared man's features to those of animals as a means of indicating character traits. Thus, sharp-tipped (doglike) noses belonged to those who were irascible; large, round noses (like those of lions) were found on the faces of magnanimous persons; thin, hooked noses (comparable to eagles' beaks) were common to people who were noble but grasping; and so on.[3]

The first step toward the ultimate development of graphology was the recognition of individuality in handwriting, and this was accomplished by the time Jewish laws were collected and written down in the Mishnah (ca. A.D. 70–200):

> These when they come of age may be believed when they testify of what they saw while they were yet minors: A man may be believed when he says, "This is my father's handwriting," or "This is my teacher's handwriting," or "This is my brother's handwriting." . . .[4]

It appears that the rudiments of graphology were also familiar to the Romans. The second-century historian Suetonius drew inferences about the character of Augustus from his examination of Augustus's handwriting.[5] As well, the Emperor Nero is said to have remarked that he was distrustful of a particular man in court because "his handwriting showed him treacherous."[6] A more emphatic endorsement of the validity of graphology came from the eleventh-century Chinese artist and philosopher Kuo Jo Hsu, who said: "Handwriting can infallibly show whether it comes from a person who is noble-minded, or from one who is vulgar."[7]

Apparently the first attempt to explicate the perceived relationship between handwriting and personality was made by a seventeenth-century Italian physician named Camillo Baldi (or Baldo, 1547–1634). In 1622, Baldi published in Capri his *Trattado come da una lettera missiva si conoscano la natura e qualita dello scriviente* (*Treatise on a Method to Recognize the Nature and Quality of a Writer from His Letters*). Baldi wrote:

> It is obvious that all persons write in their own way. . . . These . . . traits of character can be recognized in any handwriting. . . . Yet it is necessary to observe carefully whether the characteristics of handwriting recur, moreover whether they are in any way artificial. . . .[8]

Baldi initiated the analysis of handwriting by dividing it into its various elements. However, his treatise generated relatively little interest,[9] although some itinerant magicians were said to have gone "from castle to castle practicing the new art."[10]

A similar treatise was written by Marco Aurelio Severo (1580–1656), and more than a century later, J.K. Lavater (1741–1801) included a chapter on the subject in his *Physiognomische Fragmente* (*Physiognomic Fragments,* 1774–78). Still another work was produced by Johann Christian August Grohmann (1769–1847).[11]

Modern interest in graphology is attributed to a circle of the French Catholic clergy in the nineteenth century. About 1830, this group of churchmen—including the Archbishop of Cambria, the Bishop of Amiens, and Abbé Louis J.H. Flandrin—began to involve themselves in the study and interpretation of handwriting.[12] This ecclesiastical impetus, according to one commentator, "may account for the severity of judgment still to be found in some French graphology."[13]

It was a disciple of this group, Abbé Jean-Hippolyte Michon (1806–1881), who established the term *graphology,* founded the Society of Graphology in Paris (1871), and set forth the results of his studies in several treatises, including *Les Mystères de l'écriture* (*The Mysteries of Handwriting,* 1872); *System de graphologie* (*System of Graphology,* 1875); and *La Méthode pratique de graphologie* (*Practical Method of Graphology,* 1878).[14] Michon attempted to give graphology a systematic basis and to associate isolated "signs" or elements (*i*-dots, *t*-bars, flourishes, etc.) with particular character traits.[15]

Michon's *analytical* approach contrasted with the *intuitive* approach of medieval Chinese philosophers like Kuo Jo Hsu and of certain eighteenth- and nineteenth-century intellectuals and amateur graphologists like Johann von Goethe, Thomas Gainsborough, Edgar Allan Poe, and Robert Browning. In an attempt to better understand a writer's personality, these intuitive practitioners would often trace over the script, thus supposedly getting a "feel" for the person's character.[16]

Although Michon had addressed the need for systemization (a requisite for graphology to lay claim to being a science), his "fixed signs," according to one critic, "were so numerous and arbitrary that they invariably contradicted one another unless some coordinating factor was introduced, and he made no effort to resolve the contradiction by a more general theory of personality. . . ."[17]

That task fell to Michon's pupil, Crepieux-Jamin (d. 1840), who eventually broke away from his teacher's system. He took instead a more *holistic* approach, stressing that a specimen of writing must be comprehended as a whole, to which the various signs and features contributed in different degrees. As he asserted, "The study of elements is to graphology as a study of the alphabet is to the reading of prose."[18]

French researchers continued to dominate the field of graphology until near the end of the nineteenth century, when the focus shifted to Germany. Wilhelm Preyer related the physical movements of writing to mental processes and, in 1895, advanced the notion that handwriting is essentially "brain writing."[19] (This concept is discussed in chapter 14.) Georg Meyer, a German psychiatrist, argued that emotion was expressed through all psychomotor functions, not just handwriting, and he suggested the need for a new science, *characterology,* in addition to graphology. Meyer also advocated a common vocabulary for the two "sciences."[20] His suggestions were taken up by Ludwig Klages. According to Klara G. Roman, in her *Encyclopedia of the Written Word:*

> In establishing laws and principles of graphology and characterology, Klages assumed a "science of expression" that postulates two forces within man: "mind," which binds and inhibits him, and "soul," which frees and develops him creatively. According to Klages these two forces, always dynamically at variance, influence all of man's behavior and are most crystallized in his *expressive movements*—a term coined by Klages—that is to say, walk, gesture, gait, speech, mimicry, writing, and so on. All such bodily movements, actualizing the tensions and drives of the personality, have a common form *level or style that is consistent with the individual's general motor* behavior and *rhythm* of movement. It is particularly in handwriting, where the movements between the two forces are caught, that they are most accessible for study and interpretation.[21]

Klages set forth his theories in five books and was mentor to an entire generation of German graphology enthusiasts.[22]

Subsequently, Professor Max Pulver of the University of Zurich extended Klages's theories into the field of psychoanalysis. To the usual measurements of letter height and width, Pulver added depth (i.e., pen pressure), which he linked to the individual's libido. He also sought to evaluate the "symbolic" aspects of handwriting and to interpret them much as one would interpret symbols in dreams.[23] His *Symboliker der Handschrift* (*Symbolism of Handwriting*) was published in 1930. According to one author:

> Interested in the psychology of the unconscious, he saw the clean white page as world space, to be filled by entering it according to one's nature, be it quickly but hesitantly, slowly and with eyes constantly turning backward to the past, or in an eager, all-embracing rush. He noted the upward reaching of the spiritually inclined, and the downward plunging strokes made by earthy natures. But he was also aware that many of these impulses are unconscious, that we are governed as much—or more—by those thoughts and feelings which never surface, as by our conscious attitudes and decisions.[24]

Further developments took place elsewhere—including Belgium, Hungary, and the Netherlands. And in England, Robert Saudek, a Czech, sought to modify the European speculative approach by using more quantitative methods. In his experiments in the 1930s, he employed devices to measure pressure and even used slow-motion photography to study writing movements.[25]

In the United States, June Downey was one of the earliest experimenters in the field, following the lead of French and German researchers. Her book, *Graphology and the Psychology of Handwriting*, which appeared in 1919, was based on earlier German and French notions of writing as expressive movement. In 1933, Harvard's Gordon Allport and Phillip E. Vernon published their *Studies in Expressive Movement*, which presented their view that handwriting was part of a person's total expressive nature (a view stemming from the theories of Meyer and Klages).[26] (See also chapter 14, this volume.)

Today, the status of graphology reflects its somewhat checkered past, and it often seems not far removed from the time when wandering conjurers disseminated the "art." Competing theories vie for favor, nowhere more than in America where some thirty-two different graphological societies—some "using methods which are not easily combined with other systems"[27]—attempt to advance the ancient belief. Lacking significant scientific or scholarly endorsement, but attracting criticism from many quarters,[28] the various practitioners often advertise their services in tabloids and occultish publications like *Fate* magazine. Their ads in *Fate* share pages with those hawking other forms of character reading, divination, crystal power, and the like. Similarly, book catalogs often reflect graphology's kinship with the mystical. For example, a Barnes & Noble catalog advertises a graphology text under the heading "The Occult," along with such books as *The Ghost Hunter's Guide, How to Read Hands,* and *The Evidence for Visions of the Virgin Mary.*[29]

In Europe, where various French, German, Swiss, and other theories represent a patchwork system, belief in the validity of graphology is apparently much stronger among university psychology professors than it is among their North American counterparts. However, the situation there is not always as favorable to graphology as is sometimes claimed.[30] In any event, acceptance is no substitute for proof. As Martin Gardner observes in his classic work, *Fads & Fallacies in the Name of Science:*

One of the major difficulties in all forms of character reading research is that no really precise methods have yet been devised for determining whether an analysis fits the person or not. Wide margins on a written letter, for example, are supposed to indicate "generosity." Is there anyone who would not feel that such a trait applied to himself? People are generous in some ways and not in others. It is too vague a trait to be tested by empirical method, and even good friends may disagree widely on whether it applies to a given individual. The same is true of most of the graphological traits. If you are told you have them, you can always look deep enough and find them—especially if you are convinced that the graphologist who made the analysis is an expert who is seldom wrong.

After describing the need for appropriate tests of the claims made by graphologists, Gardner concludes:

> Until a character analyst can consistently score high on [such] tests . . . his work will remain on the fringes of orthodox psychology. The fact that millions of people were profoundly impressed by the accuracy of phrenological readings suggests how easy it is to imagine that a character analysis fits the person analyzed—provided you know exactly who the person is![31]

Gardner's statement—made in 1957—continues to be valid today. It is time to realize that the Emperor of Graphology has no clothes.

NOTES

1. Etymologically, graphology (from Greek words for *writing* and *doctrine*) means the study of handwriting.
2. See also Ecclesiastes 8.1.
3. "Physiognomy," *Encyclopaedia Britannica,* 1960, 17: p. 886.
4. Ketuboth, 2.10. (See Herbert Danby, *The Mishnah: Translated from the Hebrew* [Oxford: Oxford UP, 1933], p. 247).
5. Suetonius, *History* 2.87 (cited in "Graphology," *New Catholic Encyclopedia,* 1967, 6: p. 704).
6. Quoted in Huntington Hartford, *You are What You Write* (New York: Macmillan, 1973), p. 43.
7. Ibid.
8. Quoted in "Handwriting," *Encyclopedia Britannica,* 1960, 11: p. 149.
9. Werner Wolff, *Diagrams of the Unconscious* (New York: Grune & Stratton, 1948), pp. 5, 357; "Handwriting," p. 149.
10. Hartford, p. 49.
11. "Graphology," p. 704; Wolff, pp. 5, 364.
12. "History of Graphology," in Klara G. Roman, *Encyclopedia of the Written Word: A Lexicon for Graphology and Other Aspects of Writing* (New York: Frederick Ungar, 1968), p. 174; Margaret Gullan-Whur, *The Graphology Workbook: A Complete Guide to Interpreting Handwriting* (Wellingborough, England: Aquarian, 1986), p. 11.
13. Gullan-Whur, p. 11.
14. Ibid.; Wolff, pp. 5, 366; Roman, p. 174; Hartford, p. 50.
15. Roman, p. 175.
16. "Handwriting," p. 149.
17. Hartford, p. 50.
18. Roman, p. 175.
19. Ibid.
20. Ibid., pp. 175–176.

21. Ibid., 176.

22. Ibid.; Hartford, p. 52.

23. "Handwriting," p. 150; Hartford, p. 56.

24. Gullan-Whur, p. 12.

25. Roman, p. 178.

26. Ibid.

27. Gullan-Whur, p. 13.

28. Particularly vocal against the claims of graphologists has been the distinguished Committee for the Scientific Investigation of Claims of the Paranormal—a scientific watchdog group including Carl Sagan, Isaac Asimov, and others.

29. Barnes & Noble's "Winter Reading" catalog, February-March 1987, p. 49. (Other headings on the same page are "Fortune Telling" and "Astrology & Magic.")

30. See also Oskar Lockowandt, "On the Development of Academic Graphology in the Federal Republic of Germany After 1945," *The Graphologist* 4(1): pp. 2-8 (Spring 1986).

31. Martin Gardner, *Fads & Fallacies in the Name of Science* (New York: Dover, 1957), pp. 296-297.

3

By a Man's Calligraphy Ye Shall Know Him: Handwriting Analysis in China

Barry L. Beyerstein and Zhang Jing Ping

Graphologists often point to the age and ubiquity of their art as though this implies validity. They argue, for instance, that because it was widely accepted in ancient China that a writer's character could be discerned from his or her calligraphy, this counts as evidence in favor of modern graphology. Similarly, western graphologists often claim that handwriting analysis enjoys greater official acceptance in modern China than in the West, but they present little evidence that this is so or that this alleged endorsement is based on scientifically acceptable data. What proponents neglect to state is that Chinese graphology arose from the same sorts of augury and divining practices as western graphology and is thus open to the same criticisms (see chapter 9, this volume).

In fact, raising the Chinese connection actually arouses further doubts about graphology. As Barry Beyerstein points out in Chapter 14, it reduces the already low *a priori* credibility of graphology to demand that the physical substrate of each personality trait must unerringly connect with the same set of writing features in every writer of the Roman alphabet and a quite different set in every writer of an idiographic script such as Chinese. It strains credulity even further to think that not only would personality mechanisms have to modify hundreds of features of copybook letters in exactly the right pattern to reflect the individuality of every person who learns one system of written symbols, but must also be able to automatically lock their in-

30

fluences onto a totally different set if he or she should learn another arbitrary system for encoding language. It would be an interesting test to see if a Chinese graphologist analyzing the Chinese script of a group of bilingual writers would make the same attributions as a western graphologist analyzing the same writers' Roman script. Given the frequent lack of agreement among different schools of western graphology, the editors would not expect high concurrence cross-culturally.

In addition to its long and varied history of magical divination practices, China can also take credit for the world's oldest system of objective selection tests. The ancient Chinese civil service examinations represent the first attempt to select public administrators on the basis of merit rather than social standing. Graphologists have sometimes taken the fact that penmanship counted in these written exams to mean that the detection of moral stature and character from script had, at this early date, already made the transition from occultism to the realm of objective testing. Though historical accounts by westerners dispute this, the senior author of this chapter was delighted to have an opportunity to examine claims about Chinese graphology first hand when he was invited to spend part of a sabbatical year at Jilin University in the People's Republic of China. There he met a very capable collaborator, Zhang Jing Ping, who examined Chinese historical materials and surveyed modern popular sources, looking for references to handwriting analysis and any objective tests that might have escaped western critics. His search confirmed that, in accord with the western sources cited in this chapter, and contrary to some graphologists' claims, reading personality from calligraphy did not enter into the ancient Chinese civil service examinations. Divination from calligraphy does, however, form an interesting thread in the Chinese folk tradition, one that survives, as in the West, despite scientific doubts about its accuracy.

During his stay in China, Barry Beyerstein also had the opportunity to speak with various officials and academics interested in personnel selection. He found that these officials were eager to catch up on developments in western psychological testing that had previously been unavailable for political reasons and that they were quite happy to leave graphology where they feel it belongs—in the realm of folk superstition.

INTRODUCTION: PROPHECY IN ANCIENT CHINA

Although graphology as practiced in the West has not emerged as a separate profession in China, the notion that an individual's personality and future prospects are encoded in his or her handwriting has long enjoyed a place among Chinese divination practices.[1] It is part of a tradition, rooted in ancient Taoist mysticism, that assumes the magical power of written symbols to access the spiritual world and thereby to inform, to protect, or to cure (Legeza 1975).

China's ancient civilization has produced an amazing variety of occult methods for reading personality and foretelling the future (Bloomfield 1983; Loewe 1981; Needham 1956, ch. 14; Ronan 1978, ch. 10). Ronan (1978: 202) lists "glyphomancy" (augury by scrutiny of writing) as a common divination practice in ancient China. It coexisted with other methods that interpreted facial features, palms, dream imagery, geologic formations (geomancy), patterns of strewn milfoil sticks (which evolved into the hexagrams for the divinatory book, *The I Ching*), and, of course, the alignments of heavenly bodies (astrology). Some of the very earliest examples of Chinese writing are archeological relics (c. 1400 B.C.E.) that record oracles' interpretations of the surface cracks produced by roasting tortoise shells or the shoulder bones of certain large mammals (Loewe 1981; Ronan 1978: 192). Obviously, it is but a small step to interpreting the lines in writing itself.

Given this climate of belief and the visual and symbolic richness of Chinese written characters,[2] it is not surprising that interpretation of pictographs (or "ideographs" as they are also known) would emerge as a mantic practice. The rarity and power of literacy itself was so great in earlier times that it often acquired a magical aura (Zusne and Jones 1989: 196–198; 248–250). According to Legeza (1975: 9),

> a profound belief in spiritual powers of calligraphy was very probably already present even in the formative period of Chinese civilization (i.e. during the first millennium B.C.), and was largely responsible for the survival of the Chinese idiographic script. For it is significant that, despite several attempts at reform, the Chinese civilization has always shown reluctance to adopt an alphabetic script.

Like the western divining methods discussed in chapter 9, Chinese augury is based on the assumption that supernatural powers will guide intuition and free association toward the "correct" meanings of arbitrary signs or omens. The rationale for extending the mental associates of these ambiguous stimuli to people or events is the magical "law of similarity" (Ronan 1978: ch. 10; B. Beyerstein, ch. 9, this volume). Western graphology is based upon the same trust that symbolism suggested by the shapes and positions of letters will be magically reenacted in the writer's life. But while the supernatural connection was taken for granted by Chinese glyphomancers, it is strenuously denied by most European and North American graphologists. Nonetheless, as chapter 9 of this book demonstrates, claims by the latter to have abandoned their magical roots are less than convincing.

According to Loewe (1981: 40), the history of Chinese divination has followed a course familiar to observers of western graphology—the initial meanings of signs were arrived at by intuition and free association, supposedly with the aid of supernatural inspiration. But once these revelations were recorded, readings tended, thenceforth, to be a fairly mechanical process of matching an individual's signs with codified interpretations found in the sacred texts. Like the rules of modern graphology, these were passed down reverently and seldom, if ever, tested or revised.

Chinese calligraphy, like all other forms of writing, originated as pictorial representations, but the pictographs have come to represent sounds rather than objects (DeFrancis 1984: 137). DeFrancis (1984: 133) puts to rest the prevalent western misconception that modern Chinese characters remain mere facsimiles, i.e., that they portray objects and actions visually, without the restrictive intermediary of phonetics. On the contrary, modern Chinese characters represent sounds by symbolizing objects whose names sound like the phonemes (the smallest sound units of a language) they are to convey. But, although they have become highly stylized and simplified, Chinese characters are still more obviously related, visually, to their pictographic origins than are the many alphabetic systems for representing phonemes. Thus they present an even richer substrate than western alphabets for eliciting free associations and pareidolia (see ch. 9) for oracular purposes.

Bloomfield (1983, ch. 8) describes a number of descendants of ancient Chinese augury that persist in Chinese communities around the world. Among them is a procedure that can be traced back at least to 722 B.C.E. and employs methods not unlike those of western graphologists. A Taoist priest of the Tang Dynasty (618–907 C.E.), Tsui Wu Yih, is revered as a master of this technique.

> The questioner first writes down a Chinese character—anything that comes into his head. Then the fortune-teller goes on to dissect the character and tell him what it all means. This can give rise to a considerable meaning because all Chinese characters, unlike the Roman alphabet, have many elements of other words in them. It is this multiplicity of concepts in each character that makes Chinese poetry so difficult to translate. . . . Obviously a written language so rich in elements is ready made for the fortune-teller's rhetoric. (Bloomfield 1983: 143)

Paralleling the Chinese prophetic tradition is another longstanding heritage of skeptical thought (Needham 1956: 365–395). Chinese skeptics have raised doubts about glyphomancy that sound rather like western criticisms of graphology (Bloomfield 1983). The Chinese critics were chagrined, first of all, by glyphomancers' unbridled freedom to pick and choose parts of characters, realign, and reassemble them. They were further upset by the augurers' use of analogical and associative thinking to play upon the multiplicity of homophones, puns, visual resemblances, etc., in Chinese writing. Doubters charged that this meant readings were bound to be an arbitrary outpouring of the reader's (perhaps unconscious) prejudices, intuitions, and flights of fantasy.

In addition to glyphomancy and use of written incantations in hopes of securing a desirable future, China has also had a tradition of personality reading by impressionistic appraisal of calligraphy. It is to this analogue of western graphology that we now turn.

CALLIGRAPHY AND PERSONALITY

Since the writing tools of the ancient Chinese, waterbrush and prepared ink, are different from those in common use today, there are distinct differences in the calligraphy produced by traditional and modern implements. The nuances of brush technique allow more scope for personalization of characters. This, plus the effects of officially-mandated simplifications of the script in recent years, means that ancient and modern calligraphy should be considered separately. The six basic strokes used in traditional Chinese characters are the following:

一 丨 丶 丿 乙 亅

The modern, simplified characters taught today have been reduced to combinations of five basic strokes:

丶 一 丨 丿 乙

In ancient China, nearly all calligraphers assumed that their calligraphy was a precise expression of their inner nature. Calligraphy itself was regarded as much more than just a means of conveying facts. It was an important aspect of Chinese culture, essentially an art form. As with poetry, painting, music, or dance, it was taught that through subtle embellishments of brush strokes, calligraphers could express thoughts, feelings, ideals, and ambitions, independently of the semantic content of their script. It was taken for granted among the literate elite that one's temperament, sentiments, and innermost soul were revealed for all to see when one put brush to paper. As the tenth century Chinese artist and critic Liu Xi Zai remarked in his famous work *The Generalizations of Chinese Art*:

> Calligraphy is the thing that manifests man's knowledge and learning, ability and talent, ideals and aspirations; in short, just man himself in nature.

This view is neatly encapsulated in an old aphorism, well known throughout China: "By a man's calligraphy ye shall know him." In part, this simply recognizes that calligraphers may intentionally embellish their work as an artistic statement, but it also incorporates an idea more akin to western graphology, namely, that unintentional adornments of written characters reveal precise aspects of personality. As claimed by some "holistic" schools of western graphology, these qualities are supposedly conveyed to others impressionistically, by a sort of intuitive "resonance" rather than by any intellectual or analytical process.

At the very least, it is universally accepted that writers of Chinese characters impart individually recognizable qualities to their script, just as writers of the Roman alphabet do. It is this personal imprint, which emerges despite standardized instruction, that gives handwriting analysis its appeal in both the East and West. It feels as though it ought to work. But despite this surface plausibility, the assumption that writing encodes specific personality traits remains to be proved. It is not a given to be accepted merely because it seems to make sense intuitively. As B. Beyerstein points out in chapter 14, individuality in script is more likely to be due to variations in bio-mechanical factors and bio-cybernetic programs controlling writing movements than to the graphologists' assumption that precise personality traits commandeer unique writing movements.

OBJECTIVE VS. SUBJECTIVE TESTING IN ANCIENT CHINA

Regardless of how it might arise, the distinctiveness of an individual's calligraphy was of concern to the officials who set the stringent civil service exams that became formalized in China around 200–100 B.C.E. (DuBois 1965; Bowman 1989). By 622 C.E., open, competitive examinations were taking place at regular intervals. Candidates who had been previously screened for their moral stature and basic literacy were allowed to sit formal written examinations in this, the world's first attempt to select public administrators objectively on the basis of merit. In the Chinese civil service examinations we see the earliest example of a split that was to occur much later in the West, between those attempting to develop objective measures of individual differences (see chs. 10 and 11) and those who rely on subjective, intuitive, and magical means of evaluation (cf. ch. 9).

By the time of the Ming Dynasty (1368–1644 C.E.) the civil service exams had become quite standardized, with successful candidates funneling through district and provincial screenings to the national selections in Beijing.

At the district level, required compositions were evaluated on several criteria including their "beauty of penmanship and grace of diction" (Martin 1870, quoted in DuBois 1965: 31). The best and the brightest were eligible to proceed to the provincial capital where they vied for the coveted title of "Promoted Scholar."

At this level, according to Martin, each examination was marked with a cipher and re-copied by an official scribe so "that the examiners may have no clew to its author and no temptation to render a biased judgement." Interestingly, Martin's observations show that the Chinese were already aware at this early date of two prime requirements of modern psychological measurement: "blind" rating of test materials and the need to secure independent agreement among more than one rater. These are precautions western graphologists still routinely violate more than six centuries later.

The "Promoted Scholars" advanced to the pinnacle of the selection system in Beijing where the emperor himself set the themes upon which candidates were required to write. Hanging in the balance was a place in the Imperial Academy. At this stage, interpretation of the Confucian classics dominated the content of the examinations and preference was given to those exhibiting outstanding verbal cleverness and the ability to construct elegant arguments almost like those of modern word games (Bowman 1989).

Also at this rarefied level,

> [p]enmanship reappears as an element in determining the result, and a score or more of those whose style is the most finished, whose scholarship the ripest, and whose handwriting the most elegant, are drafted into the college of Hanlin, the "forest of pencils" [and] recognized as standing at the head of the literary profession. (Martin 1870, quoted in DuBois 1965)

The Chinese selection system, being open to men (and at certain times also to women) from any background and based strictly on ability, was an influential model when competitive civil service examinations were finally adopted by France, the United Kingdom, the U.S.A., Canada, and other nations. The Chinese examiners recognized that a relatively small sample of relevant behavior, obtained under controlled conditions, could yield an estimate of performance in a wider range of situations. The key word here is "relevant," for the intention was to sample behaviors that had a reasonable chance of predicting performance on the job (for a modern perspective, see Klimoski, ch. 11). Where handwriting counted in assessing candidates for the Chinese civil service, it was considered a measure of esthetic, manual, or spatial abilities, not a magical index of personality.

Though the content of the Chinese examinations was criticized at the time as being too esoteric, Huang Chi, an official of the examining board, defended the selection system in 1655. In effect, he argued that it measured certain general mental abilities of the sort that are recognizable to modern psychologists (Jang 1990). Penmanship played a part to be sure, but it was only evaluated, quite reasonably, for its own sake or as a gauge of artistic flair or proficiency on spatial or mental imagery tasks. In the days before mechanical printing (also a Chinese invention), and especially in a style-conscious court, pleasing, legible script was a reasonable part of a public official's job description.

At a more abstract level, calligraphy was also deemed useful in assessing other pertinent abilities. For instance, in addition to including the appropriate content in his or her answer, the candidate was required to make it fit a specified page format on the first and only attempt. Thus the examinations, in addition to sampling memory, verbal agility, and educational attainments, tested the candidates's spatial skills and ability to reconcile the conflicting demands of accommodating to traditional constraints while still exhibiting creativity. Though an individual's moral status was important in selection for the ancient Chinese civil service, there is no evidence that the examiners thought they could discern such attributes from the candidate's calligraphy. The admirable restraint of the examiners in this regard did not, however, deter prevalent folk beliefs in the occult powers of calligraphy. It continued to be widely supposed that personal qualities were encoded in writers' script.

It is interesting, given the differences in their idiographic and alphabetic writing systems and so many other aspects of Chinese and European culture, that many of the same folk beliefs about writing emerged, apparently independently, in both populations. As Warner and Sugarman (1986) point out, ordinary westerners who have no training in graphology exhibit some agreement in the free associations they make to certain features of handwriting. These tend to be commonsense connections such as associating a large signature with self-importance, for example. Though the validity of such attributions is questionable, there seems to be a natural tendency to extend the traits a script reminds one of to the person who wrote it. Humans everywhere seem to have a strong bent for this sort of magical attribution, as seen by the widespread appeal of the "law of similarity" (see ch. 9).

Parallels in popular beliefs about writing in China and the West suggest interesting universalities in how intuition and free-associative processes work. For instance, in both cultures it is widely felt that hard-to-read handwriting betrays the writer's antisocial tendencies and intention to stifle communication. Also in both cultures, folk diagnoses of this sort typically have built-in loopholes to save the system when its ascriptions don't fit or might prove embarrassing, i.e., verbal sleight-of-hand that renders the procedure effectively unfalsifiable. For example, the junior author of this chapter found that, despite the predominantly negative connotations ascribed to illegible writing in China, it was also believed that some indecipherable handwriting is merely the result of a hasty or energetic nature that cannot be bothered to make neat, conventional characters.[3] He also found that it is conventional wisdom in China, as in the West, that happy people will tend to accentuate their uphill strokes and that their dot-like strokes will thicken at the end.

Chinese handwriting interpreters apparently share other beliefs with western graphologists, such as the following. If bar-like strokes are wavy or dots appear more like curves, or the endings of words show an upswing, this supposedly indicates a sense of humor. Similarly, handwriting interpreters in both cultures assume that people who like to do things in a big way, to "make a splash," as it were, will write with a large hand. Small writing in both societies suggests the writer has a penchant for concentrating on details.

In China, as in the West (cf. chapter 9), it is popularly held that perusal of the calligraphy of historical figures will confirm one's casual impression that there are written correlates of personality and occupation. The calligraphy of intellectuals is believed to have a tender, delicate nature; military heroes are reputed to have bold, unconstrained calligraphy. Upright, resolute people are expected to write with a firm, vigorous hand and artists' calligraphy is said to have a picturesque, poetic quality. Scholars and professional caligraphers are thought to impart a certain profundity and academic quality to their writing.

When asked what support there is for these popular beliefs, Chinese adherents, like their western counterparts, fall back on anecdotal evidence. Best known in this regard are historical figures who are also honored as calligraphy masters and whose distinctive styles are reputed to mirror their personalities. Among those often cited are the eminent Tang Dynasty writer Han Yu (768–824 C.E.), the Song Dynasty poet Su Shi (1036–1101 C.E.), and his contemporary, the statesman and writer Ou Yang Xiu (1007–1072 C.E.).

Because of such examplars, and especially the eleventh-century artist and philosopher Kuo Jo Hsu (see ch. 2), it has long been believed in China that expert calligraphers themselves may be particularly adept at judging personality from the calligraphy of others. This is alleged to include the ability to discern noble-mindedness from vulgarity, caution from recklessness, and maturity from naivety. Supposedly, one can also divide the observant from the dull-witted, the easy-going from the irascible, and the trustworthy from the treacherous. Also revealed are liberalism versus conservatism, realism versus idealism, kindheartedness as opposed to callousness, etc. As with western graphology, some of the foregoing may seem slightly more plausible than others, but a search of Chinese sources by the junior author of this chapter revealed no empirical studies to back up any of these assertions.

Like their western counterparts, Chinese supporters of handwriting analysis make the mistake of concentrating exclusively on anecdotal evidence that is consistent with their position; i.e., they regard the fact that some people exhibit both the written sign and the putatively related behavior as "proof" the technique is valid. As Dean (ch. 12) and B. Beyerstein (ch. 9) show, a proper test must compare the incidence of these supportive cases with that of people who have the writing feature but lack the personality trait and those who have the personality trait but not the allegedly correlated written sign. The critics in this volume show that when these rules have been scrupulously followed, the result has not been flattering to handwriting analysis.

READING PERSONALITY FROM WRITING IN MODERN CHINA

Just as there is debate among western graphologists over the relative merits of "molecular" versus "holistic" ways to discern personality from writing, there have been similar disagreements in China. In the West, the trend in graphology seems to be away from interpreting small portions of letters in favor of reliance on more "holistic" impressions (see Crumbaugh, ch. 7 and Nickell, ch. 2). But in China developments seem to have followed the reverse path. While the attributions discussed in the foregoing sections could be considered "global" impressions of the overall impact of writing, more recent opinions in China regarding interpretation of calligraphy focus on individual differences in formation of the five basic strokes that comprise modern Chinese characters (see above). To some extent, this has coincided with adoption of western writing implements, replacing the more variable brush and ink, and with official attempts to simplify and standardize the characters themselves.

We have looked in vain for scientific evidence regarding handwriting analysis in China. It seems that the Chinese scientific establishment considers it a holdover from old folk superstitions, not worthy of empirical study.[4] This is significant because other traditional practices with a mystical past, such as acupuncture and herbal medicine, are being scrutinized by reputable Chinese researchers because they can demonstrate some efficacy. Occultists practicing handwriting analysis, for their part, appear to be content to remain in the mystical camp. There is no indication they are trying to acquire a gloss of authority for their divining practices by pretending to be scientific disciplines.[5]

When the senior author of this chapter was a visiting professor in China, he was unable to find any credible experts in relevant fields who believed that precise personality traits were encoded in writing. This does not preclude the possibility that some ostentatious people might choose to express their flamboyance in certain features of their writing or that artistic or meticulous people might do likewise. But evidence to support the contention that there are unique written signs of, say, sincerity, benevolence, hostility, or promiscuousness is no better in the Chinese than the western literature.

NOTES

The authors would like to acknowledge the assistance of Elsie Zhang and Elliott Marchant in the preparation of this chapter.

1. Divination is also known as augury. Diviners assume supernatural forces will guide them in interpreting signs or omens to foretell the future or discern information about individuals. Almost any random, complicated stimulus can be the starting point for the process of free association that leads to the interpretation. For a more detailed discussion of the related concept of "pareidolia," and divination in general, see chapter 9 of this volume. A good history of Chinese divinatory practices can be found in Loewe (1981).

2. To avoid confusion, we shall use the term "character" in this chapter to refer to a single Chinese ideograph, and not in its other common usage as a synonym for personality makeup.

3. Whether the more or less charitable interpretation will be deemed appropriate is usually decided by the well-known "halo effect." This is the tendency to rate someone's unknown attributes more or less favorably, depending upon how one feels about aspects of him or her that are already known. Examples of this in western graphologists' judgments can be seen in chapter 9.

4. In the recent drive to modernize the Chinese economy, identification of talent has become a priority and interest in scientifically based selection procedures has burgeoned. Contact with worldwide developments in the psychology of individual differences had previously been discouraged for political reasons. Handwriting analysis does not seem to be finding a place in this resurgent interest in testing.

5. This is quite unlike the case of other Chinese occult practices such as Qi Gong, which are actively seeking unearned respectability by developing into full-blown pseudosciences (Kurtz 1988).

REFERENCES

Bloomfield, F. 1983. *The Book of Chinese Beliefs.* New York: Ballantine Books.

Bowman, M. L. 1989. "Testing Individual Differences in Ancient China." *American Psychologist* (March): pp. 576–578.

DeFrancis, J. 1984. *The Chinese Language: Fact and Fantasy.* Honolulu: University of Hawaii Press.

DuBois, P. H. 1966. "A Test-Dominant Society: China, 1115 B.C.–1905 A.D." In *Testing Problems in Perspective,* edited by A. Anastasi. Washington, D.C.: American Council on Education, pp. 29–36.

Jang, K. 1990. "The Imperial Chinese Civil Service Examinations: Observations from a Modern Measurement Perspective." Unpublished manuscript. Dept. of Psychology, University of Western Ontario, London, Ontario, Canada.

Kurtz P. 1988. "Testing Psi Claims in China: Visit by a CSICOP Delegation." *The Skeptical Inquirer* 12(4): pp. 364–375.

Legeza, L. 1975. *Tao Magic: The Secret Language of Diagrams and Calligraphy.* London: Thames and Hudson.

Loewe, M. 1981. "China." In *Oracles and Divination,* edited by M. Loewe and C. Blacker. Boulder, Colo.: Shambhala, pp. 38–62.

Needham, J. 1956. *Science and Civilization in China.* Vol. 2: *History of Scientific Thought.* Cambridge: Cambridge University Press.

Ronan, C. A. 1978. *The Shorter Science and Civilization in China: An Abridgement of Joseph Needham's Original Text.* Vol. 1. Cambridge: Cambridge University Press.

Warner, R., and D. Sugarman, 1986. "Attributions of Personality Based on Physical Appearance, Speech, and Handwriting." *J. of Personality and Social Psychology* 50(4): pp. 792–799.

Zusne, L., and W. Jones. 1989. *Anomalistic Psychology: A Study of Magical Thinking.* Hillsdale, N.J.: Lawrence Erlbaum.

4

Handwriting: Identification Science and Graphological Analysis Contrasted

Joe Nickell

As a practicing Questioned Document Examiner, Joe Nickell shares with others in his profession the annoyance of being confused with graphologists. The concern with this widespread misapprehension goes deeper than the annoyance all professionals feel when their profession is confused with another by the public (e.g., the podiatrist who must continually tell laypeople that he or she specializes in feet, not babies).

Drawing the distinction, as Nickell does here, between questioned document examination and graphology helps to deal with one of the major reasons pseudosciences survive. People do not believe questionable or patently false notions merely out of stupidity; they believe them because they first of all accept sensible notions, and then are lulled into suspending their critical faculties; thus allowing in the nonsense which follows. We might refer to this as the principle that *"Nonsense rides piggyback on sensible things."* Most defenders of questionable practices begin their discussions by referring to truisms that everyone accepts, or facts that were discovered by legitimate sciences. It is even more difficult to separate sense from nonsense when one is confused about which professions defend which, or worse, the same professional defends both. In some jurisdictions, graphologists are recognized as Questioned Document Examiners. And graphologists do share some beliefs with the latter, as Nickell points out. But the *differences* he notes between determining common authorship and personality traits are, he argues, more important.

Following a lecture I had given on "historical investigation"—which included a segment on certain documents I had authenticated as well as several I had exposed as forgeries—an elderly woman raised her hand. What did I think of graphology, she asked. I replied, all too briefly, that I had no doubt that personality affected one's handwriting, but that I questioned whether one's personality could be gleaned from one's handwriting alone. The woman persisted, but with some confusion. Perhaps it was Graphoanalysis she was referring to. I replied that while Graphoanalysis is alleged to have a scientific basis, I was skeptical of it as well. Still she insisted— as if to prove its validity—that it is used as "evidence in court."

It was only later, as I was driving home, that I finally realized what the woman had probably intended: She was inquiring about handwriting *comparison,* the work of respected forensic experts like those she had no doubt seen on TV detective shows.

As this incident demonstrates, the lay person may not always understand the differences between the examinations conducted by the document examiner and those performed by the graphologist—instead lumping both under the imprecise heading of "handwriting analysis." Actually, the graphologist attempts to divine from handwriting the largely subjective and elusive quality of a writer's personality, whereas the questioned document examiner is concerned with a panoply of more or less objective problems, including detecting forged handwritings, uncovering alterations in documents, identifying authorship of anonymous writings, and the like. For example, I recently exposed as forgeries some notes, ostensibly by Charles Dickens for his novel *Great Expectations,* and I demonstrated that some letters received by a newspaper from supposedly different persons were authored by a single individual who had altered her handwriting to hide the fact.

Nevertheless, there *are* superficial similarities between the two approaches. The graphologist, like the scientific document examiner, studies such individual features as pen pressure, the slant and speed of writing, the form of connecting strokes, and similar characteristics.[1] Both consider the implications inherent in forged and disguised writings, such as might be found, for instance, in a "poison pen" letter.[2] States one graphological text, "It is practically impossible either to disguise one's own handwriting completely or to copy the handwriting of another person beyond the range of detection."[3] A standard text on document examination agrees with the former premise but notes that "imitation of the handwriting of another is one of the most effective disguises of one's own handwriting."[4]

In fact, both graphology and questioned-document examination share a basic concept: the individuality of handwriting. As it is expressed by a prominent graphologist, Werner Wolff, in his 1948 *Diagrams of the Unconscious:*

Both conscious and preconscious movements are learned. Even if many children have the same teacher and learn to make letters in the same way, each child's writing will nevertheless show an individual pattern. This variation cannot be explained by the immediate conditions of writing such as paper, pen, or position of the body, because the variation remains stable, allowing us to identify each child's writing in many repetitions even if we alter the conditions intentionally, as by giving different kinds of paper and pens, and changing the positions of the body.[5]

Similarly, a noted document expert, Ordway Hilton, states in his *Scientific Examination of Questioned Documents:*

Writing is a conscious act. Still, through repeated use, the actual formation of each letter and word becomes almost automatic so that the experienced writer concentrates most of his conscious thought on the subject matter rather than the writing process itself. Thus, writing comes to be made up of innumerable subconscious, habitual patterns, which are as much a part of the individual as any of his personal habits or mannerisms. Writing is more, however, than a set of subconscious habits. It is a living, gradually changing part of the writer, and is far from a mechanical reproduction prepared by the complex human mechanism of muscles and nerves which are called into play to produce it. It is influenced by a mental picture of copybook form, modified by individual taste and the writer's ability to imitate that which is in his mind. Physical and mental conditions at the time of writing may affect it. Whether it is a criterion of personality is debatable, but that it is individual to each and every person is an established fact. Therefore, it can be identified, and the identification is based upon all of the elements which combine to create its individuality.[6]

(See Figure 1.)

The fact that handwriting exhibits traits which can identify an individual has been recognized since ancient times. Indeed, as early as the third century, Roman jurists established guidelines for making legal comparisons of handwriting based on "resemblance or similitude of hands."[7] But there are other factors that reflect a person's individuality—fingerprints, for instance, and facial features—yet few graphologists would urge us to believe in physiognomy (the attempt to read character from facial features). And few would suggest that fingerprints offer any more credible basis for divining character than do the lines studied by palm readers.

Nevertheless, by analogy if not by science, handwriting has long been held to mirror personality. (See chapter 2: "A Brief History of Graphology.") What was lacking, however, according to Adrian Furnham, lecturer in psychology at London University, was "not a method of analysis so much

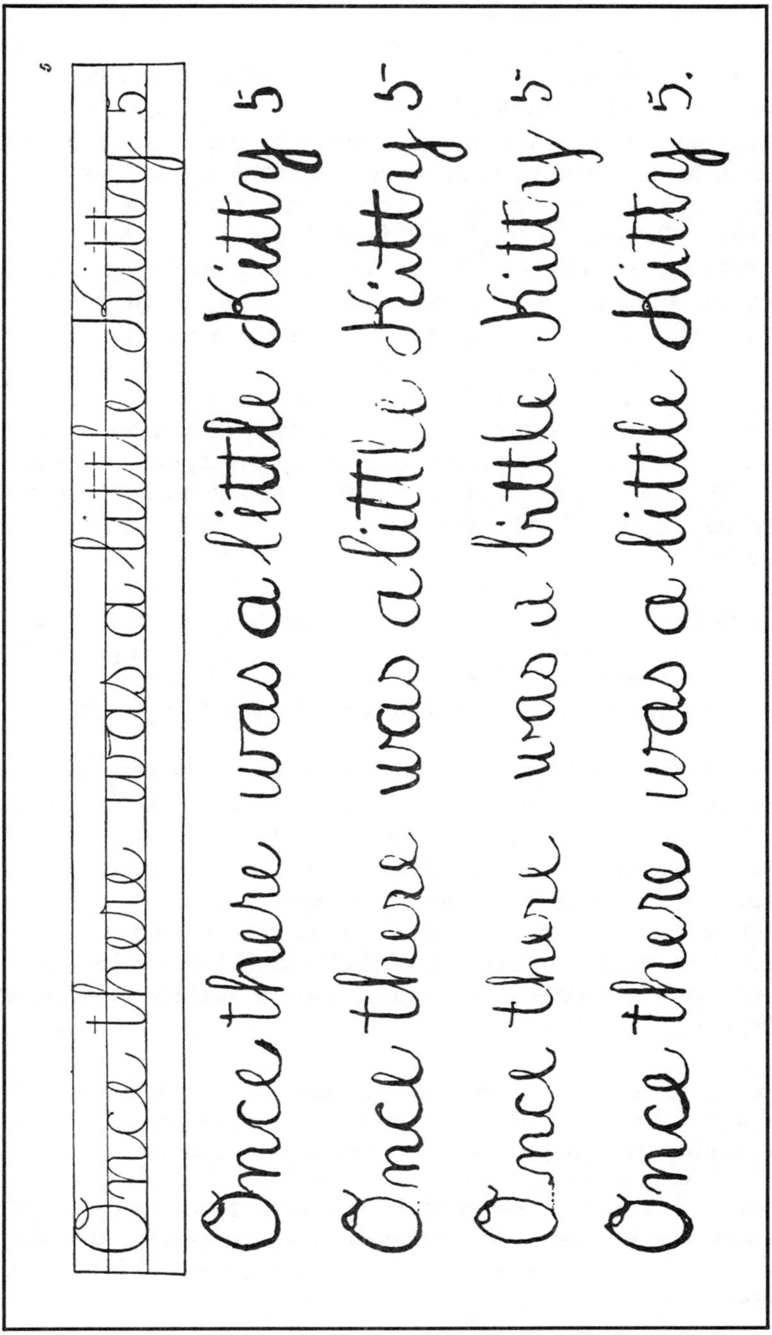

Figure 1. COPYBOOK SCRIPT. Typically, people learn to write by imitating standard models (such as this "vertical writing" that was taught in American schools from about 1890–1900). Over time, individuality increasingly develops. (Collection of Joe Nickell)

as a theory of how or why individual differences are manifest in hand-writing."[8] In any case, evidence that handwriting accurately reflects person-ality variables is at best equivocal and, in most cases, is negative.[9] (Such evidence is treated at length elsewhere in this book.)

This is not to say there is nothing that can be gleaned about a person from his or her handwriting. Although most graphologists will not attempt to do so, lay people can correctly determine a writer's sex from handwriting approximately 70% of the time.[10] And forensic texts such as Albert S. Os-born's monumental classic, *Questioned Documents,* generally agree that not only sex but a number of additional factors may be gleaned from hand-writing, though with varying degrees of certainty. For example, there are particular features that may indicate nationality, such as certain capital-letter forms that are common to German writing systems.

Then there are clues, not only from spelling and punctuation errors but also from the letter forms and certain other traits, that point to illiteracy.[11] Indeed, the alleged ability of graphologists to distinguish criminals from noncriminals by their handwriting may merely be predicated on socio-economic status.

> Criminals tend to come from lower socioeconomic classes than noncriminals, and socioeconomic class does seem to be reflected in handwriting, perhaps as a function of better education and more emphasis on good handwriting in the upper as opposed to the lower ranges of the socio-economic class structure.[12]

Other features that a scientific document detective might observe in handwriting include the tremor attributable to old age or illness (see Fig. 2),[13] as well as certain features that may suggest the writer's occupation. An obvious example is the "court hand" of old English documents—an elab-orate script used by members of the legal profession who reportedly "made something of a racket of it" because it was so difficult for the lay public to read.[14] Or a telegrapher might have inadvertently revealed his trade by a characteristic five-words-to-a-line writing, even in an anonymous letter.[15] Still other occupations might be reflected in handwriting, as Hilton observes:

> Elementary school teachers have for the most part a neat, legible hand closely imitating copybook style. Draftsmen may reveal their occupation through their numeral styles or particular letter forms. Many accountants have a small precise handwriting, while other occupational groups have writing peculiar to their profession or trade. Interpretation of these signs must of course be done with caution as within each group there is the exceptional person who fails to conform, and there are many groups which have no occupational habits.[16]

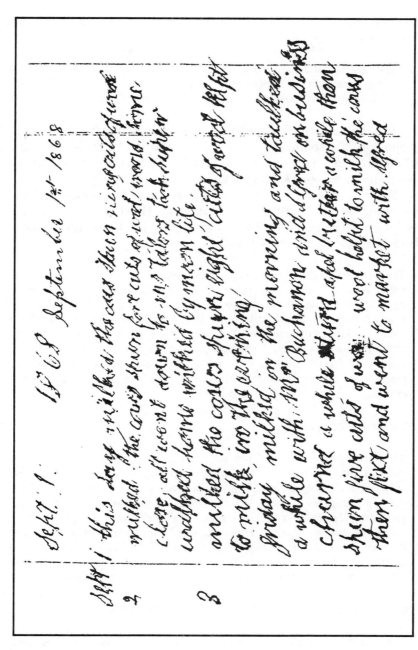

Figure 2. TREMULOUS WRITING—like this extreme example from a woman's diary of 1868—can result from a variety of causes, including illness and old age. (Collection of Joe Nickell)

Document expert Hilton is quick to note, however, that while certain aspects of an individual may be suggested by his or her handwriting,

> These findings should not be confused with a graphological analysis of writing—character and personality reading based on the individual's handwriting, an art the scientific basis of which is not clearly established.[17]

In a chapter entitled "Graphology and the Identification of Handwriting [graphology]," Osborn agreed with those who felt "there is something in it." Nevertheless, he placed graphology in the category of pseudoscience, along with phrenology and physiognomy.[18]

Some years later, a very thoughtful response to graphological claims was made by the British expert, Wilson R. Harrison, then Director of the Home Office Forensic Science Laboratory. In his *Suspect Documents: Their Scientific Examination* (1958), he stated:

> There can be no doubt that every handwriting does, to some extent at least, reflect the personality of the writer. A neat and elegant handwriting is more likely to be the work of someone who has at least a modicum of artistic ability, muscular control and careful habits than that of a person who is entirely lacking in these respects. It is when efforts are made to extend general conclusions and a detailed character analysis is attempted from the consideration of small amounts of handwriting—sometimes a single signature seems to be all that is needed—that the graphologist lays himself open to criticism.

Dr. Harrison continued:

> There are different schools of graphology, each with its adherents, who stoutly maintain that theirs and theirs alone are the true principles on which correct conclusions can be reached. Many of the books which have been written, either on graphology or on the psychology of handwriting, seem to have only one feature in common—whilst the preliminary chapters appear reasonable enough, the arguments employed become increasingly vague as they are developed in greater detail, until finally it becomes obvious that the majority of the conclusions of any graphologist must be reached by intuitive methods, since they appear to have little or no experimental foundation.

Harrison was pessimistic about the future of graphology:

> It is unlikely that graphology will ever be raised to the status of an experimental science because of the formidable difficulties certain to be encountered in assembling and analysing numerous specimens of the handwriting of a

great many people whose character and capabilities, both realised and latent, are known. This would be an essential preliminary if the principles on which character assessment is to be accomplished are to be sufficiently reliable to allow the conclusions of graphologists to be seriously considered in the courts.[19]

An interesting exchange between an advocate of graphology and a noted document expert, Ordway Hilton, took place in 1985 in the pages of the prestigious *Journal of Forensic Sciences.* Not only had Hilton spoken somewhat disparagingly of graphology in his 1956 book on questioned documents (as quoted earlier), but in 1980, he had branded it a "rather dubious art" that "has nothing to do with scientific questioned document examination as practiced in this country."[20] (The distinction is not always clear outside the U.S. and England.)[21]

The 1985 exchange began with the criticism by Dr. Niyogi, a toxicologist, of a 1983 article by Hilton.[22] Dr. Niyogi asserted:

Document examiners [have] ignored the aspect of determining personality from handwriting. Above all, the decision to write comes from brain [sic]. The hand obeys the command of brain, so we see writing on the paper. In other words, it is not only handwriting but brainwriting.[23]

In his article, Hilton had pointed out that "Any two writings by different individuals usually contain some similarities, sometimes a great number, but the differences should distinguish between the writers." Dr. Niyogi offered a suggestion. Perhaps, he thought, "personality traits in handwriting analysis" could assist the document examiner in distinguishing between the writers.[24]

Hilton responded:

Dr. Niyogi's letter shows a lack of understanding of the work of a questioned document examiner and how the identification of handwriting differs from graphological analysis. The identification of handwriting and graphological determinations of character traits are two very different disciplines that he chooses to treat as one.

The production of handwriting involves a complex physical act. Between the brain and the moving hand and fingers is an extensive muscle and nerve system that must be trained to react in a coordinated way to produce the finished writing. Thus writing is more than simply "brainwriting" as Niyogi and some graphological writers term it. Writing can be changed by intensive practice, and it can deteriorate over a period of time by lack of proper attention to its production. Physical factors such as injury to the arm or hand can change a person's handwriting.

Hilton added (in part):

Niyogi's references to personality traits and his suggestion that document examiners should apply these to handwriting identification is an easy route to error in identification problems. Graphologists find similar personality traits in very different handwritings, that is those that can easily be distinguished by the identification processes. If one is inexperienced in identification of handwriting, overdependence on these traits in an identification problem can lead to serious error.[25]

Notwithstanding such statements, there are qualified document examiners who are also practitioners of the "emerging science"[26] of graphology. In a study of data published in 1976, I found that slightly more than half of semi-professional and professional graphologists offered themselves as consultants in questioned-document identification. Only about one in four, however, were members of peer-review organizations such as the International Association of Questioned Document Examiners.[27]

Figures were not available for the number of questioned-document examiners who profess a belief in graphology, but as Osborn said, if an English or American expert who testifies in court "believes in the subject he usually conceals the fact."[28] Osborn also concluded:

As practiced at least, this alleged science has no value in identifying the author of a writing, and its exaggerations and unjustified inferences are likely to lead to loose thinking and weakening credulity. When the reports of practicing graphologists are more than mere generalities of wide application—which they usually are—they consist as a rule of positive inferences from ridiculously frail or misinterpreted data. This tendency toward exaggeration no doubt partly arises from the common tendency of devotees of various half-sciences and occult subjects to become partly self-hypnotized and self-deluded. . . .[29]

Osborne's thoughts—if not his "brainwriting"—exhibit the praiseworthy traits of critical thinking, honesty, and wisdom. If he, and his colleagues, seem harsh in judging graphology, it is not because of an unwillingness to consider the claims made in its behalf; rather, it is because those claims have not been substantiated by scientific investigation.

NOTES

1. Compare, for example, Barbara Hill's *Graphology* (New York: St. Martin's Press, 1981), pp. 5–6, with Charles E. O'Hara's *Fundamentals of Criminal Investigation* (Springfield, Ill.: Charles C. Thomas, 1973), p. 786. Of course, the *manner* in which these features are studied can be markedly different.

2. See Hill, pp. 121–27, and Werner Wolff, *Diagrams of the Unconscious* (New York: Grune & Stratton, 1948), pp. 144ff. and 178; cf. Albert S. Osborn, *Questioned Documents,* 2nd ed. (1929; reprinted, New Jersey: Patterson Smith, 1978), *passim* (see especially pp. 147 and 270ff.).

3. Huntington Hartford, *You Are What You Write* (New York: Macmillan, 1973), p. 245; Hartford is citing earlier texts.

4. Osborn, pp. 18, 212.

5. Wolff, p. 3.

6. Ordway Hilton, *Scientific Examination of Questioned Documents* (Chicago: Callaghan & Co., 1956), p. 136.

7. John I. Thornton and Edward F. Rhodes, "Brief History of Questioned Document Examination," *Identification News* (January 1986): p. 7.

8. Adrian Furnham, "Write and Wrong, the Validity of Graphological Analysis," *The Skeptical Inquirer* 13 (Fall 1988): p. 64.

9. Ibid., pp. 64–69. For a book-length study, see Abraham Jansen, *Validation of Graphological Judgments* (The Hague, Netherlands: Mouton, 1973).

10. Furnham, p. 68.

11. Osborn, pp. 410–11.

12. Terrence Hines, *Pseudoscience and the Paranormal* (Buffalo, N.Y.: Prometheus Books, 1988), p. 296.

13. Osborn, pp. 112–13; Hilton, p. 128.

14. Mary A. Benjamin, *Autographs: A Key to Collecting* (New York: Dover, 1986), p. 155.

15. Illustrated in Osborn, p. 139.

16. Hilton, pp. 129–30.

17. Ibid., p. 127.

18. Osborn, pp. 435–48.

19. Wilson R. Harrison, *Suspect Documents: Their Scientific Examination* (New York: Frederick A. Praeger, 1958), pp. 518–19.

20. Ordway Hilton, letter to editor, *Journal of Forensic Sciences* 25 (1980): p. 469.

21. Osborn, pp. 441–42.

22. Ordway Hilton, "How Individual Are Personal Writing Habits?" *Journal of Forensic Sciences* 28 (1983): pp. 683–85.

23. S. K. Niyogi, letter to editor, *Journal of Forensic Sciences* 30 (1985): pp. 6–7.

24. Ibid.

25. Ordway Hilton, letter to editor, *Journal of Forensic Sciences* 30: p. 8.

26. Hartford, p. 232.

27. I selected the 91 "professional" and "semi-professional" graphologists listed in Paul W. Landrum and Betty Tucker, *Who's Who in Graphology and Questioned Documents World-Wide* (Hixson, Tenn.: Unique Books, 1976), including an "update section." There were 52 (or 56.5%) who offered their services as questioned-document examiners, and 24 (or 26%) who were members of the International Association

of Questioned Document Examiners and World Association of Document Examiners.

28. Osborn, p. 442.
29. Ibid., pp. 442–44.

REFERENCES

Blotnick, Srully. 1985. *Otherwise Engaged: The Private Lives of Successful Career Women*. New York: Facts on File.
Chassler, Sey. 1986. "The Women Who Succeed." *Working Woman* 86–87 (January): pp. 102–103.
Gaeddert, William P. 1987. "The Relationship of Gender, Gender-related Traits, and Achievement Orientation to Achievement Attributions: A Study of Subject-Selected Accomplishments." *Journal of Personality* 55 (4): pp. 687–710.
Gallup, George, Jr., and Alec M. Gallup, with William Proctor. 1987. "What Successful People Have in Common." *Reader's Digest.*
Halcomb, Ruth. 1979. *Women Making It: Patterns and Profiles of Success*. New York: Ballantyne Books.
Harrison, A. A., M. Moore, and M. H. Rucker, 1985. "Further Evidence on Career and Family Compatibility Among Eminent Women and Men." *Archivo de Psicologia, Neurologia e Psichiatria* 46 (1): pp. 140–155.
Jacoby, Susan. 1988. "Roots of Success." *Family Circle Survey* (April 5): pp. 1–8.
Lawrence, Timothy L., and Brian H. Kleiner. 1985. "The Keys to Successful Goal Achievement." *Journal of Management Development* 6 (5): pp. 39–48.
Moch, Adrienne. 1983. "Psychologist Explores Keys to Success in Love, Money." *Profitline* 3 (9).
Roman, K. G. 1968. "The Psychogram, Its Background and Uses." In *Handwriting Analysis Workshop Unlimited,* ed. C. Cole. Campbell, Calif.: E.C.F. Cole.
Roman, K. G., with G. Staempfli. 1956. *Das Roman-Staempfli graphologische Psychogramm [The Roman-Staempfli Graphological Psychogram]*. Berne: Ausdruckstunde.
———. 1968. "The Profile-in-the-Circle: A Graphological Psychogram." In *Encyclopedia of the Written Word: A Lexicon for Graphology and Other Aspects of Writing,* ed. K. G. Roman. New York: Frederick Unger. [Reprint of 1956 article.]
Sheehy, Gail. 1981. *Pathfinders*. New York: Bantam.
Wellingham-Jones, P. 1989. *Successful Women: Their Health and Handwriting*. Tehama, Calif.: PWJ Publ.

Section Two

Graphologists Present Their Case

5

The Present Status of Research on Handwriting Psychology as a Diagnostic Method

Oskar Lockowandt

The present selection appeared first as a chapter in Muller and Enskat (1961) and was updated in 1976, translated into English, and made available in North America in the Journal Supplement Abstract Service of the American Psychological Association, volume 6 (1), 4, ms # 1172. Slight grammatical alterations have been made by the editors to the version which appears here. Since it was meant to be an overview of the literature, none of the experiments cited here are described in sufficient detail for the reader to evaluate them. However, it is interesting to compare Lockowandt's opinion of the value of certain studies which the reader knows firsthand; or to compare Lockowandt's opinion with somene else who discusses the same experiment; e.g., the reader may wish to compare what Lockowandt has to say about the study by Frederick (1968) with Dale Beyerstein's discussion of the same experiment in chapter 8.

Unfortunately, many of the papers cited here are not available in English. However, Lockowandt's discussion gives the reader an idea of the breadth of studies done by European graphologists. The reader may also wish to consult Geoffrey Dean's chapter 12, which reviews some of the same studies cited by Lockowandt. Dean's advice in that chapter is to ask how big the *effect size* is in the studies reported. Lockowandt gives us this information about some of the experiments he discusses. Where Lockowandt reports this, the reader may wish to look at what Dean has to say about how useful graphology has been shown to be. Also, the reader may wish to read Lockowandt's own assessment, given twelve years after this review was first published in English, of what has been demonstrated about the validity of graphology. That assessment appears in Lockowandt's chapter 6.

Since the first appearance of this review in 1961, the principles of handwriting psychology have been explored more intensively than ever before. This research activity has concentrated on verifying the assertions of handwriting psychology. Muller and Enskat (1965) and Muller and Mattes (1966) have addressed the issues in handwriting research in their studies and have included it in their theoretical framework. The most recent critical analyses of experimental verification studies are those of Prystav (1969, 1971a, 1971b). From these and other studies, we will present an overview of the methods and results of controlled studies of handwriting psychology.

HANDWRITING PSYCHOLOGY AS A PSYCHODIAGNOSTIC DISCIPLINE

Handwriting psychology owes the progress reflected in modern validation research to psychological diagnostics. The application of today's psychometric methods to handwriting, especially as advocated by graphometrists, rests on the same assumptions regarding the scientific and theoretical position of handwriting psychology as do other branches of psychology. In light of current developments, one can no longer safely consign graphology to the realm of expressive psychology. Many critics (such as Kirchhoff 1926, 1962, 1965, 1968) exclude graphology completely from the science of expression, on the grounds that handwriting is detached from the person and from bodily awareness of its working materials and, instead, include it in the methodological repertoire of psychological diagnostics. This viewpoint may be too extreme. Writing and the written product are similar to the self-recorded responses made to the stimulus conditions of a test; in both cases a person's attributes, psychic structure, personality development, etc., are assessed by self-recorded behavioral characteristics. The present author adopts a position midway between expressionistic and test psychology. Handwriting psychology occupies a special position within test psychology, because, unlike the testing situation, no new behavior is required, only the activation of long-practiced skills.

How the debate on the scientific and theoretical position of handwriting psychology will be resolved remains to be seen; the ultimate conclusion will depend upon the results of further research. In the overwhelming majority of controlled studies currently available, however, handwriting psychology is considered a psychodiagnostic discipline. Three principles, which hold for the entire field of psychology, characterize both the progress and direction of research: the objective reality of human behavior and experience, the ability to control research conditions, and the reduction of speculative ideas to empirically verifiable questions. The preferred methods for testing handwriting psychological statements have been defined by these principles.

PREREQUISITES FOR VALIDATING THE PRINCIPLES OF HANDWRITING PSYCHOLOGY

The most important prerequisite for validation research is the quantifiability of handwriting characteristics. Quantifiability means more than measurement in the physical sense, because only a few handwriting characteristics can be handled in this way. In psychometry, quantification has a broader meaning; it requires that each handwriting trait be assigned a definite place on a scale. The type of scale (nominal, ordinal, interval) dictates which type of statistics is used to analyze the data.

Many basic handwriting factors are easily scaled, because they appear to be unidimensional (that is, they vary along a single dimension). Other, more complex factors such as movement flow, regularity, and distribution are multidimensional (that is, they vary along several dimensions simultaneously). The number of dimensions of highly complex factors such as the expressive quality of rhythm is unknown but is probably very large. Until now, the experimental treatment of these highly complex factors, which are vitally necessary for handwriting interpretation, has been greatly oversimplified, and they have usually been scaled as if they were unidimensional, if they are scaled at all. This practice has been aptly criticized, for research methods must be suitable to the material being studied. Thus, multidimensional scales, such as those developed by Torgerson (1958), should be used for these complex factors. A simple writing factor is assigned a single point (or value) on a single unidimensional scale, whereas a complex writing factor will be assigned a single point on each of a number of dimensions and, therefore, needs to be represented as a spatial configuration.

Two further assumptions can only be touched on here: the unequivocal definition of the writing factors and their range of variability or fluctuation. Except for impression characters, it has not been difficult to define writing factors, but the scaling of very changeable handwriting samples is still problematical. Proposals for the psychometric solution of these problems have been put forward by Stein Lewinson (1956, 1964) and Lockowandt (1968). In addition, research in handwriting psychology must meet standard experimental conditions with regard to the selection of research subjects, statistical methods, and writing materials. These issues have been discussed by Wallner (1961a).

METHODS OF VALIDATING HANDWRITING PSYCHOLOGY

The following questions are commonly asked in handwriting validation research, and they must be answered scientifically if handwriting is to be recognized as a useful diagnostic instrument: Can handwriting factors be measured or evaluated accurately? To what extent do handwriting psychologists agree on the measurement or evaluation of graphic factors? Can production variables such as writing pressure and writing speed, which are recordable only in the act of writing, be reliably ascertained from an evaluation of the fixed writing picture? How confidently can factors measured from the writing picture be evaluated? Does handwriting vary with changing time and circumstances?

These questions are answered in the following review of studies of handwriting reliability. Reliability refers to the degree to which the behavior under study—in this case, handwriting—is reproducible and to the degree to which measurement or evaluation of that behavior is reproducible. It is prerequisite for validity. It can be investigated with respect to both the writing features themselves and to the meanings derived from them. As the questions posed above suggested, various aspects of reliability remain to be explored. On the graphic characteristics level, objectivity, stability, and consistency of the trait have attained particular importance in the studies done so far. On the interpretation level, it is necessary to determine the degree of agreement among several judges (interjudge reliability) and the consistency in the interpretations made by a single judge.

If the reliability of handwriting and handwriting analysis can be established, we will need to answer the following questions: Are the interpretations derived from the handwriting features valid? Have they a diagnostic use? Which areas of personality do they illuminate? Can intelligence, emotionality, and other traits be inferred from the handwriting? How confidently can these areas of personality be identified?

Validity is the degree to which a psychological diagnostic procedure, including handwriting analysis, actually measures the personality trait it purports to measure. It is the goal for which all other researches are only necessary preliminaries. Like reliability, it can be investigated either in terms of the writing characteristics themselves or in terms of the interpretations of handwriting characteristics. The validity of writing characteristics has been examined by a variety of methods, including correlation of single features with criteria, multiple correlation, factor analysis, and contrast group comparisons. Contrast group methods and fractionated and construct validation have been used to study the validity of interpretations. The statistical bases of these methods can be found in Lienert (1969), and an overview of quantitative testing methods in handwriting psychology can be found in Lockowandt (1968).

THE RELIABILITY OF HANDWRITING CHARACTERISTICS

OBJECTIVITY

If statements about the attributes of the writer are to be derived from his or her writing characteristics, then it must be possible to identify these characteristics objectively. That is, the identification of these characteristics must not be a product of wishful thinking on the part of those describing them. For a long time, the objectivity of handwriting characteristics had always been assumed, but more recent studies in handwriting psychology have addressed themselves to the problem of objective identification for both measured and evaluated characteristics. Objectivity is here operationally defined as the degree to which the measurements and/or the ratings made by several handwriting psychologists of the same graphic characteristic correlate with each other.

Birge (1954) and Wallner (1961b) investigated the metric objectivity of measurable variables. Birge had two graphologists independently measure five metric writing variables from fifty writing specimens. The correlations between the measurements made by the two graphologists were extremely high (average r = .97). Wallner had one graphologist rate and measure eleven metrically measurable writing characteristics in 107 handwriting specimens. His results were also highly favorable (average r = .90). This research shows that measurable characteristics are reliable.

Groffmann and Fahrenberg (1960) analyzed the writing speed complex and isolated three types of speed: pen speed, performance or output speed, and subjective haste. The objectivity of the ratings made of these factors by handwriting psychologists and by laymen was tested by Lockowandt (1961) and by Wollenweber (1961). Pen or speed could be objectively rated, but performance speed could not because of experimental error. Also, the handwriting psychologists reached a high level of agreement on their rankings of subjective haste.

Characteristics which are rated are less reliable (or objective) than those which are measured. Studies by Wallner (1961c, 1962) showed that the objectivity of rated or ranked characteristics is largely dependent upon their complexity; very complex characteristics can be judged objectively only with great difficulty. Nevertheless, his studies yielded unexpectedly favorable results. His five judges used a seven-point rating scale to rate flow of rhythm, an unquestionably complex characteristic, in 100 unsorted writing samples. The overall agreement among judges was high (average r = .59). Other rated characteristics, especially impression qualities, have shown a satisfactory degree of objective judgment. Nevertheless, the reliability coefficients so far reported for complex writing characteristics are too low to be used in validation studies.

Wallner's (1962) study provides further information with regard to the differences in objectivity between rated and measured characteristics. The objectivity of impression qualities was approximately .17 correlation points below that of corresponding measurable characteristics, even when the latter were judged rather than measured. A study by Hofsommer, Holdsworth, and Seifert (1965) corroborates these results. They found a substantial difference between the objectivity of measured and rated characteristics (treatment of margins: r = .98; and stiffness of pen grip: r = .41). These results provide a realistic estimate of the true differences in objectivity.

The experiments discussed so far do not, however, represent the practical work of the handwriting psychologist, who does not classify impressionistic qualities that have been chosen by others, but who makes his or her own selection from an array of impressionistic characteristics that are presented in the form of adjectives. Muller (1957) has examined this selection process in an experiment in which ten handwriting psychologists were asked to assign to twelve handwriting samples the twenty most suitable adjectives from a list of 150 impressionistic characteristics. These impressionistic qualities were divided into twenty-four groups of adjectives that were related in meaning. The inter-rater agreement of the handwriting psychologists was 42.5%; that is, on average, they agree on eight of the twenty selected qualities. It is interesting that consensual agreement—that is, agreement based on the significance of the adjective in the context of the entire handwriting sample—is higher than agreement based on the meaning of the adjective in isolation (68.5% vs. 42.5%). Searching for consensual agreement closely parallels the practice of handwriting psychologists in their everyday work. The difficulty of judging highly complex impression qualities is illustrated by a marginal finding; as a rule, male handwriting psychologists prefer different impressionistic qualities from those selected by female handwriting psychologists.

STABILITY

Handwriting psychology seeks to discern psychic attributes through hand-writing as collective signs and draws conclusions from observed and recorded writing behavior about the dispositions and attributes that determine these behaviors. In accordance with basic hypotheses of personality theory (Graumann 1960), handwriting psychology assumes that these attributes are not subject to continual, substantial alteration but are relatively, though not rigidly, constant.

It is further assumed that the relative constancy of these personality attributes corresponds to the relative intra-individual constancy of writing movements and writing characteristics. Therefore, a person's typical system of handwriting must not vary substantially if one is to draw conclusions from it about the permanent attributes of the writer. This constancy is called stability or repeated measurement (test-retest) reliability. Handwriting stability is defined as the relative constancy of handwriting characteristics over time and under different circumstances. It is, of course, a prerequisite for validity, but it can be studied independently of it.

An accurate assessment of stability can be achieved only by systematic variation of writing conditions and of time intervals. The few studies on stability which have been done to date have concerned themselves with the effects of different instructions on the constancy of handwriting characteristics (e.g., normal pace compared with increasing speed to maximum tempo) and with time intervals of ninety minutes to two months.

Harvey (1934) found, with an interval of two months between first and second writings, an average stability coefficient of $r = .77$, with values ranging from $r = .48$ for the size of capitals, to $r = .85$ for the size of middle zones. Bearing in mind that the second writing was produced under rapid dictation, these results can be considered highly favorable. Fischer (1962, 1964) reported even greater stability in handwriting samples produced a week apart ($r = .80–r = .93$). Fahrenberg and Conrad (1964) confirmed these results using an interval of ten days.

More recent research from the Psychological Institute of the University of Freiburg in Breisgen (Beiersdorf, Derleth, and Kupper, all cited in Prystav 1971a) has yielded remarkably high stability coefficients under varying experimental conditions. Most values were beyond $r = .80$, many were beyond $r = .90$. These studies used time intervals ranging from ninety minutes (Beiersdorf) to three weeks (Derleth and Kupper).

All of these studies dealt with the stability of measurable characteristics. Prystav (1969) is the only investigator to study the stability of a characteristic —writing pressure—which cannot be measured, but must be evaluated. Using an interval of six weeks and a four-point scale, he obtained an average agreement of r = .90 in the rating of this characteristic.

Lockowandt and Keller (1975) examined the stability of children's handwriting. Two handwriting specimens were collected from each of 120 male and female pupils, ranging in age from ten years to twelve years, eleven months. The interval between the first and second specimens was two years. Six handwriting psychologists and ten laymen had the task of determining which handwriting samples were written by the same child. These judges showed a significant level of agreement in matching pairs of samples, thereby demonstrating that the handwriting of children represents a stable graphometric product.

Since the birth of handwriting psychology, the individuality of handwriting has been one of the basic axioms of the discipline; and this axiom has never been seriously questioned with regard to the handwriting characteristics of the graphically mature and graphically practiced person. There was much doubt, however, that the handwriting of those who are graphically immature and unpracticed showed similar individuality. It was believed that the handwriting of children was so likely to change during their developmental stages as to render valid interpretation impossible.

The results of the Lockowandt and Keller (1975) experiment, as well as those from the first genetic stability research performed by von Bracken (1934), have shown clearly that handwriting becomes individualistic at an early stage, as early as the first year of school. This individuality can be observed during the entire period of schooling. It is more pronounced in the handwriting of boys than of girls, and it increases with age. It is particularly significant that individually shaped graphic movements are manifested during the first years of school, because they are complex characteristics of a coordinated total movement, even though this coordination is not yet fully developed. The distortion of the microdynamics of writing during puberty is not so drastic that the basic personality of the adolescent cannot be reflected in handwriting. With certain reservations, therefore, the interpretation of children's handwriting is justified (see also Ajuriaguerra and Denner 1964).

CONSISTENCY

Consistency studies address the question as to whether and to what extent the individual measurements in a *single* writing specimen are in accord with each other. Consistency is also known as split-half reliability, because the measurements or ratings from one-half of the specimen (e.g., the even-numbered) are correlated with those from the other half (e.g., the odd-numbered). Consistency determinations are particularly important for evaluating how representative of the specimen the measurements are. The more variations there are in an intra-individual characteristic, the greater the number of individual measurements required for accurate evaluation.

Studies by Timm (1965, 1967), Fischer (1962), and Prystav (1969) and those by Derleth, Kupper, and Beiersdorf (see Prystav 1971a) have yielded high consistency coefficients for metric handwriting characteristics. Almost all the coefficients reported are greater than r = .85, most are beyond r = .90. A comparison of Fischer's consistency values, based on twenty individual measurements per characteristic, and Prystav's, values based on ten measurements, clearly supports Wallner's hypothesis that ten individual measurements are sufficient to establish the consistency of metric writing characteristics. The consistency coefficients from the two studies scarcely varied from each other.

In general, lower consistency coefficients are obtained for rated or evaluated characteristics than for metric characteristics. Timm found r = .94 for measured characteristics, r = .89 for simple ratings, r = .82 for complex ratings, and r = .73 for impressionistic characteristics. Prystav's (1969) values for rated characteristics are even lower; they vary from r = .15 to r = .47 for impressionistic characteristics (lively – rigid), from r = .12 to r = .47 for complex characteristics (right-tending–left-tending), and from r = .29 to r = .86 for simple ranked characteristics (curving – straight).

Much more favorable results were obtained by Hofsommer, Holdsworth, and Seifert (1965) and by Wallner (1968), apparently because of the optimal conditions under which the research was carried out. Markedly different writing samples were selected, the samples were presented simultaneously, and forced classifications were made. Prystav reached the same conclusion: "The astonishingly high reliabilities of these writers have now mainly theoretical importance as indicating values of graphological evaluated characteristics obtainable under the best possible conditions" (1969, 127).

When measurable characteristics are compared with evaluated characteristics under research conditions similar to those of actual practice, evaluated characteristics have shown relatively little consistency. Because of their complexity and their unknown dimensional structure, the definition of these characteristics is still imprecise. Only more uniform definition of evaluated characteristics, combined with the use of comparison and model writing samples, as Muller and Mattes (1966a, 1966b) have shown, can lead to better results. Further research on the consistency of evaluated characteristics is warranted, because they appear to be very useful diagnostically (Babst 1971).

THE RELIABILITY OF HANDWRITING INTERPRETATIONS

Of all the cognitive processes used in handwriting psychology, interpretation—the assignment and judgment of meaning—is the least well understood. It involves cognitive operations by which a multiplicity of combinations and chains of reasoning are integrated in ways that are difficult to explicate and describe, so there is ample opportunity for the use of subjective judgment.

Handwriting interpretation is dependent on a multiplicity of factors. It is influenced by the size and quality of the writing specimen, by the spontaneity and evocativeness of its formation, by information concerning its origins, by the information content and semantic richness of the writing, and by conditions specific to the writer. The methods of evaluation used also affect the interpretation process, that is, by the precision with which the writing characteristics are defined, the ways in which graphic factors are combined and modified, the specificity and generality of the essential rules of interpretation, and the recognition of measurement errors such as central tendency and halo effect.

The personality of the judge has a major influence on the kind of interpretation that is made. His qualifications, his personal and practical experience, the nature of his training (e.g., pluralistic or dogmatic), and his ability to make specific judgments will all play a part in his interpretation. And finally, the purpose for which the judgment is to be used will determine how detailed and extensive the interpretation will be. The nature of the interpretation will vary depending on whether, for example, the writing psychologist is asked to evaluate specific qualifications such as leadership ability for a particular occupation or to evaluate general characteristics such as sociability or vitality.

In terms of the psychology of thought, the interpretation process itself can be regarded as a process of gathering and assimilating information, from which a global picture of the psychological attributes of the personality emerges. This global picture is then steadily differentiated and, if need be, restructured on the basis of the information gleaned from the written material (Daul 1966; see also the description of the interpretation process by Lockowandt 1973 and chapter 8 of this volume).

OBJECTIVITY: INTER-INDIVIDUAL AGREEMENT

Reliability studies of graphological interpretations are concerned with the extent to which several judges agree in their interpretation of the same handwriting sample, regardless of whether their diagnostic judgments are correct. The earliest and frequently cited work on this topic was done by Crider (1941). Two handwriting psychologists ranked eighteen handwriting samples on nine personality characteristics. Overall agreement between the judges was low (average rho = .18). Crider's study was, however, methodologically flawed; his judges were very different in their qualifications, and the written material was scanty. Although Crider's findings cannot be taken as an accurate estimate of inter-judge reliability, his study pointed up the need for better research design.

Among the small number of studies on reliability of interpretation, the works of Hofsommer, Holdsworth, and Seifert (1965), Wallner (1965, 1969), Schneevoigt (1968), Cohen (1969), Reichold (1969), and Volz (1969) are of particular importance because of their wide scope and more exacting methodology. Hofsommer and colleagues had three handwriting psychologists rate leadership ability among foremen (n = 322) on a seven-point scale. They found a high and statistically significant level of agreement among all judges (average rho = .74). This result, unusually favorable for handwriting psychology, is all the more unusual because the attribute to be judged was quite broad and the handwriting samples had not been written under standardized conditions (the candidates had written to apply for jobs using their own writing implements).

A much lower level of agreement among their three handwriting psychologists was found in their judgments of the success of technical school students (n = 57) (average rho = .39), but overall, at least four of five coefficients were significant. Their three handwriting psychologists were able to reach a highly significant level of agreement (average rho = .62) in their evaluations of the abilities of office workers.

It is usually assumed that the reliability of graphological judgments is influenced by the nature of the writing (e.g., spontaneous writings vs. those designed to be pleasing to the reader) and by the writing instrument (pen vs. pencil). However, Hofsommer, Holdsworth, and Seifert (1965) demonstrated that such influences are only slight. Handwriting psychologists generally assume that the personality of the writer is relatively constant across situations, so the special circumstances of the writing has little influence on their evaluations. The value of this expanded research for handwriting psychology cannot be overstated. It provided, for the first time, a methodologically faultless demonstration that handwriting psychologists use binding yardsticks of judgment and agreed-upon cognitive schemata in the complex process of interpretation.

The fundamental finding that handwriting interpretations are produced by something other than chance has been successfully replicated with other populations and other research techniques. Wallner (1965) had eighty-nine writing samples rated by six handwriting psychologists on 12 dimensions such as movement tempo, mood swings, perceptual faculty, temperament, and contact ability. Of the 180 rater intercorrelations, 93% were significant at or beyond the .05 level. This high reliability value, which the author achieved in later study (Wallner 1969), leaves little doubt about the stability of the judgment processes used by handwriting psychologists.

Wallner (1965) was also able to show that the effect on their interpretations of the judges' qualifications was substantial. The judge who had no university training in psychology and scarcely any practical experience deviated considerably from the combined ratings of his colleagues. Furthermore, the content of the writing specimens did not explain the high-level agreement among the judges; the one judge who did not understand the language of the writing specimens (Swedish) did not differ in his judgments from the other judges.

That handwriting psychologists can make reliable judgments of such specific attributes as intelligence has been demonstrated by Schneevoigt (1968) in a painstaking experiment. The results of two intelligence tests served as the intelligence criteria, and five out of six concordance coefficients were statistically significant. Schneevoigt also found that the more varied the expression of the intelligence in the writings of the subjects, the greater the degree of agreement among the raters—a finding of particular relevance to handwriting psychologists, many of whom prefer a broad concept of intelligence (see Lockowandt, chapter 8).

In spite of the favorable evidence currently being amassed on the objectivity of interpretation, it must be remembered that interpretative judgments are, in general, less reliable than judgments of graphic characteristics. Better results must await more analysis of the interpretation processes themselves.

STABILITY: INTRA-INDIVIDUAL CONSTANCY

How stable are the judgment processes of handwriting psychologists? If the same psychologist evaluates the same handwriting specimen at two different times, how similar are his two evaluations? Although we do not yet know how long the time interval between repeated interpretations should be in order to rule out memory effects, the results to date suggest that handwriting psychologists are constant in their judgments.

Crider (1941) presented a handwriting psychologist with the same writing sample he had rated on twelve personality traits one month earlier. Agreement between the two ratings was significant on all twelve traits (average rho = .82), including the writer's intelligence, emotional stability, and self-confidence.

Reichold (1969) has confirmed that handwriting psychologists derive their interpretations from a clear cognitive frame of reference. After an interval of three months, a handwriting psychologist evaluated ninety handwriting specimens on adjustment to the environment, self-confidence, perseverance, foresight, and maturity. Stability coefficients for the five dimensions ranged from r = .78 to r = .88. Both studies used only one judge, so more extensive studies are needed to establish the generalizability of these early results.

The interpretation of a writing sample is the product of complicated processes of selection, ordering, and combination. The studies by Crider and by Reichold indicate that the judgments of handwriting psychologists were not accidental but were based on firm methodological rules.

THE VALIDITY OF HANDWRITING ANALYSIS: GRAPHIC CHARACTERISTICS

Validity is the accuracy with which a diagnostic or assessment procedure measures what it is supposed to measure. It is usually assumed—incorrectly—that the same general concept of validity is equally applicable to every diagnostic method, including handwriting psychology. A diagnostic method is not, however, valid or not valid. On the contrary, each test of validity must be considered in terms of the research sample and the criteria used in that particular study. Accordingly, there is only a "differentiated validity" (Michel and Iseler 1968); that is, a test of handwriting is able to make valid assertions about some criteria, but not about others. Validity research, then, can be compared to exploring new territory; every study—insofar as it is methodologically sound—expands the informational and practical possibilities of a diagnostic method.

The validity of handwriting analysis is operationally defined as the degree to which the handwriting characteristics of a sample of individuals correlates with specific, precise criteria such as scores on tests, responses to questionnaires, or ratings by supervisors. It must be emphasized that negative results from such studies do not necessarily speak against the validity of handwriting psychology. A low correlation, by itself, may reflect either the low validity of the criterion employed in the study or the low validity of the handwriting analysis. A validity study can only be considered satisfactory when the reliability and validity of the criterion have been established. In the meantime, studies in which handwriting characteristics were correlated with test results must be critically evaluated (see Muller and Mattes 1966a and Prystav 1969 for critical historical reviews of validity research). Furthermore, the choice of appropriate criteria is critical. We believe that internal criteria such as test scores must be replaced by external criteria such as professional and academic success or occupational achievement.

CORRELATION OF INDIVIDUAL GRAPHIC
CHARACTERISTICS WITH CRITERIA

Secord (1948) and Wallner (1966) investigated the validity of individual handwriting characteristics by correlating them with specific criteria. Secord tried to validate the Stein Lewinson (1942) scale by using such personality characteristics as mood state and affective ability, but without success. Wallner's results were equally disappointing. These validation techniques have been dismissed by graphologists, because they do not take into account the holistic nature of handwriting, and instead cultivate an atomistic view of graphic characteristics (see Angermann 1970). In view of the results to date, it is unlikely that simple graphic variables will correlate significantly with the criteria used. Such relationships are possible, however, in the case of complex characteristics such as those used by Wallner (e.g., regularity, maturity of the writing) in his, so study of these validation procedures cannot be entirely rejected.

To date, none of the factor analytic studies (discussed in detail below) which have generated large correlation matrices (as many as 29,000 coefficients per test) has led to satisfactory results, when only the correlations between single graphic characteristics and criteria are taken into account. To be sure, many significant relationships between writing characteristics and criteria are found, but the correlations are too low (usually on the order of $r = .15$) to permit accurate prediction of criteria. There is no point, therefore, in citing the individual relationships that have been found.

There are a number of factors that may serve to reduce the correlation between handwriting characteristics and criteria. The computation of the product-moment correlation is based on statistical assumptions that are not always fulfilled. The most important of these assumptions is that the two things being correlated are related to each other in a linear fashion. When this is not true, the degree of actual relationship will be systematically underestimated. See Timm (1965) and Prystav (1969). It is not yet known whether curvilinear relationships are more frequent than linear relationships in handwriting psychology as Wallner (1970) has assumed.

It is also possible that the relationship between graphic characteristics is affected: there may be a three-sided distribution in an uncontrolled way by other (moderator) variables. The theory of "moderated regression," proposed by Saunders (1956), was used for the first time by Konttinen (1968) in the psychology of children's handwriting. In addition, the correlation can be reduced if the criterion is unreliable or if the writing characteristics are unreliable, as might be the case with a subjectively evaluated trait that is assessed by a single rater.

MULTIPLE CORRELATION

Handwriting psychology has always objected to simple correlation studies on the grounds that it is impossible to predict any criterion from a single graphic characteristic. This objection is remedied by multiple correlation techniques (also called multiple regression analysis), in which several graphic characteristics are combined in the prediction of criteria. Multiple correlation was introduced into handwriting psychology by Timm (1965, 1967) and pursued by Linster (1969), Prystav (1969), and Wallner (1970).

Linster (1969) has presented the most promising results thus far. He was able to predict an extensive spectrum of ability and personality characteristics from graphometric variables. Regression coefficients of .65–.85 were found between writing variables and specific aspects of intelligence, achievement, interpersonal behavior, relationship to environment, emotionality, and personal maturity. Intelligence was manifested as intellectual agility, theoretical ability, logical thinking, and imaginativeness. The graphometrically definable traits included both quantitative and qualitative performance. Tolerance ($r = .85$), good fellowship, restraint, and discretion were the forms of contact behavior most precisely defined. Environmental adjustment could be differentiated by handwriting psychology as openmindedness, activity, drive for dominance, passivity and adaptability, overall behavior, openness, and self-criticism. Affectivity included the distinction between robust and sensitive emotionality.

These findings show the wide range of behavior and dispositions that can be identified with confidence from handwriting, even on the level of graphic characteristics. Although the research results are still clear enough for practical application, they are plausible in terms of handwriting psychology. The use of multiple regression techniques has shown that graphological characteristics are endowed with psychological meaning.

FACTOR ANALYSIS

Factor analysis starts with the intercorrelation of a large number of characteristics and then determines which characteristics cluster together to form a smaller number of basic components or factors that are responsible for the handwriting, ability, or personality under investigation. Factor analytic studies aimed at revealing the basic dimensions or factors of handwriting have been carried out by Lorr, Lepine, and Golder (1954), Droesler (cited in Unkel 1964), Fischer (1964), Adolfs (1964), Seifert (1965), and Stein Lewinson (1968).

Attempts to use factor analytic methods to validate handwriting psychology have been made by Fahrenberg (1961), Conrad (1964), Unkel (1964), Fahrenberg and Conrad (1965), Timm (1965, 1967), Lockowandt (1966, 1968), Wallner (1971), Linster (1969), Prystav (1969), and Paul-Mengelberg (1971). This branch of research is still in flux, but several general statements can be made.

Factor analytic studies of graphometric variables have yielded many different factors that help reveal those aspects of handwriting that may be important for assessing ability and personality. Unfortunately, the task is not complete. Most writing variables occur in several factors, thereby obscuring the clear identification of independent factors. Furthermore, there is no unanimity as to the number of factors required for a complete description of handwriting. Prystav (1969, 282) concluded from his review that there are "about 10 principal factors which share importantly in coining the 'basic framework' of writing and above all in regard to movement; and around 15 specific factors, which contribute predominantly to the individual shaping of the writing picture." Although there are theories of handwriting psychology that postulate a small number of basic dimensions—or even a single basic dimension—they undoubtedly oversimplify what is actually a complex situation.

To date, factor analytic studies of handwriting have been successful in predicting the following criteria: (1) intelligence as measured by the Raven test, by the Intelligence-Structure Test of Amthauer, and by Wechsler's Full Scale Intelligence Quotient and Deterioration Index; (2) several kinds of psychomotor performance such as finger coordination, finger-hand speed, and arm movement; and (3) the psychic regulation mechanism derived from the Color Pyramid Test (Schaie and Heiss 1964), acheivement motivation, vital energy, and psychic balance. However, the vast amount of work done so far on factorial validation of handwriting is not in proportion to the still scanty results. An economical construction of future research is urgently needed.

CONTRAST GROUP PROCEDURES

The contrast group method of validation involves the selection of two groups that differ markedly from each other with respect to a particular characteristic. These groups are then tested to determine whether they can also be differentiated on the basis of the criterion variable. In handwriting psychology, these groups can be formed either on the basis of marked differences in handwriting characteristics or in personality characteristics. Both methods have been employed with varying degrees of success. The use of extremely different groups increases the likelihood that they will also differ on the criterion, but this approach has little practical application, because the extreme characteristics required for this method are not usually found in the situations in which handwriting psychology is customarily used.

Only Land (cited in Adolfs 1964) and Birge (1954) have used the contrast groups method to validate individual handwriting characteristics. Land constituted his groups on the basis of two handwriting characteristics, slant and alignment. From two hundred handwriting samples, he selected four groups of ten samples each, one with normal slant, one with extreme left slant, one with normal alignment, and one with extremely sloping alignment. The Pressey-X-O test, which identifies group differences in emotionality, served as the criterion. Land found that writers with extreme handwriting characteristics—i.e., left slant and down-sloping alignment— were more emotional than those with normal characteristics—a result in full accord with the interpretive hypotheses of handwriting psychology.

It is not clear, however, whether each of the two graphic signs chosen by Land, slant and alignment, is independently related to emotionality, or if they are the only or the most critical graphic signs associated with emotionality. Lockowandt (1966) has shown, for example, that slant is significantly correlated with the following writing characteristics: extent of upper loops ($r = -.41$), size of upper length ($r = -.38$), and distance of upper signs from the word body ($r = -.35$). Thus, the stronger emotionality reported by Land could also be attributed to the characteristics that are highly correlated with slant. It is better, therefore, to proceed not from individual graphic characteristics, but from writing factors which represent clusters of related graphic characteristics.

Birge (1954) chose the opposite route from Land and divided his research sample on the basis of personality characteristics. A total of 685 students ranked each other on five dimensions: intelligence, emotional stability, dominance, culture, and sensibility or high-strung temperament. From this sample of students, groups of twenty-four subjects were selected so that two subjects with the most extreme ratings for each dimension were to be found in each group. Thus in each group two were highly intelligent, two unintelligent, etc. Correlations of the differences among twenty-two handwriting variables for the groups judged most extreme yielded no significant relationships with the five ability and personality characteristics. It is likely, however, that this study was flawed by the use of personal judgments made by naive observers, which are known to be affected by such tendencies as the halo effect and the projection of the rater's own unconscious problems onto the person being rated.

The use of the contrast group method for validating specific handwriting characteristics has been neglected in handwriting psychology even though positive results can be obtained, as Land's experiment has demonstrated. The method would probably be more fruitful if groups were formed not on the basis of specific graphic signs, but on the basis of graphic dimensions of a higher degree of abstraction (factors). Thus, for example, contrasting groups might be formed on the basis of their Writing Expansion, a general factor which has been identified in several factor analyses and which has a generally agreed upon definition.

THE VALIDITY OF HANDWRITING INTERPRETATIONS

Contrast Group Methods. The contrast group method can also be used to study the validity of interpretations made from handwriting analyses. Much of this research had dealt with the writing of children.

The distinguished developmental theorist Gesell (1906) was the first to study the relationship between quality of handwriting and gender, school achievement, general intelligence, motor skills, and experimentally determined writing dexterity (n = 4361 schoolchildren). His results are noteworthy: (1) From the first grade on, boys showed a greater tendency than girls to uncoordinated writing. (2) From the fifth grade on, girls were more accurate than boys. (3) Sex differences manifested themselves clearly by the age of about ten and a half years. (4) The accuracy of handwriting in primary school children varied directly with school achievement. Among these primary schoolchildren, it was found that the inaccurate writer was also less accurate and less conscientious in the rest of his or her school performance. This author has used the Chi-square test to analyze Gesell's data and has found all the differences he reported to be statistically significant (Lockowandt 1970a, 310).

Oinonen (1961) divided 122 first and second graders into those with good and those with poor handwritings and found significant correlations between handwriting quality and intelligence (r = .38) and between handwriting quality and school performance (r = .60). The combined correlation of handwriting and intelligence with school performance was, predictably, even higher (r = .74 in the first grade and r = .70 in the second grade), indicating that school performance can be predicted with a high degree of accuracy by a combination of intelligence and handwriting assessment. Thus, both Gesell and Oinonen were able to demonstrate the partial validity of children's handwriting and to show that Klages's judgment regarding the "inferior handwriting form" (1927, 233) and the poverty of expression in children's handwriting was not justified.

Hueskins and Schuler (quoted in Lockowandt 1972) also tested the validity of children's handwriting using the contrast group method. Performance on the Pauli-Test served as the criterion for 295 children, age 10–12, and 299 children, age 13–16 years. The performance structure of the Pauli-Tests could be predicted with a high level of statistical significance for the younger group but not for the older group of children. The average biserial correlation coefficient for the younger group was r = .27 for boys (ranging from r = .13 to .48) and r = .44 for girls (ranging from r = .45 to .53). It is especially noteworthy that positive results could be obtained using a very specific criterion and unpracticed judges.

In contrast to these characteristic-centered studies were the group studies based on contrasting personality characteristics. Grunewald-Zuberbier (1966) used the type of contrast group procedure used by Birge (1954), in that she looked at differences in handwriting among three groups of children: children in institutions, children in correctional facilities, and normal children. She assumed that there would be substantial differences in personality among the three groups of children. One of her most important findings was a difference in the variability of writing characteristics (size, width, regularity, interval between words, and space between lines) between children in institutions and normal children. Institutionalized children who were behavior problems because of excessive impulsivity (Aggressions) showed greatly increased variability. Grunewald-Zuberbier interpreted the differences she found for the constructive writing components, Activity and Control, to mean that the children from institutions, unlike normal children, were characterized by increased Activity drive and decreased Control. She also found evidence against the dogmatic assertion of Klages (1927) that children's writings show poverty of expression.

It is difficult to find groups of adults who, because of highly unusual life histories, show clearly distinguishable personality structures. A very interesting research program involving extreme groups of people was conducted by Paul-Mengelberg (1965). She compared the qualitative and quantitative handwriting characteristics of two groups of disturbed adults with those of a normal control group. Group A consisted of persons who had returned home after long periods in Russian prisoner-of-war or labor camps; Group B consisted of politically oriented persons who had spent long periods underground or in concentration camps. Group A and B showed prominent symptoms of premature aging, which were manifested by a much higher biological age as compared to chronological age.

Paul-Mengelberg was able to differentiate the three groups on the basis of their handwriting characteristics. Groups A and B both showed a syndrome of strikingly disturbed handwriting characteristics, but Group A showed a more uniform graphic symptomatology than Group B. The author attributed the uniform symptomatology of Group A to the frequent occurrence of such disorders as organic brain damage from head injury or deterioration from the aftereffects of systemic disease like typhus. Group B was characterized by severely neurotic symptomatology, including anxiety and restlessness, fears of death, and irritability. In subsequent studies (1971a, 1972), Paul-Mengelberg added a group of compulsive personality types to her original research sample. Further analysis of the expanded sample confirmed the limited graphic performance possibilities of the brain-injured by contrast with the varied writing performance of the neurotic subjects, whose conflict structures were as varied as the circumstances underlying their neuroses.

Lockowandt (unpublished) used a contrast group procedure to compare the writing actions of children who were dyslexic with those of children who were not dyslexic. The children were asked to copy a text from the blackboard, while their writing movements and the movements of their heads were filmed. The first ninety seconds of the films were evaluated graphometrically, and significant differences were found between the two groups.

The value of handwriting psychology for the assessment of ability and personality gains further support from a very original study by Frederick (1968), carried out in collaboration with the Institute of Applied Psychology in Saltsjobaden, Sweden. Its goal was the identification of fifty-five male and female suicides from their handwriting. From the typed text of each suicide's writing specimen, three handwritten copies were prepared by control subjects. Five handwriting psychologists, five detectives, and five secretaries served as judges. Their task was to select from the four specimens presented the one that was in the suicide's own writing. All five handwriting psychologists showed highly significant percentages of successful choices, and the accuracy of their choices was clearly superior to that of the detectives and the secretaries.

The handwriting validity values obtained from comparison group studies are generally very high. Nevertheless, it must be acknowledged that the differentiation of comparison groups on the basis of handwriting interpretation is not always successful. For example, it has not been possible to discriminate psychotics from normals using handwriting psychology (Pascal and Suttell 1947, Frederick 1965). The reasons for this failure are not known, but the clinically variable ways in which psychosis is manifested makes it unsuitable as a validity criterion.

Content Validity. Early evidence for the validity of handwriting interpretation came predominantly from studies using matching procedures. In this case, handwriting psychologists would either judge the writing of persons unknown to the researchers (a procedure used by Binet 1906 and Bobertag 1929), or they would match their judgments against judgments based on clinical evaluations or the results of tests. In all these studies, global comparisons were made in accordance with the precepts of Allport and Vernon (1933): "If we are to attain the most adequate validation, the script as a whole and the personality as a whole must somehow be compared."

Eysenck reported (1961) that the interpretations of a handwriting psychologist were greater than chance performance matched with brief psychiatric descriptions. There are also well-known matching experiments of

Powers, a collaborator of Allport and Vernon, who obtained greater than chance agreement between personality judgments and handwriting interpretations. These studies were particularly welcome to traditional graphology because they supported the holistic character of graphological assessment. They have, however, been criticized by psychometrically oriented handwriting psychologists such as Fahrenberg (1961) and Prystav, because the nature of the matching process remains unclear.

Recognition of the weaknesses of holistic matching methods soon led to attempts to validate individual interpretive statements. We will pass over the early and well-known studies by Marum (1945), Eysenck (1948), and Castelnuovo-Tedesco (1948)—all of which yielded positive results, despite methodological flaws—and report some of the more recent work on the validity of handwriting psychology.

Hofsommer, Holdsworth, and Seifert (1962) investigated the accuracy with which two handwriting psychologists could predict success at a Swedish school of forestry. Fifty-four students were rated by two handwriting psychologists on a set of attributes that the authors assumed would determine success in this institution: emotional stability, vital energy, strong will power, and intellecutal versatility. The critical validation criterion was the average school report record for twenty-three subjects after one and a half years of training. The results are surprising and demonstrate that prognosis by handwriting can be very accurate. Validity coefficients for the two judges combined ranged from rho = .17 to rho = .78 (average rho = .55), and almost all of them were statistically significant. These results are particularly important because they successfully replicate the most positive early validation study by Castelnuovo-Tedesco (1948).

Hofsommer and Holdsworth (1963) reported equally favorable results from a study in which a handwriting psychologist attempted to predict from the handwritten autobiographies of 141 candidates their degree of pilot aptitude after a year and a half of basic training. The authors hypothesized that the following personality characteristics were important: ability of tolerate psychic stress, method of working, and social adaptability. At the end of the training period, the judgments of the handwriting psychologists were correlated with the dichotomous criteria "suitable for further training" or "not suitable for further training." As demonstrated by the significant biserial correlation coefficient (r = .36), the handwriting psychologists could predict the general vocational suitability of pilots with a considerable degree of confidence. They could also predict achievement in advanced training for the sixty-one candidates who had been selected for the basic course (rhotau = .41). They could not predict the training results for the twenty-four aspirants in the final stage of training, but this result is not surprising in view of the homogeneity of the group. It is astonishing that so specific a characteristic as qualification for fighter pilot could be predicted by handwriting, especially because it had not previously been known that it was determined by psychological motivation.

Relationships between single personality factors and handwriting variables have been confirmed and expanded in a series of studies reported by Wallner (1963a, 1963b, 1965). He was able to show that many psychic attributes such as temperament, distractibility, need for recognition, verbal ability, logical reasoning, ability to achieve, motivation to achieve, and intelligence could be evaluated reliably by handwriting psychology. In his studies of intelligence, Wallner achieved a triple replication of the same results with different research samples, thus demonstrating that intelligence can be reliably assessed by handwriting analysis.

It should be noted that Wallner applied rigorous standards of test construction in his experiments. He devised and standardized scales for such attributes as speed of movement, contactability, and need for recognition. He also repeated some of his experiments with different samples of subjects, following the warning by Mosier et al (1951) that validity coefficients decrease when the same tests are applied to different groups of individuals.

On the whole, the rigorous tests of content validity have demonstrated the validity of handwriting analysis. Unfortunately, however, the validity coefficients from all the studies reviewed are relatively low. The reason does not lie in the low validity of handwriting psychology but in the lack of semantic congruence between the evaluations of writing and psychological criteria.

Construct Validity. The concept of construct validity, which seems to hold out great promise for handwriting psychology, derives from Cronbach and Meehl (1955). It is not a fundamentally new method of validation but a structured combination of a number of validation methods that have in common one theoretical assumption: one proceeds not from a specific test or writing behavior to a behavior criterion, but from behaviors to attributes, psychic structures, dispositions, dimensions—from the observable to the non-observable. In other words, given an observable behavior, what are the attributes or internal psychological structures of the individual that are likely to mediate or produce that behavior?

These attributes and structures have been called constructs. No assumptions are made as to the nature of constructs except that they are not open to direct observation. They are, however, necessary for explaining the uniformity of a person's behavior.

The theoretical development of a construct requires a well-grounded theory from which several hypotheses are derived. Different behavioral characteristics are then interpreted on the basis of these hypotheses. The process of construct validity is thus a continual process of modification of the underlying theoretical system and reinterpretation of empirical findings in the light of modified constructs.

Traditional graphology, the oldest graphological diagnostic method, offers an abundance of interpretative propositions, which are derived from specific theories and which can be considered as empirically testable hypotheses. They are, however, not easily understood. For research purposes, it is important that these hypotheses be formulated as narrowly, clearly, and unequivocally as possible.

Fervers's (1948) noteworthy study of construct validity is illustrative. Twenty research subjects were injected intravenously with Eunarcon to produce sleep. Afterward, they were required to empathize in their handwriting with different groups of people—laborers, maidservants, monks, nuns, kings, and queens. The handwritings produced from the "inner person" in this way showed the typical forms and characteristics of the person with whom the writer empathized. The basic structure of the writer's script was preserved, but with an overlay of the collective features of the imagined group. The writing samples produced as if the writer were farmer were full of energy, powerful but clumsy and unrefined; the writing produced as if the writer were the monk was weak, delicate, intellectual, precise, and refined.

Fervers's study stimulated further investigation of pharmacologic effects on the motor aspect of writing. These later experiments made precise and specific predictions about the alterations in handwriting to be expected after induction of a drug with known psychological effects. They also used better quantitative methods. Grunewald (1967) carried out an exacting study of the effects of the central nervous system stimulant Peripherin and the depressant Evipann, and he described the resulting disturbances of coordinated movement. His descriptions of the changes that occur in writing after electric shock (for example, the loss of writing coordination) are especially impressive. There have also been informative studies of the effects of alcohol, such as those by Rabin and Blair (1953), Detrey (1954), Tripp, Fluckiger, and Weinberg (1959), and Gerchow and Wittlich (1960). All of these studies document the progressive deterioration of graphomotor performance with alcohol, the expansion of the writing motoric, and the decreasing precision of form.

There have been numerous handwriting studies of monozygotic and dizygotic twins. The results of work by von Bracken (1939a, 1939b), Wanscher (1943), Goldzieher-Roman (1945), Norinder (1946), and Ostlyngen (n.d.), to name only the most important thematic studies, have been contradictory. Collectively, they come to the paradoxical and surprising conclusion that monozygotic twins differ more in their handwriting behavior than do dizygotic twins. Several explanations of this phenomenon have been offered. Von Bracken proposed a sociopsychological explanation, that is, that mono-zygotic twins tend to cultivate asymmetrical social behavior; whereas Gold-zieher-Roman proposed a genetic explanation, that is, that monozygotic twins are opposite in handedness.

There have also been several studies aimed at delineating developmental changes in handwriting. Longitudinal studies by Kircher (1926), Gold-zieher-Roman (1936), Legrun (1929), and Ajuriaguerra (1964) have described evolution of the functional structure of the writing of hyperkenetics from insufficient movement control to sureness and restraint. A complete genetic validation of handwriting is, however, yet to be done (see Lockowandt 1970a for a critical overview of genetic studies).

Construct validation of handwriting has also been attempted using the theories of constitutional psychology, which posits that different personality types or attributes are associated with different body types. Steinwachs (1952) used the triadic schema of Kretschmer (1943), and Pascal (1943) used the somatotype system of Sheldon. They found not only quantitative but also structural typological differences in handwriting as a function of body type, but most of the differences were confined to measures of speed and pressure.

A number of criticisms can be leveled at much of the research on the construct validity of handwriting: that only elementary graphometric variables were used; that an oversimplified functional model of the brain physiology of writing was used as the basis for the mechanisms of activation and control; and that the writing was produced under exceptional conditions. On the other hand, the experimental precision with which these studies were conducted is impressive.

SUMMARY

The reliability of handwriting is well established for simple measured and ranked characteristics. The results of most studies have yielded values that are typical for psychological test procedures. The results are more variable for complex writing characteristics; some are adequate, some inadequate. With more rigorous attempts to specify the multidimensionality of these characteristics, higher reliability coefficients are to be expected.

The reliability of graphological interpretations is surprisingly high (Prys-tav 1969, 1971a, 1971b), indicating that handwriting psychologists have gone beyond a restricted evaluation yardstick to a unified cognitive schema of interpretation. Thematic studies have shown that an extensive analysis of the interpretation process is indispensable.

The results of validity studies correlating individual characteristics with criteria are predominantly negative, but validation studies using multiple correlation have yielded more positive results. Factor analytic research has been productive, but not uniformly so.

Contrast group studies of specific writing characteristics have led to inconclusive or conflicting results. They have been more successful at validating interpretations of handwriting. Especially noteworthy are the studies on children's handwriting (Lockowandt 1970a), on groups who had experienced extreme conditions (Paul-Mengelberg 1965), and on suicides (Frederick 1968). Accordingly, handwriting must be regarded as an efficient diagnostic instrument.

Most content validity studies have yielded positive correlations with criteria (see particularly the work of Wallner 1961–1971 and of Hofsommer, Holdsworth, and Seifert 1962, 1965). Many psychic dimensions can be diagnosed with confidence using prevailing research techniques and conditions. The unimpressive size of the coefficients can be attributed to the lack of semantic congruence between graphological and psychological judgments. Lockowandt's (1969c) critical overview of construct validity research shows that handwriting has proved itself valid in many respects and that the shortcomings found can probably be remedied.

This review indicates that the results of reliability and validity studies in handwriting psychology are not uniformly positive. There are two possible explanations for the negative findings reported. First, some authors lack sufficient knowledge of the relationships and conditions of handwriting psychology and, therefore, are misled by inadequate and unsuitable experimental procedures. They ignore the recent scientific reorganization of handwriting psychology, and they continue to attack the discipline as it existed in the early stages of its development. They continue to engage in "validation research" such as the handwriting games of Hull and Montgomery (1919), which can assume unfair importance in places such as America where the climate is already hostile toward handwriting psychology. Future researchers will avoid these fallacies if they acquire a thorough grounding in the history, methods, and practical efficiency of handwriting psychology before launching their investigations—a prerequisite for validation studies in any area of psychology.

Second, many validity studies have failed to separate the effects of the handwriting system used from the personality of the handwriting psychologist using the system. Until this is done, one cannot determine whether negative results reflect the failure of the graphological instrument or of the handwriting psychologist. It is necessary, therefore, to understand the psychologist's methods of working, the source of impression qualities, and the complicated process of interpretation. We still do not know the role played by his kinesthetic experience, his adherence to specific forms of impression, his practical experience, and his constant errors of judgment.

Despite the problems that remain to be solved, it is clear that there is no justification for the view that the findings of handwriting psychology are the result of chance or mere accident. The research reviewed demonstrates that there are orderly, lawful relationships between handwriting and personality, aptitudes, and behavior. There is no doubt that the methodology of handwriting psychology can be expanded and refined, and it is hoped that this review will help stimulate such efforts.

REFERENCES

Adolfs, K. 1964. "Faktorenanalytische Untersuchung der gebrauchlichsten Handschriftvariablen." Dissertation, University of Freiburg.

Ajuriaguerra, J. de, und A. Denner. 1964. L'ecriture de l'enfant. Neuchatel.

Allport, G., and P. Vernon. 1933. Studies in Expressive Movement. New York, Macmillan.

Angermann, Ch. 1970. "Messen und Deuten." Zeitschr. f. Menschenkunde 34: pp. 262–279.

Babst, E. 1971. "Zur Objektivität und Reliabilität der Handschrift-Beschreibung mittels Eindruckscharakteristiken." Thesis, University of Berlin.

Binet, A. 1906. Les revelations d'ecritures d'apres un controle scientifique. Paris.

Birge, W. R. 1954. "An Experimental Inquiry into the Measurable Handwriting Correlates of Five Personality Traits." J. of Personality 23: pp. 215–223.

Bobertag, O. 1929. Ist die Graphologie Zuverlässig? Heidelberg.

Bracken, H. v. 1934. "Die Konstanz der Handschriftenart bei Kindern der ersten Schuljahre." Nederlandsch Tijdschrift voor Psychologie 1: pp. 541–554.

———. 1939a. "Untersuchungen an Zwillingen über die quantitativen und qualitativen Merkmale des Schreibdrucks." Zeitschr. angew. Psychol. 58: pp. 367–384.

———. 1939b. "Das Schreibtempo von Zwillingen und die sozialpsychologischen Fehlerquellen der Zwillingsforschung." Z. f. menschl. Vererbungs- u. Konstitutionslehre: p. 58.

Broeren, W. 1964. "Über die Zuverlässigkeit der Beschreibung von Sprechstimme und Handschrift." Thesis, University of Heidelberg.

Castelnuovo-Tedesco, P. 1948. "A Study of the Relationship between Handwriting and Personality Variables." Genetic Psychol. Monographs 37: 167–220.

Cohen, R. 1969. Systematische Tendenzen bei Persönlichkeitsbeurteilungen. Bern und Stuttgart.

Conrad, W. 1964. "Untersuchung über die Faktorenstruktur der Handschrift." Thesis, University of Freiburg.

Crider, B. 1941. "The Reliability and Validity of Two Graphologists." J. Appl. Psych. 25: pp. 323–325.

Cronbach, L. J., and P. E. Meehl. 1955. "Construct Validity in Psychological Tests." Psychol. Bull. 52: pp. 281–302.

Daul, H. 1966. "Das Deuten in der Graphologie. Eine methodologische Untersuchung der Struktur und Prinzipien graphologisch-diagnostischer Interpretation." PhD Dissertation, University of Heidelberg.

Detrey, M. 1954. "Handschriftveränderungen unter Alkoholeinfluss." *Ausdruckskunde* 1: pp. 9–12.

Eysenck, H. J. 1948. "Neuroticism and handwriting." *J. of Abnormal and Social Psychology* 43.

———. 1961. *Dimensions of Personality*. London, pp. 5ff.

Fahrenberg, J. 1961. "Graphometrie." PhD Dissertation, University of Freiburg.

Fahrenberg, J., und W. Conrad. 1964. "Eine explorative Faktorenanalyse graphometrischer und psychometrischer Daten." *Zeitschr. exp. angew. Psychol.* 12: pp. 223–238.

Fervers, C. 1948. "Experimentelle Untersuchungen der Schrift nach Einführung mit Eunarcon intravenos." *Grenzgeb. der Medizin* 1: pp. 89–93.

Fischer, G. 1962. "Die faktorielle Struktur der Handschrift." PhD Dissertation, University of Vienna.

———. 1964. "Zur faktoriellen Struktur der Handschrift." *Zeitschr. exp. angew. Psychol.* 11: pp. 254–280.

Frederick, C. J. 1965. "Some phenomena affecting handwriting analysis." *Percept. and Motor Skills* 20: pp. 211–218.

———. 1968. "An Investigation of Handwriting of Suicide Patients through Suicide Notes." *Journal of Abnormal Psychology* 73: pp. 263–267.

Gerchow, J., und B. Wittlich. 1960. "Experimentelle und statistische Untersuchungen über alkoholbedingte Persönlichkeitsveränderungen in der postresorptiven Phase." *Bund für alkoholfreien Verkehr e. V.*

Gesell, A. L. 1906. "Accuracy in Handwriting as Related to School Intelligence and Sex." *Am J. Psychol.* 17: pp. 394–405.

Goldzieher-Roman, K. 1936. "Studies on the Variability of Handwriting: The Development of Writing Speed and Point Pressure in School Children." *J. of Genetic Psychol.* 49.

———. 1945. "Untersuchungen der Schrift und des Schreibens von 283 Zwillingspaaren." *Schweiz. Z. f. Psychol. und ihre Anwendung* 6.

Graumann, C.-F. 1960. "Eigenschaften als Problem der Persönlichkeitsforschung." In *Persönlichkeitsforschung und Persönlichkeitstheorie,* Lersch, Ph., und H. Thomae. Göttingen.

Groffman, K. J., and J. Fahrenberg. 1960. "Experimentelle Untersuchungen zum Problem der Schreibgeschwindigkeit." *Psychol. Forschg.* 26: pp. 114–156.

Grünewald-Zuberbier, E. 1967. "Aktivierung und Kontrolle bei verhaltensschwierigen Kindern im Bereich der Graphomotorikm." *Psychol. Beitrage* 9: pp. 503–524.

Grünewald, G. 1966. *Dynamik und Steuerung der Schreibmotorik*. Köln and Opladen.

Gubser, F. 1972. "Inwieweit sind 'Führungseigenschaften' graphologisch fassbar?" *Industrielle Organisation* 4: pp. 147–154.

Harvey, O. L. 1934. "The Measurement of Handwriting Considered As a Form of Expressive Movement." *Char. and Pers.* 2.

Heer, G. M. 1970. "Schulerfolg im Spiegel der Handscrift." Thesis, University of Zurich.

Hofsommer, W., and R. Holdsworth. 1963. "Die Validität der Handschriftenanalyse bei der Auswahl von Piloten." *Psychol. u. Praxis* 7: pp. 175–178.

Hofsommer, W., R. Holdsworth, and T. Siebert. 1962. "Zur Bewahrungskontrolle graphologischer Diagnosen." *Psychol. Beitrage* 7: pp. 397–401.

————. 1965. "Reliabilitätsfragen in der Graphologie." *Psychol. u. Praxis* 9: pp. 14–24.

Hull, C. L., and R. P. Montgomery. 1919. "Experimental Investigation of Certain Alleged Relations between Character and Handwriting." *Psychol. Rev.* 26.

Kircher, R. 1926. "Experimentelle Untersuchung der Entwicklung des Schreibens während der Volksschulzeit, besonders im ersten Schuljahr." *Arch. f. d. gesamte Psychol.* 54: pp. 313–354.

Kirchhoff, R. 1962. "Das Verhältnis von Graphologie und Ausdruckskunde." *Zeitschr. f. Menschenkunde* 26: pp. 320–337.

————. 1962. "Methodologische und theoretische Grundprobleme der Ausdruckskunde." *Stud. Gen.*

————, ed. 1965. *Ausdruckspsychologie.* Band 5 des *Handbuchs der Psychologie.* Göttingen.

————. 1968. Ausdruck: "Begriff, Regionen und Binnenstruktur." *Jahrbuch für Psychologie und Psychotherapie.*

Klages, L. 1927. *Zur Ausdruckslehre und Charakterkunde.* Heidelberg.

Konttinen, R. 1968. *Relationships Between Graphic Expansivity and Extraversion as a Function of Anxiety and Defensiveness.* Helsinki.

Legrun, A. 1929. *Die Schreibgeläufigkeit der Schulkinder.* Wien-Leipzig.

Lienert, G. A. 1969. *Testaufbau und Testanalyse.* Weinheim, privately circulated.

Linster, H. W. 1969. *Eine Validitätsuntersuchung graphometrischer Variablen.* Zul.-Arbeit: Freiburg i. Brg.

Lockowandt, O. 1961. *Reliabilitätskontrolle und Validitätsuntersuchung zum Problem der Schreibgeschwindigkeit.* Freiburg i. Brg., unveröffentl.

————. 1966. "Faktorenanalytische Validierung der Handschrift mit besonderer Berücksichtigung projektiver Methoden." PhD Dissertation, University of Freiburg.

————. 1968. "Faktorenanalytische Validierung der Handschrift mit besonderer Berücksichtigung projektiver Method." *Zeitschr. exp. angew. Ps.* 15: pp. 487–530.

————. 1968. "Quantitative Uberprüfungsmethoden in der Graphologie." *Zeitschr. f. Menschenkunde* 32: pp. 232–253.

————. 1969. "Über das Konzept einer konstruktiven Validierung der Handschrift." Part I. *Zeitschr. f. Menschenkunde* 32 (1968): pp. 426–437; Part II. *Ebendort* 33 (1969): pp. 57–83.

————. 1970a. "Die Kinderhandschrift—ihre diagnostischen Möglichkeiten und Grenzen." *Zeitschr. f. Menschenkunde* 34: pp. 301–326.

————. 1970b. "Le probleme de la garantie dans la psychologie de l'ecriture." *La Graphologie* 119: pp. 21–41.

————. 1972. "Empirische Untersuchungen zur Validität der Kinderhandschrift."

Zeitschr. f. Menschenkunde 36: pp. 293–311.

———. 1973. "Der Prozess der Urteilsbildung in der Schrift-psychologie." *Zeitschr. f. Menschenkunde* 37 (1973): pp. 135–154.

Lockowandt, O., and C.-H. Keller. 1975. "Beitrag zur Stabilität der Kinderhandschrift." *Psychol. Beitrage* 17: pp. 273–282.

Lorr, M., L. T Lepine, and J. V. Golder. 1954. "A Factor Analysis of Some Handwriting Characteristics." *J. Pers.* 22: pp. 348–353.

Marum, O. 1945. "Character Assessments from Handwriting." *J. Ment. Sci.* 91: pp. 22–42.

Michel, L., and A. Iseler. 1968. "Beziehungen zwischen klinischen und psychometrischen Methoden der diagnostischen Urteilsbildung." In *Person als Prozess.* Festschrift zum 65. Geburtstag von Prof. Dr. Phil. Robert Heiss, herausgegeben von K. J. Groffmann und K. H. Wewetzer. Bern und Stuttgart.

Mosier, Ch. I., E. E. Cureton, R. A. Katzel, and R. J. Wherry. 1951. Symposium: "The Need and the Means of Cross-Validation." *Educ. Psychol. Measmt.* 11 (5).

Muller, W. H. 1957. "Über die Objektivität von Anmutungsqualitäten in der Handschrift." *Psychol. Beitrage* 3: pp. 364–389.

Muller, W. H., and A. Enskat. 1961. *Graphologischen Diagnostik.* Bern und Stuttgart.

———. 1965. *Grundzüge der Graphologie.* In *Ausdruckspsychologie,* edited by R. Kirchoff, Göttingen.

Muller, W. H., and H. P. Mattes. 1966a. "Die Grundhypothesen graphologischer Diagnostik und der gegenwärtige Stand ihrer empirischen Überprufung." *Acta Graphologica* 17.

———. 1966b. "Zur Objektivierung der Schriftbeschreibung." *Zeitschr. f. Menschenkunde* 4: pp. 361–379.

Norinder, Y. 1946. "Twin Differences in Writing Performance: A Study of Heredity and School Training." Lund.

Oinonen, P. 1961. "Poor Handwriting as a Psychological Problem." *Acta academiae paedagogicae Jyvaskylamisis.* Jyvaskyla, 21.

Ostlyngen, E. n.d.. *Über erbliche und umweltliche Bedingungen.*

Pascal, G. R. 1943. "Handwriting Pressure: Its Measurement and Significance." *Character and Personality* 11: pp. 235–254.

Pascal, G. R. and B. Suttell. 1947. "Testing the Claims of a Graphologist." *J. Personality* 16: pp. 192–197.

Paul-Mengelberg, M. 1965. "Die Symptome der Veralterung in der Handschrift." *Zeitschr. f. Menschenkunde* 29: pp. 3–27.

———. 1971a. "Beziehungen zwischen dem Abbau-Quotieten im Hawie und der Intelligenz-Baurteilung auf Grund der Handschrift." *Zeitschr. f. Gerontologie* 4: pp. 208–216.

———. 1971b. "Schreibmotorische Störungen bei ehemaligen Kriegsgefangenen und Verfolgten." In *Spätschaden nach Gefangenschaft und Verfolgung,* edited by H. J. Herberg. Herford.

———. 1972. *Die Handschrift von ehemaligen Kriegsgefangenen und politische Verfolgten.* Bonn.

Prystav, G. 1969. "Beitrag zur faktorenanalytischen Validierung der Handschrift." Dissertation, University of Freiburg.

——. 1971a. "Reliabilität graphometrischer Schriftebeschreibung (Part I: Merkmalsebene)." *Zeitschr. f. Menschenkunde* 35: pp. 70–94.

——. 1971b. "Reliabilität graphologischer Beurteilungen. (Part II: Interpretationsebene)". *Zeitschr. f. Menschenkunde* 35: pp. 95–110.

Rabin, A., and H. Blair. 1953. "The Effects of Alcohol on Handwriting." *J. Clin. Psychol.* 9: pp. 284–287.

Reichold, L. 1969. "Die Reliabilität und Validität graphologischer Aussagen. *Zeitschr. f. Menschenkunde* 33: pp. 198–210.

Saunders, D. R. 1956. "Moderator Variables in Prediction." *Educ. Psychol. Measmt.* 16: pp. 209–222.

Schaie, K. W., and R. Heiss. 1964. *Color and Personality.* Bern and Stuttgart.

Schneevoigt, I. 1968. *Graphologische Intelligenzdiagnose.* Bonn.

Secord, P. F. 1948. "Studies of the Relationships of Handwriting to Personality." *J. Pers.* 17: pp. 430–448.

Seifert, T. 1965. "Faktorenanalyse einiger Schriftmerkmale." *Z. exp. angew. Psychol.* 11: pp. 645–666.

Stein Lewinson, Th. 1956. "Graphische Darstellung der Handschriftlichen Dynamik." *Ausdruckskunde* 3: pp. 145–180.

——. 1964. "Die dynamische Kurve und der Leistungsquotient." *Graphol. Schriftenreihe* 6.

——. 1967. "Klages in Zeitalter der Psychometrie." *Zeitschr. F. Menschenkunde* 31: pp. 1–33.

——. 1968. "Entwicklung mit Hilfe des Elektronenrechners." *Zeitschr. f. Menschenkunde* 32: pp. 393–413.

Stein Lewinson, Th., and J. Zubin. 1942. *Handwriting Analysis.* New York.

Steinwachs, F. 1952. "Konstitutionstypische Grundkurven der Handschrift und ihre pathologischen Veränderungen." *Z. Psychoth.* 2.

Sulzer, F. 1949. *Angst, Verdrängung, Hemmung und Unlust im Schriftausdruck.* Leiden.

Timm, U. 1965. "Graphometrie als psychologischer Test?" Dissertation, University of Freiburg.

Timm, U. 1967. "Graphometrie als psychologischer Test?" *Psychol. Forschg.* 30: pp. 307–356.

Torgerson, W. S. 1958. Theory and Methods of Scaling. New York.

Tripp, C. A., F. A. Fluckiger, and G. H. Weinberg. 1959. "Effects of Alcohol on the Graphomotor Performances of Normals and Chronic Alcoholics." *Percept. Mot. Skills* 9: pp. 227–236.

Unkel, H. 1964. "Eine Faktorenanalysis graphometrischer und psychometrischer Daten." Working paper, University of Freiburg.

Volz, D. 1969. "Zur Objektivität und Reliabilität graphologischer Beurteilungen." Working paper, University of Freiburg.

Wallner, T. 1961a. "Bemerkungen zu W. H. Muller's 'Untersuchungen über die Objektivität von Anmutungsqualitäten in der Handschrift.' " *Psychol. Beiträge*

5: pp. 585–596.

————. 1961b. "Experimentelle Untersuchungen über die Reliabilität direkt metrische messbarer Handschriftvariablen." *Zeitschr. f. Menschenkunde* 25: pp. 49–78.

————. 1961c. "Reliabilitätsuntersuchungen an metrisch nicht messbaren Handschrifvariablen." *Zeitschr. f. Menschenkunde* 25: pp. 1–14.

————. 1961d. "Undersokningar av tillfortitligheten i bedomningar baserade pa grafologiska metoder." Thesis, University of Stockholm.

————. 1961e. "Über Zusammenhänge zwischen Merkmalen der Handschrift." *Zeitschr. f. Menschenkunde* 25: pp. 113–121.

————. 1962. "Neue Ergebnisse experimenteller Untersuchungen über die Reliabilität von Handschriftvariablen." *Zeitschr. f. Menschenkunde* 26: pp. 257–269.

————. 1963. "Konstruktion und Reliabilität von geeichten numerisch-beschreibenden Skalen." *Diagnostica* 9: pp. 139–155.

————. 1963. "Über die Validität graphologischer Aussagen." *Diagnostica* 9: pp. 26–35.

————. 1965. "Graphologie als Objekt statistischer Untersuchungen." *Psychol. Rdsch.* 16: pp. 282–298.

————. 1966. "Zusammenhänge zwischen Prognosedaten, Handschriftenvariablen und Ausbildungsergebnissen." *Zeitschr. f. Menschenkunde* 30: pp. 380–387.

————. 1967. "Orientering i skriftpsykologins teori och forskningsresultat." *Nordisk psykologi* 19: pp. 162–173.

————. 1968. "Zusammenhänge zwischen graphischen Variablen und Persönlichkeitsbeurteilungen." *Zeitschr. f. Menschenkunde* 32: pp. 438–445.

————. 1969. "Die Reliabilität schriftpsychologischer Begutachtungen." *Zeitschr. f. Menschenkunde* 33: pp. 191–197.

————. 1970. "Der prognostische Wert von Tests und Handschriftenvariablen bei Eignungsuntersuchungen." *Zeitschr. exp. ang. Psychol.* 17: pp. 316–356.

————. 1970. "Planung und Durchführung von schriftpsychologischen Untersuchungen." *Zeitschr. f. Menschenkunde* 34: pp. 280–300.

————. 1971. "Der Unterschied zwischen Schriftpsychologie und Graphologie." *Psychol. u. Praxis* 15: pp. 1–8.

Wanscher, J. H. 1943. "The Hereditary Background of Handwriting: An Investigation of Mono- and Dizygotic Twins." *Acta Psychiat. Kbh.* 18: pp. 349–375.

Wolfson, R. 1949. "A Study in Handwriting Analysis." Ph.D. thesis, Columbia University.

Wollenweber, H. 1961. "Experimentelle Untersuchungen zur Frage der Abhängigkeit der Feder- und Leistungsgeschwindigkeit von der Schriftgrosse." Working paper, University of Freiburg.

6

The Problem of the Validation of Graphological Judgments

Oscar Lockowandt

The following chapter was originally presented at the First British Symposium on Graphological Research, held in Oxford, UK, in August, 1987. An abridgment was published in *The Graphologist,* the journal of the British Institute of Graphologists in the Summer 1988 issue (Lockowandt 1988). It was originally written by Dr. Lockowandt in German, then translated into English by Brenda James and Natalie Marby. This version relies on both the original translation of the talk and the published paper, and the editors have made some slight changes to the translation.

Lockowandt candidly admits to graphologists that in the studies he and his colleagues have conducted the validity coefficients are too low to demonstrate graphologists' abilities to predict intelligence quotients: "Here we see that graphologists, using handwriting as a basis, are clearly not capable of diagnosing the intelligence quotients (or standard values) which result from the various kinds of intelligence tests in use" (p. 92). Thus, on this point Lockowandt finds himself in agreement with the skeptics in this volume, as well as being somewhat less optimistic than he was in 1976 when he published the original version of chapter 5. However, he parts company with skeptics over what conclusions should be drawn from this.

Lockowandt offers three reasons for graphologists' failure: First of all, he maintains that graphologists mean something different by "intelligence" than what has been traditionally meant by psychologists who devised the intelligence tests that were used as the criterion in his and his colleagues' experiments. On this matter he will find a fair bit of support from psychologists, who will readily agree that ordinary language notions of intelligence are not the same as those presupposed by standard intelligence tests. To deal with this problem, Lockowandt introduces the notion of the "graphological concept of intelligence," which he equates with the German word *Bildung*. However, note that he offers no evidence in this paper that graphologists can reliably or validly measure this attribute either.

Second, he wonders whether the differentiations in intelligence measured on standard IQ tests really are measuring anything significant in the sense of our determinations of intelligence in real life. While this is an issue about which all competent psychologists are acutely aware, we shouldn't allow this *tu quoque* response to obscure the point that graphology does not allow us to make the fine discriminations about intelligence that cannot be made by standard IQ tests. If Lockowandt is right in maintaining that these differences are not worth making, the question then arises why we need to pay anyone to discern what common sense tells us about for free—and this point would apply to graphology no less than to other tests.

Third, on page 96 he suggests that graphologists may be measuring something that is independent of that which is measured by standard personality tests. Hence it would be no surprise that the validity of graphological judgments appears quite low. This is possible, but Lockowandt fails to mention a consequence of his speculation that could be tested: If these traits really were being accurately measured by graphologists, we would expect to find a fair degree of inter-rater *reliability* amongst graphologists, even though we do not find a high *validity*. (See Bowman, chapter 10 for the distinction between these.) But we do not find this.

Lockowandt distinguishes between three models of testing for validity of graphological assessments. Model 1a compares *graphological characteristics* of the writing sample being analyzed (e.g., the relative heights of capital and lower case letters) with the *criterion* (e.g., the results of a standard IQ test). It thus serves to answer the question whether there is a correlation, say, between making large capital letters and intelligence. Model 1b attempts to compare *graphological judgments* (i.e., the *judgment of the graphologist* that the *subject who produced the handwriting* is intelligent), which will (in some way, depending on the particular theory held by the graphologist) be determined by the graphologist's assessments of the graphological characteristics and the criterion. Lockowandt admits that the studies he cites in the following paper, whether following model 1a or 1b, simply demonstrate low-validity coefficients.

Lockowandt proposes a third sort of testing, which he calls *processual validation.* The basic idea is one with which Bowman (chapter 10) agrees: most ordinary language personality terms are vague, ambiguous, or otherwise unclear. So, when the graphologist produces his *judgment,* Lockowandt maintains that the reason it is not accepted may be because of this indeterminacy in meaning, and not the graphologist's inability to discern personality traits. So, the point of processual validation is essentially to clear up this indeterminacy by having the person who disagrees discuss the matter with the graphologist, until they can agree upon common meanings. Lockowandt suggests that it will often be discovered that the two parties do not disagree after all; they had just been involved in a terminological misunderstanding; and once this is resolved, they will all agree that the graphological judgment really did fit the client all along. The obvious rejoinder to this proposal is that it calls into question the standard scientific method for determining validity of tests, as outlined in chapter 8 and by Klimoski in chapter 11. Those who are familiar with the debate about psychic mediums or channelers will see a parallel: the alternate explanation for their seeming accuracy is the subjective validation effect (see chapter 13). Unless this hypothesis can be ruled out, we do not have good evidence for the validity of the technique.

Second, it appears Lockowandt has simply conflated a scientific test of graphology with the usual operation of graphologists in personnel situations: note the example that Lockowandt uses, p. 100, which is not of an experimental situation testing graphology, but an *application* of graphology. Evidence that graphology "works" that is derived from this type of "case study" approach might be valuable if graphology had already been validated in a proper scientific test; but it cannot serve as a *replacement* for such a test. See Dean et al. in chapter 13 for a discussion of the worth of anecdotal evidence.

Lockowandt's processual validation also creates problems with practical applications of graphology in personnel selection. Compare Klimoski's requirement, described in chapter 11, that a personnel psychologist must compile a job description and worker requirements *before* beginning to assess candidates for a job. The personnel psychologist should try to eliminate, from the very beginning, the sorts of ambiguity and vagueness Lockowandt discusses, and not to try to resolve them *after* the candidates are recommended for the job.

Also worthy of note is Lockowandt's discussion of the experiment he carried out, reported on pp. 90–91. He reports that he examined 690 possible correlations out of over 7,000, and found 46 of these variables to be correlated with IQ scores. Instead of beginning with a prediction, as described in chapter 8, Lockowandt was just looking for correlations in a large volume of data. If one goes on "fishing expeditions" when analyzing data, it will be no surprise that one will find positive correlations aplenty if one keeps searching long enough. In this case, Lockowandt found positive correlations between his graphological measurements and intelligence test scores 8 percent of the time.

Lockowandt realizes what the problem is here: ". . . so that even if some of the correlations should be purely by chance, the obvious correlations—about 8 percent of the total—remain significant" (p. 91). The reader should draw his or her own conclusions about whether the fact that there are some significant positive correlations out of this large sample really matters. *Some* correlations are bound to be positive by chance alone: perhaps *these* are the ones. What is required is an independent replication of this study; but Lockowandt reports no such studies that find these correlations repeated.

Last, on p. 89, Lockowandt points out that there has been no "clear, comprehensible and irrefutable" refutation of graphology. Some readers may quibble at this, depending on their definition of "clear, comprehensible and irrefutable." For example, it is arguable that the study by Karnes and Leonard in chapter 16 meets this standard, as does Klimoski's two studies done with Rafaeli, reported in chapter 11, and Dean (chapter 12) cites a number of studies that are possible candidates. However, the main point is that it is not up to the critics to offer studies refuting graphology; the onus of proof rests on the defenders of it. And Lockowandt is not prepared to state of any experiment that he discusses in this chapter or his chapter 5 that it offers "clear, comprehensive and irrefutable" evidence in favor of graphology either.

STANDARD MODELS OF VALIDATION

THE NEED FOR VALIDATION

Academic recognition of handwriting analysis has once again become problematical. Some believe that the validity of graphology must first be proved before it can gain access to the hallowed halls of the university. This view, which is shared by many of my colleagues, is not only wrong, but also short-sighted. Up to now there has never been a clear, comprehensible, and unimpeachable refutation of the claims of handwriting analysis. Daring assumptions of the past are being revived in order to discredit graphology for good. One of them is Guilford's (1964, 271ff) absurd explanation that differences in handwriting are due to the anatomy of the hand. This view was offered earlier by Carus (1938, 325–326) and later by Pawlik et al. (1973). But these criticisms are wide of the mark, and they obscure the most important reason for including graphology in the university.

If graphology is to be studied scientifically, it must be studied in the university. This point becomes especially important when we realize that, outside the university, graphology has been called upon to judge the abilities of individuals, and these graphological judgments have been used to determine status of individuals in many important ways. The social acceptance and, widespread use of graphology in nonacademic spheres make it necessary to raise it to a scientific subject. Both unquestioning acceptance of graphology's powers and outright rejection of graphology on the basis of untenable arguments are founded on irrational attitudes. What is needed is a *critical attitude of mind,* which we have taken as the basis of our work.

I shall present in this chapter some thoughts on the validity of graphological judgments. For the sake of easier comprehension, I shall mention only a few studies; but you may be sure that every one of my statements can be confirmed empirically. You will find the necessary data in chapter 5.

One theoretical approach to graphology maintains that it is unnecessary to prove the validity of graphological statements because handwriting is a form of human expression and can, therefore, be just as revealing as facial expression. It asserts that in the same way that we immediately understand laughter and a person's feelings by looking into his face, we can instantaneously determine a person's character by looking at his handwriting. This almost parapsychic ability is given the name "intuitive knowledge" (*Kennerschaft*) as if, thereby, all problems have been solved. I consider this theory to be incorrect for two reasons. First, contrary to the elaborate argumentation of Ludwig Klages, handwriting is *not* an expression, but rather an act, a work, a thing (an *ergon*) that is separated from the person (Kirchhoff 1962). Second, it is unfortunately the case that many graphological judgments of individuals are inaccurate. In going through cases in our research seminar, we have come across judgments made by fully trained graphologists which prove to be completely incorrect. Evidence of recurring misinterpretations of handwriting and the ethical issues that are raised by those mininterpretations make it absolutely necessary to carry out validity tests.

CRITERION-RELATED VALIDATION

If we acknowledge that validity tests are necessary, then we are faced with the problem of selecting or devising the most appropriate tests. The most important and most frequently used method is *criterion-related validation*. A criterion-related validation study of handwriting analysis could start, for example, with the individual characteristics (such as slant or expansion of height) of one person's handwriting, and then determine whether any of these graphic characteristics are correlated with that person's scores on various tests, such as objective tests of intelligence or projective tests of personality. We carried out such a test with 100 subjects (Lockowandt 1966). In order to determine each of 69 different graphic characteristics, we carried out a total of 28 measurements randomly throughout each handwriting sample.[1] Approximately 800 to 1,000 measurements were carried out on each handwriting sample.

Each subject took a variety of tests, including an intelligence test (Amthauer's Intelligenz-Struktur-Test) and the Holtzman Inkblot Technique, a variation of the Rorschach Test. The correlation coefficients between our 69 handwriting characteristics and the total standard score on the intelligence test ranged from 0.20 to 0.40. Of the 690 possible coefficients,[2] 46 were significant.

What conclusion can be drawn from these results? First, it is clear that there are relationships between the handwriting characteristics we measured and the intelligence test results. In the total experiment we looked at 102 criterion variables, which, when correlated with each of the 69 handwriting variables, yield a total of 7,038 correlations. Thus, even if some of the correlations occurred purely by chance, the obvious correlations—about 8 percent of the total—remain significant. It must be noted, however, that all the correlation coefficients are much too low. The largest coefficient (r = 0.35) suggests that there is a connection between the width and increasing size of the left margin and certain aspects of the intelligence test. We graphologists have always taken such a correlation for granted. The significance of the left margin is different from that of the right margin in that the left margin is indicative of reflection and conscious detachment, which are qualities relating, in a broad sense, to a person's intelligence.

I have presented this selection of results from our experiments because they are typical. Using the same number of handwriting characteristics, two of my colleagues, Timm (1965) and Prystav (1971), have correlated these handwriting characteristics with the findings from other diagnostic methods such as questionnaires. The same results were obtained repeatedly: correlations of the most varied kind were evident, the coefficients were statistically significant, but in general they proved to be far too low. It was irrelevant which criterion was chosen.

VALIDATION ON THE INTERPRETATION LEVEL

I am well aware that graphologists will be dissatisfied with the experimental studies I have described. I am a graphologist myself, and I too am dissatisfied. The graphologist is justified in criticizing them, because they do not examine the *judgment itself*, nor do they take into account the ways in in which the *overall impression* can alter the significance of individual handwriting characteristics. This shortcoming we call the *interpretation limitation*.

To remedy this shortcoming, my colleague, Michel, devised another method of validation (Michel 1969). Let us refer to the traditional criterion-related validation of graphology as *Model 1a: Validation at the graphological characteristics level.* Model 1a attempts to find correlations between selected handwriting characteristics and criteria such as test scores. The graphologist, his intuitions, his conclusions, and his thought processes are not taken into consideration. The aim of Michel's alternative, however—call it *Model 1b: Validation on the interpretation level*—is to draw special attention to these inner processes, but only in the sense that it demands from the graphologist the solution of the assessment task, without requiring that his or her processes become explicit. These two models are illustrated in Figure 1.

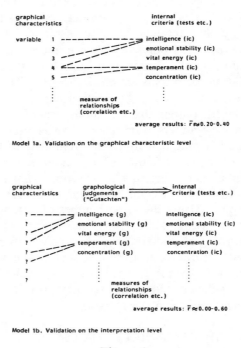

Figure 1.

Model 1a can also be criticized because it limits the array of graphic characteristics that can be studied. It is possible that we select those handwriting characteristics which are easy to work with, but which are of little diagnostic significance. This criticism does not apply to Model 1b, because here it is up to the individual graphologist to decide which characteristics will be used as the basis of his or her graphological judgment. The disadvantage of this approach is that, when negative results are obtained, it is not clear whether they are due to the handwriting (that is, the assessment instrument) or to those interpreting it.

Michel (1968) used the Model 1b approach in a series of careful studies in which he correlated graphological judgments of intelligence with data from intelligence tests, teachers' judgments, and semester reports. The handwriting samples of seven students whose intelligence quotients covered a wide range (see Table 1) were given to several graphologists to rank according to judged intelligence quotients.

TABLE 1

IQ SCORES OF SUBJECTS IN MICHEL (1968)

Subject	IQ Score
1	88
2	116
3	98
4	110
5	133
6	127
7	122

Table 2 shows the correlations (Spearman rho) between the ranking of graphological judgments of intelligence and the rankings based on intelligence tests and other sources. With the exception of the results with the Raven's test, however, the results are generally disappointing.

We can see that the results obtained with Models 1a and 1b are discouraging for the validity of graphology. There is only a single experiment —that combines both Models 1a and 1b—which has yielded more promising results (Castelnuovo-Tedesco 1948). We have tried for several years to reproduce these experiments (Lockowandt 1979). Unfortunately, we did not succeed, so we could conclude only that unknown factors, which cannot be found in the description of the experiments, must have been at work. A personal consultation with the author also failed to shed light on the subject.

But is the situation really so bleak? Let us look critically at these experiments and see what conclusions we can draw from them.

TABLE 2

	Concord-ance (rho)	IST	WAIS	Raven	Teacher's judgment	Term report
Experiment I	.25	.16	.27	–*	.27	.27
Experiment II	.59	.37	.16	.66	.46	.40
Experiment III	.64	–.36	–.09	–.18	–.08	–.19
Mean	.47	.06	.11	(.24)	.22	.16

*Raven-test not used.

Table 2. Mean concordance and validity coefficients of the graphological diagnosis of intelligence in three studies by Michel (1968).

PROBLEMS WITH CRITERIA AND PROBLEMS WITH VALIDATION

My major objection to such experiments is that they *oversimplify* the nature of the graphologists's diagnostic work. Let us take a closer look at the most widely used criteria, intelligence tests. Here we see that, using handwriting analysis, graphologists are unable to determine the intelligence quotients which result from the intelligence tests now in use. It does not necessarily follow, however, that graphologists are incapable of assessing a person's intelligence from his handwriting.

The use of intelligence test scores as criteria in studies of the validity of handwriting analysis is based on a premise which has by no means been proved—namely, that intelligence quotients are a valid measure of a person's intelligence. After many decades of research into intelligence, it has become clear that intelligence tests provide only a one-sided, limited assessment of intelligence. Therefore, it can be argued that graphologists can, indeed, determine a person's actual intelligence from his handwriting, but not the artificial intelligence scored in standard tests. In our practical and controlled examination of individual cases, we have become convinced that graphological analysis can accurately assess true intelligence.

By a detailed analysis of the diagnostic process, we increased our understanding of the *graphological* concept of intelligence. This concept can be best described with the German word *Bildung*—the sum of a person's cultural development—for which there is no English equivalent. Graphologists know from experience that it is not possible to determine very special talents and abilities from a person's handwriting; even the special talents of a genius cannot be recognized, as the handwriting of Einstein and of the artist Kathe Kollwitz have clearly demonstrated. On the other hand, it is not difficult to differentiate between an "educated" and an "uneducated" person by looking at their handwriting. As used here, the term "education" (*Bildung*) can perhaps be equated with "knowledge of life" or a "discriminating attitude to culture." What is *not* meant is the ability to complete a sequence of numbers or to create an analogous word pattern or other simple cognitive tasks. What *is* meant is a person's "general state of culture" or what Lewin called a person's "degree of differentation." Or, it may also be similar to the difference between "crystallized" and "fluid" intelligence as proposed by Cattell.

In his excellent phenomenological work on intelligence, the Swiss graphologist Pulver (1949) also presented an extended concept of intelligence, composed of five types of intellectual behavior: ordering and arranging, intentional application, abstraction and ideation, intensity and concentration (an auxiliary function), and sheer comprehension. Without going into the details of his analysis, I should like to state only that our daily systematic work has shown that graphological diagnosis can indeed be accurate and valid, if one uses this broad concept of intelligence. Although it is very difficult to find adequate measures for these components of intelligence, graphologists have been right not to shrink from or ignore such difficulties and to avoid basing validity tests, for purely methodological reasons, on limited and inadequate understanding of intelligence. When experimenters fall prey to this temptation, one can observe what Maslow (1970) called "overstress on technique": the view that a research finding has value only when it has been done "cleanly," that is, in a methodologically correct way.

The studies described above contain clear indications that the extended concept of intelligence (*Bildung*) is the one that is most suitable for graphological diagnosis. My colleague Timm (1965), for example, has found a sizeable correlation between school education (as determined by levels of school qualifications) and several arrangement characteristics of writing such as the distance between words and between lines (multiple R = .59).

In the experiment cited earlier, Michel (1964) tested only concurrent validity, that is, the extent to which the graphologists' assessment of intelligence agreed with the results of an intelligence test. In this regard, Michel has noted that:

> The concurrent validity of new tests is sometimes determined by correlation with tests with a high validity result. Here, of course, we are only checking

whether the old test can be substituted by the new. *Therefore, negative results do not necessarily go against the new test.* (Michel 1964, 53; emphasis added)

His assertion is indeed correct, and it is unfortunate that he did not apply it to his own experiment.

Formal tests cannot, of course, embrace all of reality. Each test can gain access to only a limited number of the many characteristics that constitute the whole person. Furthermore, test results are *internal* criteria for testing graphological validity, in that they are produced by the same source as the handwriting that the graphologist analyzes. But experiments conducted to date indicate that the validity of graphological analysis is best tested by using *external* criteria, such as the judgments of teachers and supervisors.

It is strange that the validity of handwriting analysis has so often been tested on the basis of characteristics which it neither wanted to assess nor pretended to be able to assess. The fact that its results so seldom agree with those of other evaluation techniques may well be an indication of its *independence* and its unique access to an individual's personality—an access which is impossible with any other method.

FAILURE TO CONSIDER THE INTERPRETATION PROCESS

Another important criticism of the usual methods of validating graphology is that research carried out to date has examined only *universal graphic characteristics* and has ignored the interpretation process of the handwriting analyst. Even if research had established the psychological significance of each graphic characteristic, it would still be necessary to understand the individualistic interpretation processes of the graphologist.

Let us assume, for example, that we wish to validate handwriting analysis by means of the Rorschach Test. Take the relationship between form and color in the Rorschach Test, which is said to reflect emotional impulse and emotional regulation. These emotional tendencies can also be determined from handwriting by analyzing the relationship between motion and form. Assume, further, that we found for a number of individuals that there was a high correlation between the overall motion-to-form characteristic of handwriting and the form-color sequence of the Rorschach. Although this result would be a valuable demonstration of the connection between handwriting and character, it would have limited practical value for the handwriting analyst, who can make use of it only to the extent that it fits into his or her individualized process of interpretation. Even in those studies, like Michel's (1964), in which the handwriting analyst has been free to use his own methods of interpretation, the results have been disencouraging, because the very process of interpretation has been ignored.

A NEW MODEL OF GRAPHOLOGICAL VALIDATION: PROCESSUAL ASSIMILATION

In order to understand and conceptualize the interpretive processes on which the processual assimilation model is based, we drew on three sources of information: (1) our observations of our own interpretive processes; (2) our observations of other qualified handwriting analysts whom we asked to "think out loud"; and (3) our process analyses of the cognitive operations used to generate model reports.

The processual assimilation model can perhaps best be introduced by an experience common in our practice. A graphologist receives instructions to analyze a person's handwriting and prepares his report, which he hands over to the head of a personnel department. To his great disappointment, he is told that his report is unfounded and incorrect. The story could end here, as would be expected by opponents of handwriting analysis. But it is possible that the graphologist or the personnel manager or both of them feel that the work had been too superficial; so they decide to discuss the entire text again, in detail. Perhaps they divide it into individual statements—a technique known as *fractional validation.* At the end of this concerted effort at mutual understanding, the graphologist and the personnel manager discover, to their surprise, that they agree to a great extent, without one having forced his ideas on the other. The conclusions they have reached constitute *objective evidence.* How is this possible?

This process—which we call *procedural agreement*—is of central significance for the validation procedure. Unfortunately, handwriting analysis is expected to reach a level of achievement which is not expected, for example, of medicine. It is expected to be speedily produced and unwavering in accuracy, like William Tell's aim at the apple. What is not appreciated is the fact that handwriting analysis requires a kind of dialectic operation to work out the actual circumstances. Every well-meaning and critical researcher realizes that the validity of statements is not of a dichotomous nature; it is not all or none, but in certain stages of the validation process —a process which can last for several years in difficult cases—it may vary considerably. Validity may be very low or even zero at the beginning of the process, but after long and deep discussion it may reach a high level. I should like to stress that these changes may arise without forced group agreement, but simply from feelings of objective inadequacy.

What has actually happened in the course of this processual change in validity and of what importance is this observation for our problem?

Both experts speak a *different language;* each codes his or her communications in a language that is very different from that of the other. It is important to emphasize that we are not dealing with a linguistic-semantic problem. These language differences are only a symptom of something different; they merely characterize the superficial aspect of the situation. In general, little would be achieved if one expert should try to explain his vocabulary to the other, but it can be used as a starting point, in order to rid language of misunderstandings and errors. Here is an example from my colleague, Mr. H. Hartmann.[3] In a graphological reference submitted by an applicant, special emphasis was placed on his vitality, which was considered to be a positive attribute. He was not given the job, however, because it was feared that this vitality would have an adverse effect on the female members of the staff. "The potential employer had thus interpreted the very general term 'vitality' in a selective manner (that is, in the sense of sexual activity) and thus completely reversed its positive connotation" (Hartmann, 1970, 78).

Let me emphasize again that it is not the differing language codes which are decisive. Rather, it is *what* is coded. The two language codes are founded on different conceptual frames of reference or different theories of personality or motivation, which have different origins. The frame of reference of the handwriting analyst has developed from his daily involvement with "curdled" or fixed individual movements that record themselves and that are *oriented from standard handwriting.* The genesis of his frame of reference is thus graphogenotic. On the other hand, the frame of reference of the personnel manager, who generates the external criterion, has evolved from his long involvement with his subordinates, his knowledge of average work rates, and his experience with the attributes that promote work effectiveness and social compatibility.

These differences among experienced experts can lead to large discrepancies in the interpretation of the same observations. Fiedler (1984) has pointed out that experts cannot always digest important observations dispassionately. Judgment may be distorted by one's conceptual schema, by selective perception, by the self-fulfilling prophecy—seeing what one expects to see—and by the dominance of the hypothesis. Thus, a hypothesis is not always abandoned, even when facts clearly discomfirm it. It is essential, therefore, that the handwriting expert be constantly aware of his or her conceptual framework and, as recommended by Dettweiler (1980, 1984), acquire psychologically believable self-experience in the diagnostic of handwriting psychology.

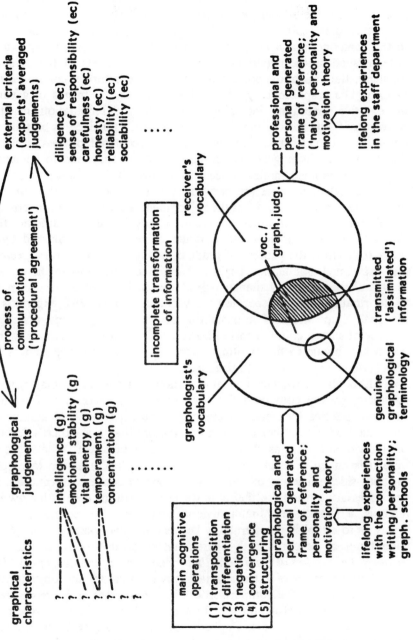

Figure 2. Validation in the form of 'processual assimilation'

Model 2 represents our current view of the process of validation. Figure 2 shows how the model works, using our example of the graphologist presenting the results of his analysis of employees' handwriting samples to the personnel manager. Once internal criteria are replaced by external criteria, such as the expert assessments and judgments of the personnel manager, the validation process involves a very complex *communication process*. The graphologist generates his judgments by means of a variety of cognitive operations, including transposition, differentiation, negation, convergence, and structuring. These are, in turn, embedded as partial operations in a broader meaning-centered and recentered process. Relations that tend to be homogeneous and configurations that tend to be syndromatic are combined in this process (Lockowandt 1973, Jager 1984). We mark the judgments that are derived by this method with the index (g), in order to separate them from those judgments based on external criteria.

Expert judgments which are diagnostically founded in different theories of personality or conceptual frames of reference are marked by the index (ec). Now, the process of gradual mediation, procedural agreement, and processual assimilation begins. Communication between the graphologist and the personnel manager produces an incomplete transformation of information—in part, because the vocabulary of the two experts is not identical. Some items of information can be exchanged and assimilated because of shared comprehension horizons. Others cannot, especially those which are unique to handwriting-psychological terminology, such as Pulver's (1949) concept of "depth-tension."

Although the transfer and assimilation of information may never be complete, we are convinced that two very different frames of reference can be connected by means of language. Thus, it is naive to assume that the validation process consists of nothing more than one expert's declaring the individual assertions of the other correct or incorrect. What is needed instead is an *intermediary process* in which a transformation takes place on both sides. In terms of radio technology: to convey information, it is first necessary to establish the same wavelength. In the case of handwriting analysis, it is necessary that individual statements be rephrased in such a way as to establish comparability between the two systems. This process should not be confused with operationalizing; *the process at issue here involves the creation of conditions that make correct judgments possible.*

These processes of externalization, transformation, and objectification that make possible the comparison of different frames of reference are idiosyncratic and, therefore, must be brought forth anew for each expert.

Consider, for example, Pophal's concept of "degree of stiffening," a handwriting characteristic that is intended to encompass the behavioral characteristics of both inhibition and disinhibition. The word "inhibition" may be part of a sales manager's vocabulary, but it does not mean the same as "degree of stiffening"; and if it is used in the lay-psychological sense, it may well obscure rather than elucidate the intended sense. In our own research we have found that the most commonly used metaphor for inhibition, the brake, fails to capture what the author actually meant. The term "inhibition" is commonly mistaken for the neurotic state of inhibition. For Pophal, however, inhibition is a normal psychological and physiological constituent of the movement of writing, without which it would not even exist. The possible psychopathological manifestations of stiffening are of only secondary interest.

In view of these conceptual differences, it may be difficult or even impossible for a sales manager to understand that a salesman's writing should show degree of stiffening III, perhaps with a tendency toward II if more indulgence is demanded, or toward IV if more power of resistance and a higher tolerance of frustration are considered necessary. If, however, the sales manager's life experiences prevent him from appreciating these distinctions, he will consider the handwriting-based psychological assessment entirely false. The discernment of the respective connection of explanation and the transformation of judgments into statements are necessary in this case in order to make a comparison at all possible.

The process of arriving at such judgments has seldom been given such extensive consideration and treatment. Only a single work with this declared aim has come to our attention, that based on Max Hall's (1928) psychotechnique, which has since fallen into oblivion. Hall's work dealt with the value of handwriting analysis as a method for selecting mercantile apprentices. He found a high level of agreement between the psychological judgments of a single handwriting psychologist and information obtained from six mercantile experts (total rho = .86; the values for the six experts ranged from .68 to .86). Hall explained the high correlations as follows: "The amount of correlation is only then clear when the mistakes, which are made by competent judges in the quantification of both items of information, are very little" (Hall 1928). These findings are particularly striking, because the judgments of the experts were completely independent of each other. It is possible that this experiment was conducted under unusually favorable conditions and that the use of a single handwriting psychologist may limit the generalizability of Hall's result. Nevertheless a close analysis and replication of this experiment would be worthwhile, especially because it is so carefully described.

CONCLUSIONS

1. Internal criteria such as the results of tests or questionnaires should not be used in attempts to validate handwriting analysis. Internal criteria fall short of the demands of handwriting analysis, either because it is not known precisely what they assess, or because it is known that they assess only limited aspects of the information provided by handwriting analysis.

2. Attempts to validate should use external criteria, which in most circumstances would be the judgments of experts in the field of practice (e.g., staff managers). The experts should function as independently of each other as possible, so that, for example, each would assess the employee's personal references independently of the others and then generate an average assessment through group discussion. The experts should go through a similar process to create an average judgment of the graphological assessments. The correlation between these two average assessments constitutes the measure of validity. It is important that the experts should not work with global reports, but with individual statements.

3. It is essential that the communication process between the experts in the field of practice and the handwriting analysts be kept free of disturbing influences. In pilot studies, we have found that failure to control such influences impedes the clear communication of judgments, not the ability to make judgments. In these situations, special attention must be paid to the way in which information is transmitted.

4. Should the judgments diverge, that is, in the absence of validity, one should first look for possible errors in the transmission of information and then recheck the experiment. As we know from initial experiments, such errors can be avoided by giving the professional expert and the handwriting analyst the opportunity to gain deeper insight into each other's perspective, so as to clarify differences in conceptual framework, views of being evaluated, and the requirements of the position to be filled.

5. Finally, we believe that such validation experiments demand a radical change of view, a shift in focus. We must direct our scientific skill toward working out an appropriate criterion for handwriting analysis. Above all, we must try to bring clarity into the communication process with all its possible obstacles. Hall's (1928) study demonstrates that such experiments are much more complicated than those that have been conducted to date on the validity of handwriting analysis. We firmly believe that, "If we are faced with the choice of dealing with either (1)

experimentally simple problems that are however trivial or invalid, or (2) experimental problems that are fearfully difficult but important, we should certainly not hesitate to choose the latter." (Maslow 1970, 21)

SUMMARY

This chapter discusses the problem of establishing the validity of psychological judgments based on handwriting analysis. After preliminary remarks concerning the need for a scientific approach to the problem, the two most commonly used models for criterion-based validation are described and criticized in detail. Their two most important defects are their lack of fit with the subject and their total dependence on internal criteria. We then suggest a recentering of the whole perspective in order to solve the validity problem. The process of passing a judgment should be cleared up in a body, and above all, external criteria should replace internal criteria, and judgments by professional experts should be made via discussion among all the experts involved. Until the new model is fully elaborated, the process of validation should be viewed as a complicated process of communication, which is susceptible to disturbance and in which clarification and transformation of information is necessary. These ideas reflect our efforts to drive back quantitative methods of examination in psychological assessment and to find the way back to qualitative methods of research.

NOTES

1. The randomizing process was as follows. In order to ensure that the measurements were random throughout the sample, we divided the sample into four quadrants, and took three measurements on the edges, the first possible measurement from the border of the page, and so on. In addition, we took four measurements from the center of the sample, for a total of 28 measurements. In order to ensure the accuracy of each measurement we used a magnifier with a scale.

2. We used Subtests 70–79 of the Intelligenz-Struktur-Test, making a total of 10 x 69 = 690 possible correlations.

3. I would like to express my thanks to Mr. Hartmann for the many important insights and items of scientific information he has provided over the years.

REFERENCES

Carus, C. G. 1938. *Symbolik der Menschlichen Gestalt.* 4th ed. Dresden.
Castelnuovo-Tedesco, P. 1948. "A Study of the Relationship Between Handwriting

and Personality Variables." *Genetic Psychological Monographs* 37: pp. 167–220.

Dettweiler, Ch. 1980. "Die Tiefenpsychologische Dimension der Schriftpsychologie." *Angewandte Graphologie und Charakterkunde* 28(2): pp. 5–21.

———. 1984. "Zum Selbstverständnis des Schriftanalytikers (Schriftpsychologen)." *Angewandte Graphologie und Charakterkunde* 32(2): pp. 46–50.

Fiedler, K. 1984. "Diagnostische Fähigkeiten und Diagnostische Erfahrung." In *Diagnostische Urteilsbildung in der Psychologie,* edited by R. S. Jager et al., pp. 303–327.

Guilford, J. P. 1964. *Persönlichkeit.* Weinheim, 1964.

Hall, M. 1928. "Die Schriftbeurteilung als Methode der Berufsauslese." *Psychotechnische Zeitschrift* 3(1): pp. 65–81.

Hartmann, H. 1970. *Psychologische Diagnostik.* Stuttgart.

Jager, R. S. et al., eds. 1984. *Diagnostische Urteilsbildung in der Psychologie: Grundlagen und Anwendungen.* Göttingen.

Kirchhoff, R. 1962. "Das Verhältnis von Graphologie und Ausdruckskunde." *Zeitschrift für Menschenkunde* 26(3): pp. 320–337.

Lockowandt, O. 1966. "Faktorenanalytische Validierung der Handschrift mit Besonderer Berücksichtigung projektiver Methoden." Ph.D. Dissertation, University of Freiburg.

———. 1973. "Der Prozess der Urteilsbildung in der Schriftpsychologie." *Zeitschrift für Menschenkunde* 37(3): pp. 135–154.

———. 1979. "Bericht über das Symposion Schriftpsychologie in Mannheim." In *Bericht über den 31. Kongress der Deutschen Gesellschaft für Psychologie in Mannheim 1978.* Vol. 2, edited by L. Eckensberger, pp. 331–350. Göttingen.

Maslow, A. H. 1970. *Motivation and Personality.* New York, p. 21.

Michel, L. 1964. "Allgemeine Grundlagen Psychologischer Tests." In *Psychologische Diagnostik,* edited by R. Heib, p. 53. Göttingen.

———. 1969. "Empirische Untersuchungen zur Frage der Übereinstimmung und Gültigkeit von Beurteilungen des Intellektuellen Niveaus aus der Handschrift." *Archiv für die gesamte Psychologie* 121: pp. 31–54.

Pawlik, K., M. Amelang, B. Heinze, and W. Beyer. 1973. "Zur Abhängigkeit graphometrischer Variablen von Merkmalen der Anatomie und Psychomotorik." *Zeitschrift für Experimentelle und Angewandte Psychologie* 20(4): pp. 630–652.

Prystav, G. 1971. "Reliabilität graphometrischer Schriftbeschreibung (Part I.)" *Zeitschrift für Menschenkunde* 35: pp. 70–94.

Pulver, M. 1949. *Intelligenz in Schriftausdruck: Eine Studie.* Zürich.

Timm, U. 1965. "Graphometrie als psychologischer Test? Eine Untersuchung der Reliabilität, Faktorenstruktur und Validitat von 84 Schriftmerkmalen." Ph.D. Dissertation, University of Freiburg.

7

Graphoanalytic Cues

James C. Crumbaugh

This chapter is a slightly revised version of Dr. Crumbaugh's contribution to the *Encyclopedia of Clinical Assessment,* volume 2 (San Francisco: Jossey-Bass Inc., 1980).

After his introduction, Dr. Crumbaugh provides a brief history of graphology up to Bunker's founding of the Graphoanalysis movement in 1929. The reader may wish to compare this section with Nickell (chapter 2). Section II outlines Graphoanalytic procedures. Dr. Crumbaugh distinguishes between two sorts of handwriting traits: *primary,* which can be determined from a single feature of handwriting, such as the position of the stroke on the *t,* and *evaluated,* which are inferred from two or more primary traits. Dr. Crumbaugh maintains that Graphoanalysis can discern emotions, optimism, loyalty, logical thinking, impulsiveness, prejudice, diplomacy, selfishness, and fears, as well as many other traits. However, he specifically asserts that Graphoanalysis cannot diagnose mental or physical disease. He also expresses doubts about graphotherapy, a movement which asserts that changing one's handwriting changes the associated personality traits.

Dr. Crumbaugh endorses the notion of holism criticized by Dale Beyerstein in chapter 8 and Dean et al. in chapter 13, as well as the idea that clinical judgment on the part of the Graphoanalyst is required to produce valid predictions of a handwriting subject's character.

Graphoanalytic cues are based on a particular system of graphology or handwriting analysis, which in turn is one form of graphokinesics or expressive movements made graphically. Interpretation of all forms of graphokinesics for the purpose of assessing the personality and character of an individual is based on the fundamental assumption in clinical psychiatry and psychology that personality is expressed by or projected into all of the individual's responses to the environment. The person may respond in either of two ways: (1) verbally, by describing a perception or interpretation of an ambiguous stimulus such as a Rorschach inkblot; or (2) manually, via such expressive movements as projective drawing or handwriting.

Projective techniques of the verbal type include: (1) the Rorschach, Holtzman, and other inkblot tests; (2) the Murray Thematic Apperception Test (TAT), which requires the person to interpret ambiguous pictures of persons and objects, and which contains more structure than inkblots but is still open to broad interpretation; (3) the Shneidman Make a Picture and Story Test (a variant of the TAT); (4) the Twitchell-Allen Three Dimensional Apperception Test, which offers small objects for both visual and kinesthetic perception; and (5) the tautophone test, which uses ambiguous recorded sounds that can be free-form like inkblots or more structured like the apperception tests—to name but a few. Most projective methods have been of the verbal type, and most of these have involved visual perception.

The chief projective techniques of the expressive movement type are the various forms of projective drawing or writing tests: (1) the Goodenough (1926) Draw-a-Person Test and the Buck (1948) House-Tree-Person Test, which require the person to draw his or her own version of persons or objects; (2) the Mira (1940) Myokinetic Test, which requires a blindfolded subject to draw free-hand different types of lines in various planes with each hand alternately; and (3) handwriting analysis. Of these, the Goodenough and the Buck tests are the most widely used, although most clinicians "crystal ball" the drawings and do little in the way of objective scoring. Nevertheless, many practitioners believe that they are among the most revealing of all projective methods, even though studies have failed to demonstrate their validity. Although responses to the Mira Myokinetic Test are scored more objectively, the test is complicated to administer and has never been widely employed. Handwriting analysis offers the advantage of being more amenable to precise measurement, while at the same time allowing the seasoned analyst to bypass detailed measurement and to make global interpretations based on a subjective fusing of the relationships among the data.

Sign interpretation, the attempt to tie specific personality traits to specific signs or features found in inkblots, drawings, or handwriting, has never been well validated for any projective technique, and it is often said that the validity is in the clinician and not in his tools. Global interpretation has consistently been superior to sign interpretation, which means that what is actually valid is the experience of the clinician in putting together in a totally unanalyzable way the overall picture of personality yielded by the complex interaction of all the signs. Since the meaning of a sign changes depending on the other signs with which it occurs, a sign cannot be interpreted in a constant manner from one person to another. (Allergists experience the same problem: a patient may not be allergic to an apple as such but may respond severely to the combination of an apple and an orange.)

Handwriting analysis not only permits the experienced clinician to make global interpretations, but it also offers the novice or the less expert practitioner adequate quantification to depend on until holistic expertise is developed. The same can be said for the Rorschach, but not for most projective methods. Handwriting analysis has other advantages: (1) The sample of writing can be taken by a clerk without expenditure of professional time. (2) It can be obtained without the person knowing what it is to be used for. (3) Samples can be obtained from most people over a span of many years, since most people have kept something they have written by hand at most key periods of their lives. Thus, longitudinal studies of personality can be carried out more easily than with other techniques of evaluation, because test data are usually not available from earlier stages of life.

Background and Current Status

Probably the first organized attempt to analyze handwriting was that of Camillo Baldi, an Italian scholar and physician.[1] While a professor at the University of Bologna in 1622, he published his *Treatise on a Method to Recognize the Nature and Quality of a Writer from His Letters*. The next published work was by Johann Kasper Lavater (1741–1801), a Swiss scholar of personality at the University of Zurich. These early publications interested many intellectuals but had little following as a possible method of personality analysis, for the simple reason that very few people could read and write.

As education became more widespread in the nineteenth century, handwriting analysis rapidly gathered interest. It was practiced far more as an art than a science, but often with amazing intuitive skill, by such figures of the period as Goethe, Poe, the Brownings, Leibniz, Balzac, Dickens, and many others. It is said that Gainsborough achieved the lifelike quality of his portraits by having before him, while painting, a handwriting specimen of his subject. He felt that the handwriting enabled him to capture the essence of the subject's personality.

In France serious study of handwriting was undertaken by Abbé Louis J. H. Flandrin and the Archbishop of Cambrai. Their real contribution, however, was the training of their assistant, Abbé Jean Hippolyte Michon, who published in Paris in 1875 the most scholarly work on handwriting up to that time. Entitled *The Practical System of Graphology,* Michon's work coined the generic term for handwriting analysis. He tirelessly studied hundreds of graphic signs which were presumed to indicate specific personality traits, and his system because known as "the school of fixed signs."

In the late nineteenth century, a discipline of Michon, Crépieux-Jamin, expanded his master's studies and modified to some degree the rigid one-to-one relationship that Michon assumed to exist between handwriting strokes and personality traits. But the basic theory of isolated signs remained dominant in French schools of handwriting analysis.

Near the turn of the century, Crépieux-Jamin interested the great French psychologist Alfred Binet (who devised the first intelligence tests) in handwriting analysis as a technique for testing personality. Binet's experiments indicated that handwriting experts could distinguish successful from unsuccessful persons by their writing with an accuracy of 61 to 92 percent, a remarkable accomplishment in view of the crude methods of the day. Binet was also able to determine, to a considerable degree, the intelligence and honesty of writers, but not their age or sex. These findings have been verified in the graphoanalytic system of handwriting analysis.

In Germany also there were serious students of handwriting during the last half of the nineteenth century. William Preyer at the University of Berlin demonstrated an essential similarity between handwriting, foot writing, teeth writing, opposite-hand writing, and even crook-of-the-elbow writing; and he noted that "all writing is brain writing." Later, psychiatrist Georg Meyer showed important differences between spontaneous writing and written material that had been copied.

The most prominent name in German handwriting analysis became —and remained for some years—that of Ludwig Klages. He coined the term *expressive movement* to refer to all motor activities performed habitually, automatically, and without conscious thought: walking, talking, gesturing, facial responding, and especially handwriting. But while Klages' influence was strong in Germany for a time it did not spread, because his system was esoteric and subjective, intuitive in the extreme, complex, and mixed with an intricate personal philosophy that made it incomprehensible and of dubious authenticity to serious scholars.

Although Klages' work was not widely followed by handwriting experts elsewhere, his name had gathered enough momentum in German circles (which were the most respected in science of the time) to cause many scholars to evaluate the validity of handwriting analysis by appraising the validity of his system. When American psychology developed from the historical foundations of German psychology, which was the cornerstone of the scientific study of the mind, many early American psychologists did the same.

Graphoanalysis, founded by M. N. Bunker in 1929, has been called a protest against both the atomistic, one-to-one sign graphology that typified the French school and the broad, sweeping, intuitive graphology of the German school. This middle-of-the-road compromise position drew heavily from the then new Gestalt school of psychology, which insisted that people must be studied as dynamic wholes and that these wholes are more than the sum of their individual parts. Bunker based this method of personality evaluation through handwriting on this fundamental Gestalt concept. Thus, he emphasized that the interplay of related traits produces an overall effect that is different from that of any single trait, and that the holistic or global personality pattern can be produced by a variety of single-trait combinations, all of which must be learned by experience.

Until his death in 1961, Bunker developed his school and continued to augment its teachings by empirical studies of the handwriting specimens of various personality types. Following Bunker's death, V. Peter Ferrara of Chicago assumed the leadership. Holding a master's degree in psychology, Ferrara emphasized sound validation research to support the concepts of Graphoanalysis and to modify those that did not prove valid.

Graphoanalysis now has certified practitioners in all states of the union and in most countries of the world. It has a wide variety of practical applications. The chief areas of use are: (1) in business and industry (Fullmer, 1971; Rast, 1966), where Graphoanalysts assist personnel specialists in selecting job applicants with specific aptitudes, in job placement and promotion, and in the determination of character in credit risks; (2) in schools (International Graphoanalysis Society, 1975), where Graphoanalysts help vocational counselors determine areas of aptitude and help teachers determine the patterns of personality that cause the student to have trouble in school or the school to have trouble with student; (3) in mental health clinics and hospitals (Root, 1966; Watanuki, 1963), where Graphoanalysts help psychiatrists and psychologists understand the personality structure, traits, and psychodynamics of patients (it should be noted that Graphoanalysts do *not* offer diagnoses of either mental or physical illnesses, and they do not do therapy); and (4) in forensic or questioned-document work, where Graphoanalysts serve as expert witnesses in authenticating legal instruments (International Graphoanalysis Society, 1975).

Graphotherapy, training the person to use in his or her writing those strokes that usually represent desirable traits and to eliminate those strokes that usually imply undesirable traits, has been explored, but it is in a strictly experimental stage at present. It is not taught in Graphoanalysis or permitted by the code of Graphoanalytic ethics except in collaboration with mental health specialists in a clinical setting. The validity of this type of therapy is questionable. Although favorable results have occurred with graphotherapy, they can also be explained as placebo effects. Further, the face validity of such therapy is poor; there is no apparent reason why traits *reflected in* handwriting but *not caused by* handwriting should yield to a manipulation that is unrelated to their cause.

CRITICAL DISCUSSION

DESCRIPTION OF GRAPHONALYTIC PROCEDURES

Graphoanalysis consists of the following steps: First, a *perspectograph*—an analysis of the first hundred upstrokes that appear in the sample of writing—is constructed. This sample is preferably a full page or more of spontaneous writing made with a pencil or ballpoint pen on unruled paper, without the individual's knowing that it is for analysis. The rules for determining and measuring these upstrokes are rather complex. The final measure is the percentage of each of seven degrees of slant found in the writing, from far forward to far backward. Each upstroke is marked and measured by a specially constructed gauge, and each of the seven degree spans of the gauge indicates a degree of emotional responsiveness of the writer. In general, far-forward writing is found in extremely emotional persons, while backward writing indicates emotional constraint and blockage (see Fig. 1). This characteristic becomes important in determining the way in which many traits found in one's writing will affect one's behavior. The percentage of each slant span is plotted on a bar graph for reference as other traits are revealed. The interpretation of slant is demonstrated in Figure 1.

Figure 1. Levels of Emotional Responsiveness

| (a) | (b) | (c) |
| Withdrawal | Objectiveness | Intense responsiveness |

The second step in constructing a Graphoanalysis is completion of a special worksheet that lists some one hundred "primary" personality traits and some fifty "evaluated" traits. A primary trait is one that can be determined from a single-stroke formation. For example, temper is indicated by t-bars made to the right of the t-stem. An evaluated trait is one that must be inferred from two or more other traits. For example, timidity is a product of low self-confidence, shyness, self-consciousness, and clannishness. It should be noted that graphoanalytic definitions of traits are often different from those most commonly employed among mental health disciplines, but personality theorists differ so much among themselves that few uniform definitions are possible. Both primary and evaluated traits are rated as to intensity in the handwriting sample on a three-point scale in which "X" is slight, "XX" is moderate, and "XXX" is strong.

The worksheet is divided into trait groups, which serve to delineate the personality. Among these groupings are:

1. Emotions, revealed by slant and depth of writing, as shown in Figure 1.

Figure 2. Mental Processes

(a)	(b)	(c)
Comprehensive thinking	Cumulative logical thinking	Exploratory or investigative thinking

2. Mental processes, revealed by such traits as comprehensive, cumulative, and exploratory thinking, as demonstrated in Figure 2. The sharp points of the *m* and *n* in 2a show comprehension: the rounded tops of the loops of the same letters in 2b show logical thinking; the wedges of the *m* and *n* in 2c show investigative thinking. Mental processes are intensified by traits like conservatism, generosity, optimism, loyalty, positiveness, broad-mindedness, and tenacity; they are reduced by such traits as impulsiveness, pessimism, prejudice, and narrow-mindedness.
3. Social behavior, supported by such specific traits as diplomacy, frankness, humor, optimism, poise, and self-reliance; negated by such traits as clannishness, selectivity, selfishness, and impatience, as illustrated in

Figure 3. Note the tight loops of the *m* and *n* in 3a, which indicate repression, and the spread loops in 3b, which indicate the opposite.

Figure 3. Social Responsiveness

(a)
Repression

(b)
Uninhibition

Fears and defenses, and the degree and type of adjustment, are indicated by such traits as caution, bluff, dignity, decisiveness, pride, tenacity, and persistence. Special aptitudes are evaluated for the fields of business (diplomacy, decisiveness, determination, and initiative), science (creativity, imagination, and analytical thinking), mechanics (manual dexterity, precision, rhythm, and the like), and other areas. Further illustrations of stroke interpretations in the determination of personality traits are shown in Figures 4 through 10.[2]

The low t-bar in Figure 4a reveals a lack of self-confidence, while the high t-bar of 4b indicates strong will power. Figure 5a shows simplicity or modesty in the small *a* of *Ann*, while 5b reveals ostentation in the large *a*. Figure 6a shows frankness in the closed *a* of *and;* 6b shows self-deception in the initial loop of *a;* and 6c shows purposive or intentional deceit in the double loop of *a*. Figure 7a demonstrates abstract imagination in the large upper loop of the letter *l*, while 7b reveals materialistic imagination in the large lower loop of the letter *g*. Figure 8a portrays depression or pessimism in the downward slope of the word *many*, while 8b indicates optimism in the upward trend of the word. Figure 9a shows strong determination in the bold downstroke of *y*, while 9b shows weak determination in the short, light downstroke of this letter. Figure 10a reveals close attention to details in the closely dotted *i*, while 10b portrays inattention in the high, removed dot of the *i*.

These cues will not be "sure fire" for any individual, but if the reader will check a given cue against the personalities of a dozen or so people whom he knows well and who show it in their writing, he will find that most of these people show the trait represented by the cue. Of course, in a given case the cue meaning may be modified by overriding counter-

Figure 4. Approach to Achievement

(a)
Lack of
self-confidence

(b)
Strong
will power

Figure 5. Levels of Social Appeal

(a)
Simplicity,
modesty

(b)
Ostentation

Figure 6. Levels of Honesty

(a)
Frankness

(b)
Self-deception or
rationalization

(c)
Intentional
deception

Figure 7. Levels of Imagination

light   *light*

(a)   (b)
Abstract   Materialistic
imagination   imagination

Figure 8. Attitude toward Life

many   *many*

(a)   (b)
Depression   Optimism
Pessimism

Figure 9. Levels of Determination

many   *many*

(a)   (b)
Strong   Weak
determination   determination

Figure 10. Levels of Attention

(a)	(b)
Close attention	Inattention
to details	

cues, and the true interpretation is based on the relationship among cues and, therefore, requires broad clinical experience. Before this experience can be acquired, the many variations of each handwriting stroke and the probable meaning of each variation are studied. After mastering these elements, the student is coached and given practice in creating from the mass of data collected a personality picture that shows the trait interactions and the effect of these interactions in producing the individual's unique personal Gestalt.

When the worksheet has been completed, the true skill of the Graphoanalyst is tested by his ability to put all the data together into a unified, meaningful Gestalt or pattern, which yields a valid picture of the personality of the writer. Graphoanalysis, like the Rorschach or any other good projective technique, is thus not a cut-and-dried mechanical process but a dynamic means of assessment that can be learned only through broadly based experience. The fundamentals and the basic procedures can be taught in school, and the neophyte must depend on them while he or she gradually accumulates the experience that is necessary for accurate clinical judgments based on intuitions about the meaning of the various patterns of traits. Here again is a demonstration of the adage that the validity of a projective technique is in the clinician and not in the instruments. The beginner can, with mastery of the instrument of Graphoanalysis, offer much helpful information about the writer's personality and style of dealing with life situations, but only years of practice will make him a master of the art.

THE QUESTION OF VALIDITY

The theory of handwriting analysis rests on solid ground as a projective technique of the expressive movement type, but historically it has been dismissed as pseudoscience, because early psychologists reacted negatively to the intuitive and imprecise systems of early graphology. Psychologists have often acknowledged in elementary textbooks that handwriting *should* reveal personality and graphology that has good face validity—it looks as if it should work. But they maintain that because empirical studies have failed to establish the validity of graphological systems, they must be classed with astrology, phrenology, and the like. Thus, the majority of psychologists turned to other projective techniques of expressive movement such as projective drawing. Projective drawings have long been a part of the armamentarium of many clinical psychologists, even though there is little evidence for their validity (Murstein, 1965). In more recent years, many authors have reexamined the evidence, particularly that for Graphoanalysis, and have concluded that graphology is not a pseudoscience. Ruch (1967, p. 117), for example, states: "Although many psychologists feel [graphology] has no more value than palmistry or reading tea leaves, it has been studied scientifically in recent years by rigorously controlled methods. The general conclusion is that graphology may eventually prove to have value in predicting personality traits." Within the last ten years, more and better validity research has appeared, and a number of psychologists, psychiatrists, and other physicians have begun to take training in Graphoanalysis.

The question of validation continues to be raised by critics, most of whom are psychologists. While some have seen the advantage of graphology and have taken the training, the majority apparently feel that the methods in which they already have been schooled are the only assessment burdens they wish to assume. Perhaps this is understandable in view of the fact that the training required to become expert in handwriting analysis is at least as demanding as that required to master the Rorschach. (It should be noted that this is the situation in America; in Germany many universities have required training in graphology as part of the work for a Ph.D. in psychology.)

The chief validation studies are cited and abstracted in a brochure published by and available from the International Graphoanalysis Society (1970). These and later studies have demonstrated a scientific basis for the assumption that handwriting can be as valid in personality assessment as other major projective techniques. The work of Eysenck (1945), Wolfson (1949), Weinberg, Fluckiger, and Tripp (1962), and Crumbaugh and Stockholm (1977) has shown that it is easier to establish the validity of global or holistic interpretations of handwriting samples than of the atomistic, molecular, or isolated sign approach to interpretation. The same is true of other projective techniques, demonstrating once again that validity is primarily in the clinician rather than in the technique. Only experience blended with good intuitive judgment makes for valid assessment, whatever instrument is used. Further validation evidence has been offered by Fluckiger, Tripp, and Weinberg (1961), Mann (1961), Naegler (1958), and Thomas (1964).

Even the infant shows personality tendencies in graphic movements, and these tendencies do not disappear in old age. While handwriting reflects the motor decline of advanced age, neither age nor sex can be assessed by handwriting. Education (beyond basic literacy), socioeconomic status, race, ethnicity, and vocation have no bearing on the ability of Graphoanalysis to determine character and personality, although vocational aptitudes and interests are reflected in handwriting.

As has been noted, neither mental nor physical disease can be diagnosed by Graphoanalysis, but handwriting often provides information that helps the physician make a better estimate of the cause of symptoms. IQ is never determined by the Graphoanalyst, but the level of intellectual efficiency can be estimated. Graphoanalysts can help those professionals who are charged with responsibility for almost all types of disorders—though they do not assume this professional responsibility themselves—by offering a picture of personality patterns that often yields helpful clues to the presence of underlying organic factors in the etiology of psychiatric disorders.

PERSONAL VIEWS AND RECOMMENDATIONS

The present state of Graphoanalytic art and science warrants its practical use by well-trained Graphoanalysts in a variety of working situations, although neither Graphoanalysis nor any other single assessment technique should ever be used alone in making important life decisions. Neither handwriting analysis nor any other psychological test of personality should determine whether one enters a certain occupation, gets credit, and so forth. Test results must be combined with clinical, educational, demographic, and all other relevant data. The validation of Graphoanalysis is neither better nor worse than that of most other projective techniques. While all of them leave something to be desired in "hard-core" validation, no experienced clinician doubts that any one of them may constitute a useful tool in the hands of a practitioner who believes in it, studies it deeply, and gains broad experience in the relationships between the responses it elicits and the patterns of behavior and personality traits it reveals.

NOTES

1. The historical material in this section is taken primarily from Lecture No. 3 of the general course of the International Graphoanalysis Society.
2. Constructed by Teresa Croteau-Crumbaugh, MGA, Master Graphoanalyst.

REFERENCES

Buck, J. N. 1948. "The House-Tree-Person Test." *Journal of Clinical Psychology* 4: pp. 151–158.

Crumbaugh, J. C., and E. Stockholm. 1977. "Validation of Graphoanalysis by 'Global' or 'Holistic' Method." *Perceptual and Motor Skills* 44: pp. 403–410.

Eysenck, H. J. 1945. "Graphological Analysis and Psychiatry: An Experimental Study." *British Journal of Psychology* 35: pp. 70–81.

Fluckiger, F. A., C. A. Tripp, and G. H. Weinberg. 1961. "A Review of Experimental Research in Graphology, 1933–1960." *Perceptual and Motor Skills* 12: pp. 67–90 (Monograph Supplement 1–V12).

Fullmer, T. P. 1971. "The Use of Graphoanalysis in Personnel Selection." *Best's Review* 72(2).

Goodenough, F. L. 1926. *Measurement of Intelligence by Drawings.* Yonkers, N.Y.: World Book.

International Graphoanalysis Society. 1970. *An Annotated Bibliography of Studies in Handwriting Analysis Research.* Catalogue No. G1059. Chicago: International Graphoanalysis Society.

————. 1975. *Field Reports from IGAS Students and Graduates: The Many Varied and Successful Uses of Graphoanalysis.* Catalogue No. G623 0475. Chicago: International Graphoanalysis Society.

Mann, W. R. 1961. "A Continuation of the Search for Objective Graphological Hypotheses." Ph.D. dissertation, University of Ottawa.

Mira, E. 1940. "Myokinetic Psychodiagnosis: A New Technique for Exploring the Cognitive Trends of Personality." *Proceedings of the Royal Society of Medicine* 33: pp. 173–194.

Murstein, B. I. 1965. *Handbook of Projective Techniques.* New York: Basic Books.

Naegler, R. C. 1958. *A Validation Study of Personality Assessment Through Graphoanalysis.* Catalogue No. 309. Chicago: International Graphoanalysis Society.

Rast, G. H. 1966. "The Value of Handwriting Analysis in Bank Work." *Burroughs Clearing House* 50: pp. 40–41ff.

Root, V. T. 1966. "Graphoanalysis—An Aid in Solving Human Relations Problems." *Hospital Topics Magazine* (July).

Ruch, F. L. 1967. *Psychology and Life.* 7th ed. Glenview, Ill.: Scott, Foresman.

Thomas, D. L. 1964. "Validity of Graphoanalysis in the Assessment of Personality Characteristics." Master's thesis, Colorado State University.

Watanuki, H. H. 1963. "Graphoanalysis: A Tested Tool in Clinical Counseling." *Journal of Graphoanalysis* 3(12): pp. 11, 13 (July).

Weinberg, G. H., F. A. Fluckiger, and C. A. Tripp. 1962. "The Application of a New Matching Technique." *Journal of Projective Techniques* 26: pp. 221–224.

Wolfson, R. A. 1949. *Study in Handwriting Analysis.* Ann Arbor, Mich.: Edwards Brothers.

Section Three

Philosophical Underpinnings
of Graphology

8

Graphology and the Philosophy of Science

Dale F. Beyerstein

In this chapter, Dale Beyerstein examines the rationale behind a scientific experiment: What *should* it be attempting to prove? This chapter complements the discussion of Dean, Kelly, Saklofske, and Furnham in chapter 13 of the biases which corrupt our common sense when we attempt to assess the efficacy of a method of personality assessment such as graphology. Dean et al. show why it is necessary to be able to minimize the chances of these biases leading our judgment astray. Beyerstein maintains that the scientific method is the best we have to acheive this end. Dean in chapter 12 provides a discussion of the concept of *effect size,* which is what we attempt to measure by a scientific experiment. Bowman in chapter 10 discusses the special pitfalls of experiments to determine personality traits. Section IV of this chapter provides the reader with a guide showing where to find the information contained in the typical scientific paper. A well-written scientific paper ought to provide the reader who is not used to reading scientific literature the information necessary to assess the argument. In Section V this guide is applied to an analysis of one of the most often cited papers providing evidence for graphology. The reader is also encouraged to apply the tools discussed here to the three original experiments discussed in this volume, Wellingham-Jones in chapter 15, and Karnes and Leonard in chapter 16.

INTRODUCTION

"Is graphology scientific?" This question surfaces almost every time graphology is discussed, but it cannot be answered until we decide what we mean by "scientific" in this context. That is the main purpose of this chapter. But before tackling this question, we should look at why people think that it is an important one to ask. Graphologists claim to discern personality traits with some degree of accuracy. Most people think that a scientific technique for determining personality traits will be more accurate than an unscientific one. So, the question whether graphology is scientific is often asked in order to throw light on the question whether graphology *works*.

If our real interest is in the latter question, we do not need to worry *directly* about whether graphologists themselves follow the scientific method, even if we do believe that a scientific assessment is generally more reliable than one which is not scientific. To say that one technique is more reliable than another does not commit us to holding either that the first is perfect, or that the second is utterly worthless. Therefore it is *possible* that graphologists may have stumbled upon an assessment technique which works, at least tolerably well, quite by accident. That is, they might not be able to *describe* what they do in terms familiar to scientists, and they might not be *aware* that their techniques are functionally equivalent to those used by a scientist. Nevertheless, at least some of the graphologists' techniques might be in accordance with the scientific method. Of course, even on this assumption, most of us would maintain that graphology would work even better if the hit-and-miss techniques used by unscientific graphologists were to be replaced with ones that are more scientific. This is the view of many people who defend graphology at the same time as they extol the virtues of the scientific method. No doubt they are embarrassed by some of the people practicing graphology, who are also practitioners of astrology or their pseudosciences, and who make pronouncements and use methods that cause scientists to cringe. But, after all, most sciences that are respectable today had their origins in pseudo- and proto-scientific practices.[1] So, the hope of many who defend graphology is that it can be put into a scientific framework; and in the meantime, we can gain from the valuable insights into personality that graphology has to offer. Note that this position is compatible with the one taken by the graphologists contributing to this volume, Crumbaugh, Wellingham-Jones, and Lockowandt.

Nevertheless, we should not allow defenders of this position to beg the question whether graphlogy does work. We must *independently verify* the judgments of graphologists. We need a "yardstick," or in technical talk, a *criterion*, by which we can measure personality traits of subjects, and with which we can compare the judgments of personality traits independently arrived at by the graphologists. Such a criterion must come from a method of personality assessment that is arrived at by the scientific method. So, we must at this stage concern ourselves with the question about what constitutes a scientific method of personality assessment, in order to determine what will serve as an adequate criterion. Again, the graphologists contributing to this volume endorse this requirement. Once we have decided on the necessary conditions for what makes the criterion a scientific measure, we can compare the criterion with the graphologists' ways of doing things, as Richard Klimoski does in chapter 11. Thus, if it does turn out that the graphologists' personality assessments measure up fairly well against the criterion, the hope is that graphologists can borrow whatever it is that makes the criterion scientific, and thereby improve their accuracy.

So much for one reason for discussing the scientific method in this chapter. A second, and more important reason is that the authors in this volume all refer to studies, done either by themselves or by others, purporting to demonstrate the validity, or lack of validity, of various types of graphology. But there is disagreement, not only amongst these experts, but also amongst most others, over which studies are properly done and which really represent any *important* evidence in favor of graphology. Many executives of companies that are considering graphology as a hiring tool, and many people who simply want to find out about graphology out of curiosity, find this disagreement amongst so-called experts bewildering. A question I have often heard from laypeople is, "If the experts cannot agree, how can the layperson hope to come to an informed opinion by reading these studies?" And the answer to this rhetorical question then serves as their justification for doing their own type of test. This usually consists of hiring the graphologist and seeing what he or she can do. But such a test is just not very reliable, for reasons outlined by Dean et al. in chapter 13 of this volume. Human reason and observation unaided by the scientific method are impotent to deal with a complex question such as the validity of graphology. Fortunately, it is not as difficult as many people suppose to read a scientific paper critically and make up one's own mind about the evidence presented. After I present the analysis of what makes a good scientific test, and an argument for why such tests are necessary, I offer a short guide to the standard format of papers in most scientific disciplines. I shall show there that, in a good scientific paper, what may appear at first to be very intimidating is really a straightforward way of presenting the information necessary for the reader to decide whether the experiment under discussion was a good test of a theory. Of course, not all scientific papers are well written; but at least my discussion should give the reader criteria which will allow the reader to discover this quickly and put the paper aside in favor of another worth his or her time. As a practical illustration of how to read a scientific paper I offer a critique of what is most often cited as one of the very best papers presenting scientific results in favor of graphology (Frederick 1968).

GOOD SCIENTIFIC TESTS

THE SCIENTIFIC, THE NONSCIENTIFIC, AND THE UNSCIENTIFIC

T. H. Huxley described science as "organized common sense." Its major virtue is to provide a method for *testing* claims about how the world works, or proposed *explanations* of these workings. For present purposes, we will call these claims or explanations *theories*. A scientific theory deals with the empirical world. This is the world that we perceive through our senses, or which *cause* things to happen that we can perceive through our senses, as in the case when a proton passes through a cloud chamber and (via a complicated causal chain) produces a blip on a monitor which can be perceived by the naked eye. However, common sense theories also attempt to describe the empirical world. Anyone can come up with claims about the empirical world, and some of these are bound to be correct. The difference between a scientific and a common-sense theory is this. When we describe a theory as scientific, we are not so much interested in the *content* of the theory—what it actually *states*—as we are in whether it is of the sort that can be tested by the scientific method. This requires qualification: of course it is thanks to what the theory states that we are able to find ways of testing it. For example, a theory about God's intentions cannot be tested by the means available to science; therefore the *content* of such a theory will not be scientific, but rather theological. But the point remains that, so long as the theory is testable by the scientific method, a theory will count as scientific, even if it contradicts previously accepted scientific theories, or seems on the face of it absurd.[2] Also, we must remember that to say that a theory is scientific is not to endorse it as *true*, since there have been, and will continue to be, many false scientific theories. And, conversely, to say that a theory is *not* scientific is not to say that it is *false*. Science is *one* method of getting at the truth, but there are disciplines other than science that state true propositions. Take logic, for example: despite some differences of opinion amongst philosophers of logic about the correct *analysis* of logical truth, they will all agree that there *are* logical truths, and furthermore, that they can be discovered independently of the methods used in the sciences.[3] So, not all truths are discoverable by science.

Note that I was careful to use the description "*not* scientific" above, rather than "*un*scientific." There is a distinction. The latter carries with it the idea of being *contrary to* science. Logic, as I just implied above, is not contrary to science; it is simply another discipline with a different methodology. Logic, the formal study of patterns of reasoning that are valid or invalid, does not use the scientific method described below to arrive at its results. Nevertheless, scientists *use* logic in their reasonings—when they reason correctly, at any rate; thus logic is *consistent with* science. On the other hand, to be *un*scientific is to be contrary to science in (at least) one of three ways.

The first way of being unscientific is to think that claims require no justification, no evidence to back them up, when obviously they do. Of course, to think this is not just to be unscientific, it is to be irrational. This mistake can be referred to as an *absence of skepticism*.

The second way is to use a method of testing a claim which is incompatible with the scientific method, *where the scientific method is appropriate*. Let us refer to this as the *alternative paradigm* approach.

The third way of being unscientific is to *abuse* the methodology of science by attempting to do science properly but failing at it. Let us refer to this as *mistaken methodology*.

Absence of Skepticism. Often skeptics will compare graphology to what most graphologists will agree are pseudosciences: phrenology, astrology, or the like. For example, see Barry Beyerstein's parallels between graphology and sympathetic magic in chapter 9. Graphologists will often take umbrage at this. They will point out that the *content* of the theory of graphology is nothing like that of, say, astrology. They will point out that astrologers assert the existence of causal relationships between the positions of planets or stars at the time of one's birth and human personality traits without having the faintest idea of what *mechanisms* might be responsible for these relationships. Or astrologers will be more precise in asserting what mechanisms are responsible, but these mechanisms are ones that are totally at variance with what modern science tells us. On the other hand, graphologists maintain that the theory behind graphology is, on the face of it, plausible and consistent with what we—and more importantly, scientifically trained psychologists—know about human personality. Handwriting, they say,[4] is a bit of behavior, which expresses personality traits, just as style of dress or characteristic facial expressions. In other words, this claim has *face validity* (see Bowman, chapter 10, and Klimoski, chapter 11). This response is problematic for two reasons. First, what seems plausible on the face of it just may not be plausible once we examine the assumptions in more detail. On this point see Barry Beyerstein's discussion in chapter 14.

Second, this response by the graphologist misses the point of the comparison the skeptic is making. The skeptic usually has in mind not the content of the theory, but the attitude toward *justification* of theories that graphologists sometimes take. The skeptic's point is that graphologists, like practitioners of pseudosciences such as astrology or biorhythms, sometimes do not see the need to look for evidence for their claims, and when they do, they are willing to settle for evidence that is not very good.

The big difference between someone with a skeptical, scientific cast of mind and someone who lacks it is in the way these two types of people deal with something that "seems obvious on the face of it." The former type will notice something that seems obvious and then ask how one might go about *testing* whether it is really so. The latter will simply assume that no further testing is required, *since* it is so obvious that it is so. The former, of course, will often discover that which appears obvious *is* in fact the case, after some further investigation. If so, she will not think that she wasted her time doing this further investigation; she will have enjoyed the testing procedure itself as a satisfaction of her curiosity, and will have gained a deeper insight into the phenomenon in question for her trouble. The latter, on the other hand, simply views further examination of "the obvious" as a waste of his time—he is too anxious to *apply* this insight to confirm it first. Furthermore, this sort of person views anyone who asks for further evidence as questioning his integrity, as obstructive, or—worst of all, in this person's view—as *negative!*

Both skeptics and believers realize *in principle* that not every immediate insight that tells us something "obvious" about the world really will pan out in the end; but it is only the person with the scientific temperament that has a chance of discovering that things really aren't this way after all. On occasion, this sort of person will be thankful to discover that she has made a mistake before wasting a lot of time. And she will certainly be thankful to someone else who takes the trouble to present her with evidence that things are not as she originally thought. The person who lacks a scientific temperament, on the other hand, has often committed himself—and his *ego*—so deeply into this insight that he will be very unhappy to find out that things are not really as he thought, and it is for this reason that he sees the skeptic as being "negative."

But it is acknowledged by almost everyone, except those in the heat of debate with a skeptic, that the best defense against the frailties of our intuition is the scientific method and the skepticism which is its underpinning. The problem is, however, that there are many defenders of the *principle* of open-minded skepticism who fail to put it into *practice* when their cherished beliefs are at stake.[5] Dealing with this sort of defender of graphology consists mainly in asking them to live up to the standards of evidence that they profess.

Alternative Paradigms. Not all graphologists share this commitment to the scientific method, however. My colleagues and I have proposed scientific tests to graphologists who have refused, offering the reason that graphology is an art, not a science. By this remark we take them to mean that their judgments are based on some kind of intuition, which is not reducible to, or duplicated by, the methods of the sciences. We have countered with the argument that using the scientific method is the best way of determining whether graphology works or not, quite apart from the question how the graphologist views the status of his or her profession. That is, the graphologists we have encountered have not yet demonstrated that they can use graphology to discern personality traits that are opaque to non-graphologists. Until they demonstrate this there is nothing that requires explanation by intuition, or non-Newtonian, non-linear, non-Western, or non-*anything* paradigms. However, some graphologists have argued that the scientific method gives us no knowledge of any value about human personality. This extreme view is, as I have just emphasized, not taken by the graphologists contributing to this volume, and it is not shared by any of the personnel managers using graphologists with whom I have had discussions. The latter have been quite insistent that they would not be using it if they did not think that it had the status of a science. So, I shall not take the time to refute this position here, because the people who are interested in this book do not really believe it. The point of this volume is to debate the scientific status of graphology. There are, I admit, people who reject the scientific method as a means of arriving at truth —or at least *probable* truth—about the empirical world. But the onus of proof is on them to describe their favored alternative to the scientific method clearly enough for me to assess it. I have no idea how to assess their usual handwaving about "intuition," "alternative paradigms," or mystical sources of enlightenment.

There are some defenders of graphology who try to hold *whichever* of the above positions that will work best. They will begin by holding that the scientific method demonstrates the validity of graphology, and thus are in a position to cash in on the rewards that can be had in this society by anyone offering a service that has been "scientifically proven," until they are confronted with the data, which they have not previously bothered to consult. Instead of examining those data, and either rebutting them or revising their views, they simply switch to the "alternative paradigm" position and maintain that scientists don't really know anything anyway. This is an obvious rhetorical trick, and I emphasize that it is

not used by the defenders of graphology in this book. Nevertheless, it
is common enough amongst defenders of graphology that I should mention
it in passing. The response to it is obvious: simply keep asking for the
evidence.

Mistaken Methodology. This is the kind of problem encountered in
orthodox science all the time. Science has evolved by refining methods
to deal with this problem: the peer review process, publication of the methods
used in experiments in order to get criticism from colleagues that will
correct methodological flaws, replication of experiments in order to uncover these flaws, and so on. Since these problems are commonly found
in orthodox science, it is not surprising that we find them in graphology
as well. But insofar as graphology really is scientific, methodological problems should be no more problematic for graphology than any other science. Scientists who criticize graphological experiments on methodological grounds are paying graphologists the respect of treating graphologists in the same way that they treat their colleagues. In the next two
sections I describe the rationale behind the methodology accepted by other
sciences, and argue that there is no reason why graphological claims, if
they are true, cannot be shown to be true by the methods consistently
practiced in orthodox psychology.

THEORIES, HYPOTHESES, PREDICTIONS, AND TESTS

Let us return to Huxley's point about science being organized common
sense. A good experiment is just one that organizes our search for evidence for or against the theories. To criticize an experimental design is
just to say that it is badly organized for that purpose. Now we shall look
at what constitutes a good experimental test of a theory, and what fails
to meet these standards.

A good scientific test is one that will provide evidence for or against
a theory. By "good test" I do not mean one that *verifies* the theory being
tested; I mean one that provides unambiguous evidence *either* in favor
of the theory *or* against it. How does a test do this? I shall take up this
question in the "Scientific Experiments" section, but first we should look
at the elements involved in a scientific test.

Theories. Since theories are complex—consider quantum mechanics,
or a theory about the mechanisms of evolution—they will consist of many
individual statements which should be true or false independently of each
other. To be more precise, the statements of a theory fit together into
subsets of statements, with entailment relations between members of the
set, but typically not between them and statements that form part of another subset.[6] It is for this reason that it is possible to *modify* a theory

by changing one part of it, while leaving other parts relatively intact. However, some statements of a theory are more central to it than others; and a rough idea of how central a given statement is in a theory is captured by seeing how many statements it entails. Roughly speaking, the more central a statement is in a theory, the more statements it[7] entails.

So whole theories cannot be tested all at once if they have any complexity; an experiment will test a *part* of a theory. If the part survives the test, this will add support to the theory as a whole, if the part fails the test, then the theory will require modification. Perhaps just that part that failed will require modification, but in some cases the entire theory will have to be revised in order to leave a consistent package. When we are devising a test of a theory, one thing that matters is what we already think of that theory. If we think that the theory is basically sound, then we usually perform tests of minor parts of a theory. We are looking to extend the theory and apply it to a new range of cases, or to "fine tune" it: to modify small details. On the other hand, if we think that the theory is mistaken, we try to test a central tenet of the theory, to get to the heart of the matter and show what is fundamentally wrong with it.

Hypotheses. In either case, the part of the theory that will be tested will be that which entails a *hypothesis*: a statement that something or other will be the case under certain conditions. For example, "Pure water freezes at 0° Celsius at air pressures normally encountered at sea level" is an hypothesis in our sense.[8] It is a common-sense assertion, but also one that follows from certain statements in the theory of thermodynamics. The verification of the hypothesis is what provides evidence—though not *conclusive* evidence, as we shall see in a moment—that the theory is true. The refutation of the hypothesis provides evidence—though, again, not *conclusive* evidence—that the theory is false. We shall come in a moment to the explanation of how this works. But the most important point for the moment is that, if the testing of the hypothesis is to play this evidential role for the theory, then the hypothesis must be one that is entailed by the theory we are ultimately trying to get evidence for. We do not want to be in the position, after the test has been conducted, of not knowing whether the experiment has provided worthwhile evidence for or against the theory. So, it is essential that we be clear before we examine the results of the experiment whether the theory really does entail the hypothesis. And in order to determine this, both have to be clearly and unambiguously stated.

Predictions. If the above hypothesis is true, then it, along with other statements will entail another statement, such as "the thermometer will read

0° at the moment this water turns to ice." Call this latter statement a *prediction*.[9]

Initial Conditions. Obviously the mere fact that water freezes at 0° C does not *by itself* entail that a given thermometer will read 0°. The thermometer must be accurate, working properly, immersed in the water in a certain way, and a whole host of other conditions must be met. Call all these conditions *initial conditions*. For our simplified present purposes, we can think of the description of the initial condition as the description of how an experiment was set up and conducted, and how the measurements are made—anything, in short, which might affect whether or not the prediction comes true in the experiment.

SCIENTIFIC EXPERIMENTS

In a scientific experiment we begin with a hypothetical statement of the form "*If* water freezes at 0° C, *and* <DESCRIPTION OF INITIAL CONDITIONS>, *then* the thermometer will read 0° C at the conclusion of the experiment."[10] Schematically, this statement looks like this:

FIGURE 1

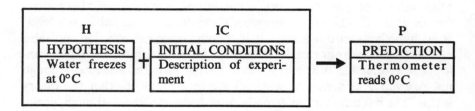

So, we assume that the hypothesis is true, and we do our best to see that the initial conditions are the way we described them, and then check to see whether the prediction turns out to be true.

Confirmation of Theories. When we get the prediction we were expecting, we take the hypothesis to be confirmed. What we have done here is to make use of an argument with the following form:

$$\begin{array}{ll} \textit{If } \mathbf{H} \textit{ and } \mathbf{IC} \textit{ then } \mathbf{P} & \qquad (1) \\ \underline{\mathbf{P}} & \\ \mathbf{H} & \end{array}$$

But now we see the reason why scientists insist that the confirmation of a hypothesis in an experiment does not establish that hypothesis with certainty: an argument of this form is invalid. A valid argument is one that satisfies the following property: *It is impossible for the premises of the argument to be all true while the conclusion is false.* If an argument is not valid, then it is invalid. The sense of *impossibility* we have in mind is that it is not just *accidental* that we happen to have true premises and a true conclusion of a given argument; this must be guaranteed by the form of the argument. However, consider another instance of an argument with the same form:

> *If* Harry visits us *and* Isabella Calls us,   (2)
> then the telePhone rings.
>
> The telePhone rings.
> _____
> Harry visits us.

Here we do have the possibility of true premises and a false conclusion: the telephone rings on occasions when Harry is not visiting us. Therefore, it is possible to have true premises and a false conclusion with this form of argument, and it is invalid. Since the scientific argument is of this form, it is invalid. That is why the truth of its premises is no guarantee that the conclusion is true also., So, using this argument, we have not established *with certainty* that the hypothesis being tested in an experiment is true just because we get the expected prediction (Giere 1984 and Hempel 1979). However, all is not lost. What this argument does for us is to *increase the probability* that the hypothesis is true; and with each succeeding replication of the experiment, the probability of the hypothesis gets successively closer to 1 (certainty), without ever reaching it. Philosophers use the admittedly horrid term *"probabilification"* to refer to the kind of support that premises offer for their conclusions in these types of arguments. The type of argument that *probabilifies* (as opposed to *entails*) a conclusion is *inductive* (as opposed to *deductive*).

Thus we can see one of the reasons why replication is important in science. Even though an experiment yields the expected prediction, and we are reasonably confident that the initial conditions were as described, we cannot be sure that the prediction came true *because* the hypothesis is true. It is always possible to construct an *alternate* hypothesis, such that it, along with these same initial conditions, will *also* entail that prediction. Fortunately, we often have reasons other than those derived from an experiment for preferring one hypothesis to a rival one. Such considerations turn on how well each hypothesis serves to explain this experimental result *as well as* other similar results and observations. For more on this, see Quine and Ullian (1978).

Disconfirmation of Theories. How do experimental results count as evidence against a theory? They do so by disconfirming a hypothesis which is entailed by the theory. In the example we used before, the hypothesis that water freezes at 0° C will be severely weakened by the experiment if we carry it out under the same initial conditions as I described previously, and find that the thermometer reads something other than 0° C. The argument for the falsity of the hypothesis makes use of the same first premise in the argument for the truth of the hypothesis. The difference in the two arguments is that in this case, the prediction is false:

$$(H \ \& \ IC) \rightarrow P \tag{3}$$

$$\underline{Not \ P}$$

$$\therefore Not \ (H \ \& \ IC)$$

This argument is valid, as the reader can see for herself by substituting another argument for the same form. However, it does not establish the conclusion we were looking for, namely the falsity of the hypothesis *simpliciter*. Our conclusion is equivalent to denying *either* the hypothesis *or* that the initial conditions in fact held (perhaps the thermometer isn't reading accurately anymore?—maybe we aren't really at sea level?). Nevertheless, if we accept the claim that the initial conditions really were as described, we do have conclusive proof that the hypothesis is false. We construct the following argument, making use of the conclusion of the previous one, and pay attention to what we are saying when we have a statement of the form "Not (H & IC)":[11]

$$\therefore \ 1. \ Not \ (H \ \& \ IC) \tag{4}$$

    2. Not H *or* Not IC

$$\therefore \ 3. \ IC$$

$$\overline{}$$

    4. Not H

This conclusion follows with the certainty of a deductive argument. Hence the oft-repeated claim that a scientific hypothesis can be refuted, but not verified. What we have seen from this discussion is that it can be verified, as long as we do not take verification to involve 100 percent certainty but rather *probabilification*; and it can be refuted as long as we are able to settle legitimate disputes about whether the initial conditions in the experiment are really satisfied.

Verification of Theories. What does the verification of a hypothesis tell us about the theory which entails it? As I said in a previous section, the degree of support that the theory receives from a verified hypothesis will depend upon how central the hypothesis is in the theory. For example, the Big Bang theory entails the claims that some photons which were released a few hundred thousand years after the Big Bang are still travelling around in the universe. Along with certain theoretical statements that the wavelength of a photon expands as the universe expands, this will yield the hypothesis that some of these presently existing photons are now of a certain wavelength. This hypothesis, along with suitable initial conditions describing the way the aerial on your TV set picks up photons, yields the prediction that you will see evidence of the Big Bang amongst the "snow" on your TV screen (Ingram 1989).

If that prediction is verified, this will lend support to the Big Bang theory. But the hypothesis that the photons will have just the wavelength that allows them to be picked up by a TV is not as central to the theory as many other parts. It is arrived at by calculations based on the age of the universe and its expansion rate. These calculations in turn could be revised if new data were to come to light; and these revisions would not significantly affect what is central to the Big Bang theory, viz., that the present universe grew out of a single, much denser collection of matter which is now expanding outwards *at some rate or other.* Therefore, the fate of this prediction about what you will see on your TV set will not determine the entire fate of the Big Bang theory though its failure might cause some revisions to it.

A second, related point that determines the degree to which a successful prediction supports a theory has to do with whether rival theories also make this prediction. For example, in the previous example, the Big Bang theory holds that only about 4 percent of the snow on your TV screen is from these photons left over from the Big Bang. Hence the vague prediction that you will see snow on your screen does little to support the theory, since other theories (accounting for the other 96 percent) also predict this snow. The success of this prediction also confirms these other theories. As I pointed out before, it is always possible to construct *inconsistent rival* theories to your favorite theory. What gives your theory the leg up against these competitors is its ability to predict something that none of the rival theories does; or, failing that, at least to make a much more *accurate* prediction than those of the rivals. This is often referred to as a *risky* prediction. The success of a risky prediction does much more to probabilify a theory than the success of a prediction which is also entailed by the rival theories. So, the kind of experiment that provides the best test for any theory will be one that determines whether a risky prediction is verified under conditions where we can be assured that the initial conditions are present.

TESTING GRAPHOLOGICAL HYPOTHESES

We are now in a position to examine what would constitute a good test of a graphological hypothesis that will in turn provide evidence for or against a theory of graphology. Our first problem is that there are many different schools of graphology, each consisting of rival theories. See Nickell (chapter 2) for an account of the three broad schools of graphology. However, our task is made easier by the fact that anything properly called a theory of graphology will consist of the claim that certain personality traits are correlated with certain features of handwriting. We need not concern ourselves with the differences of opinion amongst graphologists about *why* these traits are correlated in the way that they are, or which traits are correlated with which personality traits. All we need is a statement of a correlation entailed by that theory. That will serve nicely as a hypothesis to test. In order to tell whether the hypothesis has been demonstrated or refuted it must be stated clearly and unambiguously. For example, the hypothesis might be, "Handwriting which slants to the right at least $X°$ is correlated with *Personality Trait T* (e.g., gregariousness) in the general population at a level which is statistically significant"; where X is a precise number, so we can be clear whether this condition is satisfied or not, and T specifies some trait which we can readily measure and agree whether the trait is displayed or not.[12] If this hypothesis is true, then it, along with suitable initial conditions, will entail a prediction which we can test. In fact, there are two types of validation studies, based on different hypotheses and different predictions, commonly used in testing graphology.

Lockowandt in chapter 6 identifies three types of validation, which he calls *validation at the graphological characteristics level* (Model 1a), and *validation on the interpretation level* (Model 1b). Jensen (1973:2) draws a similar distinction. His third type, *processual validation*, does not fit the scientific methodology under discussion, so I shall defer discussion of it to my section "A Diversion." In Model 1a, what are tested are the putative correlations between handwriting traits and personality traits. Note that the claim that there are such correlations is central to graphological theory. Once it is agreed how to measure the handwriting traits, *non*graphologists could measure them just as well as graphologists. For example, it would not take a graphological theoretician to discern that the width of the margin at a certain point on the page was 1.66 centimeters. Thus an experiment of this sort provides the strongest evidence for graphology, since there will be no question whether the prediction is true or not.

In Model 1b, on the other hand, what is being tested is the hypothesis that graphologists have the ability to make reliable or valid judgments of personality traits. Note that this hypothesis *presupposes* the hypothesis involved in Model 1a: that is, we must presuppose that there really are correlations between the handwriting and personality traits, and it is *this* correlation the graphologist is noticing in order to make his or her reading of the subject. As we shall see, it is just this presupposition that is called into question in debates between graphologists and skeptics. Let us now turn to Model 1a.

VALIDATION OF GRAPHOLOGICAL TRAITS

The hypothesis being tested in Model 1a is that there are correlations between a graphological trait G (e.g., handwriting slanting upwards on the page) and a personality trait T (e.g., gregariousness). In a good scientific test, the *strength* of this correlation would be given, but we must at least be told that the correlation is *statistically significant* (which means that it is unlikely that this difference is the result of chance) if we are to have anything to test. The best test of this hypothesis would be to gather a randomly selected subset of the population at large, further divide this group into those that clearly satisfied condition of having the graphological trait of slanting handwriting (call these people "Group 1") and those who do not (call these "Group 2," or the *control* group). Then, our prediction would be that the number of people in Group 1 who were gregarious exceeded those in the control group by an amount that was statistically significant. The reason that we require merely that there be *more* gregarious people in Group 1 than in the Group 2, rather than that *everyone* in Group 1 display T, while *no one* in the control group display it, is twofold. First, the correlation between the handwriting trait and the personality trait may be less than 1—that is, less than perfect; so we would not expect everyone in Group 1 to have T. Second, T may be correlated with other graphological traits as well (perhaps fat loops on their ls), and thus if some people in the control group make fat ls, they may be gregarious as well. Here is the prediction in this sort of experiment in the form of a histogram:

FIGURE 2

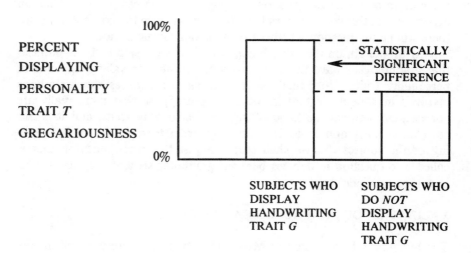

A more immediate problem is that most ordinary-language person-ality terms are vague and open-ended. You, dear reader, are gregarious some of the time, and your Presbyterian friends think that you are too much so sometimes, despite the fact that your friend Aloysius who is the profit margin at Clancy's Bar is continually telling you to loosen up and socialize more. For more on this, see Marilyn Bowman in chapter 10. In order to know whether the prediction can be verified or not, we must have a *criterion* of *T*: some independent measure of gregariousness —perhaps a psychological test which everyone agrees is unambiguous, precise, valid, and reliable enough as a measure of *T* to make a good test. If we are testing some controversial matter such as graphology, we must be especially careful to choose a criterion which is agreed upon by all parties to the dispute to be a good measure of the trait in question. Marilyn Bowman and Richard Klimoski discuss this point further in chapters 10 and 11, respectively. Once we have solved the problem of agreeing on the criterion, we would be in a position to know whether there are more gregarious people identified as belonging to Group 1 than in the control group, which would be the *prediction* of such an experiment.

The *hypothesis (H)* is that graphological trait *G* is correlated with personality trait *T*, but this by itself does not entail the *prediction (P)* that *G* will be found more frequently amongst members of Group 1 than the control group *in this test*. Whether this is so will depend upon *how G and T are measured*, and by whom (by someone competent?). Furthermore, description of how the test was done has to be added to *H* in order to entail *P*. The statement of these initial conditions has to make it clear that it is on the basis of measuring *G* that subjects were assigned to Group 1, and on the basis of measuring the *absence* of *G* that people were assigned to the control group. But often the trouble with graphological traits is that their measurement is a very subjective affair, and the only way we can ensure that the measurement is not corrupted by the person "knowing" that *G* "must" be present *because H is true*, and the writer of the specimen possesses *T*. After all, what is being tested is *H*, and this will not be tested if subjects could have been assigned to their groups on the basis of the graphologist *already knowing* whether the subjects possess *T*. Under these conditions, *whether or not H is true, P* will come true. Thus, the most important initial condition in such an experiment is that the graphologist be unaware of any test subject's score on the criterion: that is, he must be *blind*. And, in order to *ensure* this, the experimenter who determined *T* must not be in a position to pass this information on to the graphologist accidentally or unknowingly by transmitting unintentional cues.[13] The experimenters who deal with the graphologist must be blind to these results as well. We call an experiment *double blind* if both these groups lack knowledge in advance of the criterion.

The second crucial initial condition arises from the fact that the hypothesis under consideration is that it is the handwriting characteristics themselves that are correlated with the personality trait, and not other traits of the subject that happen to be revealed to the graphologist in the *content* of the handwriting. So, when we are testing *H*, we do not want to confuse the issue by allowing the graphologist to come to know of these personality traits from the meanings of the phrases in the handwriting sample itself. In our example, where gregariousness is the trait being tested for, we would not want the handwriting sample to be a personal letter, in which the subject recounts all the parties he has been to in the past few weeks. The content of the handwriting sample must be *controlled* to ensure that none of the information would allow the graphologist to determine the personality traits of the subject by good old common sense. Otherwise, the common-sense hypothesis will explain the success of the prediction as well as the graphologists' hypotheses, and we therefore derive no evidence for graphology from the test. As obvious as this requirement is, it is flouted by most of the studies cited by graphologists in support of their theory.

There are other important initial conditions, specifying how the measurements are to be made, how the criterion was selected, and so on. The following table summarizes where we are at the moment:

FIGURE 3

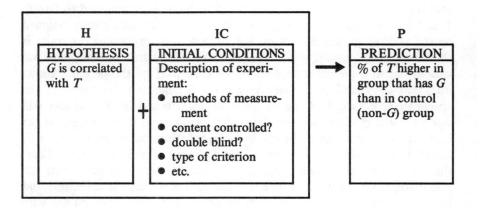

VALIDATION OF GRAPHOLOGISTS' JUDGMENTS

The second type of test, which Lockowandt calls *validation on the interpretation level* (Model 1b), involves testing the graphologist, rather than *directly* testing the claim that there is a correlation between graphological and personality traits. Of course, the assumption behind Model 1b is that the graphologist discerns personality on the basis of examining graphological traits; otherwise this kind of test would not support or provide evidence against graphology. So this type of test provides *indirect* evidence for or against the hypothesis that there are correlations between graphological and personality traits. The advantage, if it can be called that, of a 1b type test is that the particular correlation need not be specified. The focus of the experiment turns on the question whether the graphologists tested can discern any personality traits in the samples they analyze. If they cannot, then the question *what* they are analyzing is moot. But the disadvantage of this type of experiment is that if it provides evidence that the graphologists are discerning *something*, it gives us no indication of what that something might be. A further hypothesis would have to be formed about what the correlation might be, and then a model 1a-type experiment would have to be done.

The *hypothesis* being tested in a 1b-type experiment is a double-barrelled one: (1) there are certain (perhaps unspecified) correlations between graphological and personality traits; and (2) the graphologists being tested can discern these traits.

The *initial conditions* involved in the 1b test will be identical to those of 1a: in a well-designed test, they will ensure that the graphologists being tested are making their assessments of personality *only* on the basis of information contained in the handwriting samples they are working with, and not from any other source.

Given this complex hypothesis and these initial conditions, the *prediction* will be about graphologists' success at determining personality traits. But it cannot simply be that they will determine these traits: it has to be that they will do so *at a greater rate* than they would do if they did not have the graphological traits to work with. How much greater? Given the initial conditions, we are assuming that the only information available to the graphologists is the graphological traits in the sample. So, if the graphologist does *not* use these, he or she would be reduced to guessing, and in a properly run experiment we would be able to determine the rate of successful guesses we could expect by chance. For example, perhaps there are five possible traits to be guessed at, so we would expect by chance a subject would get 20% right, plus or minus the margin of error for a sample of that size. Therefore, the prediction we make in an experiment of this sort is that the graphologist will make *more correct guesses than expected by chance*, and, of course, the difference must be statistically significant.

FIGURE 4

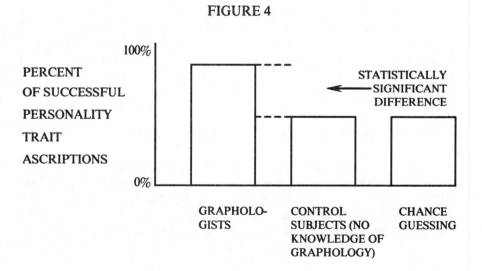

A variant of this experiment is based on the notion that, under the initial conditions assumed, a *control group* of non-graphologists would also lack any information they could use to determine personality traits. There would be no clues provided them, such as knowing that the subject who wrote the handwriting sample they are analyzing spent 25 years as a successful copy editor, which would lead to the likely guess that the subject was good at paying attention to subtle details. Also, since the control is assumed to be naive with respect to graphology, she would be unable to determine personality traits from the graphoanalytical traits in the sample. So, the control group should do no better than chance at guessing subjects' personality traits. On the other hand, as in the previous experiment, the graphologists should be able to exceed chance.[14] Therefore, the prediction in this experiment is that the graphologist should be able to do significantly better than the non-graphologist. Figure 5 shows the schema of this experiment:

FIGURE 5

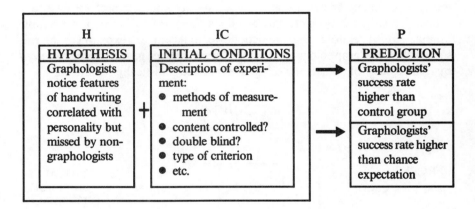

A DIVERSION: GRAPHOLOGY'S SPECIAL PLEADING

Graphologists historically did not arrive at their claims about correlations on the basis of validation studies of the Model 1a sort described in the preceding "Validation of Graphological Traits" section. Instead, as Nickell points out in chapter 2, the correlations they claim are ones that have been posited by a particular graphologist after a certain length of time observing handwriting, or that have passed down for generations by those who are members of a particular school. Given the levels of statistical sophistication in the past, this comes as no surprise. What is surprising is the paucity of these types of studies in modern times. Lockowandt (1966) is a welcome exception to this rule. This study is referred to by Lockowandt in chapter 6. There are comparatively more studies of the Model 1b sort: for example, Klimoski and Rafaeli (1983) and Rafaeli and Klimoski (1983), discussed by Klimoski in chapter 11; Karnes and Leonard in chapter 16; Wellingham-Jones in chapter 15; and Frederick discussed below. But, as Dean demonstrates in chapter 12 and Lockowandt admits in chapter 6, these studies do not offer a convincing case for graphology. Why aren't more and better studies done to settle the issue? Graphologists have two excuses for not doing either kind of study, to which we now turn.

Holism. When graphologists are criticized for not doing a model 1a-type of validation experiment, their standard defense is to argue for holism. Holism is the view that "the whole is more than the sum of its parts."[15] In graphology, this cashes out as the view that a single handwriting trait, such as the slope of the crossbar of the *t*, is not simply correlated with a personality trait such as enthusiasm or pushiness. Rather, a handwriting trait will mean one thing when associated with some other handwriting trait such as long descenders on letters such as *p* or *q* but quite another when associated with another handwriting trait such as thin loops on letters such as *l.* Therefore, some graphologists maintain that model 1a-type studies simply will not work: we cannot measure the influence of one handwriting trait in isolation; the only way of evaluating the influence of these traits is by examining the handwriting sample as a whole.[16]

But there are two problems with this line of defense. The first, explicated by Dean, Kelly, Saklofske and Furnham in chapter 13, is that if graphologists were right about this, they never would have discovered it using the methods they profess to use.

The second problem is that it is not clear what graphologists' claims to evaluate personality from handwriting samples could *mean*, unless they hold that, *everything else being equal*, a particular handwriting trait *G* will be found together with a particular personality trait *T.* That is what is meant by saying that there is a *positive correlation*, though less than 1, between *G* and *T.* And graphologists do make assertions of such correlations all the time. For example, consider Mahoney (1985:251) on the *t* crossbar: "An ascending slant connotes enthusiasm and an uplifted spirit. Those who allow their enthusiasm free reign in the world of dreams and hopes for the future exhibit this characteristic *t*." Now this certainly sounds like an unqualified assertion of a correlation, even if it isn't so clear how strong the correlation is in her view (no correlation coefficient is given), or what "enthusiasm" really amounts to and so we would be hard pressed to suggest a criterion for it.

But never mind. If we cannot get the graphologist to solve these problems for us, the problem is not holism, but simple vagueness. We will not know what hypothesis is to be tested, and we will not know whether the prediction is fulfilled or not. However, if we could get these problems solved, and if such a correlation exists, it will be possible to discover it by simply choosing a large enough group who make slanting *t* crosses, and a large enough control group who do not exhibit that handwriting trait, and measuring both groups against a criterion that operationally defines "enthusiasm" or an "uplifted spirit."[17] What constitutes "large enough" groups in this case will depend upon a number of things. First of all, the strength of the correlation: the weaker the correlation, the larger the groups will have to be for the correlation to show itself. Second, we will have to decide between two strategies about how to deal with all the other handwriting variables which might be connected with the personality trait, and which confound our problem. One strategy is to start with large enough samples of randomly chosen subjects, so that we have good reason to believe that all these other traits will be found in equal numbers in the experimental and control groups. Then it will not matter if some of these variables do mask the correlation. Remember that the claim being tested is that, *everything else being equal*, uplifting *t*s are correlated with an enthusiastic personality. The second strategy is to *ensure* that there are the same amounts of the other handwriting traits present in the control and experimental groups. Then they should cancel each other out, and a difference in frequency of enthusiasm between the two groups should be thanks to uplifting *t*s.

This is just the method called *control by random variation*, and it is successfully used for testing the efficacy or side effects of new drugs. If it works in pharmacology, despite the fact that the human body is an interrelated system with hundreds of variables compounding the picture, there is no reason that it should not work in graphology despite large numbers of interrelated variables. And this method works in orthodox psychology, despite the fact that even lower animals such as rats are integrated systems with hundreds of variables to deal with; not to mention the fact that with humans, psychologists regularly abstract from thousands of variables to find correlations between just two. Graphology simply cannot engage in special pleading—there is nothing special about handwriting variables that is not the case with the traits psychologists routinely handle. The main point here is that if holism in handwriting is true, it would not prevent us from discovering correlations between handwriting and personality traits by doing proper large-scale validity studies. In fact, if the problems were as thorny as the graphologists maintain, this would be the *only* way we could discover such correlations; they would never have come to the attention of graphologists, given the hit-and-miss methods they traditionally employ, as is pointed out by Dean et al. in this volume.

Processual Validation. Lockowandt describes a method in chapter 6 which is a rival to the two standard types of validity study discussed earlier. Its main advantage, he claims, is that it deals with the perennial disagreements over interpretation of personality characteristics that occur between graphologists and lay people such as personnel managers or supervisors. It is because of these disagreements, Lockowandt argues, that many people mistakenly come to the conclusion that graphologists fail to determine people's personalities accurately. As I described in the "Graphological Traits" section above and Klimoski describes in chapter 11, the normal way of handling this type of problem in science is to reach agreement *in advance* about what the prediction is really stating. This involves eliminating the vaguenesses in the personality judgment made by the graphologist, and in the criterion that is used to determine whether or not the prediction counts as accurate. As Klimoski shows, it is seldom a problem in industrial psychology to reach such an agreement prior to doing the study. But Lockowandt's method has the advantage for the graphologist of making it impossible for the graphologist ever to fail a validation study. Where there is disagreement between a lay person and a graphologist about a given subject's personality, what is required is:

> . . . a kind of dialectic operation in the original sense. Every well-meaning, but at the same time critical, researcher will come to the conclusion that the validity of statements is not of dichotomic nature, it is not either true or false, but in certain stages of this process—a process which can last for several years in difficult cases—it may vary considerably. At the beginning it may be very low or even zero; however, after long and deep discussion it may be high.

In other words, if the lay person accepts the graphologist's analysis, it is validated; if he does not, the process simply carries on until the lay person accepts it! As Randi says of the strategy of the psychic, "When you win, you win, and when you lose, you win." Not bad for the graphologist—but it's not science either. It is impossible to test a hypothesis without already agreeing in advance what hypothesis is to be tested and what will count as success or failure of the prediction.

WHAT A SCIENTIFIC EXPERIMENT PROVES

It might be thought that, because skeptics are "out to disprove graphology" whereas believers are "out to prove it," skeptics and believers in graphology will run entirely different experiments. In fact, the experiments themselves and the logic behind them should not differ no matter who is running them. Even if the *expectations* about the outcome of the prediction differ in the two groups, both will test *the same* hypothesis, and also the same prediction. For example, in a Model 1b-type experiment, the prediction will be that the graphologists being tested *can* discern personality traits by discerning the handwriting traits correlated with them. If the prediction turns out to be true, then skeptics and believers must both use the argument form (1) given above, along with the assertion that no other rival hypothesis would make the same prediction, to argue that the hypothesis is probabilified. If it is false, then skeptics and believers must both use argument forms 3 and 4 to argue that the test shows that the hypothesis has been disconfirmed. Of course, believers *expect* to use the argument for probabilification, while skeptics *expect* to use the argument for disconfirmation, while a person with a completely open mind would not have any idea until the data is in which arguments she will be using. However, it is highly unlikely that a person who has invested enough time to be in a position to conduct this type of experiment competently would be so unfamiliar with the issues to have an open mind *in this sense*. But this really does not matter. Unless skeptics or believers have some supernatural ability to *make* their expectations come true, any difference in the truth or falsity of the prediction of the experiment will be because of a difference in the initial conditions. Believers who are already convinced of the truth of graphology may be less willing than skeptics to entertain alternate hypotheses, and therefore may be less likely to design controls in the experiment that will rule them out. They may also be convinced by the prowess of the particular graphologists they are studying, to the degree that they do not bother to use all the care necessary to prevent the graphologists from picking up information from non-graphological sources.

Defenders of graphology often are quick to point out that "all" the skeptics have shown by showing the prediction to be false in an experiment is that *this particular* hypothesis has been disconfirmed—that *this particular (group of) graphologist(s)* could not demonstrate their abilities in *this particular experiment*. From this evidence alone, we cannot generalize to the conclusion that graphology is worthless. Of course this is true, for the reasons outlined above ("Scientific Expeirments"). But to say that "all" the skeptics have managed to prove is the above is like my admission that "all" I have been able to prove about the existence of Santa Claus is that he has never come down *my* chimney. But, given that none of my friends have reported a visit, and that I have reasons to suspect reports that he has visited other people, and that there are theoretical reasons for finding this existence claim implausible, I think that my skepticism about Santa Claus is more than just a peculiar prejudice. The main reason for this is that, properly, the onus of proof is on the believer in Santa Claus, not on me, the skeptic. And so is the onus on the defenders of graphology. Thus, the skeptic who presents negative results is presenting a very strong case, given the lack of positive results from controlled experiments from believers.

Testing an alternate hypothesis. Skeptics who are convinced by the rationale which parallels the Santa Claus reasoning just given must still confront the most ubiquitous—and, unfortunately, the *best*—argument in favor of graphology: Why do so many people, who are not fools, believe it works, *unless it does*? Dean et al. (chapter 13) discuss 23 biases that influence us toward thinking that a system of discerning personality traits, such as graphology, astrology, or phrenology, works even when it does not work. The most commonly discussed bias is the *Barnum Effect*, discussed in chapter 13, Bowman (chapter 10), and Klimoski (chapter 11). It is incumbent upon skeptics to offer experimental evidence to show that the Barnum Effect can explain people's tendency to believe that graphology works even if it doesn't. Karnes and Karnes (chapter 16) describe an experiment probabilifying the Barnum Hypothesis. In a crucial experiment, we test *the same prediction under the same initial conditions*. If the prediction comes out *true*, then this will support the graphological hypothesis; if it comes out *false*, it will support the Barnum Effect hypothesis.

So, in this type of experiment, an outcome which supports graphology cuts against the Barnum Effect, and vice versa. At least it does so on the presupposition that is defended by most graphologists, that their clients' claims to be able to match the personality profile with their own personality is evidence that graphology works. Most graphologists are not in a position to deny this, since it is the strongest argument they know of in favor of their discipline.

To sum up this section, then, there are two types of experiments that you will encounter. The first will test a hypothesis entailed by graphology. If the prediction entailed by this hypothesis is verified by the experiment, then this supports graphology; if it is falsified then this puts the ball in the believers' court: it is up to them to show other evidence that supports their belief. The second will test a hypothesis maintained by skeptics who attempt to explain why people believe in graphology despite the paucity of experiments of the first sort which support graphology.

HOW TO READ THE SCIENTIFIC LITERATURE

We turn now to the scientific literature reporting on the experiments that are offered in support of, or as evidence against, graphology. The first problem that might trouble the reader is that he or she was not there when the experiment was done, and hence must rely upon the honesty and integrity of the researchers. However, skepticism has its natural limits, and those limits are reached when further doubt is very unlikely to save one from error, and is likely to prevent one from accepting the truth. Given that authors are exposing themselves in public and placing their reputations on the line, we have some reason to have confidence in what they publish. Academics do suffer from being exposed as frauds or incompetents. Journals suffer as well, as do the reputations of their editors. So, despite the worries raised recently about fraud in science by authors such as Kohn (1988), Savan (1988), and others, we should remember that these authors were in a position to gather their data precisely because the fraud-detecting mechanisms did work, albeit more slowly than would be ideal. Thus, unless we have reasons to the contrary, we are not very likely to go far wrong by accepting the data presented in a journal that has a solid reputation.[18]

As it turns out, the usual way readers are led astray—intentionally or otherwise—is not by what *is* said that is false, but by what is *not* said about the initial conditions. The most common example of this is the lack of a clear statement about whether the test was double blind: whether the experimenter who was in contact with the graphologist being tested knew the information (e.g., the results of the criterion) the graphologist was trying to discern. Sometimes we are not given precise information about how well the graphologist knew the authors of the handwriting samples, and thus was influenced by something other than the handwriting. Usually we are told whether the handwriting samples were copied from the same source (e.g., a book or a magazine), in which case we do not have to worry about the graphologist getting information from the *content* of the handwriting (except for unintentional spelling mistakes, which can be revealing). However, many graphologists refuse to work from such samples, claiming that they are not "spontaneous," and for some reason never clearly specified, this prevents them from giving an accurate analysis. So, in many cases, graphologists work from personal letters, or, since the major interest in graphology is in personnel selection, many experiments are conducted using job application letters. This material is rich in personal information: obviously, someone applying for a job requiring an engineering degree is almost sure to have one, even if the letter doesn't say so; and age, place of birth, previous job history, and other relevant information gives the graphologist who can put two and two together, even subconsciously, an enormous edge. There is a reason why people so often resort to stereotypes about other people: they often *work*. Despite the fact that there are so many exceptions, if we follow them, we can often discern enough about a person to appear to be psychic (Hyman 1981), or to have knowledge about a person from a testing method such as phrenology or palmistry. But in journal reports, space is at a premium; and so we do not see the contents of the handwriting, and thus can only guess about how much the content influenced the graphologist's assessment.

Fortunately, the scientific journals have over the years established a standard format for papers, so it is easy to find the information that is available to evalute the experiment being reported. Psychology journals, where one is most likely to find a properly controlled study on graphology, almost universally follow this format. There are generally four sections to a scientific paper, each of which contains the elements I have discussed above.

The Introduction. The typical paper begins with an introduction, whether it is so labeled or not, which outlines the derivation and the importance of the problem being investigated, the results of other relevant research, etc. It is from this discussion that we get an idea of the theory that the authors are defending or attacking. Sometimes we have to piece together the theory from several places in the introduction and in the "Discussion" section (which I mention below), rather than finding it clearly stated in one place. We will also find here the statement of the *hypothesis* being tested, and the *prediction* that is expected, given that the hypothesis is true. This is the most important thing to look for in this section, but it is also important to ask the question raised above, whether the hypothesis being tested is really entailed by the theory being discussed. Some very good experimentalists are not as good theoreticians, and despite the fact that they go on to describe a very elegant experiment which provides very good evidence for the hypothesis, all this is for naught if the hypothesis isn't after all entailed by the theory. If this is so, then providing strong evidence for the hypothesis doesn't provide evidence for the theory being discussed.

Method Section. The introduction is usually followed by a section entitled "Method," wherein the procedures of the experiment—what I referred to above as the *initial conditions*—are described. It is here that the reader will look for conditions that would permit the prediction to come true even if the hypothesis were false—that is, if *some other* rival hypothesis were true instead. This problem is usually referred to as *confounding of variables.* As I said above, it isn't worth one's while at this stage to *simply* doubt that the initial conditions really were as described. The reader wasn't there, so he or she cannot determine this any better than the experimenters could. And, if a clever fraud took place, the experimenter can be expected to have covered his or her tracks sufficiently well that it cannot be discerned from an armchair several miles away, and several months or years later. However, what the reader can do is to ask herself whether the experimental design is inappropriate to determine whether these initial conditions are present. The "Method" section should describe the way measurements were taken, what instruments were used, and what precautions were taken to prevent the graphologist from gaining information through channels other than the handwriting. Central among these safeguards is the "double blind" condition. Questions about these procedures are relevant, and not just idle skepticism. And the most fruitful questions will be ones that will suggest modifications to the experimental design for a replication of the experiment. If there are legitimate doubts as to whether the initial conditions were as described, the modifications needed are ones that will more clearly determine this in a replication. Suggesting these modifications is therefore the positive contribution the skeptic can make, as opposed to simply doubting.

Results. In the third part, usually headed "Results," the author(s) state whether the prediction entailed by the hypothesis was verified or not. Again, as with doubts about initial conditions, doubts about whether the prediction came true are best settled by paying attention to the statements in the "Methods" section about how the effects were measured.[19]

Discussion. In the last section, the authors generally go on to discuss what they think they have proved, and careful authors point out what they have *not* proved. Also, we want to know whether what the graphologists managed to discern in the experiment was very imoprtant in two senses. First, we are interested whether the probabilification of the hypothesis being tested provides such support for graphology. Second, if it does provide theoretical support, most of us are interested in whether graphology has any *application* as a diagnostic tool—for example, in personnel selection. Careful readers will pay close attention at this point to Geoffrey Dean's advice in chapter 12: ask *how big* the effect size is. Perhaps the effect size is so small—even if it is highly statistically significant—that graphology would be useless as a selection tool. Or, perhaps the effect size is respecable, but there are a number of other methods of discerning the trait in question that are much better.

But paying attention to this question is pointless until we examine the first question about importance raised above. Even if the hypothesis is probabilified by the experimental result, the question about the centrality of the hypothesis still remains, and it is very easy for authors to overestimate this.

My examination of the literature convinces me that reports which satisfy *all* the criteria mentioned above provide negative results for the central claims of graphology. I know of no study published in English that unequivocally satisfies all the criteria, including the double-blind condition, *and* supports graphology. Lockowandt cites in chapter 5 a number of studies published in German which he advocates as examples of good tests; but he does not provide the details necessary for us to examine them here.

Since they are not available in English, the skeptical defender of graphology who reads no German, and who knows my professed position on graphology, may not want to trust my summary. So I shall present in the next section a test to which the reader may defer.

A SAMPLE SCIENTIFIC PAPER

The study which is most often cited by graphologists who pay attention to the scientific literature as one that provides strong evidence for graphology is Frederick (1968).[20] This study appeared in the *Journal of Abnormal Psychology*, a respected, peer-reviewed scientific journal. We have no difficulty in identifying the hypothesis being tested and the prediction which would probabilify it. The initial conditions are described carefully enough for us to see in general how the experiment was conducted, even if there are crucial details which I wonder about below. If all the experiments on graphology displayed *at least* this degree of rigor in their design, I would have no hesitation in describing graphology as a discipline backed up by careful scientific method. As for the degree of support this experiment provides for graphology, I have reservations which I shall outline in a moment; but I must emphasize that the criticism to follow is not directed at the author, since in his discussion section he never claims to have established a central tenet of graphology.

The hypothesis which was tested is neatly laid out in the "Discussion" section (p. 266):

> A priori, it seems reasonable to believe that there might be something operating within an individual at the time he is preparing to commit suicide which would reveal itself in a motor-expressive act such as handwriting.

In other words, if the various theories of graphology are true, Frederick maintains that the above hypothesis should be verified. Now for the *caveat* that I mentioned above: As Nickell mentions in chapter 2, the one tenet which is central to all schools of graphology is that handwriting traits are enduring qualities which correspond to long-term personality characteristics, such as nervousness or honesty. Notice that the probabilification of Frederick's hypothesis in this study does nothing to bolster this tenet of graphology. As I just said, this is not a criticism of Frederick; for he nowhere claims that it does. However, many supporters of graphology who cited Frederick to me implied that it did. What it does support is a claim only tangentially related: viz., that graphologists can detect very transitory features found in people's handwriting under extreme circumstances. Second, we should be clear about how little consolation the prob-abilification of this hypothesis provides for graphology as a practical diag-nostic tool: as a help in preventing suicides, it is of no use to be able to detect agitation or nervousness in the suicide note. If the person contem-plating suicide is available for study, the agitation or nervousness will be observable in many other ways; and if the note is all we have left to study it is too late. Frederick candidly admits (p. 266) that in an earlier study (1965) a trained graphologist could not distinguish between the handwrit-ings of hospitalized psychotic patients and those from a control group of non-hospitalized people matched for age and sex. As Frederick puts it, "[a]pparently the writing of non-hospitalized psychotics as a group is de-void of clear-cut expressive signs such as anxiety, depression, aggressive-ness, etc., which permit it to be distinguished from that of non-hospitalized persons" (ibid). Thus, a potential suicide has to be very close to the actual event before the agitation or depression will be manifested in the handwrit-ing; thus my claim to its very limited efficacy.

Thus, Frederick's two studies taken together provide evidence going against the claims usually held by graphologists, that they can discern long-term personality traits. It is at most the transitory ones that graphologists can discern. And this is bad news for those who argue for graphology's efficacy as a personnel selection tool; for it is precisely the former that they offer to tell prospective employers about, and graphologists claim that one of the virtues of their system is that it doesn't confuse the discerning personnel manager with transitory features of the person that show up in a handwriting sample because of nervousness about the job applica-tion itself, or a fight with a spouse the morning that the handwriting sam-ple is done. So, beware of a graphologist who tries to sell you a deal on personnel selection by citing Frederick. This graphologist either hasn't read it or understood it, or hopes that you won't.

Still, the above criticism says nothing about the quality of the experi-ment. So, I now turn to the question whether this hypothesis, along with the initial conditions, entails the prediction. First, the initial conditions: Frederick took 45[21] actual suicide notes, and had three independent per-sons, matched for age and sex with the suicide, copy them onto paper matched to the original suicide note, thus providing three control notes for each genuine note. The 45 sets of four notes were presented to three groups of subjects—one experimental group and two control groups. Group 1 consisted of five graphologists, and two control groups were comprised of subjects ignorant of graphology: one was comprised of five detectives, and the other of five secretaries. All subjects were to choose the genuine note from the four notes in the set, for each of the 45 sets presented. The object of these conditions was to ensure that whatever motivated the choice, it would not be the content of the note, since this was the same for all the notes of the set, nor the telltale signs that were independent of graphological characteristics. Thus the assumption was that the *only* marks that would distinguish the genuine suicide notes from the controls were graphological cues available to the graphologists but opaque to the non-graphologist control subjects. The expected frequency of hits for each subject would be between 11 and 12, if that subject were reduced to random guessing. Seventeen guesses would be statistically significant—17 or greater would occur only about twice in 100 such experiments if nothing but random variation were present.

Given these initial conditions, the prediction expected was essentially a two-part one: (1) that the graphologists' success rate would be statistically significant (i.e., 17 or better), while the non-graphologists would be in the range expected by chance 95 times in 100 (between 6 and 16 correct guesses); and (2) that the differences between the experimental and control groups would be statistically significant.

The results appear to be a very strong vindication of the hypothesis— see Table 1.[22] Both of these predictions were confirmed by the actual results. In a preceding section I said that the verification of a risky prediction— that is, one not made by the other rival theories—counts much more in favor of the theory than one which is made by all the rival theories as well. So, what we should now ask is whether some *alternate* hypothesis explains these results as well or better. That is to say, could some other hypothesis, along with these initial conditions, *also* explain these experimental results? To answer this question, we need to examine the initial conditions of the experiment a bit more closely.

As I already mentioned, the first thing to check for in the "methods" section is a statement about whether the test was conducted "double-blind." Here is what Frederick tells us (p. 264):

> In most instances, the experimenter himself was not fully aware of which note constituted the original since they were arranged by the research assistants and co-workers.

This leaves open the possibility that in *some* instances the experimenter *was* fully aware of which of the four choices was the original note— and the *really* skeptical amongst us may wonder whether in the remainder of the cases, he was *partially* aware. In any event, the possibility of the experimenter *unwittingly* cuing the graphologists toward the correct choice is there in this protocol, by Frederick's own guarded admission. Note my emphasis on "unwittingly": I am *not* suggesting anything like fraud. As some parapsychologists have finally discovered, after skeptics spent years

TABLE 1

JUDGE	NUMBER CORRECT	LEVEL OF SIGNIFICANCE
Graphologists		
1	30	10^{-8}
2	25	0000119
3	30	10^{-8}
4	28	.00000001
5	27	.00000007
Detectives		
1	16	.0753
2	14	.2159
3	15	.1327
4	11	.5911
5	15	.1327
Secretaries		
1	16	.0753
2	15	.1327
3	12	.4543
4	16	.0753
5	13	.3252

trying to convince them, many cases of supposed telepathy are more readily explained as instances of transmission of information by subtle, though wholly prosaic means that were opaque to both sender and receiver. For just one of the many discussions of this problem, see Hines (1988:82–84). A quick glance at Table 1 will reveal that these sensory cues would have to be effective in only a third of the graphologists' guesses in order to provide the difference between their success rates and those of the controls. Of course I have no idea what role subtle sensory cues played in obtaining these results. My point is that this is an alternate hypothesis not ruled out by the experimental design; and therefore Frederick's hypothesis is not shown to be superior to it by this experiment. Obviously we need a replication of this experiment, with this alternative ruled out by ensuring that it is double blind.

A second problem does not reveal itself in Frederick's discussion, although he did say something that made me want to do some more investigation. Describing the subjects, he states (p. 264):

> The graphology judges were all fully qualified professional European psychologists trained at the universities of Berlin, Freiberg, Stockholm, Basel, and Munich. One was a former university professor. American detectives and secretaries served as control judges.

So the graphologists had a further advantage over the control judges: an academic training in psychology. Does the training in psychology explain (part of) their higher success rate? We do not know, and therefore need a further study to test this alternate hypothesis. But that is not my main worry. The graphologists were European, and the controls were American.[23] So, it would appear that either the experimental or the control group was at a disadvantage because of a language barrier. Which group was it? To answer this question, we need to know the language in which the original suicide notes were written. Frederick doesn't say. Also, I *presume* that the control notes were written by people fluent in that language as well, though again Frederick does not say. So I speculate. For these speculations, it would be helpful to know where the experiment was conducted. Again, Frederick doesn't say, but Lockowandt (chapter 6) provides us with a clue. He reports that the experiment was carried out in collaboration with the Institut fur Tillampad Psykologi (Institute of Applied Psychology) in Saltsjobaden, near Stockholm, Sweden. Presumably that is where the suicide notes came from. But where did the Americans in the control groups come from? At the time Frederick worked at Patton State Hospital in Patton, California. Did he test control groups in the United States? If so, it would be no surprise that Americans, unfamiliar with Europeans' handwriting, may have missed subtle cues available to the European graphologists. Of course, these cues would be useful if the graphologists had access to other information about the subject which could be correlated with the actual person who committed suicide. And, indeed, this information was in some cases made available to the judges (p. 264):

Each note was given an identifying number with the date on each [writer of the original suicide note] such as age, sex, and method of suicide recorded on a separate sheet of paper. This was available to judges who cared to use it. In some instances, religion and place of birth were also noted; in others, they were not.

So, if the information provided to the judges suggested the nationality of the writer of the suicide note, and the control notes were written by people from a different country or region from the suicide note writer, the graphologists may have done better than the control judges by using information other than graphology. That is, the graphologists and the control judges may have both known from the information provided that the actual suicide was in her 50s, born in Stuttgart, and had access to drugs readily available to a veterinarian, since ingesting drugs prescribed only for dogs was the method of suicide. But the European graphologists, and not the Americans, might have seen a lot of samples of middle-aged European veterinarians' handwritings, and further, be aware of the writing styles taught in Stuttgart schools just after World War I. We do not have to postulate that the European graphologists were able to identify all three controls on this basis. Being able to eliminate even one control by these means increases the judge's chances of a hit on a particular trial from .25 (4 choices) to .33 (3 possible choices).

We do not even have to speculate that the graphologists were *consciously* using this information in this way. But some graphologists do pride themselves on being able to identify handwriting from the region or country where particular handwriting features are taught. Goldberg (1986) reports that he lost a case of scotch in a bet with a graphologist who claimed to be able to do just this. So, even though it is impossible to tell how much of an advantage this added information in fact was to the graphologists, the fact that it was available is enough to ask that the experiment be replicated with this source of information eliminated.

Given the above, we are not in a position to say that Frederick's hypothesis is supported in this experiment. We have equal grounds for the hypothesis that the graphologists were able to outperform the control group simply in virtue of being more familiar with the characteristic handwritings of the authors of the notes, or that they were on some trials accidentally cued toward the correct answer by an experimenter who knew the correct target. And third, I suggested (note 21) a problem with the execution of the experiment that may have magnified the differences between the graphologists and the control judges. I do not maintain that I have *proved* that any one, or any combination, of these problems suggests an alternative hypothesis that accounts for these data better than Frederick's hypothesis. But my last point about the evidence we get from scientific experiments is that I do not have to. The burden of proof is on the defender of graphology to show that Frederick's hypothesis is more probable than an alternative hypothesis suggested by my criticisms. The standard way of doing this is to replicate this experiment, changing the initial conditions to rule out these problems that I have noted, and then to see whether a similar prediction gets verified. In the 22 years since this experiment was done, no such replication has been reported.

CONCLUSION

Even non-scientists should have little difficulty in analyzing the evidence presented in a paper published in a scientific journal. The reader can test this claim by trying her hand at analyzing the two papers presented in Part Five of this volume, by Wellingham-Jones and Karnes and Leonard. The reader who lacks independent verification of the facts or results presented in the paper, or the statistical tools to calculate the results for herself, is not at the disadvantage she might feel at first blush. She can rely upon the integrity of the authors, and the perspicacity of the journal editors to catch some mistakes in the data or statistics. Anyway, the real problems in scientific papers are to be found in the *arguments from* these data.

The reader is not so fortunate, however, in dealing with most of the publications from graphological organizations or popular books touting graphology. Most of the evidence presented for graphology in these publications consists of anecdotal evidence and testimonials from satisfied customers. Or worse, many books in this *genre* offer signatures or short handwriting samples of famous people from which we are asked to "infer" their personalities. For example, Paterson (1980:21–26) shows us that we can see "reaching for the stars" in Neil Armstrong's signature, "concentration" and "efficiency" in Bertrand Russell's, and that the murderer Crippen was "headstrong, aggressive, and hard." Where data are presented, often a little digging is required to extract it. In most cases, however, no useful data at all are presented. In this case one might adopt the strategy that works very well at the used car lot: If the salesman doesn't know the answers to your questions, or seems unwilling to provide the answers, wise consumers remember that there are other cars available, even if the sales pitches do not make them sound so attractive.

NOTES

1. A reflection for a moment on this point will show us what is wrong with the graphologists' explanation for why so many psychologists, at least in North America, reject graphology. Defenders of graphology maintain that this is because psychologists are in competition with graphologists, and therefore the former have financial reasons to denigrate the latter. However, psychologists also have financial reasons to borrow anything which works. Therefore, we have reason to suspect that if graphology proves to have anything going for it, psychologists will take over graphology. The acceptance of hypnotism by some psychologists is an example of this phenomenon. Note I am not maintaining that hypnotism has much therapeutic value (see Baker (1982), Hilgard (1979), and Zusne and Jones (1982) for reasons to doubt this. My point is rather that, *despite* the suspiciousness of hypnotism, so many psychologists have demonstrated their open-mindedness (perhaps to the degree of *credulity*) on the matter, precisely because they *think* that it works. Defenders of graphology may retort that all I have shown is that the attitude toward graphology is like the attitude of many psychologists toward hypnotism before it became more widely accepted. But this response simply takes us back to the place in the argument from where this red herring sidetracked us: *how reliable is the evidence that graphology works?*

2. Of course, it is not a simple matter to state what is required to make a theory testable. Fortunately, we do not need to provide a full account of this for our purposes. Readers wishing to pursue the vast literature that has accumulated around Karl Popper's (1968) first attempt at stating the requisite conditions might wish to begin with the papers collected in Section II of Grim (1982). This section also includes the gist of Popper's orignal article.

3. The reason that there are different methodologies for different disciplines is that there are truths about different kinds of things. The majority of philosophers (though not all—for a dissenting viewpoint, the best place to start is with Mill 1970 and Quine 1960 and 1961) hold that the objects of mathematics and logic are different *kinds* of things from the objects of science. That is why different methodologies are appropriate to study them. We need not concern ourselves with the disputes in philosophy of mathematics or philosophy of logic over how similar the methods of logic are to the methods of science. Furthermore, I take it that I need not bother to justify the claim that graphology makes straightforward empirical claims: e.g., that there is a correlation between this feature of handwriting and that personality trait is about as good an example of an empirical claim as I can think of.

4. But not all of them—see the qualifications in Lockowandt.

5. As evidence of how widespread the respect for the *principle* of open-minded skepticism is, note the numbers of defenders of graphology who begin their defense with "I used to be skeptical, but . . . ," and then carry on with their evidence. But this evidence is almost always anecdotal, not the sort that would convince someone who was genuinely skeptical.

6. Another term for "theory" is "model." As an orrery or planetarium pro-

vides a *visual* representation of the solar system which demonstrates the relationships between planets, moons, etc., so an astronomical model provides a representation *in words* of these sorts of things, and also of more abstract notions such as causal or correlational relationships. See Giere (1982) chapters 5 and 6 for a more comprehensive discussion of this.

7. In conjunction with other statements—very few statements entail much by themselves.

8. Some may object to calling this statement a hypothesis, on the grounds that it is so firmly established. Indeed it is; and this points out an ambiguity with this term. (In fact, it is the ambiguity used by "Creation Scientists" in order to state that the theory of evolution is "just a hypothesis.") "Hypothesis," as defined in the *Oxford English Dictionary,* is "A supposition or conjecture put forth to account for known facts; *esp.* in the sciences, a provisional supposition from which to draw conclusions that shall be in accordance with known facts, and which serves as a starting point for further investigation by which it may be proved or disproved and the true theory arrived at." Thus, a hypothesis is *provisional,* and if it is confirmed by the facts, we should call it something else. Since the statement about water freezing (and also the theory of evolution) is so well confirmed by experimental evidence, we should call it something else. Perhaps we should; since there is a second sense of "hypothesis" which definitely does not fit: "A groundless or insufficiently grounded supposition; a mere assumption or guess." But, as I shall point out below, an experiment *never* confirms a hypothesis with certainty; so there is a sense in which all scientific claims are taken to be provisional: they are all subject to *possible* revision by further data, even if the probability of having to revise them is extremely low. (The theory of evolution fits into this category.) And there is a third sense of the term that fits the sense that it is used in the discussion below: "In *logic,* the supposition or condition forming the antecedent . . . of a conditional [If . . . then . . .] proposition." It is in order to capture this third sense that we call a statement, even when rendered highly probable, a hypothesis.

A second reason for objecting to calling the statement about the freezing point of water a hypothesis is that it is *now* counted as *true by definition*: We simply would not count a substance as water unless it froze at 0° C. This is true, but first, it was an empirical discovery (which has since been amply confirmed) that led to this definition; and second, if *per impossible,* water suddenly ceased to freeze at 0°, scientists would abandon this definition.

9. Ideally, such a prediction will be in the form of an *observation statement* (see Quine [1960:42–45]) and Quine and Ullian [1978] for a definition). Roughly, an observation statement is one that is true or false, and can be *determined to be* true or false independently of the theory that entails it. The reason why "the thermometer reads 0°" serves as an example of an observation sentence is that it can be determined to be true or false independently of the theories of thermodynamics which entail it on a particular occasion. Although there is a great deal of controversy over whether there really are any pure observational sentences, and this leads some philosophers to question whether we really can test theories by

the method described here (the problem of *incommensurability of theories*), I side-step this question here and refer the reader to Newton-Smith (1981), especially chapter 2.

10. Often this hypothetical statement is referred to as the prediction. This is a perfectly sensible use of the term, but the way we are using the term "prediction," it refers only to the *consequent* of this hypothetical statement.

11. The move from (2) to (3) in the argument below is justified by a Rule of Inference often called *Disjunctive Syllogism*. It tells us that to deny a conjunction—to say "not (H & IC)"—it is sufficient to deny *either one* of the conjuncts ("not H *or* not IC"). (This is the reason that the sign on your local transit system reads [with the logician's brackets added for clarity] "No Smoking *or* Drinking," not "No Smoking *and* Drinking." If it read the latter, you could satisfy the ordinance by smoking, as long as you refrained from drinking at the same time.)

12. Experimental psychologists call this attempt to make the personality trait measurable *operationalizing*.

13. Readers who are familiar with the skeptical literature on parapsychology are already aware of the necessity of double-blind conditions in paranormal research. Psychologists are well aware of these problems in their experiments that need to be handled by double-blind conditions, especially since the publication of Rosenthal (1966). And it is no answer to this requirement to design an experiment so that measurements are made with protractors or even more sophisticated instruments; so that despite the fact that the graphologist knows what results are expected, the measurements are "objective" and can be read only one way. Rosenthal (1966) provides numerous examples that belie this assumption. A further recent example is given in Maddox et al. (1988) of evidence for homeopathy, published in *Nature,* gathered by a simple procedure of counting tiny spots on a microscope slide that turned blue. Maddox et al. present convincing evidence that more blue spots were counted on the slide than were actually there, precisely because the experimenter *expected* there to be more.

14. Is there any necessity to design the experiment so that the control group performs at chance expectations? Could we design the experiment so that the graphologists and the controls both have access to non-graphological information about the subjects? The Frederick experiment described below does this, and we see from it why this strategy is a bad one. First, it enormously complicates the question of what the expected rate of success without using graphology should be: we must not only determine how an *ideal* subject would use this information to improve her score over chance expectation, but we must predict how successfully subjects will *actually* use it in this experiment. Secondly, if the graphologist does better than the non-graphologist, this *could* be because the graphologist is using the non-graphological informrmation better than the non-graphologist; and therefore a further experiment would be required to rule out this hypothesis.

15. For an excellent discussion of the original roots of holism in philosophy of biology, see Brandon (1985). His careful distinction between reductionism and mechanism in philosophy of science takes the wind out of arguments for holism in contemporary science; and his account of the original holism propounded by

Jan Smuts and J. S. Haldane as a *non*-vitalistic theory demonstrates how little succor New Agers can take from the position they have corrupted.

16. This line of argument is maintained not only by the gestalt school, which maintains explicitly this holistic assumption that it is not single traits that are correlated with personality, but rather global features of handwriting such as width of margins (see Nickell in chapter 1); it is also maintained by the trait school which does profess to deal with individual features of handwriting such as thinness or thickness of loops on *l*s. The latter school does hold that it is individual traits that matter, but they also fall back on holistic assumptions when asked for validation studies that demonstrate this.

17. This may not be so easy, since we would first have to get handwriting analysts to tell us what these terms *mean*. If they cannot agree, then the problem has nothing to do with the assumption of holism; it would simply be the case that they are not measuring anything at all.

18. Now, it might be held that the strictures that work to keep scientists honest when they are publishing in peer-reviewed scientific journals are not to be found, or are to be found to a lesser extent, in graphology journals. Even when they are peer-reviewed, the peers are those that are already inclined to accept the claims in question; and, in the climate of disbelief of graphology's claims found among North American psychologists and other scientists, the editors of and reviewers for graphology journals might be expected to be less critical of data which serve as good ammunition against the critics. As well, most North American graphologists are not very well educated. However, first of all, these comments apply to a *much* lesser degree to European graphology journals. Secondly, a much more important point: the skeptic who has to resort to accusations of fraud simply does not know his business. Methodological problems of the sort outlined in this chapter are sufficient to dismiss graphology's claims until better studies are done; and much of what appears in graphology journals simply isn't scientific evidence from a study. Much of what appears there consists of testimonials, anecdotal evidence, and the like.

19. One might worry about what has come to be known as the "Bottom Drawer Effect": if an experiment does not get significant results, obviously it is not going to get submitted for publication. Graphology experiments will almost always involve a prediction that a (the) subject(s) will do significantly better than expected by chance. The minimum level of above chance significance is "significance at the .05 level," meaning that if we repeated this experiment 100 times, we would expect only 5 results to be as high—*or low*—as this (we are talking about the end points on the classic "bell curve"). So, one might worry that the study you are reading is just one of the five, and the other 95 never saw the light of day. This is one reason why extraordinary claims usually have much higher levels of significance than the .05 standard. But, of course, an examination of the study itself will never settle this question for you. All you can do is to seek out further literature to determine whether this study has been replicated.

20. All page references in this section are to this article.

21. Originally 55, but 10 were discarded for what appear to be plausible reasons. One thing to be careful about, however, in evaluating a written report of an

experimental protocol, is to see whether the author clearly reveals *when* the protocol was changed to handle some sort of unforeseen problem. If one is suspicious, one might suspect unconscious selection of data in order to magnify an observed effect. For example, note Frederick's description of how these sets were determined to be unsuitable, and thus discarded:

> The control judges [i.e., the non-graphologist judges—*DFB*] were also used to assist in picking out any potential biases among the notes. For example, if the paper or blood smear on a note was thought not to be genuine, if the writing appeared on the back where it did not belong and could be noticed, etc., these could constitute a bias. Although such phenomena were not unequivocal in influencing the choices by the judges in any of the notes, to be certain that no biases were present 40 of the original 220 notes [i.e., 10 actual suicide notes and the three controls associated with each of them—*DFB*] were discarded from the final computation. (p. 264)

First of all, Frederick is to be commended for informing us of this change. For, what it suggests is that these 10 notes are ones that *were* identified correctly by (a significant number of) the control judges, and would have been identified correctly by the experimental group (graphologists) as well. Assuming that on average only 5 of the 10 notes could be identified by all subjects (graphologists *and* controls), then, from the results indicated in Table 1 (p. 265), at least 6 of the 10 control subjects would have achieved success rates significant at the .05 level, whereas without counting these notes, *none* of the control subjects did. Of course, this would not explain the highly statistically significant difference in success rates of the experimental (graphologist) group and the control group; nor would it explain the fact that the graphologists' success rate is highly statistically significant with these notes excluded. However, it raises the possibility that the graphologists noticed and made use of biases that they kept to themselves. *Of course* I do not know that this was the case; I merely raise the possibility as a reason for wanting this study replicated.

22. Those readers familiar with statistics may wish to consult Tables 1, 2, and 3 of Frederick (1968) for other statistical analyses which suggest a fair degree of inter-rater reliability amongst the graphologists, but none amongst the controls. On the other hand, those readers who are familiar with experimental design may want to examine the full description of the experimental protocols before bothering with this. The reader who agrees with my conclusion that the protocols are fundamentally flawed will agree that it wasn't chance that explains these results, but that the study doesn't demonstrate that it was noticing graphological cues either. Coming up with alternate explanations will not be aided by examining the statistics.

23. An explanation for Frederick having to go to Europe to find graphologists with a significant background in psychology is ready to hand: People with such dual training are much more common in Europe. Oskar Lockowandt, the author of chapters 5 and 6, is a psychologist trained in graphology, and is not that unusual. But, although there are notable exceptions—J. C. Crumbaugh, the author of chapter 7 is one—people trained in both disciplines in North America are pretty thin on the ground.

REFERENCES

Baker, Robert A., B. Haynes, and B. Patrick. 1982. "Hypnosis, Memory and Incidental Memory." *American Journal of Clinical Hypnosis* 25(4): pp. 253–262.

Brandon, Robert. 1985. "Holism in Philosophy of Biology." In Stalker and Glymour 1985, pp. 127–135.

Forer, B. R. 1949. "The Fallacy of Personal Validation: A Classroom Demonstration of Gullibility." *Journal of Abnormal and Social Psychology* 44: pp. 552–564.

Frederick, Calvin. 1965. "Some Phenomena Affecting Handwriting Analysis." *Perceptual and Motor Skills* 20: pp. 211–218.

Frederic, Calvin. 1968. "An Investigation of Handwriting of Suicide Persons Through Suicide Notes." *Journal of Abnormal Psychology* 73 (3): pp. 263–267.

Giere, Ronald. 1984. *Understanding Scientific Reasoning,* 2nd ed. New York: Holt Rinehart and Winston.

Goldberg, L. 1986. "Some Informal Explorations and Ruminations About Graphology." In *Scientific Aspects of Graphology,* edited by B. Nero. Springfield, Ill.: Charles Thomas, pp. 281–293.

Grim, Patrick, ed. 1982. *Philosophy of Science and the Occult.* Albany, N.Y.: State University of New York Press.

Hempel, Carl. 1979. *Philosophy of Natural Science.* Englewood Cliffs, N.J.: Prentice-Hall Inc.

Hilgard, Ernest R. 1977. *Divided Consciousness: Multiple Controls in Human Thought and Action.* New York: Wiley.

Hines, Terence. 1988. *Pseudoscience and the Paranormal.* Buffalo, N.Y.: Prometheus Books.

Hyman, Ray. 1981. "Cold Reading: How To Convince Strangers that You Know All About Them." In *Paranormal Borderlands of Science,* edited by Kendrick Frazier. Buffalo, N.Y.: Prometheus Books, pp. 79–96.

Ingram, Jay. 1989. "The Big Bang on Cable." In *The Science of Everyday Life.* Markham, Ontario, Canada: Viking.

Jensen, Abraham. 1973. *Validation of Graphological Judgments: An Experimental Study.* The Hague, Netherlands: Mouton.

Klimoski, R. J., and A. Rafaeli. 1983. "Inferring Personal Qualities Through Handwriting Analysis." *Journal of Occupational Psychology* 56: pp. 191–202.

Kohn, Alexander. 1988. *False Prophets: Fraud and Error in Science and Medicine.* Oxford: Basil Blackwell.

Lockowandt, O. 1966. "Faktorenanalytische Validierung der Handschrift mit Besonderer Berücksichtigung projektiver Methoden." Ph.D. dissertation, University of Freiburg.

Maddox, J., J. Randi, and W. Stewart. 1988. "'High Dilution' Experiments a Delusion." *Nature* 334 (28 July).

Mahoney, Ann. 1989. *Handwriting and Personality: How Graphology Reveals What Makes People Tick.* New York: Ballantine Books.

Mill, John Stuart. 1970. *A System of Logic*. London: Longman Group Limited. (Originally published 1843)

Newton-Smith, W. H. 1981. *The Rationality of Science*. London: Routledge and Kegan Paul.

Paterson, Jane. 1980. *Know Yourself Through Your Handwriting*. Montreal: The Reader's Digest Association (Canada), Ltd.

Popper, Karl R. 1968. "Science: Conjectures and Refutations." In *Conjectures and Refutations*. New York: Harper & Row.

Quine, Willard Van Orman. 1960. *Word and Object*. Cambridge, Mass: The MIT Press.

————. 1961. *From a Logical Point of View*. New York: Harper & Row. Especially "On What There Is," and "Two Dogmas of Empiricism."

Quine, Willard Van Orman, and J. S. Ullian. 1978. *The Web of Belief*. New York: Random House.

Rafaeli, A., and R. J. Klimoski. 1983. "Predicting Sales Through Handwriting Analysis." *Journal of Applied Psychology* 68: pp. 212–17.

Rosenthal, R. 1966. *Experimenter Effects in Behavioral Research*. New York: Appleton Century Crofts.

Savan, Beth. 1988. *Science Under Siege: The Myth of Objectivity in Scientific Research*. Toronto: CBC Enterprises.

Stalker, Douglas, and Clark Glymour, eds. 1985. *Examining Holistic Medicine*. Buffalo, N.Y.: Prometheus Books.

Zusne, Leonard, and Warren H. Jones. 1989. *Anomalistic Psychology: A Study of Magical Thinking*. Hillsdale, N.Y.: Erlbaum.

9

The Origins of Graphology
in Sympathetic Magic

Barry L. Beyerstein

In her book, *Crime and Sex in Handwriting* (London: Constable and Co., 1981, p. 11), Patricia Marne writes:

> Although the Ancient Chinese and Romans accepted that there was a relationship between handwriting and personality, it was not until comparatively recently that graphology could lay claim to being a science, following clearly defined rules, and producing findings accurate enough to be used in personnel work in the professions, and in commerce and industry, to assess character and suitability. Furthermore, serious practitioners have had to fight against popular misconceptions that associate graphology with fortune telling and forecasting the future.

In chapter 9, Barry Beyerstein suggests the misconception lies with Marne and her colleagues, not the skeptics. Beyerstein reminds us that there is much more to being a science than "following clearly defined rules." Tarot reading, for instance, has clearly defined rules—the crucial distinction between science and pseudoscience is the way in which their rules are derived and validated. Another fundamental difference is that a putative science must produce a plausible theory to explain *why* its objects of study are linked in lawful and predictable ways. In chapter 14 of this volume, Barry Beyerstein shows why the graphologists' preferred causal explanation (viz., the "brainwriting" rationale) is untenable on scientific grounds. What, then, *is* the underlying rationale for graphology? In the present chapter, Beyerstein shows, by examining a broad range of graphological publications, that the causal force is still—although rarely acknowledged—the ancient principle of magical corrrespondence.

*   *   *

Where any conviction remains in the existence of a supernatural order, . . . mantic practices are likely to persist. They are likely to flourish in proportion to men's recognition of their own weakness, and consequent need for help in solving problems beyond the scope of human competence.

M. Loewe and C. Blacker, *Divination and Oracles*

In chapter 14 of this volume I question the scientific status of graphology, criticizing the hypothetical mechanisms modern practitioners invoke to explain relationships that were postulated long ago between writing and personality. It is my task in this chapter to show that, scientific pretensions notwithstanding, handwriting analysis has not really abandoned its origins in ancient principles of magical correspondence.

MAGIC VERSUS SCIENCE

At the dawn of the scientific era, Francis Bacon (1561–1626) wrote that "knowledge is power." The methods he, Galileo, and others developed for realizing that power emerged from incomparably older, but similarly motivated, attempts to understand, predict, and control an often threatening world. The details of how the scientific attitude gradually distanced itself from its roots in tribal magic are lost in antiquity but the conjectures of many anthropologists, psychologists, and philosophers of science converge upon a few major themes. Though differences of opinion remain, there is little doubt that both magical and scientific thinking stems from the desire for a hedge against uncertainty by harnessing unseen but lawful forces assumed to govern worldly events.

Lacking an understanding of the true causes of weather and natural disasters, or of crop and hunting failures, accidents, illness, and death, our early ancestors were understandably desirous of ways to circumvent their apparent arbitrariness. In his classic work, *The Golden Bough* (abridged and updated by Gaster 1959), the Scottish anthropologist Sir James Frazer (1854–1941) suggested how the primitive search for such magical protections probably evolved into scientific notions of cause and effect (for good discussions, see Monte 1975, ch. 1; Alcock 1980, ch. 2; Zusne and Jones 1989, ch. 2). The scientific and magical worldviews share the belief that it is humanly possible to uncover and exploit the immutable, impersonal, and non-obvious rules that determine natural phenomena.

Based on his observations of extant non-technological societies, Frazer argued that the search for magical powers began with attempts to recognize regularities in the chaotic stream of experience. Primordial science diverged from magical thinking when it began to insist that these regularities, once intuitively grasped, must be submitted to the acid test of empirical validation. Frazer suggested that the seeds of the scientific attitude were sown when a few "shrewder minds" started to suspect the inherent unreliability of magic. Others who noticed this elasticity between rituals and their intended effects took the alternate route of inserting wilful, vain, or whimsical deities into the causal chain. They envisioned an animistic world governed by capricious spirits who must be flattered, cajoled or bribed to permit desired events. By contrast, both magical and rudimentary scientific thinkers viewed the cosmos as an orderly and non-capricious system, though their relative success in bending it to their liking it came to differ sharply.

Despite centuries of evidence attesting to the superiority of the scientific approach, the sorts of magical thinking described by Frazer are far from extinct in modern industrial societies. This has been strikingly documented by observers of popular culture (e.g., Basil 1989; Schultz 1989) and by empirical research (e.g., Shweder 1977; Marks and Kammann 1980; Rozin et al. 1986; Zusne and Jones 1989).[1]

Shweder (1977) sees this persistence of magical thinking as a result of the general disinclination of normal adults to distinguish the truly causal from the merely coexistent in their everyday experience, coupled with an equally strong bent for seeing symbolic, personally meaningful relationships between unrelated objects or events. As Dean et al. discuss in chapter 13, we are all prone to make predictable blunders of this sort when we rely on informal reasoning to infer causality in complex situations. Driving these errors are numerous mental short-cuts called "cognitive heuristics" (Tversky and Kahneman 1974; Nisbett and Ross 1980). Among other things, they contribute to the illusory validity of various pseudoscientific practices when we evaluate them subjectively rather than by formal logic and statistical tests.[2]

The penchant for seeing intentionality and meaning in random coincidence, the basis of most superstitious beliefs, is so pervasive that it is even demonstrable in laboratory pigeons (Skinner 1948), not to mention any gaming table in Las Vegas. It underlies all divination procedures[3] and attempts to sway events by magical means. At its core is the assumption that perceived similarity, in and of itself, permits physical interaction between the phenomena that are felt to be alike.[4] The fallacy here is what Zusne and Jones (1989) call "reification of the subjective," the tendency to accord causal power in the external world to symbolic or metaphorical relationships conceived wholly in one's mind.

Believers in magic are not wrong in assuming that events are subject to lawful, hidden influences, but in their conceptualization of the nature of these influences. It is these ancient but erroneous views of influence that science has discarded, but which live on in the rationales for various occult and pseudoscientific practices. These range from telepathy, water dowsing, homeopathic medicine, faith healing, and astrology to divination practices such as the I-Ching, Tarot, numerology, and palm reading—and, as I intend to show, to graphology.

MAGICAL CORRESPONDENCES

The bedrock of all magical thinking is the notion of "sympathy," the idea that "like-begets-like." This vague notion of "likeness" permeates the occult and pseudoscientific realm. Sympathy can arise from spatio-temporal contiguity (contact magic) or symbolic association in the mind of an observer (homeopathic magic).

According to the *Law of Contagion*, a mystical "essence" passes between animate or inanimate objects that come into contact. The transfer of this ill-defined influence ensures that these objects retain an affinity for one another after they are physically separated. Because of their magical "sympathy," and in defiance of all criteria listed in note 4 at the conclusion of this chapter, an action directed toward one member of the pair supposedly engenders similar effects in its now distant partner. Practices such as voodoo, for example, maintain that mutilating hair or nail clippings or an item of clothing discarded by the intended victim will similarly devastate their former owner.

Lest we think only untutored rustics are susceptible to such delusions, consider the following examples. One, beloved by the vast readership of supermarket tabloids, is the "psychic archaeologist" who claims to describe the long-dead owner of an artifact simply by holding the object and "absorbing its vibrations." Another remnant of magical beliefs (though rarely recognized as such) can be seen at "celebrity auctions" where admirers will pay a princely sum for a pair of socks once worn by Robert Redford. Even in research settings with avowedly non-superstitious people, a surprisingly large percentage say they would feel uncomfortable if asked to don Adolph Hitler's shirt (Rozin et al. 1986).

More central to the present discussion is a related staple of magical thinking, the *Law of Similarity*. Here, it is similarity in the mind of the observer that mystically connects unrelated objects, people, or events. Things that superficially resemble one another are deemed to share fundamental properties so that the image becomes interchangeable with the object. As with contagion, the image retains a magical affinity with its referent so that the vicissitudes of the image are reenacted in affiliated objects.

A classic instance is that of astrology, which began when some ancient observer of the night sky mentally connected dots of starlight to create images of bulls, rams, crabs, fish, warriors, etc. These free associations were, of course, quite arbitrary—different cultures were reminded of quite different entities by the same random patterns, just as assorted patients see diverse things in the diagnostician's inkblots.[5] In the case of astrology, these products of human imagination allegedly take on a life of their own, imprinting the attributes of each image upon people they "contact," i.e., those born when that pattern occupies the appropriate sector of the sky. "As above, so below," the old adage goes.

Operation of the law of similarity, or magical correspondence, is apparent in the traits astrologers claim these constellations impart to people. Those born under the sign of Aries (the ram) absorb ramlike impulsivity and wilfulness; Geminis (affected by the image of the twins) are infused with a vacillating, self-divided nature; and (alas!) poor Tauruses like myself are condemned to bullish lives of plodding obduracy.

It is my contention that graphology, like astrology, sprang from the same widespread tendency to assume that similarities perceived in the mind have causal force beyond one's private feelings and imagination. Psychologists have found that ordinary people with no knowledge of graphology tend to extend their impressions of total strangers' writing styles to the writers themselves (Warner & Sugarman 1986). The traits they impute are derived in the same intuitive, common-sense way that spawned graphologists' beliefs—e.g., people with big signatures are deemed to be dominant and powerful. There is, however, no reason to believe that these naive attributions, based as they are on questionable cultural stereotypes, are necessarily accurate.

These days, graphology enjoys a surface plausibility that astrology lacks because graphologists invoke, however inappropriately, mediating mechanisms that sound, at first blush, scientifically respectable. That advantage would evaporate, however, if it could be shown that the purported links between signs and personality are metaphorical rather than physiological as graphologists claim. In chapter 14, I show why we should reject the claims for a neurophysiological basis of graphology. It is time now to support my counterargument that the rationale for graphology remains today, as it was at its inception, belief in the magical potency of symbolism and allegory.

THE ORIGINS OF GRAPHOLOGY

Graphologists whom I have debated have been proud of the antiquity of their craft. They imply that its longevity attests to its validity but, of course, the durability of racism and sexism exposes the weakness of this argument. Graphologists implicitly concede this point when they reject (as they usually try to these days) any affiliation with astrology, a much older scheme for character reading than their own.[6] Nevertheless, I maintain that the underlying rationales for graphology and astrology are identical. I assert this on the following grounds. First, both systems ascribe characteristics to people by extending to them symbolic and metaphorical attributes of arbitrary signs or images. Second, those signs, their meanings, and their supposed powers of coercion, are wholly mental constructs produced by the free associative capacity of the human imagination, as shown below. In short, for both astrology and graphology, the image governs the object—the quintessence of magical thinking.

SYMBOLISM IN WRITING

Their magical lineage would count little against modern astrologers or graphologists if they had repudiated ancestral misconceptions in favor of empirically verified mechanisms—as astronomy did with astrology and chemistry did with alchemy. Many graphologists claim they have done this but, on the contrary, my survey of their books and articles reveals veneration rather than renunciation of ancestral follies. Take for instance the esteem still accorded Ludwig Klages (1872–1956), the "founder of modern handwriting psychology" (Lewinson 1986). The father of the "expressive movement" rationale I criticize in chapter 14, Klages based his "Science of Expression" on a string of dubious, unsupported assumptions about writing movements. In order to link writing movements to character, he appeals constantly to magical forces masquerading as scientific mechanisms. In the end, they boil down to the same old metaphorical correspondences. At the conclusion of the longest series of nonsequiturs in recent memory, Lewinson (1986: 7) sums up why Klages's "intuitive philosophy" for interpreting mystical symbolism in writing should be taken seriously: "The mind would not appear in action at all, if it were not coupled with the vitality of the person." Whatever this and her other equally obtuse generalities might mean, Lewinson (1986: 8) somehow thinks it supports Klages's postulate that

> [t]here is unity of character in all the volitional movements of any individual. Every personal movement will assume that manner of movement which is

characteristic of the individual. . . . Consequently, the handwriting is a volitional movement and must necessarily carry the individual stamp of any personality.

As usual, Klages asserts that which is to be proved. No definitions are given for any of the key terms and no reason to concede their existence except belief in his equally nebulous cosmic forces. One of these is "rhythm," a basic attribute of the soul, according to Klages. Lewinson explains that "Klages used rhythm as a psychic yardstick anchored in the Cosmos." On this unpromising foundation Lewinson bases her exegesis of Klages's allegorical system, starting with his idea that writing is

> formed by the personal "guiding image" and is markedly influenced by the individual's sense of space. It is a rhythmic movement condition, in which each single movement reflects the entire personality, the sum total of the writer's intellectual, emotional and physical tendencies. (p. 9)

Hard as I tried, I was unable to find any suggestion of a mechanism that could connect rhythm of writing movements to these attributes, other than a mysterious "will and feeling" of the soul that crops up regularly in Lewinson's impenetrable presentation of Klages's muddled dogma. His magical leap from written symbols to human conduct and the sweeping overgeneralizations typical of graphology are apparent in the following rendition of Klages's thought.

> Writing is systematized conduct . . . demonstrated in the regular stopping and starting of the pen. Connected writing can be considered an unnatural connection of natural life-factors, while disconnected writing can be considered unnatural disconnection of natural life-factors. The activity of logical connecting is extreme in cases of non-observance of the natural pauses in movement. The positive interpretation of connectedness is logical activity and a gift for synthesis and dialectic, deliberation, calculation, etc. (Lewinson 1986:11)

Of course, not a shred of evidence is offered to back up any of the tortured logic in this chapter in a self-proclaimed "scientific handbook" of graphology (edited by Nevo 1986).

Magical thinking is equally prevalent in the musings of the influential Swiss graphologist, Max Pulver (1889–1952). Pulver (1931) pronounced, by fiat as usual, that the mind approaches a blank page as a metaphor for the world—a testable hypothesis perhaps, but hardly something to be accepted on faith. For Pulver, ascending extensions of letters symbolized an uplifting, spiritual nature while descending ones indicated preoccupation with base motives such as material goods and sexual pleasure. Here we see a touching holdover from simpler times when pristine spirits dwelled in the heavens, far above the grubby world below.

A more recent disciple is Rose Matousek (1987) who adopts a view of the symbolic interconnectedness of the world that would have been quite acceptable to the Oracle of Delphi.[7] E.g., Matousek (1987: 10) asserts, "The performance of writing coincides with universal symbolism of moving forward and backward, into and out of, and challenging or withdrawing, just as with body gestures." As an article of faith, she accepts the graphological dogma that people whose script relates symbolically to certain maneuvers will behave in a like fashion—another clear example of assuming that which is to be proved. Matousek feels no need for proof because it is self-evident to magical thinkers that symbols command their referents in the real world (e.g., writers of open letters are open people).

Rand (1961: 44), to his credit, shows at least some minor discomfort with the looseness of this attribution process but he quickly gets over it. He agrees that graphologists' ascriptions seem like "superficial analogies" but he circumvents this to his satisfaction, though not to mine, by saying graphologists learn "to cultivate the technique [sic] known as 'empathy,' the ability to imitate various gestures, to feel the same impulses as the scriptor [i.e., writer]." Thus, he cascades one variant of sympathetic magic upon another.

Rand (1961: 45) asserts that his graphological "theory of motor tendencies" has a "sound theoretical justification." By this he means that written signs are "best understood by their general character—whether they are efficient or inefficient, progressive or retrogressive, etc." What in people's writing actually corresponds to these concepts is hopelessly vague as usual, but this does not hinder the usual leap of faith that the writer will have comparable tendencies. Rand's justification for why people's character would conform to their handwriting is that it is "palpably obvious" (i.e., he blithely trusts in face validity instead of seeking empirical evidence—see Bowman, ch. 10, and Klimoski, ch. 11, for the dangers of this approach).

Matousek (1987) realizes the need for some rationale beyond face validity, however. Oblivious to the fact that she is trying to justify magical relationships with her misconstruals of scientific data, she engages in the kind of naive neurological argument for graphology I criticize in chapter 14. She never considers what a tall order it would be to evolve a brain mechanism that could ensure someone's behavior conforms to interpretation of a symbol in his or her script which, in turn, just happened to remind someone of those behaviors (and often reminded other interpreters of something else).[8]

REVERSE CAUSALITY AND GRAPHOLOGY

A sure sign of magical thinking is that it permits the interchange of cause and effect and thus, reverse causality (i.e., effects can precede their cause). A prime example is the branch of graphology known as "graphotherapeutics" (de Sainte Colombe 1972). Not content merely to assert that character is revealed by symbolism in handwriting, this bizarre offshoot claims that altering a feature of a client's writing will eliminate the undesirable trait it represents. Once again, the author tries to justify this with an amusingly simplistic theory of brain function. As he says on p. 15:

> Character sets the individual pattern of each handwriting and is inseparable from it; consequently, a voluntary handwriting change, once achieved, produces a corresponding change of character. How is this possible? The circuit established between brain and graphic gesture by the nervous system is two-way. Thus, the ability of the brain to influence the writing hand is reversible.

De Sainte Colombe's book bristles with the pseudoscientist's love of neologisms, nonsequiturs, name dropping, reference to unpublished research, unreasonably high cure rates unsubstantiated by data, and misappropriation of scientific sounding but vacuously applied terms. The traits he attributes to writers are the usual metaphorical ones (e.g., light pressure means timidity, "no fighting spirit," or "possibly low blood pressure") (p. 117). Baselines that rise, then fall

> signif[y] a lack of perseverance. These people make a fine start . . . but their energy soon melts, and they give up easily. (p. 92)

But take heart, the remedy for this personal shortcoming is simple: straighten out the baseline and you straighten out the client.

To his credit, Crumbaugh (ch. 7) expresses doubts about the efficacy of graphotherapeutics, though he seems less concerned about graphology's metaphorical basis in general. I invite the reader to compare Crumbaugh's metaphorical interpretation of the slant of letters to that derived from de Sainte Colombe's (1972: 84) "graphometer." Whether the connection between symbol and behavior is conceived of as one-way or two-way, it is still magical if it is based on allegory and has no plausible mediating mechanisms other than scientifically discredited brain connections and the Law of Similarity.

Bunge (1984) reminds us that a reliable sign of a pseudoscience is lack of progress in a field; i.e., reverence for the founders' revelations rather than constant revising of theories in light of improved methods and new empirical data. The examples in this chapter show that, despite claims to the contrary, graphologists today are still wedded to the same metaphorical underpinnings the field has always espoused, ones modern psychology has repeatedly shown to be unreliable.

HOW NOT TO DEVELOP A PSYCHOLOGICAL TEST

As Bowman (ch. 10) and Klimoski (ch. 11) describe, psychology has learned from frustrating experience that development of valid personality and ability measures requires procedures quite the reverse of those followed by the founders of astrology and graphology. The scientific psychologist's search for a valid trait indicator starts by identifying a generally accepted criterion for the quality the test will ultimately identify. I.e., a set of attributes widely agreed to exemplify a trait such as introversion, gregariousness, leadership, or whatever. A large group of people acknowledged to possess the criterion attributes is then assembled and closely scrutinized to see what other characteristics invariably accompany the trait of interest. The hope is that some of these correlates could be used as simpler, cheaper, more convenient indicators of the desired trait.

Mathematical correlations are calculated between the criterion measure and each of these potential test items and those most strongly related to the criterion are retained for the next round. This set of provisional test items is then given to a new, randomly selected sample of people to see if those who score highly on them are in fact strong exemplars of the criterion behavior—and, of course, low scorers must lack the trait. On the basis of this information, the test battery is further refined and tried again on yet another sample of people (for details see Schmitt, Neal, and Klimoski 1991). Only after several iterations of this procedure would an ethical psychologist release the test for use in situations where it could significantly affect people's life prospects.

Contrast the foregoing with the origins of astrology and graphology where the signs came first and the empirical validation stage was skipped altogether. The originators of these character-divining schemes first noticed some symbols—in the heavens and on a page, respectively. We might ask what determined which of many possible patterns qualified as one of these signs? The answer is the subjective impression of the observer (see the section on pareidolia below). Those configurations that reminded the selector of certain actions, players, or events were assumed, by the principles of magical similarity, to have some sympathy, affinity, or predictive value with respect to their referents in the world.[9]

In later examples, culled from the graphological literature, note the nature of the disputes when graphologists disagree about what attribute a given sign indicates. The conflict never involves conflicting empirical data, but invariably stems from differing subjective preferences for one versus another of the many equally possible mental associations the sign might trigger (and hence what trait to attribute to the writer). But first, let us look at how such associations come to be formed initially.

PAREIDOLIA—THE BASIS OF GRAPHOLOGY

The kindling of imagery by random patterns is familiar to every schoolchild who gazes at billowing cloud formations in the sky and sees majestic beasts, clashing legions, or gallant ships of the line. Psychologists refer to the products of this imagination process as "pareidolia" (Zusne and Jones 1989: 77–79). They are the basis of all divining schemes. Divination involves intuiting scenarios or personal descriptors from the free associations triggered by random patterns such as lines on the palm, smoke in the air, entrails of oxen, tea leaves in a cup, or scribbles on a page.

A rejoinder I frequently encounter from believers who concede the magical origins of graphological signs is to deny that modern practitioners rely on these sorts of cues any more. Crumbaugh and other supporters of Graphoanalysis,[10] e.g., downplay the significance of single letter shapes that would suggest pareidolia directly. They prefer to derive "holistic" impressions by noting similar "strokes" that a writer employs as parts of many letters. Nonetheless, the examples of sign-trait correspondences Crumbaugh cites (ch. 7) still analogize these strokes to behaviors in ways reminiscent of the symbolic systems of Klages, Pulver, Matousek, and de Sainte Colombe, described earlier. E.g., backslanting strokes, for Crumbaugh, as for every other graphologist I've encountered, allegedly indicate people who "draw back" from social interaction.

ON WHAT DO GRAPHOLOGISTS BASE THEIR ASSERTIONS?

The many graphological publications I reviewed before beginning this chapter were depressingly similar to other areas of "pop-psychology" I have criticized elsewhere (e.g., Beyerstein 1990). I sampled, I think fairly, from a broad spectrum of graphological works, ranging across different schools and historical periods and from academic treatises to the worst of the dime-store "know thyself" paperbacks. As noted earlier, a striking feature of graphology, like other areas of "pop psychology," is the vague usage of scientific-sounding concepts such as "rhythm," "tension," "dynamics," "sensitivity," "forcefulness," and "energy." In keeping with the folk psychology out of which graphology emerged, no operational definitions of such terms are given and insufficient evidence is supplied to back up the bald assertions that they are represented in people's script.

Rand (1961: 46), in a model of pseudoscientific discourse, constantly borrows terminology from the legitimate scientific literature but uses it in idiosyncratic and inapproprite ways. Examine, if you will, his use of terms such as "pure psychomotor impulse," "kinaesthetic impressions," "psycho-physical significance." See also Matousek's use of "energy discharge," below, and Rand's (1961: 44) mutilation of the concept of "empathy," mentioned earlier.

The graphological systems I encountered were also essentially unfalsifiable.[11] They are replete with ad hoc arguments for explaining away inconsistencies and thus clearly unscientific. I leave it to the reader to decide if Lockowandt's "processual validation" procedure (see ch. 6) would pass any fair adjudication of its falsifiability as defined by Dale Beyerstein in chapter 8. Likewise, Lewinson's (1986: 9) espousal of "the criterion of double meaning (plus and minus) of every graphological sign" allows each indicator to mean one thing or its virtual opposite! Hardly a testable theory.

Several other manifestations of pseudoscience (cf. Bunge 1984) were common in the works I reviewed. These include: (1) reliance on unvalidated, "common sense" notions of traits and motives derived from everyday language and folk psychology; (2) unfamiliarity with relevant scientific research and methodologically weak[12] or non-existent empirical support for their own views; (3) lack of standardization and practitioner accreditation in the field as a whole and constant bickering over key concepts by contending factions; (4) reliance on subjective estimation in place of rigorous mathematical operations; (5) a consistent tendency to assume that which is to be proved; (6) failure to derive acceptable theoretical explanations and mechanisms; (7) highly selective use of confirming examples and ignoring of contrary evidence; and above all, (8) magical thinking and its underlying conceptual error, "reification of the subjective."

Let us now examine some representative examples of the magical underpinnings of graphology. To highlight graphologists' reifications of metaphorical correspondences, I have preserved their exact wording in quotation marks or drop quotes, where appropriate.

GRAPHOLOGICAL SIGNS OF GENERAL INTERACTONAL STYLE

Matousek (1987: 7) interprets people's scribbles as an index of how they "discharge energy," her term for irascibility. Zigzag doodlings, with their preponderance of straight lines, remind her of lightning bolts in a stormy sky. Therefore, she says, these individuals are prone to aggressive, explosive discharges of energy. This sort of doodler is supposed to be brusque, argumentative, and, like a bolt from the blue, "goes to get what he wants." For Matousek, angularity signifies tenseness, so if scribbles change direction abruptly, it means the writer is subject to similar springlike snaps of mood. Paterson (1978: 17) embellishes this theme, branding writers of "sharp" letters as lacking sensuality and possessing a "Puritan streak." In short, jerky writers are just plain jerks.

On the other hand (no pun intended), billowy, curvy scribbles remind Matousek (1987: 7) of clouds blown by soft breezes. So this doodler must release energy in "free and sweeping impulses." In place of the uptightness of the angular scribbler, this halcyon soul has a "malleable and sensitive temperament which 'rolls' with the punch." Similarly, Teltscher (1971: 22) agrees with virtually every other graphologist that writers of smooth, rounded script are amiable, kind, gentle, and yielding—obviously people with no rough edges who go with the flow.

Despite the lack of credible evidence, a few of the foregoing ascriptions might seem at least intuitively plausible (if one accepts the dubious "expressive movement" argument I have criticized in chapter 14), but it is hard to find any rationale for the following claims of script-personality correlations other than sympathetic magic.

SIGN YOUR LIFE AWAY—
ONE PICTURE IS WORTH A THOUSAND WORDS

Graphologists also like to extrapolate to people the characteristics of objects found in their doodlings. Roman (1952: 36), e.g., reads into a woman's sketch of a top-heavy pile of books evidence that "plainly reveals [her] instability." Is your employer or fiance combing your wastebasket?

In the same pictographic vein, Teltscher (1971, ch 11) provides a chapter full of delightful examples of how signatures of famous people reflect their callings. He finds resemblance to musical notation in the signatures of Mozart and Lehar and "swordlike strokes" in those of Field Marshalls von Bismarck and von Blucher. Count Ferdinand von Zeppelin's autograph has a blimp-like quality and a local bishop's has a "large upper loop [that is] formed like a mitre, and the downward stroke resembles a pastoral staff." If Teltscher's carefully selected examples represent anything more than pareidolia, he fails to convince us by showing that these people included these flourishes in their signatures *before* embarking on their careers—and that inapproprite occupational symbols could not be just as easily read into the signatures of the professionals he chose. Also, he fails to note how many high achievers' signatures bear no resemblance whatever to their occupations.

Sara (1956), Smith (1970), Paterson (1980), and Surovell (1987) join Teltscher (1971) among the worst offenders as purveyors of this sort of highly selective, after-the-fact "proof" for their craft. They present samples of handwriting of famous individuals and then proceed to pick and choose those symbols in their writing that happen to be remind them of their well-known biographies. If graphologists could identify these sorts of signs *in advance* of knowing whose writing it was (admittedly difficult if the signee is a celebrity, but lots of very high achievers are not well known outside their professions), they might gain some credibility with this sort of theatrics. What the critics of graphology in this volume amply demonstrate is that handwriting analysts cannot pass this kind of *"blind"* test, their protestations notwithstanding.

Graphologists consider the signature especially important because it is supposed to be a "perfect pen print in miniature of what a more complete sample of your handwriting would indicate" (Holder 1958: 71). But again, there's the usual bit of waffling: there may be slight inaccuracy because people sign as they would like to have others view them. They may not have quite reached their ideal state yet. But signatures can be amazingly revealing, according to Matousek (1987: 16): a married woman who signs her given name bigger than her married surname betrays an unhappy marriage.

I-WITNESS TESTIMONY

Next to the signature, the personal pronoun "I" is the graphological "ego symbol." Matousek (p. 15) calls it the "private self estimate." Just like magic, Smith (1970: 37) says, "An inflated ego is shown by the inflated upper loop which makes the *I* tower above the others." Matousek (pp. 15–16) claims that the person who makes the *I* taller than other capitals shows that his or her "ego is trying to reach commanding heights." But if we minimize our *I*s, we "don't elevate ourselves substantially. . . . self importance has a diminished value."

Ornateness is also a useful clue to self-regard. "Beware of the man or woman who makes capital letters which are very ornate. These people are vain to the point of vulgarity . . . [and] will do anything to get attention," says Smith (1970: 30). Kurdsen (1971: 89) particularly dislikes coarse, ungraceful capital *M*s, equating them with coarse, vulgar people.

GENERAL ORIENTATION AND INTERESTS—
THE TWILIGHT ZONE

Given the nature of handwriting, it is not surprising that spatial metaphors abound in graphology. A recurrent theme is the assumption that a writer's primary devotions are reflected in the proportionality of the upper, middle, and lower segments of his or her letters, the so-called "zones." The upper zone contains the stems of letters such as *d*, the lower zone the stems of letters such as *g* or *y*, and the mid zone accommodates the body of the letter. In the best traditions of sympathetic magic, clients are saddled with folk psychology labels that have no theoretical basis other than their symbolic association with the concepts of "upper" and "lower."

Roman (1952: 140) sees nothing wrong with a supposedly scientific enterprise being founded on such shaky assumptions. She justifies the three zone concept, for instance, by reference to the mystical numerological significance of the number three—after all, there is heaven, earth, and hell, the Christian Trinity, and the anatomical divisions of head, thorax and abdomen. Roman's system is the basis of the one still used by Wellingham-Jones whose work appears as a sample of modern graphologists' research in chapter 15.

Never bashful about reifying metaphysical symbolism, Rand (1961: 45) claims that prominent upper extensions reveal up-beat concerns such as intellectual pursuits, imagination, spirituality, and idealism—the "higher" aspirations, as we say. Conspicuous middle zones mean a practical, "down to earth" person, and those who exaggerate the lower zones of their letters are supposedly "low life" types who probably also try to submerge these predilections from general view. Elaborate lower extensions expose a preoccupation with material interests, physicality, sexual conduct, and social ambition—the "baser" pursuits.

In this way, graphologists type writers as imaginative vs. reality oriented or animated by idealism and spirituality as opposed to instinctual desires, physical needs, and mundane concerns. Why so? because thoughts are experienced up in the head and are supposed to be inspired by "lofty" concerns whereas folk wisdom places avarice, instincts, gut level feelings, and the gonads, conceptually as well as anatomically, in the nether regions. Imagination and intellect are up; elimination, regurgitation, and procreation are down, so look to the homologous portion of the writer's script for their manifestations.

Paterson (1978: 11) agrees that those whose swollen loops dangle too far below the line may be a bit too "sensual" for polite company but shows how to spot the solid citizenry. They are the ones whose letters exhibit copybook equality of their upper, middle, and lower zones, showing that they, like their script, are blessed with "a good sense of proportion," whatever that might mean.

Exegesis of the spatial metaphor can get quite detailed. For instance, Martin (1969: 78) asserts that long, stiletto-like lower loops indicate love of money—obviously "sharp" operators. Long, bulbous (dare I say well hung?) lower loops signify strong sexual urges. Short, pudgy lower loops, reminiscent of little paunches and lunchbags, betoken preoccupation with food. But on p. 27, Martin (1969) says these urges could be subconscious, so we needn't worry if the writer doesn't overtly conform to his or her analysis, or even disavows the reading. The system is beautifully unfalsifiable, and on that ground alone, unscientific.

Since individual letters have upper, middle, and lower zones, they too are ripe for symbolic interpretation. Crosses on *t*s can go up or down like mercury in a thermometer and are used analogously by graphologists. Smith (1970: 20) says a high *t* cross is a sure sign of an "idealist," but be careful because a weak high cross reveals a "day dreamer." Unfortunately, Crumbaugh (ch. 7) won't attend this *t*-party—he thinks high *t*-bars indicate a high degree of will power.

Whether or not this fine level of analysis is valid is one of the sources of dispute among the different schools of graphology. Though Crumbaugh's Graphoanalyst colleagues demur (see ch. 7), the vast majority of handwriting analysts say very precise attributes can be gleaned from such minute features of single letters. Despite the Graphoanalysts' deprecating attitude toward the other, "occult" schools of graphology (their president's term for the competition), my survey finds them following the same beaten paths. E.g., Stockholm (1988), publishing in *The Journal of Graphoanalysis* (the self-proclaimed "World voice of scientific handwriting analysis"), says of a young client:

> This boy has a mental quality which is usually ascribed to adults—abstract understanding. It is most clear in the tall upstrokes of the *h*s. It denotes an ability to grasp or understand abstract concepts. This gift is invaluable in working with abstract subjects. . . .[13]

At least since Heraclitus in the first century B.C., the unconscious has always been portrayed metaphorically as beneath the conscious so, naturally, one looks below the line for evidence of seething instinctual urges. Matousek (1987: 10) reiterates the justification for this assumption she shares with Pulver, Roman, Rand, and others:

> We write on a real or imaginary line, or base line, which divides conscious activities that are above from subconscious activities below. In graphology

the baseline is also considered the line of reality because all letters should "touch base" or make contact with it.

And why can we be so confident of these attributions that we might decline to hire or marry a denizen of the wrong zone, or worse yet, suspect him of pilfering from the stock room? According to Rand (1961: 45), the proof is self-evident.

It is unnecessary to cite any rhetorical expressions associating aspirations with ascent, directing thought up and away, to the firmament, or those identifying corporeality with the earth, focusing attention downward. It would not be denied that they are well-differentiated symbolical expressions everyone knows.

In poetry or figurative language the connotations of words add variety and convey subtleties of meaning. As figures of speech, metaphors and the images they invoke can be engaging and informative. But as the power by which signs or omens supposedly command their referents, they are magic, not science. Having come to the bottom of this section on the symbolism of elevation, I must share one of my favorite up-down metaphors, one Oscar Wilde with his fine ear for nonsense never intended to reify: "We are all lying in the gutter, but some of us are looking at the stars."

SIZING YOU UP—YOUR PERSONAL PERSPECTIVE

Another favorite spatial metaphor in graphology is size. According to Teltscher (1971: 29), large writing means that one's outlook on life is broad. This person thinks big, possibly to the point of pomposity. Saudek (1924: 272) warns us, "If absolutely commonplace formations are found in a conspicuously large handwriting, they express the self-important arrogance of a blockhead."

As one might expect, diminutive writing purportedly reflects modesty:

The modest person who conducts himself unostentatiously to avoid attracting attention does not need so much space, either in life or in his writing. (Teltscher 1971: 29)

But this too can have its down side. Small writing, says Teltscher, may be a sign of "a narrow outlook and lack of confidence." Paterson (1980: 9) agrees that petite letters indicate a modest person who shuns publicity, but they may also reveal feelings of inferiority. Martin (1969: 23) nicely sums up the orthodox interpretation of size: large script means the writer is interested in generalities (the broad picture); small writing reveals a person who is detail minded, i.e., one who dotes on trees rather than forests.

Smith (1970: 30) claims that wide-based, upper-case letters indicate a gullible person. Kurdsen (1971: 55) says that narrow base capitals are a sign of skepticism. Though my letters lack this feature, I certainly have the trait.

UPS AND DOWNS AND THE BOTTOM LINE

Lots of things go up and down, literally and figuratively. This provides graphologists with another of their favorite metaphors because baselines can ascend or descend. When they go downhill, so, apparently, does everything else. But when they are on the upswing, the sky's the limit (see, e.g., Crumbaugh, ch. 7, or Smith 1970: 9). For Holder (1958: 70) descending baselines mean a fretful, easily discouraged person who lacks ambition. In the extreme, lack of mental alertness and ill health are indicated. The person whose baselines are on the skids is usually subject to depression, pessimism, and despondency, but some caution is necessary before you refuse to hire or marry this alleged sad sack. That is because, as Smith (1970: 9) warns us, descending baselines could also mean nothing more than the fact that the writer penned the sample on her lap or simply needed glasses!

Sara (1956: 48) introduces another weasel factor—downsloping lines mean pessimism, as claimed, but it could just be temporary. It's noteworthy that graphologists claim that writing is so permanently fixed by personality that it cannot be disguised while they are also eager to explain away mistaken attributions by saying the trait really was there when the sign was written but it was only temporary.

The Law of Sympathy is hard at work in Paterson's (1980: 18) explication of the descending baseline: The "writer who always lets his lines slip away is possibly a pessimist, always feeling he is being dragged down." Teltscher (1971: 135) temporarily eschews magical connotations, attempting instead a bit of folksy physiologizing to account for why those in the doldrums take their baselines down with them. Pessimism, sorrow, disappointment, and resignation are accompanied by drooping of our bodies, he says—"We always think of the word 'droop' when we're depressed." This causes the arm to fall "back against the body because of its drooping posture, and the writing will . . . droop and sag."

Then there are the fortunate ones for whom it's "ever onward and ever upward." Sara (1956: 48) sees in their rising baselines evidence of a hopeful attitude. These people are ambitious, upwardly mobile, and not easily discouraged. Teltscher (1971: 135) finds exhilaration in this uphill struggle for the summit. Like a jet poised to take off, their "whole lines tend to rise," signifying their soaring moods and aspirations. But how deep are those feelings? Read on.

EMOTIONAL INTENSITY: THE PRESSURE IS ON

Matousek (1987: 12) analogizes intensity of pressure to intensity of feelings. Roman (1952: 263), in keeping with her Freudian bent, expresses this in terms of libidinal energy.[14] In general, heavy pressure means intense feelings, indelibly driven into the page, as it were. It follows (if we don't stop to ask why), that such a writer is as stubborn and difficult to change as his etched-in script. Martin (1969: 31) depicts the heavy-handed writer as the proverbial bull in the china shop, i.e., insensitive to others' reactions. Sara (1956: 69) also sees heavy pressure as a sign of forcefulness, an extrovert. For Rand (1961: 88, 90) it is proof of pugnacity, vulgarity, and willpower.

Conversely, light pressure means a flighty, changeable personality. This writer

skims across the surface . . . of the paper, emotional impacts are relatively slight so that long term prejudice doesn't set in. (Matousek 1987: 12)

For Martin (1969: 30), light pressure means a sensitive person—a lightweight who frets over every nuance and is easily swayed by others.

Exemplifying the unfalsifiability of graphology, Sara (1956: 68) makes a strong assertion and then provides herself an escape hatch. She accepts the conventional wisdom that light, threadlike writing means the writer is sensitive, easily influenced, and introverted. But her next line provides the excuse when these predictions fail to materialize. She admits one can find light writing in hard-driving, outgoing people who seek responsibility and positions of leadership. She resolves the apparent contradiction by asserting that their writing (which, by definition, cannot lie) reveals that they're really shy and retiring underneath but trying doubly hard to compensate outwardly.

THE WIDE OPEN SPACES

In one of the few graphological ascriptions that makes any non-magical sense, Teltscher (1971: 34) asserts that stingy people cramp letters, words, and lines together to save valuable paper.[15] Generous people, he says, are "prodigal of space and paper." Their letters are wide, words widely spaced, and margins generous. But the magical metaphors are not far behind.

Paterson (1980: 11) agrees narrow writers can be "economical to the point of meanness" but adds that this narrowness also reflects a tendency to "hold restricted views." She says the writer of broad letters spreads himself around. He "likes elbow room to think and move freely, and prefers to travel." If the lines run together, Sara (1956: 54) says it's thrift, but many other graphologists think it's proof of a muddled thinker whose thoughts rub together.

Rand (1961: 115) can't decide for sure whether crowding of words signifies parsimony or confusion of ideas, but Holder (1958) would opt for stinginess if there were additional negative signs such as the angularity discussed above. Absence of terminal strokes would clinch the case, for the miserly would surely be too close-fisted to finish their words properly.

Paterson (1980: 18) finds people who leave large gaps between words are "clear minded" but they can be lonely because "they don't mix easily." One wonders why such a writer wouldn't just be "spaced out" or simply an "air head." According to Paterson, small spaces between words "mean that the writer likes people around him most of the time. He can be indiscriminate about his choice of friends."

LEFT, RIGHT, AND YOUR SLANT ON LIFE

In discussing Crumbaugh's differences with de Sainte Colombe over "Graphotherapeutics" above, we encountered another favorite graphological symbol, backward and forward slant. Paterson (1980: 9) speaks for the profession in regarding left-leaning writers as passive—"unwilling to go out and fight the world." She says they stand back, hold back their emotions, and are typically found in jobs such as back-room research and work dealing with history and the past.

Right slanters, for Paterson (1980: 9), are active; they rush "forward to meet other people." They show their feelings and their "heart almost always rules the head." Stockholm (1988: 8), of the more-scientific-than-thou Graphoanalytic School, adopts her inferiors' interpretation of slant, finding evidence of "emotional withdrawal" in a client's backhand script. Roman (1952: 184) ascribes the same general significance to slant, but prefers to equate left slant with defiance, upright writing with self-reliance, and rightward slant with a compliant nature.

ISN'T IT TIME YOU WROTE?

Rand (1961: 48) maintains the canonical view of slant but adds a time dimension (time, for some reason, always progresses from left to right). Rand analogizes right-leaning writing to progressiveness: "freedom from restrictive ties with past experience." As we saw above, Paterson thinks historians' interest in the past is coded in their back-slanting letters. For Matousek (1987: 11), any suggestion of horizontal movement also symbolizes a time line:

> where we are, where we're heading and where we've been. Going back [leftward] symbolically represents a return to the past, to ourselves, and to the comfort of home.

Longstanding cultural superstitions and biases against leftness are common in graphology (see Roman 1952: 145). They are particularly prominent in Rand's (1961: 48) treatise. He finds leftward motions retrogressive, "unnatural, time-consuming, inefficient." Quite the opposite are right-slanting, right-thinking writers.

VARIABILITY—NOT THE SPICE OF LIFE

For most graphologists, irregularity in writing is bad because variable writers are variable people. Such a writer is "disorderly, lacks discipline," and is unsure of what he wants to do (Paterson 1980: 13). But again the hedge: these may be highly original thinkers. Regularity in writing indicates a steady, disciplined, orderly individual—it is typically found among members of the armed forces and civil servants, says Paterson. Paterson's magical underwear shows when she tells us (1980: 10) that varying slant means "an unpredictable person with *changing inclinations*" [emphasis added].

FOLK PSYCHOLOGY AND GRAPHOLOGY

Modern psychology only began to achieve real explanatory and predictive success when it replaced vague everyday language and folk explanations with operationally defined, empirically validated constructs. Old folk nostrums are able to explain little, in part because of their excessively symbolic nature but mainly because they offered little beyond old adages and aphorisms as after-the-fact rationalizations. The fact that mutually contradictory aphorisms are available to cover any and all situations seriously limits their explanatory utility: e.g., "Look before you leap" vs. "He who hesitates is lost"; or, "Absence makes the heart grow fond" vs. "Out of sight, out of mind"; or, "Birds of a feather flock together" vs. "Opposites attract." Reading the graphology texts I did, I was constantly reminded of this kind of "wise old uncle" advice, which, as Krebs and Blackman (1988) demonstrate, is satisfying but notoriously unreliable.

Some areas of psychology, notably Freudian psychoanalysis, have not gone as far in purging this sort of post hoc reasoning as more scientifically minded practitioners would like. However, authors following Ellis (1956) are aware of this shortcoming and are making strong efforts to operationalize key psychoanalytic concepts and tie them to empirical observations.

The constant use of folk psychology terms and concepts in the graphological literature, and especially the way they are allegorically linked to written signs, allows graphologists to fudge the value to be placed on any given interpretation. Everyday language can be a delightfully slippery thing. After all, as Bertrand Russell reminded us, "I am firm; you are obstinate; he is pig-headed."

Not only are graphologists' trait descriptors ambiguously defined, but the signs that supposedly indicate them are open to the same freedom of interpretation. Oddly, Rand sees this as a virtue rather than a weakness.

> The fact that several meanings are given one sign does not indicate vagueness and uncertainty, but rather discriminating distinction. (1961: 40)

For instance, in some of the many sample analyses I read, vertical writing was considered evidence of an upright, upstanding, self-controlled citizen. In others, it signified a repressed, uptight martinet. On de Sainte Colombe's (1972: 84) graphometer, when the needle, like the letter slant, is vertical, the writer is poised, calm, and self-reliant, and has "a neutral attitude toward most things." Disinterest or rigidity? Admirable self-control or stifling repression? Take your pick.

Kurdsen (1971: 53) provides another example of the nonfalsifiability of graphological judgments. He toes the party line at first—backhand means aloof, reserved, self-contained, and undemonstrative, BUT slanting too far left means the writer is really highly emotional but has suppressed it. What counts as "too far" is left to the subjective opinion of the graphologist. Martin (1969: 20) also admits she encounters left-slanting writers who are unexpectedly dynamic, friendly, and outgoing. But she can see that it's obviously a facade designed to keep people from really getting close to the repressed recluse within.

MIXED MESSAGES: SIGNS IN COMBINATION

The ability to modify interpretations when combining signs is another source of graphology's unfalsifiability, especially because the combinatorial rules are so loose. E.g., Rand (1961: 91) concedes that there's more art than science in determining the meanings of signs taken together. According to Rand (1961: 40):

> It will be realized when interrelationships are studied that a group, or cluster, of related signs is a more specific indicator of behavior than any single sign. In the process of analysis the graphologist does not evaluate one sign without searching for another corroborating sign or opposing ones. It is nevertheless true that many single graphic signs manifest quite definite, if not absolutely specific, traits.

Crumbaugh (ch. 7) also advocates forming a "holistic" impression of the client by merging several indicators from a sample of writing because, in combination, a sign might suggest something different from what it would by itself. However, a recent publication of the Graphoanalytic school he represents asserts, "The dot above the letter *i*, if firm and round, tends to indicate loyalty; if circled, it's a sign of independence."[16] Despite their "holistic" rhetoric, the "strokes" Graphoanalysts interpret seem to me just as molecular as other analysis schemes I reviewed. Stockholm (1988: 9), for instance, can apparently detect "fear of ridicule" in the fact that a client's "second *l* [in the word *still*] extends up a little higher than the first *l*." Ultimately, though, the "molecular versus global" debate is a red herring because, as Dean et al. (ch. 13) point out, a holistic impression, if it is to have any reliability at all, must be a lawful synthesis of influences contributed by individual signs. The possibility that, in combination, signs might indicate something different than they do individually is not at issue. Such interactions are often found in orthodox psychology. But if the global impression of the Graphoanalyst is not based on a repeatable recognition and integration of the components that contribute to the overall impression, then the holistic technique is even more open to the criticism that its pronouncements are merely pareidolia foisted upon the client. This leaves us with the question of where the presumed meanings of Graphoanalysts' "strokes" came from originally, for even if the same combination of signs repeatedly elicits the same character sketch, it could still be invalid because the signs themselves were based on magical correspondences to begin with.

As we have seen, graphologists typically say single signs are only suggestive but then go on to discuss single signs they obviously consider conclusive—until someone points out counterexamples. Then the post hoc excuse making begins. As with astrology, there's a built-in fudge factor—if the applicable descriptor doesn't fit, it's because there's another interacting sign that modifies the first. Rand admits many people's writing contains contradictory signs that must be individually weighted (to his credit, he admits this is a source of bias). Advocates of "holistic" approaches rely on the graphologist's intuition to form the necessary synthesis. But even if the individual sign meanings were valid, Dean (ch. 12) presents evidence that the human cognitive apparatus cannot accurately track the effects of that many interacting variables simultaneously. Computers might help here, but only if the initial assumptions are valid. Otherwise, no amount of correct data processing will save faulty input—it's G.I.G.O. ("Garbage In, Garbage Out"), the computer scientist's nightmare.

Let us now turn to some examples of how the magical attributions of graphology can most easily damage innocent reputations, namely, imputations of sexual and criminal misconduct.

SEXUALITY AND SEXUAL ORIENTATION— THROWN FOR A LOOP

There being specialists within every calling these days, it's not surprising that some graphologists concentrate on matters carnal. In her graphological guide to the amorous, called *Lovestrokes*, Harriette Surovell (1987: 57) endorses the widespread conviction that hanky-panky is revealed by what goes on below the line (e.g., "peculiar loops" mean sexual "kinkiness"). Hannah Smith (1970: 30) concurs that "a great variety of, and irregularities in, lower loops indicte sex [sic] deviation." Smith also informs us that if one of the lower strokes of a y or f is stronger than the other, this shows a temporary lack of interest in or ability to enjoy sex—something common in the writing of those contemplating divorce, she says. But Surovell notes that the gender of the writer must also be taken into consideration. Unclosed lower loops in a woman's script indicate orgasmic dysfunction but in males they mean unfulfilled sexual fantasies. If lower loops descend into the upper zone of the next line, this suggests inability to control sexual impulses (Surovell 1987: 58). Before you chuckle, remember these people offer advice to the police!

It's always seemed odd to me that graphologists presume to pass on total strangers' sexual orientation and practices when they decline to guess their gender—something ordinary citizens can guess from writing at a greater-than-chance level. Could this have something to do with the fact it's hard to prove or disprove allegations about highly personal sexual tastes, but a graphologist's ascription of gender is patently easy to check?

Surovell (1987: 120), in typical good taste, shows that a savvy graphologist would not have been deceived by the late Rock Hudson's facade of heterosexual panache. The clear indications of homosexuality she finds in Hudson's signature would have been more impressive if they had been noticed *before* the details of his tragic life and death became common knowledge. A similarly after-the-fact approach to classification is seen in Smith (1970: 34). The court's wisdom in incarcerating a "criminal homosexual" was confirmed by Smith who found obvious evidence of his "perverted excitement" in the "tangled loops" in his writing. Again, with 20:20 hindsight, Smith (p. 152) finds "crooked shapes below the baseline show the emergence of perversion."

All of this would be but a humorous example of human gullibility if there were not such dire consequences that could befall those labeled in such a cavalier fashion. A Vancouver graphologist recently offered to help weed out—surreptitiously, of course—the practicing (and potential!) pederasts in the local teaching ranks. He claimed 100 percent accuracy for a method that he would not even disclose to me. More shocking yet, he actually received a favorable hearing from several school district bureaucrats (for details, see ch. 1)! Increasingly, we also find graphologists making irresponsible attributions of dishonesty and violent tendencies based on nothing more than the magical correspondences discussed above.

DISHONESTY, CRIMINALITY, AND VIOLENCE— THE PEN MIGHT REVEAL THE SWORD

Graphologists' attributions of these disreputable tendencies are as ill-founded as their sexual lore, but there is much more disagreement among individual analysts as to what to look for when blackening someone's reputation in this area. Let us hope that if your employer hires a graphologist, you benefit from the luck of the draw. Rand (1961: 115), for instance, says an undulating (i.e., serpentine) baseline reveals a snake-in-the-grass. But for Martin (1969: 18), a wavy baseline means only a moody person who has his ups and downs. Similarly, for Smith (1970: 24) lack of dots on *i*s denotes nothing more sinister than absentmindedness, but Rand (1961: 116) regards undotted *i*s as among the "chief signs" of a "treacherous thief."

In presenting this argument, Rand demonstrates the preferred way of dealing with disconfirming facts in a pseudoscience. Along the way, he has to account for why the sample he reproduces has incriminating *i*s but also contains open-topped *o*s. He and others regard the latter as a sign of trustworthy openness (like "Little open mouths," says Sara [1956: 111]). Kurdsen (1971: 96) agrees; open-top *a*'s and *o*'s mean both a talkative and a generous person (the letters remind him of open purses). Because Rand's sample criminal had been demonstrably secretive, devious, and avaricious, he decided that, in this case, the inconveniently open os must mean "he would, under conditions safe to himself, be frank, but at other times mislead by pretending to be candid." Postdiction is a wonderful thing.

Similarly, Rand (1961: 116) has to explain away the long terminal endings on words in a sample of "criminal handwriting." That is because he had previously dubbed such extensions a sign of generosity. He waffles by saying that this miscreant "would be generous for the end-purpose of getting more than he gave."

For Saudek (1924: 244), ovals closed at the top but open at the bottom are a mark of dishonest, insincere persons—something is definitely rotten beneath the surface. To be fair, Saudek, of all the authors I reviewed, relied least on blatant pareidolia and metaphor in his scheme. He also tried to introduce some degree of quantification of actual writing behavior by measuring muscle movements. However, he devised a cumbersome, convoluted system for translating strokes into speed values that he then proceeded to interpret in highly questionable ways. For all his commendable attempts at experimental rigor, I found no evidence that Saudek's work has influenced modern experts on the psychomotor control of handwriting (see ch. 14). Even graphologists today seem only to pay homage to his memory while they continue to apply their much more simple-minded metaphorical interpretations.

Saudek listed ten general indicators of dishonesty in writing, any four of which he though were sufficient to impugn the writer's trustworthiness. In addition to the aforementioned ovals, they included such sins as (1) evidence of "a slow act of writing," (2) writing that conveys "a very unnatural impression," (3) "decomposing, spineless structure," (4) "touching up the letter formations," (5) pen frequently lifted from paper, (6) important parts of letters omitted, and so on. The evidence he presented in favor of his scheme looks impressive at first glance, but would never pass by today's methodological standards. Nonetheless, Saudek is to be commended for at least attempting to validate his techniques empirically, something all too rare in a field founded on subjectivism and free association.

Knowing in advance the details of someone's felonious background is a great advantage in ferreting out "obvious" signs of their criminality. Many of the books I reviewed presented samples of convicts' scripts with analyses that showed that the signs were so clear that we should have locked them up before they committed their crimes—or at least denied them jobs in our organizations. Teltscher (1971: 231) found indisputable signals in a proven malefactor's wavy baseline, backhand slope ("standoffishness"), cramped style ("pettiness, narrow mindedness"), long lower loops ("extreme materialism"), and weak *t*-bars ("opportunistic, given to following the path of least resistance"). Smith (1970: 19) also thinks weak *t*-bars mean weak wills—and thus susceptibility to temptation.

None of these authors thought it necessary to present anything but supportive examples. The need to determine the percentage of non-criminals who have "criminal" signs and criminals who lack the definitive signs seems to have escaped them. Such evidence probably wouldn't faze graphologists anyway, for if the signs were found in a non-criminal's writing, they would claim he had larceny in his heart that just hadn't manifested itself yet.

Such is the quality of thought that could cost you your job and your reputation. Every graphologist I've debated, and most of the ones I've read, has had his or her anecdotes about detecting employees with their hands in the till. None had demonstrated this under the kind of controlled conditions one would think the gravity of the charge would demand.

When the *Vancouver Province* (January 26, 1988) alleged that Hannah Smith had been offering graphological advice to the Canadian National Parole Board, she strenuously denied it. But her 1970 book reveals a keen interest in alleged signs of criminality in handwriting. She proudly reprints (1970: 7) acknowledgments of her help from high officials in the Canadian penal system (who presumably do influence parole decisions) and her own admission, on page 35, that she had supplied "complete analyses" of the writing of an accused bank robber and murderer for her sister, Simma Holt. Holt was then a reporter for the *Vancouver Sun,* doing a story on the accused, and wanted to know his "real character" before championing his cause in western Canada's largest newspaper. Holt was subsequently appointed to the National Parole Board where she claims to have stopped relying on her sister's insights into the criminal mind when deciding which convicts were worthy of release. Let us examine the quality of these insights.

We can rest easy knowing that those rehabilitating the rapists and murderers in our penal institutions are getting the finest psychological advice available when they consult someone who believes, as Smith (1970: 22) apparently does, that double crosses on *t*'s are diagnostic of "a schizophrenic or split personality." Though readers of the popular press might confuse schizophrenia with a split personality, those who scrape through my introductory psychology course never do. Why a split personality would double its (their?) *t*-bars remains a mystery to all but the magically inclined. The real mystery to me is why a double crosser wouldn't be a con artist instead.

In a book marketed by Canada's most prestigious publishing house, and containing little else but symbolic interpretations, Smith (1970: 28) displays her forensic acumen:

Although I do not care for symbolic interpretations in graphology, there is an *f* that resembles a gun and which was found extensively in the writings of Jesse James. It can mean a killer, if the accompanying writing is illiterate, brutal, immature, or angry. The self-same *f* can also be found in the writing of a very depressed intellectual who is becoming suicidal.

Smith (1970: 49) also says having *t*-bars shaped like clubs "shows an ability to be brutal" and "whiplash" *t*-bars mean viciousness and sadism (p. 146). But there's still hope; Kurdsen (1971: 106) says writers of whip-shaped *t*-bars are just practical jokers. Rand (1961: 154) takes Kurdsen's side on this one: wavy *t*-bars just mean humor. Elsewhere, though, Kurdsen does find sadistic signs in the written arsenal. On p. 127, he suggests that arrows in doodlings indicate a calculating, cruel temperament.

Toting up the sinister manifestations, Surovell (1987, p. 105) informs us that

> [t]he graphological indicators for violent tendencies are: lots of angles, excessive pressure, sudden stoppages, changes in direction, increased pressure at the end of a stroke. . . .

LEGIBILITY

Of course, anyone so cruel would not wish it to be widely known, so suspicion is immediately cast upon those whose writing is illegible, especially if his or her signature is a scrawl. That is because legibility supposedly indicates a desire to be clear and a lack of concealed or ulterior motives. But, for graphologists, illegible writers are dead as the employment office doornail: ". . . *illegible formations not attributable wholly to haste or care-lessness or physiological defects, are attributable to deception, concealment, dissimulation*" (Rand 1961: 49, emphasis in original). But before we pass sentence in absentia, Holder (1958: 54) charitably interjects that illegibility might merely indicate a "less accurate thinker."

Nonetheless, an illegible signature would be the proof we await. The writer is thereby hiding his or her true self—engaging in a "cover-up" or laying a "graphic smokescreen." This according to Matousek (1987: 16) who seconds Teltscher (1971: 231) on this vital matter.

GRAPHOLOGICAL SIGNS OF HEALTH AND AGE

It is obvious that any disease that affects sensory-motor coordination, produces fatigue or tremor, or lowers attentiveness can lead to deterioration in handwriting. However, the evidence that specific syndromes or symptoms are symbolically represented in script is about as good as that for sign-personality correspondences.

Though all graphologists seem to think they can spot mental illness, criminality, philandering, pederasty, closet alcoholism, and real or potential drug abuse, fewer of those I encountered claimed to diagnose physical illnesses. Those who did were far from timid, however. E.g., Kurdsen (1971: 93) and Holder (1958: 147) assert that ragged or broken upper loops are a symptom of heart trouble. Kurdsen (p. 94) also says broken lower loops indicate infirmity of the legs or feet. Smith (1970: 31) regards a complete break between upper part of the letter and its lower loop as a sign of weakness in the lower back or legs. De Sainte Colombe (1972: 117) asserts that low writing pressure is diagnostic of low blood pressure. The magical connection is too obvious to require comment.

Another basic disagreement among graphologists concerns signs of aging. Hanna Smith (1970: 13) says age isn't evident in writing but Graphoanalyst Emilie Stockholm (1988) claims it is. Rose Matousek (1987: 17), in siding with the nays, exemplifies the verbal sleight of hand so typical of graphology: ". . . it is not possible to determine age from writing because there are mature young people and immature older people." As with graphologists' refusal to guess gender, it's too easy to check an age estimate and very easy to weasel with an amorphous concept like maturity.

DO CHARACTER READINGS BASED ON MAGICAL CORRESPONDENCES REALLY WORK?

It is incumbent upon purveyors of services, before money changes hands, to document their efficacy. Consumers demand truth in advertising from toaster manufacturers, why not from those who offer to reveal their aptitudes, personalities, or state of health? This is especially true when people's reputations, personal relationships, and livelihoods are at stake and they may not even know they are being assessed.

In this chapter, I have cast doubt on graphology because, like astrology, it is essentially a divination process where metaphorical interpretations are attributed to people by magical means. Nonetheless, if graphology could substantiate its claims of efficacy, its supernatural origins would be irrelevant. If it cannot pass fair scientific tests of validity, we must also ask why so many people believe it can?

As the critics in this volume show, in properly controlled studies where clients are asked to find the reading done specifically for them in a stack of anonymous astrological or graphological sketches, they are no more likely to select their own than anyone else's. Moreover, giving an identical, randomly chosen, astrological or graphological description to a large number of people who assume it was done specially for them elicits a remarkably high estimate of its apparent specificity and accuracy from everyone. This has been shown repeatedly in well-controlled experiments such as that by Karnes and Leonard (ch. 16). When the opportunity for capitalizing on this so-called "Barnum effect" is eliminated, it becomes clear that the illusion of accuracy in non-scientific character readings stems from subtle embellishments the client unintentionally reads into the actual text (see Dean et al., ch. 13).

The mental operations that contribute to the "Barnum effect" are a by-product of the habitual modes of thought we use in making sense of the ambiguities of everyday experience; i.e., they are similar to the cognitive biases that spawned astrology and graphology in the first place. It is a fundamental drive of human cognition to "make sense" out of whatever we encounter —so strong is this urge that we often perceive relevance and meaning where none exists. This tendency to produce a plausible interpretation of the facts at hand is so ingrained that when we encounter a character reader's description we are unaware that we are unconsciously infusing the meaning and significance into the bare bones of the reading (see Hyman 1977, Dickson and Kelly 1985, and Dean et al., ch. 13). I invite you to see for yourself whether the relatively few publications in respectable, refereed scientific journals that support graphology[17] incorporate the stringent controls described in the foregoing references. That is, do they have the necessary controls to prevent these subtle cognitive biases, in graphologist as well as client, from spuriously making the reading seem accurate and revealing?

P. T. Barnum attributed his success to the fact that he "had something for everyone." Likewise, as we've seen, graphologists' readings tend to be sufficiently vague, broad, and inconsistent to encompass anyone. Take for instance the double-speak in a pre-employment assessment I recently received, done by the Handwriting Resource Corporation of Phoenix, Arizona. On page 3 of HRS's slick, no doubt computerized, "Comprehensive Profile" one finds client 264-84-1259 described as possessing the following strengths "to a very high degree (Intensity 90–100)": "task-oriented, motivated by projects and work assignments." Only to a slightly lesser degree is he/she "persistent and steadfast." But on the next page, under "weaknesses," we see the same person also rated in the highest possible category for "unstable and unpredictable emotions" and undisciplined, uncontrolled behavior." Also among #1259's purported strengths are that he/she is "direct and outspoken" and "truthful, honest and sincere [and] will not mislead others." But under "weaknesses" HRC finds that #1259 "exaggerates and distorts the truth" and engages in "unkind and inconsiderate treatment of others" . . . "to a high degree (Intensity 80–90)." For some reason, the "very high degree" of "advanced conceptual skills" and "clever problem solving capabilities" revealed in his/her script apparently doesn't prevent him/her from having "poor concentration skills" and "unsystematic disorganized thinking" and paying "little attention to details" . . . "to an above average degree." On one page it's "flexible thinking" (good), on the next it's "disorganized thinking" (bad). Under strengths, he/she is listed as highly "logical and reasonable." Under weaknesses, his/her "judgment is subjective, based on emotional reactions." HRC finds #1259 "adventurous," "challenge oriented" and eager to "consider risky opportunities" but simultaneously racked by "feelings of uncertainty" and anxiety and "too concerned with self protection." He/she is also "outgoing and friendly" on page 3, but becomes "unkind and inconsiderate of others," and "lack[ing] in tact and diplomacy" by page 4. I'm sure all of these contradictions could be explained away given enough pop-psychology bafflegab, but that would be small comfort to the job candidate or the prospective employer who paid good money for this mass of contradictions.

Astrologers, Tarot readers, palmists, phrenologists, mediums, and graphologists counter scientific demonstrations of their inadequacies by parading legions of satisfied customers. Such reliance on personal testimonials and the subjective impressions of practitioners has been shown repeatedly to be a weak currency, as research on the "Barnum effect" clearly demonstrates. Unless there is valid research to support the sign-behavior attributions and the Barnum-type sources of illusory validity have been scrupulously eliminted with appropriate "blind" controls, testimonials count for nought.

COULD PROPERLY DONE STUDIES OF HANDWRITING REVEAL VALID CORRELATES OF PERSONALITY?

I have never maintained that it is impossible, in principle, that some aspects of writing could correlate with certain personality traits, just that this has not been satisfactorily demonstrated—for the various reasons cited by the critics in this volume. Nevertheless, I do have strong a priori doubts that any existing school of handwriting interpretation could ever withstand proper scientific scrutiny. That is because the putative sign-trait correlations of all extant schools were and remain rooted in magical thinking. The meanings they ascribe to signs were derived from unvalidated free associations—pareidolia triggered by crude resemblances between script configurations and the various human attributes they supposedly indicate. Extension of these attributes from sign to writer in the absence of empirical evidence and a believable causal mechanism is pure sympathetic magic.

As I have shown, the arbitrariness and subjectivity of the pareidolia process accounts for the disagreements among warring schools of graphology. All disputants leap to the conclusion, however, that their particular interpretation is the true predictor of how the writer will behave. They can't all be right, but they can all be wrong.

As long as subjective interpretation of symbols remains the basis of graphology, it cannot claim scientific status. Furthermore, until graphologists produce a plausible, scientifically testable physical mechanism that could mediate the connection between symbol and behavior (along the lines I describe in chapter 14) they will remain open to charges of occultism or pseudoscience. And finally, until graphologists eschew folk psychology and become cognizant of the methods and data of modern scientific personality research they will continue to be relegated to the fringes.

To the extent that the graphologists included in this volume have tried to demonstrate empirical relationships between writing and personality, their attempts to improve upon "pop-psychology" handwriting analysis are commendable. While I still see major methodological problems in the graphologists' best research to date, their attempts to abide by the rules of scientific personality research are to be encouraged. It remains my prediction, however, that valid correlations, if any, that might eventually emerge from improved research methods will not be strong enough or specific enough to justify the use of graphology in job selection, criminal detection, marriage counselling, and the like (cf. Dean, ch. 12). The relationships, if any, will be modest, common-sense ones, apparent to anyone, and will hardly require graphological training to notice them. E.g., careful, neat writers might, as a group, tend to be more fastidious than messy writers. Even so, I doubt that such a restricted sample of behavior would be a reliable indicator of a global personality type, and the weakness of the correlation would make it doubtful as a predictor for any particular individual. I certainly know many neat people with atrocious handwriting and neat writers whose homes and offices look like disaster areas. Obviously, it is bad enough when one tries to extrapolate from a little sample of behavior to something straightforward like neatness but, as I show in chapter 14, traits such as kindness, promiscuity, and suspiciousness that have no obvious correlate in script or unique control center in the brain could hardly be represented in writing unless one engages in the magical fallacy of reifying the subjective. I will accept graphologists' data to the contrary if it meets the methodological criteria set by the best experts in psychological measurement. To date, this has not been the case.

SUMMARY AND CONCLUSION

To reiterate, in constructing a valid psychological test, researchers start with a pool of potential test items and no preconceptions about what the eventual battery will look like. They choose, by rigorous empirical methods, those items from a large pool that happen, for whatever reason, to correlate reliably with carefully measured criterion behavior—no matter how irrelevant or counterintuitive the items finally selected may seem. Graphologists' reliance on intuitively satisfying pareidolia to diagnose traits immediately brands them as holdovers from the pre-scientific era of sympathetic magic. Far from enhancing their believability, the fact that graphologists' and astrologers' signs bear an explicit symbolic resemblance to the traits they purportedly indicate actually detracts from their credibility. Modern psychology and physiology provide no reason to think valid correlates of complex traits should be so transparently obvious.

A field that exhibits so many of the attributes of pseudoscience listed by Bunge (1984) and lacks credible mediating mechanisms as outlined in note 4 of this chapter cannot claim scientific status. If it is founded on allegorical interpretation of signs, it is all the more suspect. Above all, such divination is unscientific because it is uncheckable—there is no objective way of resolving interpretational disputes. The Danish physicist and poet Peit Hein had this fatal flaw in mind in his *Ode to Freud:* "Everything is concave or convex; so everything has something to do with sex."

NOTES

1. It is ironic that the success of the scientific method has been so great that even the most blatantly antiscientific practices today feel they must claim scientific status (see, e.g., Seckel 1988).

2. See also the discussion of the "subjective validation" effect by Marks and Kammann (1980). A demonstration of its ability to create a false sense of accuracy in graphologists' assessments is provided in the experiment by Karnes and Leonard in chapter 16. A good discussion of how widespread deficiencies in quantitative reasoning skills lead to popular acceptance of unsupportable claims is contained in Paulos (1988).

3. "Divination" refers to any practice of augury, the attempt to foretell events, select persons for particular tasks, etc., by subjectively interpreting symbols, signs, or omens ordained by a "higher power" (Loewe and Blacker 1981). Graphologists

claim they do not foretell the future; however they ascribe traits to people that would be of no interest or use whatsoever if having them did not predict how their possessor would act in a job, marriage, ethical dilemma, etc. They also say what they do is not supernatural, but in this chapter I document the magical basis of graphologists' extrapolation of signs to people. Whether practitioners realize it or not, the interpretations of signs in handwriting were not arrived at in a scientifically acceptable manner, but by processes of augury.

4. According to scientific canons, an event occuring at one time and place cannot produce an effect, locally or elsewhere, unless a finite period elapses between the two events and unless that interval is occupied by a causal chain of physical mechanisms operating successively and continuously between the two times and two places (Broad 1949). Pseudosciences and magical thinking are almost defined by their misappropriation of scientific terms such as "ether," "resonances," "vibrations," "energies," "balances," "planes," and "dimensions" in order to make it sound as if their mysterious influences meet these scientific criteria. At present, the only scientifically accepted forces that can cause interactions among physical entities are the strong and weak nuclear forces, gravity, and electromagnetism. For a good discussion of these limitations on magical interactions, see Rothman (1988). It is axiomatic among occultists, nevertheless, that mental power can affect things in the world without any mediation by these physical forces (B. Beyerstein 1988). A characteristic feature of magic is that there is no conceivable physical mechanism to mediate physical effects—they "just happen" by wishing and expressing the right incantations.

5. Unreliable as the Rorschach ("inkblot") test is as a diagnostic tool, at least all its users claim is that, because there is no inherent meaning in the pattern, the patient's free associations might reveal preoccupations, turmoils, fears, etc., that could be worth exploring. No claim is made that there is only one "right" association to the pattern or that answers reveal anything beyond that patient's state of mind *at the time*.

The serious objections to the Rorschach test arise when diagnosticians insist on reading unprovable symbolic interpretations into patients' overt utterances—much as graphologists routinely do with writers' scripts. Graphologists often compare what they do to Rorschach testing. Seeking support from such a questionable technique hardly seems prudent, but even the alleged parallels are doubtful. That is because, while it is conceivable (though not well documented) that triggering free associations with random stimuli might cause *ideas* of special concern to the patient to "pop up," there is no reason to believe learned patterns of muscle activity in the hand and arm would go to the trouble of acting out subtle, symbolic representations of the writer's character, any more than hair growth would. This would be doubly so if the "true meaning" could only be revealed by a highly trained graphologist. Why did the human species supposedly go to the trouble of encoding all this hidden material in script if there was no one to recognize it between the time writing emerged and the first graphologists came upon the scene?

6. Though most graphologists today wish to be seen as scientific practitioners, and thus downplay any affiliation with astrology, the two professions have long been closely intertwined in Europe, particularly in Germany (Howe 1984; Sklar 1977). Perusal of the classified ads in "New Age" tabloids or a visit to any "Psychic Fair" reveals continuing alliances between these two disciplines on this side of the Atlantic. Prominent graphologists such as Stephen Kurdsen (1971) who invite mediums like Jeane Dixon to write the foreword to their books or Dorothy Sara (1956) (former president of the American Graphological Society) who write books touting both graphology and occult phenomena show that magical interests remain close to the surface in the profession.

Until graphologists do more than simply deny this occult connection and replace the magical allegories that still underlie their craft with plausible mechanisms that meet the criteria I outline in chapter 14 and in note 4 above, they have only themselves to blame if they are held in low esteem by the scientific community. The graphologists invited to appear in this volume were selected because they have adopted the scientific approach by attempting to validate their methods empirically.

7. Lest I be accused of picking unrepresentative exemplars to criticize, I should note that at the time we debated in a public forum in Chicago in 1988, Rose Matousek was president of the American Association of Handwriting Analysis. Likewise, Dorothy Sara, Emilie Stockholm, and Klara Roman, whom I cite frequently, are establishment figures in their field. Sara served as president of the American Graphological Society, Stockholm is Dean of Instruction of the International Graphoanalysis Society, and Roman is highly touted by most graphologists because she is one of the few in a field generally taught in brief mail-order and night school courses who ever lectured at a large American university. In the examples cited throughout this chapter, the reader will see that they and the others mentioned indeed represent the mainstream of graphological thought.

8. Of course, graphologists could maintain that the causal arrow points in the opposite direction (e.g., open people are compelled to make open letters), but a mechanism that could assure that is equally improbable on neurological gounds, as I discuss in ch. 14.

9. Some of the early drafters of the rules for handwriting analysis probably reversed the process, starting with a subjective sense of the person and then looked for symbolic correspondences in his or her writing; e.g., "He seems to be a forward person, so what features in his script remind me of forwardness?" The metaphorical nature of the search is the same whether it was the script or the person that was examined first. It is the lack of empirical validation of the perceived likenesses and the slavish adherence to "the tried and true ways of the old masters" that disqualifies graphology as a scientific pursuit.

10. Graphoanalysis is a registered trademark that refers exclusively to the proprietary method of handwriting analysis taught by the "Chicago School" founded by M. N. Bunker. For further information on this school and its scathing denunciations of the other "unscientific" schools of handwriting analysis, see note 16.

11. For a definition of falsifiability and an explanation of why it is a crucial

requirement for a scientific theory, see Dale Beyerstein's discussion of graphology and the philosophy of science in chapter 8.

12. The most glaring and widespread shortcoming is the lack of proper "blind" control conditions. These include shielding the graphologist from knowledge of who the writer is and from other sources of information about the writer, including the often-revealing content that might be in a sample to be analyzed if it is part of a job application, for instance.

13. This passage also reveals the graphoanalyst's unfamiliarity with a vast body of research on cognitive development stemming from the work of Jean Piaget. It indicates that adolescents of this boy's age *are* usually capable of comprehending abstract concepts. One has to question the advisability of taking psychological advice from someone unaware of the work of the most cited developmental psychologist of the century.

14. Most of the criticisms directed at graphology for "reifying the subjective," i.e., assuming that symbolic relationships explain or determine psychological mechanisms, apply with equal force to the systems of Freud and his disciples. Freudian psychoanalysis has frequently been attacked for similar pseudoscientific attributes, including unfalsifiability. See Ellis (1956) regarding attempts to salvage useful insights in Freud's work while eliminating these shortcomings.

15. Even if utilizing every corner of a sheet might suggest economical use of paper, it would still be a huge leap of faith to assume that someone who is parsimonious in this situation would necessarily be equally tight-fisted in any or all other settings. See Bowman (ch. 10) regarding the problem of generalizing from small samples of behavior to broad behavioral dispositions. It is such generalizations that most need the kind of empirical validation that graphologists rarely provide.

16. From the 1982 promotional pamphlet by the International Graphonanlysis Society, Inc., *Enjoy the Rich Rewards of Graphoanalysis*. In an accompanying letter, the society's president, V. Peter Ferrara, dismisses all other schools of graphology as "non-scientific," "hit-or-miss" systems that disagree among themselves. He dubs the competition "guesswork" and "a kind of parlor game." Ferrara goes on to say that the founder of Graphoanalysis, M. N. Bunker, "one of the authentic geniuses of our age, . . . recognized that handwriting is a basic symbolism which reflects the writer's individual rhythm." Here we see the same old assumption that symbolic relationships determine real events. What a "writer's individual rhythm" might mean is anybody's guess, but it sounds rather like a bit of borrowing from the "unscientific" system of Klages discussed earlier.

In a 1988 symposium I was asked to organize, we tried to include a representative sample of prominent critics and proponents of graphology. The Graphoanalysts (who, as we've seen, pride themselves on their scientific status) were the only major school to refuse our repeated requests to send a spokesperson to this scientific forum. This despite the fact that the session was held in their hometown of Chicago.

17. Even fewer of the published studies favoring graphology are found in the highest quality journals with the most stringent peer-review standards and which do not charge authors for publication.

REFERENCES

Alcock, J. 1980. *Parapsychology: Science or Magic?* Oxford: Pergamon Press.
Basil, R., ed. 1988. *Not Necessarily the New Age: Critical Essays.* Buffalo, N.Y.: Prometheus Books.
Beyerstein, B. L. 1988. "The Brain and Consciousness: Implications for Psi Phenomena." *The Skeptical Inquirer* 12(2): pp. 163–173.
———. 1990. "Brainscams: Neuromythologies of the New Age." *Intl. J. of Mental Health* 19: pp. 27–36.
Broad, C. D. 1949. "The Relevance of Psychical Research to Philosophy." *Philosophy* 24: pp. 291–309.
Bunge, M. 1984. "What Is Pseudoscience?" *The Skeptical Inquirer* 9(1): pp. 36–46.
de Sainte Colombe, P. 1972. *Graphotherapeutics: The Pen and Pencil Therapy.* New York: Popular Library.
Dickson, D. H., and I. W. Kelly. 1985. "The 'Barnum Effect' in Personality Assessment: A Review of the Literature," *Psychological Reports* 57: pp. 367–382.
Ellis, A. 1956. "An Operational Reformulation of Some of the Basic Principles of Psychoanalysis." In *Minnesota Studies in the Philosophy of Science,* edited by H. Feingel and M. Scriven. Vol. 1, pp. 131–154,
Gaster, T. H. 1959. *The New Golden Bough: A New Abridgement of the Classic Work by Sir James George Frazer.* New York: New American Library.
Holder, R. 1958. *You Can Analyze Handwriting.* Englewood Cliffs, N.J.: Prentice-Hall.
Howe, E. 1984. *Astrology and the Third Reich.* Wellingborough, U.K.: Aquarian Press.
Hyman, R. 1977. " 'Cold Reading': How to Convince Strangers That You Know All About Them." *The Zetetic* 1(2): pp. 18–37.
Krebs, D., and R. Blackman. 1988. "The Science of Psychology and the Psychology of Common Sense." In *Psychology: A First Encounter,* pp. 27–31. San Diego, Calif.: Harcourt Brace Jovanovich.
Kurdsen, S. 1971. *Graphology: The New Science.* New York: Galahad Books.
Lewinson, T. S. 1986. "The Classic Schools of Graphology." In *Scientific Aspects of Graphology,* edited by B. Nevo, pp. 5–46. Springfield, Ill.: Charles Thomas.
Loewe, M. and C. Blacker, eds. 1981. *Oracles and Divination.* Boulder, Colo.: Shambhala Publications.
Marks, D., and D. Kammann. 1980. *The Psychology of the Psychic.* Buffalo, N.Y.: Prometheus Books.
Martin, R. C. 1969. *Your Script is Showing.* New York: Golden Press.
Matousek, R. 1987. *Graphology and the Phenomenon of Writing.* Self-published, 820 West Maple Street, Hinsdale, Ill. 60521.
Monte, C. F. 1975. *Psychology's Scientific Endeavor.* New York: Praeger.
Nevo, B., ed. 1986. *Scientific Aspects of Graphology: A Handbook.* Springfield, Ill.: Charles Thomas.

Nisbett, R., and L. Ross. 1980. *Human Inference: Strategies and Shortcomings of Social Judgement.* Englewood Cliffs, N.J.: Prentice-Hall.

Paterson, J. 1980. *Know Yourself Through Your Handwriting.* Montreal, Quebec: Reader's Digest Assn.

Paulos, J. A. 1988. *Innumeracy: Mathematical Illiteracy and its Consequences.* New York: Hill and Wang.

Pulver, M. 1931. *Symbolik der Handschrift.* Zurich: Orell Füssli.

Rand, H. A. 1961. *Graphology: A Handbook.* Cambridge, Mass.: Sci-Art Publishers.

Roman, K. G. 1952. *Handwriting—A Key to Personality.* New York: Pantheon Books.

Rothman, M. A. 1988. *A Physicist's Guide to Skepticism.* Buffalo, N.Y.: Prometheus Books.

Rozin, P., L. Millman, and C. Nemeroff, 1986. "Operation of the Laws of Sympathetic Magic in Disgust and Other Domains." *J. Personality and Social Psychology* 50(4): pp. 703–712.

Sara, D. 1956. *Handwriting Analysis.* New York: Pyramid Books.

Saudek, R. 1929. *Experiments with Handwriting.* New York: William Morrow.

Schmitt, J., J. Neal, and R. Klimoski. 1991. *Research Methods in Human Resources Management.* Cincinnati: South-Western Publ.

Schultz, T. 1989. *The Fringes of Reason.* New York: Harmony Books.

Seckel, A. 1988. "A New Age of Obfuscation and Manipulation." In *Not Necessarily the New Age,* edited by R. Basil. Buffalo, N.Y.: Prometheus Books, pp. 386–395.

Shweder, R. A. 1977. "Likeness and Likelihood in Everyday Thought: Magical Thinking in Judgments About Personality." *Current Anthropology* 18(4): pp. 637–658.

Skinner, B. F. 1948. "Superstition in the Pigeon." *J. Experimental Psychology* 38: pp. 168–172.

Sklar, D. 1977. *The Nazis and the Occult.* New York: Dorset Press.

Smith, H. M. 1970. *Between the Lines: The Casebook of a Graphologist.* Toronto: McClelland and Stewart.

Stockholm, E. 1988 (January). "Comparison of Traits Typical of 'Juniors' and 'Seniors.' " *Journal of Graphoanalysis:* pp. 3–10.

Surovell, H. 1987. *Lovestrokes: Handwriting Analysis for Love, Sex and Compatibility.* New York: Harper and Row.

Teltscher, H. O. 1971. *Handwriting—Revelation of Self.* New York: Hawthorne Books.

Tversky, A., and D. Kahneman. 1974. "Judgment Under Uncertainty: Heuristics and Biases." *Science* 185: pp. 1124–1131.

Warner, R., and D. Sugarman. 1986. "Attributions of Personality Based on Physical Appearance, Speech, and Handwriting." *J. Personality and Social Psychology* 50 (4): pp. 792–799.

Zusne, L., and W. Jones. 1989. *Anomalistic Psychology: A Study of Magical Thinking.* 2nd ed. Hillsdale, N.J.: L. Erlbaum Assoc.

Section Four

Critiques of Graphology

10

Difficulties in Assessing Personality and Predicting Behavior: Psychological Tests and Handwriting Analyses Contrasted

Marilyn L. Bowman

In chapter 10, Marilyn Bowman tackles one of the most controversial issues in psychology: the nature of personality. Although the scientific literature in this field has been plagued by misconceptions and false starts, Bowman shows that there are increasing areas of consensus. As these well-established data have emerged, they have cast increasing doubt upon various character-reading schemes that originated in the pre-scientific era of folk psychology. Modern research has revealed subtleties and complexities in the seemingly straightforward concept of a personality trait that "pop-psychologists," relying on overly simplistic, intuitive views of personality, have failed to address. This isolation, plus their failure to provide supporting research of their own, has seriously damaged their credibility in the scientific community. The pop-psychologists' lack of motivation to familiarize themselves with the latest personality research is partly due to its highly technical, mathematical nature and partly to the fact that the old folk-psychology notions of personality seem so plausible despite their inability to withstand empirical scrutiny. Heavy reliance by popular character readers, including most graphologists, on these dubious conceptual holdovers challenges their claim to describe people and predict their behavior accurately. A prime shortcoming, discussed by Bowman, is their failure to note the degree to which situational factors can modify the effects of internal dispositions.

Bowman also shows that pre-scientific character-reading schemes have paid insufficient heed to the conceptual pitfalls and measurement problems inherent in deriving accurate personality scales. She raises these methodological issues in her discussion of the two most fundamental requirements of a scientifically acceptable psychological test: reliability and validity. She then assesses the published research on graphology in light of these standards and deals with the question of why personality readings that fall far short of those standards can still seem remarkably accurate (the "Barnum Effect," examined in greater detail in chapter 13 by Dean et al. and chapter 16 by Karnes and Leonard). In the present chapter, Bowman also emphasizes the dangers of relying solely on the face validity of personality measures, the strongest selling point of most non-scientific assessment techniques.

In arriving at his or her own conclusion about the scientific credibility of graphology, the reader should compare the critiques in Bowman's chapter and Klimoski's (chapter 11) with the defenses offered by Lockowandt in chapter 6 and Crumbaugh in chapter 7, as all of these chapters revolve around the key issues of reliability and validity of psychological measurements.

*   *   *

Personality, the pattern of a person's stable and enduring psychological traits, is a common-sense idea. Most of us believe that we can describe the personalities of ourselves, our friends, and our family with some degree of accuracy. We ascribe to the people we know such traits as honesty, friendliness, sociability, or anxiety. We form our impressions from everyday behavior that we have seen or heard about; from the ideas, plans, hopes, and fears that we have heard expressed; from our observation of the impressions made on others; and from our knowledge of personal histories. Most of us believe that we can describe some of our friends more accurately than we can others and that, of the qualities we discern in a particular person, some are more central than others to the personality of that person. Furthermore, we often try to predict the behavior of people we know from what we have discerned about their personality traits.

The qualities that we use to describe ourselves and others are similar to the qualities used both by graphologists and psychologists in their formal assessments of personality. Hundreds of such personality attributes have been formally studied by personality psychologists in the twentieth century, and from these studies we have learned that descriptions of personality that seem intuitively simple and obvious are, in fact, complicated and readily influenced by many subtle factors.

The Stability of Personality

Despite the conviction most people hold that they *know* what kind of person they are and that they *know* that one friend is stubborn and another is generous, it turns out that some attributes are less enduring than they appear, and that they appear to be stable mainly because we usually interact with people only in a narrow range of specific situations. Behaviorist psychologist Walter Mischel, in his famous book *Personality and Assessment* (1968), showed that behavior can be significantly changed by situational conditions. At its most extreme, this position suggests that there may be no stable personality traits of any significance. This challenge to the conventional idea of personality as a conglomerate of relatively enduring traits stimulated two decades of active investigation into the stability of personality and the predictability of behavior.

Mischel's analysis raised the possibility that some of the qualities we observe and assume are stable might be illusions of our own need for cognitive consistency and predictability in our interpersonal relations. It suggested that we may conveniently ignore certain behaviors in our friends if we think they are not typical of them. If Mischel's ideas are correct, they also mean that if we use our current ideas about a person to predict his or her behavior, we would often be wrong, because that person's behavior would be more strongly influenced by situational forces than by his or her personality traits. For example, a person might be scrupulously honest in all matters dealing with personal income tax, and yet engage in petty pilfering in a particular job setting. If Mischel were asked the question: "How honest is this person?" he might reply, "It depends upon the circumstances," and he might decline the invitation to draw any conclusions about that person's *trait* of honesty.

Mischel was able to demonstrate that for many of the personality attributes traditionally studied by psychologists, the observed behavior was readily altered by situational influences. Thus, he forced researchers to look more closely at the stability of behavior across time and the consistency of behavior across situations. Two decades of complex research have taught us that there are individual differences in behavioral stability, that some behaviors are more responsive to situational influences than others, and that some situational forces have a greater influence upon behavior than do others. We have learned that there is no simple one-to-one relationship between a personality trait and behavior. John Doe may be generally an extroverted person, but how extroverted he will be will depend on whether he is at a party with close friends or at a formal dinner with his boss.

Nevertheless, our intuitive notions about our ability to identify the personality traits of our friends and family have not been invalidated. Kenrick and Funder (1988) concluded from their review of two decades of research that many personality traits are indeed powerfully related to behavior and that many criticisms of personality stability have been tested and been found wanting or limited in effect. Mischel's own attempts to understand these complexities have contributed important evidence that key or prototypic aspects of behavior appear to be consistent across both situations and time (1976). The cumulative effect of this vigorous research activity has been to identify more clearly several of the factors affecting behavior: most importantly, personality, abilities, and situational features. Predictions about behavior that are based solely on personality descriptions will be less accurate than those based on all three elements, and this will be equally true for psychologists and graphologists.

We have learned that certain attributes of the environment interact with personality to influence the actual behaviors that occur in specific situations. If environmental features are powerful (i.e., visible and well-defined), then individual differences in behavior are generally reduced. For example, in a place of worship during a formal service, behavior is largely constrained by the demands of the situation, and the behavior of most individuals will be predicted more accurately by knowing the nature of the situation than by knowing the personality attributes or mental abilities of the people there (Mischel 1976). If, in contrast, situational forces are weak (i.e., ambiguous as to the participants and the events unfolding), then it is more likely that individuals will call upon their own memories, and thoughts, and propensities to create their own interpretations of the event and that they will react in line with their individual interpretations. Under these circumstances, there will be much greater variation in behavior among individuals, and the behavior will depend more on internal, enduring personality and mental ability attributes than on situational influences.

We have also learned that certain psychological attributes are more enduring and stable than others. Decades of research indicate that general *mental ability* is a stable and consistent human trait. Kangas and Bradway (1971) showed, for example, that IQ scores obtained at age fourteen correlated .85 with scores obtained at age thirty and .68 with scores obtained at age forty-two.

Individual *interests* represent another family of psychological attributes that has shown significant long-term stability. Correlations in the .80s have been reported for scores obtained at three-year intervals on tests of vocational interests (Campbell 1977), and correlations as high as .40 have been reported between scores obtained as long as thirty-six years apart (Campbell 1971). Similarly, satisfaction with life at age thirty is strongly predictive of occupational and life satisfaction as much as thirty years later (Sears 1977).

Stability has also been established for a number of personality traits. Paul Costa and Robert McCrae (1985), researchers with the National Institute of Aging, concluded from their extensive longitudinal studies that there are five broad and basic dimensions of personality that are stable across time and consistent across situations: Neuroticism, Extroversion, Openness, Agreeableness, and Conscientiousness. Scores measuring these qualities may be obtained from a wide range of psychological tests, such as the Minnesota Multiphasic Personality Inventory (MMPI), the State-Trait Personality Inventory, and the Myers-Briggs Type Indicator. Other personality traits, such as impulsivity, shyness, social anxiety, and attitudes to authority, turn out to be less stable or consistent.

In describing personality, it is necessary to distinguish between a person's current, transient, psychological state and a deeper, more enduring trait. By knowing a person's state (e.g., depressed), we can often make accurate short-term predictions about the behavior that will ensue, but prediction over the long term will be poor. In contrast, by identifying an enduring personality trait, we can make (on average) accurate predictions over long time spans, but we would be less accurate in predicting behavior in single, specific situations. For example, a person might customarily be extroverted, but on a particular day might feel worried about an upcoming examination. If we assessed his or her personality on that day, it would be important to identify both the state of anxiety and the more enduring trait of extroversion, even though extroversion might not be prominent in that person's behavior or attitudes that day.

The importance of differentiating between transient and enduring aspects of behavior applies equally to conventional personality assessment and to graphology, although graphology has focused on enduring personality traits as the basis for predicting behavior. Thus, studies of the long-term consistency or reliability of personality traits are particularly important in evaluating the analyses and predictions made by graphologists. At the time Mischel first raised these issues, it was not clear if all traits were equally susceptible to environmental influences. We now know that some personality traits are, indeed, more stable than others.

We also know that the behavior of some individuals is more stable than is the behavior of others. This means that scores on a reliable and valid personality test will generate relatively accurate predictions about behavior for those individuals whose behavior is stable, but relatively inaccurate predictions for those whose behavior is changeable (Bem and Allen 1974). For example, a major longitudinal study that followed young people from adolescence to adulthood showed that the more stable individuals were those who had been particularly well-adjusted from the start. In contrast, those whose behavior was changeable had shown high tension and disequilibrium from the earliest time onward, and the nature of the changes they went through was unpredictable (Block 1971).

For truly adaptive functioning, individuals should be flexible enough to choose from their repertoires of personality and ability characteristics those behavioral responses that best match the needs of the situation. They should not be entirely driven either by situational or personality factors. Difficulties in matching behavior to environmental constraints are found, for example, in people with schizophrenia. Their behavior is described as overdetermined in that their internal preoccupations and their behavioral predispositions are so powerful that they determine behavior without reference to important environmental cues, with the result that their behavior is sometimes inappropriate. Any personality assessment procedure, including graphology, that focuses primarily on static personality attributes and ignores the complicated ways in which environmental influences interact with personality to produce behavior will be relatively inaccurate in predicting behavior.

To summarize: We know that behavior is largely the outcome of a person's mental abilities, personality traits, and the situations the person is in at the moment; that some situations have a stronger effect on behavior than do others; that some personality traits are more stable than others; and that the behavior of some persons is more stable than is the behavior of others.

Difficulties in Predicting Behavior

Personality descriptions form part of the more challenging task of predicting behavior, and predicting complex human behavior is a notoriously difficult task. How accurate are we likely to be if we want to predict the behavior of a specific person, whom we will call Jane Doe?

If the behavior is one that occurs frequently among people like Jane Doe (e.g., premarital celibacy in some religious sects, anorexia nervosa in ballet dancers), we could accurately predict Jane Doe's sexual or eating habits if she came from either of these groups, simply because those habits have high *base rates* in those groups. Furthermore, we would not even have to see Jane Doe or know anything about her (except her group membership) in order to make accurate predictions about these kinds of behavior. The same principle applies if we are trying to predict for an individual group member a kind of behavior which occurs rarely in that group (e.g., fraud among nuns). In other words, for behaviors that occur either with high or low base rates in identifiable groups, we can, on average, predict with good accuracy whether a member of the specified group is likely to engage in that behavior.

Prediction of individual behavior from group or population base rates becomes much more difficult when the behavior we are interested in occurs with a moderate rate of frequency (e.g., divorce) or when the behavior is one that is considered undesirable by society (e.g., drug abuse, violent behavior). Predicting on the basis of population frequency alone that a specific married couple will divorce will be accurate only 30–40% of the time. Predicting that a specific person will engage in undesirable behavior, even when that behavior has a high base rate in the group from which the individual comes (e.g., drug abuse in certain inner-city groups) has such potentially damaging consequences for the individual that, fortunately, psychologists are reluctant to predict from group base rates alone.

We can improve the accuracy of our predictions if we know something about the individual's own base rates for the behavior we are interested in. It is here that personality assessment techniques can play an important role. If we know, for example, that Jane Doe is a chronically anxious person, we can predict with reasonable confidence that she will be anxious in a job interview or a courtroom appearance. Conversely, if we know that Jane Doe is not depressed, has never entertained thoughts of suicide, and, indeed, considers suicide immoral, we can predict with reasonable confidence that she is not at significant risk for suicide.

This is not to say that knowledge of the personality of the person whose behavior we are trying to predict will insure that our predictions will be accurate. As we have seen, personality is not the sole determinant of behavior. It has been shown that, even when we know something about the personalities of the people whose behavior we want to predict, we are often inaccurate in predicting such behaviors as suicide among institutionalized mentally disturbed patients, violent behavior among incarcerated criminals, or theft among employees (see Farberow 1981; Mulvey and Lidz 1985; Saal and Knight 1988). Nevertheless, the use of reliable and valid techniques for assessing personality can lead to more accurate predictions of individual behavior than those based on group base rates alone.

Graphology: Stability of Behavior and Reliability of Assessment

Graphology uses a specific type of expressive behavior, handwriting, as the source of inferences about current personality traits and as the basis for predictions about behavior. In a sense, handwriting samples are analogous to the response individuals make on standardized personality tests. And, just as with personality test responses, we need to know how reliable over time and how consistent over situations an individual's handwriting is.

Documenting the stability of a person's responses is a standard procedure in the development of personality tests. A common method for determining the stability or reliability of responses to personality tests is to administer the same test to a number of people at different times and then examine the correlations for each person among his or her responses to the same test at different times (test-retest reliability). For example, the California Psychological Inventory (Gough 1957) has eighteen scales with test-retest reliabilities ranging from .57 to .77.

To determine the test-retest reliability of the graphic features of handwriting, multiple handwriting samples should be obtained from the same individuals at a number of different times. Each sample should be blind-scored (i.e., without knowledge of the author of each sample) according to formal script criteria; and, finally, correlations should be calculated between the scores for the different samples from each individual. Because handwriting analysis involves detailed judgments about script features, individual differences in judgment contribute error which usually results in lower test-retest reliabilities than are obtained for objectively scored tests, a common finding in all assessment situations where scores are based on human judgments.

The reliability of the graphic features of scripts can also be assessed by obtaining multiple script samples from each person on a single occasion, scoring these samples blind, and then correlating the scores from the different samples produced by each person. This method would give us an index of the *internal consistency* of the individual's writing, another type of reliability that is routinely determined for personality and mental ability tests. The 1955 Wechsler Adult Intelligence Scale, for example, has internal consistency (reliability) values ranging from .93 to .97. Saudek (1929), one of the classic writers on handwriting analysis, insisted that the analyst must examine many samples of an individual's writing, thus implicitly recognizing the need for internal consistency and test-retest reliability long before there was a scientific literature on these psychometric issues. In his own work on forgery detection, he used numerous samples before making his judgments.

What is the evidence that a given individual writes in an identifiably similar manner under different circumstances and at different times? Fluckiger, Tripp, and Weinberg (1961) reviewed almost three decades of research on the use of such physical measures as pressure of pen on the paper, grip pressure, and speed of writing for identifying individual handwriting characteristics. They noted that many devices had been invented to measure these physical aspects of writing but that, in fact, few studies had ever been done to determine if they were reliable in the writing of any given individual. They were able to locate several early studies that showed that handwriting can vary if the subject's central nervous system was strongly influenced (e.g., by alcohol or drugs, or after electroshock or hypnosis), but these extreme conditions do not speak directly to handwriting consistency under normal conditions. More recent studies of handwriting (e.g., Sovik, Arntzen, and Thygesen 1986) have shown that handwriting can change significantly with training. In addition, Rafaeli and Drory (1988) suggest that both individual and group or demographic characteristics may affect the consistency of an individual's handwriting.

Despite this modest evidence that the characteristics of an individual's handwriting can be altered, Klimoski and Rafaeli (1983) concluded from their review of many studies that, overall, a person's handwriting is reasonably stable across time. Reliability values have ranged from .77 to beyond .90, indicating that a person's handwriting can be reliably identified from the graphic features of his or her script. This graphic stability makes possible the forensic analysis of scripts for investigations of forgeries (see chapter 4).

Typical graphological analyses are not based solely on objective scores, but also on subjective judgments of specific script characteristics. These judgments may be of the yes/no variety; that is, a particular script feature is either present or absent; or they may be quantitative ratings of the size, intensity, etc., of specific features. Error will be introduced into the scoring of script characteristics if the person making the judgments is inconsistent in assigning scores or if different judges assign different scores to the same characteristic. These problems of intra- and interjudge reliability occur not only in handwriting analysis, but in all assessment procedures which cannot be scored objectively.

Such procedures, known in psychological assessment as projective techniques, customarily allow the person being evaluated much latitude in responding. For example, a person might be asked to describe "What might this be?" when shown a series of inkblots (Rorschach Inkblot Test, Rorschach 1942); or a person might be asked to create a dramatic story for each of a series of pictorial scenes (Thematic Apperception Test, Murray 1943). The relatively unstructured responses people make are then examined in order to identify and score features that are believed to be psychologically meaningful. In contrast, objective psychological tests markedly limit the range of responses allowed, and many well-established personality tests allow only Yes/No or True/False responses or numerical ratings of specific traits and behaviors.

In the case of handwriting analysis, the reliability of scoring judgments can be improved if the graphologist uses formal measurement devices to score features: rulers can measure letter size, protractors can measure slant, charts can provide prototype examples. Although some systems of graphological analysis accept the use of objective scoring aids, others reject them on the grounds that the best analysis is based on a holistic interpretation of many factors, including subtle qualities that do not lend themselves easily to objective measurement. To the extent that a graphology system does not assess specific features, scoring reliability cannot be determined, although the reliability of interpretations can be tested.

Intrajudge reliability in handwriting analysis can be assessed by determining the consistency with which a judge makes the same judgments of the same handwriting samples at different points in time. Most studies of the reliability of individual judges have examined the consistency of the inferences about personality made from the scripts, rather than the consistency in judging specific graphic features such as pressure or speed, or specific script features such as long loops or circles for dots. For example, Sonneman and Kernan (1962) reported highly consistent intrajudge reliability (correlations of .64–.85) for five ratings of psychological attributes inferred from two handwriting samples collected at two different times. In general, however, intrajudge reliability of handwriting analyses is rarely assessed or reported either for script features or for inferences about the personality traits of the writers. It is of interest that several of the early studies reviewed by Fluckiger, Tripp, and Weinberg (1961) were able to identify several personal characteristics of graphologists (e.g., experience in the visual arts, gender) that were associated with intrajudge consistency.

Interjudge reliability is the degree to which different judges make the same judgments of the same scripts. It has been studied more extensively than has intrajudge reliability. The results of early studies suggest that the greatest agreement among judges occurs when judgments are based on a small number of broad categories or on well-defined script features (Fluckiger, Tripp, and Weinberg 1961).

Furnham and Gunter (1987) found correlations as high as .89 between two raters of three highly specific script features. Galbraith and Wilson (1964) reported an interrater reliability of .78 between the ratings made by three handwriting judges of five personality traits, but Rafaeli and Klimoski (1983) found a median interjudge correlation of only .45, when inferred personality traits were rated. Jansen (1973) found interjudge reliability of trait inferences equally low both within and among several groups of handwriting analysts, including a group of trained graphologists. Similarly, Vestewig, Santee, and Moss (1976) reported significant differences among six experienced Graphoanalysts in their judgments of ten of the fifteen traits assessed, indicating low interjudge reliability. Keinan, Barak, and Ramati (1984) also reported low interjudge reliabilities, .20–.37 for six graphologists' ratings on thirteen scales. Overall, the range of interjudge agreement found in these studies indicates that graphologists often differ substantially in their ratings and interpretations of the same handwriting samples.

If judges, even those trained to a level of proficiency in a standardized training program such as Graphoanalysis (a registered trademark name), fail to agree with each other on the important psychological inferences to be made from script samples, what is to be done? Rafaeli and Drory (1988) point out that it is possible to reduce the statistical error that is associated with differences in ratings among judges, simply by using a single judge in each study. They do not recommend this practice, however, because if such a study generated significant results, we would never know if they were the result of the graphology method or of that graphologist's particular talents. If the graphology method is the source of the promising findings, then the results of the study could be generalized to others trained in that method. In contrast, if the results were an artifact of one graphologist's special talents, then they cannot be generalized.

Improvement in interjudge agreement on psychological rating scales can be achieved if specific names and descriptions are provided for the features important for each judgment to be made. For example, if anxiety is being rated on a 5-point scale, high interjudge agreement can be attained if the relevant behaviors for each of the five points on the scale are clearly described, and if judges are trained to reach high levels of agreement using these criteria. These techniques have been used in the development of many assessment procedures (including psychiatric diagnostic evaluation) with considerable success and with high levels of interjudge agreement. Standardized scoring criteria for handwriting analysis have not been developed to the same degree, although some commercial graphological services now use privately developed templates to classify some script features for later computerized summing. The use of computers to sum scored features does not, of course, improve the reliability of the total scores, since scores for individual features are still based on human judgments. The use of script templates should, however, improve the reliability of those judgments.

In summary: The graphic features of handwriting are stable enough that a given person's handwriting can be identified with good reliability by a well-trained judge. Psychological inferences derived from handwriting are less reliable because of error introduced by both intra- and interrater variation.

Validity of Assessment Procedures

All methods of assessing personality, abilities, interests, or temperament must be reliable, but reliability alone is not sufficient to make an assessment procedure an effective one. It is also necessary to demonstrate that the technique is valid; that is, that it measures what it purports to measure, whether it be extroversion, intelligence, anxiety, or an interest in music. Validity is usually established by demonstrating that there is an orderly relationship between the results of the assessment (e.g., test scores) and an independent index of the personal quality in question. A ruler, for example, is a reliable instrument for measuring the length of an earlobe, but we could not claim that it is a valid instrument for measuring creativity, unless we could show that there is an orderly relationship between earlobe length and creativity. In 1891, the Italian criminologist Lombroso claimed that geniuses and madmen were both characterized by short height, crooked bones, and pallor. All these qualities can be reliably measured, but none has ever been shown to be related either to genius or to mental disorder.

If we take an arithmetic test, score high, and are then told that we have a high level of arithmetic skill, what we are told makes good common sense. In more formal terms, the arithmetic test has high *face validity,* because it measured what it appeared to be measuring. But suppose we take the same arithmetic test, score low, and then are told that we have a high level of anxiety. The arithmetic test would have low face validity, because it appears to be measuring arithmetic skill, not anxiety. In fact, performance on tests of mental arithmetic does tend to decline as anxiety increases (Knox and Grippaldi 1970), so arithmetic tests may be more valid as tests of anxiety than their low face validity would suggest.

The degree to which a test does or does not measure what it appears to measure can only be determined empirically. This is especially true in personality assessment where it is known that scores may be distorted by many factors such as unconscious habits or deliberate bias. It is also known that personality test items sometimes measure the opposite of what they appear to be measuring. On the MMPI, for example, certain items with a paranoid quality contribute to the paranoia score if they are *denied,* while others contribute to that score if they are *endorsed* (Dahlstrom, Welsh, and Dahlstrom 1972). Some personality tests include items that are designed to detect deliberate bias on the part of subjects; these items look as if they are measuring one attribute when they are in fact validly measuring something quite different. Thus, it is important to distinguish between the face validity of an assessment technique and its real validity.

Handwriting analysis has a high claim to face validity. It is intuitively appealing to think that the expressive behavior of writing bears a meaningful relationship to our psychological attributes. I have noted earlier that a person's handwriting is reliable across time and consistent across situations. Also, writing is closely linked with our use of language, an important behavior for revealing many dimensions of our inner life. At first glance then, psychological descriptions based on handwriting analysis have a reasonable kind of appeal, and it is easy to believe that important personal qualities are revealed in our writing. The face validity of handwriting analysis is one of the reasons why graphology continues to be of interest in the general population, why personality reports based on handwriting analysis are often enthusiastically received by the script writers, and why it has been repeatedly studied by personality psychologists in the hope of using it in research and clinical assessment.

Gordon Allport and Philip Vernon, leading twentieth-century researchers and theorists in personality, published their investigations of handwriting analysis in their classic book *Studies in Expressive Movement* in 1933. In it, they expressed their disappointment with the lack of validity in handwriting analysis. Guilford, another major personality researcher, came to a similar conclusion more than twenty years later (Guilford 1959), and a more recent review of the literature (Klimoski and Rafaeli 1983) yielded no evidence for the validity of graphological analysis. Nevertheless, the technique has such a strong appeal to face validity that interest in it continues. Face validity often plays such a troublesome role in personality assessment research, by distracting us from the necessary empirical evidence, that one personality researcher has even suggested that "It may . . . be beneficial for any test *not* to have high face validity" [my emphasis] (Furnham 1986: 392).

The face validity of graphological analysis is also enhanced by the "Barnum effect," so named because of the readiness with which people suspend disbelief and accept the exaggerated claims of circus hawkers. In personality research it refers to the willingness with which people accept descriptions of their personalities when they believe the descriptions were made especially for them. The effect is robust if the accounts include mildly negative comments, followed by flattering comments. Paterson, who was the first to report the Barnum effect (see Blum and Balinky 1951), gave the same standard personality report to a group of businessmen, on the pretense that each report was based on observations and findings specific to each man. The men almost invariably accepted the reports as valuable, accurate, and specific descriptions of their own individual personalities.

The Barnum effect has been extensively studied ever since and is a well-established phenomenon. Snyder (1974), for example, confirmed the Barnum effect in experimental studies in which descriptions that were random and independent of the participants were presented to them in the form of horoscopes. Similarly, Karnes and Leonard (chap. 16, this volume) have shown that both authentic graphologists' reports and invented Barnum reports are accepted by subjects with equally high levels of credulity and that both are preferred to reports based on data from reliable and valid personality tests. Karnes and Leonard attribute this finding to the ambiguity and the generality of both the fictitious and the genuine graphology reports. Vestewig, Santee, and Moss (1976) also found that subjects were unable to differentiate bogus reports from Graphoanalysts' reports. A review of similar findings appears in chapter 13 of the present volume

Cognitive dissonance is another phenomenon that may contribute to the readiness with which people ascribe truth and accuracy to graphological reports. Cognitive dissonance (Festinger 1957) refers to the tendency people have to experience psychological discomfort if there is a discrepancy, or dissonance, between two attitudes a person holds or between an attitude and that person's behavior. The inclination, then, is to reduce the dissonance and the accompanying discomfort by changing one of the attitudes or by changing the discrepant behavior.

Take the case, for example, of a couple who marry despite great family opposition and then gradually realize they are badly suited to one another. Cognitive dissonance theory predicts that they will tend to distort or deny their true negative feelings in order to reduce the dissonance between their behavior (marrying in defiance of opposition) and their true feelings (unhappiness).

Cognitive dissonance has been widely studied in experimental and real-life situations, and it is a robust phenomenon. Because handwriting analysis is looked upon with some skepticism in North American culture, a person who goes against negative public opinion and submits to an analysis has in effect set the stage for possible cognitive dissonance. Thus, even if some parts of the report seemed to be incorrect, the person would be inclined to accept the analysis as a whole, because he would need to reduce the discrepancy between his initial decision and the actual, partly unsatisfactory outcome.

Personality research has demonstrated that certain personality qualities are regarded more favorably than others. For example, extroversion is viewed more positively than introversion, and high emotionality is considered an undesirable quality (Furnham 1986). To the extent, therefore, that personality analysis ascribes well-regarded personality attributes, it is likely to be well received.

We also know that a report that identifies psychological attributes that occur with a high frequency in the population will be (accurately) perceived as accurate, even though the attributes identified may be trivial. This phenomenon has been labeled the "Aunt Fanny effect" (Tallent 1958), because a skeptic reading such a report would be justified in saying, "Yes, and so's my Aunt Fanny, and so what?" The naive reader sees correct information but does not stop to think how general it is.

As we noted earlier, once it has been shown that an assessment technique (whether it be handwriting analysis or a personality test) generates reliable responses, it is necessary to demonstrate that the responses or the scores assigned to those responses are related to actual behavior in a regular and and meaningful way. It is the actual behavior, either current or future, that is the criterion against which the validity of the test procedure is measured. Thus, before we can use any assessment technique with confidence, we have to determine its *criterion-related validity*.

The personality tests that are commonly used have been developed to meet specific standards of test construction. The validity of a new personality test can be established by examining the relationships between responses from the new test and the responses obtained from other tests whose reliability and validity have already been established. Ideally, the responses from the new test should be highly correlated with the responses from other tests that measure the same traits or behaviors and poorly correlated with those from tests that measure different traits and behaviors. Furthermore, these relationships should hold whether or not the new and old tests are similar in format.

This system of test validation (the multi-trait–multi-method matrix) was devised by Campbell and Fiske in 1959, and it represents an ideal for psychological test construction. An assessment procedure that meets these criteria is said to show both convergent and discriminant validity, because it yields scores that converge with measures with which they should agree and that differ from measures with which they should disagree.

Further validation procedures include studies designed to determine whether demographic variables such as age, gender, or ethnicity significantly affect test scores, and studies designed to relate scores on the new test to past life experiences, real world behaviors, or self-reports of feelings, attitudes, and ideas. The results of these validation studies are then used to construct tables of normative scores from which one can determine, for example, whether the score of a particular person indicates a level of anxiety that is within the normal or the pathological range for a person of that age, gender, etc.

In concurrent validity procedures, the scores of individuals on the new personality assessment procedure can be correlated with their scores on a theoretically relevant psychological test, with ratings made by people who know the individuals well, or with behavior observed in a standard setting. Predictive validity procedures use such criteria as subsequent performance in a training program, sales productivity in a company, or response to drug treatment.

In general, objective psychological tests yield higher correlations with behavioral criteria than do projective assessment techniques. Because handwriting analysis shares many features with projective personality tests, it is not surprising that similar problems in establishing validity are found with both techniques.

Projective tests can be scored using well-defined scoring systems such as those devised for the Rorschach by Klopfer et al. (1954) or by Exner (1974), or they can be interpreted in an impressionistic, holistic way by a person experienced with the technique. If holistic methods of interpretation are used, the intra- and interjudge reliability of the interpretations can be evaluated, but the validity of the assessment technique is difficult to determine. To the extent, however, that formal scores are generated, these scores can be studied for both reliability and validity. Furthermore, if formal scoring methods have been developed, judges can be trained to a standard of reliability in scoring. A similar process could easily be applied to training judges to make reliable handwriting judgments so that they identify script features with a high level of agreement.

It is at the stage of relating test scores to psychological criteria (i.e., establishing criterion validity) that projective techniques often meet with difficulty. From 1930 to 1960, projective techniques were widely used to generate hypotheses about personality features, usually conceptualized in terms of Freudian or other instinct-oriented theories. Decades of studies, however, encountered major difficulties in validating these interpretations; as a result, many psychoanalytic hypotheses were abandoned. More recent work has attempted to use the Rorschach and other projective techniques to identify different perceptual styles in information processing, and there is evidence to suggest they may be useful for identifying perceptual problems associated with brain damage (e.g., Lezak 1983).

Because handwriting analysis is essentially a projective technique, validation studies are equally necessary to test its claim to validity. First, however, we have to consider the characteristics of the writing sample from which inferences about the personality or behavior of the writer will be drawn.

There are several kinds of handwriting samples, each with its advantages and disadvantages. If the sample is obtained from spontaneous writing, it may be written quickly and carelessly, whereas if it is copied or dictated text, it is usually produced more slowly and carefully (Saudek 1929). Also, spontaneous script contains idiosyncratic rather than standardized material, and it often includes autobiographical information or other material that reveals much about the writer's thought content and facility with language. In contrast, if the text is copied, the content can be limited to neutral material that is the same for everyone. These differences in script content have been found to affect graphological interpretations.

Jansen (1973) found that psychologists who read only *typed* versions of spontaneous scripts were significantly better in predicting eighteen ratings than other judges (including experienced graphologists) who were given the actual writing, which included useful biographical information. This finding implies that the graphic features of the spontaneous samples actually reduced the accuracy of interpretation. Nevertheless, the accuracy of prediction was poor for all groups of judges. Keinan, Barak, and Ramati (1984) reported that psychologists who relied heavily on the autobiographical content of handwritten samples were as accurate in predicting officer training success as were graphologists who based their predictions on both the form and content of the spontaneous scripts. Again, neither group was able to predict success with significant accuracy. Ben-Shakhar et al. (1986) also studied the predictive value of autobiographical content by comparison with graphological analysis of script features. They too found that predictions based on content or on style were equally poor in predictive validity. They did identify several features of the writing samples that did improve prediction, but they were not formal script features. They were language usage qualities such as grammar, aesthetic use of language, and articulateness, all of which can be identified from typed script as easily as from handwritten samples. Rafaeli and Klimoski (1983) reported that autobiographical content did not increase predictive accuracy. In their study, handwriting analyses were equally poor in predicting sales productivity whether the scripts had neutral or autobiographical content and whether the judgments were made by experienced graphologists or by naive students.

Neter and Ben-Shakhar (1989) performed a meta-analysis of seventeen validity studies of handwriting analysis and concluded that graphologists performed at essentially random levels when using scripts with neutral content. Their judgments improved marginally when they used samples containing autobiographical content, but, even here, their predictions were not significantly different from those made by non-graphologists.

In summary, the preponderance of evidence indicates that more useful information is obtained from the autobiographical content and the language features displayed in handwriting samples than from formal script features. These non-graphic features can be determined equally well from typewritten or handwritten materials. Analysis of script features does not increase accuracy, and it may reduce the accuracy of judgments made on scripts that include biographical information.

Graphologists assert that validity studies of handwriting analysis should use well-trained, experienced graphologists. Some recommend that graduates of a particular training program such as Graphoanalysis be used in order to provide the most valid test of the interpretive system. This is a legitimate requirement if judgments are based on a variety of subtle features used in complex combinations that cannot easily be quantified for objective scoring and that, therefore, require both training and experience with the method of analysis. Similar recommendations have been made for validation studies of other projective techniques. If this claim is legitimate, then carefully designed validation studies should show that judgments made by well-trained, experienced judges are substantially more accurate than those made by naive, untrained judges.

Jansen (1973) reported that trained graphologists were no better than psychologists or laymen in predicting high- or low-energy levels from handwriting samples, and none of the groups showed significant accuracy. Vestewig, Santee, and Moss (1976) found that there were significant differences in the judgments made by six experienced graphologists on ten of fifteen criteria. The most experienced analyst failed to produce a single significant correlation out of fifteen, and no two analysts were in significant agreement on the same trait. Ben-Shakhar et al. (1986) used autobiographical writing samples and found no significant differences between the judgments made by personnel graphologists and a psychologist; both were equally poor. Keinan, Barak, and Ramati (1984) reported that experienced graphologists and psychologists made equally poor predictions from handwriting samples, although they used different features of the writing as the basis for their judgments. Both groups were somewhat better than lay judges who had no experience in assessing personality. Rafaeli and Klimoski (1983) found significant agreement (reliability) between naive students and experienced graphologists on three of ten possible judgments, but the judgments of both groups were equally faulty in predicting real estate work performance. The meta-analysis of seventeen studies by Neter and Ben-Shakhar (1989) showed that trained graphologists were no better than non-graphologists in making predictions from scripts with biographical content, and they were usually worse. Their predictions from scripts with neutral content were even more unsatisfactory.

In summary: there is no convincing evidence that lack of training in graphological analysis is responsible for failures to establish the validity of graphology as a technique for assessing personality and predicting behavior.

Some graphologists have argued that the personality concepts they are required to use in formal studies are often different from those they would normally use (e.g., Crumbaugh 1977a). This implies that graphologists are sometimes forced to make judgments in which they have little confidence and that the accuracy of their judgments should increase as their confidence increases. Vestewig, Santee, and Moss (1976) found, however, that although the six trained Graphoanalysts in their study expressed high confidence in their judgments, these judgments showed unacceptably low levels of predictive validity. Similarly, Eysenck and Gudjonsson (1986) found no correlation between the confidence ratings of a Graphoanalyst and the validity of her judgments. Thus, the evidence to date does not indicate that the validity of graphological judgments is related to the confidence with which they are made.

It is also of interest that, although naive judges can sort handwriting samples by gender with about 70 percent accuracy, handwriting analysts are reluctant to use gender as the basis for sorting script samples. For example, Crumbaugh (1977b) cites the following statement from *The Encyclopedic Dictionary for Graphoanalysts:* "And Graphoanalysis firmly teaches that it is absolutely impossible to determine reliably the sex of the writer by handwriting (1964, 192)." To which he adds: "Especially is this true today because of the blurring of sexual role differences in our current society." If graphologists who are trained in formal systems of handwriting analysis were unable to achieve the 70% accuracy rate of naive judges, serious doubt would be raised as to the validity of their systems of analysis.

Determining the validity of handwriting analysis and of other projective techniques is complicated by the fact that different systems of interpretation are used by different practitioners for inferring personality characteristics and predicting behavior. Therefore, the validity of each interpretive system must be tested independently. Klimoski and Rafaeli (1983) described three general approaches to the analysis of handwriting: (1) a trait or atomistic approach that ascribes specific personality attributes to specific graphic features; (2) a holistic approach that requires the analyst to generate an integrated, global view of the writing, from which the personality of the writer is inferred; and (3) the Graphoanalytic approach that combines both atomistic and holistic features.

The atomistic approach was used by Linton, Epstein, and Hartford (1962), who studied the personality correlates of two kinds of beginning strokes. They reported a significant correlation between the frequent use of a primary beginning stroke and psychological test indices of social conformity. Unfortunately, their study suffered from so many flaws in research design and data analysis that the significance of their findings is in doubt.

It may be the case that graphologists find some kinds of predictions easier to make than others. For example, it may be easier to sort handwriting samples into a few broad categories (e.g., psychotic, neurotic, normal) than to predict ratings of specific personality traits. However, if the sorting categories used represent an extreme contrast (e.g., between hospitalized psychotic patients and normal, healthy people), graphologists might be able to reach a high level of sorting accuracy simply by attending to gross signs of abnormality. The usefulness of an analytic system lies, however, not in its ability to distinguish extremes but in its ability to distinguish groups or individuals who are fairly similar to each other. Furthermore, sorting procedures can be carried out without specifying the bases on which the handwriting samples are placed in one or another category, so it may not be possible to determine whether sorting is based on clearly identifiable and reproducible criteria or on global, nonspecific intuitions.

Similar drawbacks are found in matching procedures, another relatively crude approach to validation. A judge, for example, might be given handwriting samples and work samples from each of four employees, his task being to match the handwriting sample to the work sample produced by the same employee. In addition to the problems inherent in sorting procedures, matching procedures are further limited, because the judgments made are not independent of one another. With each match that is made, the number of work samples left to be matched is reduced, thus, a correct match increases the probability of further correct matches, and an incorrect match reduces the probability of further correct matches.

Even when such crude validation methods are used, graphologists have failed to distinguish themselves. In Frederick's study (1965), writing samples were sorted into two extreme categories: hospitalized psychotic patients and normal controls. He found that the sorting accuracy of an experienced graphologist was no better than that of an untrained undergraduate, even when the graphologist made use of the content of the writing samples, whereas a clinical psychologist achieved a significant level of accuracy. The poor performance of the graphologist in this study echoes similar findings from a study by Pascal and Suttell (1947), in which the task was to discriminate psychotic from normal subjects.

More recently, Zdep and Weaver (1967) reported that the Graphoanalysts in their study were inaccurate in sorting the handwriting samples of successful and poor salesmen. Jansen (1973) also used a two-category sorting procedure in his studies, and he found that, with practice, graphologists, psychologists, and laymen alike could sort with an accuracy better than chance, but they were not accurate enough for the procedure to be used on an individual basis. This raises an important point: a method may show statistically significant results for *groups* of individuals, but the effects may be so small as to preclude its use in making predictions for a *particular* individual. In other words, an effect may be statistically significant but clinically insignificant, a common problem in personality assessment research. The literature dealing with the issue of effect size in graphology is reviewed by Dean in this volume (chap. 12).

Nevo (1989) used an improved matching procedure, in which close friends of ten writers were asked to match the handwriting samples of their friends to the interpretations derived from them, and then to rank the accuracy of their matches. Although Nevo reported positive findings, he warned that "Significant as the results of the matching were, it does not seem that the validity of the graphological analysis was very high. On the basis of these findings the practical application of graphology as a single psychodiagnostic tool cannot, in fact, be recommended: too many 'misses' are involved and the probability of getting a distorted personality description is too high" (1989, 1335). To date, sorting and matching approaches to handwriting validation have failed to show that sorting, even into extreme groups, can be made at an acceptable level of validity.

Predictions from handwriting samples to rating scores on specified dimensions of behavior are to be preferred to the use of matching or sorting techniques, because they allow for a more finely differentiated set of comparisons and for more sophisticated data analysis. Whereas sorting judgments are limited to inclusion or exclusion from several broad categories, ratings can cover a wider range of variation that reflects greater subtlety in human behavior. They are not without their disadvantages, however. The rating scales which are used to generate the criterion scores must be designed well enough to allow for high interjudge reliability before the scores derived from them can be used to test the validity of handwriting judgments. Thus, if supervisor ratings of job performance are used as the criterion for handwriting judgments, it must be established in advance that supervisors use their rating scales with high levels of intra- and interjudge reliability. If this is not done, it is not possible to determine whether the results of a study reflect the low reliability of the rating scale or the low validity of the handwriting analysis, or both. Most of the graphological studies that have used rating scales as criteria have not documented the rater reliability of the rating scales they have used. Nevertheless, these studies are worth considering.

Eysenck (1948) asked a graphologist to predict two measures of neuroticism from 176 handwriting samples obtained from army hospital patients: a neuroticism rating based on aggregated psychological test scores and neuroticism identified in psychiatric diagnoses. The graphologist was able to predict the aggregated test scores at a statistically significant level, but not the diagnosis of neuroticism. Zdep and Weaver (1967) used thirteen ratings in their attempt to validate the use of Graphoanalysis for identifying competent life insurance salesmen. As noted earlier, they found no evidence of validity in two of three studies, and the modest level of validity they reported for the third study was in error (their two Graphoanalysts failed to detect half the members of a criterion group for whom correct detection had a probability of 50 percent, thus failing to achieve even chance levels of correct judgment).

In an informal account, Sonneman and Kernan (1962) reported that the ratings made by a graphologist of the work performance of executives correlated significantly (.36–.48) with ratings made by their supervisors. Unfortunately, their study was flawed in a number of respects (e.g., writing samples were taken from personnel files that may have contained biographical information; ratings were made by only one graphologist), so their results should be viewed with caution. Drory (1986) reported significant correlations on ten of thirteen scales between supervisor ratings of work performance and judgments of sixty script samples that had been evaluated by a single, experienced graphologist. This study suffers from the same shortcoming as the Sonneman and Kernan study. When judgments are made by a single graphologist, one never knows whether it is the graphological method or the special talents and skills of the graphologist that have been validated.

In an attempt to validate handwriting predictions of the work performance of real estate salesmen, Rafaeli and Klimoski (1983) used twenty experienced graphologists to predict ratings on ten dimensions and four objective sales productivity measures. None of the forty relevant correlations reached significance. Keinan, Barak, and Ramati (1984) used graphologists' ratings to predict success in officer training in Israel and found that both graphologists and psychologists were equally inaccurate in predicting from handwriting samples.

Wellingham-Jones (1989) attempted to identify specific script features and clusters of features that would discriminate successful from unsuccessful women (subjectively defined). She reported thirty-seven correct predictions out of a possible sixty, but she failed to control statistically for the large number of comparisons she made. Furthermore, most of the differences found, even the statistically significant ones, were too small to be useful for discriminating among the individual women in her study. A revised version of this study appears as chapter 15 of the present volume. Neter and Ben-Shakhar (1989) found in their meta-analysis that graphologists and nongraphologists were equally poor in predicting such things as work performance and socio-psychological attributes from handwriting samples. The performance of the graphologists in their study was even worse when they had to base their judgments on scripts lacking autobiographical content.

Nor does the accuracy of prediction improve if graphologists are allowed to define the qualities they feel are most appropriate for the ratings. In the study by Zdep and Weaver (1967), graphoanalysts specified thirteen personality traits that they believed to be important for work in life insurance sales. When their ratings on these scales were compared with actual sales performance, no significant correlations were found. The graphoanalysts then studied the writing samples of the top three salesmen in order to identify important script features associated with the success. Using these features, they tried to select successful salesmen from the remaining pool of subjects, again without success. Finally, they identified script features associated with failure from the scripts of four failing salesmen and again searched the scripts of the remaining forty-six salesmen to identify successes and failures (i.e., those above and those below the cutoff point on the three traits associated with failure). Less than 50 percent of the actual failures were correctly identified, even though a hit rate of 50 percent would have been expected on the basis of chance. Thus, even when the graphologists were able to define their own criteria, the accuracy of their predictions did not reach acceptable levels.

A number of investigators have assessed the validity of handwriting analysis by examining the relationship between graphological judgments and scores obtained from psychological tests. One disadvantage that graphologists may report in using psychological test scores as validity criteria is that they require the use of psychological concepts or personality traits that are not commonly used by handwriting analysts, a problem previously noted when ratings are used as validity criteria. Graphologists may thus be forced to adapt their interpretations to categories that seem to be artificial or unnatural. Low levels of association between graphological analyses and psychological test scores may then be attributed to these conceptual problems rather than the inaccuracy of graphological analysis.

The extensive procedures previously described for validating psychological tests of personality have not been used in assessing the validity of handwriting analysis. Nor do graphological systems provide tables of normative scores with which the handwriting analyst can determine where in the range of observed handwriting features the handwriting features of each individual can be placed. There are, however, a number of studies that have attempted to relate the results of handwriting analyses to scores from well-established psychological tests.

A few studies have shown significant correlations between handwriting analyses and performance on standard personality tests. Linton, Epstein, and Hartford (1962) reported significant relationships between the use of a particular beginning stroke and a number of psychological test indices of social conformity. As noted earlier, however, their research was seriously flawed. In 1971, Lemke and Kirchner used fifty-nine specific script features to predict personality and mental ability measures from psychological tests. They reported "slightly significant" results for some measures and a significant correlation between vertical size of script and extroversion. Their results are problematic because they found only ten significant relationships from a total of 160 prediction formulas, a result no better than chance. Similarly, Williams, Berg-Cross, and Berg-Cross (1977) reported correlations between several graphic features and extroversion, introversion, and reflectivity, but they were unable to confirm other predicted relationships, and their study was compromised by the use of a sample that was too small for the analysis that was done.

In contrast to these (flawed) studies that report modest evidence for the concurrent validity of handwriting analyses with psychological tests, numerous other studies have been unable to document significant correlations between graphologists' conclusions and psychological test scores. Jansen (1973) found no significant correlations between graphological judgments and either a composite psychological test score or a personnel rating score. Vestewig, Santee, and Moss (1976) were unable to find significant correlations between the judgments of six graphoanalysts and fifteen variables on the Edwards Personal Preference Schedule. Similarly, Lester and McLaughlin (1976) and Lester, McLaughlin, and Nosal (1977) were unable to show significant correlations between graphological analyses and test scores of neuroticism and extroversion.

Extroversion became a popular trait for study by graphologists, following the early research by Cohen (1973), which suggested that it might be readily identified by handwriting analysis. Rosenthal and Lines (1978) were unable to find evidence of a connection between three script features and extroversion as measured by the Eysenck Personality Inventory. Furnham and Gunter (1987) studied three script features commonly identified in graphology texts as indicators of extroversion. They found a high level of interjudge reliability (.89) on the scoring of these features, but the predicted relationships to extroversion were not found, and in the matrix correlating thirteen theoretically important script features and four scores from the Eysenck Personality Questionnaire (EPQ), fewer correlations were significant than would be expected by chance.

Eysenck and Gudjonsson (1986) attempted to relate graphoanalystic predictions to scores on the EPQ, but they found a significant relationship for only one of four measures. Karnes and Leonard (chap. 16 in this volume) used an unusual validation procedure, in which they obtained judgments of colleagues from individuals who had known them for a long time and then had each person select the graphological reports that they believed were accurate descriptions of themselves and of their colleagues. They found that the frequency with which participants selected graphological reports as true was no greater than chance. In contrast, reports based on valid psychological tests are generally identified correctly at rates significantly better than chance.

In summary: the results of the many studies conducted to date provide little evidence for the validity of handwriting analysis as a means of assessing personality and predicting behavior. For the most part, these studies have shown little relationship between the results of graphological analyses and: (1) actual behavior, such as sales performance or success in training programs; (2) subjective ratings of work performance or psychological attributes; or (3) objective, reliable, and valid measures obtained from psychological tests. The few studies that do report significant relationships are, unfortunately, so flawed in research design that we can accept their findings only with serious reservations.

Despite the empirical evidence, reviewers who favor graphology often come to conclusions at variance with the very evidence they have reviewed. For example, Lockowandt (1976) examined a wealth of evidence concerning the reliability and validity of handwriting analysis and concluded that "The results of validity studies correlating individual characteristics with criteria are predominantly negative" (p. 28). Nevertheless, he ended his report on a hopeful note, suggesting that the particular graphologists used in validation studies may have been a major source of the difficulty in demonstrating validity, rather than the graphology method itself.

While differences among graphologists may indeed be part of the explanation, it is important to remember from the studies reviewed earlier that trained graphologists did not produce more accurate judgments or predictions than did untrained judges. Thus, lack of training in the techniques of graphology does not appear to be responsible for the failure to establish validity, although other significant differences among graphologists may be a contributing factor. Also, research that has investigated the possible role of other mitigating factors (such as type of validation procedure used, types of personality traits to be identified, or types of behavior to be predicted) have failed to identify a set of conditions under which graphological judgments have consistently proved valid.

Our reading of the empirical evidence, therefore, compels us to the conclusion that the ability of handwriting analysis to identify personality characteristics or to predict individual behavior has not been demonstrated.

REFERENCES

Allport, G. W., and P. E. Vernon. 1933. *Studies in Expressive Movement.* New York: Macmillan.

Bem, D. J., and A. Allen. 1974. "On Predicting Some of the People Some of the time: The Search for Cross-Situational Consistencies in Behavior." *Psychological Review* 81: pp. 506–520.

Ben-Shakhar, G., M. Bar-Hillel, Y. Bilu, E. Ben-Abba, and A. Flug. 1986. "Can Graphology Predict Occupational Success? Two Empirical Studies and Some Methodological Ruminations." *Journal of Applied Psychology* 71: pp. 645–653.

Block, J. 1971. *Lives through Time.* Berkeley, Calif.: Bancroft.

Blum, M. L., and B. Balinky. 1951. *Counselling and Psychology.* Englewood Cliffs, N.J.: Prentice Hall.

Boring, E. G., ed. 1950. *A History of Experimental Psychology.* New York: Appleton-Century-Crafts.

Campbell, D. P. 1971. *Handbook for the Strong Vocational Interest Blank.* Stanford, Calif.: Stanford University Press.

———. 1977. *Manual for the Strong-Campbell Interest Inventory.* Stanford, Calif.: Stanford University Press.

Campbell, D. T., and D. W. Fiske. 1959. "Convergent and Discriminant Validation by the Multitrait-Multimethod Matrix." *Psychological Bulletin* 56: pp. 81–105.

Cohen, R. 1973. *Patterns of Personality Judgment* trans. D. Schaeffer. New York: Academic Press.

Costa, P. T., and R. R. McRae. 1985. "Concurrent Validation After 20 Years: The Implications of Personality Stability for Its Assessment." In *Advances in Personality Assessment,* edited by J. Butler and C. D. Spielberger. Vol. 4. Hillside, N.J.: Lawrence Erlbaum Associates.

Crumbaugh, J. C. 1977a. "A reply to 'Validity and Student Acceptance of a Graphoanalytic Approach to Personality' by Vestewig, Santee, and Moss." *Journal of Personality Assessment* 41: pp. 351–352.

———. 1977b. "Comment on the Graphological Studies of Lester, McLaughlin and Nosal." *Perceptual and Motor Skills* 45: p. 494.

Dahlstrom, W. G., G. S. Welsh, and L. E. Dahlstrom. 1972. *An MMPI Handbook.* Vol. 1, revised. Minneapolis: University of Minnesota Press.

Drory, A. 1986. "Graphology and Job Performance: A Validation Study." In *Scientific Aspects of Graphology,* edited by B. Nevo, pp. 165–174. Springfield, Ill.: Charles C. Thomas.

Epstein, S. 1979. "The Stability of Behavior: I. On Predicting Most of the People Much of the Time." *Journal of Personality and Social Psychology* 37: pp. 1097–1126.

———. 1980. "The Stability of Behavior: II. Implications for Psychological Research." *American Psychologist* 35: pp. 790–806.

Exner, J. E. 1974. *The Rorschach: A Comprehensive System.* Vol. 1. New York: Wiley.

Eysenck, H. 1948. "Neuroticism and Handwriting." *Journal of Abnormal and Social Psychology* 43: pp. 94–96.

Eysenck, H. J., and G. Gudjonsson, 1986. "An Empirical Study of the Validity of Handwriting Analysis." *Personality and Individual Differences* 7: pp. 263–264.

Farberow, N. N. 1981. "Assessment of Suicide." In *Advances in Psychological Assessment.* Vol. 5, edited by P. P. McReynolds. San Francisco: Josey Bass.

Festinger, L. 1957. *A Theory of Cognitive Dissonance.* Evanston, Ill.: Row, Peterson.

Fluckiger, F., C. A. Tripp, and G. H. Weinberg. 1961. "A Review of Experimental Research in Graphology, 1933–1960." *Perceptual and Motor Skills* 12: pp. 67–90 (Monograph Supplement 1-V12).

Frederick, C. J. 1965. "Some Phenomena Affecting Handwriting Analysis." *Perceptual and Motor Skills* 20: pp. 211–218.

Furnham, A. 1986. "Response Bias, Social Desirability and Dissimulation." *Personality and Individual Differences* 7: pp. 385–400.

Furnham, A., and B. Gunter, 1987. "Graphology and Personality: Another Failure to Validate Graphological Analysis." *Personality and Individual Differences* 8: pp. 433–435.

Galbraith, D., and W. Wilson. 1964. "Reliability of the Graphoanalytical approach to Handwriting Analysis." *Perceptual and Motor Skills* 19: pp. 615–618.

Guilford, J. P. 1959. *Personality*. New York: McGraw.

Gough, H. G. 1957. *The California Psychological Inventory*. Palo Alto, Calif.: Consulting Psychologists Press.

Jansen, A. 1973. *Validation of Graphological Judgements: An Experimental Study*. Paris: Mouton.

Kangas, J., and K. Bradway. 1971. "Intelligence at Middle Age: A Thirty-eight Year Follow-up." *Developmental Psychology* 8: pp. 506–520.

Keinan, G., A. Barak, and T. Ramati. 1984. "Reliability and Validity of Graphological Assessment in the Selection Process of Military Officers." *Perceptual and Motor Skills* 58: pp. 811–821.

Kenrick, D. T., and D. C. Funder. 1988. "Profit from Controversy." *American Psychologist* 43: pp. 23–34.

Klimoski, R. J., and A. Rafaeli. 1983. "Inferring Personal Qualities through Handwriting Analysis." *Journal of Occupational Psychology* 56: pp. 191–202.

Klopfer, B., M. D. Ainsworth, W. G. Klopfer, and R. C. Holt. 1954. *Developments in the Rorschach Technique*. New York: Harcourt, Brace & World.

Knox, W. J., and R. Grippaldi. 1970. "High Levels of State or Trait Anxiety and Performance in Selected Verbal WAIS Subtests." *Psychological Reports* 27: pp. 375–379.

Lemke, E. A., and J. H. Kirchner. 1971. "A Multivariate Study of Handwriting, Intelligence and Personality Correlates." *Journal of Personality Assessment* 35: pp. 584–592.

Lester, D., and S. McLaughlin. 1976. "Sex-deviant Handwriting and Neuroticism." *Perceptual and Motor Skills* 43: p. 770.

Lester, D., S. McLaughlin, and G. Nosal, 1977. "Graphological Signs for Extroversion." *Perceptual and Motor Skills* 44: pp. 137–138.

Lezak, M. 1983. *Neuropsychological Assessment*. 2nd ed. New York: Oxford University Press.

Linton, H. B., L. Epstein, and H. Hartford. 1962. "Personality and Perceptual Correlates of Primary Beginning Strokes in Handwriting." *Perceptual and Motor Skills* 15: pp. 159–170.

Lockowandt, O. 1976. "Present Status of the Investigation of Handwriting Psychology as a Diagnostic Method." *J.S.A.S. Catalogue of Selected Documents in Psychology* 6(1): p. 4.

Lombroso, C. 1891. *The Man of Genius*. London: W. Scott; New York: Scribner.

Mischel, W. 1968. *Personality and Assessment*. New York: Wiley.

————. 1976. *Introduction to Personality.* 2nd ed. New York: Holt, Rinehart & Winston.

Mischel, W. 1984. "Convergences and Challenges in the Search for Consistency." *American Psychologist* 39: pp. 351–364.

Moore, M. 1985. "About the Sad State of Scientific Graphology." *Psychological Documents* 15(2): p. 2676.

Moss, H. A., and E. J. Susman. 1980. "Longitudinal Study of Personality Development." In *Constancy and Change in Human Development,* edited by O. G. Brim and J. Kagan, pp. 530–595. Cambridge, Mass.: Harvard University Press.

Mulvey, E. P., and C. W. Lidz. 1985. "A Critical Analysis of Dangerous Research in a New Legal Environment." *Law and Human Behavior* 9: pp. 209–219.

Murray, H. A. 1943. *Thematic Apperception Test Manual.* Cambridge, Mass.: Harvard University Press.

Neter. E., and G. Ben-Shakhar, 1989. "The Predictive Validity of Graphological Inferences: A Meta-Analytic Approach." *Personality and Individual Differences* 10: pp. 737–745.

Nevo, B. 1989. "Validation of Graphology through Use of a Matching Method Based on Ranking." *Perceptual and Motor Skills* 69: pp. 1331–1336.

Pascal, G. R., and B. Suttell. 1947. "Testing the Claims of a Graphologist." *Journal of Personality* 16: pp. 192–197.

Rafaeli, A., and A. Drory. 1988. "Graphological Assessments for Personnel Selection: Concerns and Suggestions for Research." *Perceptual and Motor Skills* 66: pp. 743–759.

Rafaeli, A., and R. J. Klimoski. 1983. "Predicting Sales Success through Handwriting Analysis: An Evaluation of the Effects of Training and Handwriting Sample Content." *Journal of Applied Psychology* 68: pp. 212–217.

Rorschach, H. 1942. *Psychodiagnostics,* translated by P. Lemkau and B. Kronenberg. New York: Grune & Stratton.

Rosenthal, D. A., and R. Lines. 1978. "Handwriting as a Correlate of Extroversion." *Journal of Personality Assessment* 42: pp. 45–48.

Saudek, R. 1929. *Experiments with Handwriting.* New York: William Morrow.

Sears, R. R. 1977. "Sources of Life Satisfaction of the Terman Gifted Men." *American Psychologist* 32: pp. 119–128.

Snyder, C. R. 1974. "Why Horoscopes Are True: The Effects of Specificity on Acceptance of Astrological Interpretations." *Journal of Clinical Psychology* 30: pp. 577–580.

Sonneman, U., and J. P. Kernan. 1962. "Handwriting Analysis—A Valid Selection Tool?" *Personnel* (Nov.–Dec.): pp. 8–14.

Sovik, N., O. Arntzen, and R. Thygesen. 1986. "Effects of Feedback." In *Graphonomics: Contemporary Research in Handwriting,* edited by H. S. R. Kao, G. P. Van Galen, and R. Hoosain. Amsterdam: North-Holland.

Tallent, N. 1958. "On Individualizing the Psychologist's Clinical Evaluation." *Journal of Clinical Psychology* 14: pp. 243–244.

Vestewig, R. E., A. H. Santee, and M. K. Moss. 1976. "Validity and Student Acceptance of a Graphoanalytic Approach to Personality." *Journal of Personality*

Assessment 40: pp. 592–597.

Wellingham-Jones, P. 1989. "Evaluation of the Handwriting of Successful Women through the Roman-Staempfli Psychogram." *Perceptual and Motor Skills* 69: pp. 999–1010.

Wiggins, J. S. 1973. *Personality and Prediction*. Reading, Mass.: Addison-Wesley.

Williams, M., G. Berg-Cross, and L. Berg-Cross. 1977. "Handwriting Characteristics and Their Relationship to Eysenck's Extroversion-Introversion and Kagan's Impulsivity-Reflectivity Dimensions." *Journal of Personality Assessment* 41: pp. 291–298.

Zdep, S. M., and H. B. Weaver. 1967. "The Graphoanalytic Approach to Selecting Life Insurance Salesmen." *Journal of Applied Psychology* 51: pp. 295–299.

11

Graphology and Personnel Selection

Richard J. Klimoski

Richard Klimoski begins this chapter by discussing what a consultant advising in the area of personnel selection must determine *before* testing of applicants can begin. Assembling a detailed *job description* is the consultant's first task, in order to identify the precise traits that are relevant to the job. After reading Klimoski's account of the complexity of this preliminary stage, the reader may wish to contrast this standard procedure among industrial psychologists with the *processual validation* approach suggested by Oskar Lockowandt in chapter 6. Nevertheless, the reader might ask whether the problems Dr. Lockowandt addresses in his chapter would arise in the first place if graphologists carefully and routinely followed the procedures described by Dr. Klimoski herein.

In the second part of his chapter, Klimoski reviews the accepted standards of industrial/organizational psychologists for determining the appropriateness of any personnel selection tool. The reader may wish to look also at Marilyn Bowman's treatment in chapter 10 of similar issues in the development of personality measures. Note that the standards Dr. Klimoski advocates in this chapter are the ones shared, in principle, by all the contributors to this volume—both graphologists and their critics. The dispute between the two groups really comes down to whether or not graphology meets these standards.

In his final section, Klimoski applies these standards to graphology. He cites a number of studies that test how well graphology meets these standards, including two studies conducted by himself and Anat Rafaeli, a practicing graphologist.

Note that scientific personnel selection employs multiple convergent measures and an ethical consultant would virtually never base a decision on a single indicator, graphology or any other.

INTRODUCTION

This chapter examines the application of graphology to personnel decisions in work organizations. Its focus is on the extent to which graphology is capable of assisting managers and personnel specialists in predicting and understanding performance on the job. In the context of personnel selection, this usually means trying to estimate the likely success of people who are applying for work. The overarching goal of the chapter is to prepare the reader to make more informed choices when offered graphological services in the personnel arena.

The main premise of the chapter is that, when offered for use in work organizations, graphological services should be viewed as any other potential device or program (e.g., selection testing or interviews) and subject to the same scrutiny. Thus, the first part of the chapter reviews the basic logic of personnel decision making. This will provide the context for comparing graphology. The second section will describe the standards that human resource specialists use to evaluate the appropriateness of any personnel selection device (including graphology). The third section reviews the evidence regarding the usefulness of graphology for personnel selection in light of these standards. A final section presents conclusions and offers recommendations for both proponents and opponents of graphological applications to personnel work.

THE NATURE OF PERSONNEL SELECTION

Scientifically based personnel selection principles have been available for over 70 years. By the second decade in this century in the United States, industrial/organizational psychologists such as Munsterberg (1913) and Scott (1911) were working with a variety of companies to improve the accuracy of personnel selection. Scott was later to use his expertise in advising the U.S. military during the First World War on the processing and screening of over 1,700,000 men. In the years since, a great deal of empirical research has been carried out on approaches to personnel selection. Moreover, a great deal of practical wisdom has also accumulated. Thus, by the 1980s, Schmidt, Hunter, and their colleagues (Schmidt and Hunter, 1981; Schmidt, Hunter, McKenzie, and Muldrow, 1979; Schmidt, Hunter, and Pearlman, 1982) were able to point out both the real (i.e., scientifically established) and financial benefits of systematic, professionally based personnel selection practices. For details, see Schmitt, Neal, and Klimoski (1991).

THE LOGIC OF PERSONNEL SELECTION

The logic of personnel selection is based on the very nature of modern complex organizations and on the notion of division of labor and job responsibilities (specialization) that has evolved over the years. It is also related to the practicalities and logistics of recruiting and hiring people.

Worker Requirements. Modern organizations, whether large or small, public sector or private enterprise, generally reflect the fact that products or services can best be produced or delivered if specific individuals are assigned to particular duties or tasks. Once assigned, various individuals' work activities or products are then integrated or coordinated by management policies or rules. The division of labor and the amount of specialization will vary, of course, and will depend upon such things as the particular goods or services involved, the tools or technology required, and, especially, management's beliefs about individual workers' capabilities and needs. As a result, in most organizations, different people do different things. To perform well at these various tasks, individuals must have appropriate capacities or capabilities. These factors are usually referred to as worker requirements.

Whether the job involved is that of a salesperson or a neurosurgeon, there will be a set of worker requirements. These include the knowledge, skills, abilities, needs, motives, and personality dispositions needed to perform. In other words, these are the important attributes of the people who are likely to be successful on the job.

There will be differences as to just which worker requirements are important from job to job. Some jobs place a heavy intellectual demand on incumbents. Others emphasize physical capacities or strong interpersonal skills. This means that, prior to recruiting or selecting individuals, personnel psychologists, or anyone else in the human resource area, must establish the particular set of requirements involved.

The preferred starting point for identifying worker requirements is to conduct a job analysis. There are a variety of ways to do this (Levine et al., 1983) but usually it involves a personnel specialist who will observe workers performing the job in question, examine the content of the job, conduct interviews with workers and their bosses, and occasionally make use of a specially constructed questionnaire to be completed by incumbents. A good job analysis is systematic, makes use of a variety of techniques, and is carried out by a qualified individual. The objective is to get as complete and valid a picture of a job as possible. Without this, efforts to recruit and select people will be seriously flawed.

The output of a job analysis is both a complete job description and a list of worker requirements. The former tells us what the person does on the job. The latter, as noted, are insights as to what it takes to do the job well.

Worker requirements can take various forms. They can involve particular types of knowledge, skills, or abilities, or they might reflect key aptitudes needed to attain or develop the former (through training or supervision).

In addition, requirements may include particular interests, values, needs, or motives. Thus, they describe the type of personality necessary to do the job on a day-to-day basis. An important point to remember is that worker requirements are determined by the type of work to be performed. They will exist and affect the likely success of individuals, whether we try to uncover them or not. The prudent organization usually makes an effort to get at them systematically.

Although a wide variety of worker requirements has been identified, for purposes of this chapter, it will be convenient to cluster them into two types. Personnel specialists often distinguish between what might be called "can do" requirements vs. "will do" requirements (Porter, Lawler, and Hackman, 1975). As you might surmise, the "can do" requirements are the knowledge, skills, and abilities which determine whether or not a person is likely to be ABLE to do the job, assuming that he or she puts out the necessary effort. This can be thought of as the capacity to perform. In fact, "can do" requirements limit the potential of an individual for effective job performance in important ways.

In contrast, other characteristics might be important for success because they determine how motivated a person is likely to be if placed on the job. Extensive research has established that interests, values, or needs must be fulfilled on the job for people to be motivated (Wanous, 1980). Thus, "will do" requirements describe the potential of the job to satisfy certain needs or, alternatively, the needs of certain types of individuals.

Any given job will typically have a mixture of "can do" and "will do" requirements. To be effective, a newly hired person will usually have to meet both criteria. In other words, if a person can't do the job (for lack of ability) it is unlikely that high levels of motivation alone will be sufficient. And, as you might expect, even if the individual does have the ability to do the job, he or she may not demonstrate the motivation or the inclination to do the job once placed there. There is ample evidence that fully capable individuals, hired into a job which fails to meet their needs, are very likely to quit in short order (Wanous, 1980).

MEASURING WORKER REQUIREMENTS

In staffing positions in work organizations, in general, we usually attempt first to establish the nature of worker requirements and then find ways of measuring both capacity and motivational requirements. Over the years, personnel specialists have developed different ways of measuring or estimating the extent to which applicants meet or exceed job requirements. Some of these approaches are more appropriate for assessing a candidate's capabilities, others his or her needs and values. Figure 1 lists some examples.

Type of Information Obtained	Type of Measure
Maximum Performance "Can Do"	Cognitive Tests
	Aptitude Tests
	Work Sample Tests
	Physical Ability Tests
	Assessment Centers
Both	Employment Interview
	Reference Checks
Typical Behavior "Will Do"	Biographical Data
	Personality Measures

Fig. 1. Measuring worker requirements.

A common approach to the "can do" assessments is to use what are called work samples and work sample tests. When staffing the position of a graphic artist or illustrator, we often ask to see the artist's previous work or portfolio. If most applicants are presumed to have relatively little actual job experience, the personnel specialist might design and develop a work sample test to get at key aptitudes (e.g., color perception) or skills (e.g., use of water colors) or both (Campion, 1972). Work samples and work sample tests are designed to index the candidates' capacity to perform important aspects of the job in question. Aptitude and ability tests are other common ways to measure capacity to perform.

The measurement of the candidate's suitability for a job in terms of needs and values has often involved the use of interest inventories and personality tests. In this regard, there are numerous standard measures that might be applied to the selection of personnel (e.g., the 16PF test). Occasionally, the job analysis might uncover special worker requirements for which there is no standard measure. Under these circumstances, profession- als might be used to develop a new device. For example, Bernardin (1987) discovered that the job of telephone service representative required that the incumbent be able to tolerate a fair amount of pressure and hostility from irate customers (even verbal abuse). Because there was no standard measure for the personality that could deal with this kind of situation, he had to develop his own measure. This took the form of a self-report measure, part of which is reproduced in Figure 2.

Discomfort Sale

For each of the 20 sets of four situations listed, respondents were asked to circle the letters of the two situations—and only two—that would cause them the most aggravation or discomfort. Valid items are indicated with a (v).

1. a. You are shopping, can't find what you want and there isn't a salesperson in sight.
   b. You can't go out and party on weekends. (v)
   c. Having to listen to someone's point of view with which you disagree. (v)
   d. It rains the day you scheduled a picnic at the beach.
2. a. You must be indoors on a sunny day. (v)
   b. You are stood up for an appointment.
   c. You hear your neighbors argue. (v)
   d. You are the only employee to forget to get the boss a birthday card.
3. a. You are in an eight item express lane at the grocery and the person in front of you has 14 items.
   b. You have a long wait in a line before your number is called.
   c. Your boss yells at you about another person's mistake. (v)
   d. You have an 11:00 P.M. curfew on weekends. (v)
4. a. You are ill and have to miss work. You are docked for the time you missed. (v)
   b. A friend borrows something of yours and does not return it.
   c. You must get up at 6:00 A.M. and go to work. (v)
   d. The expressway is bumper to bumper and you are late for work.
5. a. You go to a theater and find the movie is sold out.
   b. You are required to work in a crowded, noisy room with no privacy. (v)
   c. Your work is closely monitored. (v)
   d. You are required to work in a room by yourself.
6. a. You are driving down the highway; someone cuts in front of you with only inches to spare.
   b. You work with someone who frequently uses obscenities. (v)
   c. Waiting at a railroad crossing for a long freight train.
   d. You have to repeat instructions several times. (v)
7. a. You have to be polite to a rude person. (v)
   b. Your charge account bill includes charges you did not make.
   c. Someone tries to tell you how to do something you know how to do very well.
   d. Circumstances require you to be indoors when you had scheduled a trip to the beach. (v)

Fig. 2.Assessing tolerance for stress in the job of a
telephone customer service representative (from Bernardin, 1987).

Often, a given selection technique is used to get at a wide range of applicant qualifications. That is, it attempts to get at both the can do and will do aspects of the job. Thus, in most organizations, a selection interview is involved in the screening of candidates. In fact, in a carefully designed and conducted interview, a wide range of qualities may be assessed (Campion, Pursell, and Brown, 1988). An organization might use a test battery made up of different kinds of tests (ability and personality) to get at critical factors. Life history information (in the form of an application blank or a specially constructed questionnaire) and reference checks are also popular. When selecting from internal candidates, even co-worker descriptions have been found to be useful. All these approaches, when carefully developed and executed, have the potential to provide insights into both the capacity and the motivation of individuals.

One might consider graphology as a potential selection device, and apply the logic developed here. Based on the claims of proponents and current practices, it might best be classified as a way to assess personal dispositions and inclinations (i.e., the will do part of a person's qualifications). That is, graphology is frequently used as an attempt to get at a person's willingness to perform and the suitability of his or her temperament for the job. However, practitioners occasionally will use graphology in an attempt to index intellective qualities (e.g., critical thinking ability) as well. Other graphologists claim they can also predict absenteeism, pilfering, and drug use on the job.

ASSESSING THE SUITABILITY OF CANDIDATES

In practice, organizations stress key worker requirements in their advertisements for job openings and in their recruiting. By doing so, the goal is to generate sufficient interest among individuals who would potentially qualify as employees. The people who actually apply for the job are referred to as the applicant pool. If recruiting is successful, there will be many individuals in the applicant pool. A subset of these will indeed have the necessary qualifications. It is important that such a pool exists because the logic of personnel selection dictates that the organization must have the opportunity to pick and choose among individuals. They must have what is called a favorable selection ratio (number of job openings/number of applicants). To the extent that there are too few applicants, no selection device or program, no matter how good, will be of much use. The organization would have to take just about all of those available simply to have the jobs covered. Thus, in general, most companies will strive to enlarge the applicant pool as much as possible.

Assuming a favorable selection ratio, scientific selection procedures usually involve several phases. Each of these phases makes use of some assessment or screening mechanism; those candidates who compare favorably are then allowed to move up to the next phase. In this regard, the process is sequential and analogous to requiring a candidate to clear a number of hurdles before being given the status of a regular employee (see Fig. 3). To illustrate, one public utility company in the U.S. sends recruiters to college campuses to identify suitable candidates. In 1985 representatives of the company conducted 687 interviews (the first hurdle) at 14 schools. Out of this initial effort they found 220 acceptable. But for a variety of reasons (e.g., scheduling) only 50 were invited for a visit to the company's headquarters (a second hurdle). Fourteen individuals were offered a job. Once on the job, the new recruit would be reviewed and assessed each quarter (a third hurdle) and was only taken off probationary status (a fourth hurdle) after a period of 18–24 months.

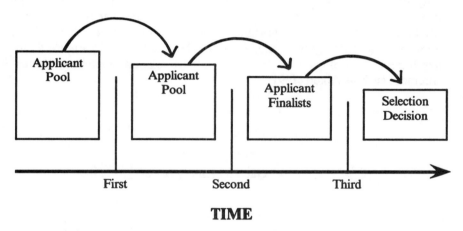

Fig. 3. Hurdles to overcome on the way to regular employee status.

Assessments at each point might involve any of a variety of tools or methods. In the example given, reference checks, resumes, tests, interviews, and ratings of on-the-job performance were all used at different stages in the process. To reiterate, the particular technique used at each hurdle was related to the worker requirements which had been previously identified as important to the job (in this case, being a manager). The stage in the sequence that a particular device was used was also determined (in part) by the belief that it was the best place to assess specific qualities with that technique. Thus, the organization in the example felt that certain skills (oral communications, decision making) and particular dispositions (being a self-starter, showing adaptability/flexibility) were basic to job performance in most jobs in the company. These were necessary (but not sufficient) qualities. Consequently, these were assessed early, at the time of the campus interview (and by relying on life history information, references, and insights gained in the interview itself). Only then did the company scrutinize the finalists for the characteristics important to specific jobs to be filled (usually during the visit to the job site).

ESTABLISHING THE USEFULNESS OF A SELECTION DEVICE

Prior to actually implementing a particular selection approach or adopting a specific device, it is important to establish that it will, in fact, be useful. This is the essence of personnel research in most organizations. Personnel specialists will do this by comparing what is known about the device to a set of standards. Several of these standards will be mentioned only briefly as they are detailed elsewhere in this book. Others will be given greater attention because they are somewhat peculiar to the personnel area. However, it is important to list them together as they will be applied to graphology in a later section. These are listed in Figure 4. In-depth treatments of each can be found in textbooks on psychological measurement such as Aiken (1991).

1. Reliability

2. Content Validity

3. Construct Validity

4. Criterion-Related Validity

5. Utility

6. Freedom from Bias

7. User Acceptance

Fig. 4. Establishing the usefulness of the selection device.

Reliability. The essence of reliability is consistency of measurement. More technically, reliability refers to the extent that data or information obtained with a particular measurement tool or selection device is free from errors (Schmitt, Neal, and Klimoski, 1991). There is a variety of ways to estimate reliability, several of which will be illustrated in a later section.

Content Validity. Whenever we want to be certain that a selection device is getting at all of the important worker requirements, we raise the issue of content validity. Technically, content validity refers to the degree to which the responses required by the test or measure are a representative sample of the whole domain of behaviors or knowledge of interest to us.

In the case of personnel selection, it means that we really are getting at the key traits or qualities needed for job performance.

Construct Validity. In many instances we assume that a selection device or measure is getting at some underlying theme, or, as professionals would call it, a "construct." Thus, an intelligence test is presumed to be measuring intelligence; an honesty test, honesty, and so on. Alternatively, an interview may or may not be used to assess the candidate's level or score on a construct. It would depend on what questions were asked and the kinds of inferences that are made. Establishing construct validity is somewhat of an inductive process whereby scores on a measure must be shown to relate in ways predicted by theory or logic to other scores or measures (Chronbach and Meehl, 1955). Equally important, a measure with good construct validity is expected to produce scores that are unrelated to other measures in a manner consistent with logic or theory. Thus, a valid measure of intelligence should produce scores that correlate with a standard or accepted measure of intelligence and, at the same time, be uncorrelated with measures of, say, physical strength.

Criterion-Related Validity. This refers to empirical evidence that the scores obtained with an assessment device are related to some important set of behaviors or some level of functioning. In personnel selection, persuasive evidence of criterion-related validity would be to show that scores on a selection device are, in fact, related to such things as job performance, regular work attendance, or longer job tenure.

Utility. Most selection devices are intended to be used for personnel decision making. The assumption is that by using the device, the organization is improving the likelihood that those people who are recommended for hire will be better than those who are rejected. But we expect even more. We assume that among those who are selected we will find a larger proportion of individuals who will be viewed as successful, once on the job, compared to what we are currently getting by using traditional methods. Utility refers to the extent that a measure does indeed fulfill this promise. We usually establish utility by demonstrating that we are making fewer selection errors by using the selection device than we would by not using it.

In personnel work there will always be some chance of making a decision error. No known system exists where this is not the case. In utility analysis, the particular kinds of errors made when using a selection device are examined.

There are two kinds of decision errors that may occur. One involves selecting someone for hire who, it is discovered later, is not a suitable employee. In fact, the individual may have to be fired. This kind of error is referred to as a "false positive" error. Alternatively, a manager or decision maker may, based on the evidence produced with a selection device, reject an individual who would have been a good employee. This is a "false negative" error.

An organization would have to determine which type of error is more important to avoid. This is, in part, a matter of business philosophy. But, it is also a matter of economics. That is to say, utility analysis will involve a computation of the expenses associated with recruiting, training, and terminating personnel relative to the benefits of average, below average, or superior performance from employees. It will also consider the "lost opportunity costs" of the excellent candidates who were turned away. Thus, a selection device with high utility is one that provides the appropriate balance between correct decisions with respect to these two types of errors (Schmitt, Neal, and Klimoski, 1991).

When selecting personnel, mistakes can indeed be costly. For example, a recent survey of U.S. personnel officers of large private companies revealed that, on average, it costs over $18,000 to dismiss an employee (Fowler, 1990). It is thus possible to estimate the money saved by using a particular device. However, a utility analysis would not only involve this figure (the benefits of avoiding mistakes) but also consideration of the actual expenses incurred in developing the measure and the recurring expenses associated with its use.

To be complete, estimating utility would also require us to consider the relative costs and benefits of alternatives. For instance, there might be some other, very inexpensive approach to selection that works almost as well.

Another aspect of cost/benefit analysis relates to just when in the selection process a given device might be used. That is to say, a more valid but expensive-to-administer device might be applied later in the recruiting/ selection sequence where there are fewer candidates to consider (semi-finalists). A somewhat less valid, but very inexpensive measure might be administered at an earlier point as a screening device.

Freedom From Bias. In the United States today it is public policy to insure equal employment opportunities for all people, regardless of religion, gender, nationality, or ethnic background. It is also against the law to unfairly discriminate in employment practices. Thus, the impact of a selection device must be scrutinized to see if there are disproprtionate numbers of individuals in these protected classes who are adversely impacted (see chs. 17 and 18 for discussions of graphology in this context).

User Acceptance. Most of the standards listed, so far, have a strong technical component. In the case of user acceptance, we are simply stating that a selection device must be perceived as appropriate and fair to the people involved. This would include the larger pool of job applicants, those people ultimately hired, the current workers and managers of the organization, as well as the personnel specialists involved (recruiters, trainers). User acceptance is very often a function of the care taken in the development of the device. It is affected by the kind of evidence (quality and quantity) that exists for its validity. But, perceptions of fairness and appropriateness will also be related to how and by what means the selection tool was implemented or put into practice. Unilateral imposition of new hiring standards and/or the use of a particular screening program (e.g., drug testing via urine samples) is likely to reduce acceptance, irrespective of whatever validity or utility evidence exists.

The foregoing standards can be applied to any potential personnel-selection device or program. Usually, all would be relevant to some degree. An exception might be where we are not concerned with personnel constructs. Under these circumstances we would have less interest in construct validity. We might substitute instead evidence of content or criterion-related validity.

GRAPHOLOGY AND PERSONNEL SELECTION

After reviewing the claims of graphology with respect to personnel decisions and some of the assumptions made in its application to personnel work, its status will be assessed by applying the standards that have just been outlined. The emphasis will be on making use of research evidence published in refereed scientific journals (as opposed to personal testimonials, self-published promotional materials, or articles in journals in which authors can place anything by paying a fee).

CLAIMS OF THE PROPONENTS OF GRAPHOLOGY

Graphology has been proposed for or used in most areas of human endeavor. Klimoski and Rafaeli (1983) reviewed published research on the application of graphology to the areas of mental health, personality assessment, and intelligence measurement. Other chapters in this book attest to the variety of contexts in which it has been used. This section will focus on its use in personnel work and especially employee selection.

Applications to Personnel Work. As early as 1965, Thayer and Antoinetti reported that the insurance industry in the U.S. was experimenting with the use of handwriting analysis in personnel work. Jaekle (1974) lists several major U.S. firms (such as GE, Firestone, U.S. Steel, Southern Bell, and even the IRS) as involved with the practice. Somewhat later, Levy (1979) estimated that over 3,000 American firms had made use of graphology in personnel matters. He also wrote that 85 percent of all European companies routinely consider the recommendations of handwriting experts. Radar (1988) describes applications by a personnel search firm (Dunhill, in Boston) and a Houston-based firm (Greensheet, Inc.). Arnett (1989) reports on the use of handwriting analysis in the auto rental business (Thrifty Rent-a-Car). He also feels that there is increasing interest in handwriting analysis in personnel work as a result of the U.S. government's restrictions on the use of the polygraph in pre-employment screening.

It should be noted, however, that the claims regarding the extent and location of use of graphology are most often found in the popular press and such claims are often based only on opinions of those being interviewed. To put it another way, at this time there is very little in the way of systematic and documented evidence on prevalence of usage. It is fair to say, however, that the perception exists among many authors and managers that the application of handwriting analysis to personnel work is widespread.

The actual purpose for using handwriting analysis in personnel matters seems to be quite varied, at least if you take popular reports at face value. Shiela Kurtz, a graphologist practicing in New York City, is reported to offer services to screen job candidates, evaluate employees for promotion, determine an individual's compatibility for particular settings or assignments, and evaluate individuals as credit risks (Anonymous, 1979). Arnett (1989) sees applications of graphology to the assessment of job-relevant personality traits, the identification of a candidate's strengths and weaknesses, establishing the overall suitability of an individual for a job, and the estimating of risk or propensity to health disorders. Lynch (1985) concurs with the above lists of applications and includes most of them in his essay.

When it comes to charging for these services, the price appears to vary widely. Taylor and Sackheim (1988) report a cost of $30 to $300 per assessment. Gorman (1989) cites a range from $100-$500 per case. Arnett (1989) offers the largest variability of fees from $25-$1,000, depending on the amount of detail required.

It would seem reasonable that charges for graphological services to organizations could differ considerably. Personnel assessments using other, more traditional approaches (e.g., multi-aptitude test batteries) also vary in their costs to organizations. Charges usually depend on such factors as the quality or reputation of the firm supplying the assessments, the skill level of the individuals actually providing the analysis, the number of cases involved (there is usually a volume discount), the amount of detail requested by the company, the type of personnel (e.g., sales, management) to be assessed (and hence the risks associated with making a decision error), and the speed of reporting needed (there is usually a premium for rapid turn-around). Thus, costs for traditional assessments can range from $5 a case (for a self-administered, computer-scored, pre-qualifying quiz used in large numbers) to $2,000 (where a specially developed Assessment Center program is involved).

The wide variety of applications of graphology notwithstanding, the usual focus is the assessment of personality traits or dispositions. The review by Klimoski and Rafaeli (1983) uncovered an emphasis on the use of graphology to estimate such traits as determination, diplomacy, initiative, energy level, passivity, empathy, and sales drive. Braverman (1986) adds to this list such qualities as intuition, fluidity of expression, ambition, determination, susceptibility to influence, fear of failure, shallowness, and self-deception. Gorman (1989) stresses the use of handwriting analysis to assess honesty or dishonesty, although he refers to the possible detection of 20 different personal characteristics. Finally, Radar (1988) reports that there are potentially 300 traits that can be measured through handwriting.

In summary, graphology is used in support of a wide variety of personnel matters, but especially in screening applicants. Its costs vary considerably. But the focus is usually on the measurement of personal traits.

Working Assumptions. When graphology is used in personnel selection, there are a number of implicit or explicit assumptions that are made by proponents. At this point, it might be appropriate to review these briefly.

The most fundamental assumption is discussed throughout this book. That is, it is believed by proponents and disputed by skeptics that an individual's nature or personal qualities are reflected in handwriting. Proponents also believe that individuals trained in graphology can infer these traits from an analysis of handwriting. However, in applying graphology to the personnel area, additional things are assumed.

The first is that *job-relevant* traits or qualities are among those revealed in handwriting. Thus, the manager seeking advice from a graphologist usually wants insights with regard to a particular set of traits. These are what we have been calling worker requirements. A second assumption is that it is possible to estimate with some degree of accuracy a person's standing or "score" on each of these worker requirements. That is, it's not sufficient merely to determine that a person does or does not possess a particular quality, but it is necessary to know that he or she has more of certain qualities than others (or, at least, enough to do the job well). Proponents also believe that graphologists, as personnel consultants, have a good idea of how requirements combine to comprise the criterion behaviors of interest. To phrase it differently, they know what combination of qualities, and what particular levels of these qualities produce (for instance) good performance on the job. Finally, given that these key traits are estimated for a candidate, it is assumed that the graphologist can integrate the assessments in such a manner so as to accurately predict some criterion (job performance, absenteeism, theft, or likely job tenure).

When and Where Is Graphology Used? Personnel decision making has been characterized as a multistage or multiple-hurdle process. Candidates for jobs are usually evaluated at several points before they are given a job offer. A given selection device can be used at any stage of this process. Despite all that is written on handwriting analysis in the workplace, it is not clear just when and where in the sequence of things the graphologist gets involved. Yet, this would seem to be important not only to the graphologist but also to evaluating the impact of his or her service.

This point might be clarified by considering alternative scenarios. It is possible for the graphologist to be contracted to produce an initial screening of applicants. He or she would see script samples from all applicants for a job. The effective task here is, essentially, to eliminate those candidates who are not worthy of further consideration. All that's required is a fairly coarse estimate of the requisite traits or qualities. Alternatively, the graphologist might be asked to evaluate the finalists in the competition for a job. Here it is necessary to make fine-grained distinctions regarding the key traits. This is because the finalists are likely to be fairly similar in their qualifications.

These two situations also differ with regard to the amount of information available to the graphologist. While it is true that many graphologists claim to consider only the nature (not the content) of the candidate's handwriting sample, consultants to organizations usually have access to other records (Taylor and Sackhiem, 1988; Radar, 1988). In an extreme case, the graphologist, as personnel consultant, might not only have access to the candidate's application materials, but know something about the hiring manager's impressions, even his or her preferences among candidates. Thus, the assessments provided to the organization and the recommendations or predictions made regarding future job success could easily become affected by (or even based on) this extra-script information. When and how graphologists are used as consultants will affect the way we might want to evaluate the usefulness of graphology itself in the context of personnel work.

THE USEFULNESS OF GRAPHOLOGY IN PERSONNEL SELECTION

It is unfortunate that we have so little representative descriptive data on the actual practice of graphology in industry. Thus, the critique offered below will be based on research which has focused on looking at graphology in isolation, where inferences made from script samples alone have been studied. The evidence that is reported in scientific journals and reviewed here is, at most, relevant to establishing the potential value of graphology. It has less to say about the actual impact of graphological consulting, where other information may be available to the practitioner.

The evidence relative to the usefulness of graphology to personnel work will be organized around the standards described in an earlier section of this chapter. As will become clear, we really have very little good research on graphology in many key areas.

RESEARCH EVIDENCE ON RELIABILITY OF GRAPHOLOGICAL INFERENCES

Reliability is a necessary attribute for measurement in any area. In personnel research and practice, levels of reliability effectively set limits to the usefulness of a selection device. Operationally, lack of reliability makes a measure worthless. We would not be able to take scores or recommendations at face value. Such a deficiency also calls into question the very nature of the measurement area itself. That is to say, lacking evidence of reliability, the scores that we get on a measure must be thought of as arbitrary, in fact, without foundation.

Other chapters in this book have addressed the issue of reliability of graphological inferences in the general case. In this section, what is known about reliability from studies in the personnel area will be summarized.

Before this is attempted, however, it will be useful to distinguish among several types of reliability of importance to the application of graphology to personnel selection. While reliability can be defined as consistency of measurement, there are many ways that this can be operationalized. When discussing the reliability of graphological data in personnel work, we need to know what type is involved.

Intra-Judge Reliability. By intra-judge reliability we mean that the individual doing the analysis, the graphologist or graphoanalyst, is in fact, consistent in his or her assessments and predictions or decisions for the single case.

Figure 5 illustrates one approach to establishing reliability in the intra-judge sense. Script samples are first obtained from a group of individuals (e.g., applicants). The identity of the writers should not be known to the analyst. The researcher or manager would then obtain inferences or recommendations from the graphologist for this same group on two occasions. Note that the same script samples are used in this approach. To deal with the possibility of the influence of memory (which would serve to increase the similarity of inferences from the same scripts across the two occasions and hence increase apparent reliability) there would need to be a reasonable interval (e.g., one week) between the first and second attempt. Traditionally,

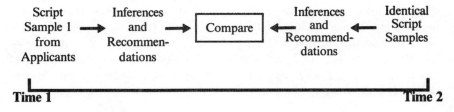

Fig. 5. Establishing intra-judge reliability: Type A

in this approach, the order of the presentation of the scripts is also varied between the two attempts. The investigator would then compare the assessment made by the graphologist of each writer, based on the same script sample. If the inferences are very similar, even exact, high intra-judge reliability could be claimed.

A second form of intra-judge reliability can be estimated. This is illustrated in Figure 6. In this case only one measurement period is involved. But two different samples of a script written by each applicant are used. In this method, the graphologist would be asked to assess both sets. This could be done simultaneously (i.e., the two sets are co-mingled) or sequentially (set one is done before set two but with little time between the work). Once again, the investigator would compare the inference from the first with those from the second set. A high correspondence would indicate high reliability.

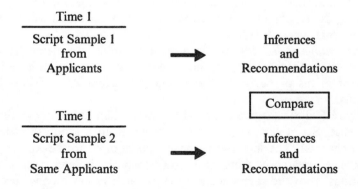

Fig. 6. Establishing intra-judge reliability: Type B.

One point that is implied by the above descriptions is that both approaches could be used to estimate the reliability of a particular graphologist. That is to say, graphologist "X" could be asked to provide evidence of both types. Alternatively, because many researchers are interested in the reliability of graphological inferences in general, a sample of graphologists would be asked to go through these exercises. In this case we would report (or ask to see) the average levels of inter-judge reliability.

There is very little empirical evidence with regard to the intra-judge reliability of graphological inferences in the personnel field. However, what little there is would seem to support the conclusions that such inferences are indeed reliable. For example, Neter and Ben-Shakhar (1989), in their review of the literature, summarize the work of Lockowandt and report intra-judge reliabilities ranging from .78–.88 (maximum r = 1.00).

It may be that the level of reliability would be affected by the nature of the inferences being made, however. For example, Nevo (1986) distinguishes script assessments that involve graphometric factors (e.g., letter size, letter shape, spacing); graphoimpressionistic characteristics (e.g., roundness, rhythm, pressure); and graphodiagnostic inferences (e.g., ego strength, honesty). It is quite likely that intra-judge reliabilities will be higher for the former type assessments than for the latter.

Still another factor to affect reliability would be the nature of the decision or recommendation being sought by the manager from the graphologist. If the latter is merely to recommend between two finalists, reliability is likely to be very high. But, if the manager is seeking elaborate diagnostic information (relative to a number of traits) for several candidates, we would expect poorer reliability.

Inter-Judge Reliability. Far more work has been done on examining the extent to which two graphologists, upon evaluating the same script sample(s), agree with one another. The paradigm for estimating inter-judge reliability is illustrated in Figure 7.

Overall, the evidence for the inter-judge reliability of graphological inferences in personnel research is supportive. Hofsommer, Holdsworth, and Seifert (cited in Neter and Ben-Shakhar 1989) found that inferences of "leadership ability" among 322 foremen estimated (on a 7-point scale) by three graphologists produced an average inter-judge agreement level of .74. Lockowandt, also cited in the same source, reported far lower agreements (average r = .39) among three graphologists estimating the likely success of technical school students. Galbraith and Wilson (1964) had three graphologists assess five attributes (e.g., persistence, dominance) from the script samples provided by 100 students. The median correlation was .78 (range from .61 for obstinacy to .87 for dominance). Rafaeli and Klimoski (1983)

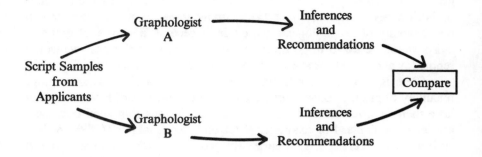

Fig. 7. Establishing inter-judge reliability.

in a study of real estate sales agents found a median correlation across 10 graphologists and 32 writers on ten factors of .45. An interesting aspect of this latter study is that, as a result of using so many graphologists (10), it was possible to contrast the levels of inter-judge agreement for analysts who used different analytic approaches. Somewhat surprisingly, it turned out that agreement levels among graphologists did not vary much as a function of the analytic paradigm involved.

Another aspect of the Rafaeli and Klimoski (1983) study that is worth mentioning is that they systematically examined the effects of script content. They questioned the assertion that graphologists only rely on script features and not script sample content. Thus, the real estate sales agents in this study were asked to provide two samples. One, of a traditional sort, was autobiographical in nature. The second was designed to be neutral with regard to the writer's background. Inter-judge agreement scores were then computed for the two types of scripts. Contrary to predictions, script content had only a modest effect on levels of agreement; even then, it was in the direction opposite to expectations. The median correlation for inferences from neutral scripts was .54; for the autobiographical scripts, .34. Finally, Nevo (1986) did find that inter-judge agreement levels were affected by the kind of assessment made. As discussed in the section on intra-judge reliability, the lowest ranges of reliabilities in his review were found for graphodiagnostic inferences (r= .30–.60). The highest for assessments of script features (r=.70–.90).

In summary, numerous studies have attempted to estimate the levels of inter-judge reliability that exists for graphologists working in the personnel area. The evidence implies that modest levels of this kind of reliability can be obtained. However, it also seems to be the case that the kind of assessment to be made by the graphologist will affect the results. Finally, at the present time there does not seem to be any research on the reliability of the actual employment recommendations made as a result of inference from handwriting.

EVIDENCE FOR CONTENT VALIDITY

Content validity issues have been largely ignored in research on applications of graphology to personnel work. In this context, content validity would be reflected in the degree of correspondence of the dimensions or factors assessed by the graphologist with those that are felt to be relevant to the job for which a candidate is being considered. In most of the available studies, the traits or factors to be assessed seem to have been chosen arbitrarily. They may have been selected based on tradition (e.g., past practice). Or the traits may reflect the preferences of the graphologists involved. Thus, the traits are ones that the graphologist feels that he or she can deal with. Recently, there appears to be an increasing amount of attention given by organizations to issues of honesty and integrity. As pointed out in an earlier section, handwriting analysts often are asked to focus on this area.

Theories of job effectiveness imply that the focus of graphological analysis for personnel selection should be on job-relevant traits. This can be accomplished by having the analyst use a set of traits that are somewhat universal to job success. For example, Drory (1984) obtained inferences on factors such as initiative, motivation, perseverance, etc., in an attempt to predict job performance for a sample of individuals working in a variety of jobs (machine operators, maintenance, clerical). While the traits were not specifically derived from an analysis of each of the jobs in question, they were job relevant, nonetheless. To put it another way, Drory's approach would seem to ensure some degree of content validity.

Far more appropriate, however, would be to have the graphologist work with only those traits that are indeed relevant to performance on a particular job. In the Raefeli and Klimoski (1983) study, this is exactly what was done. A single job, that of a residential real estate sales agent, was involved. A job analysis was performed and ten personal traits or characteristics were identified as important. These included such things as social confidence, sales (ego) drive, work management skills, vitality, and empathy. Each of these were defined and given to the graphologists as the focus of their work.

Notice that several of these factors are similar to those which have been traditionally assessed by graphologists (e.g., vitality). However, still others were peculiar to the job in question and consequently were new to the analysts involved.

There are clearly trade-offs involved in stressing content validity as a requirement for graphology as applied to personnel work. However, at the very least, graphologists should be asked to attend to those traits that they feel that they can assess and that are also job relevant. More will be said about this in the discussion of criterion related validity below.

EVIDENCE FOR CONSTRUCT VALIDITY

When a graphologist, relying on script samples, characterizes an individual in terms of traits, qualities, or dispositions, he or she is making use of constructs. A personnel manager does the same thing when discussing most job requirements or, for that matter, particular candidates for a job. Thus, it is important to know if, in fact, two such individuals are dealing with the same things. More fundamentally, we need to know if there is any evidence that particular constructs are involved in the assessment/ selection process.

Establishing construct validity for a measure or for the output from a particular measurement device like graphology is not easy. Usually processes of induction are involved (Schmitt and Klimoski, 1991). Typically we look for patterns of evidence that ultimately convince us that the measure is really getting at the constructs (factors) of interest.

More operationally, the manager or investigator relates scores from a group of people obtained from a device (e.g., graphology) with information already known about this group. We would also look to see if such data are related to what we might obtain using well established and ostensibly valid instruments. Support for construct validity would exist when the information from the new measure (graphology) parallels what would be obtained from the traditional sources.

In such an analysis not only is it necessary that scores on the same traits or factors on the two sets of measures from the same group of people correspond to one another. Scores on factors believed to be different also should not relate to one another. Thus, we seek evidence of convergence (where appropriate) and divergence (discriminability). Clearly, to establish the construct validity of a measure or scores from a device requires that we have clear definitions of just what the constructs are and how various constructs should or should not inter-relate.

As noted in some of the other chapters in this book, there is a fair amount of research which has attempted to connect inferences or scores provided by graphologists to scores on standard tests or measures. For example, Lester, McLaughlin, and Nosal (1977) studied the relationship of 16 handwriting characteristics to the trait of extraversion as measured by a standard personality measure, the Edwards Personality Inventory. This approach was followed by Jansen (1973) and Rosenthal and Lines 1972). Alternatively, investigators might relate ratings or inferences made by graphologists to assessments made by other types of judges. Lomonaco, Harrison, and Klein (1973) used this strategy. They had graphologists examine script samples of individuals for whom they had personality descriptions. The latter had been derived by clinical psychologists using a standard projective test called the TAT.

The results of studies like this are summarized in other chapters in this book. Suffice it to say, there is only weak evidence (at best) for the construct validity of graphology. To put it another way, if a graphologist asserts that a person is high on a particular trait or quality, this may or may not be the case.

The research evidence available to evaluate the construct validity of trait inferences from handwriting applied to personnel work is very limited. What does exist is not very supportive. To illustrate, Rafaeli and Klimoski (1983) obtained from a group of 20 graphologists trait ratings based on script samples of nine factors relevant to the job of a residential real estate salesperson. They then related these ratings to a similar set made by the sales managers of the people who supplied the script samples. No significant correlations were found. In this same study, when graphologists' ratings were compared to self-assessments made by the writers of the script samples on the same trait dimensions, essentially, the same results were obtained. No correspondence could be established.

In a fairly elaborate and carefully controlled experiment, Ben-Shakhar, Bar-Hillel, Bilu, Ben-Abba, and Flug (1986) tried to assess the construct validity of script inferences in two ways. Similar to the Rafaeli and Klimoski study, these investigators examined the relationship of inferences regarding traits (job compliance and human relations) and of on-the-job performance that were made by three graphologists in their study to similar ratings made by managers of a sample of bank employees. They also got a set of evaluations from a psychologist as well. While the results are complex, they did find some pattern of correspondence for the graphologists' ratings with the standard they were using (supervisor assessments). However, this group did less well than the psychologist in the study. It is interesting to note that an employee selection test battery used by the bank at the time did the best job of predicting actual performance. Both the graphologists and the psychologist were less successful than this traditional method. As in the Rafaeli and Klimoski study, no data on discrimination validity was presented, however.

In the second part of the Ben-Shakhar et al. (1986) study, five graphologists received 40 scripts. They were asked to analyze them and to match each writer to one of eight professions. It was known to the investigators that each writer was actually very successful in one (and only one) of these. The matchings were statistically analyzed. It was found that the graphologists were not able to do any better at making correct matches than would be expected to be done by chance. As a side note, there was also low inter-rater agreement among the graphologists with regard to the matches. It too didn't differ from what would be expected by chance.

In conclusion, what little evidence exists with regard to the construct validity of graphology applied to personnel work does not support the claim for construct validity. But parametric studies of particular traits or of types of inferences have not been reported.

EVIDENCE FOR CRITERION-RELATED VALIDITY

This is a major factor in assessing the usefulness of a device in personnel work. In the context of personnel selection, we are usually interested in the criterion of job performance or effectiveness. Clearly, if graphology can be used to estimate future job performance, it would be valuable to managers of organizations.

As in the case of estimating reliability, there are a number of options for doing this for criterion-related validity. Three types will be characterized here: predictive, concurrent, and postdictive strategies. Generally, the differences in approach revolve around times at which predictor and criterion data are obtained. This distinction is highlighted in Figures 8, 9, and 10.

When it comes to personnel research, a predictive approach to establishing criterion-related validity would involve obtaining graphologists' script assessments at one point (time one), waiting for a period, and then collecting criterion (job performance) data. The two sets of data would then be related and checked for correspondence. The length of time required to wait will depend on the nature of the work and work performance. For instance, a manager might be able to tell just how effective a person is as a data entry clerk after only a few weeks. However it might take years to determine if a person will be a successful scientist.

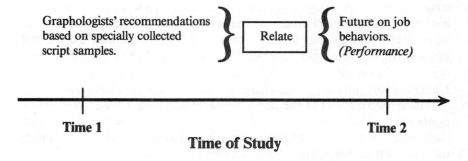

Fig. 8. Establishing predictive validity.

It is important to note that in a pure form of predictive strategy, all individuals in a validation study would be allowed to come onto the job. This would provide the maximum opportunity for an analysis to detect signs of validity. In most cases however, an organization cannot or will not permit this to happen. Instead, some screening will take place. Even in a validation study, individuals may be selected for employment based on traditional means (e.g., an interview). Those who do not do well in the interview will not be hired. As a result, the people who remain in the study (and for whom there would be job performance data) will only be a subset of the original group. More importantly, it is not a randomly established group but one that is likely to be better (on average) than the original. More technically speaking, this group will exhibit what is called a restriction of range in criterion scores. In effect, the poorest performers are, more likely than not, not represented, so the full range of possible performance is not manifest. The net result of all of this is that the potential for establishing criterion-related validity is reduced.

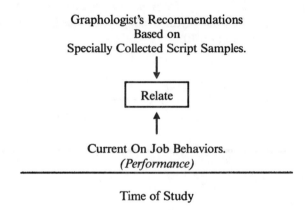

Fig. 9. Establishing concurrent validity.

There is a third circumstance where individuals in a validation study may be selected, not only using traditional means, but information from the test or device being evaluated may also be involved. Thus, in a validation study of graphology, some individuals might be rejected for employment based on the graphological inferences themselves. In this situation, the people allowed on the job and for whom there would be job performance data are not only a select group, they got their job, in part, because of their handwriting scores! This is a weak design for a validation study. An analysis of the data from such a group would tend to reveal higher than warranted correspondence between predictor (graphology) and criterion (job performance) measures. But this would be misleading. The results would be spurious and stem from what is essentially criterion contamination. (The same thing would occur if a supervisor knew of employees' graphology scores and allowed this knowledge to influence his or her ratings of job performance which are to serve as the criterion in the study.)

In a concurrent strategy, script samples would be taken from individuals currently on the job. Job performance information would be obtained at the same time. Inferences would then be analyzed and related to current performance (Figure 9). While criterion information would be known to investigators, it would not be known by the graphologist. If it were and such knowledge were allowed to influence the graphologist's assessments, we would have another form of criterion contamination.

A third form of a criterion-related validity study is possible. Because the bases of graphological inferences are script samples, it is feasible for the latter to be obtained for validation studies when, in fact, they were not intended for that purpose. Thus, in the postdictive strategy, handwriting samples from archives (e.g., from personnel files), ones that had been created at some point earlier in time, can be retrieved and related to current job performance. (Figure 10)

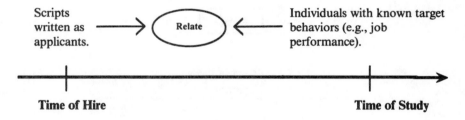

Fig. 10. Establishing postdictive validity.

All three validation approaches require some data regarding job effectiveness or job performance. This is an aspect of personnel research that has received a great deal of attention by industrial psychologists (Schmitt, Neal, and Klimoski, 1991). Thus, it is a topic of some complexity and cannot be fully developed here. What is important for the present discussion, however, is that in designing or implementing a validation study, or even in reviewing research evidence on criterion-related validity, the quality of the criterion measures themselves should not be taken for granted. Productivity data, supervisor ratings, peer ratings, customer reactions data are all options that can be used. Their appropriateness for a validation study and, once obtained, their quality should be scrutinized. Numerous techniques exist to do this (Schmitt, Neal, and Klimoski, 1991).

All three approaches to criterion-related validity also involve some mechanism for relating predictor and criterion scores. In some cases, this can take the form of a classification analysis. This would show to what extent a graphologist's assessments or recommendations correspond to discrete outcomes. If the assessment implies success, we would want to establish that the writer actually is (or will be) a success. If a failure is predicted, this also should indeed be the case. Thus, correspondence or validity can be represented in terms of "hits" or "misses." This type of analysis was performed by Ben-Shakhar et al. (1986), as described in the section on construct validity (see Figure 11).

		Actual Job Success	
		Yes	No
Graphologist's assessments, prediction of performance, or recommendation.	Hire	Hits	Misses
	Reject	Misses	Hits

Fig. 11. Classification analysis.

More commonly, however, investigators use correlational analysis to establish the degree of correspondence involved. As a result, criterion-related validities are usually reported in terms of correlation coefficients.

The absolute size of correlation coefficients can range from .00 to 1.00, with the latter reflecting a perfect alignment of predictor scores (e.g., graphological recommendations for hire) and criterion scores (levels of job performance). In personnel selection research in general, it is unusual to obtain coefficients larger than .40 (Hunter and Hunter, 1984; Schmitt, Gooding, Noe, and Kirsch, 1984; Reilly and Chao, 1982). Note that uncovering a negative or a positive value of a given size would have equal practical utility (Figure 12).

Most rigorous research studies will not only report the size of a validity coefficient, but will also provide some indication that the obtained values are not likely to have occurred by chance. Usually this takes the form of conducting and reporting a test of statistical significance. The outcome of such tests are largely a function of the size of the sample of workers involved in the validation study. Thus, a coefficient of a given

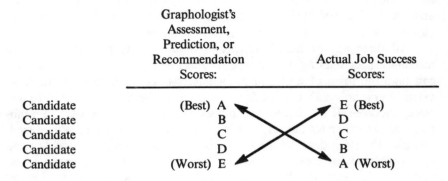

Fig. 12. Correlation analysis (r = +1.00 ⟷ 0 ⟷ -1.00)*

size (e.g., r = .35) for a small sample of cases (e.g., 25) is not given the same status as one for a larger sample as the values of a correlation coefficient are known to be unstable when the number of cases is small. Statistical tests involve an adjustment for sample size. (As an aside, most of the anecdotal arguments for and a great deal of the evidence in the popular press on the validity of graphology for personnel selection are based upon instances where small numbers of cases are involved. Thus the findings, positive or negative, are likely to be spurious.)

Most of the research on criterion-related validity has made use of the concurrent validation paradigm. This may reflect the fact that it is an easier and less time-consuming strategy to follow. Thus, Zdep and Weaver (1967), Rafaeli and Klimoski (1983), and Drory (1984) all collected script samples and criterion information at about the same time. To illustrate, Rafaeli and Klimoski (1983) visited real estate firms and arranged for sales agents to meet at a conference room where script samples were collected under controlled conditions (e.g., using pen on unlined paper in pad form). While this was being done, managers were rating each salesperson on a set of traits and on a scale of overall effectiveness. On the same visit, data on sales productivity for each agent (e.g., number of sales, dollar value of commissions earned, number of homes "listed") were recorded from company files.

The analysis of the relationship between graphological assessments and job effectiveness in the Rafaeli and Klimoski (1983) study revealed little support for claims of criterion-related validity. The trait inferences made by the 20 graphologists in the study were unrelated to the sales productivity

---

*As printed, the orders of predictions and clients' scores constitute a perfect negative correlation (r = -1.00). If the order of the righthand column were reversed, it would be a perfect positive correlation (+ 1.00).

and commissions data (median r = .06). Because the researchers were sensitive to the possibility that the traits to be rated might be unfamiliar to the graphologists (they had been derived from a job analysis), the latter were allowed to use what ever system they wished in order to directly estimate the effectiveness of each writer. They did not fare much better at this task either. Direct estimates of the effectiveness of the agents in the study made by the graphologists were also unrelated to actual productivity (median r =.04).

In their review of the more rigorously designed studies on the validity of graphology, Klimoski and Rafaeli (1983) reported at that time, ". . . given the evidence that we have, great reliance [for personnel work] on inferences based on script must be considered unwarranted" (p. 200). These authors could not find supportive scientific evidence for applying graphology to organizational problems. In a somewhat later effort, Nevo (1986) accumulated all the validity studies on graphology that he could locate that had been conducted in Israeli organizations. From the studies at his disposal, Nevo estimated the average validity coefficient (adjusting for differences in the sizes of the samples involved in each study) to be r =.14.

This is a more optimistic finding for proponents of graphology. If true, a value of this magnitude compares favorably to what has been uncovered for other, more traditional selection devices. Moreover, according to personnel selection theory, even a coefficient of this modest order of magnitude can have practical utility under certain circumstances (a favorable selection ratio—see Schmitt, Neal, and Klimoski, 1991). More recently however, Neter and Ben-Shakhar (1989) have convincingly reaffirmed the opposing position taken by Klimoski and Rafaeli (1983).

Neter and Ben-Shakhar conducted a statistical summary of all the studies that they could find that reported evidence of criterion-related validity in personnel work. All together, they uncovered 17 studies that met their standards for inclusion (e.g., they had to be empirical studies, report the results in the form of validity coefficients, clearly specify sample size and the type of criterion measures used). In this investigation, these authors used the technique called meta-analysis to control for such things as sample size and lack of reliability in order to reach conclusions regarding the best estimate of the validity of graphology as a predictor of job effectiveness (see also ch. 12, this volume). They examined the data for evidence of the validity of assessments made by others who were not graphologists (e.g., psychologists, lay people). They looked at differences in results associated with the type of job effectiveness criterion that investigators used. Finally, they contrasted studies conducted in a regular work versus a training setting.

In the 17 studies, a total of 63 graphologists and 51 non-graphologists were found to have evaluated 1223 scripts. Across all types of scripts and criteria, the predictive validities for graphologists were in the range of .14–.18. This is similar to Nevo's findings. However, if the type of script is considered, when graphologists were working with neutral (without biographical content) scripts, the predictive validity of their inferences was reduced to zero. Just as important, it was discovered that psychologists, with no knowledge of graphology ". . . outperformed the graphologists on all dimensions" (p. 737).

It was true that some graphologists were better at estimating performance than others. But this occurred in the case of non-graphologists as well. Neter and Ben-Shakhar (1989) argue that this has little to do with the validity of graphology. Finally, the type of setting also made a difference, but in complex ways. Essentially, the different groups of analysts (graphologists, psychologists, lay people) were differentially accurate in their predictions in the two settings.

In summary, there is little convincing evidence of the criterion-related validity of graphology when applied to personnel work.

EVIDENCE FOR UTILITY

To this writer's knowledge, there have been no studies which have attempted to demonstrate the utility of graphology, either in terms of reduced decision errors or of economic benefits. There are, however, a few studies comparing the performance of graphologists or graphology to alternative approaches to personnel decision making. Some of these have been alluded to already.

To illustrate, Rafaeli and Klimoski (1983) asked lay people (undergraduate students) to assess traits and estimate the effectiveness of the script writers in a manner that paralleled the task of the graphologists in their study. They found the interjudge agreement among students was less than among the graphologists. However, the data from both groups reflected the similar and low relationships with the various job performance criteria used in that study. Ben-Shakhar et al. (1986) contrasted the judgment of a clinical psychologist with those made by three graphologists. The clinician performed as well as the graphologists with regard to predicting supervisor ratings in specific areas. But she was somewhat better at estimating some of the global evaluations. These authors also contrasted the performance of all four human judges with predictions made based on the information that existed in organization's test files. It turned out that test data predicted performance as well as any of the judges.

In one final comparison, information extracted and coded from the scripts themselves (which were autobiographical in nature), when treated as a "test" of a person's background, outperformed all three graphologists in predicting a general evaluation and (in two of the three cases) in predicting the average of the ratings given each script writer by his or her supervisor. This "script content" index did about as well as the test battery information in predicting these criteria. Finally, the meta-analysis of Neter and Ben-Shakhar (1989), as pointed out above, found that graphologists possessed no special capability for predicting job performance and training criteria when compared to psychologists and lay-persons.

While these studies give us some insights regarding the comparative effectiveness of graphologists, it should be stressed that they do not really answer the essential questions about utility. We still don't know what kind of errors (if any) are reduced by using graphology to aid personnel decisions. This remains as a challenge for future work.

EVIDENCE OF FREEDOM FROM BIAS

To this writer's knowledge, there are no published studies of the differential impact of recommendations or decisions based on graphological inferences for different subgroups of people (e.g., males/females, native born/foreign born). For example, Reilly and Chao (1982) had nothing to say about graphology in their review of the fairness of various selection devices. While most graphologists wish to know the gender and the native language of the script writer (Klimoski and Rafaeli, 1983), there seems to be little evidence one way or another that this knowledge affects their trait ratings or their recommendations.

EVIDENCE REGARDING USER ACCEPTANCE

If one takes at face value the reports in the popular press, it would appear that the use of graphology by organizations in Europe and Israel is widespread and that its application to personnel work by U.S. companies is on the increase. On this basis, it would be tempting to assert that the acceptance of graphology for personnel decisions is great. However, to do so would be a mistake.

It has already been cautioned that reliable survey data on the use of graphology in industry does not exist. Moreover, just because so many managers may make use of a device or program does not mean that all the parties involved in the hiring process are amenable to it. The fact is, we don't know. There don't seem to be any studies on this issue.

There may be strong cultural differences which moderate the acceptance of a technique or service like graphology. In the United States, at least, there is an increased concern for the rights of potential and actual employees. This includes the rights to privacy (Stone and Stone, 1990). The surreptitious use of script samples would seem to violate most Americans' sense of propriety and fair play. And, even if an organization does make public its reliance on graphology, it is possible that individuals in the U.S. will challenge its relevance to personnel decisions, particularly if they felt disadvantaged in the process (see also chs. 17 and 18, this volume). Courts in the U.S. are currently willing to hear such challenges (Arvey, 1979). Thus, it would seem that an organization should have some persuasive reasons to use any non-traditional (for the U.S.) approach as a basis for selection. And, if it does make use of one, it will need to have the data to back up any claims of "business necessity."

The last point may be a key to user acceptance. Personal preferences or national values notwithstanding, it is likely that acceptance of graphology as part of a personnel selection program, like in any other case (e.g., honesty testing, drug testing), will be strongly influenced by evidence that it is needed (there are not more conventional alternatives), and that it is effective (there is convincing evidence that decisions based on graphology are related to job behaviors or performance). Based on the published literature reviewed above, such a case cannot be made.*

OVERALL CONCLUSIONS

There are several points that have been made throughout this review. In this section, the more important ones will be recapitulated in order to make clear the status of graphology as a method for aiding personnel decisions.

1. Proponents of graphology are strong advocates for its application to organizations, particularly in the realm of personnel decision making.

2. There is the perception, in the popular press at least, that an increasing number of companies are using graphology and the services of graphologists as consultants.

3. There is a well-developed theory and a technology available for making and assessing the quality of personnel decisions. This in-

---

*The editors of this volume have seen several cases where the professional reputations and career advancement of personnel managers have been harmed by the public outcry that arose when it was revealed that they were employing "unscientific" graphological services that have not passed the validation tests described in this chapter.

cludes a set of standards that can and should be applied to the analysis of claims made for any tool, device, or program to be used for personnel work.

4. As a rule, proponents of graphology do not offer credible empirical evidence to support claims of the usefulness of graphology for personnel work. When data or analysis are forthcoming, they are usually of insufficient completeness or scope to assess graphology relative to these standards.

5. When the credible empirical evidence is reviewed, summarized, and analyzed relative to these standards (as was done in this chapter), most claims for graphology as applied to personnel decisions are not supported.

A skeptic reading this chapter could reasonably conclude that there is little value to graphology for personnel work. Given the available evidence, he or she would be correct. For example, there is very little support for the construct, content, and criterion-related validity of graphological inferences. More importantly, there is no research on the utility of graphology relative to other approaches to personnel decision making. Thus, a "business case" for graphology cannot be made.

On the other hand, a proponent of graphology might find some solace in some of the findings that have been summarized. For example, modest levels of inter-judge agreement among graphologists have been documented. If they concur, however, in making invalid inferences from people's script, this agreement is hardly of much value. More importantly, it appears that some graphologists are able to estimate some organizationally relevant criteria (such as job performance and success in training) and do it about as well as others who would claim professional status (e.g., psychologists). The evidence that it is use of graphology per se that permits *some* graphologists to exceed chance in their estimates is insufficient at this time.

All things considered, at this period in time, a manager receiving solicitations for graphological services or seeking assistance in personnel decision making would be wise to heed the American credo "Caveat Emptor" —let the buyer beware. The prudent manager would examine claims closely and require documentation regarding these claims. Toward this end, the standards described and used in this chapter, and the data summarized relative to these standards, will provide a useful point of reference. To put it bluntly, careful empirical analysis, not personal beliefs or positive personal experiences, should guide the decision to adopt graphology as a solution to personnel problems.

PROBLEMATIC ISSUES

There are several questions that have been raised throughout this chapter that need to be resolved before the advocate of graphological services can hope to be credible in the eyes of the prudent manager:

A. What is graphology (as applied to personnel work)?

B. Who is qualified to offer services to industry?

C. What is the role of script sample features?

D. What is the nature of involvement of graphologists in personnel decisions?

E. Are graphologists willing to use better research designs to try to document the validity of graphology?

Fundamentally, just what is graphology? As outlined in other chapters, there are a variety of philosophical orientations, epistemologies, and techniques that are covered under the rubric. Just how this question gets answered has numerous implications for both research and practice. For example, Rafaeli and Klimoski (1983) had at least three approaches reflected in the work of the 20 graphologists in their study. However, most investigators use only one or two graphologists. And, rarely is the notion of professional orientation to graphological analysis (i.e., the particular school of handwriting analysis being employed) stressed in the published research.

In a related vein, another issue is to resolve just who is qualified to offer such services. As highlighted elsewhere in this book, there are very few barriers to entry into the field of graphology. Any number of individuals may claim to have expertise in this area. More specifically, it would seem that, as is the case in most fields, competency in one domain will not ensure the same in another one. That is to say, graphologists with no experience or expertise in personnel matters may nonetheless offer services of this type. While a number of certification programs for graphologists exist, there is no evidence that these do in fact insure competence in consulting for organizations.

With regard to the technology of graphological analysis, the issue of script sample features deserves special attention. As a rule, many graphological texts are quite specific regarding the conditions that should exist in order to obtain high-quality samples for analysis. For instance, script samples should be spontaneous (not represent copied work), they should be of sufficient length, the work should be done in pen on unlined paper from a pad or tablet, etc. However, it's not clear that this is what happens in practice. The conditions of script sample derivation are rarely described in testimonials. They are often poorly described in research. The point is that if graphological analysis is to be fairly characterized and to be offered on a regular basis as a service to organizations, some element of standardization must exist.

A particular concern with regard to script samples has to do with the nature of their content. Rafaeli and Klimoski (1983) make a strong a priori case that the content of scripts, usually of a biographical nature, could be contributing to whatever validities might be obtained in studies of graphology. Their study did reveal some impact of script content on the assessments made by the students in their research but not for the graphologists. But, it might be recalled that both groups showed little capacity to predict the actual job performance of script writers. In contrast, in their extensive review Neter and Ben-Shakhar (1989) make a convincing case that script content does make a difference, and in the direction theorized by Rafaeli and Klimoski (autobiographical content facilitates prediction). Clearly, the content issue needs to be resolved.

The nature and point of involvement of the graphologists who are offering services to organizations has already been characterized in this chapter as problematic. As consultants to organizations, graphologists can assist managers in personnel decision making in any number of ways. But, therein lies a dilemma. When assessing the usefulness of graphology for personnel work, it is difficult to separate the technique and what it can offer from the effectiveness of the consulting habits and skills of the practitioner. In particular, graphologists, as consultants, often have access to a great deal more information regarding candidates than what can be inferred from script samples. They may review an application form. They may meet the candidate. They may know the impressions and opinions held by the hiring manager of the candidate. It is quite reasonable to assume that their recommendations are affected by this non-script intelligence. The prudent manager needs to evaluate the claims of the graphologist in light of his or her "modus operandi." And the manager must scrutinize the evidence offered to see if it comes from studies of graphological analysis per se, or from studies where graphology just happened to have been used.

In this regard, it may be that the best design for research on the effectiveness of graphology as applied to personnel matters might not be the relational study, but the field experiment (Schmitt, Neal, and Klimoski, 1991). Thus, data on the correlations between graphological inferences and job performance (the type of data reviewed in this chapter), even if it were to be reassuring to proponents, would not be accepted as definitive. Instead, what would be more appropriate is a rigorously designed and executed demonstration that graphological services, when delivered in a standardized way, really do improve the quality of personnel decisions, relative to alternatives in use. Given that the work lives and careers of individuals are at stake, demonstrated effectiveness of this sort is what the prudent manager should require before adopting graphology as a solution to staffing problems. At this time such demonstrations have not yet been reported.

REFERENCES

Aiken, L. R. 1991. *Psychological Testing and Assessment.* 7th ed. Boston: Allyn and Bacon.

Anonymous. 1979. "Reading between the Lines—What Your Handwriting Reveals." *Credit and Financial Management* 81(1): pp. 14–15.

Arnett, E. 1989. "For More Employers, the Scrawl Is All." *Washington Post,* July 14.

Arvey, R. D. 1979. *Fairness in Selecting Employees.* Reading, Mass.: Addison Wesley.

Bar-Hillel, M., and G. Ben-Shakhar. 1986. "The A Priori Case against Graphology." In *Scientific Aspects of Graphology,* edited by B. Nevo. Springfield, Ill.: Charles Thomas.

Ben-Shakhar, G., M. Bar-Hillel, Y. Bilu, E. Ben-Abba, and A. Flug. 1986. "Can Graphology Predict Occupational Success? Two Empirical Studies and Some Methodological Ruminations." *Journal of Applied Psychology* 71(4): pp. 645–653.

Bernardin, H. J. 1987. "Development and Validation of a Forced Choice Scale to Measure Job Related Discomfort among Customer Service Representatives." *Academy of Management Journal* 30(4): pp. 162–173.

Braverman, Louis L. 1986. "Graphonanalysis—Let It Help You More." *Life Association News* 81(6): pp. 131–132.

Campion, J. R. 1972. "Work Sampling for Personnel Selection." *Journal of Applied Psychology* 56(1): pp. 40–44.

Campion, M., E. Pursell, and B. K. Brown. 1988. "Structured Interviewing: Raising the Psychometric Properties of the Employment Interview." *Personnel Psychology* 41(1): pp. 25–42.

Cronbach, L. J., and P. E. Meehl. 1955. "Construct Validity in Psychological Tests." *Psychological Bulletin* 52: pp. 281–302.

Drory, Amos. 1984. "Validity of Handwriting Analysis in Predicting Job Performance." Unpublished manuscript.

Fowler, E. M. 1990. "Careers: Personnel Executives on the Rise." *New York Times,* May 9.

Galbraith, D., and W. Wilson. 1964. "Reliability of the Graphoanalytic Approach to Handwriting Analysis." *Perceptual and Motor Skills* 19(2): pp. 615–618.

Gorman, C. 1989. "Honestly, Can We Trust You?" *Time,* January 23: p. 44.

Hunter, J. E., and R. F. Hunter. 1984. "Validity and Utility of Alternative Predictions of Job Performance." *Psychological Bulletin* 96: pp. 72–98.

Jaekle, L. 1974. "The Write Approach." *Pacific Business* 64(1): pp. 36–38.

Jansen, A. 1973. *Validation of Graphological Judgments: An Experimental Study.* Paris: Mouton.

Kalogerakis, G. 1984. "Enthusiasm Is Sweeping the T-Bars." *Commutator's Journal* 2: pp. 2–34.

Klimoski, R. J., and A. Rafaeli. 1983. "Inferring Personal Qualities through Handwriting Analysis." *Journal of Occupational Psychology* 56: pp. 191–202.

Lester, D., S. McLaughlin, and G. Nosal. 1977. "Graphological Signs for Extroversion." *Perceptual and Motor Skills* (44(1): pp. 137–138.

Levine, E. L., R. Ash, H. Hall, and S. Sistrunk. 1983. "Evaluation of Job Analysis Methods by Experienced Job Analysts." *Academy of Management Journal* 26(2): pp. 339–347.

Levy, L. 1979. "Handwriting and Hiring." *Dun's Review:* pp. 72–79.

Lomonaco, T., R. Harrison, and F. Klein. 1973. "Accuracy of Matching TAT and Graphological Profiles." *Perceptual and Motor Skills* 36: pp. 703–706.

Lynch, B. 1985. "Graphology—Towards a Hand-picked Workforce." *Personnel Management* 17(3): pp. 14–18.

Munsterberg, H. 1913. *Psychology and Industrial Efficiency.* Boston: Houghton-Mifflin.

Neter. E., and G. Ben-Shakhar. 1989. "The Predictive Validity of Graphological Influences: A Meta-Analytic Approach." *Personality and Individual Differences* 10(7): pp. 737–745.

Nevo, B., ed. 1986. *Scientific Aspects of Graphology.* Springfield, Ill.: Charles Thomas.

Porter, L., E. Lawler, and J. Hackman. 1975. *Behavior in Organizations.* New York: McGraw-Hill.

Radar, E. 1988. "Hire-oglyphics." *U.S. Air Magazine* (January): pp. 12–15.

Rafaeli, A., and R. J. Klimoski. 1983. "Predicting Sales Success through Handwriting Analysis: An Evaluation of the Effects of Training and Handwriting Sample Content." *Journal of Applied Psychology* 68(2): 213–217.

Reilly, R. R., and G. T. Chao. 1982. "Validity and Fairness of Some Alternative Employee Selection Procedures." *Personnel Psychology* 35: pp. 1–62.

Rosenthal, D. A., and R. Lines. 1978. "Handwriting As a Correlate of Extroversion." *Journal of Personality Assessment* 42: pp. 45–48.

Schmidt, F., and J. Hunter. 1981. "Employment Testing: Old Theories and New Research Findings." *American Psychologist* 36(10): pp. 1128–1137.

Schmidt, F., J. Hunter, and K. Pearlman. 1982. "Progress in Validity Generalization: Comments on Callender and Osburn and Further Developments. *Journal of Applied Psychology* 67(6): pp. 835–845.

Schmidt, F., J. Hunter, R. McKenzie, and T. Muldrow. 1979. "Impact of Valid Selection Procedures on Workforce Productivity." *Journal of Applied Psychology* 64(6): pp. 609–626.

Schmitt, N., R. F. Gooding, R. A. Noe, and P. M. Kirsch. 1984. "Meta-Analyses of Validity Studies Published between 1964 and 1982 and the Investigation of Study Character Clusters." *Personnel Psychology* 37: pp. 407–422.

Schmitt, N., J. Neal, and R. J. Klimoski. 1991. *Research Methods in Human Resources Management.* Cincinnati: South-Western Publ.

Scott, W. D. 1911. *Increasing Human Efficiency in Business.* New York: Macmillan.

Stone, E. F., and D. L. Stone. 1990. "Privacy in Organizations: Theoretical Issues, Research Findings and Protection Strategies." In *Research in Personnel/ Human Resources Management,* vol. 8, edited by G. Ferris and K. Rowland.

Taylor, M. S., and K. L. Sackheim. 1988. "Graphology." *Personnel Administrator* 33(5): pp. 71–76.

Thayer, P. N., and J. A. Antoinetti. 1965. "Graphology." *The Industrial Psychologist* 2: pp. 33–34.

Wanous, J. P. 1980. *Organizational Entry: Recruitment, Selection, and Socialization of Newcomers.* Reading, Mass.: Addison-Wesley.

Zdep, S., and H. Weaver. 1967. "The Graphoanalytic Approach to Selecting Life Insurance Salesmen." *Journal of Applied Psychology* 51(3): pp. 295f.

12

The Bottom Line: Effect Size

Geoffrey A. Dean

In this chapter, Dean explains what evidence is required to reasonably conclude that graphology "works." He begins by pointing out that our real question is *how well* graphology works, since when we decide to use graphology, we always have alternatives—if nothing else, we have our common-sense methods of assessing personality. So, what we want to know is whether graphology works better than the competitors. He explains, without excessive use of technical statistical terms, the notion of *effect size,* which gives us a way of measuring the effectiveness of one method of generating predictions against another. We often lose sight of the fact that a statistically significant result merely tells us that the effect was unlikely to be due to chance. It does not tell us what the non-chance factor is, nor does it tell us whether the effect is large enough to be useful in any practical sense. Thus Dean warns us not only to beware of falsely claimed effects, but also of "true-but-trivial" effects.

The reader may wish to examine also Dale Beyerstein's discussion of the rationale behind the scientific method in chapter 8, as well as Dean, Kelly, Saklofske, and Furnham in chapter 13 for a discussion of the biases which lead our common sense astray when we attempt to examine the efficacy of a method of personality assessment such as graphology. The evidence presented in the latter chapter makes a case for the need for the more sophisticated measures of efficacy discussed here by Dean.

Dean applies these standards to a discussion of a broad spectrum of studies of graphology. The results are summarized in Appendix B. He also comments on other surveys of graphological studies *(meta-analyses).* The reader can compare Dean's observations and conclusions with those of Lockowandt in chapter 5.

INTRODUCTION: LIFE ON THE BOTTOM LINE

> Scientists have known for centuries that a single study will not resolve a major issue. Indeed, a small sample study will not even resolve a minor issue. Thus, the foundation of science is the cumulation of knowledge from the results of many studies.
>
> —Hunter, Schmidt, and Jackson

This chapter goes straight to the bottom line. To what extent does graphology work? It looks at the technicalities of testing graphology, surveys over 200 experimental studies, and compares the results with those of other approaches such as personality tests, peer ratings, and astrology. The conclusions are summarized in the last section. For technical readers the more important technical details are covered by notes.[1] First a look at what the books have said over the years.

VIEWS OF GRAPHOLOGISTS

Graphology books leave you in no doubt that graphology works:

> There can be no doubt that . . . certain peculiarities of handwriting run so unfailingly and so unexceptionally parallel to certain traits of character that from them we may by analogy assume the corresponding traits of character.[2] (Saudek 1925:42)

> An accurate picture of the *real* you. . . . You will be surprised how successful you will be [at graphology] after even a small amount of practice. (Holder 1958:3,13)

> A sure-fire way of getting the real low-down . . . will give you true pictures of what they [people] really are. . . . an aid in vocational guidance . . . personnel selection . . . marriage [guidance]. (Olyanova 1960:9,15)

> Long ago reputable scientists admitted the unmistakable relationship between one's handwriting and one's character. (Jeanne Dixon in Kurdsen 1971:5)

> Discover traits . . . find immediate clues to the personality . . . Even a strange signature at the bottom of an official letter can tell you whether the writer is kind, timid, aggressive or sexy. Graphology is a recognized aid to psychology in many countries. (Lowengard 1975:3,8)

> A wonderful potential for help and personal exploration . . . an objective evaluation of personality strengths and weaknesses . . . covers aspects of personality not covered in other tests. (Paterson 1976:20,87–88)

The range of potential interpretative capacities is already much larger through graphology than through other psychological methods. (Schwieghofer 1979:10)

[Graphology] brings into focus the secrets of your basic character, emotional makeup, intellectual gifts, creative abilities, social adjustment, material values, neurotic conflicts, parental hang-ups, sensuality, sexuality, and much, much more. (Surovell 1987:11)

Your handwriting is all-revealing. To the trained eye it lays open your secret mind. Every whirl or line you pen exposes your true character and personality to the graphologist. . . . Handwriting analysis can help you in your search for whatever it is you want out of life. (Marne 1988:7)

In short, graphology is objective, accurate, true, internationally recognized, quick, easy, helpful, all-revealing, wider-ranging than other tests, confirmed by reputable scientists, and much, much more. Or so the books lead us to believe. Now for a word from reputable scientists.

VIEWS OF SCIENTISTS

Scientists have been investigating graphology since the 1900s:

The claims of the graphologists are frequently very extravagant. . . . The more pretentious works are predominantly *a priori* deductions from very general principles. (Hull and Montgomery 1919:63–64)[3]

The average graphological analysis is especially difficult to validate . . . Verbal self-contradictions appear frequently . . . and the terms employed often seem to obscure rather than reveal the personality. (Allport and Vernon 1933:210–211)

Every text on graphology examined by the author presents the analysis of handwriting as a test of personality; yet not one of them offers norms, not one of them presents figures showing the reliability and validity of their test, not one of them bothers to define their personality variables. (Pascal 1943:124)

The boundlessness of the graphologist's faith, the enormity of his claims, must make the cautious scientist hesitate . . . much of the evidence . . . cannot be regarded as more than suggestive. Too frequently the controls have been insufficiently stringent, the number of handwritings used too small to give results free from serious sampling errors, and the criteria for validation themselves too much lacking in both reliability and validity to make comparisons fruitful. (Eysenck 1945:70,72)

Research in the area of handwriting and personality has lingered long and prospered rarely. Scattered studies have continued to appear through the years, yet somehow we have not progressed very far towards reaching decisions concerning the nature of relationships between the two. (McNeil and Blum 1952:476)

[Graphologists] claim that the usefulness of graphology is proved if the writers themselves, or their acquaintances, accept their personality sketches as accurate. This is quite unconvincing to the psychologist. (Vernon 1953:58)

A vast number of articles have been written on handwriting in many languages, but few rigorous experimental studies have been done. . . . it is difficult to draw many conclusions since the methods used and the criterion variables investigated have been highly diversified. (Fluckiger et al. 1961:67)

With few exceptions, the quality of research in the area is not high. . . . when researchers are more rigorous . . . the results have not been supportive of the usefulness of inferences based on script. (Klimoski and Rafaeli 1983:200)

There is a growing body of empirical research literature on graphology. It is almost uniformly negative as regards graphologists' claims. (Hines 1988:294)

It seems there are two sides to every story. But why should the two sides be so conflicting?

RESOLVING THE CONFLICT

How can graphologists be so sure that graphology works if the empirical research literature is "almost uniformly negative"? Two reasons are given in the next chapter:

1. Human cognitive skills are not equal to the task graphologists have set themselves. Human judgmental biases have created false beliefs. (Here bias means *systematic error* not *prejudice*.)
2. There are many non-graphological reasons why graphology seems to work, none of which requires that graphology be true.

Another reason is that, as any graphology book will show, graphologists seem generally unaware of the empirical research, whereas their critics are not. So what *is* the empirical research? Is it really "almost uniformly negative"? To answer these questions we start by looking at how the research was done in the first place, that is, at how graphology is tested. This occupies the next two sections.

MEASURING EFFECT SIZE:
THE TECHNICALITIES OF TESTING GRAPHOLOGY

APPROACHES TO TESTING GRAPHOLOGY

Handwriting is said to indicate ability and behavior. In other words to see the script is to know the person. To determine more precisely what graphology claims to do, Jansen (1973) read graphology books (in English, Dutch, and German); talked to graphologists; and examined 62 graphological analyses selected at random. He concluded that:

> the claims of graphology extend to practically all character aspects and cover at least all major personality areas. (Jansen 1973:13)

To test such claims there are two basic approaches to assessing scripts and people, namely subjective (guessing) and objective (measuring):

1. Subjective. Uses *impressions* of things such as rhythm and energy. Why measure when you can guess?
2. Objective. Uses *measurements* of things such as slant and E (extroversion). Why guess when you can measure?

Figure 1. *Four Ways of Testing Graphology*

Two approaches (subjective and objective) to two target areas (scripts and human behavior) give four ways of testing graphology. Each combination except top right has been widely used, the most popular by a small margin being bottom left.

On the left generally is holistic graphology, based on the whole script, approached by tests that include matching handwriting interpretations to their owners. On the right generally is analytic graphology, based on individual signs, approached by tests that include testing the sign interpretations listed in graphology books.

BEHAVIOR

Subjective impressions, e.g., case history

S		Which script fits which case history?	Does slant relate to case history?	
C				
R	Subjective impression			Measurements
I		Which script has highest E score?	Does slant relate to E score?	e.g., slant
P				
T				

Objective measurements, e.g., E score

The two approaches combine to give four ways of testing graphology, as shown in Figure 1, of which all but one have been widely used. The choice of approach has traditionally been embroiled in an analytic-holistic controversy over the best way to assess scripts, with pros and cons briefly as follows:

Analytic approach (tests isolated script features)

> Pro: Test is readily defined and standardized. All researchers can do it the same way, so we know what is happening.
> Most graphology books list isolated features.
> Modern multivariate techniques allow for interaction.
> Accuracy is readily determined.
> Con: Isolated features play no part in modern graphology.

Holistic approach (tests the whole script)

> Pro: This is the way modern graphologists work.
> Con: Test is impossible to define or standardize. No two graphologists work the same way, so what is happening?
> Not more than five scripts can be compared at one time.[4]
> Success is influenced by external cues, atypical differences, stereotypes that happen to fit, and small samples.
> Success could mean subjective impressions are 10 percent accurate or 100 percent accurate, but there is no way of telling which.

In their everyday work most graphologists favor the holistic approach to assessing scripts and abhor the analytic approach. Fair enough. But for *testing* graphology the above cons against the holistic approach are so severe that Brengelmann (1960) could conclude "the holistic-analytic controversy is a pseudo-problem." That was thirty years ago, yet today the controversy still continues. For the present purpose we will accept that both approaches are necessary for a balanced testing of graphology.

ASKING THE RIGHT QUESTIONS

To test graphology we must ask the right questions. We should not ask *is graphology true?* (Answer: what is truth?) Or *does it work?* (Answer: can thousands of graphologists be wrong?) Or *is it real?* (Answer: you sound like a blind man feeling an elephant.) Instead we should ask about *extent*. To what extent is graphology true? To what extent do graphological judgments agree with each other? To what extent do they predict behavior?

To what extent does graphology do better than other tests? In short, we should ask about *effect size.*

An effect size is a number that, unsurprisingly, tells us how big the effect is. A big effect, like a bucket of water on a cigarette butt, is useful. A small effect, like the same bucket in a city blaze, may be of no use at all. Unfortunately effect sizes are conspicuously missing from graphology books, whose authors generally behave like used-car salesmen—yes, lady, this beauty is for you, gleaming chrome, dazzling paint job, never mind the engine.[5] In this chapter we are taking a long hard look under the hood.

MEASURING EFFECT SIZE

An effect size indicates the extent to which one thing is associated with another. It is commonly expressed as a *correlation,* a number between +1 and -1, defined as follows:

+1 perfect correlation
 0 no correlation
-1 perfect inverse correlation

All correlations have the advantage of being independent of the original units of measurement. So they can be directly compared with other correlations.[6] Box 1 shows how it works.

To obtain an effect size, someone has to test graphological indications against reality, using procedures as described in any book on experimental design, e.g., Miller (1984). This is hard and demanding work, which is one reason why busy graphologists have better things to do. Depending on the test, the outcome will be either an effect size or something that can be converted to an effect size. Whether it means anything depends on your controls and sample size, coming up next.

CONTROLS TELL THE STORY

Controls are what stop you generating nonsense. They are called *controls* because they control the possibility of mistaking spurious effects for the real thing. Predicting sunshine with an amazing 90 percent accuracy means nothing if you live in the desert. Neither does matching pairs of writers with 100 percent accuracy if one is sober and the other is blind drunk. So tests of graphologists and their readings need controls which repeat everything using nongraphologists and bogus readings. Otherwise you cannot tell whether the results are due to graphology or to something else.

Box 1. *Examples of Effect Sizes*

r	Example	Source
1.00	Feet vs. meters or 100% hits	
.95	Arm length right vs. left	1
.70	Adult height vs. weight	1
.60	Educational attainment } husbands	2
.50	Physical attractiveness } vs. wives	2
.40	City size vs. incidence of jaywalking	3
.30	Height of husbands vs. wives	1
.20	IQ vs. appreciation of music	4
.10	IQ vs. head size	5
.00	Coin tossing or 50% hits	

Sources: 1. Jensen (1984); 2. Feingold (1988); 3. Mullen et al. (1990); 4. Williams et al. (1938); 5. Van Valen (1974); Passingham (1979).

At top, an effect size of 1.00 means the correlation is perfect, as between feet and meters. You always get 100 percent hits. At bottom, an effect size of .00 means there is no correlation at all, as between the tosses of two coins. You average 50 percent hits or exactly chance. So an effect size of .00 is rock-bottom useless.

In between are the effect sizes observed in human affairs, rounded to simplify comparison. At .95 is the near-perfect correlation between right and left arm lengths, which supports our everyday observation that any difference is small. At .70 is the less-perfect correlation between height and weight—heavyweights tend to be tall and lightweights tend to be short, but there are individual exceptions. And so on, down to the almost negligible correlations for IQ vs. music appreciation and head size, where one variable is not a useful guide to the other. A negative effect size means that more of one gives less of the other, such as -.20 for job satisfaction vs. absenteeism (Hackett 1989), and -1.00 for daylength vs. nightlength.

In technical terms effect size r has a simple interpretation. If x and y are measured in standard deviations, then r is the slope of the line relating y to x, namely $y = rx$. In practical terms this means that an effect size of .40 is 40 percent as useful as an effect size of 1.00, or perfect prediction (Hunter and Schmidt 1990:200–201). The symbol r was first used over a century ago when it stood for regression.

If you find effect sizes inscrutable, try this easy conversion to hit rates. Rosenthal and Rubin (1982) show that, for tossing a coin, the hit rate corresponding to correlation r is $(50 + 50r)$ percent, which gives the conversions used above:

Effect size	-.60	-.40	-.20	.00	.20	.40	.60
Hit rate (50% expected)	20%	30%	40%	50%	60%	70%	80%

Thus an effect size of .40 is like averaging $(50 + 50 \times .40) = 70$ percent heads all the time. An effect size of .00 is like averaging $(50 + 50 \times .00) = 50$ percent heads all the time, or exactly chance.

For example, a study may show that authentic readings are seen as accurate, but so what? So are bogus readings. For sobering examples see Crowley (1991), McKelvie (1990), Vestewig et al. (1976), and the second experiment by Karnes and Leonard in chapter 16, where authentic graphoanalytic readings were found to be even more Barnum than Barnum. Box 2 will give you a feel for this sort of thing.

Box 2. *Pick the Genuine Graphoanalysis*

One statement in each pair is from a handwriting analysis by a master graphoanalyst which the subject rated as "quite startling in its accuracy" (Warner and Swallow 1989). The other is from the classic set of Barnum statements, i.e., statements of universal validity, assembled by Forer (1949) largely from a newstand astrology book. Forer's aim was "to demonstrate the ease with which clients may be misled by a general personality description into unwarranted approval of a diagnostic tool." Can you tell which statements are from the genuine graphoanalysis?

Kind and considerate with an apparent optimistic outlook, you nevertheless keep yourself and your emotions under control.	At times you are extroverted, affable and sociable, while at other times you are introverted, wary, and reserved.
While you have some personality weaknesses, you are generally able to compensate for them.	You feel deeply, but you prefer to hide your feelings and find it difficult to express them.
You seek to maintain dignity and poise in situations where you feel inferior. This can lead to tension.	Disciplined and self-controlled outside, you tend to be worrisome and insecure inside.
At times you have serious doubts as to whether you have made the right decision or done the right thing.	Some incidents affect you deeply while others of a similar nature hardly do so at all.
You tend to be reticent, but you do need people, and want to lead a life of some significance.	You have a great need for people to like and admire you. Security is one of your major goals.

You probably found it impossible to choose with any confidence, which illustrates the need for controls when assessing the accuracy of graphological interpretations. For the answers look under Warner and Swallow (1989) in the list of references. Chance score is 2.5 hits. One reader in 32 should get 0 or 5 hits by chance alone.

SAMPLE SIZE IS CRUCIAL

A sample that is too small can ruin everything before you even start. Try this simple exercise:

1. Imagine that half the population writes large, and half writes small, regardless of sex.
2. Imagine collecting a sample of 20 handwritings.

Owing to chance variations your sample will not contain *exactly* the same proportions (50 percent male and 50 percent large) as the population, any more than 20 coin tosses always gives 10 heads. If it happens to contain an excess of males and large writings, you would wrongly conclude that males tend to have large writing. Furthermore your chance of being wrong increases as the sample size N decreases. For example, to get a proportion in the range 45–55 percent for both sex and size, your chance is a reassuring 92 percent at N = 200 but only 25 percent at N = 20. The last means that on average 75 percent of such samples would give wrong answers.

In other words sampling variations are like magic—out of nothing they can produce results that are interesting, exciting, full of promise, and totally spurious. The sample size needed to avoid spurious results depends on the effect size and can be calculated.[7] For graphology the answer is typically over 200, which almost no studies manage to achieve. As we shall see later, this has predictable consequences. Next we come to a tiresome but necessary distinction between reliability and validity.

RELIABILITY VS. VALIDITY

Reliability and validity have special meanings in experimental work:

Reliability= *consistency,* the agreement between repeated measurements.
Validity = *accuracy,* the agreement between measurement and reality.

If we cannot agree on how slanted a handwriting is, then looking at slant is a waste of time, like planning a holiday but disagreeing on where to go. If we agree on slant but not on the interpretation, we are no better off. Disagreement means the measure is *unreliable*—we never get the same answer twice. By contrast a *reliable* measure gives us the same answer nearly every time. Obviously when testing graphology we want as much reliability as possible.

But reliability is not everything. The number of coins in your pocket can be measured very reliably (you get the same answer every time) but is useless for predicting the weather. So high reliability does not necessarily mean high validity. On the other hand low reliability *always* means low validity, because an unreliable test gives us different answers every time, so we cannot be sure they mean anything. Thus graphologists who disagree on what slant means are useless for interpreting slant, just as tipsters who disagree on their tips are useless for winning bets.

Now comes the clever part. If we measure both reliability and validity as a correlation, the maximum possible validity is the square root of the reliability. If the reliability of tipsters is .25, the maximum possible validity in using their tips is $\sqrt{(.25)}$ or .50—a useful finding because it sidesteps the problems of validation (agreement is easy to measure, but truth is something else).[8] On the other hand, the validity so calculated is only an upper bound (the tipsters may agree but still be wrong), so it tends to greatly overestimate the validity actually observed.[9]

In general, validity means the same as effect size. A tipster with a validity of .50 has an effect size of .50, meaning his tips correlate .50 with the winners. The terms are interchangeable, but effect size is easier to understand.[10]

RELIABILITY: HOW RELIABLE IS RELIABLE?

To be acceptable, how reliable must a test be? In general no psychological test becomes widely accepted unless its reliability exceeds .80. But it depends on the situation. Meehl (1972:159) points out that doctors still measure blood pressure despite a poor test-retest reliability caused by instrumental defects, differences in resting state, and individual differences in technique. It is simply more useful to know blood pressure with a reliability of say .65 than it is to know wrist width with a reliability of say .98. On the other hand doctors must offset the unreliability by taking many measurements, say three times a day for a week, before believing what they see. Also .65 would be unacceptable if .80 were available elsewhere. So it depends on the situation.

Nevertheless for the psychological testing of *individuals* (are you prone to anxiety?) .80 is a good starting point. For making decisions about *groups* (are old people generally more anxious than young people?), reliabilities down to .50 may be acceptable. Anything below .40 is generally regarded as useless, because the error rate is then too high for the results to mean anything.[11] As shown next, the key word is *individuals*.

EFFECT SIZE: HOW USEFUL IS USEFUL?

To be useful, how large must an effect size be? Again, it depends on the situation. If you are laying carpet, a correlation of .90 between your tape measure and reality would give dimensions accurate to only ±20 percent. So .90 would be far too low. But if you are betting at roulette, an effect size of .20 in your favor would on average take all of one hour to convert twenty dollars into a million. So .20 could be needlessly high.

Furthermore, it depends on whether the situation involves individuals or groups. For *individuals,* if you are testing personality or ability, the minimum effect size generally regarded as being useful is around .40. Also .40 is the minimum correlation that the average person can detect between columns of figures or shapes, which needs .85 before nearly everyone can detect it, see next chapter. So as a guide we can reasonably adopt .40 as the minimum useful effect size for any technique applied to individuals.

For *groups* the thinking is different. Here applying an effect size is like detecting it in reverse. Just as a small effect needs a large sample to reliably *detect* it, so it needs a large sample to reliably *apply* it. If we have a single situation such as buying a car, we need a large effect size (i.e., between our information and reality) to maximize the chance of getting a hit (i.e., not buying a lemon). But if we have many situations such as planting seeds, we can accept a smaller effect size because the large sample evens out the impact of individual misses. To put it another way, it is safer to play Russian roulette once with two chambers loaded than many times with one chamber loaded.

So what is the minimum useful effect size for groups? If the group is big enough the answer is *anything larger than zero.* Thus tests which have effect sizes too small for individual use can still be usefuly applied to groups. For a company that hires many people each year, hiring on the basis of such tests (as opposed to hiring at random) has substantial dollar value.[12]

So far so good. Now comes the frustrating part, where among other things we catch up with the predictable consequences of using small samples.

THE FINE PRINT: OR THE HIDDEN DELIGHTS OF SURVEYING EXPERIMENTAL STUDIES

YES, GRAPHOLOGY IS PLAUSIBLE, BUT SO WHAT?

In principle graphology is eminently plausible. Unlike astrology and palmistry, it relies on an actual sample of behavior. And if the differences are large enough, it would be unreasonable *not* to see them reflected in handwriting. Take the two biggest single determinants of human behavior and destiny, namely, sex and intelligence. Many studies have shown that non-graphologist judges can pick sex from handwriting with 60 to 70 percent accuracy (effect size .20 to .40), or even more when only their most confident judgments are counted, as in the following examples:

Author	Sample	No. of judges	Mean % correct	Ditto, confident judgments only
Downey 1910	200 envelopes	13	67.4%	75.1%
Young 1931*	50 brief lists	50	61.0%	
Goodenough 1945	115 same paragraph	20	69.6%	81.0%

*Cues: Careless untidy angular = male. Careful tidy rounded = female.

Similarly many studies have shown that lay and graphologist judges can judge intelligence from handwriting with comparable accuracy, the effect size averaging around .30 (Michel 1969). As expected, it gets easier as the IQ differences increase, leading to an increase in the effect size:

Author	Judges	Subjects	IQ	r
Michel 1969:44	7 rankers	7	91–128	.27
Castelnuovo-Tedesco 1948	6 raters	100	68–132	.59

Studies of sex and IQ are summarized in Appendix D.

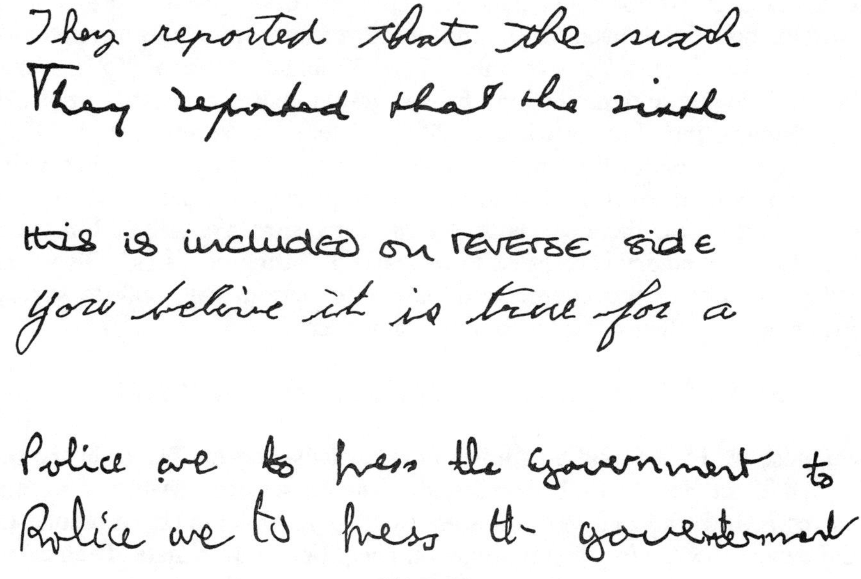

Figure 2.

Big differences are just as detectable in other areas. Thus it is unsurprising that people prematurely aged by concentration camps should have a disturbed handwriting, typically oversized or complicated, with breaks and tremors (Paul-Mengelberg 1956, Ratzon 1986). Figure 2 shows how easy it is to distinguish between extreme IQs, between the artistry of the artist and the tremor of the alcoholic, and between being sober and blind drunk. (Here I will ignore the problem that it is even easier face to face, in which case it is pointless to look at handwriting.) Furthermore, from the bottom example in Figure 2, it is easy to understand why poor handwriting gets you lower marks. It is also easy to understand this interesting 1930 court case from Germany:

> A farmer was living on bad terms with his neighbour. To offend him he deliberately sowed seeds on his neighbour's field in the form of libellous words. The seeds grew to plants which were in the exact pattern of the offender's handwriting. The court accepted this as evidence and legal proof of the offender's identity, and he was convicted. (Singer 1974:27)

If graphologists had no greater claims than these, then nobody could complain. But there is a huge leap of faith between a teacher's failing of a pupil whose handwriting she cannot decipher, and a graphologist's conclusions about your honesty, leadership, musical ability, performance in marriage, and so on, if only because there is no reason to believe such qualities find expression in handwriting. Even neat appearance and neat writing, both clear products of motor movement, seem poorly related— the observed correlation was only .23 for 30 females (Brown 1921), Neat-in-Dress scores and predictions by six graphologists correlated only .32 for 13 males and, disconcertingly, -.28 for 35 females (Vestewig et al. 1976), while 200 doctors in their neat surgeries had significantly *less* legible writing than 500 nondoctors, the corresponding correlation being -.20 (Goldsmith 1976).[13] So there seems little hope for claims like Albert Einstein's "prodigious memory is revealed in the careful dotting of his i's" (Olyanova 1960:193). But in this chapter ours is not to reason why, only to survey the evidence. Which is not as easy as it may seem.

SURVEYING EXPERIMENTAL STUDIES BY META-ANALYSIS

Suppose we have found 50 studies of a particular effect. Typically the reported effect sizes will all be different. How do we decide which ones are correct? Until the mid-1970s it was usual to attribute such variations to differences in *situation,* like testing males here but females there. Then came a revolution in thinking. It was realized that much of the variation between studies was due to differences in *statistical variables* such as sample size and measurement reliability. As a result a special method of analysis, called meta-analysis (rhymes with better), was invented to tackle this problem. Meta-analysis quickly became the preferred method for surveying research results, and by 1984 about 300 meta-analyses had been conducted in diverse areas from medical research to finance (Hunter and Schmidt 1990:41). Entering the keyword *meta-analysis* into the PsycLIT computerized database would have returned 0 titles in 1976, 50 in 1983, and 900 in 1991— and that is just for psychology. Meta-analysis is used later to survey graphology research.

Meta-analysis takes a set of effect sizes and removes the statistical variability. It then tests any remaining variability to see if it is genuine. If it is, further tests can be made to identify the underlying causes, and thus track down the variables which matter. The whole point of meta-analysis is that it reaches better conclusions than those reached in individual studies. Which is why it is used here. The first step is to retrieve all relevant research studies, which is easy to say but not easy to do.

RETRIEVING GRAPHOLOGY RESEARCH STUDIES

To retrieve research studies the usual approach (followed here) is a computerized search of literature databases, a methodical gleaning of references from the works thus uncovered, and so on down the line until nothing further appears, plus writing to people. Then it is off to the university library to photocopy the cited studies from the original journals, and (at least in theory) you are up and running. For popular orthodox subjects like personnel testing this can produce hundreds of studies based on a total of many thousands of subjects, sometimes even hundreds of thousands (Schmidt et al. 1981). Such data bases are so large that the indications become extremely trustworthy. But in graphology it is not so easy:

1. Computerized data bases rarely extend much before 1970 and therefore do not cover the important early work in graphology. Nor do they cover studies reported in graphology journals, which are excluded for the same reason that astrology journals are excluded, namely, the general absence of even minimum standards of scientific reporting.

2. Studies of graphology are so highly scattered across journals and countries that retrieval is difficult. Not even national libraries can subscribe to every scientific journal (all 100,000 of them, somewhat more than in 1700 when the total was 8). So knowing a study exists is no guarantee you can retrieve it. For example, in their reviews of reliability Lester (1981)

cites 12 studies and Nevo (1986a) cites 25 studies. Both authors tried to be comprehensive, but only 3 studies are common to both. In principle any study can be retrieved given enough resources like money and someone to do all the work, but we may then discover it suffers from the next three problems.

3. Many studies are not relevant. For example, Eysenck (1945) cites 30 studies that are "the most important 10%" to have appeared since 1933, but only 10 report effect sizes. You cannot tell from the title. Similarly, Miller's (1982) bibliography of 2321 graphology items (roughly 40 percent English, 30 percent German, and the rest mostly French), including books and journals, is of no use because he does not identify research studies reporting effect sizes.

4. Many studies are impossible to assess. For example they omit important details, or omit controls, or, as Klimoski and Rafaeli (1983) put it, they suffer from "significant methodological negligence." Examples are given in note 14.

5. Journals may tend to reject studies with negative findings. Or they may favor the better-designed studies. Either way, the retrieved studies may be a biased sample of the studies actually carried out, in the same way that shiny maggot-free apples in the supermarket are a biased sample of those on the trees. This is called the *file-drawer problem* (Rosenthal 1979), after the file drawers supposedly crammed with negative studies rejected by cruel editors.[15]

Despite these problems I managed to retrieve over 60 reliabilities and nearly 140 effect sizes, usually directly from published studies but occasionally secondhand from reviews. To give you a feel for what lies behind the dry-as-dust figures ahead, next are a few selected details from these published studies, most of them reflecting the delights of small sample sizes.

NOW YOU SEE IT, NOW YOU DON'T

Small sample sizes ($N < 100$) are common in graphology studies because they are quick and easy. They also give erratic and unreliable results, which means that for every study with a particular result there is usually another which contradicts it. For example:

Does heavy writing pressure indicate an aggressive nature? The answer is *no* according to Hull and Montgomery (1919) but *yes* according to Downey (1919), a difference which is easily explained by small sample sizes:

Hull and Montgomery 1919	Light = aggressive	r = .17	p = .53	N = 17
Downey 1919	Heavy = aggressive	r = .23	p = .25	N = 28

What size of handwriting indicates emotionality? The answer is *small* according to Taft (1967) but *large* according to Furnham and Gunter (1987):

Taft 1967	Small = emotional	r = .2	p = .07	N = 86
Furnham and Gunter 1987	Large = emotional	r = .19	p = .13	N = 64

Here the sample sizes are larger than in the previous case, but not enough to give reliable results. For even larger samples the effect size approaches zero (Crowley 1991, Stabholz 1981), which supports the view that the disagreement is mostly due to sampling variations:

Crowley 1991	Small = emotional	r = .03	p = .78	N = 93
Stabholz 1981	Large = emotional	r = .01	p = .86	N = 316

Do artistic people have artistic writing? The answer is *yes* according to Meloun (1935), who gives only sketchy evidence, but *no* according to Lester (1981:75), who gives no evidence at all despite having complained about Meloun's sketchy evidence.

Can nongraphologists judge emotionality? Middleton (1941) found they tended to get the *right* answers, but Vine (1974) found they tended to get the *wrong* answers, both at an impressive level of significance:

Middleton 1941	5 levels of emotionality.	r = .31	p = .006	N = 78
Vine 1974	6 levels of emotionality.	r = -.4	p = .001	N = 63

Do confident writers omit i-dots? Lemke and Kirchener (1971) found *yes* for 103 students, r = .20, one of the better results in a study that generated 160 effect sizes, only a handful of which are reported. But two years later Kirchener and Lemke (1973) found *no* for 72 alcoholics and schizophrenics, conveniently referring the reader to their Figure 1 for details—except there is no Figure 1.

Take twenty close friends and have a graphologist interpret five of their handwritings. Can the others tell which interpretation is which? The answer is *yes* according to Bobertag (1929) but *no* according to De Groot (1947), a difference which is entirely explained by the tiny sample size:[16]

Bobertag 1929	15 others averaged 81% hits	}	hits expected
De Groot 1947	13 others averaged 23% hits	}	by chance = 20%

Does confidence increase the accuracy of graphological judgment? Eysenck (1945) found *yes* for his graphologist filling out a personality test for 50 handwritings, whereas Eysenck and Gudjonnson (1986) found *no* for another graphologist doing the same for 99 handwritings. However others tend to find *yes,* e.g., Jansen (1973) and Vestewig et al. (1976), which is as it should be if there is something in it, even though the correlation between confidence and hit rate averaged only about .30.

When is an expert not an expert? Rafaeli and Klimoski (1983) tested 20 graphologists, of whom "Twelve had previous experience in personnel selection . . . All were considered experts in the field." But Rafaeli and Drory (1988), referring to the same study, say most of them "had little if any experience with graphology as a selection tool." So now you see it, now you don't. Perhaps the answer lies in the popular definition of expert, where x is the unknown and spurt is a drip under pressure.

Can poor results be made to look good? Of course they can. As already noted in note 14, there are numerous strategies, for example, you can toss out your controls or, in an emergency, your entire results. More subtly, you can focus on significance and ignore effect size. Less subtly, you can make unsupported assertions, as do LoMonaco et al. (1973) when they rate the empirical literature on graphology (whose bad press was aired earlier) as "predominantly favorable."

The good news is that the above problems are what meta-analysis is designed to cope with. Meta-analysis cuts through the confusion and gets straight to the bottom line. In what follows we look at the results, reliability first. For technical readers the technicalities of meta-analysis are described in note 17, the correction for artifacts in notes 18–21, and the interpretation of meta-analytic results in note 22.

THE BOTTOM LINE: THE RESULTS OF EXPERIMENTAL STUDIES OF EFFECT SIZE

RELIABILITY OF GRAPHOLOGY

Reliability is the agreement between repeated tests. By searching the literature I managed to locate 23 articles that reported reliabilities, plus a further 18 articles and dissertations whose results were obtained secondhand, mostly from the reviews by Lester (1981) and Nevo (1986a). These yielded a total of 66 reliabilities; see Appendix A. The mean reliabilities (weighted by sample size) obtained by meta-analysis are shown below. Details of how each study was processed are given in note 23.

Feature tested	Mean reliability, same scripts			No. of scripts	
	Test-retest same judges	Agreement diff judges	All	Mean	Total
Objective e.g. slant*	.87 (5)**	.85 (12)	.86 (17)	58	989
Subjective e.g. rhythm	.69 (3)	.60 (3)	.64 (6)	94	566
Interp e.g. extrovert	.59 (4)	.42 (15)	.44 (19)	40	756
Interp, lay judges	.66 (4)	.30 (16)	.36 (20)	46	923

*Based on the mean of typically ten or more instances of each feature.
**Mean is .74 (4) if retested using *fresh* scripts within two months.

( ) = number of studies

The above results show that when two or more people measure *objective* features such as slant or slope in a sample of handwriting, the correlation between their results is quite high. So such measurements tend to be reliable. As expected, the correlation drops somewhat for *subjective* features such as rhythm and connectedness, and drops still further for *interpreted* features such as extroversion. So while judges may agree closely on the degree of slant or slope, they agree less closely on what it means, which of course is what matters. As expected, the agreement between different judges is consistently worse than between repeats by the same judge.[24] Similarly, compared with lay judges, graphologist judges show better agreement on interpretation, but not much better (.42 vs. .30).

For a graphological consultation the relevant reliability in the above table is .42, or close to useless (see "Reliability: How Reliable Is Reliable?" above). It is based on 15 studies, so it cannot be easily dismissed as unrepresentative. In which case, unless graphologists improve their reliability, graphology will remain unacceptable for use with individuals.

EFFECT SIZE OF GRAPHOLOGY IN PERSONNEL SELECTION

A meta-analysis of graphology in personnel selection has been performed by Neter and Ben-Shakhar (1989). By searching the literature, and by contacting active researchers, they managed to locate 13 articles and dissertations that investigated effect size at an acceptable standard. To be acceptable the work had to:

1. Compare graphological predictions of work performance with an independent criterion such as supervisor ratings or training success.
2. Report correlations or enough data for their calculation.

3. Report sample size.
4. Report the content of the handwriting sample.

In most cases the script used for the handwriting analysis was part of a job application, whose content may have influenced the graphological judgment. So Neter and Ben-Shakhar were careful to analyze separately all studies using neutral scripts. By further searching I managed to locate another 3 articles to make a total of 16, which yielded a total of 35 effect sizes; see Appendix B. Meta-analysis gave the following mean effect sizes, the categories being those of Neter and Ben-Shakhar:[25]

| Test | Neutral scripts? | Handwriting judged by | | | | No. of scripts | |
		Graph	Psych	Lay	All	Mean	Total
Whole script { No		.158 (17)	.178 (5)	.173 (4)	.165 (26)	68	1758
vs work perf { Yes		.086 (6)	.11 (1)	.022 (2)	.073 (9)	102	920
( ) = number of studies		Weighted mean			.134 (35)	77	2678

Each effect size is the mean correlation (weighted by number of scripts) between work performance as predicted from the handwriting (by graphologists, psychologists, or laypersons), and reality as determined by supervisor ratings or success during job training. Not surprisingly they are very similar to those found by Neter and Ben-Shakhar (1989).[26] The above results show that:

1. Effect sizes are too low to be useful.
2. Nongraphologists are generally as good as graphologists.
3. Effect size is much reduced by using neutral scripts.

The last suggests that much of any validity is due to information in the scripts and not to graphology. In other words, contrary to what graphologists say, content *does* influence judgment.[27]

EFFECT SIZE OF GRAPHOLOGY IN PREDICTING PERSONALITY

To date no meta-analysis of graphology in predicting personality has been reported. Therefore I repeated the previous meta-analysis, this time on studies that compared graphological predictions of personality with an independent criterion such as self-ratings, peer-ratings, or personality test scores. Studies of sex and IQ were excluded (these yielded 10 and 14 effect sizes respectively; see Appendix D).

By searching the literature I managed to locate 47 articles and dissertations that investigated effect size at the same acceptable standard as before, plus 6 more from secondhand sources, total 53, of which 4 are shared with the previous section. These yielded a total of 72 effect sizes; see Appendix C. To be more than fair to graphology, studies were included even when methodological shortcomings could reasonably be suspected of inflating the success rate, e.g., Eysenck (1945), Crumbaugh and Stockholm (1977), and Wellingham-Jones (1989).[28] About ten works cited in reviews could not be obtained and therefore could not be included. Half were dissertations not accessible through Dissertation Abstracts International and the rest were pre-1930 German articles. However, according to the reviews they were as frequently negative as positive, so their omission should be of little consequence. Meta-analysis gave the following mean effect sizes for the same categories as before:[29]

Test	Neutral scripts?	Handwriting judged by				No. of scripts	
		Graph	Psych	Lay	All	Mean	Total
Signs vs. predicted trait			.082 (11)		.082 (11)	76	835
Whole script vs. personality {	No	.139 (14)	.269 (4)	.064 (5)	.135 (23)	60	1386
	Yes	.066 (10)	−.05 (1)	.106 (7)	.068 (18)	47	854
Match to { Script	Yes	.205 (2)	.076 (2)	.044 (3)	.076 (7)	15	107
personality { Interp	Yes			.146 (13)	.146 (13)	19	244
( ) = number of studies			Weighted mean		.104 (72)	48	3426

Each effect size is the mean correlation (weighted by number of scripts) between personality as predicted from the handwriting (by graphologists, psychologists, or laypersons), and the actual personality as determined by self-ratings, peer-ratings, or personality tests. The above results show that:

1. Effect sizes are too low to be useful.
2. Nongraphologists are generally as good as graphologists.
3. Effect size is reduced by using neutral scripts.
4. Signs (individual features) are no worse than neutral scripts.
5. Sample sizes for matching tests are dismally low.

Included in Appendix C, but not shown above, are 7 omnibus studies of signs where large numbers of signs were correlated with large numbers of traits in the hope of finding something. A total of 1519 correlations were observed but the number reaching significance at the p≤.05 level is slightly less than chance (74 vs. 76).[30] This suggests that, if effective signs exist, there are not many of them.

The results of this and the previous section show consistently that nongraphologists are generally as good as graphologists. Isn't this the worst possible news for graphology? Answer: not if the traditionally impoverished researcher could afford to test only inexperienced amateur graphologists of dubious repute. For how can you test graphology properly if you don't use *real* graphologists? A good point. Now read on.

ARE PROFESSIONALS BETTER THAN AMATEURS?

As it happens, most studies did *not* use inexperienced amateurs. Instead they used only experienced professional graphologists, typical descriptions being "well-known" (Bobertag 1929, Eysenck 1948); "experienced" (Cox and Tapsell 1991); "years of experience" (Drory 1986); "better qualified than most" (Eysenck 1945); "ample experience of personnel selection and [according to their peers] all able" (Jansen 1973); "highly experienced certified graphologists" (Kimmel and Wertheimer 1966); and "professional" (LoMonaco et al. 1973, a modest description for the then president of the American Association of Handwriting Analysts).

Furthermore, the graphologists often helped in designing the experiment to make it as realistic as possible. For example, Kimmel and Wertheimer (1966) held a joint conference among the graphologists, raters, and experimenters "to decide *which* particular personality characteristics would be rated, and precisely *how* they were to be defined and rated." For his four lengthy experiments (they took seven years), Jansen (1973) had a panel of four graphologists and four psychologists establish the initial approach, criticize each experiment when it was finished, and suggest improvements for the next (for the record the results were consistently dismal). To select a mutually acceptable task, Goldberg (1986) and his graphologist "spent a day together examining each of the tests, inventories, and questionnaires that were available."

In other words, researchers generally *have* been careful to test real graphologists under realistic conditions, so their poor results cannot be explained by lack of expertise. Similarly we cannot conclude that professionals are generally better than amateurs. Here is an example:

In one of the few studies that used amateurs, Nevo (1989) had judges match 10 persons to interpretations by student graphologists, and obtained an encouraging mean effect size of .34. But when Nevo and Benitta (1991) repeated the experiment with 12 persons and 3 professional graphologists, the mean effect size dropped to only .01. As usual the sample sizes are too small for comfort, but the results illustrate the point.

This poor performance by professionals is consistent with the findings of Garb (1989), who reviewed 55 studies of validity vs. experience in the clinical assessment of personality. In general, experienced clinicians were no more accurate than students across a wide variety of judgments including interviews, therapy sessions, biographies, and personality test results. Which sets the tone for what comes next.

IS GRAPHOANALYSIS BETTER?

Graphoanalysis is the trademarked name of a particular U.S. school of graphology founded in 1929. It is a strongly holistic method in which the graphologist converts a multitude of cues into a global whole. According to Crumbaugh and Stockholm (1977) it "has been more systematically developed, presented in greater detail, more effectively taught, and better researched, than any other method of handwriting analysis." Peeples (1991) found that 13 Graphoanalysts were slightly less in agreement with each other (mean r=.29) than were 13 psychogrammists (r=.36) and 11 gestaltists (r=.46), but since this was based on a single script no general conclusion is possible.

Of the 35 personnel selection studies and 61 non-sign personality studies surveyed here, 9 involve Graphoanalysts. Matching these studies in design are 21 involving other kinds of graphologists. Meta-analysis of these 9 Graphoanalytic studies (7 with neutral scripts) and the 21 equivalent non-Graphoanalytic studies (18 with neutral scripts) gave the following mean effect sizes and standard deviations:

9 Graphoanalytic studies	.071 sd.049 (387 scripts) }	by t-test
21 non-Grapholanalytic studies	.101 sd.121 (853 scripts) }	t=.71, p=.48

The difference is nonsignificant and in the wrong direction to suggest that Graphoanalysis has advantages over other kinds of graphology.

ARE EXTERNAL CRITERIA BETTER THAN INTERNAL CRITERIA?

In chapter 6 Lockowandt concludes that:

1. *Internal* criteria (e.g., personality and IQ tests) are of questionable validity. Therefore,
2. Only *external* criteria (e.g., peer and supervisor ratings) should be used to validate graphology.

When you see the validity comparison in my Tables 2 and 3 you may be inclined to disagree with Lockowandt's first point. And if you noted Lockowandt's own dismissal of ratings in chapter 5 to explain the disappointing results of Birge (1954), you may be inclined to disagree with his second point also. No matter. If internal criteria really are useless, then the effect sizes for studies using personality tests (*internal* criteria) should be consistently worse than those for studies using peer and supervisor ratings (*external* criteria). Since the studies surveyed here contain plenty of both, Lockowandt's claim can be put to the test.

Accordingly, I extracted every study where judgments by graphologists were compared against an independent criterion. Studies involving individual signs or nongraphologists were of course excluded. I then segregated the extracted studies into those using personality tests vs. those using peer and supervisor ratings. Excluded were matching tests, and tests where the criterion was not clearly one or the other, e.g., psychiatric diagnoses, examination grades, and success in training. The result was 15 studies using tests (6 with neutral scripts) and 16 studies using ratings (3 with neutral scripts). Meta-analysis gave the following mean effect sizes and standard deviations:

15 studies with internal criteria	.115 sd.093 (806 scripts) ⎫	by t-test
16 studies with external criteria	.102 sd.137 (794 scripts) ⎭	t=.31, p=.76

The difference is nonsignificant and in the wrong direction to support Lockowandt's claim.

OVERALL MEAN EFFECT SIZE

The results so far have shown no significant difference in effect size between predicting work performance and predicting personality, or between graphologists and nongraphologists, whereas there is a significant difference between neutral and non-neutral scripts.[31] Therefore for convenience they can be combined as follows:

Test	Neutral scripts?	Effect size sd	No. of scripts	
			Mean	Total
Signs vs. predicted trait		.082 (11) .075	76	835
Whole script vs. work ⎧	No	.152 (49) .111	64	3144
performance or personality ⎩	Yes	.080 (47) .114	45	2125
( ) = number of studies	Weighted mean	.117 (107) .114	57	6104

The above results are based on 107 studies (from 65 published and unpublished articles over the period 1905–1991), over 6100 scripts, nearly 200 graphologists, and nearly 600 psychologists and laypersons. At the going rate for everyone's time this represents over a million dollars just for looking at scripts. The above results are displayed visually in Figure 3 using the plots suggested by Light and Pillemer (1984).

Figure 3. *Visual analysis of 107 graphological effect sizes.*

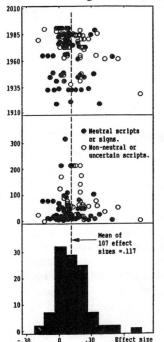

Effect size vs. year of study. As methods improve over time, so the results should converge on the truth with a corresponding decrease in scatter. But no such convergence or decrease is evident, suggesting that future studies will be equally dismal.

Effect size vs. number of scripts. As sample size increases, sampling errors decrease, so the plot should resemble an inverted funnel. And it does. There are fewer extreme results on the left than on the right, suggesting that some publication bias exists.

Distribution of effect sizes. The distribution is orderly, suggesting that most of the variability is due to sampling error, which of course agrees with the meta-analytic results. The bar width is too coarse to resolve the neutral/non-neutral difference (discernible in the other plots), so there is a single peak only.

The above results suggest that the best representative effect size for graphology using neutral scripts, and corrected for a criterion reliability of .60, is $.080/ \sqrt{(.60)} = .10$, or say .12 to allow for range restriction and other attenuating artifacts. This (at last) is the bottom line. Of course many studies used test criteria more reliable than .60, and had no range restriction (or were already corrected for it where it was extreme). Furthermore, no allowance has been made for publication bias.[15] So this estimate may be optimistic.

So what does a corrected effect size of .12 tell us? It tells us that, in general, when used for predicting personality and work performance, graphology delivers 50 + 50 ×.12 = 56 percent hits vs. 50 percent expected by chance—hardly a dazzling performance. Any null studies stashed away in file drawers will make the results even worse. Unretrieved studies may or may not improve things, but to save the day many dozens would be needed, all with effect sizes approaching 1.00—hardly something that over the years would have escaped notice by reviewers. So on balance it seems that an effect size around .12 is here to stay.

However, in fairness we must ask whether other techniques do any better. If selection interviewers, clinicians, IQ testers, inkblot readers, astrologers, palmists, and so on have no more success at this sort of thing than graphologists do, then we can hardly point the finger at graphology. So let us find out.

GRAPHOLOGY VS. THE REST OF THE WORLD

RELIABILITY: GRAPHOLOGY VS. OTHER TECHNIQUES

Table 1 shows how graphology compares in reliability with 14 other techniques. For use with individuals, tests in the top half of Table 1 are generally acceptable while those in the bottom half are not. The results show that graphology is roughly comparable with the Rorschach test (what do you see in this inkblot?), of which Jensen (1964:75) concluded as follows:

> . . . the 40 years of massive effort which has been lavished on the Rorschach technique [over 3,000 published studies by 1964] has proven unfruitful, at least so far as the development of a useful psychological test is concerned. [Therefore] . . . it seems not unreasonable to recommend that the Rorschach be altogether abandoned in clinical practice, and that students of clinical psychology not be required to waste their time learning the technique.

The same would now seem to apply to graphology. For the record, Jensen's 1964 comments about the Rorschach test had no effect, at least not in North America, where if anything the Rorschach's popularity in graduate clinical psychology courses rose between 1974 and 1984; see Ritzler and Alter (1986).[32] For recent comments about the future of the Rorschach test, and why it is unlikely to be abandoned, see Howes (1981) and Hertz (1986).

PREDICTING WORK PERFORMANCE: GRAPHOLOGY VS. OTHER TECHNIQUES

Table 2 shows how graphology compares in effect size with 15 other techniques for predicting work performance, such as cognitive tests, assessment centers, peer ratings, and interviews. The values for graphology are

Table 1. *Reliability. Graphology vs. Other Techniques.*

Technique	Mean agreement between judges		Source
Rating sex with 1% error	.98		
Achievement batteries	.92 (32)		1
Cognitive ability (IQ) tests	.90 (63)	Test-retest	1
Self-ratings of ability	.90 (24)	agreement on	2
Aptitude batteries	.88 (22)	same subjects	1
Personality inventories	.85 (43)		3
Structured interviews	.82 (25)		4
Rankings of ability	.80 approx.[33]		5
Unstructured interviews	.61 (9)		4
Ratings of ability	.48 (23)[34]		2
Mean agreement on:	*Interpretation*	*Features*	
Graphology	.42 (15)	.85 (12)	
Rorschach (inkblots)	.36 (7)	.84 (24)	6
TAT (ambiguous pictures)	–	.70 (45)	7
Palmistry	.11 (1)	.89 (4)	8
Astrology	.11 (27)	–	9

( ) = number of studies.

Sources: 1. Helmstadter (1966); 2. Harris and Schaubroeck (1988), Rothstein (1990); 3. Eysenck and Eysenck (1964), Helmstadter (1966); 4. Wiesner and Cronshaw (1988); 5. Kane and Lawler (1978), Nathan and Alexander (1988); 6. Jensen (1959, 1964), Reznikoff et al. (1982), Parker et al. (1988); 7. Murstein (1963); 8. Dean (1985), Symaniz (1980); 9. Dean (1986), Kelly et al. (1990).

taken from the preceding section "Effect Size of Graphology in Personnel Selection." The results show that graphology is outperformed by almost everything. Only predictions based on age are worse.

PREDICTING PERSONALITY AND IQ: GRAPHOLOGY VS. OTHER TECHNIQUES

Table 3 shows how graphology compares in effect size with 10 other techniques for predicting personality and IQ, such as the Eysenck Personality Inventory, IQ tests, Rorschach inkblots, and astrology. The values for graphology are taken from the preceding section "Effect Size of Graphology in Predicting Personality." Also included in the lower half are some related effect sizes for general interest. The results show that, compared to graphology, some techniques (astrology, phrenology) do worse, while others

Table 2. *Predicting Work Performance:*
Graphology vs. Other Techniques

Effect size	N	Technique	Source	Sample
.43 (.70)	61	Cognitive test vs. success in training[35]	1	31535
(.53)	425	Cognitive test plus psychomotor test	2	32124
.35 (.45)	27	Assessment center	3,4	c.1700
.35 (.63)	32	Structured individual interview	5	7873
.32	48	Work sample or biography or peer rating	4	5771
.24 (.50)	144	Cognitive test	1	10564
.23 (.35)	47	Self-ratings	6	4941
.21	32	Personality test[36]	4	4065
.18 (.26)	8	References from previous employers	2,7	5389
.18	5	Projective technique vs. various criteria	7	335
.17	26	Graphology using non-neutral scripts		1758
.11 (.20)	19	Unstructured individual interview	5	2303
.10	3	SVIB vocational interest inventory	2	1789
.07	9	Graphology using neutral scripts		920
−.01	425	Age (adults only)	2	32124

N = number of studies. Effect size is the mean correlation between prediction and actual work performance, the latter being measured by supervisor ratings unless otherwise indicated. ( ) = effect size corrected for attenuation by the original authors.[37] Cognitive tests (same as IQ tests) measure mental ability. Psychomotor tests measure mostly dexterity and coordination. Structured interviews use pre-set questions and associated rating scales. Work sample tests measure performance on a sample of work, e.g., typing a letter. The listed effect sizes usually hide individual variations. Thus biographies (akin to CVs) are better at predicting wages, and worse at predicting tenure, than the .32 above. For the present purpose these variations do not affect the broad indications.

Sources: 1. Schmidt et al. (1981); 2. Hunter and Hunter (1984); 3. Cohen et al. (1974) via 2; 4. Schmitt et al. (1984); 5. Wiesner and Cronshaw (1988); 6. Harris and Schaubroeck (1988); 7. Reilly and Chao (1982).

(all recognized tests) do better, usually much better.[38] For predicting personality, even physiognomy has a higher effect size than graphology, suggesting that a single glance at the face is generally more useful than several hours spent analyzing the handwriting.

The comparison in Table 3 confirms our earlier suspicion, namely, that the effect size of graphology is too small to be useful. Interestingly, contrary to the unanimous claims of graphologists,[39] graphology's best performance is in predicting sex, no doubt helped by good criterion reliabil-

Table 3. *Predicting Personality and IQ: Graphology vs. Other Techniques*

Effect size	N	Technique	Source
.65	5	Wechsler IQ test vs. high school grades	1
.56	13	Eysenck Personality Inventory vs. self/peer ratings	2
.52	8	Wechsler IQ test vs. college grades	1
.46	30	MMPI vs. clinical ratings	3
.34	726	Law School Ability Test vs. 1st year law grade	4
.34	13	Rorschach vs. IQ, personality test, clinical ratings	3,5
.29	14	Graphology vs. IQ test	6
.15	17	Physiognomy vs. IQ, personality test, peer ratings	7
.14	23	Non-neutral scripts ⎰ Graphology vs. personality	
.09	38	Neutral scripts ⎱ test, ratings, matchings	
≤ .05	79	Astrology vs. IQ, personality test, case histories	8
.00	1	Phrenology measures vs. peer ratings	9
−.05	9	Palmistry vs. personality test, self-ratings	10
		Some related effect sizes:	
.90	10	Social desirability of trait vs. perceived accuracy	11
.75	19	Readability score vs. grade required for comprehension	12
.72	119	IQ scores between identical twins	13
.51	116	IQ scores between nonidentical twins	13
.50	122	Personality scores between identical twins	13
.48	134	Behavioral therapy vs. outcome	14
.32	10	Graphology vs. sex (lay predictions from handwriting)	6
.30	23	Improving teamwork vs. job satisfaction (corrected r=.58)	15
.22	119	Personality scores between nonidentical twins	13
.19	16	Humanistic therapy vs. outcome	14
.10	21	Sun sign effect (role playing) vs. EPI extroversion	2
.0003	597	ESP vs. random number generators	16

N = number of studies. Effect size is the mean observed correlation between prediction and the indicated criterion. MMPI = Minnesota Multiphasic Personality Inventory. Rorschach = inkblot test. Physiognomy = judging from appearance, not body build, for which the effect size is slightly higher.[40] Astrology = individual features (signs, houses, aspects) and the birth chart as a whole, not Gauquelin planetary effects, for which the effect size is typically .05 (Kelly et al. 1990). Phrenology = judging from head shape. Humanistic therapy includes psychodynamic, client-centered, encounter, and gestalt therapies. When corrected for attenuation the effect sizes in the upper part of this table are about 10 to 30 percent larger. The listed effect sizes often hide considerable individual variations but for the present purpose this does not affect the broad indications.

Sources: 1. Frank (1983); 2. Summarized in Dean (1986); 3. Parker et al. (1988); 4. Linn et al. (1981); 5. Jensen (1964); 6. See Appendix D; 7. Dzida and Kiener (1978), Estes (1938), Hull (1928), Landis and Phelps (1928), Mason (1957), Michel (1969), Pinter (1918), Ray (1958), Vernon (1953); 8. Dean (1986), Kelly et al. (1990); 9. Cleeton and Knight (1924); 10. Dean (1985), Misiak and Franghiadi (1953), Seifer (1977), Symaniz (1980), Wilson (1983), Wolff (1941); 11. Edwards (1967); 12. Klare (1974); 13. McCartney et al. (1990); 14. Shapiro and Shapiro (1982); 15. Neuman et al. (1989); 26.

Box 3. *Not All Effect Sizes Are What They Seem*

The *criterion* is the yardstick used to measure the effect size. Because all criteria are imperfect, the observed effect size will be less than its true value, in the same way that wearing boxing gloves worsens dexterity with chopsticks. So an observed effect size will be misleading unless its associated imperfections are kept in mind. In other words, not all effect sizes are what they seem. The main imperfections to be considered are as follows:

Criterion reliability, or the agreement between repeated test scores, or ratings, or whatever. Examples are given in Table 1. This imperfection typically reduces the observed effect size to between 75 and 95 percent of what it would otherwise be.[16]

Range restriction. Samples in real life are often restricted in range, e.g., to the top 20 percent of job applicants. This reduces the overall signal without necessarily reducing the noise, which reduces the observed effect size. Range restriction is visible in Table 3, where IQ vs. high school grades has a higher effect size than IQ vs. college grades, due to selection of college students. Conversely in the laboratory the middle 30 to 90 percent of samples may sometimes be chopped out. This enhances the variation between ends, which increases the observed effect size. Range restriction can be more important than criterion reliability.[17]

Mismatch. If the criteria cover many traits or many aspects of work performance, but the test measures only some of these, then the test cannot possibly correlate highly with the criteria. Mismatch is visible in Table 2, where age cannot possibly correlate with *everything* (or even most things) relevant to work performance.

Owing to the above imperfections, observed effect sizes may be only 50–70 percent of the true effect size. For example in Table 3, efforts to improve teamwork vs. resulting job satisfaction (r=.30) seems to have a slightly smaller effect size than graphology vs. sex (r=.32). But because the criteria involved are subject to all of the above, whereas sex is not, the true effect size is much superior (r=.58). To facilitate comparison, any important obstacles like this one have been noted in the tables.

---

ity; see Box 3. But as Loewenthal (1982:85) notes, "it is hard to think of situations where this would be really useful."

ARGUMENTS OF THE GRAPHOLOGISTS

The preceding results are undeniably dismal. When faced with such results, supporters of graphology have traditionally never lacked arguments to explain them away. Their main arguments, with counterarguments in parentheses, are as follows:

- Methodology may be suspect (only sometimes true).

- Experimenters may be hostile. (Some were graphologists.)

- Graphologists may be inexperienced. (Some were world famous.)

- Traits are not enough—the whole picture must be looked at. (Many studies have done exactly that.)

- Criteria are a problem. (But not enough to hinder discovery of graphology in the first place.)

- Criteria may not be valid. (Does not worry other techniques.)

- We need *better* criteria. (Like what?)

- Graphology reaches areas inaccessible by other methods. (Nonfalsifiable.)

- Client does not understand the graphologist. (Find another graphologist.)

- Situation was unrealistic. (Now you tell us.)

- More experiments are needed. (Only if results are inconsistent, but they are not.)

- Only graphologists can judge graphology. (So who judges murder?)

However, in this case it is hardly plausible to suppose that, across 107 effect sizes, such factors could consistently attenuate a *useful* effect to the extent implied. If graphology was as good as graphologists claim, it should shine through regardless. But it does not.

COMPARISON WITH OTHER REVIEWS

How do the present results compare with those of other critical reviews? Over the years the following English-language books (denoted by *) and articles have critically reviewed the status of graphology in detail:

Allport and Vernon (1933)	59	references
Bell (1948)	137	references
Wolfson (1951)	55	references
Fluckinger et al. (1965)	105	references
Lockowandt (1976)	123	references
Lester (1981)*	240	references
Klimoski and Rafaeli (1983)	45	references
Nevo et al. (1986)*	310	references

Three of the above review articles were quoted in the Introduction, where they showed increasing negativity over the years as the number of experimental studies increased. This trend is in agreement with the present results. However, in striking disagreement is the review by Lockowandt (1976), reprinted with minor editing in chapter 5, who concludes: "With strict methodology, however, handwriting has shown itself to be highly valid in many different respects." Ironically this optimism is immediately dispelled in chapter 6, where Lockowandt notes that "While going through individual cases in our research seminar, we keep coming across judgments of fully trained graphologists which prove to be completely incorrect." Nevertheless there is disagreement. To resolve it, consider the following:

To assess a particular study the minimum information needed is sample size, observed correlation, number of judges, and type of script (neutral or non-neutral). Lockowandt cites over 20 reliability studies but gives sample size and correlation for only 6 vs. my 66. For a similar number of validity studies including sex and IQ he gives sample size and correlation for only 3 vs. my 138. For around 30 other studies such as twin studies he gives none at all. On such crucial points as sampling error, type of script, cross-validation in factor analytic studies, and range restriction in extreme groups, there is a deafening silence. These points are crucial because each can artificially inflate the observed correlation. Furthermore, other than one of his own works, there is no reference more recent than 1972, so in effect the last 20 years of research (in graphology, in psychology, in everything) are ignored. Also ignored is the general superiority of other techniques, as documented earlier. In other words Lockowandt is highly selective, and *this* is why our conclusions differ. If the result is favorable he spells out the detail. Otherwise the result is merely "greater than chance performance" or "positive" or "informative" or hidden by galloping prolixity. Your choice of conclusion about validity will depend on whether you prefer 2 percent of the evidence (chapter 5) or as near 100 percent of the evidence as possible (this chapter).[41]

Now for the books. After surveying some 200 studies, Lester (1981:122) concludes: "At the present time, it does not appear that handwriting will be a useful tool in diagnosis." However, *if* it were proven valid, it would have "a potentially great future in psychological and psychiatric assessment." It is hard to disagree. But so would reading tea leaves.

After editing his 19-author anthology, Nevo (1986:241) is equally ambivalent: "After nearly one hundred years of investigating the psychodiagnostic value of handwriting behavior, and after almost two hundred years of the practical application of graphology, it is still unclear whether these methods are, or could be, valid." But in a review of Nevo's book, Hirsch (1987:842) was not convinced: ". . . any job-related information that a graphological analysis could extract can probably be obtained more directly by other measures, which also provide additional job-related information not contained in the handwriting sample."

Similarly, to an informed and impartial observer, the research results summarized in this chapter will seem consistent and not at all unclear. The conclusion they point to will seem glaringly obvious and very simple, as indicated next.

CONCLUSION: SPELLING OUT THE BOTTOM LINE

The results of this meta-analysis of over 200 graphology studies can be summarized as follows:

Yes, graphology *is* valid . . .	(there *is* an effect, but at least some of it is due to content not graphology)
. . . but not valid enough . . .	(the representative effect size of .12 for neutral scripts is not nearly big enough)
. . . or reliable enough . . .	(the mean agreement on interpretation of .42 is not nearly good enough)
. . . to be useful.	(other methods are better)

This does not of course deny the possibility that some as yet untested graphological technique may work, or that certain graphologists may achieve success in tests where others have failed. In which case the onus is on graphologists to demonstrate it. Nor does it deny the therapeutic utility of graphological beliefs—if invalid beliefs worked for something as invasive as bloodletting, they will certainly work for graphology. What *is* denied is the practical utility of graphology as practiced by most graphologists. In terms of adequate effect sizes, the claims made in graphology books are mostly false. In other words it seems that graphology has much in common with the Emperor's New Clothes.

Should graphologists wish to challenge the above conclusion, all they need do is present a meta-analysis of properly controlled tests that demonstrates an adequate effect size. Nothing else will do.

Before leaving this chapter you may like to re-read the views of graphologists and scientists quoted in the Introduction, and draw your own conclusions.

NOTES

1. About these notes. These notes provide technical details for technical readers, and useful information for anyone wishing to test graphology, especially those without access to a university library. However they do not provide basic information such as how to calculate a correlation coefficient, which can be found in any introductory book on statistics. In addition, some references are annotated where this would be helpful. There are another 40 notes, so a bookmark will help you whizz to and fro.

2. Unfailing parallels. As an example, Saudek notes how pasty writing (thick and blurred due to holding pen far from nib) *always* indicates sensuality. "For the last seventy years graphologists of all countries have recognized this sign as unfailing, and . . . [it] has certainly been verified in hundreds of thousands of cases without exception" (Saudek 1925:42).

3. A pioneering study. The study by Hull and Montgomery (1919) was among the first to test individual features and raised a storm of protest. It had "only remote relation to most of the claims of graphologists and practically none at all to their methods of work" (Allport and Vernon 1933:186). It had "the obvious intent of debunking graphology" (Castelnuovo-Tedesco 1948:171). So it was "unscientific from the viewpoints of graphological and experimental theory alike" (Sonnemann 1950:11), being merely "not-to-be-taken-seriously handwriting games" (Lockowandt 1976 and in summary to chapter 5 of this book).

But inspection of the actual study tells a different story. Hull and Montgomery begin with a survey of existing studies, and conclude that "we may not . . . safely ignore the claims of graphologists" because there is "at least a weak relation between handwriting and certain traits of character." They noted that previous studies had tested the skill of graphologists, so by contrast they set out to test "the truth of certain graphological theories, i.e., certain correlations alleged to exist between specific traits of handwriting and traits of the writer's character." Their test involved 17 male university students, all members of the same medical fraternity, who copied the same 108-word paragraph and ranked each other on six traits (ambitious, proud, bashful, forceful, persevering, reserved). The mean rankings for each trait were then correlated with the relevant ranked measure such as slope and the thickness and width of t-bars. In hindsight the sample size is too small, otherwise the test is as carefully done as any recent test.

According to the above critics, the theories tested were merely straw men. In fact they were chosen because they involved traits "susceptible of objective measurement and being among the less improbable of the relations alleged," and each is supported by typically 2–5 references to reputable works (with page numbers) where the theory is advanced. The three most widely held of the theories tested are still widely held, but the observed correlations were neither significant nor even in the right direction, namely, –.20 for upward sloping lines = ambitious, –.06 for heavy t-bars = forceful, and –.02 for closed a's and o's = reserved. The authors end cautiously by noting that tests of theories are not the same as tests of graphologists, so their results are not necessarily in conflict with the positive results cited in their introduction. Despite which they were accused of rampant debunking.

4. Ways of matching. As N the number of cases increases, the number of possible matches increases as N^2, rapidly increasing the processing load and rapidly decreasing the average difference between each match. For this reason judges find it difficult to match more than 5 cases at a time, whether as 5 descriptions to be matched to another 5 descriptions (Crumbaugh and Stockholm 1977:404) or as 5 descriptions to be matched to people you know (LoMonaco 1973:705). So the total sample is best divided into sets of no more than 5 cases each.

However this reasonable conclusion is not supported by Allport and Vernon (1933:229), who used scripts from 23 college freshmen selected for diversity of background. They matched the 23 script interpretations with information from peer-ratings, test scores, and interviews, and then rematched them after dividing the 23 interpretations at random into three roughly equal subsets. The hit rate (as effect size kappa, see below) of 1st, 2nd, and 3rd choices showed no clear improvement over using the undivided set:

Choices	1st	1st+2nd	1st+2nd+3rd	Mean
Undivided set	.05	.13	.08	.09
Three subsets	.11	.09	.00	.07

Weinberg et al. (1962) suggest a new matching technique in which the judge selects not one but several matches for each case, the number being chosen by the judge and then kept the same for each case. Used matches are not eliminated and may be re-used without limit. When finished, the judge selects the best single match for each case, but this time without re-use. The difference between the two results allows cues to be identified much more easily than with the standard matching method. However, their actual results for 15 scripts showed no improvement over matching one sketch to each script:

	Judge A		Judge B	
Sketches matched to each script	1	3	1	4
Effect size as kappa	.21	.21	.14	.13

Usually the results of a matching test are given as observed vs. expected hits, in which case they can be converted to an effect size known as *kappa* (Cohen 1960), given by kappa = $(O-E)/(N-E)$, where O = observed hits, E = expected hits, and N = number of matches. Thus if 5 interpretations matched against 5 subjects gives 2 hits, and expected hits = 1, then kappa = $(2-1)/(5-1)$ = .25. Actually kappa is a measure of *agreement* rather than *association*, but for hits and misses they are identical. If near misses can be defined (which is seldom the case), they can be allowed for by a related measure known as *weighted kappa* (Cohen 1968), whose calculation is too complex to be summarized here. Ordinary kappa ignores near misses, so when near misses can be counted it gives a somewhat smaller effect size than weighted kappa.

A method due to Halevi (1965) automatically generates near misses and takes them into account. For each target the interpretations are ranked in order of fit, where best fit = rank 1, second best = rank 2, and so on. The effect size g is given by $g = 1 - 2 \times$ (sum of $(k-1)$ / $N(N-1)$) where k = rank of the correct match for each target, and N = number of targets. Like a correlation, g can take any value between +1 and –1. However, like biserial r and tetrachoric r, its associated variance differs from that for Pearson r, which means that too many of them (not a problem here) will bias an analysis of variance as used in meta-analysis (Hunter and Schmidt 1990:206). According to my computer simulations, this defect does not apply to kappa.

Recently Cox and Tapsell (1991) have proposed an ingenious alternative that avoids all the above problems. The scripts are paired with their matching sketches, then half of them are re-paired by sex and age but otherwise at random. Each judge rates the similarity of each pair on a 7-point scale, where 1 = certainly two different people, and 7 = certainly the same person. This allows large samples to be used without exhausting the judges. The judges' ratings are then compared with reality using point biserial r. Cox and Tapsell tested this approach on 50 scripts using 3 nongraphologist judges, and obtained mean point biserial r = .09. For a useful survey of matching methods see Swentzell and Roberts (1964).

5. Blind eyes. Nobody should be surprised to learn that the hardest things to find in graphology books are facts, although to be fair some psychology books are just as bad. Even scientific graphologists keep quiet about effect sizes. Thus Fluckiger et al. (1961) survey over 100 studies, while Bradley (1988, 1989) presents a one-page summary of each of 199 studies, both without citing a single effect size even though plenty were available. Crumbaugh (1986:56), reprinted in chapter 7, refers to the "substantial validation evidence" offered by several studies but stops short of quoting an actual effect size. This seeming inability to be specific exists even at the top. Thus Moore (1985) wrote to seven international graphology organizations asking for details of controlled studies which validated the use of graphology in personnel selection. Only four replied, namely Handwriting Analysts International [USA], the American Association of Handwriting Analysts, Societa Internazionale di Psicologia della Scrittura, and the Israeli Graphological Institute. Not one provided the requested details.

6. Types of correlation. There are various measures of correlation depending on the type of data. For example *Spearman rho* for ranked data, *kappa* (see note 4) for hits and misses, *Pearson r* (product moment) for two continuous variables, *point biserial r* if one is dichotomized, and *phi* if both are dichotomized. Their calculation is explained in any statistics textbook. Rosenthal (1984:24–26) gives methods of estimating Pearson r from reported data when no correlation is given.

7. Calculation of sample size. The calculation is complicated if exact results are required; see Schmidt et al. (1976) for Pearson r and Donner (1984:201) for phi. But as an approximation the minimum sample size N required to detect effect size E is given by $N = K/E^2$ where E is the effect size you hope to observe, not the one obtained after correcting for attenuation, and N is variously the number of pairs (Pearson r), a+b+c+d (phi), or number of observations (kappa with an

expectancy of .5, otherwise $N=K/E^2 \times P/(1-P)$ where P=expectancy).

The value of K depends on how certain you want to be of detecting E. To detect E in 4 out of 5 tests at a two-sided significance level of .05, which is the normal criterion, put K=9. To detect E in 19 out of 20 tests at a two-sided significance level of .01, put K=18. For example to detect phi=.20 using the normal criterion, minimum N is about $9/.20^2$ or 225, the exact value being 214. In technical terms K is roughly 15 percent more than $(z_\alpha+z_\beta)^2$, where z_α and z_β are the corresponding standard scores, e.g., z_α=1.96 and z_β=.84 for the above normal criterion.

Later we will find that graphological sample sizes are typically N=60 or less, which is too small for comfort. But small sample sizes are not unique to graphology and may be the most common failing in validation research generally. For example, the median of N=68 found for 427 published studies of employment tests is barely adequate to detect the typical effect size of around .30 (Lent et al. 1971).

8. Sidestepping the problems of validation. Here is an example. In note 2, graphologists were agreed that thick, pasty writing *always* indicates sensuality, which suggests excellent validity. However, pasty writing is variously characterized by *heavy* pen pressure (Sonnemann 1952:48, Olyanova 1969:123) or *light* pen pressure (Roman 1952:265, Paterson 1976:49), so judges guided by pen pressure could not possibly agree. In other words the guideline could not be more unreliable, so it cannot be valid. I could find no study of thickness vs. sensuality, but Hull and Montgomery (1919) found that thickness correlated .45 with shyness for 17 male university students. If sensual university students tend not to be shy, then this result is in the wrong direction.

9. Deriving an upper bound to validity. The true validity of a test, as measured perfectly by a perfect criterion, is given by $v/(\sqrt{r} \times k)$, where v = observed validity, r = test reliability, and k = attenuation as explained in notes 18–21. Simple arithmetic shows that only if true validity = 1 and k = 1 will the observed validity approach $\sqrt{r}$, which is therefore an upper bound. In practice both true validity and k are typically 1, and the criterion is never perfect nor perfectly measured. So the upper bound tends to be more like $\sqrt{r}/2$.

10. Misrepresenting effect size. With crooked thinking it is easy to make the use of effect sizes look ridiculous. Thus Yeaton and Sechrest (1981) note that the observed effect size of .13 between job punctuality and Type A people (who tend to be late) is quite tiny. But for a company employing 1000 people at $10 per hour, this supposedly tiny lateness translates into lost time worth about $140,000 a year. Which they suggest is not tiny at all. Therefore effect size is not a practical measure because it "fails to convey any sense of practical worth." However, they fail to mention that the total wages bill is $90 million a year, of which $140,000 represents 0.15 percent, a genuinely tiny figure compared to say annual inflation.

11. Interpreting reliability. Reliability affects the confidence we can have in a test score. Suppose there is a difference of D between the scores of two individuals on the same test. Let r be the test reliability and sd be the test standard deviation, i.e., the standard deviation of the test scores for a large sample of people. The standard deviation of D is given by $\sqrt{(2 \times (1-r))} \times sd$, provided sd does not vary with test score. From this we can calculate the standard score z = D/(standard

deviation of D) and hence the probability that D is real. Some example probabilities in percent are shown below:

Reliability	.20	.40	.60	.80	.90	.95
D/sd = 0.5	31	35	42	57	74	89
D/sd = 1.0	57	64	74	89	97	>99
D/sd = 2.0	89	93	97	>99	>99	>99

Suppose a personality test has a standard deviation of 5 points. If two individuals have scores 5 points apart, then $D/sd = 5/5$ or 1.0. If the test reliability is .80, then from the above table it is 89 percent probable that the difference is real.

12. Dollar value of an effect size. In personnel selection a number of methods have been devised to relate dollar value to effect size. From Hunter and Hunter (1984), the annual saving in dollars due to hiring people on the basis of tests, as opposed to hiring at random, is given by annual saving in dollars = Ntrsz where N=number of persons hired each year, t=average tenure in years, r=true effect size (i.e., corrected for attenuation), s=standard deviation of job performance in dollars (typically 40 to 70 percent of annual wage), and z=average standard score for the proportion of applicants who are hired. Thus if 10 percent are hired, z will be the average standard score beyond p=.10 one-sided, given by (ordinate of the normal curve at p)/p, here .176/.10 = 1.76. If 100, 50, 20, 5 percent are hired the value of z is 0, .80, 1.40, 2.08. For the U.S. federal government in 1980, N=460,000 persons, t=6.52 years, and s=.40 × $13,598. Roughly the top 10 percent of applicants are hired, so z=1.76. Entering these values into the equation shows that the saving in 1980 due to hiring via tests with an effect size r, as opposed to hiring at random, was about $28 billion. The mean effect size of U.S. government ability tests is .55, so the saving was about $15 billion, or 4 percent of the total federal budget. Cascio and Ramos (1986) present a simple method of estimating s, the most difficult component to estimate. Other approaches allow for overheads, taxes, the cost of assessment, and so on; for example, see Cronshaw and Alexander (1985) and Burke and Frederick (1986).

A related concern is productivity. Hunter et al. (1990) found that in low complexity jobs like package wrapping the top 10 percent of workers are twice as productive as the bottom 10 percent. As job complexity increases so does the difference in productivity. Thus in medium complexity jobs like claims evaluation the ratio is four times, and in high complexity jobs like law the ratio is ten times or more, always assuming that the bottom 10 percent can learn the job in the first place. Large differences will of course increase the benefits of valid selection tests.

13. Handwriting legibility. Fifty years earlier Kirk (1926) had 20 judges rate 1000 Philadelphia handwritings against standard legibility examples from the Ayres Measuring Scale for Handwriting, scaled 10 (perfectly illegible) to 90 (perfectly legible) in steps of 10. The distribution of the resulting 100 legibilities was bell-shaped and symmetrical, mean 47.1 sd 12.9. The worst writers were 20 clergymen

(mean 35.1) and 42 doctors (35.9). The best writers were 7 housekeepers (51.4) and 202 teachers (51.1). Overall 606 females (49.7) were neater than 394 males (43.0), thus supporting the sex differences noted by others. Only 186 of the 1000 (and only 3 of the 42 doctors) met the minimum standard of 60 judged acceptable for social correspondence.

14. Examples of studies impossible to assess. Lester et al. (1977) claim their results are nonsignificant but give no actual results. In their matching test Cantril and Rand (1934) use only scripts that matched in the first place. Good agreement is reported between handwriting indications and teacher ratings (Von Kügelgen 1928), therapist descriptions (Wells 1946), and personality scores (Pang and Lepponen 1968), but in each case there are no controls to establish chance agreement. Williams et al. (1977) factor-analyzed a sample of 46 scripts, which is far too small for such analysis (Comrey 1988). They also omit essential information like observed correlations and which method they used. In Wellingham-Jones (1989), reprinted in chapter 15, the graphologist knew some of the subjects, the subjects were selected by graphologists (in fact 23 percent *were* graphologists), the script content was not controlled, and scoring was not done blind. Peeples (1990) uses a sample size of 1. Oosthuizen (1991) uses 10 graphological signs of *noncognitive* personality to predict *cognitive* exam results by multiple regression, but overcomes this fatal handicap by not testing his results on a fresh sample. Such studies (many more could be cited) are impossible to assess. One wonders why anyone bothered.

15. File-drawer problem. The number of missing studies (new, unreported, or unretrieved) with null results needed to bring the retrieved studies to overall nonsignificance (p.>05) is shown by Rosenthal (1979) to be roughly 19 × number of significant studies $p \le .05$ – number of nonsignificant studies $p > .05$, Rosenthal suggests that bias is unlikely if the answer exceeds (10 + 5 × number of retrieved studies). This makes the plausible assumption that file drawers throughout the world are unlikely to have more than five times as many studies as the reviewer. For example if we retrieved 100 studies, all of them significant at $p \le .05$, we would need 19×50=950 null studies stashed in file drawers to reduce them to nonsignificance, or rather more than the plausible limit of 10+5×100=550. However, Hunter and Schmidt (1990:512) note that this approach looks at *significance* whereas the real issue is *effect size*. Therefore it is more useful to know how many missing null studies are needed to reduce the mean effect size to inutility. If we have retrieved k studies whose mean effect size is r, the number n of null studies needed to reduce r to some critical level c is given by $n = k (r/c - 1)$. For example, if our 100 studies have mean r=.40, and we adopt c=.20 as indicating inutility, then $n = 100(.40/.20-1) = 100$ null studies are needed to reach it, a much smaller number than the 950 based on significance.

But is the file-drawer problem a *real* problem? Hunter and Schmidt (1990:507) examined many hundreds of effect sizes in personnel selection, and found no difference between unpublished reports and articles published in journals. Rosenthal (1984:41–45) found much the same for many hundreds of effect sizes in 12 areas of education and psychology, although dissertations and theses (which are usually classified as unpublished) averaged 40 percent lower. Glass (1980) surveyed nine meta-analyses involving over 2000 effect sizes in education and psychology, and in every case theses were lower than journal articles, averaging 25 percent lower. For academic achievement research, theses averaged 15 percent lower (White 1982). Greenwald (1975) took the direct approach and surveyed 36 authors and 39 referees of articles submitted to the *Journal of Personality and Social Psychology* during three months in 1973. He found that, compared to researchers with negative results, those with positive results were *four times* as likely to simply give up, and were *eight times* as likely not to submit them for publication. So the better the results the more likely they are to be published. As an extreme case he cites parapsychology, which is so plagued by publication bias that "no reasonable person can regard himself as having an adequate basis for a true-false conclusion."

So, depending on the area, the file-drawer problem can indeed be a real problem. For graphology and personnel selection, the data of Neter and Ben-Shakhar (1989) show a mean effect size of .24 for 10 published studies (most with non-neutral scripts, mean N=61), significantly larger than the mean of .07 for 7 unpublished studies (all with non-neutral scripts, mean N=77). The samples are too small to be sure but they suggest that, for graphology at least, published studies do tend to have better results. This is compatible with the findings given later in Figure 3. On this basis the mean effect sizes reported later are likely to be optimistic.

16. **More on Bobertag.** Actually Bobertag (1929) gave the five scripts to six graphologists, and each of the 15 others matched the resulting 30 sketches to the subjects. Of the 450 matchings, 80.7 percent were correct. When the five writers had to pick their own sketch, three got everything right. At first sight this is a remarkable result. However, although the sketches from each graphologist were randomized, no graphologist was mixed with another. So the matchings were not independent. Furthermore the results are inflated by having *many* graphologists, *many* raters, and *few* scripts, when what is required is *many* scripts. In reality there are only 5 matchings, not 450, of which about 4 are correct—a result easily caused by atypical cues. Unfortunately Bobertag gives no details of how the subjects were selected, or how the matchings were done, so it is impossible to judge what might be happening.

17. **How meta-analysis works.** Meta-analysis can take several different forms, some of which do not consider sampling error. My procedure was the bare-bones procedure of Hunter and Schmidt (1990:107–112), which includes small improvements on Hunter et al. (1982:41–47). It begins by establishing an effect size r and sample size N for each study. It then calculates the following:

Weighted mean r	= sum of (N × r for that N) / total N
T Total variance	= sum of (N × (r – mean r)^2) / total N
S Sampling error variance	= (1 – (mean r)^2)^2 / (mean N – 1)
Vr percent variance remaining after removing sampling error	= 100 × (T–S)/T.

Ideally the effect size we want from each study is the correlation between predictor and reality, not reality as measured by imperfect criteria. But imperfect criteria (test scores, ratings, whatever) are all we have. In principle we can correct for these imperfections, in which case the subsequent calculations differ from those above, but in practice the necessary data are usually unavailable. To show how it works, corrections are described in the next four notes. Corrected effect sizes are usually described as "corrected for artifacts" or "corrected for attenuation." Many other imperfections exist such as typographical and computational errors, but they are generally (not always) minor; see Hunter and Schmidt (1990:43ff).

18. Correction for criterion reliability. The *criterion* (test scores, ratings, whatever) is the yardstick used to measure the effect size. Suppose a test correlates .50 with a criterion that happens to be measured with reliability .60. Then instead of observing r=.50 we will observe r=.50 × $\sqrt{(.60)}$, or .39. Reversing the arithmetic converts observed r=.39 into corrected r=.39/$\sqrt{(.60)}$ =.50. Examples of criterion reliabilities are given later in Table 1.

19. Correction for range restriction. Suppose an *unrestricted* sample shows effect size r. Restrict the sample by chopping subjects from one end of the range or from the middle. The observed effect size for the *restricted* sample will then be rk, where k is roughly as follows (calculated from Schmidt et al. 1976):

k for % of range lost	=10%	30%	50%	70%	90%	True r
Lost from one end	0.85	0.75	0.65	0.55	0.45	.1 to .6
Lost from middle	1.05	1.20	1.35	1.55	1.95	.1 to .3
Lost from middle	1.05	1.15	1.25	1.35	1.55	.4 to .6

Valid only if the variable is normally distributed.

Chopping from one end *reduces* r. Chopping from the middle *increases* r. For example, in the general population the effect size for predicting IQ from handwriting vs. actual IQ is around .30. Suppose we chop over 50 percent from the low end, as we do when using university students as subjects. The expected effect size is now reduced to .30 × .65 =.20, where .65 is the value of k for a loss of 50 percent from one end. Reverse the arithmetic to obtain true r = observed r/k.

20. Correction for criterion coarse grouping. A reduction in r akin to range restriction also occurs if a *continuous* criterion is chopped into a discrete N-point scale, but not if the criterion is naturally discrete, eg left-right or male-female. Here true r = observed r/g, where g is as follows (Guilford 1965:353):

N	2	3	4	5	7	11
g	.816	.859	.916	.943	.970	.988

Valid only if the variable is normally distributed.

Thus if the continuous criterion is measured on a 3-point scale, true r = observed r/.859. If in addition the criterion reliability is .60, and half the range has been chopped from one end (so k=.65), overall true r = observed r/(.859 × $\sqrt{(.60)}$ ×

.65) = 2.3 × observed r, a substantial difference. For practical purposes it is of course meaningless to apply further corrections for *predictor* reliability and coarse grouping, since no such predictor could actually exist.

21. Effect of extreme base rates. If one or both of our measures (of behavior, of handwriting) are dichotomized, then extreme base rates (e.g., the incidence of using green ink) can cause the calculated effect size to be too low, leading us to wrongly conclude that nothing important is happening (MacLennan 1988). Fortunately this is not a consideration in the studies surveyed here, but it could have been. In general if both variables are dichotomized into a 2×2 table, i.e., where phi is the measure of effect size, then if any cell = 0, or if the ratio largest/ smallest >5, the underestimation by phi may be severe. No formal corrections have been proposed, but the possibility of underestimation in a particular case can be checked by determining the maximum possible phi. If phi is positive and abcd are the cell frequencies:

1. Calculate $x = \sqrt{((c+d)/(a+b))}$ and $y = \sqrt{((b+d)/(a+c))}$.
2. If $b \geq c$, maximum possible phi is x/y.
3. If $b < c$, maximum possible phi is y/x.

If phi is negative, swap a with c, and b with d. Then proceed as above and make the answer negative. The more the answer differs from 1 the greater the underestimation. If there is underestimation then we can replace phi by a more robust measure such as Yule's colligation, given by $(k-1)/(k+1)$ where $k = \sqrt{(ab/bc)}$, see Alexander et al. (1985). Ideally we should have avoided extreme base rates by designing the experiment properly in the first place.

22. Interpretation of meta-analysis results. To help track down the variables which matter, Hunter and Schmidt (1990:68) provide this useful rule-of-thumb approach. Look at your results (calculated as in note 17) and ask: Is the sampling error variance more than 75 percent of the total variance? (Put another way, after removing the sampling error variance, is the remaining variance less than 25 percent of the total variance?) If *yes*, the variation among r's is due to sampling fluctuations (i.e., chance) and other artifacts, not to differences between studies. If *no*, there is a genuine difference between studies, in which case we can divide the studies into two groups to maximize a particular difference. If this eliminates the within-group variation (i.e., the variance of the individual groups is now less than the variance of the combined groups), then that particular difference is the culprit. However, as noted by Hunter and Schmidt (1990:449), this approach is not very sensitive, so it is better to divide the data on rational grounds in advance to see if the outcomes differ. This is the approach used here.

For a detailed and very readable discussion of meta-analysis, see Schmidt et al. (1985a), with further points in Hunter and Schmidt (1990). Another readable discussion appears in Green and Hall (1984), and in Light and Pillemer (1984), who also cover other methods of reviewing research including visual displays. For an intriguing test of meta-analysis see Schmidt et al. (1985b), who divided a large database of N=1455 into individual "studies" of N=30 and N=68. The overall r for N=1455 was .22, yet the individual rs for N=30 varied all the way from –.16 to .61, showing the enormous variation caused by small sample sizes. Meta-analysis correctly estimated the original effect size and sampling errors whereas traditional techniques failed.

23. **How each study was processed.** Ideally we want to know how reliability and effect size varies with:

1. Type of judge. Are graphologists better than psychologists?
2. Type of judgment. Is the whole script better than signs?
3. Type of script. Are content scripts better than neutral scripts?
4. Type of source material. Are originals better than photocopies?

And so on. But authors vary enormously. Some give breakdowns, some give means, others give medians. Some measure slant in degrees, others as present or absent. Some measure personality by ratings, others by tests. In general this makes it impossible to combine studies other than broadly by type of judge, type of judgment, and type of script, thus ignoring type of source material, and even then each category averages only half a dozen studies. The procedure I followed for each study was as follows:

1. Identify the particular combination of judge, judgment, and script types. Many authors look at more than one combination.
2. Take the given mean or median (reliability or effect size as the case may be), or compute a mean if several results are given.

Thus each study is represented for each combination by one reliability or one effect size, and the term *number of studies* means the number of handwriting samples, not the number of published articles. If results for three separate samples are given in the same article, they count as three studies, not one. If the same sample is judged by graphologists and again by laypersons, it counts as one study under *graphologists* and one study under *laypersons*.

No correction was made for *criterion reliability* because the required data was mostly unavailable. Occasionally there was extreme *range restriction,* usually by chopping out the middle to improve sensitivity, in which case it was corrected; see note 19. Otherwise no correction was made. In principle making a correction changes the calculation of sampling error variance as given in note 17, but the number of corrected cases were too few to make much difference.

Choice of data: Some authors report only a single effect size, so no choice is possible. Others may report effect sizes for several scales and for a single global judgment, in which case is the latter taken or the mean of the former? Generally I took the global one provided it was representative. It is here that subjective judgment becomes necessary in what should ideally be a nonsubjective procedure. Since graphologists will suspect negative bias, while debunkers will suspect positive bias, all effect sizes used in the meta-analyses are listed in the Appendices to allow independent scrutiny.

24. Reliabilities and sampling error. My meta-analysis of these reliabilities found significant differences between studies in about half of the categories. That is, of the reliabilities listed in Appendix A, half have Vr values exceeding 25 percent (Vr = percent variance remaining after removing sampling error), suggesting that genuine differences exist between studies; see note 22. But rating slant and slope is more precise than rating arcades and garlands, and 7-point scales are more precise than present-absent scales. So when such diverse techniques are lumped together, as here, it is hardly surprising that meta-analysis detects the difference.

25. Origin of categories. Neter and Ben-Shakhar (1989), in advance of meta-analysis, divided their studies into the categories shown. That is, the categories were set by them, not by their meta-analysis. To allow comparison I used the same categories. Would meta-analysis of the 35 personnel studies lumped together have produced the same categories? No, because it detected no true difference between studies, the Vr value being zero, showing that all the variance was accounted for by sampling error. This would normally suggest caution when interpreting the difference between neutral and non-neutral scripts. However, as detailed in note 31, a t-test shows that the difference is significant (p=.03). Apart from confirming the greater sensitivity of dividing studies in advance, see note 22, this means we can have some confidence that the difference is real.

Many other categories are possible. For example Rafaeli and Drory (1988) suggest looking at types of: graphologists, writers (sex, age, race, handedness, personality), jobs, context (culture, situation), and criteria. It sounds wonderful, but there are problems. (1) Testing all possible combinations would require a sample exceeding the total world population. (2) Even if graphology was thus shown to be optimum for young non-smoking gentlemen graphoanalysts, elderly left-handed neurotic Israeli ladies, middle management jobs in equal-opportunity engineering companies, and numerical scores on the Myers-Briggs Type Indicator, on past performance it is unlikely that working graphologists would take the slightest notice. (3) Such fine tuning is justified only if graphology seems likely to compare favorably with other techniques. But it does not; see Tables 1-3. (4) Nevertheless, Neter and Ben-Shakhar (1989) did meta-analyze across individual judges to see if breakdown by setting (work vs. training) and by graphologist (Israeli vs. other) had any effect. The last is of interest because the Israeli graphologists worked with scripts in Hebrew, written from right to left, whereas the other graphologists worked with scripts in English, Dutch, or German. However, the results were too ambiguous to allow a conclusion. The only breakdown with clear results was neutral vs. non-neutral scripts.

Which is not to say that looking at particular other categories may not be productive, and in later sections this is put to the test. Recently, Crowley (1991) looked at 91 female writers divided into high and low social desirability, and found that those wishing to be seen favorably by others had markedly flamboyant handwriting, i.e., large and regular like the script often used in ads to promote a prestigious product. This suggests that they had adjusted their style to project the desired image, a skill also noted by Lowenthal (1975). The correlations between handwriting and various personal qualities (personality, verbal reasoning, occu-

occupational interests, work values) were significantly different between the two groups, suggesting that those wishing to be seen favorably used flamboyance to project a good image, especially if they were also extroverted, non-anxious, and low on verbal reasoning, whereas those who were indifferent used flamboyance to signal their independence, love of freedom, and rejection of work-related values. These results suggest that image-projection may be a major source of contamination in graphology studies. If so, then graphologists can hardly use it in reverse, because the personality thus revealed by the handwriting is actually fabricated, not authentic, and therefore is precisely what graphology claims *not* to indicate. Unfortunately no other study divided writers on social desirability, so this promising lead could not be examined further.

26. Comparison with Neter and Ben-Shakhar (1989). Both our meta-analyses followed the bare bones procedure of Hunter et al. (1982), but we differed in two respects: (1) They used the median effect size from each study, whereas I used the mean effect size. (2) They did not correct for extreme range restriction. However, their results (shown below for the general evaluation dimension from their Table 3) are very close to mine (if anything my effect sizes tend to be larger), showing that the differences are of little consequence:

	Neutral scripts?	Graph	Psych	Lay
Whole script vs. work prof {	No	.153 (16)	.180 (5)	.136 (5)*
	Yes	.033 (2)		
Difference, mine – theirs {	No	.005	–.002	.037
	Yes	.053		

*Sic. But only 4 studies are listed in their Table 1.

Neter and Ben-Shakhar also meta-analyzed the effect size for each individual judge instead of averaging them as here. The mean effect sizes were slightly higher by an average of .02, and their comparison made graphology look even worse, otherwise the outcome was unchanged.

27. More on content. One detail from Experiment 4 by Jansen (1973:173–174) is of interest here. Six psychologists matched *typewritten transcripts* of nine scripts with supervisor ratings on 18 personality variables. Their mean effect size was .21, whereas another six psychologists who matched the *original scripts* averaged only .06, little different from six graphologists who averaged .09. In this case it seems that handwriting hindered more than it helped. The subjects were adults who had been selected for extreme ratings from a large parent group.

28. Examples of inflated results. Eysenck (1945) had a graphologist fill out a personality test from the handwriting of each of 50 neurotics. The result was 62 percent hits vs. 50 percent expected by chance, effect size as kappa = .23. However, Wolfson (1951:423–424) notes that the test contained many items related to neuroticism (e.g., Easily startled? Easily rattled? Mood ups and downs?), and that

these scored the most hits. This suggests that success was inflated by knowing the subjects were neurotic, especially as a repeat experiment using non-neurotics, i.e., where such cues could not apply, gave chance results (Eysenck and Gudjonsson 1986). Crumbaugh and Stockholm (1977) had an independent graphologist select most of their subjects and obtain the scripts, which immediately introduces the opportunity for selection bias (would *you* knowingly select cases that disproved *your* pet beliefs?). For Wellingham-Jones (1989) see note 14. Further sobering examples of inflation due to faulty procedures are given by Secord (1949) and Nevo (1986:203–215).

29. Effect sizes and sampling errors. Meta-analysis of the 72 studies lumped together showed that the Vr value was zero, showing that all the variance was accounted for by sampling error. As detailed in note 31, a t-test between neutral and non-neutral scripts was only marginally significant (p=.09), whereas it was significant (p=.03) for the personnel results. This reduced sensitivity is explained by the smaller sample sizes, which averaged N=48 vs. N=77 for personnel tests. In other words they were almost too small to detect any difference.

30. Significance of one result among many. Perform 1000 tests on random data and count the number of results that are significant at the .05 level. Even though the data are random, we can expect on average to obtain .05 × 1000 = 50 such results purely by chance. Only if we get significantly more than 50 such results can we claim that something special is happening. As a guide, if you make N tests then your best result will not be genuinely significant unless it is significant at the p=.05/N level. See Wilkinson (1951). In recent years this approach (and variations thereof) has become known as the Bonferroni method.

31. Differences between effect sizes. By t-test the two-sided significance of the differences between the means are as follows. For this test we use the observed standard deviations (sd), i.e., uncorrected for sampling error:

Personnel vs. personality: no significant difference.

Neutral scripts?				
	No	.165 sd.119 (26) vs. .135 sd.098 (23)	t=0.96	p=.34
	Yes	.073 sd.046 (9) vs. .068 sd.149 (18)	t=0.10	p=.92

Neutral vs. non-neutral scripts: significant difference.

Personnel	.073 sd.046 (9) vs. .165 sd.119 (26)	t=2.24	p=.03
Psychology	.068 sd.149 (18) vs. .135 sd.098 (23)	t=1.73	p=.09

Signs vs. matching tests: no significant difference.

	.082 sd.075 (11) vs. .146 sd.141 (13)	t=1.35	p=.19

32. Rorschach reliability. But all may not be lost. Weiner (1991), editor of the *Journal of Personality Assessment* (originally the *Rorschach Research Exchange and the Journal of Projective Techniques*), noted that clear criteria can produce reasonable agreement on Rorschach scores. Therefore "Reports of Rorschach research that . . . indicate less than 80% agreement . . . will be returned for further

work before being accepted for publication." The corresponding correlation is .60–.80, depending on the agreement expected by chance, somewhat less than the .84 reported in Table 1.

33. Reliability of rankings. Kane and Lawler (1978) reviewed the literature on peer evaluation and found only two studies that examined the reliability of rankings by the same judge (mean .92), and none for the reliability between judges. Nathan and Alexander (1988) surveyed the validity of ratings, rankings, and other criteria from hundreds of studies of clerical occupations. They give no reliabilities, but their results indicate that the mean reliability of rankings is nearly twice the mean reliability of ratings (.48 in Table 1), i.e., about .80 to .90.

34. Inter-rater reliability. Ratings of personality are about the same. Many things affect inter-rater reliability, for example halo effects (bias due to liking or attractiveness), how visible the characteristic is, how well each rating point is described, and especially length of acquaintance. Rothstein (1990) analyzed performance ratings for 9975 supervisors and found that reliability rose rapidly during the first six months of acquaintance. It was effectively constant after one year, although small increases occurred even after five years, the asymptotic limit being .60. The mean for all ratings was .52, in good agreement with the Table 1 figure of .48. After surveying many hundreds of occupational studies, Ghiselli (1966) suggested that reliabilities were typically .70 to .80, which a few years later he amended to .60 to .80 (Ghiselli 1973). Currently .60 is commonly used when actual reliabilities are unavailable (Schmidt et al. 1985a).

The reliability of ratings can be increased by having teams of raters. If r is the reliability between individual raters, the reliability between teams of n raters is $nr/(1+(n-1)r)$, which is known as the Spearman-Brown formula. Thus an r of .45 increases to .62 for n=2 and to .80 for n=5. Useful practical hints about the use of ratings are given by Cronbach (1970:571ff).

35. Prediction of success in a training course. The effect size for cognitive tests vs. success in training (.70 corrected for attenuation) is larger than vs. work performance (.50 corrected). This is because training puts more emphasis on cognitive skills such as learning and remembering, which are of course directly tapped by the cognitive test. Indeed, when Ree and Earles (1991) looked at the training success of 78,041 U.S. Air Force enlistees in 82 jobs, they found that nine specific ability tests such as arithmetic reasoning and mechanical comprehension added little to the prediction affored by cognitive ability alone. Such findings further weaken the case for graphology.

36. Work performance and personality tests. Personality tests are generally poor predictors of work performance, see Guion and Gottier (1965). But they can be good predictors of other work-related qualities. For example McHenry et al. (1990) found that cognitive ability tests were best at predicting general work performance for 4039 enlisted soldiers (r=.47 vs. .15 for personality tests, or .65 vs. .25 corrected for attenuation), while personality tests were best at predicting responsibility, perseverance, and capacity for hard work (r=.31 vs. .11 for cognitive ability tests, or .32 vs. .16 corrected). Similarly, Barrick and Mount (1991) found that conscientiousness is a consistently valid predictor regardless of occupation.

37. Correction of effect sizes in Table 2. Typically only 10 percent of studies report criterion reliability and range restriction. So meta-analysts correct for these artifacts by assuming the delinquent 90 percent are no different, which may or may not be the case. This means that the corrected effect sizes in Table 2 are somewhat uncertain, especially when N (number of studies) is small.

38. Other methods are better. Whether predicting aptitude or personality, the best pencil-and-paper tests are invariably more accurate, quicker and cheaper than graphology, which in the U.S.A. costs $35–$300 per assessment (cost is from Taylor and Sackheim 1988:74), or in the U.K. around £200 for a Graphoanalysis covering personality, thinking patterns, imagination, goals, fears, defenses, integrity, social traits, and aptitudes (Warner 1991). For example, in his review of several dozen graphological studies of IQ, Michel (1969:52) notes that IQ "is traced more economically and with higher validity by other techniques, since evaluation of intelligence on the basis of graphology hardly seems to be of any usefulness." And Eysenck (1948) notes that the emotionality judgments for 176 subjects by Mrs. F, a famous long-established European graphologist, bore no relation to psychiatric diagnoses (r=.02), whereas individual objective tests showed good agreement up to .57, and a battery of 17 tests showed .73. These objective tests are now largely obsolete, but they included things like measuring dark vision, persistence (write S's and reversed S's as fast as you can for two minutes), and body sway when blindfolded, all of which correlate with emotionality. He comments "When it is further remembered that these objective tests are of short duration (2 to 5 minutes each), and that they can be combined and multiplied at will [to improve accuracy], while the graphological analysis is extremely time-consuming, the relative superiority of the tests as opposed to the analysis will perhaps become apparent." And that was in 1948, when such tests were inferior to the pencil-and-paper tests available today.

Recent developments in testing methods promise to widen the gap still further. For a readable review see Murphy (1988). For example, computerized tests can measure abilities difficult to measure by pencil-and-paper tests, such as basic information processing and spatial visualization. Other computerized tests can generate narrative reports (Butcher et al. 1985), although unsurprisingly they are not universally popular among clinicians (Matarazzo 1986). Computers can also generate psychodiagnoses from interview questions administered by laypersons without any clinical experience, thus greatly reducing costs (Robins et al. 1981). Finally the computerized development known as Item Response Theory is having a major impact in the laboratory if not yet in the workplace. Classical test theory is based on test scores, that is, on the overall response to a number of individual items. From the scores comes the model of personality. By contrast IRT is based on *providing* responses to individual test items, and takes into account random disturbances. From the model of personality comes the individual item responses. In effect IRT allows tests to be separated from people, thus delivering personality freed from the quirks of a particular test (Hambleton and van der Linden 1982).

39. No, we cannot predict sex. For example, Olyanova (1960:15) says "The *sex*—whether male or female—is not revealed in handwriting. Neither is the *age* of the writer." Paterson (1976:90) says "'No graphologist or handwriting expert

can tell the age or sex of a writer." Roman (1952:5) says "Neither the chronological age nor the sex of a writer can be ascertained from his [sic] script." Bar-Hillel and Ben-Shakhar (1986:274) make the pointed comment that, because even lay persons can diagnose a writer's sex with some accuracy, "It would therefore seem reasonable to expect graphologists to be willing—and able—to predict a writer's sex from handwriting. That they refuse to do so reflects, under a charitable interpretation, their preference for predicting deep-lying unobservables to their observable correlates and perhaps even a disavowal of the relevance of behavioral criteria to the evaluation of their assessments."

40. Physiognomy in Table 3. Body build correlates around .10 with IQ (Rees 1960:375–376) and .20 to .30 with extroversion and emotionality (Eysenck 1970:346), so that unstable introverts tend slightly to be tall and narrow while stable extroverts tend slightly to be short and wide. Correction for attenuation increases the latter effect size to around .30 to .50, or large enough to be visible, which may explain the old English saying "Fat and merry, lean and sad." But then so does starvation. Conversely, the correlation of .10 between body build and IQ is not large enough to be visible, so it is unremarkable that the old Italian proverb "Fat heads, lean brains" is in the wrong direction. Secord et al. (1954) found that, as expected, people showed good agreement when judging purely physical features such as *light-dark complexion* or *height of eyebrows*. Interestingly, they showed equally good agreement when judging inferred traits (i.e., stereotypes) such as *honest face* or *intelligent look*. As a result the correlation between physical appearance and the inferred traits reached a dramatic .60 or more, thus confirming the power of stereotypes. But as shown by the physiognomy effect size of .15 in Table 3, these powerful stereotypes are powerfully inaccurate. For a review of the prominent role of appearance in forming stereotypes, and of recent trends toward an ecological theory of physiognomy (childlike faces are perceived to have childlike qualities such as warmth, honesty and submissiveness), see Berry and McArthur (1986).

41. Help wanted. If you know of any study that has been missed, please send details to the editors, if possible enclosing a photocopy of the original study, for which postage and photocopying expenses will be reimbursed. If the study is a lengthy one, just the title page and results pages will do, in which case make sure they include the details indicated by the headings in the relevant Appendix. The study will then be included in an updated meta-analysis in the second edition of this book, and your help will be acknowledged. Write to: Dr. Barry L. Beyerstein, Department of Psychology, Simon Fraser University, Burnaby BC, Canada V5A 1S6. Fax 604-291-3427.

REFERENCES

Alexander, R. A., G. M. Alliger, K. P. Carson, and G. V., Barrett. 1985. "The Empirical Performance of Measures of Association in the 2×2 Table." *Educational and Psychological Measurement* 45: pp. 79–87.

Allport, G. W., and P. E. Vernon. 1933. *Studies in Expressive Movement.* New York: Macmillan. Graphology is reviewed on pages 185–211, with 59 references, plus another 142 unrelated to graphology.

Anderson, L. D. 1921. "Estimating Intelligence by Means of Printed Photographs." *Journal of Applied Psychology* 5: pp. 152–155.

Bar-El, N. 1984. "Interrelations among Graphological Judgments, Psychological Assessments and Self-Ratings of Personality." MA thesis, Tel Aviv University. Cited by Nevo (1986a).

Barnes, G. E. 1984. "A Brief Note on Two Often Ignored Principles That Tend to Attenuate the Magnitude of Correlations." *Personality and Individual Differences* 5: pp. 361–363.

Barrick, M. R., and M. K. Mount. 1991. "The Big Five Personality Dimensions and Job Performance: A Meta-Analysis." *Personnel Psychology* 44: pp. 1–26.

Bayne, R., and F., O'Neill. 1988. "Handwriting and Personality: A Test of Some Expert Graphologists' Judgements." *Guidance and Assessment Review* 4(4): pp. 1–3. Additional data kindly supplied by Dr. Rowan Bayne.

Bell, J. E. 1948. "The Analysis of Handwriting." Chapter 14 in *Projective Techniques: A Dynamic Approach to the Study of the Personality.* New York: Longmans, Green, pp. 291–327. 137 references.

Ben-Shakhar, G., M. Bar-Hillel, Y. Bilu, E. Ben-Abba, and A. Flug. 1986. "Can Graphology Predict Occupational Success? Two Empirical Studies and Some Methodological Ruminations." *Journal of Applied Psychology* 71: pp. 645–653. The same study but with additional reliability coefficients appears in G. Ben-Shakhar, M. Bar-Hillel, and A. Flug. "A Validation Study of Graphological Evaluation in Personnel Selection." In Nevo (1986: pp. 175–191).

Berry, D. S., and L. Z. McArthur. 1986. "Perceiving Character in Faces: The Impact of Age-related Craniofacial Changes on Social Perception." *Psychological Bulletin* 100: pp. 3–18.

Binet, A. 1906. *Les révélations de l'écriture d'après un contrôle scientifique.* Paris: Alcan. Cited by Downey (1910).

Birge, W. R. 1954. "An Experimental Inquiry into the Measurable Handwriting Correlates of Five Personality Traits." *Journal of Personality* 23: pp. 215–223.

Bobertag, O. 1929. *Ist die Graphologie zuverlässig?* Heidelberg: Kampmann. Cited by Allport and Vernon (1933:201).

Borenstein, Y. 1985. "The Utility of Graphological Assessment As a Selection Tool in the Israeli Defence Forces." MA thesis, University of Haifa. Cited by Keinan (1986) and by Neter and Ben-Shakhar (1989).

Bradley, N. 1988. "99 Studies in Handwriting and Related Topics." Published by the author, 91 Hawksley Avenue, Chesterfield, Derbyshire S40 4TJ, England.

———. 1989. "100 Studies in Handwriting and Related Topics." Published by the author, see above. In preparation is a further volume "101 Studies in Handwriting and Related Topics."

Brandstatter, H. 1969. "On Diagnosing Integration of Personality from Handwriting." *Psychologische Rundschau* 21: pp. 159–172. Cited by Nevo (1986:257).

Brengelmann, J. C. 1960. "Expressive Movements and Abnormal Behavior." In *Handbook of Abnormal Psychology,* edited by H. J. Eysenck. London: Pitman, pp. 62–107. Graphology is reviewed on pages 82–85.

Briggs, D. 1970. "The Influence of Handwriting on Assessment." *Educational Research* 13: pp. 50–55.

Broom, M. E., B. Thompson, and M. T. Bouton. 1929. "Sex Differences in Handwriting." *Journal of Applied Psychology* 13: pp. 159–166.

Brown, L. E. 1921. "An Experimental Investigation of the Alleged Relations between Certain Character Traits and Handwriting." AB thesis, University of Wisconsin. Cited by Hull (1928: pp.. 149–151).

Burke, M. J., and J. T. Frederick. 1986. "A Comparison of Economic Utility Estimates for Alternative SD Estimation Procedures." *Journal of Applied Psychology* 71: pp. 334–339.

Burnup, R. H. 1974. "Handwriting Characteristics as Predictors of Personality Patterns." Thesis, University of Missouri, Kansas City. Cited by Stabholz (1981: p. 59).

Butcher, J. N., L. S. Keller, and S. F. Bacon. 1985. "Current Development and Future Directions in Computerized Personality Assessment." *Journal of Consulting and Clinical Psychology* 53: pp. 803–815.

Cantril, H., H. A. Rand, and G. W. Allport. 1933. "The Determination of Personal Interests by Psychological and Graphological Methods." *Character and Personality* 2: pp. 134–143.

Cantril, H., and H. A. Rand. 1934. "An Additional Study of the Determination of Personal Interests by Psychological and Graphological Methods." *Character and Personality* 3: pp. 72–78.

Cascio, W. F., and R. A. Ramos. 1986. "Development and Application of a New Method for Assessing Job Peformance in Behavioural/Economic Terms." *Journal of Applied Psychology* 71: pp. 20–28.

Castelnuovo-Tedesco, P. 1948. "A Study of the Relationship Between Handwriting and Personality Variables." *Genetic Psychology Monographs* 37: pp. 167–220.

Cleeton, G. U., and F. B. Knight. 1924. "Validity of Character Judgments Based on External Criteria." *Journal of Applied Psychology* 8: pp. 215–231.

Cohen, J. 1960. "A Coefficient of Agreement for Nominal Scales."*Educational and Psychological Measurement* 20: pp. 37–46.

———. 1968. "Weighted kappa: Nominal Scale Agreement with Provision for Scaled Disagreement or Partial Credit." *Psychological Bulletin* 70: pp. 213–220.

Comrey, A. L. 1988. "Methodological Contributions to Clinical Research." *Journal of Consulting and Clinical Psychology* 56: pp. 754–761.

Cox, J., and J. Tapsell. 1991. "Graphology and Its Validity in Personnel Assessment." Paper presented at the BPS Occupational Psychology Conference, Cardiff, January 1991.

Crider, B. 1941. "The Reliability and Validity of Two Graphologists." *Journal of Applied Psychology* 25: pp. 323–325.

Cronbach, L. 1970. *Essentials of Psychological Testing,* 3rd ed. New York: Harper and Row.

Cronshaw, S. F., and R. A. Alexander. 1985. "One Answer to the Demand for Accountability: Selection Utility as an Investment Decision." *Organizational Behaviour and Human Decision Processes* 35: pp. 102–118.

Crowley, T. 1991. "The Influence of Social Desirability on the Relationships Between Handwriting and Personal Qualities." *Personality and Individual Differences* 12: pp. 881–885.

Crumbaugh, J. C. 1986. "Graphoanalytic Cues." In Nevo (1986: pp. 47–58).

Crumbaugh, J. C., and E. Stockholm. 1977. "Validation of Graphoanalysis by Global or Holistic Method." *Perceptual and Motor Skills* 44: pp. 403–410.

Dean, G. 1985. "Can Astrology Predict E and N? 2. The Whole Chart." *Correlation* 5(2): pp. 2–24. Palmistry test is on page 20. A total of 14 palmists made 1–2 yes/no judgments of personality on each of 13 color slides showing the hands of extreme personalities.

————. 1986. "Can Astrology Predict E and N? 3. Discussion and Further Research." *Correlation* 6(2): pp. 7–52. A detailed survey of the evidence, including a comparison with palmistry, graphology and orthodox methods. 110 references, most of them annotated.

De Groot, A. D. 1947. "Een experimenteel-statistische toetsing van karakterologische (grafologische) rapporten." *Nederlands Tijdschrift van Psychologie* 2: pp. 380–473. Cited by Jansen (1973:3).

Donner, A. 1984. "Approaches to Sample Size Estimation in the Design of Clinical Trials—A Review." *Statistics in Medicine* 3: pp. 199–214.

Downey, J. E. 1910. "Judgments on the Sex of Handwriting." *Psychological Reviews* 17: pp. 205–216.

————. 1919. "Character and Handwriting." *Psychological Bulletin* 16: pp. 28–31.

Drory, A. 1986. "Graphology and Job Performance: A Validation Study." In Nevo (1986: pp. 165–173).

Dzida, W., and F. Kiener. 1978. "Strategien der Verwertung nonverbaler Informationen zur Persönlichkeitsbeurteilung." *Zeitschrift für experimentelle und angewandte Psychologie* 25: pp. 552–563.

Edgell, S. E., and S. M. Noon. 1984. "Effect of Violation of Normality on the *t* Test of the Correlation Coefficient." *Psychological Bulletin* 95: pp. 576–583.

Edwards, A. L. 1967. "The Social Desirability Variable: A Review of the Evidence." In *Response Set in Personality Assessment,* edited by I. A. Berg. Chicago: Aldine, pp. 48–70.

Eisenberg, P. 1938. "Judging Expressive Movement: I. Judgments of Sex and Dominance-Feeling from Handwriting Samples of Dominant and Non-dominant Men and Women." *Journal of Applied Psychology* 22: pp. 480–486.

Esroni, G., A. Rolnik, and E. Livnat. 1985. "Studies Evaluating the Validity of Graphology in a Voluntary Military Unit." A paper presented at the 20th Israeli Psychological Association Conference. Cited by Neter and Ben-Shakhar (1989).

Estes, S. G. 1938. "Judging Personality from Expressive Behavior." *Journal of Abnormal and Social Psychology* 33: pp. 217–236.

Eysenck, H. J. 1945. "Graphological Analysis and Psychiatry: An Experimental Study." *British Journal of Psychiatry* 35: pp. 70–81.

———. 1948. "Neuroticism and Handwriting." *Journal of Abnormal and Social Psychology* 43: pp. 94–96.

———. 1960. *Handbook of Abnormal Psychology: An Experimental Approach.* London: Pitman.

———. 1970. *The Structure of Human Personality.* 3rd edition. London: Methuen.

Eysenck, H. J., and S. B. G. Eysenck. 1964. *Manual of the Eysenck Personality Inventory.* London: University of London Press.

Eysenck, H.J., and G. Gudjonsson. 1986. "An Empirical Study of the Validity of Handwriting Analysis." *Personality and Individual Differences* 7: pp. 263–264.

Feingold, A. 1988. "Matching for Attractivness in Romantic Partners and Same-Sex Friends: A Meta-Analysis and Theoretical Critique." *Psychological Bulletin* 104: pp. 226–235.

Feldt, L. 1962. "The Reliability of Measures of Handwriting Quality." *Journal of Educational Psychology* 53: pp. 288–292. Concerned with, e.g., clarity of form and size in the handwriting of elementary school children. Of little relevance to graphology.

Fischer, G. 1962. "Die faktorielle Struktur der Handschrift." Doctoral dissertation, Vienna University. Cited by Nevo (1986:255).

———. 1964. "Zur faktorielle Struktur der Handschrift. *Zeitschrift für experimentelle und angewandte Psychologie* 11: pp. 254–280. Cited by Nevo (1986:255).

Fluckiger, F. A., C. A. Tripp, and G. H. Weinberg. 1961. "A Review of Experimental Research in Graphology 1933–1960." *Perceptual and Motor Skills* 12: pp. 67–90, 105 references.

Flug, A. 1981. "Reliability and Validity of Graphology in Personnel Selection." MA thesis, Hebrew University of Jerusalem. Cited by Nevo (1986:258).

Forer, B. R. 1949. "The Fallacy of Personal Validation: A Classroom Demonstration of Gullibility." *Journal of Abnormal and Social Psychology* 44: pp. 118–123. The Barnum statements used in Box 2 are those numbered 11, 4, 6, 7, and 1+13.

Frank, G. 1983. *The Wechsler Enterprise: An Assessment of the Development, Structure, and Use of the Wechsler Tests of Intelligence.* Oxford: Pergamon.

Frederick, C. J. 1965. "Some Phenomena Affecting Handwriting Analysis." *Perceptual and Motor Skills* 20: pp. 211–218.

Furnham, A., and B. Gunter. 1987. "Graphology and Personality: Another Failure to Validate Graphological Analysis." *Personality and Individual Differences* 8: 433–435. Additional details including resolution of conflict between table and text were kindly supplied by Dr. Adrian Furnham.

Galbraith, D., and D. Wilson. 1964. "Reliability of the Graphoanalytic Approach to Handwriting Analysis." *Perceptual and Motor Skills* 19: pp. 615–618.

Garb, H. N. 1989. "Clinical Judgment, Clinical Training, and Professional Experience." *Psychological Bulletin* 105: pp. 387–396.

Gesell, A. L. 1906. "Accuracy in Handwriting, as Related to School Intelligence and Sex." *American Journal of Psychology* 17: pp. 394–405.

Ghiselli, E. E. 1966. *The Validity of Occupational Aptitude Test.* New York: Wiley. Important comments on this and the next reference appear in Pearlman et al. (1980).

————, 1973. "The Validity of Aptitude Tests in Personnel Selection." *Personnel Psychology* 26: pp. 461–477.

Goldberg, L. R. 1986. "Some Informal Explorations and Ruminations About Graphology." In Nevo (1986: pp. 281–293).

Goldsmith, H. 1976. "The Facts on the Legibility of Doctors' Handwriting." *Medical Journal of Australia* [no vol. nos.], part 2: pp. 462–463.

Goodenough, F. L. 1945. "Sex Differences in Judging the Sex of Handwriting." *Journal of Social Psychology* 22: pp. 61–68.

Green, P. E., V. R. Rao, and D. E. Armani. 1971. "Graphology and Marketing Research: A Pilot Experiment in Validity and Inter-judge Reliability." *Journal of Marketing* 35: pp. 58–62.

Greene, B. F., and J. A. Hall. 1984. "Quantitative Methods for Literature Reviews." *Annual Review of Psychology* 35: pp. 37–53.

Greene, J., and D. Lewis. 1980. *The Hidden Language of Your Handwriting.* London: Souvenir Press, p. 252.

Greenwald, A. G. 1975. "Consequences of Prejudice against the Null Hypothesis." *Psychological Bulletin* 82: pp. 1–20.

Guilford, J. P. 1965. *Fundamental Statistics in Psychology and Education,* 4th ed. New York: McGraw-Hill.

Guion, R. M., and R. F. Gottier. 1965. "Validity of Personality Measures in Personnel Selection." *Personnel Psychology* 18: pp. 135–164.

Hackett, R. D. 1989. "Work Attitudes and Employee Absenteeism: A Synthesis of the Literature." *Journal of Occupational Psychology* 62: pp. 235–248.

Halevi, H. 1964. "Studying Graphology via Matching Technique." MA thesis, Hebrew University of Jerusalem. Summarized in Nevo (1986: p. 244).

Helevi, H. 1965. "An Alternative Approach to the Method of Correct Matching." *Psychometrika* 30: pp. 67–90.

Hambleton, R. K., and Q. J. van der Linden. 1982. "Advances in Item Response Theory and Applications: An Introduction." *Applied Psychological Measurement* 6: pp. 373–378.

Harris, M. M., and J. Schaubroeck. 1988. "A Meta-Aanalysis of Self-Supervisor, Self-Peer, and Peer-Supervisor Ratings." *Personnel Psychology* 41: pp. 43–62.

Harvey, O. L. 1933. "The Measurement of Handwriting Considered as a Form of Expressive Movement." *Character and Personality* 2: pp. 310–321.

Helmstadter, G. C. 1966. *Principles of Psychological Measurement.* London: Methuen, p. 85. The values cited are those obtained by Helmstadter in the early 1960s "by simply recording reported reliabilities for well known tests in each of several areas."

Hertz, M. R. 1986. "Rorschachbound: A 50-Year Memoir." *Journal of Personality Assessment* 50: pp. 396–416.

Hines, T. 1988. "Pseudoscience and the Paranormal: A Critical Examination of the Evidence." Buffalo, N.Y.: Prometheus Books.

Hirsch, R. H. 1987. "Review of Nevo (1986)." *Personnel Psychology*, 40: pp. 838–842.

Hoepfner, R. 1962. "An Empirical Study of the Contents of Handwriting." Thesis, University of Southern California. Cited by Stabholz (1981: p. 53).

Hofsommer, W., R. Holdsworth, and T. Seifert. 1962. "Zur Bewahrungskontrolle Graphologischer Diagnosen." *Psychologische Beitrage* 7: pp. 397–401. Cited by Neter and Ben-Shakhar (1989).

Hofsommer, W., and R. Holdsworth, 1963. "Die Validität der Handschriftenanalyse bei der Auswahl von Piloten." *Psychologie und Praxis* 7: pp. 175–178. Cited by Neter and Ben-Shakhar (1989).

Holder, R. 1976. *You Can Analyze Handwriting*. North Hollywood: Wilshire.

Hönel, H. 1977. "Grundrhythmus und Kriminelle disposition in der Handschrift." *Zeitschrift für Menschenkunde* 41: pp. 1–55. Re-analyzed by Nevo (1986: pp. 203–215).

Howes, R. J. 1981. "The Rorschach: Does It Have a Future?" *Journal of Personality Assessment* 45: pp. 339–351. The answer was yes.

Hull, C. L. 1928. *Aptitude Testing*. London: Harrap.

Hull, C. L., and R. B. Montgomery. 1919. "An Experimental Investigation of Certain Alleged Relations between Character and Handwriting." *Psychological Reviews* 26: pp. 63–74.

Hunter, J. E., and R. F. Hunter. 1984. "Validity and Utility of Alternative Predictors of Job Performance." *Psychological Bulletin* 96: pp. 72–98.

Hunter, J. F., and F. L. Schmidt. 1990. *Methods of Meta-Analysis: Correcting Error and Bias in Research Findings*. Newbury Park, Calif.: Sage. An updated and enlarged version of next reference.

Hunter, J. E., F. L. Schmidt, and G. B. Jackson. 1982. *Meta-Analysis: Cumulating Research Findings Across Studies*. Beverly Hills, Calif.: Sage.

Hunter, J. E., F. L. Schmidt, and M. K. Judiesch. 1990. "Individual Differences in Output Variability as a Function of Job Complexity." *Journal of Applied Psychology* 75: pp. 28–42.

Jansen, A. 1973. *Validation of Graphological Judgments: An Experimental Study*. Paris and The Hague: Mouton.

Jensen, A. R. 1959. "The Reliability of Projective Techniques: Review of the Literature." *Acta Psychologica* 16: pp. 108–136.

———. 1964. "The Rorschach Technique: A Re-evaluation." *Acta Psychologica* 22: pp. 60–77. Repeats much of the data in the previous reference but includes validity and an update.

———. 1981. *Straight Talk about Mental Tests*. London: Methuen, pp. 19–34.

Kane, J. S., and E. E. Lawler. 1978. "Methods of Peer Assessment." *Psychological Bulletin* 85: pp. 555–586.

Karnes, E. W., and S. D. Leonard. 1991. "Graphoanalytic and Psychometric Personality Profiles: Validity and Barnum Effects." Chapter 16 in this book.

Keinan, G., A. Barak, and T. Ramati. 1984. "Reliability and Validity of Graphological

Assessment in the Selection Process of Military Officers." *Perceptual and Motor Skills* 58: pp. 811–821.,

Keinan, G. 1986. "Graphoanalysis for Military Personnel Selection." In Nevo (1986: pp. 193–201).

Kelly, I. W., G. A. Dean, and D. H. Saklofske. 1990. "Astrology: A Critical Review." In *Philosophy of Science and the Occult,* edited by P. Grim. 2nd ed. Albany, N.Y.: State University of New York, pp. 51–81. 80 references. Page 55 updates the survey by Dean (1986).

Kimball, T. D. 1973. "The Systematic Isolation and Validation of Personality Determiners in the Handwriting of School Children." Thesis, University of Southern California. Cited by Stabholz (1981: pp. 58–59). Summarized in *Dissertation Abstracts International* 34: pp. 6450–6451.

Kimmel, D., and M. Wertheimer. 1966. "Personality Ratings Based on Handwriting Analysis and Clinical Judgment: A Correlational Study." *Journal of Projective Techniques* 30: pp. 177–178.

Kinder, J. S. 1926. "A New Investigation of Judgments on the Sex of Handwriting." *Journal of Educational Psychology* 17: pp. 341–344.

Kirchner, J. H., and E. A. Lemke. 1973. "I-dots in the Handwriting of a Clinical Sample." *Perceptual and Motor Skills* 36: pp. 548–550.

Kirk, J. G. 1926. "Handwriting Survey to Determine Grade Standards." *Journal of Educational Research* 13: pp. 181–188 and 259–272.

Klare, G. R. 1974. "Assessing Readability." *Reading Research Quarterly* 10: pp. 62–102.

Klimoski, R. J., and A. Rafaeli. 1983. "Inferring Personal Qualities through Handwriting Analysis." *Journal of Occupational Psychology* 56: pp. 191–202. 45 references.

Kurdsen, S. 1971. *Graphology The New Science.* New York: Galahad.

Landis, C., and L. W. Phelps. 1928. "The Prediction from Photographs of Success and of Vocational Aptitude." *Journal of Experimental Psychology* 11: pp. 313–324.

Lemke, E. A., and J. H. Kirchner. 1971. "A Multivariate Study of Handwriting, Intelligence, and Personality Correlates." *Journal of Personality Assessment* 35: pp. 584–592.

Lent, R. H., H. A. Aurbach, and L. S. Levin. 1971. "Predictors, Criteria, and Significant Results." *Personnel Psychology* 24: pp. 519–533.

Lester, D., S. McLaughlin, and G. Nosal. 1977. "Graphological Signs for Extraversion." *Perceptual and Motor Skills* 44: pp. 137–138.

Lester, D. 1981. *The Psychological Basis of Handwriting Analysis: The Relationship of Handwriting to Personality and Psychopathology.* Chicago: Nelson-Hall. 240 references of which 40 are nongraphological. Very readable but summaries of published articles often lack detail and are sometimes inaccurate.

Light, R. J., and D. B. Pillemer. 1984. *Summing Up: The Science of Reviewing Research.* Cambridge, Mass.: Harvard University Press.

Linn, R. L., D. L. Harnisch, and S. B. Dunbar. 1981. "Validity Generalization and Situational Specificity: An Analysis of the Prediction of First-Year Grades in Law School." *Applied Psychological Measurement* 5: pp. 281–289.

LoMonaco, T., and R. Harrison. 1973. "Accuracy of Matching TAT and Graphological Personality Profiles." *Perceptual and Motor Skills* 36: pp. 703–706.

Lockowandt, O. 1976. "Present Status of the Investigation of Handwriting Psychology as a Diagnostic Method." *JSAS Catalog of Selected Documents in Psychology* 6(1): p. 4. Reprinted with minor editing in chapter 5 of this book.

Lowenthal, K. 1975. "Handwriting and Self-presentation." *Journal of Social Psychology* 96: pp. 267–270.

———. 1982. "Handwriting as a Guide to Character." In *Judging People: A Guide to Orthodox and Unorthodox Methods of Assessment,* edited by D. M. Davey and M. Harris. London: McGraw-Hill, pp. 83–96.

Lorr, M., L. T. Lepine, and J. V. Golder. 1953. "A Factor Analysis of Some Handwriting Characteristics." *Journal of Personality* 22: pp. 348–353.

Lowengard, M. 1975. *How to Analyze Your Handwriting.* London: Marshall Cavendish.

Mabe, P. A., and S. G. West. 1982. "Validity of Self-Evaluation of Ability: A Review and Meta-Analysis." *Journal of Applied Psychology* 67: pp. 280–296.

MacLennan, R. N., 1988. "Correlation, Base-Rates, and the Predictability of Behavior." *Personality and Individual Differences* 9: pp. 675–684.

Mann, W. 1961. "A Continuation of the Search for Objective Graphological Hypotheses." Thesis, University of Ottawa. Cited by Stabholz (1981: p. 53).

Marne, P. 1988. *The Concise Graphology Notebook.* Slough: Foulsham.

Mason, D. J. 1957. "Judgments of Leadership Based upon Physiognomic Cues." *Journal of Abnormal and Social Psychology* 54: pp. 273–274.

Matarazzo, J. D. 1986. "Computerized Clinical Psychological Test Interpretations: Unvalidated Plus All Mean and No Sigma." *American Psychologist* 41: p. 96. With subsequent debate in 42: pp. 192–193.

McCartney, K. M., M. J. Harris, and Bernieri. 1990. "Growing Up and Growing Apart: A Developmental Meta-Analysis of Twin Studies." *Psychological Bulletin* 107: pp. 226–237.

McHenry, J. J., L. M. Hough, J. L. Toquam, M. A. Hanson, and S. Ashworth. 1990. "Project A Validity Results: The Relationship Between Predictor and Criterion Domains." *Personnel Psychology* 43: pp. 335–354.

McKelvie, S. J. 1990. "Student Acceptance of a Generalized Personality Description: Forer's Graphologist Revisited." *Journal of Social Behavior and Personality* 5: pp. 91–95.

McNeil, E. B., and G. S. Blum. 1952. "Handwriting and Psychosexual Dimensions of Personality." *Journal of Projective Techniques* 16: pp. 476–484.

Meehl, P. E. 1972. "Reactions, Reflections, Projections." In *Objective Personality Assessment: Changing Perspectives,* edited by J. N. Butcher. New York: Academic Press, pp. 131–189. For the technical problems of blood pressure measurement see O'Brien and O'Malley (1979).

Meloun, J. 1935. "Does Drawing Skill Show in Handwriting?" *Character and Personality* 33: pp. 194–213.

Michel, L. 1969. "Empirische Untersuchungen zur Frage der Übereinstimmung und

Gültigkeit von Beurteilungen des intellektuellen Niveaus aus der Handschrift." *Archiv für die gesamte Psychologie* 121: pp. 31-54. For a shorter updated version in English, but without physiognomy results, see L. Michel, "Intellectual Abilities and Handwriting," in Nevo (1986: pp. 217-229).

Middleton, W. C. 1941a. "The Ability of Untrained Subjects to Judge Neuroticism, Self-Confidence, and Sociability from Handwriting Samples." *Character and Personality* 9: pp. 227-234.

———. 1941b. "The Ability of Untrained Subjects to Judge Intelligence and Age from Handwriting Samples." *Journal of Applied Psychology* 25: pp. 331-340.

Miller, J. H. 1982. *Bibliography of Handwriting Analysis: A Graphological Index.* Troy, N.Y.: Whitson, 432 pages. An annotated list of 2,321 references, not 100 percent comprehensive.

Miller, S. 1984. *Experimental Design and Statistics,* 2nd ed. London: Methuen. Readable and inexpensive.

Misiak, H., and G. J. Franghiadi. 1953. "The Thumb and Personality." *Journal of General Psychology* 48: pp. 241-244.

Moore, M. 1985. "About the Sad State of Scientific Graphology." *Psychological Documents* 15 (2), MS No. 2676.

Mullen, B., C. Copper, and J. E. Driskell. 1990. "Jaywalking as a Function of Model Behavior." *Personality and Social Psychology Bulletin* 16: pp. 320-330.

Murphy, K. R. 1988. "Psychological Measurement: Abilities and Skills." In *International Review of Industrial and Organizational Psychology 1988,* edited by C. L. Cooper and I. T. Robertson, pp. 213-243. New York: Wiley.

Murstein, B. I. 1963. *Theory and Research in Projective Techniques (emphasizing the TAT),* pp. 139-148. New York: Wiley.

Nathan, B. R., and R. A. Alexander. 1988. "A Comparison of Criteria for Test Validation: A Meta-Analytic Investigation." *Personnel Psychology* 41: pp. 517-535.

Neter, E., and G. Ben-Shakhar. 1989. "The Predictive Validity of Graphological Inferences: A Meta-Analytic Approach." *Personality and Individual Differences* 10: pp. 737-745. See note 26.

Neuman, G. A., J. E. Edwards, and N. S. Raju. 1989. "Organizational Development Interventions: A Meta-Analysis of Their Effects on Satisfaction and Other Attitudes." *Personnel Psychology* 42: pp. 461-489.

Nevo, B. 1986. *Scientific Aspects of Graphology: A Handbook.* Springfield, Ill.: Thomas. An anthology of 19 authors including Nevo. About 310 references not counting those duplicated between chapters, of which about 190 are on validity and methodology.

———. 1986a. "Reliability of Graphology: A Survey of the Literature." In Nevo (1986: pp. 253-261).

———. 1986b. "Graphology Validation Studies in Israel: Summary of 15 Years of Activity." Paper presented at the 21st International Congress of Applied Psychology, Jerusalem.

———. 1988. "Yes, Graphology Can Predict Occupational Success: Rejoinder to Ben-Shakhar et al." *Perceptual and Motor Skills* 66: pp. 92-94.

———. 1989. "Validation of Graphology through Use of a Matching Method Based on Ranking." *Perceptual and Motor Skills* 69: pp. 1331–1336. Same study as reported briefly in B. Nevo and H. Halevi (1986). "Validation of Graphology through the Use of Matching Method Based on Ranking." In Nevo (1986: pp. 241–246).

Nevo, B., and R. Benitta. 1991. "Rank-Ordered Matching in Validity Studies of Personnel Selection Devices: A Proposed Model and Some Empirical Results." Pre-publication draft kindly supplied by Professor Baruch Nevo.

Newhall, S. M. 1926. "Sex Differences in Handwriting." *Journal of Applied Psychology* 10: pp. 151–161.

O'Brien, E. T., and K. O'Malley. 1979. "ABC of Blood Pressure Measurement." *British Medical Journal* 1979 (2): pp. 851–853.

Olyanova, N. 1960. *The Psychology of Handwriting.* New York: Sterling.

———. 1969. *Handwriting Tells.* London: Peter Owen.

Oosthuizen, S. 1990. "Graphology as Predictor of Academic Achievement." *Perceptual and Motor Skills* 71: pp. 715–721.

Pang, H., and L. Lepponen. 1968. "Personality Traits and Handwriting Characteristics." *Perceptual and Motor Skills* 26: p. 1082.

Parker, K. C. H., R. K. Hanson, and J. Hunsley. 1988. "MMPI, Rorschach, and WAIS: A Meta-Analytic Comparison of Reliability, Stability, and Validity." *Psychological Bulletin* 103: pp. 367–373. Their five Rorschach studies came from the *Journal of Personality Assessment* 1970–1981. I added three more studies by extending the survey to 1990. There is no overlap with Reznikoff et al. (1982).

Pascal, G. R. 1943. "The Analysis of Handwriting: A Test of Significance." *Character and Personality* 12: pp. 123–144.

Pascal, G. R., and B. Suttell. 1947. "Testing the Claims of a Graphologist." *Journal of Personality* 16: pp. 192–197.

Passingham, R. E. 1979. "Brain Size and Intelligence in Man." *Brain, Behavior and Evolution* 16: pp. 253–270.

Paterson, J. 1976. *Interpreting Handwriting.* London: Macmillan.

Paul-Mengelberg, M. 1965. "Die Symptome der Veralterung in der Handschrift." *Zeitschrift für Menschenkunde* 29: pp. 3–27. Summarized by Lockowandt in chapter 5 of this book.

———. 1986. Personal communication to Nevo (1986: p. 257).

Pearlman, K., F. L. Schmidt, and J. E. Hunter. 1980. "Validity Generalization Results for Tests Used to Predict Job Proficiency and Training Success in Clerical Occupations." *Journal of Applied Psychology* 65: pp. 373–406.

Peeples, E. E. 1990. "Training, Certification, and Experience of Handwriting Analysts." *Perceptual and Motor Skills* 70: pp. 1219–1226.

Perron, R., and H. De Gobineau. 1957. "Study on Identification and Diagnosis of Epilepsy by Means of Handwriting Analysis." *Travail Humain* 29: pp. 323–338. Cited by Nevo (1986: p. 256).

Pinter, R. 1918. "Intelligence as Estimated from Photographs." *Psychological Review* 25: pp. 286–296.

Powers, E. 1933. "Matching Sketches of Personality with Script." Chapter 10 in Allport and Vernon (1983: pp. 212–223).

Prystav, G. 1969. "Beitrag zur faktoren analytischen Validierung der Handschrift." Doctoral dissertation, University of Freiburg. Cited by Nevo (1986: 256).

Rabin, A., and H. Blair. 1953. "The Effects of Alcohol on Handwriting." *Journal of Clinical Psychology* 9: pp. 284–287. Scripts were obtained from 28 adult males before and after drinking to a blood alcohol level of .05–.17 percent, and each pair was judged by 8 nongraphologists. The mean number judged correctly was 26.9 or 96 percent, range 26–28.

Radin, D. I., and R. D. Nelson. 1989. "Evidence for Consciousness-Related Anomalies in Random Physical Systems." *Foundations of Physics* 19: pp. 1499–1513. A meta-analysis of random number generator studies.

Rafaeli, A., and A. Drory. 1988. "Graphological Assessments for Personnel Selection: Concerns and Suggestions for Research." *Perceptual and Motor Skills* 66: pp. 743–759.

Rafaeli, A., and R. J. Klimoski. 1983. "Predicting Sales Success through Handwriting Analysis: An Evaluation of the Effects of Training and Handwriting Sample Content." *Journal of Applied Psychology* 68: pp. 212–217. Additional data kindly supplied by Professor Richard Klimoski.

Ratzon, H. 1986. "Handwriting Analysis of Holocaust Survivors." In Nevo (1986: pp. 127–139).

Ray, W. S. 1958. "Judgments of Intelligence Based on Brief Observations of Physiognomy." *Psychological Reports* 4: p. 478.

Ree, M. J., and J. A. Earles. 1991. "Predicting Training Success: Not Much More than g." *Personnel Psychology* 44: pp. 321–332.

Rees, L., 1960. "Constitutional Factors and Abnormal Behavior." In Eysenck (1960: pp. 344–392).

Reilly, R. R., and G. T. Chao. 1982. "Validity and Fairness of Some Alternative Employee Selection Procedures." *Personnel Psychology* 35: pp. 1–62.

Reznikoff, M., E. Aronow, and A. Rauchway. 1982. "The Reliability of Inkblot Content Scales." In *Advances in Personality Assessment*, Vol. 1, edited by C. D. Spielberger and J. N. Butcher. Hillsdale, N.J.: Erlbaum. There is only a small overlap with Jensen (1959, 1964).

Ritzler, B., and B. Alter. 1986. "Rorschach Teaching in APA-approved Clinical Graduate Programs: Ten Years Later." *Journal of Personality Assessment* 50: pp. 44–49.

Robins, L. N., J. E. Helzer, J. Croughan, and K. S. Ratcliff. 1981. "National Institute of Mental Health Diagnostic Interview Schedule." *Archives of General Psychiatry* 38: pp. 381–389.

Roman, K. G. 1952. *Handwriting: A Key to Personality*. New York: Pantheon.

Rosenthal, D. A., and R. Lines. "Handwriting as a Correlate of Extraversion." *Journal of Personality Assessment* 42: pp. 45–48.

Rosenthal, R. 1979. "The 'File Drawer' Problem and Tolerance for Null Results." *Psychological Bulletin* 86: pp. 638–641.

———. 1984. *Meta-Analytic Procedures for Social Research*. Beverly Hills, Calif.: Sage.

Rosenthal, R., and D. B. Rubin. 1982. "A Simple, General Purpose Display of

Magnitude of Experimental Effect." *Journal of Educational Psychology* 74: pp. 708–712.

Rothstein, H. R. 1990. "Interrater Reliability of Job Performance Ratings: Growth to Asymptote Level with Increasing Opportunity to Observe." *Journal of Applied Psychology* 75: pp. 322–327.

Saudek, R. 1925. *The Psychology of Handwriting*. London: Allen and Unwin.

Schmidt, F. L., J. E. Hunter, and V. W. Urry. 1976. "Statistical Power in Criterion-related Validation Studies." *Journal of Applied Psychology* 61: pp. 473–485.

Schmidt, F. L., J. E. Hunter, and K. Pearlman. 1981. "Task Differences as Moderators of Aptitude Test Validity in Selection: A Red Herring." *Journal of Applied Psychology* 66: pp. 166–185.

Schmidt, F. L., J. E. Hunter, K. Pearlman, and H. R. Hirsch. 1985a. "Forty Questions about Validity Generalization and Meta-Analysis." *Personnel Psychology* 38: pp. 697–798. Includes comments from others and authors' replies.

Schmidt, F. L., B. P. Ocasio, J. M. Hillery, and J. E. Hunter. 1985b. "Further Within-Setting Empirical Tests of the Situational Specificity Hypothesis in Personnel Selection." *Personnel Psychology* 38: pp. 509–524.

Schmitt, N., R. Z. Gooding, R. A. Noe, and M. Kirsch. 1984. "Metaanalyses of Validity Studies Published Between 1964 and 1982 and the Investigation of Study Characteristics." *Personnel Psychology* 37: pp. 407–422.

Schweighofer, F. 1979. *Graphology and Psychoanalysis: The Handwriting of Sigmund Freud and His Circle*. New York: Springer. Comments on the handwriting of Freud and about 40 others.

Secord, P. F. 1949. "Studies of the Relationship of Handwriting to Personality." *Journal of Personality* 17: pp. 430–448.

Secord, P. F., W. F. Dukes, and W. Bevan. 1954. "Personalities in Faces: 1. An Experiment in Social Perceiving." *Genetic Psychology Monographs* 49: pp. 231–279.

Seifer, M. 1977. "Dominant Personality Characteristics and Their Relationship to Thumb Size." *Journal of Occult Studies* (later *Metascience Quarterly*, now defunct) 1: pp. 242–256. Summarized in Dean (1986).

Shapiro, D. A., and D. Shapiro (1982). "Meta-Analysis of Comparative Therapy Outcome Studies: A Replication and Refinement." *Psychological Bulletin* 92: pp. 581–604. Therapy outcome is a hotly debated issue, so see also the debate in *Psychological Bulletin* 1990, 107: pp. 106–113.

Shilo, S. 1979. "Prediction of Success on a Moshav According to Graphological Scores as Compared to Prediction of the Same Criterion by Psychological Scores." Internal Research Report, Hadassa Institute for Career Guidance Counselling, Jerusalem, Israel. Cited by Nevo (1986b).

Singer, E. 1969. *A Manual of Graphology*. London: Duckworth.

Smith, M .L. 1980. "Publication Bias and Meta-Analysis." *Evaluation in Education* 4: pp. 22–24.

Sonnemann, U. 1950. *Handwriting Analysis as a Psychodiagnostic Tool*. London: Allen and Unwin.

Sonnemann, U., and J. P. Kerman. 1962. "Handwriting Analysis—A Valid Selection Tool?" *Personnel* 39: pp. 8–14.

Stabholz, M. S. 1981. "Individual Differences in the Handwriting of Monozygotic and Dizygotic Twins in Relation to Personality and Genetic Factors." MPhil Thesis, Institute of Psychiatry, University of London.

Strolovitch, I. 1980. "Impact of Personal Variables and Job Variables on the Predictive Validity of Some Personnel Selection Practices for Scientific-Technical Positions." MA thesis, the Technion, Israel. Cited by Neter and Ben-Shakhar (1989).

Super, D. E. 1941. "A Comparison of the Diagnoses of a Graphologist with the Results of Psychological Tests." *Journal of Consulting Psychology* 5: pp. 127–133.

Surovell, H. 1987. *Lovestrokes. Handwriting for Love, Sex, and Compatibility.* New York: Harper & Row.

Sussams, P. 1985. "Graphology and Psychological Tests: Part 2—The Correlation Experiment." *The Graphologist* [UK] (1)3: pp. 10–12.

Swentzell, R., and A. H. Roberts. 1964. "On the Interaction of the Subject and the Experiment in the Matching Model." *Psychometrika* 29: pp. 87–101.

Symaniz, A.J. 1980. "A Study Concerned with Investigating the Potential Diagnostic Value of Palmar-analysis." Honors psychology thesis, University of Adelaide, South Australia. Summarized in Dean (1986).

Taft, R. 1967. "Extraversion, Neuroticism, and Expressive Behavior: An Application of Wallach's Moderator Effect to Handwriting Analysis." *Journal of Personality* 35: pp. 570–584.

Taylor, M. S., and K. K. Sackheim. 1988. "Graphology." *Personnel Administrator* (5)33: pp. 71–76 (May 1988). [Each month starts from page 1].

Van Valen, L. 1974. "Brain Size and Intelligence in Man." *American Journal of Physical Anthropology* 40: pp. 417–424. The correlation with *brain* size is larger than that with *head* size.

Vernon, P. E. 1953. *Personality Tests and Assessments.* London: Methuen.

Vestewig, R. E., A. H. Santee, and M. K. Moss. 1976. "Validity and Student Acceptance of a Graphoanalytic Approach to Personality." *Journal of Personality Assessment* 40: pp. 592–598.

Vine, I. 1974. "Stereotypes in the Judgement of Personality from Handwriting." *British Journal of Social and Clinical Psychology* 13: pp. 61–64.

Von Kügelgen, G. 1928. "Graphologie und Berufseignung." *Industrielle Psychotechnik* 5: p. 311.

Wallner, T. 1961. "Reliabilitätsuntersuchungen an metrisch nicht messbaren Handschriftvariablen." *Zeitschrift für Menschenkunde* 25: pp. 1–14 and 49–78. Cited by Nevo (1986: 257).

———. 1962. "Neue Ergebnisse experimenteller Untersuchungen über die Reliabilität von Handschriftvariablen." *Zeitschrift für Menschenkunde* 26: pp. 257–269. Cited by Nevo (1986: p. 257).

———. 1963. "Über die Validität Graphologischer Aussagen." *Diagnostica* 9: pp. 26–35. Cited by Neter and Ben-Shakhar (1989).

Warner, L. 1991. Information kindly supplied by Lawrence Warner, President of the International Graphoanalysis Society in the UK.

Warner, L., and J. Swallow. 1989. "Graphoanalysis: Can It Save You Money and Help to Increase Effectiveness?" *Sundridge Park Management Review* [UK], Summer 1989: pp. 11–18. From the top, the graphoanalysis statements are LRLRL. The statements received minor editing, e.g., to substitute "you are" for "the writer is"; otherwise their original sense and order is unchanged. Although the excerpt presented by Warner and Swallow is only two paragraphs from a 3-page interpretation, it is clearly intended to show what graphoanalysis can do, so some generalization is warranted. Both authors are qualified graphoanalysts.

Weinberg, G. H., F. A. Fluckiger, and C. A. Tripp. 1962. "The Application of a New Matching Technique." *Journal of Projective Techniques* 26: pp. 221–224.

Wellingham-Jones, P. 1989. "Evaluation of the Handwriting of Successful Women through the Roman-Staempfli Psychogram." *Perceptual and Motor Skills* 69: pp. 999–1010. Reprinted in chapter 15 of this book.

Wells, F. L. 1946. "Personal History, Handwriting and Specific Behavior." *Character and Personality* 14: pp. 295–314.

White, K. R. 1982. "The Relation between Socioeconomic Status and Academic Achievement." *Psychological Bulletin* 91: pp. 461–481.

Wiesner, W. H., and S. F. Cronshaw. 1988. "A Meta-Analytic Investigation of the Impact of Interview Format and Degree of Structure on the Validity of the Employment Interview." *Journal of Occupational Psychology* 61: pp. 275–290. The reliability and validity of *unstructured* (i.e., traditional) interviews is much lower at .61 (9 studies) and .11 (19 studies), respectively.

Wilkinson, B. 1951. "A Statistical Consideration in Psychological Research." *Psychological Bulletin* 48: pp. 156–158.

Williams, E. D., L. Winter, and J. M. Woods. 1938. "Tests and Literary Appreciation." *British Journal of Educational Psychology* 8: pp. 265–284. See page 282. Sample was 256 schoolgirls aged 11–17.

Williams, M., G. Berg-Cross, and L. Berg-Cross. 1977. "Handwriting Characteristics and Their Relationship to Eysenck's Extraversion-Introversion and Kagan's Impulsivity-Reflectivity Dimensions." *Journal of Personality Assessment* 41: pp. 291–298.

Wilson, G. D. 1983. "Finger-Length as an Index of Assertiveness in Women." *Personality and Individual Differences* 4: pp. 111–112.

Wolff, C. 1941. "Character and Mentality as Related to Hand-Markings." *British Journal of Medical Psychology* 18: pp. 364–382.

Wolfson, R. 1951. "Graphology." In *An Introduction to Projective Techniques, and Other Devices for Understanding the Dynamics of Human Behavior,* edited by H. H. Anderson and G. L. Anderson. New York: Prentice-Hall, pp. 416–456. 55 references of which only about a dozen are on validity.

Yeaton, W. H., and L. Sechrest. 1981. "Meaningful Measure of Effect." *Journal of Consulting and Clinical Psychology* 49: pp. 766–767.

Young, P. T. 1931. "Sex Differences in Handwriting." *Journal of Applied Psychology* 15: pp. 486–498.

Zdep, S. M., and H. B. Weaver. 1967. "The Graphoanalytic Approach to Selecting Life Insurance Salesmen." *Journal of Applied Psychology* 51: pp. 295–299.

APPENDIX A

RELIABILITY OF GRAPHOLOGY

All the studies meta-analyzed in the text are summarized below. Reliability is expressed as a correlation, decimal point omitted.

Blank	=	source gives no details.
Judges	=	graphologists unless otherwise indicated.
Signs	=	individual handwriting features tested, e.g., slant.
Traits	=	traits established by ratings or personality tests.
Wtd mean	=	mean weighted by number of scripts.

a	Assumed equal to the mean to avoid wasting a useful result.
e	Estimated from range or other source details.
sd	Standard deviation of mean before removing sampling error.
Vr	Variance remaining after removing sampling error; see note 17.
*	Data obtained from secondary sources; see annotated reference.

Reliability of Objective Features (e.g., slant)

	Source	Scripts	Signs	Judges	Range	Mean	Interval
		\-\-\-\- Number of\-\-\-\-			Reliability		
Test-retest	**DIFFERENT SAMPLES, DIFFERENT TIMES**						
agreement	Fisher 1964*	25a			80 93	84	1 week
for same	Harvey 1933	20	15	1	47 85	73	2 months
judges	McNeil & Blum 1952	40	9	2	26 80	64	1 month
	Nevo 1986 vs. global	15		15		89	1 week
	4 studies mean N=25	100 total		18	Wtd mean	75 sd 10 Vr 17%	
	SAME SAMPLE						
	Fischer 1962*						
	Timm 1967*	74a				90	split half
	Prystav 1969*						
	Mann 1961*	30	4	1		89	test-retest
	Hoepfner 1962*	100	1	1		80	test-retest
	Rosenthal & Lines 1978	58	3	1	82 92	90	split half
	Wallner 1975*&	107	11	1		90	test-retest
	5 studies mean N=74	369 total		4	Wtd mean 87 sd 04 Vr 59%		
Agreement	Birge 1954	50	5	2	94 99	97	
between	Furnham & Gunter 1987	64	13	2		89	
different	Galbraith & Wilson 1964	100	5	3	46 91	78	
judges	Hoepfner 1962*	100	1	2		87	2 weeks
	Kimball 1974*	32	61	2		73	
	McNeil & Blum 1952	20	7	2	40 99	85	
	Nevo 1986:256	15	11	2	85 99	95	
	Oosthuizen 1991	69	10	2		89	
	Perron & de Gobineau 1957*	2	12	6		90	
	Rosenthal & Lines 1978	58	3	2	91	93e	
	Williams et al. 1977	47	11	2	92	95	
	Zdep & Weaver 1967	63	13	2	50 85	64	
	12 studies mean N=52	620 total		29	Wtd mean 85 sd 10 Vr 84%		

Reliability of Objective Features (e.g., rhythm)

	Source	Scripts	Ftres	Judges	Range	Mean	Interval
		── Number of ──			Reliability		
Test-retest	Honel 1977*	111	2	1	81 82	81	10 months
agreement	Prystav 1969*	56	3	1	15 86	39e	
for same	Timm 1967*	83a				73	
judges							
	3 studies mean N=83	250 total		2	Wtd mean 69 sd 16		Vr 88%
Agreement	Honel 1977*	111	2	5	25 63	44	
between	Paul-Mengelberg 1986*	105a	3		70 85	78e	
different	Wallner 1961, 1962*	100	1	5		59	
judges							
	3 studies mean N=105	316 total		10	Wtd mean 60 sd 14		Vr 80%

Reliability of Interpretation (e.g. extroversion)—For IQ see Appendix D

	Source	Scripts	Traits	Judges	Range	Mean	Interval
		── Number of ──			Reliability		
Test-retest	GRAPHOLOGIST JUDGES						
agreement	Crider 1941	12	16	1	64 94	82	1 month
for same	Goldberg 1986	21	32	1		17	1 month
judges	Jansen 1973:58 Expt 1+2	5	1	6		54	1 year
	Sonnemann & Kerman 1962	37	5	1	64 85	77	15 years
	4 studies mean N=19	75 total		9	Wtd mean	59 sd 27	Ve 68%
	LAY JUDGES						
	Dzida & Kiener 1978	45	1	22		56	4 weeks
	Goldberg 1986	21	32	2	18 29	24	1 month
	Jansen 1973:58 Expt 1+2	5	1	10		41	1 year
	Reichold 1969*	90	5	1	78 88	83e	3 months
	4 studies mean N=40	161 total		35	Wtd mean 66 sd 21		Vr 82%
Agreement	GRAPHOLOGIST JUDGES						
between	Bar-El 1984*	10	14	8	33 64	51	
different	Ben-Shakhar et al. 1986	80	4	3		40	
judges	Borenstein 1985*	214	1	3	33 58	46e	
	Brandstatter 1969*	84	24	2		71	
	Crider 1941	9	16	2		18	
	Flug 1981*	58	1	3		30	
	Green et al.1971	7	20	7	–24 51	21	
	Hofsommer et al.1965*	57	1	3		39	
	Jansen 1973:34 Expt 1	15	1	10		21	
	Jansen 1973:57 Expt 2	20	1	10		14	
	Jansen 1973:90 Expt 3	20	1	10		32	
	Jansen 1973:173-4 Expt 4	9	18	6		45	
	Keinan et al.1984	65	13	6	21 37	29	
	Peeples 1990	1	16	37	07 63	37	
	Rafaeli & Klimoski 1983	32	11	2	23 51	42	
	15 judges mean N=45	681 total		112	Wtd mean	42 sd 14	Vr 19%

LAY JUDGES

Study						
Bar-El 1984*	10	14	8			18
Borenstein 1985*	214	1	3	16	28	22e
Dzida & Kiener1978	45	1	22			31
Jansen 1973:57 Expt 2	20	1	10			17
Jansen 1973:90 Expt 3	20	1	10			19
Jansen 1973:173–4 Expt 4	9	18	6			14
Kienan et al.1984	65	13	6	09	20	14
Middleton 1941a	10	3	72	27	63	44
Middleton 1941b	20	1	98			36
Vine 1974	6	2	63	31	60	46

10 studies mean N=42   419 total 298   Wtd mean 23 sd 07 Vr Nil

PSYCHOLOGIST JUDGES

Study						
Borenstein 1985*	214	1	3	46	48	46e
Jansen 1973:34 Expt 1	15	1	10			29
Jansen 1973:57 Expt 2	20	1	20			24
Jansen 1973:90 Expt 3	20	1	10			28
Jansen 1973:173–4 Expt 4	9	18	6			30
Keinan et al.1984	65	13	6	17	36	25

6 studies mean N=57   343 total 55   Wtd mean 39 sd 10   Vr Nil

APPENDIX B

EFFECT SIZE OF GRAPHOLOGY IN PERSONNEL SELECTION

All the studies meta-analyzed in the text are summarized below. Effect size is expressed as follows, decimal points omitted:

cc	contingency coefficient		ph	phi coefficient
g	Halevi's g		r	Pearson r
ir	intraclass correlation		rp	point biserial r
k	Cohen's kappa		rs	Spearman rho for ranks
kw	Weighted kappa		rt	r by $r=\sqrt{(t^2/t^2+df)}$

c   Corrected for range expansion.
e   Estimated from significance level.
sd Standard deviation of mean before removing sampling error.
u   Uncorrected value (if available).
Vr Variance remaining after removing sampling error, see note 17.
x   Scripts not identical but content cues deleted.
?   Source gives no details.
*   Data obtained from secondary sources, see annotated reference.
†   Graphologists were graphoanalysts.

Under criterion, tr = trainees, ratings = supervisor ratings.

	—Number of—				Effect size			Neutral	
Source	Scripts	Judges	Sample and criterion	Type	Range	Mean	scripts?	Method	
GRAPHOLOGIST JUDGES									
Ben-Shakhar et al. 1981	58	3	Bank–global ratings	r		21	n		
Borenstein 1985*	214	3	Military tr–grades	r		14	n		
Drory 1986	60	1	Drinks plant–ratings	r	13 55	36	n		
Esroni et al. 1985*	23	1	Military–success	ph		19	n		
Esroni et al. 1985*	125	1	Military–ratings	ph		01	n		
Esroni et al. 1985*	49	1	Military–rtgs & success	r		03	n		
Esroni et al. 1985*	45	1	Military–ratings	r		06	n		
Hofsommer et al.1962*	54	?	Forester tr–grades	rs		55	n		
Hofsommer&Holdsworth 1963*	141	1	Pilot tr–success	rp		20	n		
Jansen 1973:91 Expt 3	20	10	Commercial–ratings	ph		23c	n		
Jansen 1973:173–4 Expt 4	9	6	Administration–ratings	rs		09	n		
Keinan et al.1984	65	6	Military tr–success	r	06 36	23	n		
Rafaeli & Klimoski 1983	55	20	Real estate–sales	r	-15 25	03	n		
Shilo 1979*	15	?	Moshav–success	?		18	n		
Sonnemann & Kerman 1962	37	1	Executives–ratings	r	35 48	43	n		
Strolovitch 1980*	25	2	Technical–ratings	r		-19	n		
Wallner 1963*	89	2	Executive tr–ratings	r		05	n		
17 studies mean N=64	1084	61+			Wtd mean 158 sd 147			Vr 30%	
Ben-Shakhar et al. 1981	36	5	Successful professionals	k	01 18	08	y	Pick profession	
Borenstein 1985*	214	3	Military tr–grades	r		12	y		
Cox & Tapsell 1991	50	2	Exec–9 assessment rtgs	r	-20 22	00	y		
Rafaeli & Klimoski 1983	55	20	Real estate–sales	r	-09 26	09	y		
Super 1941	24	1	Students–SVIB	ph		-02	x	Pick vocation	
Zdep & Weaver 1967†	63	2	Insurance–sales	r	01 12	08	y	6 success traits	
6 studies mean N=74	442	33			Wtd mean 086 sd 045			Vr Nil	
PSYCHOLOGIST JUDGES									
Ben-Shakhar et al.1981	58	1	Bank–global ratings	r		24	n		
Borenstein 1985*	214	3	Military tr–grades	r		16	n		
Jansen 1973:91 Expt 3	20	10	Commercial–ratings	ph		21c	n		
Jansen 1973:173–4 Expt 4	9	6	Administration–ratings	rs		06	n		
Keinan et al. 1984	65	6	Military tr–success	r	11 26	19	n		

	N		Task				
5 studies mean N=73	366	26				Wtd mean 178 sd 035	Vr Nil
Borenstein 1985*	214	3	Military tr–grades	r		11	y
1 study means N=214	214	3				Wtd mean 11 sd 000	
LAY JUDGES							
Borenstein 1985*	214	3	Military tr–grades	r		20	n
Jansen 1973:91 Expt 3	20	10	Commercial–ratings	ph		23c	n
Jansen 1973:173–4 Expt 4	9	6	Administration–ratings	rs		07	n
Keinan et al. 1984	65	6	Military tr–success	r	–12 17	08	n
4 studies mean N=77	308	25				Wtd mean 173 sd 053	Vr Nil
Borenstein 1985*	214	3	Miitary tr–grades	r		02	y
Cox & Tapsell 1991	50	3	Exec–9 assessment rtgs	r	–18 39	03	y
2 studies mean N=132	264	6				Wtd mean 022 sd 004	Vr Nil

APPENDIX C

EFFECT SIZE OF GRAPHOLOGY IN PREDICTING PERSONALITY

All studies meta-analyzed in the text are summarized below. Symbols are the same as in Appendix B.

Key to Method

Rate script	= rate script vs personality ratings or test scores.
Decide A or B	= subject is A or B, judge must decide which.
Fill out test	= graphologist uses script to fill out personality test.

Key to Personality Tests:

ACL	Adjective Check List
AS	Allport's Ascendance-Submission
CPI	California Psychological Inventory
EdPI	Edwards Personality Inventory
EPI	Eysenck Personality Inventory
EPQ	Eysenck Personality Questionnaire
MBTI	Myers-Briggs Type Inventory
SV	Study of Values
SVIB	Strong Vocational Interest Blank
TAT	Thematic Apperception Test

Test Objective Signs (e.g. slant)

Source	—Number of— Script	Signs	Tested vs these traits	Type	Effect size Range	Mean	Number of results Total	Sig*	Exp
TEST MANY SIGNS, NO PREDICTED DIRECTION, MEAN IS ABSOLUTE MEAN									
Birge 1954	56	22	6 peer-related extremes	rt	19c		132	10	6.6
Furnham & Gunter 1987	64	13	E,N,P,L, by EPQ	r	-19 24	09	52	1	2.6
Harvey 1933	20	15	E by AS test	r	-24 19	11	15	0	0.8
Lemke & Kirchener 1971	103	16	10 by unspecified test	r			160	9	8.0
Lester et al. 1977	111	16	E,N by EPI	rp			16	0	0.8
McNeil & Blum 1952	119	17	11 by projective test	ph	24e		352	17	17.6
Pascal 1943	22	22	36 by clinical ratings	r	-56 60		792	37	39.6
7 studies mean N=71	495	121	Mean number of signs=17		Absolute mean 095		1519	74	76.0
TEST SPECIFIC SIGNS, A POSITIVE EFFECT IS IN PREDICTED DIRECTION									
Brown 1921*	30	5	5 by peer ranking	rs	-05 23	11			
Burnup 1974*	83	1	MZ size vs E by EPI	r		19			
Crowley 1991	93	4	E by EPQ	r		07			
Downey 1919	28	9	5 by peer ranking	rs	23 61	38			
Furnham & Gunter 1987	64	4	E by EPQ	r	03 15	09			
Lester et al. 1977	111	1	Slant vs E by EPI	r		08			
Harvey 1933	20	4	E by AS test	r	-17 08	-04			
Hull & Montgomery 1919	17	6	6 by peer ranking	rs	-45 38	-02			
Rosenthal & Lines 1978	58	3	E by EPI	r	-13 11	01			
Secord 1949	15	11	11 by peer rating	r	-39 30	-05			
Stabholz 1981:105	316	6	Size vs E by EPQ	r	-05 19	06			
11 studies mean N=76	835	54			Wtd mean 082 sd 075			Vr Nil	

*Sig = Number of significant results with 2-sided p ≤ .05, Exp = expected number.

Judge Whole Script for Particular Traits

Under criterion, t = traits or scales.   For judgment of sex and IQ see Appendix D.

Source	Scripts	Judges	Criterion	Type	Range	Mean	Neutral scripts?	Method
GRAPHOLOGIST JUDGES								
Bar-El 1984*	28	?	Personality tests	?		16	n	Rate script
Ben-Shakhar et al. 1981	58	3	Supervisor ratings 24t	r	06 42	21	n	
Crider 1941	18	2	Test scores 16t	rs	15 27	20	n	
Goldberg 1986	170	1	ACL,CPI,SVIB results 54t	r		02	n	
Green et al.1971	7	7	Self-ranked traits 20t	rs	-21 51	24	n	
Keinan 1986†	56	3	State anxiety score	r		13	n	
Peeples 1990	1	37	16PF scores 16t	r		-13	n	
Rafaeli & Klimoski 1983	70	20	Supervisor ratings 10t	r	-16 20	08	n	
Wellingham-Jones 1989	112	1	Recognized success	rt	-16 64	20	n	
Bayne & O'Neill 1988	16	6	6 clear MBTI-peer types	k	-40 14	20	n	
Eysenck 1948	176	1	Neurotic or normal?	r		21	n	
Frederick 1965	80	1	Psychiatric case or not?	k		20	n	Decide A or B
Jansen 1973:36 Expt 1	15	10	Energetic-lethargic	ph		01c	n	
Jensen 1973:59 Expt 2	20	10	extremes by test	ph		10c	n	
14 studies mean N=59	827	102				Wtd mean 139 sd 081		Vr Nil
Cantril et al. 1933	50	1	SV test scores 5t	r	-06 40	21	y	Rate script
Kimmel & Wertheimer 1966†	22	1	Peer ratings 5t	r	-27 53	06	y	
Rafaeli & Klimoski 1983	70	20	Supervisor ratings 10t	r	-10 10	00	y	
Vestwig et al. 1976†	48	6	EdPI scores 15t	r	-23 21	00	y	
Frederick 1965	80	1	Psychiatric case or not?	k		-10	y	
Lester et al. 1977†	39	1	EPI E extremes = 1t	k	(08u)	05c	y	Decide A or B
Pascal & Suttell 1947	20	1	Psychotic or normal?	k		20	y	
Eysenck 1945 Method 1	50	1	N by personality test	k		24	y	
Eysenck & Gudjonsson 1986†	99	1	E,N,P,L by EPQ = 4t	r	-06 22	05	y	Fill out test
Sussams 1985	20	4	E,N by EPI = 2t	r	23 38	30	y	
10 studies mean N=50	498	37				Wtd mean 066 sd 117		Vr Nil
PSYCHOLOGIST JUDGES								
Ben-Shakhar et al.1981	58	1	Supervisor ratings 24t	r	-08 42	28	n	Rate script
Frederick 1965	80	1	Psychiatric case or not?	k		35	n	
Jansen 1973:36 Expt 1	15	10	Energetic-lethargic	ph		06c	n	Decide A or B
Jansen 1973:59 Expt 2	20	20	extremes by test = 1t	ph		07c	n	
4 studies mean N=43	173	32				Wtd mean 269 sd 107		Vr Nil
Frederick 1965	80	1	Psychiatric case or not?	k		-05	y	Decide A or B
1 study means N=80	80	1				Wtd mean -050 sd 000		
LAY JUDGES								
Goldberg 1986	170	2	ACL,CPI,SVIB results 54t	r		02	n	Rate script
Keinan 1986	56	6	State anxiety score	r		13	n	
Eisenberg 1938	60	10	Dominant/nondominant?	k	(15u)	11c	n	
Frederick 1965	80	1	Psychiatric case or not?	k		08	n	Decide A or B
Jansen 1973:59 Expt 2	20	10	Energetic or lazy?	ph		05c	n	
5 studies mean N=77	386	29				Wtd mean 106 sd 197		Vr Nil
Castelnuovo-Tedesco 1948	104	6	Rorschach scores 3t	cc	29 37	33	y	Rate script
Dzida & Kiener 1978	45	22	Aggression test scores	r		10	y	
Lowenthal 1975	11	5	Self-rated traits 5t	rs		13	y	
Middleton 1941	20	72	Extreme test scores 3t	r	-15 31	05c	y	(08u)
Vine 1974	6	63	E&N extreme scores = 2t	rs	-40 30	04c	y	(05u)
Frederick 1965	80	1	Psychiatric case or not?	k		-15	y	Decide A or B
Pascal & Suttell 1947	20	25	Psychotic or normal?	k	-60 60	02	y	
7 studies mean N=39	276	194				Wtd mean 106 sd 197		Vr 34%

Match Script or Interpretation to Person or Sketch

Under method, int = graphological interpretation, scr = script, sketch = personality description by close acquaintance, sometimes supported by tests or interviews, gr = graphologists.

Source	—Number of—		Method	Effect size			Neutral scripts?	Items per matching
	Scripts	Judges		Type	Range	Mean		
GRAPHOLOGIST JUDGES MATCH SCRIPTS								
Cantril & Rand 1934	6	26	Match scr to extreme type	k		28c	y	(56u)	6
Powers 1933	10	17	Match script to sketch	k	-11 44	16	y		10
2 studies mean N=8	16	43			Wtd mean 205 sd 058			Vr Nil	
PSYCHOLOGIST JUDGES MATCH SCRIPTS								
Eysenck 1945 Method 5	10	10	Match script to sketch	k		-08	y		5
Weinberg et al. 1962	15	2	Match script to sketch	k	14 21	18	y		15
2 studies mean N=13	25	12			Wtd mean 076 sd 127			Vr Nil	
LAY JUDGES MATCH SCRIPTS								
Cantril & Rand 1934	6	26	Match scr to extreme type	k		00c	y	(01u)	6
Powers 1933	10	168	Match script to sketch	k	-11 56	09	y		10
Secord 1949	50	5	Match script to TAT	k		04	y		5
3 studies mean N=22	69	199			Wtd mean 044 sd 023			Vr Nil	
LAY JUDGES MATCH INTERPRETATIONS								
Bobertag 1929*	5	15	Match int by 6gr to person	k		76	?		30
Cox & Tapsell 1991	50	3	Pick matches in 100 pairs	rp	-05 23	09	y		2
Crumbaugh & Stockholm 1977†	30	3	Match int to person	k	-17 58	18	y		5
De Groot 1974*	5	13	Match int to person	k		04	?		5
Eysenck 1945 Method 4	50	8	Match int to person	k		18c	y	(11u)	4-6
Halevi 1964*	7	7	Rank 7 int to fit person	k		50	x		7
Karnes & Leonard 1991†	9	9	Pick own int from 9	k		-02	n		9
LoMonaco & Harrison 1973	10	85	Match int to TAT	k		25	y		5
Nevo 1989	10	10	Rank 10 int to fit person	g		34	y		10
Nevo & Benitta 1991	12	24	Rank 6 int by 3gr to fit p	g		01	n		6
Allport & Vernon 1933:228	23	1	Match int to sketch	k		12	x		23
Allport & Vernon 1933:231	12	8	Pick own int from 12	k		-10	x		12
Vestewig et al.1976†	21	21	Rate two int (one yours)	rt	-11 35	09	y		2
13 studies mean N=19	244	207		Wtd mean		146 sd 141		Vr Nil	

APPENDIX D

EFFECT SIZE OF GRAPHOLOGY IN JUDGING SEX AND IQ

The studies of sex and IQ meta-analyzed in Table 3 are summarized below. Effect size is expressed as kappa with decimal point omitted. Symbols are the same as in Appendix B. Unlike in Appendices A–C, no attempt has been made to be exhaustive.

Judgment of Sex from Handwriting

Source	Handwriting sample	No. of judges	Mean % correct	Effect size
Binet 1966	180 envelopes	10	69.8	40
Broom et al.1929	40 same sentence	24	69.9	40
Castelnuovo-Tedesco 1948	100 same two paras	6	68.1	36
Downey 1910	200 envelopes	13	67.4	35
Eisenberg 1938	60 same passage	10	71.7	43
Gesell 1906	50 high school	16	62.6	25
Goodenough 1945	115 same paragraph	20	69.6	39
Kinder 1926	100 same sentence	20	68.4	37
Newhall 1926	200 addresses	92	57.0	14
Young 1931	50 brief lists	50	61.0	22
10 studies mean N = 110	1095 total, Vr=23%	261	Wtd mean	323

Judgment of IQ from Handwriting (all studies are from Michel 1969)

Source	Handwriting sample	No. of judges	Neutral scripts?	Effect size
RELIABILITY, GRAPHOLOGIST JUDGES				
Mields 1964	24 women	18	n	60
Schneevoight 1968	18 men	12	?	75
RELIABILITY, PSYCHOLOGIST OR LAY JUDGES				
Michel 1969	20 adults	7	n	57
Schneevoight 1968	18 men	12	?	52
INDIVIDUAL SIGNS				
Lockowandt 1966	100 children vs IQ tests		?	20–35
Oinonen 1961	122 children extreme IQs (38u)		?	29c
Timm 1967	80 adults vs IQ tests		?	24–37
GRAPHOLOGIST JUDGES				
Michel 1969	20 adults vs. WAIS/ratings		n	16
Mields 1962, 1964	24 adults vs. WAIS		n	33
Rasch 1957	114 adults vs. ratings		?	29
Schonfeld & Simon 1935	100 children vs. IQ tests		n	34
Schneevoight 1968	18 men vs. IQ tests		?	36
Von Foerster 1927	70 children vs. IQ tests		?	29
Wallner 1965 Expt 1	118 adults vs. IQ tests		?	20
Wallner 1965 Expt 2	88 adults vs. IQ tests		n	20
Wallner 1965 Expt 3	91 adults vs. IQ tests		n	23

PSYCHOLOGIST OR LAY JUDGES

Castelnuovo-Tedesco 1958	100 adults IQ 68–132 (59u)	y	43c
Schneevoight 1968	18 men vs. IQ tests	?	40
14 studies mean N=76	1063 total, Vr=Nil	Wtd mean	286

13

Graphology and Human Judgment

G. A. *Dean*, I. W. *Kelly*,
D. H. *Saklofske*, *and* A. *Furnham*

In this paper the authors are concerned with the kinds of biases in perception and judgment that can make us think that we know something when we do not. Many of these biases are responsible for false beliefs in ordinary life. However, the most interesting problems with our reasoning identified here are the ones that lead us to posit correlations between two things—such as backward-slanting handwriting and a certain personality trait—whether or not these correlations actually exist. Many points made here that apply to graphology can be generalized to both pseudosciences and bad science. Almost all scientific claims involve correlations.

The authors argue that most of the correlations regularly claimed by graphologists *could not* be discerned by graphologists. First of all, some of the correlations reported in the scientific literature as vindications of graphological claims are so small that they simply would not have been noticed prior to controlled statistical studies on quite large populations. (Further evidence for this claim is to be found in Dean's chapter on effect sizes that precedes this one.) So how did graphologists come to make these claims for years, prior to these tests being done? The present authors, as well as Barry Beyerstein in chapter 9, provide an answer to this.

Dean et al.'s second reason why graphologists were not in a position to notice these correlations depends upon the fact that graphologists usually examine at least 15, and sometimes as many as 55, features of handwriting in order to make a judgment about the writer; and they maintain that these features mean different things when they are found along with other features on their list. (This is the presupposition of "holism" discussed in chapter 8.) Thus they do not examine features one by one, they must juggle all the features on their list at the same time. But the simple fact is that research has shown that people are not capable of keeping a list of all these features in their heads as they examine features of handwriting, let alone keeping straight all the combinations and permutations of them that would seem to be necessary if graphology were really correct. Graphologists, despite their often-made claims to the contrary, must be selecting from the data they examine, and they do not usually report using an algorithm to weigh these factors in their judgments. They instead talk of "intuition" and the "clinical judgment" used by the skilled clinical diagnostician. The authors of chapter 13 make their most disturbing point here: they make use of the results of over 100 studies which show that experts in a wide range of fields do not use the procedures they *think* they are using to select and weigh the conflicting criteria involved in their judgments; and that they are often outperformed in making these judgments by simple algorithms of the sort a computer can use. So, graphologists, as well as many other practitioners whose reputations depend on these supposed abilities involved in "clinical judgment," have food for thought.

INTRODUCTION: VIEWS OF JUDGMENT AND HOW GRAPHOLOGISTS DO IT

Given the extraordinary ability of the human mind to make sense out of things, it is natural occasionally to make sense out of things that have no sense at all.

—Richard Furnald Smith

This chapter is about how graphologists and their clients make judgments. Not *what* they do, but the judgment processes *underlying* what they do. We look at three crucial areas, namely, (1) detecting correlations (which is how graphology arose); (2) combining correlations into predictions (which is how graphology is applied); and (3) human biases (which graphologists don't tell you about) in assessing the predictions. The results throw new light on systems like graphology and astrology that claim to indicate your character without necessarily making your acquaintance. On the way we discover how easy it is to be fooled, so we end with hints on protecting yourself from the known ways of fooling yourself. But first a quick peek at human judgment then and now.

HUMAN JUDGMENT THEN AND NOW

Around 1600 William Shakespeare gave this rousing view of human judgment (taken from Slovic 1972):

> What a piece of work is man! How noble in reason! How infinite in faculties! In form and moving, how express and admirable! In action, how like an angel! In apprehension, how like a god! The beauty of the world! The paragon of animals! (*Hamlet,* Act 2, Scene 2)

Three centuries later the 1978 Nobel prizewinner in economics, Herbert Simon (1957), gave this somewhat different view:

> The capacity of the human mind for formulating and solving complex problems is very small compared with the size of problems whose solution is required for objectively rational behaviour in the real world—or even for a reasonable approximation to such objective rationality.

On these two views Armstrong (1978:74) comments:

> On almost any basis one would choose Shakespeare! He is more poetic than Simon; he is more widely read; and his position is more popular. The only thing that Simon has going for him is that he is right.

Unfortunately we act as if Simon were wrong. We act as if human judgment was always accurate. But the primary aim of human judgment is not accuracy but the avoidance of paralyzing uncertainty (hence the popularity of religion). We hate uncertainty so much that our judgment processes are geared to speed and confidence—but at a price. They work well in simple situations like deciding who won the ball game or what hat to buy. But they fail in complex situations like deciding the chance of a recession or the validity of a graphology reading. To see why, we look first at how graphologists make their judgments.

HOW GRAPHOLOGISTS MAKE THEIR JUDGMENTS

A serious handwriting analysis may take several hours. Typically the aim is to describe either the client's entire personality or the part relevant to a given area such as employment. There is no single method or approach, but having considered pen, paper, age, sex, handedness, nationality, and aim of the analysis, the graphologist typically proceeds in three broad steps as follows:

1. Gain an initial overall impression.[1]
2. Examine each of typically 20 features such as size and slant.
3. Combine the indications into a global assessment.

The most important step is the last. A golden rule in graphology is that no one graphological feature means anything by itself. In fact Singer (1969:39) says "It should be printed three times at the beginning and end of each chapter in every book on graphology." Thus whatever is suggested by feature A may be modified by features B and C. So each feature must be carefully juggled against everything else before judgment is made. The final judgment is thus a synthesis of isolated features or discrete signs into a meaningful whole or gestalt.

But even that may be simplistic. Some graphologists hold that each feature has a double meaning (basically good vs. bad, such as generous vs. extravagant) depending on the standard of writing. An original and harmonious hand is good. A trite and discordant hand is bad. Other graphologists hold that each feature has many meanings depending on the area involved, such as physical, intellectual, social, or spiritual—in which case the juggling process must be repeated for each area (Singer 1969:81–84).

Never mind. What matters is that graphologists say that handwriting features *interact*. So the whole is more than the sum of its parts, which means it is futile to study isolated features.[2] McNeil and Blum (1952) give a selection of quotes to illustrate such views, and make the following pithy comment:

> While we are quite willing to grant that the whole may represent more than the sum of its parts, it is difficult to see how discrete signs, valueless in themselves, can suddenly be transformed by artful intuition into a highly functional, significant gestalt.

That was in 1952. Since then research into human judgment (which is what this chapter is all about) has thrown much light on what may be happening. We look first at detecting correlations, that is, at how graphologists derived their discrete signs in the first place.

DETECTING CORRELATIONS: OR HOW DO YOU KNOW FORWARD SLANT MEANS EXTROVERTED?

IS YOUR CORRELATION REALLY NECESSARY?

If systems like graphology, astrology, and palmistry are used as entertainment or as an excuse for unburdening your soul, it hardly matters whether extroversion is *really* indicated by forward-slanted writing or Sagittarius rising or short fingers. But if they are presented as being not merely helpful but also true (which is usually the case) then the system *requires* a correlation between each feature and the person; Otherwise the system is pointless, for without such a correlation no feature could mean anything.

In graphology the correlation between each feature and the person is said to be based on observation, despite occasions when this process "was surrendered to metaphysics and armchair speculation" (Roman 1952:9), to say nothing of the huge difficulty, generally unrecognized by graphologists, of assessing the person; see chapter 10 in this book. For our purpose it does not matter whether the feature is a discrete sign or a motor pattern or an overall gestalt or whatever. What matters is that everything begins by detecting a correlation. So how good are we at detecting correlation? And exactly what do we detect? We start with the simplest case, namely detecting correlation in yes/no data using slant as an example.

DETECTING CORRELATION IN YES/NO DATA

When reduced to yes/no data, forward-slanted writing and extroversion can combine in four possible ways as follows:

Forward slant	Extrovert		Example	
	Yes	No	Yes	No
Yes	a	b	35	20
No	c	d	10	10

Correlation phi = (ad-bc) / $\sqrt{((a+b)(c+d)(a+c)(b+d))}$

On the left, abcd are the observed totals for each of the four combinations. As shown by the equation, the correlation between slant and extroversion cannot be determined unless *all* of the four cells are considered. And all four cells are equally important. But most people consider only cell a, while a few consider cell a and one other. Hardly anyone considers all four *even when all four are provided* (Smedslund 1963, Ward and Jenkins 1965, Arkes and Harkness 1983). Look at the (fictitious) example on the right. Does extroversion go with forward slant? The high total of 35 in cell a gives the impression that the correlation is high and useful. But the other cells indicate otherwise—while nearly 80 percent of extroverts have forward slant, so do nearly 70 percent of introverts. In fact the correlation is only .12, which for practical purposes is quite useless.

In other words, without formal training we are hopeless at detecting correlations in yes/no data. If asked whether redheads are hot tempered, or prayers are answered, hardly anyone considers even-tempered brunettes or non-prayed-for answers. Yet no special correlation can exist unless redheads differ from brunettes in the incidence of temper, and praying from not praying in the incidence of answers.[3]

Faust and Nurcombe (1989) point out that the utility of any sign (in this case the graphological indication) depends on two things, namely, (1) the correlation, and (2) the base rate, the rate of occurrence in the base population. Thus for 2000 members of the British Mensa the base rates are 2 percent for colored ink (red, green, or purple), 8 percent for left-handedness, 14 percent for left-slanted writing, and 52 percent for right-slanted writing (Paterson 1976). For areas of graphological interest like managerial ability, the base rate in the general population is typically 10 percent or less. For such low base rates a sign may increase accuracy only if the correlation between sign and managerial ability exceeds about .4 or .5. If it does not, as is invariably the case (see preceding chapter), then *using graphology may make the prediction worse*. This is such an unexpected but crucial point that we explain it at length in note 4.

DETECTING CORRELATION IN PAIRED DATA

When the data are *not* neatly summarized in a table, our ability to detect correlation is even worse. Does giving Tom an apple make him happy? We can detect correlation between these two events only if they occur less than a few seconds apart, they are quantifiable, and the correlation is high enough (Holyoak and Nisbett 1988:61–62). Figure 1 suggests that correlations in paired data are not reliably detected until they exceed about .4, which is rather higher than the correlations of .3 typically observed between trait and behavior in comparable data, i.e., for a group of people in a single situation.[5] Even correlations around .7, which are considered strong by psychologists, are missed by one person in four. Only when the correlations reach .85 and above are they detected by almost everyone.

At this point a problem arises. As shown in the preceding chapter, the observed correlations between personality and graphological features (whether discrete or global) are typically around .2 or less, far too small to be reliably detected. So how did graphologists discover them in the first place? How can countless graphology books imply that the correlations are strong when they are not? The answer is next.

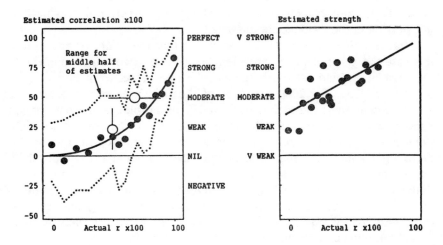

Figure 1. How Good Are We At Detecting Correlation?

Left: Detecting correlation in numbers, drawings, and timing. Jennings et al. (1982) asked 64 undergraduates to look at 16 sets of paired data whose correlation varied from 0 to 1. Each set contained 10 items, either pairs of simple numbers, or drawings of men holding walking sticks. In each case the subjects could study the data for as long as they liked. There was also a spoken letter followed by a tone. The subjects had to estimate on a scale of 0-100 the correlation between the numbers, between the figure height and stick length, and between the alphabet position and tone duration. The results showed no consistent differences so they are plotted together. For each of the 16 actual Pearson r correlations (horizontal axis) there is a black dot showing the mean correlation estimated by the 64 subjects (vertical axis).

The two open circles show the results of a similar study by Oakes (1982). *Lower circle:* 30 psychologists guessed the correlation between two sets of numbers 1-12, whose correlation was .50. *Upper circle:* Another 30 psychologists arranged two sets of numbers 1-12 to give a guessed correlation of .50. The bars indicate the standard deviation.

The main features are as follows: (1) The two studies are in reasonable agreement. (2) The range of individual estimates is very large, showing that judgment was difficult and uncertain. (3) Correlations are consistently *under*estimated, i.e., poorly detected. The relationship seems to be non-linear, albeit less so in the Oakes study, so that weak correlations are proportionately much harder to detect than strong ones. Thus the correlations typically observed in graphology (.0 to .2) are generally beyond unaided detection.

Right: Detecting correlation in behavior. Epstein and Teraspulsky (1986) asked 88 undergraduates to estimate the correlation between various behaviors on a scale of 1 = very weak to 5 = very strong. The correlations had been previously determined for a separate sample of 63 students or 51 problem boys, and ranged from .00 to

.73, e.g., general high activity vs. fights readily (.18), neat desk vs. neat notes (.44), number talked to at lunch vs. number talked to at dinner (.63). For each of the 21 observed Pearson r correlations (horizontal axis) there is a black dot showing the mean strength as estimated by the 88 subjects (vertical axis).

The main features are as follows: (1) Zero correlations are rated weak to moderate, which is probably due to illusory correlation; i.e., the subjects believed the behaviors were correlated when in fact they were not. This is confirmed by the lefthand graph, where the data sets are not subject to illusory correlation, and the curve shows no inflation at zero correlation. (2) The dots are scattered due to the small sample sizes for criteria and estimates, but there is no obvious curvature as in the lefthand graph, probably because the vertical scale is not tied to actual numbers. (3) Nevertheless the vertical scales of both graphs are broadly similar, as are their mean slopes. So the two graphs are broadly consistent. Overall their message is clear, namely, *we are generally poor at detecting correlation.*

Box 1. *Test your skill*

Below are six sets of 10 number pairs similar to those used by Jennings et al. (1982 in Figure 1). Look first at the 10 vertical pairs in the AA row and estimate the correlation between them. That is, how well does one A row keep in tune with the other A row? Then do the same for the BB and other rows. Which row has the highest correlation, AA or BB, CC or DD, EE or FF? All correlations are positive and between 0 and .7, so in each case your answer should be between 0 and .7.

```
A 5 5 1 8 2 2 5 7 2 4      C 5 6 5 5 5 6 3 4 9 4      E 5 1 5 2 1 8 2 6 9 3
A 4 4 8 5 1 4 2 6 4 6 B    C 2 9 4 6 9 9 8 4 5 1 D    E 2 8 3 3 3 8 1 4 4 4 F
  1 7 8 6 1 5 1 6 9 4 B      6 1 9 1 7 4 9 4 3 3 D      2 9 5 9 1 7 5 9 7 7 F
```

For the record, the Pearson r correlation for paired data is given by $r = (a - bc/n) \sqrt{(d-b^2/n)} \sqrt{(e-c^2/n)}$, where abcde = sum of xy, x, y, x^2, y^2 respectively, x and y = values of each pair, and n = number of pairs. Because we cannot juggle so many variables, it will not escape your notice that knowing this equation is no help at all.

Now test your skill at picking randomness with this example from Wagenaar (1988:92). A coin is tossed 50 times. Which of the following five sequences is the most likely? Answers to both tests are given in note 6.

1. hxhxhxxhxhxhxhxxhxhxhxxhhxhxhxhhxhxxhhxxhxhxhxhxxx
2. hxhhxhhxxhhhxxxhxxxhxxhxxhxhxhhxhhhxhhhxxhxxhxhxhx
3. hxhxhhxhhhhhxxxhhxhxhxxhxhhxxxxhxhxxxhhhxxhxxxhxxh
4. xhhhxxhxhxxhxhxhhhxhhxxxhxhhhhhxhhhhhhxhhxxhxxxxxxh
5. xxhhhhhxhxxxhhhhxxhhhxxhxxxxxxxhhhhhxxxxxxhhhxxhhh

DETECTING CORRELATIONS WHERE NONE EXISTS

We make up for our poor ability to detect a real correlation by a spectacular ability to see correlation where none exists. The only requirement is that we know (or think we know) the answer in advance regardless of whether true or not. It also helps if our data is ambiguous and vague, as it will be if nothing is *measured*. For example, if we believe that redheads are hot tempered, then ambiguous behavior can be seen as hot tempered, and vaguely red hair can be seen as red—or the opposite, depending on what we want to see. Confirmation of our belief then follows automatically, especially as we are not disposed to consider even-tempered brunettes.

Consider the Draw-a-Person technique (Machover 1951). You draw a person on a sheet of blank paper, and its size, detail, clothing, etc. supposedly reveal your inner conflicts. Thus close-set eyes mean you have a suspicious nature, big eyes indicate paranoia, and a big head means you worry about intelligence. However, dozens of studies have found these to be stereotypes which are in fact false—*people with such features do not draw such pictures* (Chapman and Chapman 1971, Aiken 1989). The point is that such stereotypes are pervasive and almost impossible to eradicate.[7] In other words if we think we know the answer then accurate judgment is impossible. That is why scientific blind trials (i.e., where experimenters are deliberately not told what is being tested) are necessary when the outcome is crucial, as in testing new drugs.

The phenomenon of believing-is-seeing is called *illusory correlation*.[8] Less illusory are the problems it can cause (see Figure 2). The belief or stereotype can come from anywhere—myths, superstition, rumors, something we read, even experience (see below). . If we believe that forward slant or Sagittarius rising or short fingers indicates an extrovert, then our observations will confirm it even if our belief is false.[9,10] So no matter what others may say, our belief is here to stay, as for this clinical psychologist quoted by Chapman and Chapman (1971):

> I know that paranoids don't draw big eyes in the research labs, but they sure do in my office.

We say more about stereotypes later. In the meantime, if it still seems preposterous that your judgment could be biased by knowing the answer in advance, try the simple test given in note 11.

But what if no stereotypes exist? Does this free us from the tyranny of illusory correlation? Unfortunately not, for this is where *experience* can generate illusory correlations due to a learning process that works like this. Suppose we try our hand at graphology, and our first reading is successful. Since the outcome is good, we try more readings. Even if we tend to be unsuccessful, the occasional success is enough to keep us trying. This process is called *operant conditioning,* where a behavior (graphology)

Figure 2. How Illusory Correlation Can Be Bad for You

The eminent graphologist Nadya Olyanova was consultant to many American psychiatrists and businesses. Two former pupils describe her as having

a highly developed ability to sift the wealth of data, and to coordinate and summarize it. In finding common denominators and arranging them by order of importance, she demonstrates the remarkable capacity of the human mind at the height of alertness. (Olyanova 1969:x)

Perhaps the most important characteristic of Miss Olyanova's techniques in general is that they are so largely a product of her long experience analyzing not hundreds, but thousands of handwritings. (Olyanova 1960: 220)

Her pupils imply that an alert mind and huge experience are sufficient to guarantee accuracy. So what about her neglect (common to nearly all graphologists) of the scientific approach?[12] Olyanova gives this diagram showing the relation of slant to extroversion:

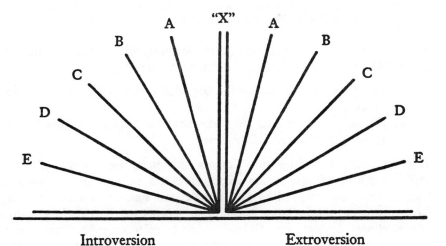

EXTROVERTS AND INTROVERTS

Introversion   Extroversion

Extroverts are "social, gregarious, impulsive, and demonstrative." Introverts are "undemonstrative, reticent, and withdrawn. . . . they . . . usually reflect before taking action." These descriptions are a close match to the extroversion measured by personality tests such as the Eysenck Personality Inventory, so we confidently expect a sizable correlation between slant and test scores. But what we actually get is very close to chance:

Source	Subjects	Mean age	Correlation	p
Harvey (1933)	20 students	21 years	.02 vs. AAS	.93
Lester et al. (1977)	111 students	22 years	.08 vs. EPI	.41
Rosenthal and Lines (1978)	58 students	19 years	-.13 vs. EPI	.33
Furnham and Gunter (1987)	64 adults	early 30s	.10 vs. EPQ	.44

These results indicate that if you judge extroversion by slant, your accuracy is no better than that of tossing a coin. But it gets worse. Olyanova asserts that two people are compatible only if their slants are alike:

There can seldom be compatibility when one person writes leftward and the other rightward. . . . they would have too little in common emotionally, temperamentally, and in interests to ensure a lasting relationship in marriage. . . . Attractions between extroverts and introverts rarely jell. (Olyanova 1969:92)

No hedging here with the futility of looking at isolated features! But compatibility is unrelated to extroversion. For married couples the correlation is around .5 for intelligence and .3 for height, but only .1 at most for extroversion (Eysenck and Wakefield 1981). So even if slant did indicate extroversion, it would be irrelevant to compatibility. In other words the above assertions, delivered with all the authority of an alert mind and huge experience, are wrong twice over. The point is, Olyanova had thousands of clients. How many relationships suffered needlessly from her illusory correlations and neglect of the scientific approach?

is closely followed by something good (success), thus reinforcing the behavior (Alcock (1982:94–97). The crucial points are:

1. The outcome must follow the behavior without delay but need not be related to it.
2. The behavior becomes very resistant to change if reinforced *intermittently* rather than all the time.

Thus intermittent winning on a slot machine encourages further play because we see that frequent non-success does not deny occasional success, whereas ten wins followed by ten losses encourages us to leave believing the machine is broken. Since intermittent success will happen in graphology by chance anyway, we will tend to see correlations even if none actually exist. Here we are concerned only with the conditioning *process* and not with the many ways (of which illusory correlation is only one) of being persuaded that graphology works, for which see later.

Operant conditioning is a powerful process. No reasoning ability is required (even the lowest animals learn in this way), which can cause problems. For when the time interval between two events is short, *learning* occurs automatically, so if no actual relation exists we have to make a conscious effort to overcome such learning. Alcock (1982:16-20) suggests that operant conditioning plays a major role in the development of magical beliefs and superstition generally.

Having observed our correlations, real or illusory, we are now ready for the next step, namely combining them into a prediction.

COMBINING CORRELATIONS INTO PREDICTIONS

HOW MANY CORRELATIONS ARE WE LOOKING AT?

To obtain a judgment, graphologists have to juggle many features at once. So do astrologers, palmists, and orthodox clinicians. According to the books the number of features to be juggled is considerable, as shown below:

Graphology	15–55, typically 20	Number of
Astrology	20–120, typically 40	features to
Palmistry	27–70, typically 40	be juggled
Phrenology	27–92, typically 39	before proper
Rorschach	5×10, i.e., from 10 blots	judgment
Personality tests	1–20, typically 5–10	can be made.

However, our short-term memory cannot juggle more than about 7±2 features at a time, as is apparent whenever we try dialing an unfamiliar 10-digit telephone number.[13] If the features have little in common, we have trouble in juggling even *two* of them. For example, when people are asked to compare circles of various sizes containing spokes at various angles, they tend to look at size *or* angle but not both (Shepard 1964). As a result the information content of the above techniques (except personality tests with few scales) *always* exceeds our capacity to handle it.

This means that practitioners cannot possibly do what they say they do, namely, juggle all relevant features. Even with a memory aid such as pencil and paper, which would always be used in serious work, their task is not much easier. Instead they are forced to do what their golden rule expressly forbids, namely, be selective.[14] For the moment we will ignore this problem and look at the ways in which we transform parts into wholes, starting with intuition.[15]

INTUITION: APPREHENSION BY MEANS UNKNOWN

Common to the first five systems listed above is the supposed faculty of intuition, also called insight or hunch or gut feeling, which is frequently assumed by experts and generously attributed to the entire female sex. Its key features are (1) everything happens in your head, and (2) answers pop up out of nowhere.

However, since the 1930s there has been evidence that intuition comes not from nowhere but from previous experience.[16,17] The relevant experience may not be quickly remembered or its existence even recognized, in which case the incubation process so helpful in problem solving may merely reflect the time needed for (unconscious) retrieval. Similarly the supposed effortless, unanalyzable, and instant nature of intuition means nothing; driving a car requires endless decisions of exactly this nature, but from our first fumbling steps at learning to drive they clearly owe nothing to intuition as traditionally conceived.

For these reasons most cognitive psychologists discount intuition. For example Dawes (1988:204), a leading expert in judgment psychology, comments that unless the person relying on intuition has good evidence for its validity, meaning sound experimental data rather than plausible arguments, then the use of intuition "is in my view arbitrary, stupid, and unethical."

A useful clarification is provided by Cook (1982), who points out that the confusion surrounding intuition would disappear if it was redefined as "a skill so thoroughly learned that one is not conscious of its operation." The alternative to intuition is inference.

INFERENCE: APPREHENSION BY THINKING

Human inference is made on the basis of (1) what we see, and (2) what we know. We see that Mary Lou wears glasses. We know that people who wear glasses are brainy. Therefore Mary Lou is brainy.

However there are problems. What we see may be wrong (the glasses are only safety spectacles) or what we know may be wrong (not everyone who wears glasses is brainy). Actually nearsightedness *is* associated with high IQ but the correlation is only around .2 (Jahoda 1962, Karlsson 1978), which emphasizes our next point.[18] Co-occurrences in real life are far from perfect, so we should always think in tendencies and in shades of gray. But there is abundant evidence that we cannot do this (Kahneman and Tversky 1973). Instead we use black and white, and persist in using our favorite information long after we have evidence of its inutility. For example, we tend to see smoking vs. lung cancer not as a gray tendency but as either black (cancer cures smoking) or white (grandma smoked 50 a day and lived to be 95).

Our attempts to combine information can lead to peculiar judgments, especially when its relevance is uncertain. Is a man likely to assault his friends if he is aggressive when drunk? Probably. If he is aggressive but a good darts player? Probably not! (from Bromley 1986:247).

Our problems do not end there. People are good at picking predictors but bad at combining them. As explained next.

COMBINING PREDICTORS: PEOPLE VS. EQUATIONS

A predictor is something we use to predict something else. Thus wrinkles, false teeth, and gray hair are predictors of old age. When we have many predictors we combine them in clever ways. For example, we ignore wrinkles if caused by sunbathing, ignore false teeth if due to an accident, suspect hair dye if an old person's hair is not gray, and so on. This cleverness sets us apart from machines, or so we like to believe.

But we are wrong. In reality people are so bad at *combining* predictors that their results are consistently worse than simply *adding* predictors.[19,20] This remarkable finding has been tested in over 100 studies involving all kinds of judgment from people to economic trends, and in all but 6 cases (mostly medical) the finding has been confirmed (Dawes et al. 1989). When equation is pitted against expert using the same codable predictors,[21] the equation is always as good and usually better. Table 1 gives examples. In fact, the findings are so controversial yet so consistent that a former president of the American Psychological Association could comment:

> There is no controversy in social science that shows such a large body of qualitatively diverse studies coming out so uniformly in the same direction as this one. When you are pushing 90 investigations, predicting everything from the outcome of football games to the diagnosis of liver disease, and when you can hardly come up with half a dozen studies showing even a weak tendency in favor of the clinician, it is time to draw a practical conclusion, whatever theoretical differences may still be disputed. (Meehl 1986)

Naturally the findings are an affront to vested interests. Who would dare imagine that an equation could outperform the experience, sensitivity, and intuitive skills of the human expert? Certainly not the expert.[22] Related findings (Dawes et al. 1989) add to the affront. Minimally-trained people do as well as experts (see also Faust and Ziskin 1988, and Garb 1989, for reviews relevant to personality assessment). Accuracy is unrelated to confidence. When equation judgments are partialled out of expert judgments, the result is usually close to zero, indicating that experts have noth-

Table 1. Examples of expert judgments vs. equations.

Area	N	Judgment	No. of experts	Correlation with Experts	Equation
Academic	90	Student performance.	80	.35.	60
Astrology	120	Extroversion and emotionality.	45	.01	.14*
Economics	60	Which firm will go bankrupt?	43	.50	.64
Graphology	52	Job performance.	3	.19	.30**
Medical	193	How soon will patient die?	3	.00	.42
MMPI	861	Neurotic or psychotic?	29	.28	.34
Shapes	180	Ellipse size and color.	6	.84	.97

*Vs. age   **Vs. 9 variables such as army rank and neatness of writing.

The above table shows the correlation between actual outcome and the outcome predicted by (1) experts and (2) an equation using the same data. No matter what area is involved, the equation outperforms the experts in each case. MMPI = Minnesota Multiphasic Personality Inventory, a widely-used test of disturbed personality.

From top, sources are Wiggins and Kohen (1971), Dean (1985), Libby (1976) and Goldberg (1976), Ben-Shakhar et al. (1986), Einhorn (1972), Goldberg (1965), Yntema and Torgerson (1961).

ing useful to add. Indeed, letting experts revise the equation judgment usually makes it worse. This does not make experts redundant—they are still needed to select the predictors. Armstrong (1978:85) suggests that the place of experts "is in saying how things are (estimating current status), rather than in predicting how things will be (forecasting change)."

But what if no equation is available? Can anything be done to improve the experts? Shanteau (1988) studied experts recognized by their peers as being the best (in auditing, business management, livestock judging, nursing, personnel selection, or soil judging) and found several characteristics that set them apart from lesser experts. For example, they could home in on the relevant information, were always right up to date with the latest developments, and knew which problems to tackle and which to avoid. *They also used strategies designed to overcome cognitive limitations.* For example, they sought feedback from associates, learned from past successes and failures, used aids such as written records to aid judgment biases, focused on avoiding really bad mistakes rather than on being exactly right, and solved large problems by dividing into parts and then reassembling the partial solutions. Shanteau suggests that novices will become genuine experts only if their natural thinking patterns match the above. Some of these patterns may be teachable, others such as those requiring creativity may not. Nevertheless, the general failure of experts when pitted against equations suggests that, for most of us, equations are the best option. For a review of how to choose between using experts and equations or both, with many examples and helpful suggestions, see Kleinmuntz (1990).

Even the crudest of equations can be surprisingly effective. Thus Dawes (1979) could predict marital happiness by lovemakings/week minus arguments/week, whereas neither predictor was effective alone. The trick is to pick the right predictors and know how to add. But why should equations perform better than people?

WHY SHOULD EQUATIONS PERFORM BETTER THAN PEOPLE?

Let us be clear what these studies are telling us. They tell us that two basic patterns underlie apparently complex human judgments:

1. Judges do not use the process they think they use.
2. Simply adding the predictors usually outperforms the judges.

Judges think they use more than simple weighting and adding. For example, if A then X=Y, but if B then X=Z. But tests reveal a different story. For example, analysis of the way physicians diagnose ulcers from X-ray photos (Hoffman et al. 1968), or decide to release patients (Rorer et al. 1967), showed that most of the time they just added up their favorite cues, despite their claims to the contrary. The problem of course is that judges seldom agree on the relevant cues and on their weighting.[14]

We can now see why equations perform better than people. They simulate what we actually do, i.e., add up our favorite cues. But they do it more consistently. When people make complex judgments as in graphology, the proliferation of cues overwhelms their capacity to be consistent. Give us more than one or two interrelated cues to juggle and we are lost. Indeed it is difficult not to get lost even when the cues are *not* interrelated (Slovic 1974). By contrast an equation never gets lost. It is always consistent. It can handle any degree of complexity, never gets tired, and is never distracted by irrelevant cues. So it is not surprising that equations outperform experts using the same cues.

Having combined our correlations into a prediction, we are now ready for the final step, namely assessing the results. At this point we take on board a staggering number of biases, discussed next. We start with a look at some testimonials on graphological judgments.

BIASES IN HUMAN JUDGMENT: OR HOW TO BE WRONG WITHOUT EVEN TRYING

TESTIMONIALS: CAN COUNTLESS CLIENTS BE WRONG?

Graphologists believe in graphology because it seems to work. Their belief is not based on scientific evidence, for if it were, there would be little or no belief. Instead their belief rests on face validity, where graphology *looks* like it should work, and on the satisfaction of clients, a process called *personal validation* (Bar-Hillel and Ben-Shakhar 1986, Ben-Shakhar et al. 1986). Not surprisingly, opinions on the result are divided. On the one hand there are opinions like this one from John Mansfield, a British producer of TV documentaries on personality assessment:

> . . . graphologists are still their own worst enemy as far as gaining recognition goes. Much of their published work is based on little, if any, experimentally proven evidence; remarkably few scientifically controlled studies have been undertaken; and many books and articles purporting to be written by qualified, responsible graphologists are so crammed with wild generalizations that, however titillating they may be, they deter serious study. . . . Tragically for the prestige of graphology, it is precisely because everyone has a sneaking belief that it makes sense that charlatans have found it an easy way to make a living, particularly when they present their findings in the ambiguous terms of a newspaper horoscope wherein every reader can see some element of truth. (Mansfield 1975:73)

On the other hand there are testimonials from satisfied clients:

> "[The graphologist] told me some things that were of such a personal nature I was surprised he would know. . . .He said 'Here are some things you might be afraid of. . . . here are some situations you're going to run into.' " (Purvis 1987)

> The president of a savings and credit union says, "We find [the graphologist] very, very accurate, uncannily so." (Purvis 1987)

> The personnel director of another credit union says, "At first I thought it was black magic . . . but after seeing it work, it's obviously not." (Griffin 1988)

> A seventeen-year-old youth on the brink of suicide says, "I thought no one cared; I knew no one would believe me. Couldn't talk about it to anybody. Then somebody looked at my handwriting and told me what was going on in my head." (Hollander and Parker 1989)

The managing director of a British employment agency which uses graphology says the analysis of his own handwriting "was remarkably accurate. It also added to self-knowledge and has since contributed to greater effectiveness in doing my job." (Reid 1983)[23]

Furthermore there are testimonials from eminent men such as these taken from Severn (1913:6) and Hungerford (1930):

Thomas Edison: "I never knew I had an inventive talent until graphology told me. I was a stranger to myself until then."

Andrew Carnegie: "Not to know yourself graphologically is sure to keep you standing on the Bridge of Sighs all your life."

Alfred Russel Wallace: "The graphologist has shown that he is able to read character like an open book . . . with an accuracy that the most intimate friends cannot approach."

Edgar Allen Poe: "Graphology is no longer to be laughed at. . . . it has assumed the majesty of a science and as a science ranks among the most important."

Impressive stuff. After all, these people have been there. *They know.* Despite what Mansfield says, are you not convinced that graphology works? Before you answer, be aware that we have doctored the eminent quotes—every reference to *graphology* is actually to *phrenology,* a system of reading character from brain development as shown by head size and shape. The point is, the claims of phrenology are now known to be wrong.[24] So a bulge here or a depression there cannot mean what it is supposed to mean. If eminent men of the highest standing can testify to nonexistent effects, then what price testimonials?

More to the point, how can an invalid system like phrenology *seem* valid? The answer is simple—*personal validation is hopelessly unreliable.* The validity we perceive can be due to many factors, none of them related to the factor supposedly responsible (Hyman 1977, Marks and Kammann 1980). As a result the system can be totally invalid yet totally accepted.[25] The factors actually responsible are generated by our judgment biases, discussed next. Some apply to judgment in general. Others apply to the judgment of personality descriptions. We look at these in turn.

BIASES IN GENERAL JUDGMENT

We cannot attend to everything, so our judgment must be selective to avoid overload. Otherwise we would drift forever in a sea of possibilities so vast that the idea *fire causes burns* would be no more likely than the idea *ice causes baldness*. What happens is that we attend to a manageable subset selected by our ideas (which may be wrong), by our problem (which makes us look here rather than there), and by our cognitive ability (which may be inadequate), all of which generate bias.[26] Here bias means *systematic error* not *prejudice*.

People are quite good at things that require only counting. As marbles are drawn at random from a bag, we can estimate their average size or the proportion of red quite well. But once we start using *data drawn from memory* we become subject to the following biases:

1. *Vividness*. We attend more to things that are noticeable or vivid. You decide to buy car X because 1000 readers of *Consumer Reports* liked it. By chance you meet someone who hates their X. It leaks, rattles, belches smoke, guzzles gas, and is always breaking down. Suddenly you decide against buying X, even though your database of 1000 has been incremented by only one. Tornadoes make the headlines whereas asthma does not, so you guess that tornado deaths are more common than asthma deaths. You are wrong (Fischoff 1988:177). Vivid images always have more impact, and we remember them for reasons other than their actual frequency (which is what matters). This is known as the availability heuristic (*heuristic* comes from the Greek and means an *aid to discovery*).

It has an interesting corollary. To us our situation is more vivid than our personality, whereas the personality of others is more vivid than their situation. So we attribute *our* behavior to situation but *their* behavior to personality (Jones 1976). This is called the fundamental attribution error. Among other things it is a further complication for those claiming to see personality in handwriting.

2. *Representativeness*. We go by looks and ignore base rate, the rate of occurrence in the base population. At the Massachusetts Institute of Technology you meet Tom, who looks like a poet. Is he a poet or a physicist? To answer poet is to ignore base rate—physicists are much more common at MIT than poets. Are you amazed by psychic predictions? To answer yes is to ignore base rate—the incidence of fraud among psychics is high (Brandon 1983). You toss four coins and get HTTH. Is this more likely than HHHH? It looks more likely but in fact both are equally likely. The apparent representativeness blinds us to the actual frequency (which is what matters). This is known as the representativeness heuristic.

3. *Stereotypes.* Once we perceive a person as old or Irish or having neat writing, or a car as expensive or a good runner or a lemon, then a great number of attributes follow *automatically,* some right, some wrong. Such preconceptions of what to expect are called stereotypes, useful short-cuts that we use to avoid our pet hates of uncertainty and having to think. Thus there are stereotypes for almost everything from laundry detergents to restaurants. And they work. Coke and Pepsi stereotypes prevail over taste differences (Woolfolk et al. 1983). Ada and Mason are seen as better therapists than Gladys and Fritz (Gladding and Farrar 1982). Lisa and David get 5 percent better marks than Bertha and Hubert for the same essays (Harari and McDavid 1973). Neat writing gets 15 percent better marks than untidy writing for the same essays (Briggs 1970). Mouth curvature is seen as kind, friendly and easygoing, and thin lips as conscientious (r= .7 for both, Secord et al. 1954). A dramatic example of visual stereotypes was discussed earlier in note 7.

The important features of stereotypes are as follows: (1) They are part of the human way of judgment. (2) They do not arise from our observations, because our ability to detect correlation is too poor. Instead they arise from what some person (or book, newspaper, TV program, song, or joke) told us. (3) Even if the stereotype is totally false, we always meet confirming cases in cell a by chance alone, so the stereotype is almost impossible to eradicate. Especially as confirmation of any *part* of it will be seen as evidence for *all* of it—one red hot momma in a sea of tight-lipped matrons is all we need. (4) Explanations (male chauvinists are pigs because . . .) serve to maintain the stereotype. (5) Like other beliefs, stereotypes are acted on (see above examples). For all these reasons, stereotypes are pervasive and a potent source of bias. All too easily are we like the psychoanalyst who accused clients who came late of hostility, those who came early of defensiveness, and those who came on time of compulsiveness (from Nisbett & Ross 1980:242).

4. *Sample size.* We recognize that people are more variable than peas, and that to make a reliable judgment we need more people than peas (Nisbett et al. 1983). But once past the first few, we think that a small sample of 10 is as good as a larger one of 100 (it is not), and that the difference between a random sample and one selected to prove a point is unimportant (it is hugely important). This failing is sarcastically called the law of small numbers (Tversky and Kahneman 1971), in distinction to the statistical law of large numbers which says the bigger the sample the better it represents the population it came from.

5. *Inflation of coincidence.* In a Paris hotel we are amazed to meet a long-forgotten school friend. The co-occurrence of *this* city, *this* place, and *this* friend seems wildly improbable. But in reality the co-occurrence of *a* city, *a* place, and *a* friend is not so unlikely (Marks and Kamman 1980:165, Falk 1981). A woman won the New Jersey lottery twice in four months, for which *her* chance was an amazing 1 in 17 million million. But many millions of people buy U.S. lottery tickets, and the chance that *some* person will win twice in their lifetime is better than 50:50 over a 7-year period (quoted by Diaconis and Mosteller 1989).[27] There is also a strong egocentric influence—we find our coincidences more amazing than your coincidences, and our coincidences amaze us more than they amaze others, even when they are between random numbers and are therefore truly meaningless (Falk 1989).

6. *Order.* We try to create order even when it does not exist. If we take a fair coin and toss 5 heads in a row, we feel the next toss is bound to redress the balance. But we are wrong. This is called the gambler's fallacy, because the probability of heads is a constant .5 regardless of what went before (Yackulic and Kelly 1984).

7. *Overconfidence.* We tend to be overconfident in our judgments. Thus we can be 100 percent confident in our reply to general-knowledge questions even though our accuracy averages only 80 percent (Fischoff et al. 1977). This overconfidence applies even in physics, where current values for several constants such as the speed of light lie well beyond one standard deviation of many earlier values (Fischoff 1988:173–175). For a long time the British national electricity supply suffered from its engineer's overconfidence in predicting the time taken to overhaul electric generators, even though the predictions were made long after each overhaul had started. It now multiplies their predictions by two (Kidd 1970).

Box 2. *De-biasing your data analysis*

If you snoop around in data looking for something interesting then your biases are bad news. Diaconis (1988) suggests you try the following remedies:
- Graph the results so you can *see* what is happening.
- If you tried N tests, multiply your individual p values by N.
- Test the findings from one half of the sample on the other half.
- Compare your results with those of similar or nearly similar studies.
- Replicate on fresh data, or if unavailable, on random data.

BIASES IN JUDGING DESCRIPTIONS OF PEOPLE

Whatever the system, be it graphology, astrology, palmistry, or a personality test, the end result is a prediction of what we are like. If it seems accurate, then we are persuaded that the system works. What could be simpler? How could we possibly be wrong? As we shall see, the answer is *very easily*. Such judgments are subject to so many biases that a detailed description of just some of them has occupied entire books, for example (in order of decreasing readability) Armstrong 1978, Dawes 1988, Hogarth 1987, Sternberg and Smith 1988, Kahneman et al. 1982, Nisbett and Ross 1980. So what follows is a brief survey only. An overview with some additional biases appears in Table 2.

Before we start, two points need to be made. First, the biases apply to person descriptions from any source, not just graphology. Second, each bias varies in effectiveness depending on the situation and the people involved. So in a particular case some may be trivial and others may be irrelevant. However, they *all* operate in the direction of reinforcing belief, with *no* opposing biases other than the informed critical mind, which of course is not a bias in the sense used here. For convenience we list them in alphabetical order.

1. *Asking the wrong questions.* Or how we accentuate the positive. If graphology says a person is extroverted, we tend to test it with extroverted questions (do you go to parties?), rather than introverted questions (do you read books?). Since introverts occasionally do extroverted things, the answer (yes I go to parties) will necessarily confirm graphology. In other words we tend to test graphology with strategies that are bound to *confirm* it (Glick and Snyder 1986), whereas it would be more efficient to use strategies that would *disconfirm* it.[28] This is the same as "not considering all four cells" discussed earlier in "Detecting Correlation in Yes/No Data."

2. *Aunt Fanny effect.* Or bigger is better. Superfluous statements that say nothing (you have trouble performing optimally under stress; you have unconscious hostile urges) should prompt the alert reader to think "So has my Aunt Fanny!" (Tallent 1958). This is similar to the Barnum effect (see next) except the intent is not to satisfy the reader but to pad out the reading. If size impresses, then we will be impressed.

Table 2. Twenty-six ways to convince clients that graphology works.

Principle	Factor	How it works
Cues	Cold reading	Let body language be your guide.
	Hot reading	Let the content give the game away.
Disregard for reality	Illusory validity	Sound argument yes, sound data no.
	Procrustean effect	Force your client to fit his writing.
	Regression effect	Winter doesn't last forever.
	Selective memory	Remember only the hits.
Faith	Placebo effect	It does us good if we think it does.
	Predisposition	Preach to the converted.
Generality	Barnum effect	Statement has something for everybody.
	Variability	Everybody has something for statement.
Gratification	Client misfortune*	The power of positive thinking.
	Rapport*	Closeness is its own reward.
Invention	Illusory correlation	Know the answer in advance.
	Non-falsifiability	Safety in numbers.
Packaging	Aunt Fanny effect	Bigger is better.
	Dr. Fox effect	Blind them with science and humor.
	Face validity	It works if it looks like it should.
	Halo effect	The importance of first impressions.
	Social desirability	I'm firm, you're obstinate, he's !!!
Self-fulfilling prophecies	Hindsight bias	Once seen, the fit seems inevitable.
	Projection effect	Find meaning where none exists.
	Self-attribution	Role play your handwriting.
Self-justification	Charging a fee*	The best things in life are not free.
	Cognitive dissonance	Reduce conflict—see what you believe.
Testing	Missing out cells	Ask only confirming questions.
	Ignorance	Yes we have no way of checking validity.

*Not discussed in text but mechanism will be self-evident.

The above table shows there are many non-graphological reasons why clients should be satisfied by a graphology reading, none of which require that graphology be true. But if clients are going to be satisfied, then graphologists can hardly fail to believe in graphology. In this way a vicious circle of reinforcement is established whereby graphologists and their clients become more and more persuaded that graphology works. A graphologist typically spends years learning to read handwriting and thus has ample chance to respond to such reinforcement. (Adapted and enlarged from Dean 1987).

3. *Barnum effect*. Or how we accept vague statements as being specific for us when in fact they apply to everybody. Named after P. T. Barnum's circuses which had a little something for everybody. A typical Barnum statement is "You tend to be critical of yourself." Sundberg (1955) identified the most readily accepted types of statement as follows:

Favorable:	You are forceful and well-liked by others.
Vague:	You enjoy a certain amount of change and variety.
Double-headed:	You are generally cheerful and optimistic but get depressed at times.
Typical:*	You find that study is not always easy.

The Barnum effect is pervasive and has attracted over 60 studies; for reviews see Dickson and Kelly (1985) and Furnham and Schofield (1986). Not unexpectedly, the result of accepting Barnum statements is an increase in belief. For example, McKelvie (1990) gave the same set of Barnum statements to 108 students as a supposed interpretation of their handwriting. As a result their belief in graphology rose from 3.6 to 4.7 (mean standard deviation 1.5) on a 7-point scale of 1 (not at all) to 7 (completely).

In general the acceptance of Barnum statements is strongly increased if: (1). the *reading* is general, favorable, and short, and is said to apply specifically to the client. (2) The *favorability* suits the client's personality. Beware unfavorable items (you are not an independent thinker) unless the client is introverted, emotional, or fatalistic (Furnham 1989). However, the occasional unfavorable item adds plausibility provided it is also very general (Hyman 1977:31). (3) The *client* is naive and insecure. (4) The *situation* is intimidating, as for students in class or when the reading is expensive.

Acceptance is weakly increased if: (1) The *reader* is confident and of high status. This works only if the statements are favorable. (2) The *method* is mysterious. Thus a projective test (what do you see in this inkblot?) is more mysterious than an interview. (3) The *data required* are as exact as possible. Thus statements supposedly based on month of birth are accepted less readily than those supposedly based on year, month, day, and minute of birth (Snyder 1974). (4) The reading contains *qualifiers* such as "but", "nevertheless", and "in spite of" (Rim 1981).

Acceptance is little affected by the sex of the participants, and by whether the reading is oral or written or computerized.

Many of the above features fit graphology exactly. But why are Barnum statements so readily accepted? The answer is not because we are gullible but because the statements fit—and if they fit they will be accepted.

---

*In this case of students.

Here it is vital to distinguish between *accurate* statements and *trivial* statements.[29] Barnum statements are accurate but trivial; i.e., they say nothing really important or specific. They do not tell us how we differ from others, which is what matters. If we judge only on accuracy, then Barnum statements tend to win when pitted against interviews (Gage 1952) and personality tests (Sundberg 1955). But if we also judge on triviality, they lose (Furnham and Schofield 1986:175). So we are not completely gullible. That is the good news. The bad news is that we tend *not* to judge on triviality unless prompted.

In graphology, individual-feature interpretations may appear specific, such as *cautious* or *wasteful* or *shy* or *vain*, but in combination they tend to become Barnum statements. Note also that we have all been each of these things at some time or another. However, the problem is not unique to graphology. Due to the universality of human traits it is difficult to avoid at least some Barnum statements in any personality description. The trick is to focus on traits that make a person different (Tallent 1958) and to distinguish between accuracy and triviality.

4. *Client predisposition.* Or preaching to the converted. A predisposition to believe in graphology must already exist among clients or they would not have contacted a graphologist in the first place. Furthermore, it is a common experience among graphologists that their clients tend to be uncritical. Hence there will be little to stop the predisposition becoming a reality.

5. *Cognitive dissonance.* Or the need to justify our decisions. If we believe in graphology, then it is painful to find discrepancies between our belief and reality, especially when graphology readings cost us money. So we search (unconsciously or otherwise) for personal attributes to match the graphology. Given the variability of human nature, the search can hardly fail. Cognitive dissonance is among the most potent of the effects listed here (Dean 1987:259–260).

6. *Cold reading.* Or how body language tells the story. Here the graphologist uses cues (e.g., pupil dilation and hand movements) leaked by the client to home in on the truth (Hyman 1977, Dutton 1988). Such cues may be used quite unwittingly. Thus Neher (1980) concluded from observations of astrology/palmistry/Tarot/etc. readers that they were often "astute, sensitive individuals who pick up subtle clues leaked by the client. Usually neither the reader nor the client is consciously aware of this communication process, which therefore can result in a reading that seems mysteriously perceptive." The point is that a skilled cold reader can produce

a totally convincing reading very similar to a graphology reading (and probably more accurate) but without using graphology (Nelson 1971).[30] In which case it cannot be claimed that graphology plays an essential part in the reading process. This would not of course apply to readings written down before the client arrives, or to readings by mail order, especially if addressed to specific abilities.

7. *Dr. Fox effect.* Or how style can be more important than content. Dr. Fox was an actor who was coached to give a meaningless one-hour talk on games theory to 55 psychiatrists and social workers (Naftulin et al. 1973). He looked distinguished, sounded authoritative, and lectured charismatically with much jargon, enthusiasm, jokes, and references to unrelated topics. His talk was highly entertaining but deliberately meaningless. Yet the audience found it to be clear and stimulating, and nobody realized it was nonsense. In other words an expressive presentation can persuade us to see meaning where none exists. The Dr. Fox effect explains why Evans (1973) could remark of L. Ron Hubbard (whose style was exactly that of Dr. Fox) that "one gets the feeling that were Hubbard to stand on the platform and recite the telephone directory backwards he would still receive a standing ovation." To the extent that a graphologist is authoritative, witty, and entertaining, clients will be seduced into believing what they hear. The Dr. Fox effect also extends to writing, where perceived prestige increases with increasing unintelligibility (Armstrong 1979).

8. *Face validity.* Or if it looks right, then it is right. Thus a new radio looks functional even if its batteries are dead. Graphology certainly has face validity, with features that look like they *should* work, a lengthy history, impressive jargon, national organizations, national and international conferences, and a huge literature.[31] To the unwary the effect is dazzling.

9. *Halo effect.* Or how one favorable trait causes us to infer the presence of others. Numerous studies have shown that we are more likely to believe a person if they are warm rather than cold, if they are authoritative rather than indecisive, if they are well-dressed rather than dowdy, and if they are encountered in prestigious surroundings rather than non-prestigious ones. In other words packaging can work wonders for graphologists, their claims, and their products (Cooper 1981, Kelly and Renihan 1984).

10. *Hindsight bias.* Or the I-knew-it-all-along effect. Once we know the answer we find plenty of evidence to support our judgment, so we feel we knew it all along when in fact we did not (Fischoff 1982). Once a match has been found between handwriting and person, it will be hard

to see how it could be any other way. In which case the graphologist gains a strong impression that the match was inevitable, and thus gains unwarranted confidence in graphology. Once a match has been found, the rest of the sequence from bias to conviction follows automatically. Hindsight bias is important because we are unaware of it, it affects everybody, it limits our ability to learn from experience, and it is not affected by strategies designed to reduce it, such as providing prizes or advance warnings. The last means that any graphologists who read this are unlikely to be influenced by it.

Of course for hindsight bias to operate a match must exist between handwriting and person. But given the large number of features that can be seen in handwriting, and the variability of personality (most of us have been everything at one time or another), some match is inevitable. No matter whether our slant indicates we like or dislike people around us, we can always find instances where it is true.

11. *Hot reading.* Or with all this input who needs graphology? Graphologists need to know in advance the client's age, sex, handedness, and nationality. Some may also require brief medical, educational, and social details as well. Such data alone can lead to predictions of modest validity, especially if the writing sample contains personal data, as is usually the case if it forms an application for employment. Thus a survey of 17 studies of personnel selection showed that graphologists were generally outperformed by psychologists using the same writing, even though both did poorly, suggesting that any validity was due to content alone (Neter and Ben-Shakhar 1989). This point is examined further in the preceding chapter.

12. *Ignorance is bliss.* Or believing what you cannot prove. Large-scale clients of graphologists, such as companies and organizations, are seldom able to check each reading against the truth (Bar-Hillel and Ben-Shakhar 1986). Criteria for predictions such as honesty may be unavailable, there may be no time for checks, the candidate may be rejected out of hand, and so on. In which case the reading cannot fail to be accepted provided it sounds good and matches our ideas of what people are like.

13. *Illusory correlation.* Or seeing only what we want to see because we know the answer in advance. This most potent effect was discussed earlier in "Detecting Correlation Where None Exists."

14. *Illusory validity.* Or making ostensibly sound judgments from unsound data. If a graphologist is judging whether a person should be a librarian, his confidence is determined by how well the handwriting fea-

tures happen to match his librarian stereotype, even though the features and stereotype may lack validity. A good fit will thus produce an illusion of validity (Tversky and Kahneman 1974). The important point is that the illusion persists even when we should know better. Thus a psychologist can feel confident about projective tests or unstructured interviews even though a vast literature shows both to be highly fallible. Similarly, after reading a graphological description of personality, we feel we know the person and can predict his behavior, even though graphology is unproven and personality is generally a poor predictor of behavior in a specific situation.

But if the validity is an illusion, why don't we notice it? One good reason is illusory correlation (see previous item). Another is that even though a stereotype may be unsound it can boost accuracy as well as confidence. Asked to say what Tom will do, we invoke the stereotype and say what people in general will do—meaning we play with Barnum statements. As noted under *Barnum effect,* the result is usually more accurate than a specific prediction (Gage 1952). So the illusion will persist. Conversely, if we are prevented from using stereotypes, our accuracy is drastically reduced. The effect of stereotypes can be minimized by rating all subjects on one trait at a time, so later ratings will be less influenced by earlier ones.

15. *Nonfalsifiability.* Or why graphology cannot possibly be wrong. Should the graphologist make a wrong statement he has an endless supply of plausible explanations as follows:

Client does not know himself. Graphologist is not infallible.	This shifts the blame from graphology to the participants.
Another feature is responsible. Manifestation is nontypical.	This puts the blame on the ambiguity of the indication.

In an emergency he can always turn to his bookshelf. For example, depending on whether you believe Lowengard (1975) or Greene and Lewis (1980), red ink indicates *vitality and affection* or a *disturbed personality,* and green ink indicates *harmonious and adaptable* or *different and nonconforming.* Such strategies make the whole process nonfalsifiable. Once the reading has begun, the end result can hardly fail to support graphology. No matter what the client now believes, the graphologist's belief in graphology remains unassailed.

16. *Placebo effect.* Or how anything will do us good if we think it will. From the Latin *I will please.* Thus a gelatine capsule filled with table

salt, and given with the assurance that it will bring sleep, will actually do so for about 1 person in 3 (Melzack and Wall 1983). Here it is the faith itself, not the doctrine, which is the effective agent (Prioleau et al. 1983). Placebos are effective even when people know they are receiving them (Levine and Gordon 1984). In fact, the effect is so potent (whether in medicine or psychotherapy or graphology) that entire books have been written about it and the special experimental strategies needed to cope with it (e.g., Spiro 1986). If people have a strong need to believe in graphology, then that alone will be enough to convince them of its validity.

17. *Procrustean effect.* Or forcing the client to fit his handwriting. After the mythical Procrustes who stretched his guests' limbs or lopped them off to fit his bed. Much easier than you might think.[10] It can also work over time. Knowing that a person should be X (when in reality they are not), we behave in a way that elicits X, thus producing a self-fulfilling prophecy. For example, a waiter who suspects you are a poor tipper may give poor service, thus helping his suspicion come true.

18. *Projection effect.* Or finding meaning where none exists. Hyman (1977) points out that in order to comprehend anything we have to make sense out of what is normally a disorderly array of inputs. Because the inputs are so numerous, to survive we have to be selective. The problem with this necessary process occurs when no actual message is being conveyed, because we then manage to find meaning where none exists, as when we see images in clouds or in vague interpretations. Ironically, the vulnerability to being led astray may increase with the ability to comprehend and hence with intelligence. But the problems do not end there. As Hyman (1981) and Connor (1984) point out, words and sentences do not exist like chunks of rock but have to be interpreted before they mean anything. Thus the message we receive is determined by our previous programming, that is, by the experiences and expectations we draw on to give it meaning. Thus normally trivial statements (you have problems with money) may seem deeply meaningful.

19. *Regression towards the mean.* Or the natural alternation of ups and downs. If today is very windy, it will most likely be less windy tomorrow. So the natural tendency is for extreme situations to become less extreme, i.e., to regress towards the mean (Tversky and Kahneman 1974). Thus football players who do poorly in one game will tend to do better in the next (so our criticism will seem to work), whereas those who did brilliantly will tend to do worse (so our praise will seem premature). Similarly, if clients consult a graphologist when their fortunes are low, they

are likely to improve anyway. Because regression is generally unrecognized, clients will tend to attribute their improvement to graphology.

20. *Role playing effects.* A variant of the self-fulfilling prophecy. If we write with a forward slant, and we know this supposedly indicates extroversion, we tend to see ourselves as more extroverted than would otherwise be the case (see Jones 1986). The effect probably varies greatly from one person to the next, but overall it is important because it can affect independent measures such as personality tests (Delaney and Woodyard 1974, Layne and Ally 1980). Thus the effect is sufficient to explain the apparent correlation of about .1 between test scores and astrological signs (Eysenck and Nias 1982). The effect is also known as self-attribution.

21. *Selective memory.* Or remembering the hits and not the misses. Here our memory is selective not because of inherent bias (although this can occur; see previous section and note 26) but because we think that striking coincidences cannot occur by chance (Marks and Kamman 1980:165; Falk 1981). In a graphology reading the number of things that can exist in both handwriting and person are so large that some kind of striking hit is more than likely. This will not be recognized as a statistical artifact and so will be remembered as evidence for graphology. The misses will of course be forgotten or explained away. Assisting our selective memory is the operant conditioning process discussed earlier, where behavior becomes resistant to change if reinforced intermittently rather than all the time. Since intermittent success will happen in graphology by chance anyway, our chances of becoming hooked are excellent, leaving selective memory to finish the job.

22. *Social desirability effects.* Or the nicer the statement the greater its acceptance. People agree very closely on what they see as desirable or undesirable, and this agreement is maintained across age groups, class, and culture (Edwards 1967: 48–70). On average, social desirability is roughly equal in effect to the statement itself, and the correlation between desirability and acceptance is around .9, which is extremely high. Thus to make people believe what you say, tell them they are *cautious, self-controlled, and thrifty* rather than *timid, inhibited, and stingy*. In other words be positive rather than negative. Since a golden rule in graphological counseling is *be positive*, this can be an unexpectedly potent influence. For example Green et al. (1971) got 7 graphologists and 7 adult subjects to rank themselves on 20 traits such as cautious, conceited, dependable, and stubborn (note the differences in social desirability). The graphologists then ranked each subject on the same traits using graphology. The results showed that

the graphologists' self-ranking matched the subjects' self-rankings better than the rankings based on graphology (the mean correlations were .49 and .24). Green et al. conclude that an approach based on social desirability "appears to do better than the one based on training and experience in graphology."

23. *Variability effects.* Or how we can usually find something to match any statement. All people have a rich repertoire of behavior, and how they behave at any given time depends on experience, situation, and personality. Everyone is shy in one situation and bold in another, and so on. Thus we can usually find aspects of ourselves that will match almost any statement within a broadly qualified range, thus reducing the chance of it being wrong (Marks and Kammann 1980:189). The effect is aided by the imprecision of language. Are we shy because we dislike crowds or shy because we are scared?

*   *   *

We end this survey with two points. First, the word *gullibility* does not appear above because it implies an element of wanton frailty, whereas most of the biases reflect fundamental human qualities. Second, our survey has revealed many reasons why people should see graphological readings as valid, none of which require that there be any truth in graphology as such. Of course these reasons do not mean that graphology is invalid. They mean only that a large number of variables have to be controlled before conclusions are possible. In other words, graphologists have to show that their results have an adequate effect size, and that they cannot be accounted for by non-graphological factors.[32]

At this point there will be an obvious question in readers' minds. If we are so hopelessly biased, how do we ever get to Friday, let alone walk on the moon? A good point. However, as noted by Hogarth (1987), our judgment skills are perfectly adequate for cooking meals r o playing chess, but not for the information explosion.[33] Once the information becomes complex as in graphology, or the outcome becomes *really* important as in to bomb or not to bomb, then we need help. Which brings us to our final section.

HOW TO PROTECT YOURSELF FROM
THE KNOWN WAYS OF FOOLING YOURSELF

ASSESSING WHAT YOU SEE

Short of running your own controlled experiment, try this:

1. Be aware of your biases. Do not believe what you see.
2. Consider your emotional involvement. Hell hath no fury like a cherished belief under attack.
3. Ask where the sample came from. If small or non-random, forget it, i.e., suspend judgment.
4. Ask what all four cells look like. If not available forget it. If available, look at effect size. See preceding chapter.
5. Consider base rates, then use control groups to provide an objective basis for comparison. If not possible, forget it.

For example, apply the above to the previous testimonials, and their bias will be apparent. As another example, consider the following claims:

> Extroverts are right slanted.
> Graphology readings describe the person.
> Clients are satisfied.

Here we need to know the sample source and size, how the variables were measured, and the following:

Whether introverts are also right slanted
    (so there is nothing special about extroverts).
Whether wrong graphology readings also describe the person
    (so there is nothing special about authentic readings).
Whether clients can be dissatisfied.
Whether there are non-graphological explanations for client satisfaction
    (so there is nothing special about graphology).

Until such questions are answered, no conclusions are possible.

HOW TO BE CRITICAL

Marks and Kamman (1980:223–226) suggest that you ask the person advocating an idea the following questions:

1. Why do you believe in it? This puts the burden of proof on the claimant.
2. What evidence would you accept as proving your idea wrong?
3. Are there other explanations that could produce the same result?
4. Where did your idea come from? Is the source credible?

Such questions should be asked at all graphology lectures. Bear in mind that the aim is not to win but to learn.

Hyman (1987) makes the following suggestions:

1. Do your homework. Know what you are talking about.
2. Examine your aims. Is it the truth or your ego at stake?
3. Be fair and honest. Attack the claim, not the claimant.
4. Avoid emotion. Let the facts speak for themselves.
5. Above all, be constructive. Specify improvements.

Truzzi (1987) makes the following comments:

1. In science the burden of proof lies with the claimant.
2. The more extraordinary the claim, the stronger the evidence required.
3. If your verdict is *not proved,* meaning that the claimant's evidence is insufficient, you make no claim and have no burden to prove anything. But if your verdict is *disproved,* you make a claim and must bear the burden of proof.
4. Be as critical of the ordinary as of the extraordinary. For example, consider not only graphology but also personality tests, and make a truly scientific comparison.

CONCLUSION: THIS CHAPTER IN A NUTSHELL

For graphology as traditionally practiced, we conclude that:

1. Graphological effects are too small to have been reliably observed.
2. Graphological features are too numerous to be reliably combined.
3. Assessment of the match between graphology and the person suffers from too many biases to allow valid conclusions.

In other words, from start to finish the system is beyond unaided human judgment. Human cognitive skills are simply not equal to the task graphologists have set themselves and routinely claim to have accomplished. So what we read in graphology books deserves disbelief. The remedy is clear —graphologists need appropriate strategies such as the scientific approach to control judgment errors. But from what we have said about human biases, we predict that graphologists will be unconvinced.[34,35] Paraphrasing Dean and Mather (1985), we can say:

> Graphologists are like phrenologists. Their systems cover the same ground, they apply them to the same kinds of people, they turn the same blind eye to the same lack of experimental evidence, and they are convinced for precisely the same reasons that everything works. But despite glowing testimonials from eminent people the phrenologists were wrong. So why shouldn't critics conclude for precisely the same reasons that graphologists are wrong? This is an honest question that graphologists have yet to answer.

Perhaps the issue facing graphology is not whether graphological beliefs are true, but whether the beliefs *need* to be true. If they do not need to be true, as is suggested by present evidence, then graphology will be left without a leg to stand on.

NOTES

1. For example, strong or weak, harmonious or unbalanced. However, having specified this first step, even to the extent of holding the script upside down to avoid bias by its contents, the graphologist Klara Roman (1952:119–124) notes that such initial judgments "prove to be the main sources of error in graphological analysis." So the value of this first step is unclear.

2. If it is futile to study isolated features, it is not clear how their meanings (which fill the pages of graphology books) could have been derived in the first place. According to Olyanova (1960:13): ". . . over a period of many hundreds of years, men and women of intellect and intuition used handwriting as a means of judging character. From their intuitive findings a set of rules developed and it is by these that the student of graphology is guided today." However, to claim individual knowledge of so many *interacting* variables is like claiming to know the effect of each of 20 chemical elements on every feature of every plant in your garden regardless of climate. The task is clearly beyond unaided human ability. The good news is that interaction can be tested directly using ANOVA techniques (short for analysis of variance), which reduce the variation in a set of data to components whose relative importance we wish to assess. The bad news is that such tests provide no evidence for interaction. Thus for 13 features such as size and slant in the handwriting of 64 adults vs. personality test scores for extroversion and emotionality, there was no evidence that interaction improved the fit (Furnham and Gunter 1987). Furthermore, different features that supposedly indicate the same

thing should tend to cluster, i.e., correlate with each other. Letter size (area) and width are physically related, so it is hardly surprising they correlate about .60 (Taft 1967). But the correlations between three physically unrelated features (letter width, letter slant, line slope), all supposedly indicative of extroversion, are all close to zero and thus show no evidence of clustering:

	Width vs. slant	Width vs. slope	Slant vs. slope	
Lorr et al. 1953	.06	–.03	–.03	N=200
Rosenthal and Lines 1978	.16	.07	–.08	N=58

So these features *cannot* be indicating the same thing, be it extroversion or anything else, which suggests that the general interaction of handwriting features may be a myth. However, for the present purpose this is of no conseuqence.

3. A good example of error due to missing out cells is biorhythms, the idea that people are subject to cycles of 23, 28, and 33 days starting from birth. Despite the impressive counts in cell a promoted by proponents, a review of 13 studies involving a massive 25,000 events and all four cells showed no hint of a biorhythm effect (Hines 1979).

4. In the absence of signs the best predictor is the base rate itself, given by $(a+c)/n$, where $n=a+b+c+d$. If the base rate exceeds 50 percent, the best prediction is *yes;* otherwise the best prediction is *no.* The base rate for literacy exceeds 50 percent, so in the absence of signs our best prediction is *yes this person can read.* The base rate for murder is much less than 50 percent, so our best prediction is *no this person is not a murderer.*

Enter signs. Surprisingly, the best predictor may still be the base rate, and using graphology may only make our prediction worse. To see why, suppose we are using graphology to distinguish between 90 innocent people and 10 murderers. In terms of cells abcd their handwriting will either set them free or send them to jail as follows:

			Murderer	Innocent
Graphological indication	{	Murderer = Jail	a	b
		Innocent = Free	c	d

correlation between graphology and murder
$$= (ad-bc)/\sqrt{((a+b)\,(c+d)\,(a+c)\,(b+d))}$$

Method. We can play the base rate for murderers, which in our sample is 10 murderers per 100 people, so $a+c=10$. Or we can use graphology, for which we will pretend there are correlations of .00 to 1.00 between handwriting features and murder. Now when we use graphology, we must send 10 people to jail, so $a+b=10$. Since $a+b+c+d=100$, we can calculate the remaining unknowns a and d by working backwards from our pretend correlations, which gives the following results:

		Hits		Misses		
Method		Murderers in jail a	Innocents set free d	Murderers set free c	Innocents in jail b	Total errors c+b
Base rate		0	90	10	0	10
Graphology	.00	1	81	9	9	18
where correlation	.11	2	82	8	8	16
between writing	.44	5	85	5	5	10
and murder is	1.00	10	90	0	0	0
perfect result						

In the first line we play the base rate. Since the base rate is 10 percent, and 10 percent is less than 50 percent, our best prediction is *this person is not a murderer.* We jail no innocent people, but we jail no murderers either. Overall we make 10 errors, all of them unjailed murderers.

In the remaining lines we use graphology. Here we can make two kinds of errors, namely a *wrong no* (setting murderers free) and a *wrong yes* (jailing innocent people). If we care only about jailing murderers (too bad if we jail innocent people as well), then column a shows that any increase in correlation increases the number of mailed murderers, so even a tiny correlation can help.

But if we also care about not jailing innocent people, tiny correlations do not help at all, for using graphology will increase accuracy only if the error rate (c+b)/n is less than the base rate (a+c)/n, that is, *only if b< a.* As shown in column c+b, this occurs only when the correlation between handwriting and murder exceeds about .44; otherwise we make more errors than by playing the base rate. Similarly if the base rate is 1 percent or less, we need correlations exceeding about .50; otherwise using graphology will make our predictions worse. These findings apply equally to astrology, palmistry, and any other technique that uses signs.

In this sample the incidence of handwriting features indicating murder has to be 10 percent because graphology has to jail 10 people in our sample of 100. If the incidence happened to be less than 10 percent, then graphology would of course jail fewer murderers and fewer innocents, and the opposite if it was more than 10 percent.

5. Two points are important here. First, if we are sneaky about sampling then we can get any correlation we like. For example, a graphology test for the position of psychology professor would presumably report higher correlations if the applicants were a professor, a schoolboy, and a dog than if they were three professors. So the correlations cited here assume an unbiased sample. Second, the typical correlation of .3 between trait and behavior in a single situation is low because behavior nearly always depends on more than one trait. Our going to a particular party depends not only on our fondness for parties but also on the kind of party, our availability, our good nature (which is why we were invited), our inter-

est in a concurrent movie, and so on. It is a property of correlation that, as the number of things which determine our behavior increases, the correlation with any one of them must decrease to leave room for the others. Thus if there are 3 or 4 independent determinants, then the maximum possible correlation with any one of them is generally around .5 or .45 respectively (Ahadi and Diener 1989).

6. Answers to *Test Your Skill*. The highest correlation in each pair is BB, CC, FF. The difficulty increases from left to right, and you probably noticed how juggling even ten pairs of numbers is an impossible task. Alternatively you may have stored mental pictures of each set divided into pairs and trios, which makes juggling easier. All correlations are in the nil-to-weak range of Figure 1, but in each case the highest correlation is much higher than those typically observed between personality and graphological features. The actual Pearson r correlations are AA.04 BB.63, CC.29 DD.00, EE.20 FF.51. Only BB is statistically significant with p=.05 exactly, df=8.

In the coin-tossing test, the correct answer is sequence 4. Sequences 1–3 have too many short runs. Sequence 5 has too many long runs. When Wagenaar (1988:92–93) gave an extended version of this test to 203 subjects, the preference for sequences 1,2,3,4,5 was 4,29,37,27,3 percent respectively. When the responses were divided into above or below the correct answer, a large majority of 86 percent preferred too many short runs. This suggests that we tend to see long runs as non-random (and therefore due to some outside factor) when in fact they are genuinely random, thus generating erroneous beliefs.

7. In one famous study (Chapman and Chapman 1967) groups of 56 college students were given 45 Draw-a-Person drawings each with six personality statements. The students had to work out the meaning of features such as head size. But unknown to them the statements involved stereotypes that were deliberately unrelated to the drawings. For example, the statement "worried about intelligence" appeared just as often for small heads as for big heads. However, nearly every student saw the stereotype relationships even though they did not exist, and continued to see them despite anti-stereotype strategies such as repeating the exercise, sorting the drawings into piles for closer study, and being offered money for accuracy. Even when the statements totally opposed the stereotype, so that "worried about intelligence" appeared *only* for small heads, the students still saw the stereotype relationship, albeit to a somewhat lesser extent. In other words, they saw only what they expected to see. The same result was observed for ink blots and in verbal studies. The important point is that these experiments made it easy to avoid stereotypes. But the students failed miserably, so there is no reason to suppose we do any better in daily life.

8. Being fooled by illusory correlation is a fundamental human quality that has perpetrated all kinds of false beliefs such as N–rays and polywater (Kohn 1986). N–rays were a new type of radiation supposedly emitted by a very hot platinum wire enclosed in an iron tube. Polywater was a supposedly new form of water produced by condensing ordinary water in quartz capillaries. Initially both received support from dozens of independent studies. Interest ran high until further studies showed they did not exist, whereupon they were abandoned. Despite

these crushing findings, the discoverer of N–rays kept going for 25 years until his death (Hines 1988). Such is the power of illusory correlation. Anastasi (1988) comments, "Illusory correlation is a special example of the mechanism that underlies the survival of superstition . . . This mechanism may actually interfere with the discovery and use of valid diagnostic signs in the course of clinical observation by clinicians who are strongly identified with a particular diagnostic system."

9. This would not apply if the correlation was enormously high, like .9 between not-slanted and not-extroverted, because our belief would then be too frequently and too obviously wrong. Thus nobody believes that weight is unrelated to height, for which the correlation is about .7. But such an argument does not apply here, because the whole point of illusory correlation is that the true correlation is near zero.

10. Relevant here is our ability to link any trait to any behavior. Gergen et al. (1986) asked university students how a given trait could explain a given attitude or behavior, both of which (unknown to the students) had been picked at random. The results showed that any trait could plausibly explain any attitude and any behavior including opposite behaviors. For example, the *hostile* person *avoids social groups* because he hates people, and *seeks social groups* because he needs people to attack. There were typically 3–6 plausible explanations for a given link. For example, the *lonely* person agrees that *luck determines who is boss* because he is covering up (why admit to social inadequacy?), logical (luck is the easy way), or incapacitated (not familiar with social processes).

11. This test is from Marks and Kamman (1980:178) and shows how a single casual cue can organize an entire performance. The following poem is from Dooling and Lachman (1971). Read it carefully and try to make sense of it:

> With hocked gems financing him
> Our hero bravely defied all scornful laughter
> That tried to prevent his scheme
> Your eyes deceive he said
> An egg not a table correctly typifies
> This unexplored domain.
> Now three sturdy sisters sought proof
> Forging along sometimes through calm vastness
> Yet more often over turbulent peaks and valleys
> Days became weeks
> As many doubters spread fearful rumors
> About the edge
> At last from nowhere winged creatures appeared
> Signifying momentous success.

If you found no satisfactory meaning, go to note 36. But beware—after note 36 this poem will never be the same again.

12. The *non*scientific approach is the way graphologists have always done it, namely: (1) Examine handwritings. (2) Find interesting features like slant. (3)

Conclude it means something, like extroversion. By contrast the scientific approach is much more systematic and rigorous. It also recognizes and controls our biases. The steps are: (1) Define problem. Is slant related to extroversion? (2) State hypothesis. Forward slant = extroverted. (3) Collect data, e.g., 200 handwritings and personality test scores. (4) Analyze results statistically. To what extent is the hypothesis supported? Scientific and nonscientific approaches differ not in their ideas but in the methods used to test them.

13. Our short-term memory can hold only about 7±2 items at a time, whether numbers, letters, or words (Miller 1956). Some people manage only 4–5 while others manage 10 or more. Alternatively, we tend to manage only as much as we can say in 1.5 seconds (Baddeley 1982). Unless continuously rehearsed, half the items are gone after about 7 seconds, and all are gone after about 20 seconds (Peterson and Peterson 1959, Murdock 1961). Adding new items displaces existing ones. So give us more than about 7 items to juggle and we are lost. For example, with your eyes shut to stop inadvertent cheating, try multiplying 52×9 in your head. This involves storing 7 digits (namely 52,9 and the two intermediate products 18,45), which is just within the 7-item limit. So most people can do it. Now try 52×49. This involves storing about twice as many digits, or well beyond the 7-item limit. So most people fail. Stage mentalists succeed by using special techniques, for example 52×49 is seen as 52×7×7 or as (52×50)–52.

14. Graphologists stress the interaction between cues and the need for combining individual cues. So do astrologers and palmists. But when Dean (1985:19) submitted birth charts or hand prints to live panels of astrologers (total N=39) or palmists (total N=14), together with questions like *extrovert or introvert?* it was clear that they were swayed by the presence or absence of relatively few cues. And because they used different cues, disagreement was the rule. Thus it was not uncommon for alternate panel members to vote alternate ways, or for half the audience to vote one way and the other half to vote the other way, which incidentally had no evident effect on their faith in their craft. For the record, their overall accuracy was no better than chance.

15. Here we use intuition in the popular sense of a quasi-psychic process. This differs from psychology, where *intuitive* means *done in your head.*

16. Birch (1945) describes an interesting test of insight. Six laboratory-raised chimpanzees are put one at a time into a cage containing a stick. Outside beyond reach there is food. Will they use the stick to get it? Each animal is given half an hour. The first four have no history of stick-using, and in each case the answer is no. The fifth has used sticks before and gets the food within 12 seconds. The sixth has no history of stick-using and reaches for the food without success. After four minutes his thrashing arm brushes the stick and moves the food slightly. He stops, pushes the stick against the food, and sees it move. A few more trials and the food is his. The four unsuccessful animals are then given sticks to play with for the first time in their lives. After three days the use of sticks is old hat. The food test is then repeated, and all get the food within seconds. Conclusion: there is no insight that does not go back to actual experience. As you might imagine, the bigger the similarity between problem and experience the better the in-

sight (Holyoak and Koh 1987). And the insight that brings a truly creative achievement may come only after months or years of uneventful labor and general floundering. Thus Newton did not suddenly happen on the law of gravitation in his mother's orchard. Instead it came "by thinking on it continually." See Ochse (1990:252–256).

17. But what about leaps of imagination, like predicting life on other planets? Surely they transcend the need for prior experience? Yes indeed. Since the time of the visionary scientist Emanuel Swedenborg (1688–1772), many hundreds of intuitives have documented such leaps in hundreds of books. The results are generally glowing descriptions of exotic landscapes, undiscovered moons, and abundant life (usually humanoid), most of them conflicting and all of them wrong (see Gardner 1988). Such is the penalty for transcending experience. Furthermore, if we really could leap there would be no casinos, because our leaping would put them out of business. We know this because the mathematics professor E. O. Thorp (1966) noticed that the odds on blackjack made no allowance for the decrease in the card deck as the game progressed. By keeping a tally of the cards played he was able to win consistently, just as if he could leap on demand. This led to a crisis among casinos, and ultimately he was banned from playing. Casinos were forced to change the game (e.g., by using multiple decks and more frequent shuffling) to foil those who used his methods. Interestingly, despite these changes, there remains a widely-publicized optimal strategy that should allow players to win in the long run. But due to their judgment biases (which favor other strategies), players refuse to believe the optimal strategy will work (Wagenaar 1988:15). So in casinos at least, chance is alive and well, and leaping is conspicuous by its absence.

18. Furthermore, farsightedness is associated with lower IQ and is roughly twice as prevalent as nearsightedness at age 16. In general only nearsighted people need glasses in the street, and only farsighted people need glasses in the library. So the relationship glasses = brains should apply in the street but not in the library—except that libraries tend to attract high verbal IQs, thus confounding the issue. Interestingly, people wearing glasses are perceived *initially* as being more intelligent (Thornton 1944), but the effect of glasses wears off as we collect a larger sample of behavior (Argyle and McHenry 1971).

19. Adding predictors will not work unless (1) the predictors are roughly proportional to the quality predicted, which is nearly always the case (if not, e.g., due to skew, they can be transformed to suit); (2) they are scaled in the same direction; and (3) they are converted to standard scores to eliminate differences in scaling. The standard score of a predictor is (actual value − mean value)/standard deviation. The accuracy is remarkably insensitive to weighting, so it is usual to give each predictor equal weight to avoid bias from measurement error. If there are N predictors, then (sum of the N standard scores)/N = standard score of the quality predicted. Optimal weights can be derived by regression analysis but will generally not improve accuracy unless (number of cases/number of predictors) exceeds 20. See Dawes (1979).

Alternatively the predictors can be adjusted to avoid the use of standard scores. If each predictor is given equal weight, then predicted rating = k + sd of ratings

$\times$ $(a_1/s_1 + a_2/s_2 + \ldots)/N$ where k = mean rating – sd of ratings $\times$ $(m_1/s_1 + m_2/s_2 + \ldots)/N$, s = sd of predictor, m = mean value of predictor, a = actual value of predictor, and N = number of predictors

For example, Dawes (1971) looked at the evaluation of 384 applications for entry to graduate courses in the University of Oregon. Although the Admissions Committee considered many variables including letters of recommendation, their admission rating was well predicted by

admission rating = .0032 graduate exam score + 1.02 mean grade +
.0791 crude index of undergraduate institution.

Other coefficients (of .0006, .76 and .2518 respectively) produced even better predictions of subsequent graduate performance than the Committee ratings. Dawes suggested that, if this represented a policy which the Committee endorsed, then much effort would be saved by publicizing the equation and discouraging people with low scores from applying.

20. If we have lots of predictors to choose from, how many should we use? The usual approach is to assemble as many predictors as possible, and then identify the best combination by multiple regression analysis. It sounds easy but there is a tricky problem—due to measurement errors and sampling fluctuations, the sample *always* contains false correlations that can grossly bias the overall result. False correlations exist even when the sample consists of random numbers, i.e., pure noise. For example, Freedman (1983) analyzed ten sets of random data, each having 50 predictors and a sample size of 100. The mean overall correlation between criterion and combined predictors (i.e., between noise and noise) should have been zero, but thanks to false correlations it was a staggering .69. This agrees with the expected value of .70 given by $\sqrt{((k-1)/(N-1))}$, where k = number of predictors and N = sample size (Kachigan 1986:230). Similarly, an overall correlation of .60 with graphology would normally delight any graphologist, but it would mean nothing if obtained using 20 handwriting features and 50 subjects, because on average we would expect $\sqrt{(19/49)}$ = .62 by chance alone. If we have tested k predictors and pick the best n, the correlation expectd by chance is not much less than if we use all k, being very roughly $\sqrt{(a/(N-1))}$, where a=(k+n)/2.

Because a sample always contains false correlations, the top predictors found by our analysis may be in error. So they must always be checked against a fresh sample. Furthermore, predictors are useful only if they add something new. Suppose we predict the area of playing fields by measuring their length with a steel tape. Obviously we do not include length estimated by eye, because it adds nothing new and would reduce accuracy. By contrast, we might include *width* estimated by eye, because it adds something new and could increase accuracy. However, predictors tend to correlate with each other. Playing fields tend to be of standard shape, so length tends to be strongly correlated with width. So as we add more and more predictors, starting with the strongest, we usually get more and more error but less and less new information, with the whole picture being continuously biased by false correlations due to measurement errors and sampling fluctuations. Consequently we can never be sure that the weaker predictors are not adding more error than they are worth. For this reason it is usually not practical to use more than 4 or 5 predictors, especially when predictors cost time and effort to obtain (Baggaley 1964:54).

The above considerations are bad news for those who defend graphology by saying they use it only with other evidence. When we add graphology to other predictors such as personality tests that have a higher validity, we *lower* rather than *raise* the overall accuracy, in the same way that eyeball estimates lower the accuracy of our steel rule. So unless graphology is known to be more valid than our other predictors, or is known to cover a new area, its use can only reduce the overall accuracy of our predictions.

21. If expert judgments occasionally appear superior to an equation, this is because the experts use more predictors than the equation. So the qualifier *using the same codable predictors* is important.

22. If equations are better than experts, why are they not more used? Meehl (1986) suggests seven reasons—sheer ignorance, threat of unemployment, threat to dignity, we don't do it that way, it is inhuman, my way feels better, and I hate computers. Kleinmuntz (1990) adds a further reason—in many cases no equation is available.

23. Reid (1983) also presents selected anecdotes from his employment agency files after 15 years of using graphology. For example, a manager saved by graphology after a bad interview was a great success in his new job, an executive whose malpractice was indicated by graphology was removed in the nick of time, an older candidate had his references and medical condition confirmed by graphology, and graphology pointed to deceit by a consultant that was subsequently confirmed.

24. In the brain there are modules that do highly specific things like recognize speech or recognize faces (Fodor 1983), but they are quite different from the faculties such as acquisitiveness, vanity, and veneration modularized by phrenology. The faculties do not correspond to the way the brain works, nor does personality break down in the way required by phrenological theory. So the whole thesis of phrenology is illusory. For example, a fundamental claim of phrenology is that size is a measure of power. Leading textbooks such as Fowler (1895) and Sizer and Drayton (1893), both of which sold over 100,000 copies, vigorously assert that, other things being equal, brain size indicates mental power. Severn (1913:20), who in over 25 years as a practicing phrenologist examined over 100,000 heads, says "Persons of commanding mentality invariably have heads above the average size." Who would dare question such intimidating sources? Yet scientific studies of IQ vs. brain size, estimated from *head* size just as a phrenologist would, have consistently found the correlation to be around .1, or effectively zero, although the true correlation between *brain* size and IQ, i.e., after correction for the unreliability of the measures, may be higher (Van Valen 1974, Passingham 1979). So the claimed association between size and power could not possibly have been observed by phrenologists. Indeed, their observations should have denied it. That it persisted was another triumph for illusory correlation.

Nevertheless, in the 1830s phrenology was far more popular in the U.S.A. and Britain than graphology is today. Like graphology, it attracted people of intelligence and a vast literature wherein every criticism was furiously attacked. Flugel (1965) comments, "The failure of phrenology, with the implied immense amount of misdirected effort and ill-informed enthusiasm, was the price that had to be paid for this neglect of scientific caution." Unfortunately, this neglect of scientific caution is raging out of control among graphologists and their teaching institutions. For example, fifty years ago Jacoby (1939) could say, "There are graphologists who allow of no objection whatsoever to graphology, discard all criticism, and will never admit that there are limitations to the work of a graphologist. They are inclined to treat anybody doubting the one or the other point in graphology as their personal enemy." More recently, in an address to the British Institute of Graphologists, the psychologist Pamela Sussams (1984) could say, "you have decided to be a scientific body, yet some of you, sometimes, have appeared to me to speak and behave as if it is a religious one . . . [which says] we have the way, the truth and the light, only believe and all will be revealed to you."

25. Personal validation is validation by subjective experience, not by scientific tests. We see that the reading fits and conclude that graphology works. What could be simpler and more convincing? But as shown in this chapter, it is not nearly that simple, and our convincing conclusion can be dead wrong. Graphology (and astrology, palmistry, phrenology, the Tarot, and so on) rest entirely on personal validation, never on scientific tests, whereas for properly devised personality tests the opposite applies. Beware the difference.

26. These findings arose from the cognitive revolution of the 1950s and the birth of artificial intelligence. Before then the talk was on stimulus and response. Now it is on things like the selective filtering of experience, and strategies for handling information. Perception is seen as a set of ideas and models on which we act until they are proved wrong, in which case we change them. That is, we do not merely receive experience, we use it selectively to test models. These models are basically labor-saving devices that collapse the information into manageable chunks. They determine to some extent what we see and how much. For example, in a given landscape the geologist will see rocks, the developer will see building sites, and the artist will see meaning. So what is more important in determining perception, the model or the information input? The answer is the model. For example, suppose we see a slippery wet road ahead. Because the image on our retina is neither slippery nor three-dimensional, the perception must be generated by selecting the model that best fits the cues. So perception is not simply seeing. Instead it is a matter of guessing followed by adjustments if we find the wrong model was chosen, as for example when the shadowy figure in our bedroom turns out to be a coat hanging behind the door. This explains hindsight bias—once the choice of models has been biased by the experience, it reintroduces itself into the original perception. The problem is that guessing from inadequate data can go off the rails, as when it generates fiction, because the fiction is not easily dispelled by knowing the truth. Although we may know when our perception is wrong, this does not correct the perception. In other words, intellect and perception are almost separate processes. No wonder we need the scientific approach to keep us on the rails. (Miller 1983)

27. Suppose two people meet and compare notes. Coincidences could involve countless topics such as same birthday, same job, same car, and so on. If a topic has N categories, e.g., for birthdays N = 365, there is a 50 percent chance of at least one coincidence if the sum of $1/N$ for each topic exceeds 0.35, and a 95 percent chance if it exceeds 1.5 (Diaconis and Mosteller 1989). If all N's are the same, e.g., 10 makes of car and 10 brands of toothpaste, only 0.35N topics are needed for a 50 percent chance of at least one coincidence, and 1.5N topics for a 95 percent chance. Because possible topics can be multiplied almost indefinitely (same color dress, same make, same style, same size, same number of buttons, and so on), this makes coincidences of one kind or another almost inevitable. For a lengthy discussion of coincidences with many examples and much useful data, see Watson (1981).

28. The surprises do not end there. Studies have shown that if we are basically skeptics, our belief will be modified by subsequent evidence. But if we are believers, our belief will persist because positive evidence will be remembered, whereas negative evidence (like much of this book) will be ignored (Russell and Jones 1980, Glick et al. 1989). On this basis, regardless of the evidence, graphology is not going to go away. On the other hand, we should not underestimate the power of really vivid facts. As Bertrand Russell (1952) cogently observed, "We were told that faith could remove mountains, but no one believed it; we are now told that the atomic bomb can remove mountains, and everyone believes it." Nor should we underestimate the cunning of psychologists. Suppose we believe that men make better bosses than women. If our belief is entrenched, contrary questions (why do women make better bosses than men?) will have no effect. So Swann et al. (1988) use questions that are simply more extreme (why do men *always* make better bosses than women?). Because we resist change, we think up reasons against this extreme view—and unwittingly change our beliefs in the opposite direction. Interestingly, the authors show that the change is a true shift in position, not just a recognition that more extreme views exist. So the next time you meet an entrenched graphologist, ask questions like: Why are isolated features always so accurate? Why do small differences in pen and paper have such enormous effects? Why is it possible to make judgments from a photocopy? Why do different approaches always give the same result? Why is it impossible to judge sex? Why does graphology deny free will?

29. Accuracy and triviality can combine in four ways as shown below:

	Trivial and general	*Important and specific*
Accurate:	You have two legs.	Your verbal IQ is way above average.
Inaccurate:	You hate chocolate.	Yesterday you committed suicide.

The effect of triviality and generality is well illustrated by an experiment conducted in 1928 by Meili, supervisor of the Rousseau Institute in France, long before the Barnum effect was named. Meili set out 68 very diverse items such as will, fear of storms, aptitude for maths, sense of color, response to weather, aptitude for teaching, and respect for the opinion of others. He wrote the 68 items on 50 sheets of paper, giving each item a score (1–5) picked at random, but taking care that the middle scores occurred more frequently than the extremes. Without looking at the results, he wrote on the back of each sheet the name of a psychology student at the Institute. He then gave the sheets to the students as a test of graphology: "A sample of your handwriting was sent to a graphologist. Here are the results. Please give your opinion, and your own rating for each of the items."

The results showed that over half the students found most of the items to be perfectly accurate. Of the 2516 random items, 53 percent agreed perfectly with the self-ratings, while a further 25 percent were only 1 point apart, the mean difference being 0.73 points. Only 6 percent were 3 or more points apart. Meili concludes pithily, "Fictitious diagnoses, determined by chance, will satisfy subjects to a large extent if one follows the following rules: Give the interpretation in the vaguest possible terms; always prefer poorly-defined and difficult-to-check qualities; choose the most uniform qualities possible, i.e., where individual differences are the least marked. . . . One will thus find a certain number of qualities which would be of no risk in an interpretation." (Quoted by Ferrière 1946:66–67.) In other words, in modern terms, they would be ideal Barnum statements.

30. Steiner (1989), a magician and expert cold reader, gave fake Tarot card readings at a party. Someone who was impressed asked if he could also read palms. His answer, although crude, makes the point. "I have studied the craft of cold reading and am skilled in the art. With equal grace and confidence, I can read buffalo shit."

31. For example, Miller (1982) gives a 430-page annotated list of 2321 references to books and journals in over 6 languages, and Gille-Maisani (1989) gives a 60-page bibliography covering books and journals from eight countries. The latter does not include the several hundred articles that have appeared in scientific journals.

32. This need not be difficult. For example, if wrong profiles (whose nature is of course concealed) are accepted as readily as correct profiles, it cannot be claimed that graphology plays much part in the process. Kelly and Saklofske (1989) gave three graphological profiles to each of 10 female subjects aged 21 to 42. One was theirs, the other two were matched on age and chosen at random. The graphologist claimed that his profiles were always accurate. But only three subjects picked the correct profile, which is no better than guessing. By contrast, people do tend to pick the correct profile when based on a valid personality test; see Furnham and Schofield (1986:175).

33. Funder (1987) gives this useful visual analogy. The two horizontal segments are the same length. On paper the lower segment *appears* shorter, but on a real railroad track it *is* shorter. Without this bias we would misjudge real size and distance, so we would crash airplanes and cars and trip over railroad tracks. Similarly, without our judgment biases we would be overloaded by the need for  (usually unavailable) data, so everyday life would grind to a halt. In general our biases lead us seriously astray only when we enter non-everyday areas like rail-

road tracks on paper or evaluating graphology.

34. Just as Rorschach (inkblot) testers remain unconvinced despite published studies showing the test to be unreliable and invalid—the correlation with independent measures is typically .3 at best (Jensen 1964). Furthermore, such tests can reveal more about the judge than about the subject (Hamilton and Robertson 1966). Nevertheless, in the USA about six milllion Rorschach tests were given in 1964. Dawes (1988:234), a former user, comments that "the use of Rorschach interpretations in establishing an individual's legal status and child custody is the single most unethical practice of my colleagues. It is done, widely. . . . it violates what I believe to be a basic ethical principle in this society—that most people are judged on the basis of what they do, not on the basis of what they feel, think, or might have a propensity to do. And being judged on an *invalid* assessment of such thoughts, feelings, and propensities amounts to losing one's civil rights on an essentially random basis." Graphologists please note.

35. Dawes (1988:243–253) suggests that the Rorschach test persists because plausibility is more powerful than disconfirming evidence. For example, a clinical psychologist quoted by Chapman and Chapman (1971) said, "I'll trust my own senses before I trust some journal article." This is especially true when vested interests are involved (note 22). So Dawes suggests that the best way to attack a belief based on plausibility is not to provide disconfirming evidence but to provide a *new* plausible hypothesis. Thus the Draw-a-Person test has been largely abandoned because the hypothesis *unusual person = inner conflicts* was displaced by the more plausible (and better supported) *unusual person = lack of artistic ability*. Dawes (1988:240–243) notes that graphology too is based on plausibility. However, the hypothesis *handwriting = personality* has no accepted rival such as *handwriting = hand shape*, which tends to be implausible because foot or mouth writing show features similar to hand writing—the correlations are around .6 or .2 respectively (Lyons 1964). But without a rival hypothesis we tend to brush aside any evidence against our cherished beliefs. So what can we do? Dawes suggests the trick is to estimate two probabilities, namely pT, the probability of getting the existing evidence if *handwriting = personality* were *true*, and pF, the corresponding probability if it were *false*.

Here pT and pF will be between 0 and 1, and the evidence should be *reliable* evidence, meaning scientific tests and not personal validation. If pT>pF, then we think the hypothesis is more likely to be true than false, and vice versa if pT<pF. For example, if the hypothesis were true to the extent claimed by graphologists, we might estimate the probability of getting the existing dismal evidence as fairly low, say pT=.2. If the hypothesis were false, or at least not true to the extent claimed by graphologists, we might estimate the same probability as fairly high, say pF=.8. Since pT>pF, we think the hypothesis is more likely to be false than true.

36. Read the poem in note 11 again but this time ignore the fact that it is about Christopher Columbus. You will find that you cannot, neither now nor in a year's time. Your judgment is totally affected by knowing the answer in advance. Also, it now seems impossible that anyone could not identify Christopher

Columbus from the poem. No wonder graphologists find that handwriting perfectly reflects the person.

REFERENCES

Ahadi, S., and E. Diener. 1989. "Multiple Determinants and Effect Size." *Journal of Personality and Social Psychology* 56: pp. 398–406.

Aiken, L. R. 1989. *Assessment of Personality*. Toronto: Allyn & Bacon.

Alcock, J. E. 1981. *Parapsychology: Science or Magic?* Oxford: Permagon. A readable account of the fallibility of human judgment is on pp. 90–104.

Anastasi, A. 1988. *Psychological Testing*. 6th ed, p. 260. New York: Macmillan.

Argyle, M., and R. McHenry. 1971. "Do Spectacles Really Affect Our Judgements of Intelligence?" *British Journal of Social and Clinical Psychology* 10: pp. 27–29.

Arkes, H. R., and A. R. Harkness. 1983. "Estimates of Contingency between Two Dichotomous Variables." *Journal of Experimental Psychology: General* 112: pp. 117–135.

Armstrong, J. S. 1978. *Long-range Forecasting: From Crystal Ball to Computer*. Wiley: New York. Extremely readable, nearly 800 rated and annotated references, essential reading for anyone interested in human judgment.

———. 1979. "Unintelligible Research and Academic Prestige: Further Adventures of Dr. Fox." Paper presented to the 1979 TIMS/ORSA conference in New Orleans.

Baddeley, A. 1982. *Your Memory: A User's Guide*, p. 175. London: Sidgwick & Jackson.

Baggaley, A. R. 1964. *Intermediate Correlational Methods*. New York: Wiley.

Bar-Hillel, M., and G. Ben-Shakhar. 1986. "The *A Priori* Case against Graphology: Methodological and Conceptual Issues." In *Scientific Aspects of Graphology*, edited by B. Nevo, pp. 263–279. Springfield, Ill.: Thomas.

Ben-Shakhar, G., M. Bar-Hillel, Y. Bilu, E. Ben-Abba, and A. Flug. 1986. "Can Graphology Predict Occupational Success? Two Empirical Studies and Some Methodological Ruminations." *Journal of Applied Psychology* 71: pp. 645–653.

Birch, H. G. 1945. "The Relation of Previous Experience to Insightful Problem-Solving." *Journal of Comparative Psychology* 38: pp. 367–383.

Brandon, R. 1983. *The Spiritualists: The Passion for the Occult in the 19th and 20th Centuries*. Buffalo, N.Y.: Prometheus Books.

Briggs, D. 1970. "The Influence of Handwriting on Assessment." *Educational Research* 13: pp.50–55.

Bromley, D. B. 1986. *The Case-Study Method in Psychology and Related Disciplines*. New York: Wiley.

Chapman, L. J., and J. P. Chapman. 1967. "Genesis of Popular but Erroneous Psychodiagnostic Observations." *Journal of Abnormal Psychology* 72: pp. 193–204.

Chapman, L. J., and J. Chapman. 1971. "Test Results Are What You Think They Are." *Psychology Today* (November 1971): pp. 18–22, 106–110. Reprinted in Kahneman et al. 1982, pp. pp. 230–248.

Connor, J. W. 1984. "Misperception, Folk Belief, and the Occult: A Cognitive Guide to Understanding." *Skeptical Inquirer* 8 (Summer): pp. 344–354.

Cook, M. 1982. "Perceiving Others: The Psychology of Interpersonal Perception." In *Judging People: A Guide to Orthodox and Unorthodox Methods of Assessment,* edited by D. M. Davey and M. Harris, pp. 67–82. Maidenhead Berks, UK: McGraw-Hill. See p. 77.

Cooper, W. H. 1981. "Ubiquitous Halo." *Psychological Bulletin* 90: pp. 218–244.

Dawes, R. M. 1971. "A Case Study of Graduate Admissions: Applications of Three Principles of Human Decision Making." *American Psychologist* 60: pp. 180–188.

———. 1979. "The Robust Beauty of Improper Linear Models in Decision Making." *American Psychologist* 34: pp. 571–582.

———. 1988. *Rational Choice in an Uncertain World.* New York: Harcourt Brace Jovanovich.

Dawes, R. M., D. Faust, and P. E. Meehl. "Clinical versus Actuarial Judgment." *Science* 243: pp. 1668–1674.

Dean, G. 1985. "Can Astrology Predict E and N? The Whole Chart." *Correlation* 5 (2) (1985): pp. 2–24.

———. 1987. "Does Astrology Need to Be True? Part 2: The Answer Is No." *Skeptical Inquirer* 11: pp. 257–273. See p. 263.

Dean, G., and A. Mather. 1985. "Superprize Winners Part I: And a New Prize to Challenge the Critics." *Astrological Journal* 28(1): pp. 23–30.

Delaney, J. G., and H. D. Woodyard. 1974. "Effects of Reading an Astrological Description on Responding to a Personality Inventory." *Psychological Reports* 24: pp. 1214.

Diaconis, P. 1988. "Theories of Data Analysis: From Magical Thinking through Classical Statistics," pp. 1–36. Suggested remedies are from pp. 12–22.

Diaconis, P., and F. Mosteller. 1989. "Methods for Studying Coincidences." *Journal of the American Statistical Association* 84: pp. 853–861.

Dickson, D. H., and I. W. Kelly. 1985. "The 'Barnum Effect' in Personality Assessment; A Review of the Literature." *Psychological Reports* 57: pp. 367–382.

Dooling, J. D., and R. Lachman. 1971. "Effects of Comprehension on Retention of Prose." *Journal of Experimental Psychology* 88: pp. 216–222.

Dutton, D. L. 1988. "The Cold Reading Technique." *Experientia* 44: pp. 326–331.

Edwards, A. L. 1967. "The Social Desirability Variable—A Review of the Evidence." *Response Set in Personality Assessment,* edited by I. A. Berg. Chicago: Aldine.

Einhorn, H. J. 1972. "Expert Measurement and Mechanical Combination." *Organizational Behavior and Human Performance* 7: pp. 86–106.

Epstein, S., and L. Teraspulsky. 1986. "Perception of Cross-Situational Consistency." *Journal of Personality and Social Psychology* 50: pp. 1152–1160.

Evans, C. 1973. *Cults of Unreason,* p. 70. New York: Farrar Straus and Giroux.

Eysenck, H. J., and D. K. B. Nias. 1982. *Astrology: Science or Superstition?* pp.

50–60. New York: St. Martin's Press.

Eysenck, H. J., and J. A. Wakefield. 1981. "Psychological Factors as Predictors of Marital Satisfaction." *Advances in Behavior Research and Therapy* 3: pp. 151–192 (a study of 566 couples).

Falk, R. 1981."On Coincidences." *Skeptical Inquirer* 6(2): pp. 18–31.

———. 1989. "Judgment of Coincidence: Mine versus Yours." *American Journal of Psychology* 102: pp. 477–495.

Faust, D., and B. Nurcombe. 1989. "Improving the Accuracy of Clinical Judgment." *Psychiatry* 52: pp. 197–208.

Faust, D., and J. Ziskin. 1988. "The Expert Witness in Psychology and Psychiatry." *Science* 241: pp. 31–35.

Ferrière, A. 1946. *L'Influence des Astres.* Tome 1 de Typocosmie. Nice: Editions des Cahiers Astrologiques.

Fischoff, B. 1982. "Debiasing." In Kahneman et al. 1982.

———. 1988. "Judgment and Decision Making." In Sternberg and Smith 1988, pp. 153–187.

Fischoff, B., P. Slovic, and S. Lichtenstein. 1977. "Knowing with Certainty: The Appropriateness of Extreme Confidence." *Journal of Experimental Psychology: Human Perception and Performance* 20: pp. 159–183.

Flugel, J. C. 1964. *A Hundred Years of Psychology,* 3rd ed., p. 37. London: Duckworth.

Fodor, J. A. 1983. *The Modularity of Mind.* Cambridge: Cambridge University Press.

Fowler, L. N. 1895. *Fowler's New Illustrated Self-Instructor in Phrenology and Physiology,* p. 39. London: Fowler.

Freedman, D. A. 1983. "A Note on Screening Regression Equations." *American Statistician* 37: pp. 152–155.

Funder, D. 1987. "Errors and Mistakes: Evaluating the Accuracy of Social Judgment." *Psychological Bulletin* 101 pp. 75–90.

Furnham, A. 1989. "Personality and the Acceptance of Diagnostic Feedback." *Personality and Individual Differences* 10: pp. 1121–1133.

Furnham, A., and B. Gunter. 1987. "Graphology and Personality: Another Failure to Validate Graphological Analysis." *Personality and Individual Differences* 8: pp. 433–435.

Furnham, A., and S. Schofield. 1986. "Accepting Personality Test Feedback: A Review of the Barnum Effect." *Current Psychological Review of Research* 7: pp. 162–178.

Gage, N. L. 1952. "Judging Interests from Expressive Behavior." *Psychological Monographs* 66(18): whole no. 602.

Gage, H. N. 1989. "Clinical Judgment, Clinical Training, and Professional Experience." *Psychological Bulletin* 105: pp. 387–396.

Gardner, M. 1988. *The New Age: Notes of a Fringe Watcher,* pp. 252–263 on "Psychic Astronomy." Buffalo, N.Y.: Prometheus Books.

Gergen, K. J., A. Hepburn, and D. C. Fisher. 1986. "Hermeneutics of Personality Description." *Journal of Personality and Social Psychology* 50: pp. 1261–1270.

Gille-Maisani, J-C. 1989. *Psychologie de l'Ecriture.* Paris: Payot. 347 pp.

Gladding, S. T., and M. K. Farrar. 1982. "Perceptions of Common and Unusual First Names of Therapists." *Psychological Reports* 50: pp. 595–601.

Glick, P., and M. Snyder. 1986. "Self-Fulfilling Prophecy: The Psychology of Belief in Astrology." *Humanist* (May/June): pp. 20–25, 50.

Glick, P., D. Gottesman, and J. Jolton. 1989. "The Fault Is Not in the Stars: Susceptibility of Skeptics and Believers in Astrology to the Barnum Effect." *Personality and Social Psychology Bulletin* 15: pp. 572–583.

Green, P. E., V. R. Rao, and D. E. Armani. 1971. "Graphology and Marketing Research: A Pilot Experiment in Validity and Inter-Judge Reliability." *Journal of Marketing* 35: pp. 58–62.

Greene, J., and D. Lewis. 1980. *The Hidden Language of Your Handwriting,* p. 252. London: Souvenir Press.

Goldberg, L. R. 1965. "Diagnosticians vs. Diagnostic Signs: The Diagnosis of Psychosis vs. Neurosis from MMPI." *Psychological Monographs* 79. 28 pp.

———. 1976. "Man versus Model of Man: Just How Conflicting Is That Evidence?" *Organizational Behavior and Human Performance* 16: pp. 13–22. A re-analysis of Libby (1976).

Griffin, K. 1988. "What They See Is What You Write." *Enterprise* (November 1988): pp. 22–25. See p. 23.

Hamilton, R. G., and M. H. Robertson. 1966. "Examiner Influence on the Holtzman Inkblot Technique." *Journal of Projective Techniques and Personality Assessment* 30: pp. 553–558.

Harari, H., and J. W. McDavid. 1973. "Name Stereotypes and Teachers' Expectations." *Journal of Educational Psychology* 65: pp. 222–225.

Harvey, D. L. 1933. "The Measurement of Handwriting Considered as a Form of Expressive Movement." *Character and Personality* 2: pp. 310–321.

Hill, B. 1981. *Graphology.* London: Hale, p. 56.

Hines, T. 1979. "Biorhythm Theory: A Critical Review." *Skeptical Inquirer* 3(4): pp. 26–36.

———. 1988. *Pseudoscience and the Paranormal: A Critical Examination of the Evidence,* p. 11. Buffalo, N.Y.: Prometheus Books.

Hoffman, P. J., P. Slovic, and L. G. Rorer. 1968. "An Analysis of Variance Model for the Assessment of Configural Cue Utilization in Clinical Judgment." *Psychological Bulletin* 69: pp. 338–349.

Hogarth, R. M. 1987. *Judgement and Choice: The Psychology of Decision.* 2nd ed, pp. 1–3. New York: Wiley.

Hollander, P. S., and R. Parker. 1989. "Handwriting: Fingerprints of Character." *The World and I* (June 1989): pp. 244–251.

Holyoak, K. J., and K. Koh. 1987. "Surface and Structural Similarity in Analogical Transfer." *Memory & Cognition* 15: pp. 332–340.

Hungerford, E. 1930. "Poe and Phrenology." *American Literature* 2: pp. 209–231.

Hyman, R. 1977. "Cold Reading: How to Convince Strangers That You Know All About Them." *The Zetetic* (now *The Skeptical Inquirer*) 1(2): pp. 18–37.

Hyman, R. 1981. "The Psychic Reading." In *The Clever Hans Phenomenon: Communication with Horses, Whales, Apes, and People*, edited by T. A. Sebeok and R. Rosenthal, pp. 169–181. New York: New York Academy of Sciences.

———. 1987. "Proper Criticism." *Skeptical Briefs* 3: pp. 4–5. Reprinted in Hyman, R. *The Elusive Quarry: A Scientific Appraisal of Psychical Research*, pp. 437–441. Buffalo, N.Y.: Prometheus Books 1989.

Jacoby, H. J. 1939. *Analysis of Handwriting: An Introduction into Scientific Graphology*, p. 44. London: Allen and Unwin.

Jahoda, G. 1962. "Refractive Errors, Intelligence and Social Mobility." *British Journal of Social and Clinical Psychology* 1: pp. 96–106.

Jennings, D. L., T. M. Amabile, and L. Ross. 1982. "Informal Covariation Assessment: Data-Based versus Theory-Based Judgments." In Kahneman et al. 1982, pp. 211–238.

Jensen, A. R. 1964. "The Rorschach Technique: A Re-evaluation." *Acta Psychologica* 22: pp. 60–77.

Jones, E. E. 1976. "How Do People Perceive the Causes of Behavior?" *American Scientist* 64: pp. 300–305.

———. 1986. "Interpreting Interpersonal Behavior: The Effects of Expectancies." *Science* 234: pp. 41–46.

Kachigan, S. K. 1986. *Statistical Analysis*. New York: Radius Press.

Kahneman, D., and A. Tversky. 1973. "On the Psychology of Prediction." *Psychology Review* 80: pp. 237–251.

Kahneman, D., P. Slovic, and A. Tversky. 1982. *Judgment under Uncertainty: Heuristics and Biases*. New York: Cambridge University Press.

Karlsson, J. L. 1978. *Inheritance of Creative Intelligence*. Chicago: Nelson-Hall.

Kelly, I. W., and P. Renihan. 1984. "Elementary Credibility for Executives and Upward Mobiles." *The Canadian School Executive* 3(10): pp. 16–18.

Kelly, I. W., and D. H. Saklofske. 1989. "Small Scale Study of a Graphologist Using Wrong Profiles." Unpublished study, Dept. of Educational Psychology, University of Saskatchewan, Saskatoon, Canada S7N 0W0.

Kidd, J. B. 1970. "The Utilization of Subjective Probabilities in Production Planning." *Acta Psychologica* 34: pp. 338–347.

Kleinmuntz, B. 1990. "Why We Still Use Our Heads Instead of Formulas: Toward an Integrative Approach." *Psychological Bulletin* 107: pp. 296–310. A comprehensive review with 231 references.

Kohn, A. 1986. *False Prophets: Fraud and Error in Science and Medicine*, pp. 18–20 and 26–30. Oxford: Basil Blackwell.

Layne, C., and G. Ally. 1980. "How and Why People Accept Personality Feedback." *Journal of Personality Assessment* 44: pp. 541–546.

Lester, D., S. McLaughlin, and G. Nosal. 1977. "Graphological Signs for Extroversion." *Perceptual and Motor Skills* 44: pp. 137–138.

Levine, J., and N. Gordon. 1984. "Influence of the Method of Drug Administration on Analgesis Response." *Nature* 312: pp. 755–756.

Libby, R. 1976. "Man versus Model of Man: Some Conflicting Evidence." *Organizational Behavior and Human Performance* 16: pp. 1–12 and 23–26.

Lorr, M., L. T. Lepine, and J. V. Golder. 1953. "A Factor Analysis of Some Handwriting Characteristics." *Journal of Personality* 22: pp. 348–353.

Lowengard, M. 1975. *How to Analyze Your Handwriting,* p. 26. London: Marshall Cavendish.

Lyons, J. 1964. "Recognition of Expressive Patterns as a Function of Their Mode of Expression." *Journal of Consulting Psychology* 28: pp. 85–86.

Machover, K. 1951. "Drawing of the Human Figure: A Method of Personality Investigation." In *An Introduction to Projective Techniques,* edited by H. Anderson and G. Anderson. New York: Prentice-Hall.

Mansfield, J. 1975. *Selfscape,* p. 73. London: Weidenfeld and Nicolson.

Marks, D., and R. Kammann. 1980. *The Psychology of the Psychic.* Buffalo, N.Y.: Prometheus Books.

McKelvie, S. J. 1990. "Student Acceptance of a Generalized Personality Description: Forer's Graphologist Revisited." *Journal of Social Behaviour and Personality* 5: pp. 91–95.

McNeil, E. B., and G. S. Blum. 1952. "Handwriting and Psychosexual Dimensions of Personality." *Journal of Projective Techniques* 16: pp. 476–484.

Meehl, P. E. 1986. "Causes and Effects of My Disturbing Little Book." *Journal of Personality Assessment* 50: pp. 370–375.

Melzack, R., and P. Wall. 1983. *The Challenge of Pain.* New York: Basic Books.

Miller, G. A. 1956. "The Magical Number Seven, Plus or Minus Two: Some Limits on Our Capacity for Processing Information." *Psychological Reviews* 63: pp. 81–97.

Miller, J. 1983. *States of Mind: Conversations with Psychological Investigators.* London: British Broadcasting Corporation.

Miller, J. H. 1982. *Bibliography of Handwriting Analysis: A Graphological Index.* Troy, N.Y.: Whitston.

Murdock, B. B. 1961. "The Retention of Individual Items." *Journal of Experimental Psychology* 62: pp. 618–625.

Naftulin, D. H., J. E. Ware, and F. A. Donnelly. 1973. "The Doctor Fox Lecture: A Paradigm of Educational Seduction." *Journal of Medical Education* 48: pp. 630–635.

Neher, A. 1980. *The Psychology of Transcendence,* p. 230. Englewood Cliffs, N.J.: Prentice-Hall.

Nelson, R. A. 1971. *The Art of Cold Reading, and A Sequel to the Art of Cold Reading.* Calgary: Hades.

Neter, E., and G. Ben-Shakhar. 1989. "The Predictive Validity of Graphological Inferences: A Meta-Analytic Approach." *Personality and Individual Differences* 10: pp. 737–745.

Nisbett, R. E., and L. Ross. 1980. *Human Inference: Strategies and Shortcomings of Social Judgment.* Englewood Cliffs, N.J.: Prentice-Hall.

Nisbett, R. E., D. H. Krantz, D. Jepson, and Z. Kunda. 1983. "The Use of Statistical Heuristics in Everyday Inductive Reasoning." *Psychological Review* 90: pp. 339–363.

Oakes, M. 1982. "Intuiting Strength of Association from a Correlation Coefficient."

British Journal of Psychology 73: pp. 51–56.

Ochse, R. 1990. *Before the Gates of Excellence: The Determinants of Creative Genius.* Cambridge: Cambridge University Press.

Olyanova, N. 1960. *The Psychology of Handwriting*, p. 220. New York: Sterling Publishing.

———. 1969. *Handwriting Tells.* London: Peter Owen.

Passingham, R. E. 1979. "Brain Size and Intelligence in Man." *Brain Behavior and Evolution* 16: pp. 253–270.

Paterson, J. 1976. *Interpreting Handwriting*, pp. 61, 78, 79, 81. London: Macmillan.

Peterson, L. R., and M. J. Peterson. 1959. "Short-Term Retention of Individual Verbal Items." *Journal of Experimental Psychology* 58: pp. 193–198.

Prioleau, L., M. Murdock, and N. Brody. 1983. "An Analysis of Psychotherapy versus Placebo Studies." *Behavioral and Brain Sciences* 6: pp. 275–310.

Purvis, A. 1987. "Right Writing the Key to Right Choice." *Vancouver Sun* (6 October): p. D1.

Reid, J. 1983. "Use of Graphology." *Personnel Management* (October 1983): p. 71.

Rim, Y. 1981. "Who Believes in Graphology?" *Personality and Individual Differences* 2: pp. 85–87.

Roman, K. G. 1952. *Handwriting: A Key to Personality.* New York: Pantheon.

Rorer, L. G., P. J. Hoffman, H. R. Dickman, and P. Slovic. 1967. "Configural Judgments Revealed." *Proceedings of the Annual Convention of the American Psychological Association.* Washington, D.C.: APA.

Rosenthal, D. A., and R. Lines. 1978. "Handwriting as a Correlate of Extraversion." *Journal of Personality Assessment* 42: pp. 45–48.

Russell, Bertrand. 1952. *The Impact of Science on Society*, p. 25. London: Allen and Unwin.

Russell, D., and W. H. Jones. 1980. "When Superstition Fails: Reactions to Disconfirmation of Paranormal Beliefs." *Personality and Social Psychology Bulletin* 6: pp. 83–88.

Saudek, R. 1925. *The Psychology of Handwriting*, pp. 1–4. London: Allen and Unwin.

Secord, P. F., W. F. Dukes, and W. Bevan. 1954. "Personalities in Faces: I. An Experiment in Social Perceiving." *Genetic Psychology Monographs* 49: pp. 231–279.

Severn, J. M. 1913. *Popular Phrenology*, p. 6. London: Rider.

Shanteau, J. 1988. "Psychological Characteristics and Strategies of Expert Decision Makers." *Acta Psychologica* 68: pp. 203–215.

Shepard, R. D. 1964. "On Subjectively Optimum Selections among Multivariate Alternatives." In *Human Judgments and Optimality*, edited by M. W. Shelly and G. L. Bryan, pp. 257–281. New York: Wiley.

Simon, H. A. 1957. *Models of Man: Social and Rational*, p. 198. New York: Wiley.

Singer, E. 1969. *A Manual of Graphology.* London: Duckworth.

Sizer, N., and H. S. Drayton. 1893. *Heads and Faces, and How to Study Them.*

A Manual of Phrenology and Physiognomy for the People, p. 7. New York: Fowler & Wells.

Slovic, P. 1972. "From Shakespeare to Simon: Speculations—and Some Evidence —about Man's Ability to Process Information." Revised version of a paper presented at the Ninth Meeting of the Institute of Management Sciences, Houston, Tex., April 1972. Copies available from Oregon Research Institute, P.O. Box 3196, Eugene, OR 97403.

———. 1974. "Hypothesis Testing in the Learning of Positive and Negative Linear Functions." *Organizational Behavior and Human Performance* 11: pp. 368–376.

Smedslund, J. 1963. "The Concept of Correlation in Adults." *Scandinavian Journal of Psychology* 4: pp. 165–173.

Smith, R. F. 1975. *Prelude to Science: An Exploration of Magic and Divination,* p. 24. New York: Scribner.

Snyder, C. R. 1974. "Why Horoscopes Are True: The Effects of Specificity on Acceptance of Astrological Interpretations." *Journal of Clinical Psychology* 38: pp. 577–580.

Spiro, H. 1986. *Doctors, Patients and Placebos.* New Haven: Yale University Press.

Steiner, R. A. 1989. *Don't Get Taken! Bunco and Bunkum Exposed: How to Protect Yourself,* p. 57. El Cerrito, Calif.: Wide-Awake Books.

Sternberg, R. J., and E. E. Smith, eds. 1988. *The Psychology of Human Thought.* Cambridge: Cambridge University Press.

Sundberg, N. D. 1955. "The Acceptance of 'Fake' versus 'Bona Fide' Personality Test Interpretations." *Journal of Abnormal and Social Psychology* 50: pp. 145–147.

Sussams, P. 1984. "Graphology and Psychological Tests: Part 1—Some Pitfalls in Personality Assessment." *The Graphologist* 2(4): pp. 3–5.

Swann, W. B., B. W. Pelham, and T. R. Chidester. 1988. "Change through Paradox: Using Self-Verification to Alter Beliefs." *Journal of Personality and Social Psychology* 54: pp. 268–273.

Taft, R. 1967. "Extraversion, Neuroticism, and Expressive Behaviour: An Application of Wallach's Moderator Effect to Handwriting Analysis." *Journal of Personality* 35: pp. 570–5874.

Tallent, N. 1958. "On Individualizing the Psychologist's Clinical Evaluation." *Journal of Clinical Psychology* 14: pp. 243–244.

Thornton, G. R. 1944. "The Effect of Wearing Glasses upon Judgments of Personality Traits of Persons Seen Briefly." *Journal of Applied Psychology* 28: pp. 203–207.

Thorp, E. O. 1966. *Beat the Dealer.* New York: Vintage Press.

Truzzi, M. 1987. "Zetetic Ruminations on Skepticism and Anomalies in Science." *Zetetic Scholar* 12/13: pp. 7–20. Comments are from pages 16–19.

Tversky, A., and D. Kahneman. 1971. "Belief in the Law of Small Numbers." *Psychological Bulletin* 76: pp. 105–110.

———. 1974. "Judgment under Uncertainty: Heuristics and Biases." *Science* 185: pp. 1124–1131.

Van Valen, L. 1974. "Brain Size and Intelligence in Man." *American Journal of Anthropology* 40: pp. 417–424.

Wagenaar, W. A. 1988. *Paradoxes of Gambling Behaviour*. Hillsdale: Lawrence Erlbaum. Contains many examples of judgment biases among casino and other gamblers, with a useful review on pp. 107–114.

Ward, W. C., and H. M. Jenkins. 1965. "The Display of Information and the Judgment of Contingency." *Canadian Journal of Psychology* 19: pp. 231–241.

Watson, P. 1981. *Twins: An Investigation into the Strange Coincidences in the Lives of Separated Twins*. London: Hutchinson, pp. 101–190. Very readable but no index.

Wiggins, N., and E. Kohen. 1971. "Man vs. Model of Man Revisited: The Forecasting of Graduate School Success." *Journal of Personality and Social Psychology* 19: pp. 100–106.

Woolfolk, M. E., W. Castellan, and C. I. Brooks. 1983. "Pepsi versus Coke: Labels, Not Tastes, Prevail." *Psychological Reports* 52: pp. 185–186.

Yackulic, A., and I. W. Kelly. 1984. "The Psychology of the 'Gambler's Fallacy' in Probablistic Reasoning." *Psychology* 21: pp. 55–58.

Yntema, D. B., and W. S. Torgerson. 1961. "Man-Computer Cooperation in Decisions Requiring Common Sense." *IRE Transactions of the Professional Group on Human Factors in Electronics* HFE-2(1): pp. 20–26.

14

Handwriting Is Brainwriting. So What?

Barry L. Beyerstein

In debates between skeptics and proponents of handwriting analysis, one of the most frequent defenses offered by graphologists is that "handwriting is brainwriting." In this chapter Barry Beyerstein provides a critique of that argument from the perspective of a physiological psychologist. Physiological psychology is the interdisciplinary field that seeks to elucidate the brain mechanisms involved in psychological phenomena such as cognition, perception, memory, emotions, personality, motor movements, arousal, etc. This chapter provides a review of research in the neurosciences and psychology that shows why the "brainwriting" argument not only fails as a plausible rationale for handwriting analysis, but in fact weakens the graphologists' case because its central assumptions are questioned by modern research into the neural substrates of personality and writing.

INTRODUCTION

Graphologists often defend their craft with the assertion that "handwriting is brainwriting" (e.g., Lockowandt, this volume, chap. 5; Matousek 1987, 1). If by advancing this truism they were claiming nothing more than the undeniable fact that handwriting is controlled by the brain, I would have no objection. But by use of this rhetorical device, graphologists obviously wish to imply much more, namely, the non sequitur that because the brain is responsible for our psychological makeup as well as our writing, script formation necessarily reveals deep secrets about our personal habits, talents, and predilections.

Despite its surface plausibility, closer inspection reveals that this gambit merely asserts that which is yet to be proved. The burden of proof for the claim that minute details of writing correlate with psychological, social, or medical phenomena remains firmly with those who promote graphology as an evaluative or predictive tool, and on this point skeptics find the evidence insufficient.[1] The introduction by graphologists of the true but misleading assertion that "handwriting is brainwriting" diverts attention from the real issue: the paucity of methodologically adequate research supporting their techniques. The mere proclamation that writing is controlled by the brain provides no reason to believe that particular signs on a page are related to unique neurophysiological entities and, therefore, to highly specific personal qualities (especially when different schools of graphology disagree as to what the same signs mean).

"THOSE WHO IGNORE HISTORY ARE CONDEMNED TO RELIVE IT"

The attempt by the graphological community to cloak itself in neurological garb is reminiscent of a long line of questionable diagnostic and self-improvement schemes whose authors have tried to enhance their credibility by claiming unearned affiliation with brain research (Beyerstein 1990). Naive "neurologizing" is so prevalent among "pop-psychologists' seeking a patina of authority for unproven speculations that Miller (1986) coined the term "neurobabble" for those attempts to usurp the prestige of neuroscience without understanding its principles. In placing themselves in such unenviable company, graphologists do little to advance their claim to scientific respectability.

In this chapter, I contrast the tacit assumptions underlying the "handwriting is brainwriting" justification with current neurological perspectives on personality and writing. In so doing, I question whether neuroscience does indeed offer an acceptable rationale for graphology. It is ironic that by appealing to neuroscience, graphologists actually weaken their case, for in order for handwriting analysis to draw support from brain research, the cerebral mechanisms responsible for writing, cognition, and personality would need to be organized in ways that clash with well-established principles of neurophysiology and neuroanatomy.

A THEORETICAL BASIS FOR GRAPHOLOGY?

Among the reasons critics cite for doubting the validity of graphology are the failure of its proponents to produce an acceptable theory to account for why it appears to work, and the fact that graphology neither draws upon nor contributes to progress in related fields such as psychology, neurophysiology, biomechanics, biocybernetics, and graphonomics.[2] One of the hallmarks of a legitimate science is that its data and theory mutually support (rather than contradict) those of related disciplines (Bunge 1984).

If graphologists wish to be taken seriously by the scientific community, they will first have to:

(a) present replicable, methodologically sound research to document the links they postulate between writing and psychological variables;
(b) account satisfactorily for the large number of careful studies that have failed to find such relationships (cf. Karnes and Leonard, this volume, ch. 16; Neter and Ben-Shakhar 1989; Furnham 1988);
(c) adequately rule out alternative explanations[3] for graphology's apparent successes in everyday settings; and then, *and only then,*
(d) provide a plausible and falsifiable theory to explain their findings.

Only if robust correlations between written signs and psychological attributes could be empirically established would it be worth attempting a theoretical explanation by reference to brain mechanisms. But even then, such attempts are likely to founder because the kind of personality constructs used by graphologists are not only questionable in themselves (see Bowman, this volume, ch. 10), but are of a sort that is difficult, if not impossible, to relate to mechanisms at the neural level.

In fields such as graphology, where supporting data are equivocal at best, plausibility of the underlying theory and compatibility with established research become the paramount arbiters of scientific status. Though graphologists have not, to my knowledge, tried to develop (or test) the implications of their "handwriting is brainwriting" argument, it and the related "expressive movement" rationale (discussed below) come as close to theoretical statements as I have found in this essentially ad hoc field. Thus it is worth unpacking and examining these assertions to see if they could constitute an acceptable theoretical rationale for graphology.

WHAT DOES THE BRAINWRITING ASSERTION IMPLY?

It should be emphasized that although the brainwriting argument is true as far as it goes, it cannot, by itself, sustain the explanatory burden graphologists place upon it. The fact that handwriting is controlled by the central nervous system is necessary, but not sufficient, for their purpose, as can be seen from the following.

No educated person seriously doubts that handwriting is controlled by the brain, but so are coughing, yawning, spitting, and vomiting. Why, then, should writing deserve special status as a putative window on character and talent? The reason many have accorded it this distinction in advance of the usual verification is, I submit, that writing seems as though it *ought* to correlate with personality, whereas so many other behaviors controlled by the brain do not.[4] Writing is multifaceted, as is personality; it exhibits the kind of variation across and consistency within individuals that makes it an intuitively attractive candidate for character reading. Moreover, handwriting offers a wealth of detail for metaphorical generalization to behavior, the "pop-psychologist's" stock in trade (see B. Beyerstein, ch. 9, this volume). Moreover, it does not seem unreasonable that sloppy, artistic, or even bold people might reveal some of these qualities in their handwriting. As a source of testable hypotheses these inferences may not be inherently absurd, but their truth or falsity is an empirical question to be established by research, not proclaimed by fiat. And, to date, the evidence is questionable. Furthermore, what quirks of penmanship could distinguish the deceitful from the honest, the cold from the compassionate, or the promiscuous from the faithful? And why?

The brainwriting argument allays the unease many laypersons might feel when such questions arise because it appears to carry the imprimatur of legitimate research. It impresses the neurologically untutored because it is easy to imagine that writing movements and personality could somehow be linked (because of their common reliance on the brain), whereas it is more difficult to conceive of plausible mechanisms to link character with lines on the palm or the position of the stars. Nonetheless, for those of us directly involved with the neurosciences, the brain-writing–personality nexus is extremely dubious, a priori, for reasons discussed below. Before pursuing those objections, brief mention should be made of a related graphological claim to legitimacy, the "expressive movement" argument.

EXPRESSIVE MOVEMENTS AND GRAPHOLOGY

Graphologists also seek credibility by analogizing their practices to ortho-dox research that suggests that some gestures are related to broad aspects of comportment. Though the strength of the relationship remains contro-versial, a few very general correspondences between mannerisms and other social tendencies have been noted (Kirkcaldi 1985). While these studies are valid within their own domain, the support they lend to graphology is tenuous. The weak and rather indefinite relationships reported in the ex-pressive-movement literature cannot be stretched to justify the fine-grained character depictions produced by graphologists.

In his review of the expressive-movement research, Brebner (1985) noted modest correlations between certain gestures and very general inclinations such as extroversion and introversion.[5] However, he found that even these frail relationships could be overridden by transient emotional states and situational factors. Such clues to personality as could be inferred from movements were far too inexact to justify the willingness of graphologists to label people potential thieves, child molesters, or drug abusers. In fact, it is extremely unlikely that such complex behavioral patterns have a particular neuroanatomical locus that could reliably evoke specific gestures, or, for that matter, specific writing features.

In the only study reviewed by Brebner that involved graphic behavior, it was found that outgoing, sociable people tended to fill more of a page with their "doodlings." However, there was no suggestion in his extensive review that more subtle attributes like honesty, loyalty, or benevolence ex-press themselves gesturally.[6] Brebner also noted that untrained people can glean all there is to infer from expressive movements simply by observ-ing them for a few minutes. Thus there is no need to hire graphologists to uncover such readily obtainable information, and its precision is hard-ly sufficient to justify the involvement of graphologists in marital, employ-ment, or parole decisions.

Even if the correlations between personality and expressive movements were stronger and more specific, the onus would still be on graphologists to show how minute facets of handwriting relate to these global gestures, let alone to highly specific personality traits. This they have notably failed to do. It goes without saying that the willingness to pronounce someone sexually deviant, violence prone, or a security risk based on such flimsy extrapolations from gestures to writing behavior is unconscionable and is not condoned by the expressive-movement researchers.

Graphologists might be tempted to claim as support for their endeav-ors the research on facial expressions that has demonstrated relatively pre-cise ties between muscle configurations and psychological qualities. But here too they would encounter serious obstacles. Distinctive facial expressions are produced by activity in brain systems that mediate anger, disgust, happiness, etc. (Ekman 1980). The basic facial code is innate and similar across many diverse cultures. Presumably, it was favored by natural selection because this way of broadcasting inner feelings promoted survival by enhancing social cooperation (Buck 1985). But, as with the gestural behaviors discussed earlier, no professional training is needed to read facial signals. Furthermore, they evolved to indicate moment-to-moment emotional changes, not the enduring personality styles that graphologists wish to infer. Support from other superficial similarities between handwriting and facial expressions crumbles with the realization that the usefulness of facial expressions depends upon the invariance of the inborn facial code across individuals, whereas it is minute idiosyncrasies in the acquired skill of writing that graphologists insist are revealing.

Similar arguments arise with regard to brain mechanisms that imbue speech with its recognizable emotional timbre. Inasmuch as this must involve connections between emotional mechanisms of the brain and the musculature of speech, could this finally be the elusive prototype for graphology? To see why not, we must look more closely at how this brain system works.

Loss of right temporal lobe function can strip a person's speech of its emotional tonality while leaving its meaningfulness intact (Dimond 1979; Sacks 1985, 83).[7] Lesions of the left temporal lobe spare the ability to recognize the emotional qualities in the speech of others but devastate the ability to understand its content. The fact that no training is required for normal production and recognition of these speech qualities and that identifiable areas of the brain are devoted to them are obvious differences vis-a-vis graphology. Discerning graphological signs requires formal training, and I know of no reports of specific brain lesions that obliterate the ability to make graphological judgments and nothing else. A final reason for doubting facile analogies between graphology and this aspect of oral communication arises from the fact that the brain's emotional apparatus blends the same affective flavoring unformly across any given utterance, rather than differentially modulating one morpheme for aggressiveness and another for kindliness, and so on. The latter would need to be the case for graphologists to derive any comfort from this research.

Before leaving this section, we should be reminded how convincingly skilled actors and manipulative sociopaths can learn to mimic body language, facial expressions, and tone of voice so as to create false personas. This should give pause to graphologists who invoke the expressive-movement rationale to support the claim that they can "see through" a writer's attempts to disguise his or her script in order to mask unsavory tendencies (assuming that writing could expose them in the first place.)[8] That said, let us return to the central assumptions of the "handwriting is brainwriting" argument.

THE BRAIN AND PSYCHOLOGICAL PROCESSES

Graphologists and their critics can agree that individual differences in personality, abilities, and dispositions derive from structural and functional relationships in the brain.[9] Some of these are innate, others are learned and stored as permanent modifications in brain circuitry. The field of physiological psychology provides ample evidence that the attributes of concern to graphologists are—like all thoughts, feelings, motives, skills, memories, perceptions, and movements—products of brain states (Carlson 1986; Oakley 1985). Even though the central programming of writing and the psychological traits that graphologists claim to discern are both due to brain states, the question remains as to whether specific writing movements are matched in a one-to-one fashion with any other personal attributes.

For the statement "handwriting is brainwriting" to offer any meaningful support for graphology, several preconditions would need to be satisfied. First, every psychological dimension upon which graphologists pass judgment (e.g., optimism, conservatism, piety) would need to be associated with a unique entity in the brain.[10] This was once a popular view in neurology but has long since been abandoned (as will be discussed shortly). Each of these anatomical representations of a trait, unlikely as they are, would in turn need to be hard-wired to a neural program that executes a particular set of writing movements. Granting for the moment this improbable scenario, it would still be necessary, in order for graphology to be a useful diagnostic tool, that these connections be invariant across all people in a given culture. Otherwise, there would be no reason to expect the same pen strokes from everyone who shares the psychological trait in question.[11] As we shall see, the sort of brain organization necessary to satisfy these conditions is hard to reconcile with current data on how psychological functions are mapped out in the brain. In fact, as Ben-Shakhar et al. (1986) remind us, if reliable relationships were found between handwriting and personality traits, they would pose a major theoretical challenge for modern psychology and neurology to accommodate them.

Though proponents of the brainwriting argument seem unaware of it, their thesis presupposes a particular position with respect to the age-old debate about localization of functions in the brain (Krech 1962; Rosner 1974). As it shares this tenet—and its attendant problems—with a once popular, but now discredited, school of trait assessment, a brief historical digression seems in order.

LOCALIZATION OF FUNCTION—A FALSE START

In the last century, a widely acclaimed character-reading system emerged from the discovery that different mental operations are handled by separate parts of the brain. Phrenology, the most egregious overextension of this legitimate notion of functional specialization, was the handiwork of Franz Joseph Gall (1758–1828). Gall was a leading neurophysiologist of his day whose many worthwhile discoveries have, unfortunately, been overshadowed by his phrenological follies.[12] He tried to explain personality by postulating circumscribed "organs" in the brain, each devoted to a "faculty" such as "secretiveness," "reverence," "self-esteem," or "benevolence" (Leahey and Leahey 1983, ch. 4). It is my contention that, in order for writing to correlate with psychological dispositions, a similarly dubious allocation of traits to isolated brain sites would be required.[13]

Gall proceeded logically from flawed premises: viz., that "faculties" were innate, possessed in varying degrees by everyone, and that each was segregated in a unique brain region. One's outstanding endowments were thought to stem from enlargement of the responsible "organs" which, in turn, should be marked by protuberances of the overlying skull. Thus, anyone's intimate makeup could be established by "reading" the shape of his or her cranium.

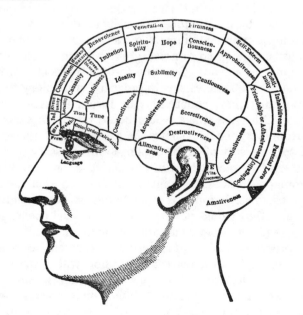

Figure 1. Thirty-seven faculties: the phrenological "organs"

Gall's initial assumptions were not unreasonable for his time, but he (and especially his overzealous followers) carried them to absurd lengths. Their unshakable faith in the theory led them to see confirmation where there was none and to discount the negative evidence provided by others.[14] In addition to their failure to subject their ideas to rigorous testing, the phrenologists were doomed by several other misapprehensions. One was the assumption that common-sense, essentially literary, depictions of human peculiarities could adequately describe and explain the complexities of human personality. Another was their belief that such depictions would be sufficiently stable across social situations to permit reliable predictions of behavior. Similar assumptions have not fared well at the hands of modern researchers (see Bowman, this volume, ch. 10), but they remain central to most graphological notions of personality. Even if the phrenologists had not erred in their conceptualization of traits and in their assumption that they live in little islands of enlarged cortex, their head-reading system would have been rendered useless by the fact that the outer shape of the cranium does not follow exactly the contour of the underlying brain.

Doubtful as the phrenologists' program was, it still left them better off than the graphologists in one respect—an enlarged phrenological organ simply had to produce an excess of its associated feelings. These urges could then be expressed in a variety of voluntary or involuntary ways. Thus, the phrenologists were spared the difficulty of suggesting a plausible mechanism whereby each "organ/faculty" could be invariably fixed to an output as specific as a unique writing movement.

Graphologists who rely on testimonials from famous supporters could do well to ponder the impressive list of those who staunchly defended phrenology in its heyday (cf. Edwardes 1977, pp. 131–138; Leahey and Leahey 1983, chs. 3 and 4; and Dean et al., this volume, ch. 13). The fact that intelligent people can be easily misled when they stray beyond their fields of expertise makes this sort of endorsement much less impressive than it might otherwise seem.

Despite its abandonment by mainstream physiological psychology, phrenology continues to enjoy devoted adherents, largely because its all-encompassing simplicity appeals to the impatient and its anti-establishment flavor attracts the envious and uncredentialed. Anyone offering the average citizen an allegedly powerful tool for manipulating others by exposing "what they are really like" invariably attracts an eager clientele (Beyerstein 1990). If vendors offer benefits shunned by scientific experts and even promise to evaluate people without their knowledge, so much the better for sales.

LOCALIZATION OF FUNCTION— THE CONTEMPORARY VIEW

Cerebral localization of function is a well-documented fact, but the brain's functional units in no way correspond to the "faculties" proposed by the phrenologists and implicitly assumed by graphologists (Krech 1962; Posner et al. 1988; Gazzaniga 1989). Studies of brain damage and experiments using electrophysiological, imaging, and cerebral bloodflow measures of brain structure and activity indicate that the functions localized in the brain are narrow subcomponents of psychological processes rather than the global attributes and dispositions dear to prescientific character readers. Graphologists could sidestep this difficulty if it did not immensely complicate any brain theory that could account for their alleged trait-writing correspondences.

Modern brain research shows that the elementary operations underlying complex mental functions are strictly localized and that these dispersed subroutines are assembled into different temporary networks as their contributions are required. The brain can be thought of as a collection of modules, each performing a fragment of tasks such as facial recognition or linguistic analysis (Gazzaniga 1989; Posner et al. 1988). In other words, broad abilities and dispositions do not reside in any single area of the brain, but their constituent operations do. Evidence for this kind of dynamic organization poses grave difficulties for the simplistic assumption of graphologists that minute features of writing could denote complex abilities, because there is no single, enduring center devoted exclusively to each of these abilities or traits. In other words, there is nothing that could easily be hard-wired to writing movements. This is essentially the same problem that thwarted neurosurgeons who naively thought violent behavior could be eliminated by surgically removing an allegedly overactive "aggression center" in the brain; no such convenient target exists (Valenstein 1973). We turn next to a consideration of the implications for graphology of this modular organization of the brain.

BIOLOGICAL THEORIES OF PERSONALITY

There is much reason to doubt the outmoded notion that people possessed of, say, a compassionate nature are so inclined because of a hyperactive "compassion center" in their brains. If, as I believe, personality differences do ultimately reflect brain differences, they must be much more subtle than the one center–one trait model proposed by the phrenologists and implied by graphologists of the brainwriting persuasion.

These days, students of the biological bases of personality think the plethora of overt character types reflects various blends of activity from a more modest number of temperamental systems in the brain (see, e.g., Mangan 1982; Derryberry and Rothbart 1988). Just as all colors of the spectrum can be produced by appropriate mixtures of a few primary hues, dissimilar personalities can result from varying strengths of a few neural systems, in a manner akin to the cognitive networks described in the preceding section. These temperament modules evolved to regulate physiological states and to motivate appropriate survival behaviors. Though their aggregate effect is the biological substrate of personality, the actual function each module performs bears little resemblance to any recognizable personality style. The sum of genetically determined "set points" in the different systems produces characteristic emotional responses to novelty, threat, deprivation, reward, and other biologically significant stimuli. These interact with learned attitudes to produce the behavioral consistencies we call personality.

Given their more primitive arousal, motivational, and emotional responsibilities, these temperament networks are found mainly in subcortical limbic areas (i.e., the evolutionarily older core of the brain that is most similar in human and infrahuman species). The cognitive modules are mostly cortical and serve perceptual awareness and the planning and execution of voluntary actions that satisfy limbic urgings.

Although theorists differ on specifics, they broadly agree about how idiosyncratic mixtures of these temperament systems could affect personality. Jeffrey Gray (1982), for instance, shows how individual differences in a "behavioral inhibition" system found in limbic areas can interact with arousal and motivational mechanisms in ways that could explain the personality dimensions proposed by Hans Eysenck (see Brody 1988, ch. 5). These interactions affect general orientation to the environment and increase the probability of certain kinds of responses to threat, novelty, punishment, and reward. They also set general excitability levels and affect readiness to learn about particular stimuli. Externally, they appear as inclinations to be impulsive, anxiety prone, or introverted as opposed to extroverted.

Tucker and Williamson (1984) have related neurochemical aspects of these subcortical activation and arousal systems to individual differences in specialization of the right and left cerebral hemispheres. They show how personal styles could be affected by interactions among subsystems governing response to novelty and reward, rate of habituation, filtering extraneous stimuli, maintaining vigilance, and the like. These subsystem interactions bias the relative importance of internal versus external controls on behavior, with obvious consequences for personality.

Extrapolating from studies of drug effects, brain damage, genetic selection, and other manipulations in animals, Cloninger (1986) argues that various human typologies can be derived from responsiveness in three separate but interacting subcortical systems. The novelty-seeking system, mediated by the neurotransmitter dopamine, regulates exploratory drives and the level of arousal generated by new stimuli. Those high in activity of this system are strongly motivated to avoid monotony. The second system, controlled by the neurotransmitter serotonin, mediates self-protectiveness. People with a robust harm-avoidance system generally choose their options with an overriding concern for averting punishment and unpredictable situations. The "harm-avoider" thus learns to inhibit behavior that might lead to punishment, excessive novelty, or loss of reward. Reward dependency, characterized by low activity in the norepinephrine tracts of the brain, is associated with a strong need to please others and a low tolerance for delay of gratification. Among other things, a reward-dependent person finds it difficult to abandon previously rewarded behaviors.

Cloninger has speculated about the types of personality that might result from various "set points" in his three systems. For instance, a person dominated by need for novelty but less driven by a need for constant reward might appear opportunistic and unconventional, whereas someone high in both needs might be an impassioned, self-indulgent attention seeker. Similarly, one low in need for both novelty and frequent reward would tend to be modest, unimaginative, and reclusive.

Kagan and colleagues (1988) extended a similar biological perspective to explain shyness, a human trait that remains quite stable throughout life. Faced with unfamiliar events or persons, some people typically become timid and withdrawn, whereas others are gregarious and affectively spontaneous. Kagan et al. drew upon research showing that animals who become cautious and socially avoidant when they encounter unexpected changes have hypothalamic-limbic mechanisms that are innately easy to arouse. They predicted that socially inhibited children might have similar hair triggers for certain sympathetic nervous system reactions, muscle tensions, and neuro-hormone secretions involved in the fight-or-flight response. The expected patterns, consistent with inherited differences in limbic arousability, were found to distinguish shy from outgoing children, further supporting a biological basis for the widely studied traits of extroversion and introversion.

It is clear that the biological component of personality is derived from *quantitative* interactions among several diverse brain systems possessed by everyone, not from *qualitatively* different trait controllers that some possess and others do not (and which could more easily command their own unique writing programs). Even if a temperament module could become linked with a writing trait, the link would be very difficult for a graphologist to discern because what any given module is actually doing for the individual bears little resemblance to the various overt behaviors it affects. Two people equally high in activity in one module could have quite different personalities because they differed in the quantitative inputs from a second or third. These two individuals would display the same written sign, but appear quite unalike nonetheless. The quantitative nature of these multiple contributors to a trait also makes it difficult to see how they could determine something as qualitative as an embellishment of a letter.

Of course, people's idiosyncratic experiences contribute importantly to their adult personality as well, creating a further problem for graphological theorists to explain: how can life's vicissitudes lead to modifications in writing in the first place, let alone produce the same modifications in everyone with a shared background?

In this section we have seen that the kinds of character traits portrayed by graphologists are not controlled by unitary centers that could easily be attached to specific writing movements. Having writing traits determined by quantitative interactions among the dispersed motivational and emotional mechanisms that actually underlie personality would represent a neural control problem of horrendous magnitude and no conceivable evolutionary value. For the brainwriting justification to make sense, graphologists would have to point to neural pathways that could lock these farflung temperament systems onto equally dispersed control systems for handwriting. It is to the latter that we now turn.

BRAIN MECHANISMS AND WRITING

Writing is a secondary, graphic representation of language, or, a re-encoding of another more basic code.

> As a code, language symbolizes experiences. This code can then be represented through a system of sounds combined to form words and sentences. However, these sounds (which are themselves a code) can be rerepresented as visual, rather than auditory, symbols. That is, reading and writing are codes for hearing and speaking, which themselves are codes for the actual experience or ideas (the referents). (Reed 1986, 17)

Reed (1986) classifies linguistic communication according to the receptive and expressive modalities employed. The auditory-oral system, comprised of hearing and speech, is the most common way of using language. It supplies the foundation for the visual-graphic system, the derivative ability to read and write.

Evolutionarily and developmentally, speech predates writing. Constructing visual signs to stand for auditory symbols emerged from primitive picture writing as recently as three to five thousand years ago (Ellis 1985). Long before that, the neural substrates of the auditory-oral system evolved as genetically organized features of the brain's cognitive apparatus—as evidenced by the fact that normal children require only minimal exposure to the arbitrary codes of a particular linguistic community to become proficient in their native tongue. By contrast, writing and reading must be laboriously taught and practiced, long after the auditory-oral system has attained a high level of sophistication. Even today, the power of manipulating written symbols remains a minority accomplishment (Critchley 1970, 1263).

Like all complex motor skills, writing demands painstaking attention to individual movements as it is being learned. With practice, writing comes to require little conscious monitoring and as this automatization progresses, letter formations become personalized. This process raises another problem for any theory of graphology because it must explain why a student's personality mechanisms supposedly force him or her, unconsciously, to deviate from the teacher's standard strokes in exactly the same way as all psychologically similar persons. Non-graphologists offer a much more convincing and parsimonious explanation for why individual differences in script formation emerge as we learn to write. For example, in their mathematical model of writing, Edelman and Flash (1987) show how slight biases in biocybernetic brain/ muscle programs could interact with biomechanical factors to individualize writing strokes in ways that graphologists would insist are personality driven. The biocyberneticists require none of the convoluted inputs from motivational systems that the graphologists do in order to account for individual differences in writing. Furthermore, biocyberneticists show how the same control modules could contribute to different writing strokes that would need to be controlled separately if—as graphologists believe—they derive from quite different trait mechanisms.

If writing is a learned extension of the brain's cognitive apparatus, one would expect that its neural control systems would receive their input from perceptual, linguistic, and memory areas rather than the motivational/personality ones suggested by graphology. This is supported by the fact that writing disorders (other than those resulting from damage to systems controlling the hand and arm) are most likely to accompany disruption of linguistic areas. These can include the mechanisms that imbue the strokes with meaning or the translational functions that encode acoustic, visual, or semantic information into motor commands (cf. Luria 1970, 328). The resulting syndromes are known as "agraphias" or "dysgraphias," depending on the type and severity of the deficit (Critchley 1970, ch. 22). The fact that dysgraphia is usually, though not inevitably, associated with receptive or expressive speech disorders shows that they share some, but not all, neural substrates.

If writing were linked to peculiarities of personality as graphologists maintain, brain damage that alters personality should have predictable consequences for writing, and vice versa. My search of published clinical case reports revealed no support for this notion. On the contrary, brain damage that profoundly alters personality can leave a patient's writing unchanged and gross disruptions of writing can occur in the absence of personality changes. In cases where both personality and writing are affected, there is no systematic relationship between losses of one kind and the other. Damage to the frontal lobes or their limbic connections is most likely to alter global personality (Damasio and Van Hoesen 1983), whereas it is injury to motor or language systems or to the parietal regions toward the rear of the cortex that disrupts writing.

Ogle (1867, in Roeltgen and Heilman 1985) was a pioneer in classifying writing disorders produced by injury to higher brain centers. By relating specific deficits to sites of damage, he derived the first comprehensive neurological model of writing. Recent technological advances have improved the precision of his picture of the distributed brain networks that serve writing.

The writing system, like the other brain networks discussed earlier, is dispersed and modularized (see Luria 1970; Ellis 1982; Roeltgen and Heilman 1985; Paradis 1987). Since there are visual, auditory, cognitive, linguistic, and motor subcomponents to the act of writing, it is not surprising that there can be a variety of partial deficits, depending upon which modules or interconnecting pathways are damaged. For instance, it is not unusual for a brain-injured patient to be able to spell a word orally but not in writing, even if he or she retains the ability to form individual letters. Other patients can write letters and words dictated to them but are unable to copy them from visual examples.

Some brain lesions affect the translation of acoustically stored information into the basic graphemic units[15] used by motor programs for writing. These patients are unable to write pronounceable nonwords (e.g., "blarg") but can still write irregular words such as "knife" that cannot be spelled by converting their auditorily stored form to its graphemic equivalent. Other patients, whose injuries disconnect hand/arm control from the memory banks that contain these atypical spellings (but spare access to phonetic systems), might hear and understand the word "laugh" but only be able to write it as "laf" (Ellis 1982). Roeltgen and Heilman (1985) have developed a comprehensive model of writing control in the brain by correlating dysfunctions such as these with specific anatomical sites of damage.

Since graphologists claim to look only at script formation and distribution, we can concentrate on modules that control these features. Dysfunctions of the pyramidal motor system (cortical muscle control areas and their efferent pathways) and extrapyramidal motor systems (basal ganglia, cerebellum) can cause writing to become undecipherable, even if the perceptual/cognitive input is normal (Roeltgen and Heilman 1985). In these cases, performance on other tasks requiring manual dexterity will be similarly degraded.

When perceptual input to the motor systems for writing is interrupted by localized damage to the brain, different problems arise. Disruption of brain mechanisms that process spatial relationships drastically affects writing (Ellis 1982; Luria 1970, ch. 8; Roeltgen and Heilman 1985). Parietal lobe damage on the nonlinguistic side of the brain affects orientation of letters and lines on the page, including various combinations of irregular slants and baselines, duplication of strokes (particularly the vertical strokes of the letters *m*, *n*, and *u*), sequestering of script to one side of the page, inappropriate insertions of spaces in words, abnormally small or large script, pressure variations, and difficulty in combining correctly formed strokes into proper letters. Effects such as these are of particular interest because they show that the sorts of features upon which graphologists base their judgments are sensitive to alterations in spatial perception systems, not systems related to personality.

Injury to the parietal area on the linguistic side of the brain produces quite different dysgraphias, characterized by difficulty in producing graphemes, the basic units of writing. Letters are adequately formed, but their sequence, and hence the meaning they convey, is jumbled.

Graphologists I have debated are impressed by the fact that a person's writing on a page and on a blackboard are recognizably similar (as, allegedly, are the same person's writing done with either hand or even, some say, by hand and foot!). This, they assert, indicates that there are idiosyncratic central programs for writing, as indeed there are. However, what this individuality of script most likely indicates is that the complex programming of biomechanical relationships, speeds of movement trajectories, etc. (Edelman and Flash 1987) is performed at a relatively high level, before the command sequence is fed into one of several possible motor output systems. Once again, graphologists point to an interesting phenomenon that prejudges nothing one way or the other about their hypothetical personality-writing correspondences.

GRAPHOLOGY AND OTHER AREAS OF SCIENCE

In this chapter I have argued that concern for consistency with relevant scientific research has been sadly lacking in graphological thought. Graphologists' unfamiliarity with reliable, easily obtainable information on the psychophysiology of personality and writing has led them to base their major theoretical justification upon outmoded concepts. This sort of insularity must cast serious doubt upon the scientific pretensions of the field. If this criticism seems unduly harsh, I could point to further evidence: e.g., the failure of graphologists to anticipate evolutionary arguments against their implicit brain theory.

Given that the structure of the human brain is the culmination of a long series of selective pressures (cf. Oakley and Plotkin 1979), we must ask what survival advantage would have been conferred by specifying an elaborate system of interconnections between control routines for minute aspects of writing and the motivational/emotional networks that underlie personality. The amount of genetic information, structural material, and metabolic resources required to develop and maintain the required "labeled lines" in the brain would be enormous. As nature has been notoriously loathe to squander investments of that magnitude for minimal evolutionary payoffs, it is incumbent upon graphologists to suggest how such a costly and cumbersome arrangement would have enhanced fitness. Theorists who propose intricate connections between the facial musculature and limbic mechanisms, or similar connections that infuse speech with its emotional timbre, were able to point to just such a payoff—improved social communication. How would natural selection have worked to fashion neural substrates for writing-personality correspondences so subtle that they only became apparent to specially trained observers in the last few hundred years? For what purpose was this alleged arrangement in place before our ancestors first devised the art of writing and before there were graphologists to supply the needed exegesis?

And, finally, because writing is a learned, arbitrary rerepresentation of a similarly arbitrary auditory code, it is twice removed from any genetically determined cognitive function—hardly an ideal arena for natural selection to work. Is it not more reasonable to think of writing as one of many possible uses to which this general purpose, user-programmable part of the brain can be put?

The kind of lockstep control by ancient parts of the brain over more recent additions implied by graphology's trait-writing correspondences also flies in the face of another well-established evolutionary trend. As vertebrate species developed increasingly elaborate brains, they began to rely correspondingly less on automatic, stereotyped behaviors to satisfy motivational states. Using trial and error to select the most efficient approaches proved to be a more effective survival strategy for higher mammals than the kind of hard-wired links between motives and micromovements suggested by graphology. Phylogenetically recent cortical additions that allow us to generate a mental representation of the environment greatly broadened the range of strategies for achieving goals. The result, as someone once put it, is that "our ideas can die in our stead." The cerebral cortex with its symbolic representational systems, of which writing is a learned expression, is the culmination of a trend that has loosened the bonds between motivational/emotional/personality mechanisms and any particular behavior fragments that could express them. Tying our most recently evolved and uniquely human capacities to older brain systems in the unyielding way graphology demands would mitigate the flexibility brain evolution has made possible. Inasmuch as writing is a quite recent acquisition—and a learned, conventional one at that—it seems odd that the human brain, the only one to have evolved the necessary substrate, would have saddled it with exquisitely deterministic links of such dubious value.

Now, it might be countered that writing itself exhibits just this sort of rigidity within individuals, which of course is true. But that rigidity is typical only within functional modules, and we have seen that in this instance it results from automatization of carefully practiced routines. What these stereotyped behavioral routines become temporarily attached to is anything but rigid in our highly plastic species.

Of course, if people with certain personalities chose voluntarily to express their predominant characteristics by means of certain writing conventions, the foregoing would be less problematic, but this would not sit well with the expressed belief of most graphologists that writing movements are unconscious and automatic.[16] Furthermore, this view hardly jibes with our subjective experience that few of us actively chose to write the way we do. And, finally, if the putative personality-script correspondences are not innate and unconscious, it strains credulity even further to accept the notion that everyone with a given trait would learn to express it via the same arbitrary writing convention.

CONCLUSION

In deciding among conflicting claims, it is often worth asking what must be abandoned as well as what will be accepted if we embrace one alternative over another. Other chapters in this collection have presented data in favor of and against the practical utility of graphology. Here, I have argued that in order to accept graphology as a valid method of discerning human strengths and weaknesses, one would have to consign a century of well-documented data in psychology and the neurosciences to the rubbish heap. The fact that so much of what we have learned about the neurological underpinnings of personality must be wrong if graphology is right does not automatically rule out graphology's claims. But, surely, it makes the gravity of accepting them such that a prudent observer would demand a specially high standard of proof before concluding that graphology is valid and that the whole edifice of psychobiological research, which serves us so well in so many areas, is in need of drastic revision. In my opinion, that standard has not been met.

It is ironic that so many graphologists should think the "handwriting is brainwriting" argument is one of their best lines of defense when it represents some of the most tempting chinks in their armor.

NOTES

1. See, e.g., chapters by Bowman, Dean, Dean et al., Klimoski, and Karnes and Leonard in this volume.

2. "Graphonomics" is the name chosen by the recently founded association of psychologists, physiologists, bioengineers, educators, and computer scientists devoted to research on handwriting. It is significant that this interdisciplinary taskforce invited no graphologists to join, cited no work by graphologists in its conference proceedings (Kao et al., 1986), and, despite demonstrations by members of the group that certain errors in children's writing predict later academic problems, did not even mention the possibility that handwriting might correlate with personality. Perusing graphologists' works, I have been unable to locate any who seem conversant with the published research of this highly relevant scientific organization.

3. One important alternative is "the Barnum Effect"—see Dean et al., and Karnes and Leonard, this volume.

4. See chapters by D. Beyerstein, Bowman, Dean et al., and Klimoski in this volume for discussions of the dangers of relying on this kind of "face validity" to justify psychological testing methods.

5.. Furnham and Gunter (1987) tested the ability of graphology to discern extroversion and introversion. They found that the results did not exceed chance expectancy. For a review of many other graphological failures to detect these most robust of all personality dimensions, see Furnham (1988).

6. In a related vein, it is a prevalent misconception that sexual orientation is discernible from body language (e.g., the stereotypes of the "swish" gay male or "butch" lesbian), but research shows that attributions based on this kind of folk-psychology are inaccurate most of the time (Krajeski 1981).

7. With respect to graphological claims, it is worth noting that therapists who work with these patients typically find no alterations in their handwriting

despite profound changes in personality. This underscores the fact, discussed above, that writing is a learned re-representation of speech. As such, its neural mechanisms are not innately intertwined with the emotional/motivational systems in the brain that affect personality and the emotional qualities of speech.

8. And would not this alteration of writing eliminate the undesirable behavior anyway? According to many highly touted "graphotherapists" (e.g., de Sainte Colombe 1972, pg. v): "You can correct your worst faults and strengthen your character by changing your handwriting."

9. By this, I do not mean to deny that many consistencies in behavior that might be called personality traits are, in fact, under control of regularities in the environment. But even these reactions are mediated by perceptual, motivational, memory, and motor systems of the brain.

10. Even if, say, "perseverance" could be said to have a unique brain locus, why would the property of "being a security risk" be any more likely than "vegetarianism" to have a brain area devoted to it and thus to command writing features all its own?

11. This sort of invariance is unlikely enough, but there is a further problem. How would this dubious "trait mechanism" in the brain "know" that it should become wired to neural programs for forming a particular letter, line arrangement, etc. in every writer of the Roman alphabet and attached to quite different features in programs for pictographic writing (which, as Paradis [1987] shows, are located in different brain sites) in those who happened to be born in another culture? Even within writers of Roman script, there are characteristic writing conventions in different countries and historical periods (Goldberg 1986). Obviously, these differences must be learned—otherwise, why would immigrants display the characteristics of their homelands and their children write with the national markings of their adopted lands? How could a group of hypothetical "personality neurons" unerringly sort out this myriad of demands, and why would they bother?

12. Though his own construal of the relationship between brain structure and mental endowment was fatally flawed, Gall deserves credit for promoting popular acceptance of the notion that individual differences are rooted in specializations of the brain. For equating mental states with brain states, Gall endured many attacks from religious leaders who assumed mind was a property of the immaterial soul.

13. I grant that one could conceive of a way in which numerous sites contributing to nonlocalized personality traits could be rigidly linked to equally dispersed writing mechanisms (if graphologists' accuracy were good enough to demand an explanation at the neural level). But such an arrangement would be far-fetched indeed. There is no independent evidence for it, and the required number and specificity of nerve tracts would be staggering. And we would still have to ask what purpose such a profligate use of genetic information and brain tissue would serve. Before graphologists invoke the brainwriting argument, they should at least show how such a cumbersome substrate could be laid down during brain development, long in advance of acquiring one of many possible learned programs for writing. If these dubious but necessary interconnections are not specified by

genetic instructions during early development, why would the brain bother to enshrine them later?

14. Once again, this demonstrates the necessity of "blind" measurements in situations where judgments of this sort are being made (see Dale Beyerstein's discussion in ch. 8).

15. Graphemes are the written equivalents of phonemes in spoken language.

16. To abandon the claim that writing unconsciously conforms to inner aspects of character would undermine the graphologists' contention that they can see through attempts to disguise writing because we inadvertently reveal these attributes in our script.

REFERENCES

Ben-Shakhar, G., M. Bar-Hillel, Y. Bilu, E. Ben-Abba, and A. Flug. 1986. "Can Graphology Predict Occupational Success? Two Empirical Studies and Some Methodological Ruminations." *J. of Applied Psychology* 714(4): pp. 645–653.

Beyerstein, B. L. 1990. "Brainscams: Neuromythologies of the New Age." *Intl. J. of Mental Health.* 19(3): pp. 27–36.

Brebner, J. 1985. "Personality Theory and Movement." In *Individual Differences in Movement,* edited by B. D. Kirkcaldy. Lancaster, U.K.: MTP Press.

Brody, N. 1988. *Personality: In Search of Individuality.* San Diego: Academic Press.

Buck, R. 1985. "Prime Theory: An Integrated View of Motivation and Emotion." *Psychological Review* 92(3): pp. 389–413.

Bunge, M. 1984. "What Is Pseudoscience?" *The Skeptical Inquirer* 9(1): pp. 36–46.

Carlson, N. R. 1986. *Physiology of Behavior.* 3rd ed. Boston: Allyn & Bacon.

Cloninger, R. 1987. "A Systematic Method for Clinical Description and Classification of Personality Variants." *Archives of General Psychiatry* 44: pp. 573–588.

Critchley, M. 1970. *Aphasiology and Other Aspects of Language.* London: Edward Arnold.

Damasio, A. R., and G. W. Van Hoesen. 1983. "Emotional Disturbances Associated with Focal Lesions of the Limbic Frontal Lobe." In *Neuropsychology of Human Emotions,* edited by K. Heilman and P. Satz. New York: Guilford Press.

Derryberry, D., and M. Rothbart. 1988. "Arousal, Affect, and Attention as Components of Temperament." *Journal of Personality and Social Psychology* 6: pp. 958–966.

de Sainte Colombe, P. 1972. *Grapho-therapeutics: The Pen and Pencil Therapy.* New York: Popular Library.

Dimond, S. 1979. "Symmetry and Asymmetry in the Vertebrate Brain." In *Brain, Behaviour and Evolution,* edited by D. Oakley and H. Plotkin, pp. 189–218.

Edelman, S., and T. Flash. 1987. "A Model of Handwriting." *Biological Cybernetics* 57: pp. 25–36.

Edwardes, M. 1977. *The Dark Side of History: Magic in the Making of Man.* New York: Stein and Day.

Ekman, P. 1980. *The Face of Man: Expressions of Universal Emotions in a New Guinea Village.* New York: Garland STPM Press.

Ellis, A. W. 1982. "Spelling and Writing (and Reading and Speaking)." In *Normality and Pathology in Cognitive Functions,* edited by A. W. Ellis. New York: Academic Press, pp. 113–146.

Furnham, A. 1988. "Write and Wrong: The Validity of Graphological Analysis." *The Skeptical Inquirer* 13: pp. 64–69.

Furnham, A., and B. Gunter. 1987. "Graphology and Personality: Another Failure to Validate Graphological Analyses." *Personality and Individual Differences* 8: pp. 433–435.

Gazzaniga, M. S. 1989. "Organization of the Human Brain." *Science* 245: pp. 947–952.

Goldberg, L. 1986. "Some Informal Explorations and Ruminations about Graphology." In *Scientific Aspects of Graphology,* edited by B. Nevo, pp. 281–293. Springfield, Ill.: Charles Thomas.

Gray, J. A. 1982. *The Neuropsychology of Anxiety: An Inquiry into the Functions of the Septo-hippocampal System.* Oxford: Clarendon.

Kagan, J., R. Reznick, and N. Sidman. 1988. "Biological Bases of Childhood Shyness." *Science* 240: pp. 167–171.

Kao, H. S. R., G. P. van Galen, and R. Hoosain. 1986. *Graphonomics: Contemporary Research in Handwriting.* North Holland: Elsevier.

Kirkcaldi, B. D., ed. 1985. *Individual Differences in Movement.* Lancaster, U.K.: MTP Press.

Krajeski, J. 1981. "Identifying Homosexuals by Mannerisms." *Medical Aspects of Human Sexuality* 7: p. 52.

Krech, D. 1962. "Cortical Localization of Function." In *Psychology in the Making; Histories of Selected Research Problems,* edited by L. Postman, pp. 31–72. New York: Knopf.

Leahey, T. H., and G. E. Leahey. 1983. *Psychology's Occult Doubles: Psychology and the Problem of Pseudoscience.* Chicago: Nelson-Hall.

Luria, A. 1970. *Traumatic Aphasia: Its Syndromes, Psychology, and Treatment.* The Hague: Mouton.

Mangan, G. L. 1982. *The Biology of Human Conduct: East-West Models of Temperament.* Oxford: Pergammon Press.

Matousek, R. 1987. *Graphology and the Phenomenon of Writing.* Self-published. 820 W. Maple St., Hinsdale, Ill. 60521.

Miller, L. 1983. "Neurobabble." *Psychology Today* (April): pp. 70–72.

Neter, E., and G. Ben-Shakhar. 1989. "The Predictive Validity of Graphological Inferences: A Meta-Analytic Approach." *Personality & Individual Differences* 10(7): pp. 737–745.

Oakley, K., ed. 1985. *Brain and Mind.* London: Methuen.

Oakley, K., and H. Plotkin, eds. 1979. *Brain, Behaviour and Evolution.* London: Methuen.

Paradis, M. 1987. "The Neurofunctional Modularity of Cognitive Skills: Evidence from Japanese Alexia and Polyglot Aphasia." In *Motor and Sensory Processes of Language,* edited by E. Keller and M. Gopnik. Hillsdale, N.J.: Lawrence Erlbaum, pp. 277–289.

Posner, M. I., S. E. Peterson, P. T. Fox, and M. E. Raichle. 1988. "Localization of Cognitive Operations in the Human Brain." *Science* 244: pp. 1627–1631.

Reed, V. A. 1986. *An Introduction to Children with Language Disorders.* New York: Macmillan.

Roeltgen, D. P., and K. M. Heilman. 1985. "Review of Agraphia and a Proposal for an Anatomically-Based Neuropsychological Model of Writing." *Applied Psycholinguistics* 6: pp. 205–230.

Rosner, B. 1974. "Recovery of Function and Localization of Function in Historical Perspective." In *Plasticity and Recovery of Function in the Central Nervous System,* edited by D. Stein, J. Rosen, and N. Butters. New York: Academic Press.

Sacks, O. 1985. *The Man Who Mistook His Wife for a Hat and Other Clinical Tales.* New York: Harper and Row.

Tucker, D., and P. Williamson. 1984. "Asymmetric Neural Control Systems in Human Self-Regulation." *Psychological Review* 91(2): pp. 185–215.

Valenstein, E. S. 1973. *Brain Control.* New York: Wiley.

Section Five

Representative Research by Graphologists and Critics

15

Evaluation of the Handwriting of Successful Women Through the Roman-Staempfli Psychogram

Patricia Wellingham-Jones

This study is included as an example of a recent attempt to validate the methods of a particular graphological school, as published in a refereed psychology journal. This chapter is a modified version of Dr. Wellingham-Jones's paper published originally in *Perceptual and Motor Skills* 69 (1989):999–1010.

As with the experiment published in chapter 16, the reader should carefully scrutinize the methodology. The hypothesis tested in this experiment is that successful women write differently from not-so-successful women. Thus, the prediction to be tested is: "[S]ignificant differences between the two groups would be found for six syndromes. . . ." (p. 425) Of course, if graphology is worth anything as a predictor of personality traits, we would expect that graphology by itself could predict these traits in advance of the graphologist knowing them. But this claim is not tested in the experiment reported here: "Several of the participants were known to the investigator, but not closely acquainted." (p. 427). Note that nothing is said in the paper about the graphologist reviewing the handwriting samples *blind*—that is, without knowing the identities of the writers. And we should never simply assume that this is the case, just because a properly controlled experiment would be done this way. Also, this study provides no evidence for the central claim of graphology that it is the features of the *handwriting* itself that provide the graphologist with the information used to construct the personality profile. Note on p. 425 that the subjects wrote about success or on random topics, but composed the passages themselves: "It was stressed that voluntary (noncopied or dictated [sic],[1] informal) writing was needed." Thus there was a wealth of cues—spelling, grammar, style—in the content of the writing, which could be used to determine the personal attributes quite irrespective of what the graphological theory in question has to say about the actual features of the handwriting. Those readers who are not trained in any version of graphology may wish to try an informal "experiment" to demonstrate how information supposedly irrelevant to graphology can provide information for guesses about a writer's personality: Read the two handwriting samples in Figure 2A and 2B on p. 428, without reading the captions below the samples. Guess which is the example of the successful, and which is the unsuccessful person's handwriting. Also, make a list of traits you associate with each writer. Now, read the captions below the samples. Look at the samples again, and try not to see the traits mentioned in these captions! (For another example of this *illusory correlation,* see note 9 of chapter 13 by Dean, Kelly, Saklofske, and Furnham).

Previous studies have shown that such personal qualities as adaptability, asseriveness, common sense, creativity, independence, intelligence, resourcefulness, leadership drive, and risk-taking are more highly developed in people who achieve their goals in life than in those who do not (see References for a selection of relevant articles, and Wellingham-Jones, 1989, for a complete bibliography). The present study was designed: (1) to discover what, if any differences exist between women who are considered successful and women from the population at large; and (2) to determine whether qualities that are important for achieving success are relevant to self-judgments of success. Personality characteristics of the participants in the study were determined by handwriting analysis, using the Roman-Staempfli Psychogram.

THE ROMAN-STAEMPFLI PSYCHOGRAM

The Roman-Staempfli Psychogram was developed in the 1950s by the European graphologist and psychologist Klara G. Roman and her associate, George Staempfli. The Psychogram was designed to show the functional interrelatedness of graphic characteristics, which may be interpreted as a profile of personality (Roman 1968: 516–524). The Psychogram provides a scoring system and a "map" of the personality. It allows the graphologist to make objective ratings and to integrate material in a meaningful way. The charting system assembles individual components of the handwriting sample into groups or syndromes of functionally related graphic indicators. Although significant in its own right, each syndrome is actually inseparable from every other syndrome, and each is subordinate to the overall pattern of the Psychogram. Roman referred to this pictorial rendering of a writer's personality as the "Profile-in-the-Circle."

The circular Psychogram is divided into segments which reflect the visual pattern of writing. They correspond to the symbolic use of space, and they are placed so as to be symbolically meaningful. Mental characteristics and the corresponding graphic indicators are in the upper half of the circle. Biologically rooted characteristics appear in the lower half of the circle. Introversion, the self, mother, past, and tension are represented in the left half of the circle. Extroversion, the world, father, future, and release appear in the right half of the circle. See Figure 1 on the next page.

Some indicators can be measured to a fairly refined degree by instruments such as the graphodyne, a device developed by Roman to measure pressure; some can only be matched to standard forms. Some indicators have accepted standards of judgment, such as 3 mm for the height of middle-zone letters in a writing sample. Indicators are rated on a scale of 1 to 5, from zero expression to average performance at 2.5, to over-expression at 5 (Roman 1956, 1961). These raw scores are doubled to obtain a total score.

The result is a synthesis of graphic indicators and their corresponding personality traits which yields a personality profile. The Psychogram depicts the personality of the writer as a dynamic whole. The qualities of achievement and success reported in the literature are also measured in the Psychogram both directly and indirectly.

HYPOTHESIS

It was hypothesized that the Psychogram scores of successful women would be significantly different from those of less successful women along some dimensions, but not all. In addition, it was predicted that significant differences between the two groups would be found for six syndromes: Intellect, Ego, Emotional Release, Inhibitions/Overcontrol, Repression, and Control, but not for two others: World Directedness and Libido-Vitality-Drives.

METHOD

There were two criteria for participation in this study. To be included in the successful group, a woman had to see herself as successful or she had to be considered successful by others. The expression "high achiever" was deliberately avoided, because a secondary object of the study was to learn what women themselves consider success to be. Dictionary definitions of personal success focus on outcomes such as the attainment of wealth, fame, or position. In this study, friends or family members nominated women

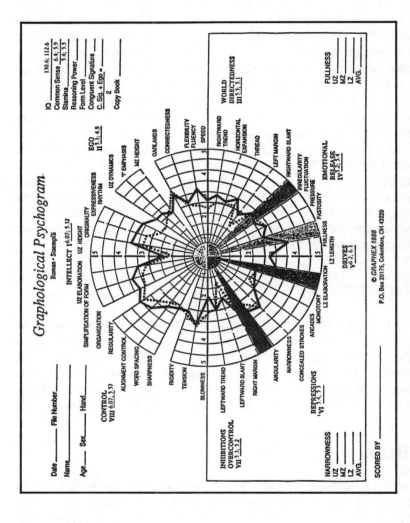

Fig. 1. Psychogram showing mean scores of successful women (—) and the comparison group (· ·). Note: Graphological Psychogram by Roman-Staempfli. © 1988 by Graphex. Permission to reprint by Ellen Bowers, Ed.D. and Graphex. Where no dots appear, the mean scores of the two groups were the same.

for the successful group, because they had achieved recognition, competence, or power in their work or personal lives; because they were considered to function better than average; or because they seemed to handle their lives competently. When questioned, the women themselves agreed with these observations but said they felt that success was an inner glow of satisfaction with their lives rather than external evidence of achievement. Success meant different things to different women. For some, success meant raising healthy children, for others it was linked directly to job satisfaction, and for still others inner tranquility was the criterion. Only two women in the group volunteered for the project.

The women in the comparison group were chosen either because they did not see themselves as markedly successful, or because they were considered by others to lead lives of only average or less than average success. Some of the women in the comparison group were identified by acquaintances; others were the authors of handwriting samples in the author's collection or in the collections of other psychologists.

Handwriting samples were either volunteered by the participants or were collected from their acquaintances in response to requests at graphological meetings, in graphological journals, and in correspondence. The samples came from women located across North America and from all walks of life. The content of the samples varied; some women wrote about success, others on a variety of topics. It was stressed that informal, spontaneous (noncopied or dictated) writing was needed. Examples are shown in Figure 2A and 2B. Several of the participants were known to the investigator, but not closely acquainted. The investigator had not previously analyzed any of the writings.

Table 1 shows the demographic characteristics of the 70 successful and 42 comparison women. All were Caucasian, and ages for both groups ranged from 19 to 80 yrs. The women were married, divorced, or single. Economic status ranged from welfare recipient through moderate wealth. Some were employed; some were not. Some had children; some did not. Many in the successful group were well known and respected in their fields; others were not known outside their immediate area.

One graphologist (the author) analyzed the handwriting samples of all participants in the study using the Roman-Staempfli Psychogram and nine additional graphological indicators:

Personal pronoun I	t-bar	t-stem
Baseline garlands	ovals	e
Buckles (k,s,p)	j and LZ loops	f

The measurement criteria of the Roman-Staempfli Psychogram indicators are generally well known to graphologists. Other qualities, such as IQ, common sense, and stamina, are calculated by combining and averaging scores from

There, you have my 'print' hand which I use often.
On occasion, I will get off formal notes or presentations
with a vertical script:

A mixed-up kid...

May good things
be yours
always!

The reverse side a note I just
wrote to the current director of Filoli (with check),
and a 'typical' example of my letter writing

Fig. 2A. The handwriting of a 74-yr.-old woman reflects her artistic temperament (she is an active landscape designer, artist, and author) in its high form level, individuality, and aesthetic placement on the page. The rhythmic writing swings with health, vigor, and enthusiasm, hallmarks of the successful woman.

Dear Grandma:
Hello honey, I hope this
Card finds you ok. I'm
sure sorry about you
haveing to be there. I
tried to call you but
there wasn't an answer.
So I called Dad.
I think of you often.
I was very sad to
hear you were there.
I'll write you very
often. And try to visit

Fig. 2B. The writing of an unhappy and insecure 30-yr.-old woman accurately depicts her inner fears and tension in angular forms, leftward tendencies, jerky rhythm, and variable spacing. Her strong dependency needs are seen in right slant, excessively full and looped ovals, exaggerated but weak personal pronoun I, and the clinging to the left margin with some long initial strokes. She has a history of failed relationships and alcohol.

TABLE 1

DEMOGRAPHIC CHARACTERISTICS OF 70 WOMEN IN
SUCCESS GROUP AND 42 IN COMPARISON GROUP

Characteristic		Success	Comparison
Age, yr.	18—19	1	0
	20—29	1	6
	30—39	19	9
	40—49	13	11
	50—59	15	7
	60—69	15	4
	70—79	3	4
	80 and over	2	0
	Unknown	0	1
Marital Status	Married	46	20
	Single	12	13
	Divorced	7	4
	Unknown	5	5
Children	Have children	42	26
	Do not have children	16	9
	Unknown	12	7
Handedness	Right	61	30
	Left	4	2
	Unknown	5	10:
Occupation	Artist	5	0
	Banker	1	2
	Editor	2	0
	Educator	6	1
	Executive	3	0
	Graphologist	16	1
	Health	2	2
	Homemaker	7	9
	Horticulturist	2	2
	Librarian	0	2
	Manager	4	0
	Own Business	11	0
	Retired	0	1
	Student	1	0
	TV personality	2	0

TABLE 1 (CONTINUED)

DEMOGRAPHIC CHARACTERISTICS OF 70 WOMEN IN
SUCCESS GROUP AND 42 IN COMPARISON GROUP

	Characteristic	Success	Comparison
Occupation	Welfare recipient	0	4
	Worker	3	12
	Writer	5	0
	Unknown	0	6

the Psychogram. The nine additional indicators were adapted from the graphometric system of graphology and were graded for width, height, and exaggeration of form on a 5-point scale. Data were analyzed statistically using the one-way analysis of variance program in the Statistical Package for the Social Sciences.[2]

RESULTS

The data presented in Tables 2 and 3 indicate that of the 38 graphological indicators on which successful and less successful women were expected to differ, significant differences were found for 24 indicators. More predictions were confirmed for those indicators on which successful women were expected to score *higher* than the comparison group (22 of 27, or 81.5%) than for those indicators on which they were expected to score *lower* (2 of 11, or 18.2%). Of the 14 indicators for which no significant differences were expected, the hypothesis was confirmed in 10 cases (71.4%; see Table 4). In the remaining four cases, successful women scored higher than the less successful women.

Of the six syndromes (clusters of graphological indicators) on which the two groups of women were expected to be significantly different, only three predictions were confirmed: Intellect, Ego, and Control. On all three of these syndromes, successful women scored higher than the women in the comparison group (see Table 5). For the other three syndromes (Emotional Release, Inhibitions, and Repressions), there were no differences between the groups. Of the two syndromes on which successful and less successful women were expected not to differ, one (Libido-Vitality-Drive) was confirmed; the other (World-Directedness) was not. In the latter case, successful women again scored higher than the less successful women.

TABLE 2

SCORES PREDICTED TO BE SIGNIFICANTLY HIGHER FOR THE SUCCESSFUL GROUP THAN FOR THE COMPARISON GROUP

Graphological Indicator	Success		Comparison		F
	M	SD	M	SD	
Organization	6.5	.94	6.0	1.15	6.98†
Simplification	6.6	.97	5.9	1.09	13.98†
Originality	6.7	.87	5.9	.73	26.67†
Expressiveness	6.7	.93	5.8	1.11	18.81†
Rhythm	6.1	1.01	4.6	1.06	57.56†
Upper Zone Dynamics	5.6	.79	4.6	.76	39.81†
"I" Emphasis	5.4	.72	4.9	.76	10.49†
Flexibility/Fluency	6.1	1.29	4.8	1.21	27.57†
Right Trend	5.6	1.12	5.1	1.22	4.61*
Speed	5.3	.83	4.7	1.00	10.49†
Pressure	5.4	.77	5.6	.69	2.81
Fullness	7.1	1.10	7.1	1.16	.01
Angularity	6.2	1.08	5.6	1.10	8.23†
Sharpness	5.3	.59	5.0	.81	5.39*‡
Word Spacing	5.5	.72	5.1	.97	6.55†
Alignment Control	6.5	.90	5.8	1.13	13.28†
Regularity	7.0	1.14	6.4	1.61	5.14*‡
IQ	130.6	11.31	112.6	8.82	77.83†
Common Sense	6.4	.61	5.8	.72	17.54†
Stamina	5.4	.76	5.5	.96	.03
PPI	5.6	1.18	5.1	1.12	5.83*
t-bar	6.2	1.27	5.4	1.58	8.98†
t-stem	6.2	.88	5.6	.94	10.93†
f	6.4	1.09	5.8	1.26	6.88†
j	6.9	1.74	6.6	1.96	.62
e	5.3	.97	4.7	1.04	8.77†
Ovals	5.5	1.09	5.6	1.15	.14

$*p < .05.$
$†p \le .01.$
‡Violated homogeneity of variance assumption although considered reportable.

TABLE 3

SCORES PREDICTED TO BE SIGNIFICANTLY LOWER
FOR THE SUCCESSFUL GROUP
THAN FOR THE COMPARISON GROUP

Graphological Indicator	Success		Comparison		F
	M	SD	M	SD	
Irregularity, Fluctuation	5.0	1.13	5.3	1.44	1.60
Narrowness	6.4	1.21	6.4	1.30	.03
Monotony	4.6	.83	5.0	1.29	3.64
Right Margin	5.3	1.53	5.3	2.05	.01
Left Slant	4.0	2.62	2.8	2.95	4.95*
Slowness	4.8	.83	5.3	1.05	8.13†
Tension	6.3	.88	6.4	.79	.27
Rigidity	5.3	.75	5.5	.92	2.31
Left Trend	5.9	1.19	5.8	1.34	.56
Buckles	5.4	1.09	5.0	1.45	2.37
Baseline	5.2	.97	5.1	.97	.33

$*p < .05$ †$p < .01$.

TABLE 4

SCORES PREDICTED TO SHOW NO SIGNIFICANT DIFFERENCES
BETWEEN THE SUCCESSFUL GROUP
AND THE COMPARISON GROUP

Graphological Indicator	Success		Comparison		F
	M	SD	M	SD	
Upper Zone Elaboration	5.9	.64	5.4	.77	13.51†
Upper Zone Height	3.9	1.21	3.6	1.53	1.08
Middle Zone Height	5.0	1.40	5.2	1.66	.31
Garlands	6.7	.88	6.9	1.16	1.76
Connectedness	5.1	1.58	5.2	1.79	.01
Horizontal Expansion	5.2	1.17	5.1	1.54	.00
Thread	6.0	1.13	5.3	1.35	7.96†
Left Margin	4.5	1.98	3.7	1.61	4.49*
Right Slant	5.2	2.27	5.4	2.66	.23
Pastosity	5.1	.62	5.1	.84	.00
Lower Zone Length	5.4	1.40	5.3	1.93	.21
Lower Zone Elaboration	6.0	.88	5.9	1.14	.33

TABLE 4 (CONTINUED)

SCORES PREDICTED TO SHOW NO SIGNIFICANT DIFFERENCES
BETWEEN THE SUCCESSFUL GROUP
AND THE COMPARISON GROUP

Graphological Indicator	Success		Comparison		F
	M	SD	M	SD	
Arcades	4.7	.75	4.5	.77	3.82*
Concealed	5.0	.58	5.2	.55	1.78

*$p < .05$.
†$p \leq .01$.

TABLE 5

MEAN SCORES OF GROUPS BY SYNDROME

Syndrome	Success		Comparison		F
	M	SD	M	SD	
Control	6.1	.62	5.6	.87	12.74†
Ego	5.3	.65	4.9	.53	14.42†
Emotional Release	5.2	.60	5.4	.62	2.15
Inhibitions	5.3	.70	5.2	.90	.41
Intellect	6.1	.46	5.3	.40	75.53†
Repressions	5.4	.37	5.3	.41	1.20
Libido-Vitality-Drive	6.2	.85	6.1	1.17	.22
World-directedness	5.5	.71	5.1	.78	6.43†

*$p < .05$.
†$p \leq .01$.

The Roman-Staempfli Psychogram shown in Figure 1 presents the mean scores of both groups of women.

DISCUSSION

The results of this study suggest that the qualities found by other investigators to be important in the perceived achievement of success are indeed expressed in the writing samples of highly achieving women and that they can be measured by the Psychogram plus other graphological indicators. Scores for such qualities as originality, expressiveness, rhythm, flexibility, organization, and simplification of form were significantly higher in the writings of the successful than of the less-successful women. Successful women also showed less rigidity and slowness. Other characteristics such as pastosity, fullness, lower zone length, and narrowness were shared by both groups (see Figure 1).

The four graphological indicators which were expected to be similar for the two groups but which were actually different were: (a) The successful group used far more personal flourishes and dynamics (upper zone elaboration). (b) Signs of diplomacy and ability to handle awkward situations (thread) were more evident for the successful group. (c) Although both groups scored lower than average on arcades (a dignified and self-protective connecting stroke), the comparison group used this form less often than the successful group. (d) Both groups scored lower than average on width of left margin, indicating a certain need for security or caution before starting a project, but hesitancy to proceed was somewhat greater in the comparison group than in the successful group.

There were 14 indicators for which the predicted differences between the groups were not confirmed. These findings indicate that personality or behavioral qualities such as energy and stamina (pressure and lower zone length), and tension and self-protectiveness (narrowness, tension, left trend) are observed in equal degree in both groups. However the reasons for these similarities may be quite different for the two groups of women (e.g., socioeconomic pressures, self-esteem needs, achievement motivation).

In addition, the data identify areas of personality functioning that do not seem to be associated with perceived success or failure; at least, not as indicated by these women. Personality characteristics which both groups shared include physical and psychic energy, tension, rigidity, defenses against fears, traditional female amiability and receptiveness, need for feedback, curiosity, and emotional release.

The results of this study suggest that achievement or success can be inferred fairly easily from measures used in graphological analysis. Specific behavioral traits, such as assertiveness, decisiveness, and risk-taking, are associated with perceived success, and they are readily apparent in handwriting samples. The actual feelings of success, however, are more subtle, and they are not necessarily accompanied by those outward signs which others consider as indicative of achievement. Further, these perceptions of success and well-being are not independent of life's fears and problems. For successful women, these fears and problems may be overridden by the drive to push ahead, whereas low-achieving women (who nonetheless may view themselves as relatively successful) may find life's challenges more problematic.

This study was subject to several limitations that follow-up studies should seek to avoid. First, many of the handwriting samples included signatures. Although signatures are important for complete analyses, they may introduce bias into analyses conducted for research purposes, and they should be omitted or hidden until the analyses have been completed. Second, in order to collect a sufficiently large number of handwriting samples, it was necessary to admit to the study women who were known to the graphologist. The graphologist also knew whether the samples came from women in the successful or the comparison group. Future studies should use blind scoring of handwriting samples; that is, scoring without knowledge of the group membership of the writer. And, finally, the writing samples were scored by only one graphologist, because there are few research-trained graphologists in the United States who can spend the many hours required for scoring.

This study suggests intriguing possibilities. It indicates that personality and behavioral characterisitics associated with achievement and success can be identified by properly trained graphologists and that other aspects of personality functioning can be similarly detected. Such information could be used in psychological counseling, personnel profiles, vocational counseling, assessment, monitoring of behavior, and in other areas where knowledge of perceived success would be useful.

NOTES

1. Meaning "not copied and not dictated."—Eds.

2. Fisher's exact method was used to address whether agreement with the predictions was as a result of chance or not. Because the test is specifically designed for a small number of comparisons and this study involved many, the results were inconclusive. Jeanette Alosi's help in the statistical analysis is gratefully acknowledged.

16

Graphoanalytic and Psychometric Personality Profiles: Validity and Barnum Effects

Edward W. Karnes and S. David Leonard

Chapter 16 presents two experiments prompted by the senior author's curiosity about a news report concerning several prominent local citizens who expressed great satisfaction with a graphoanalyst's personality reading based on their handwriting. Knowing that the so-called "Barnum Effect" can produce a strong but illusory sense of accuracy in such readings (see also Bowman, chapter 10, and Dean et al., chapter 13) he suspected that this might have been responsible for the graphoanalyst's rave reviews. From this conjecture came several predictions discussed in this chapter. First, if graphologists can depict personality accurately as they claim, clients should be able to exceed chance in correctly selecting their own character sketch from an anonymous batch of such analyses. Second, people who know these clients well should also be able to identify their friends' profiles in a similar "blind" test. Third, it is reasonable to assume that if graphologists' descriptions are in fact specific to the individuals for whom they were done, they should be less acceptable as personality portrayals if given to randomly selected individuals than intentionally vague, global sketches that are known to be acceptable to virtually everyone.

In Experiment One, Karnes and Leonard compare their subjects' success rates in identifying their own graphological profiles with those when they tried to identify their own profiles derived from two standard psychological tests. The authors also compare subjects' confidence in the accuracy of their identifications when they make correct as opposed to incorrect identifications.

In Experiment Two, the authors ask whether graphological profiles contain enough unique information about the client that they would not serve as equally good descriptors for anyone else. They compare subjects' ratings of applicability to themselves when they receive a randomly selected personality sketch from one of four different sources. One group received standard psychometric profiles that had been prepared for someone else, other groups received graphoanalytic profiles that were done for people in Experiment One or for the people in the Denver newspaper "test," and the remainder received vague "Barnum-type" personality descriptions. The group given the profiles derived from valid psychological tests rated them the poorest match with themselves (because they contained specific descriptions that apply to another individual), whereas those who received the graphoanalytic and Barnum-type profiles rated them much more accurate descriptions of their own personality (because of their widely applicable generality). In fact, the graphoanalytic profiles proved just as universally acceptable as the Barnum sketches. This was true whether or not the subjects thought the sketch they had just read was their own or that it had been intended for someone else. Interpretations of these findings are presented along with a discussion of their implications for use of graphology as a diagnostic or job placement tool. (cf. Klimoski, chapter 11).

As with Wellingham-Jones' study in chapter 15, the reader is encouraged not only to examine the authors' conclusions, but also to pay close attention to the methodological details of the experiments (see Dale Beyerstein's evaluative criteria in chapter 8 and Geoffrey Dean's in chapter 12). A single study practically never settles a scientific controversy and since the two studies in Section Five of this book come to different conclusions about the value of graphology, the reader will have to decide which carries the greater weight. Note that Wellingham-Jones was testing the hypothesis that graphologists can discern personality traits from script, whereas Karnes and Leonard were testing the aforementioned hypotheses which could account for customer satisfaction with graphology even though it cannot pass properly controlled tests. Because support for Karnes and Leonard's hypotheses would cast doubt on Wellingham-Jones' conclusions, the reader must examine each chapter on its own merits and in light of how it is supported or contradicted by research reviewed elsewhere in this book. One's provisional decision, pending further research, should be based on a number of methodological considerations.

First, do the statistical procedures meet the criteria listed by Geoffrey Dean in chapter 12? Karnes and Leonard used a relatively small sample size of nine subjects in their first experiment and found that people could not exceed chance in identifying their own or their acquaintances' graphological profiles. Subjects did better in identifying their own psychometric profiles, but this difference did not quite reach statistical significance. While the direction of this result is consistent with many similar studies that did reach statistical significance, the experiment should be replicated with a larger group of subjects before definitive conclusions can be drawn. However, testing with a large group of subjects whether or not close colleagues can recognize each other's profiles would present another problem. On the one hand, in order to find subjects who satisfy the "familiarity" criteria for inclusion in the test, the sample size cannot be very large (how many people do you know that intimately?) But, on the other hand, statisticians would prefer the sample size to be much larger. Karnes and Leonard discuss ways around this problem for future research. Their second experiment has the sort of sample size recommended by Dean in chapter 12 and provides much more telling evidence against graphology.

Other elements to compare (where applicable) in weighing the conclusions of chapter 16 against those of chapter 15 are the following. How were the key variables in the experiment chosen and operationalized? How were the subjects, the graphologists, the psychometric measures, and the handwriting samples selected? What steps were taken to prevent "leaking" to the graphologist relevant information other than what might be contained in the scripts themselves? (E.g., were the ratings done "blind" and was the evaluated material stripped of all useful biographical cues?) How was the criterion of accuracy determined for the different procedures being evaluated? What controls were in place to minimize the effects of unintentional bias on the part of the experimenter and/or subjects?

In choosing sides in the graphology debate, it is insufficient merely to tally up the "box score" of papers reporting positive versus negative results. As Dean (chapter 12) emphasizes, the methodological soundness of each study must be evaluated first to see if it can count as evidence at all.

INTRODUCTION

Handwriting analysis is once again the subject of public controversy because an increasing number of businesses have begun to consult graphologists in personnel matters. This use of graphology has been particularly offensive to civil libertarians who see it as an evasion of laws that have restricted the use of invalid tests in the workplace. After successfully opposing the use of polygraphs on the grounds of unreliability, opponents see "lie detectors" being replaced by an assessment technique with even less scientific credibility, graphology.

As the critics in this volume show, the overwhelming majority of scientific experts consider graphology unproven; e.g., few reputable texts in the field of psychological measurement even mention graphology, let alone accept it as a valid science. Nonetheless, many non-scientists working in personnel selection feel that graphology has demonstrated its worth in everyday settings. Frequently, this conviction is based on a graphological sketch of the personnel manager that seemed "amazingly accurate." Sometimes it also stems from satisfaction with employees hired on the recommendation of a graphologist. Althoughs anecdotes of this sort may be true as far as they go, they do not constitute scientifically acceptable evidence for the validity of graphology. To see why they cannot count, we must consider how the rules for obtaining and evaluating data in scientific disciplines differ from those of everyday decision making.

The scientific method evolved to help discern real from apparent relationships in the world. It accomplishes this by ensuring that samples to be studied are representative, observations are systematic, and possible alternative causes for the phenomena under study are eliminated. It demands that putative effects be repeatable under controlled conditions. These rules are necessary in order to counter our strong tendency to perceive illusory relationships in complex situations, simply because we wish or expect them to be there. The scientific method also allows us to distinguish causality from mere coincidence. While it cannot claim infallibility, it is certainly the most reliable way of gaining knowledge we have, and it has the additional advantage of being self-correcting over time. The reader may wish to pursue these issues further by consulting Dale Beyerstein's discussion in chapter 8.

Proponents of graphology (see Section Two, this volume) assert that their methods are sufficiently like those of psychology, particularly in the area of projective testing, that graphology deserves to be considered a branch of psychology. The critics counter that while the two disciplines bear certain superficial similarities, graphology is essentially a pseudoscience. They base this on the magical underpinnings of handwriting analysis (see chapters 2, 3, and 9), the failure to produce a plausible theory of graphology (see chapters 8, 9, and 14), and, above all, the shortage of methodologically sound evidence for its validity (see Section Four of this volume).

A PRIORI DOUBTFULNESS OF GRAPHOLOGY

There are many aspects of graphology that strike critics as implausible from the outset. These doubts have supplied the impetus to seek alternate explanations for graphologists' apparent successes (e.g., the Barnum Effect discussed below). One of these sore points is the lack of a credible theory to account for the posited correspondences between writing and personality. Evaluating graphological claims is made difficult by this lack of a unified theoretical position and by the frequent factional disputes over meanings of various signs and the relative merits of interpreting individual components of letters to specific traits versus relying on the graphologist's "holistic" impressions. Thus a study demonstrating the inadequacy of one type of graphology is often endorsed by rival schools who still claim that their own brand of analysis would have passed.

The "Brainwriting" Rationale. The graphologists' main attempt at theorizing has been the so-called "brainwriting hypothesis." This is the assumption that because personality and writing are both controlled by the brain, writing necessarily reveals character. As Barry Beyerstein points out in chapter 14, no competent neurophysiologist would deny that both writing and personality depend on brain functions. But this is no different from any other human activities. If we carry the "brainwriting" argument to its logical conclusion, we might just as reasonably claim to read details of someone's character from the way he or she walks down the street. Certainly, different people have recognizable ways of walking (see next paragraph). Should we therefore refer to walking as "brainstepping"? The mere fact that the brain controls writing movements offers no guarantee that writing is a valid indicator of personality. The burden of proof that it is rests with the graphologists, whose evidence to date has been quite unconvincing.

The "Uniqueness" Argument. Graphologists also trade on the undeniable individuality of a person's script by assuming that the uniqueness of both writing and personality implies some sort of correspondence between the two (see Nickell, chapter 4). Appealing though this leap of faith may be, readers with a historical bent will recall the failures of several other systems that attempted to read character from equally unique attributes; e.g., Caesar Lombroso (1831–1901) thought he could recognize criminal tendencies from distinctive facial features. Modern criminologists and psychologists have completely abandoned Lombroso's theories because research found that facial features, despite their uniqueness, are useless as predictors of character. Extending our earlier walking analogy to the graphologists' "uniqueness" argument, consider the following. In his graduate student days, one of the authors used to surprise fellow students by addressing them by name before they entered his field of view. He was able to recognize them from the distinctive sounds of their gait as they traversed the hallway leading to his office. This obviously unique behavior provided no basis for inferring the walker's honesty, piety, or conscientiousness, however.

"You're as bad as we are." Another ploy used by graphologists to deflect attacks is to concede that their procedures lack empirical support but to argue that they are no worse than those of orthodox psychologists and psychiatrists. This is misleading because there are degrees of wrongness. To admit that the diagnostic methods of psychology and psychiatry are not perfect provides no support for graphology, which must stand or fall on its own merits.[1] The claims of psychologists and psychiatrists to discern traits and syndromes should be, and are, rigorously tested (see chapters 10, 11, and 12). Their professional journals are replete with experiments

providing evidence for and against various theories and practices. As a result, many once-popular tests in psychology and psychiatry have been abandoned and others continue to undergo extensive modification. Despite the fact that some questionable methods have not yet been abandoned by all mainstream practitioners, this does not abrogate the requirement for psychological techniques to prove their effectiveness empirically. As pointed out in chapter 9, it is the fact that graphologists have virtually never abandoned any of their oldest precepts that makes the field most suspect. Sciences progress, pseudosciences remain stagnant.

"We play by different rules." When all else fails, graphologists often fall back on the argument that empirical verification is unnecessary because graphology is an art rather than a science. If graphology were only a parlor game like a ouija board, or a harmless foible like belief in the Easter Bunny, this argument could be tolerated, but it is unacceptable for several reasons. First, whether it be art or science, graphology makes claims about relationships in the world and is therefore required to back them up with evidence. Second, graphologists sell their services to the public for purposes that seriously affect people's happiness and welfare. Citizens whose livelihoods or reputations are at stake have a right to demand proof of competence from any professional who can stigmatize them in this way. And finally, those who pay for graphologists' services have the right to know that they are not being victimized by flim-flam artists or by sincere but deluded pseudoscientists. What standards could reasonably decide these issues, other than those of empirical validation?

Graphologists also alienate the scientific community with their ad hominem responses to criticism, such as branding critics as narrow minded or claiming that detractors are simply protecting their own turf. In chapter 8, Dale Beyerstein deals with such failures to answer the substance of principled criticisms. The scientists' rejoinder is that until graphologists meet conventional standards of proof, they have no right to demand acceptance by the scientific community—the burden of proof is always with the claimant.

"Caveat emptor." It is odd that people who have grown wary of financial institutions that promise unbelievable returns often fail to extend this skepticism to the sphere of psychological and medical services. Here, as elsewhere, the maxim of the consumer advocate David Horowitz applies: "If it sounds too good to be true, it probably is." The more a technique promises, the closer it should be scrutinzed, and the extravagance of graphologists' claims puts them squarely in this category. E.g., their ads proclaim, "It opens up the entire personality like an X-ray photograph," and "It is a technique to scrutinize the unconscious." Such claims are vague but seem to promise a great deal. Other statements such as the one that eight to ten lines of writing can reveal someone's mental abilities, business

aptitude, personal fears and foibles, moral shortcomings, and how well he or she will interact with the boss are more precise but are presented without even the standard of proof one would normally demand of a used car salesman. Such grandiose claims immediately arouse suspicion in those who have seen similarly overblown assertions fail consistently in the past.

CONCERNS FROM SCIENTIFIC TEST DEVELOPERS

Chapters 10, 11, and 12 of this volume specify the requirements for a scientifically valid psychological test, so our treatment here can be brief. When the distribution of scores on a test that claims to predict how well people will perform on some task (called "the criterion") turns out to correlate well with their eventual performance on that task, we say the test has demonstrated validity. It can thenceforth be used in good conscience, where applicable, to help decide among competing job candidates, provide marital advice, make parole decisions, etc. But assessing the validity of a test is much more complicated than it may seem at first glance.

Let us assume, for instance, that we are to hire six persons from a pool of twenty-four applicants. Suppose that we hire the six highest scorers on Test Z and find that they perform well on the job. Does this prove that Test Z is a good selection device (i.e., is a valid predictor of criterion performance)? To see why the foregoing scenario provides necessary but not sufficient grounds for approving the test, we must also consider the possibilities of "the road not taken." In other words, how would the rejected applicants have performed, had they been given the opportunity? Cost considerations usually preclude such a test in the corporate world, but in the development stage that should precede any application of a test in the real world, this kind of evaluation is absolutely necessary. Without such evidence, simple satisfaction with a test on the part of a personnel manager is no proof of its validity. The following example shows why.

The matrices of Table 1 provide a range of possible results for all 24 applicants had they been hired for a trial period. Note that the outcomes depicted in matrices a, b, c, and d would provide the same evidence if only the six high-scoring individuals were hired. Clearly, the usefulness of Test Z also depends on how the low scorers perform, not just on how well the high scorers do. Yet, if only the latter are hired, as is typically the case when companies consult graphologists, we will never know if the test tells us anything about the adequacy of the applicants for the job. As Dean et al. emphasize in chapter 13, it is essential in determining the presence or the absence of a relationship that we note the cases of non-occurrence as well as cases of occurrence. It is at this stage of basic research, prior to any application, where graphologists have failed to prove their worth.

Table 1

*Possible Matrices of Number of Successful Cases When Hiring
Individuals Scoring High and Low on "Test Z"*

Test Scores	Job Performance							
	Scenario a.		Scenario b.		Scenario c.		Scenario d.	
	Good	Poor	Good	Poor	Good	Poor	Good	Poor
High	6	0	6	0	6	0	6	0
Low	18	0	15	3	9	9	0	18

Note that for the cases in matrix *b* of Table 1, a very minor change in the performance of the high scorers would make the probability of success the same for high and low scorers. That is, if one of the high scorers performed less well on the job, the ratios of good to poor among both high and low scorers would be identical. Thus there would be serious doubts about the relationship of scores on Test *Z* to performance on the job. Even in set *c,* a numerically small change in performance would result in questions about the validity of the test. This raises the question of how it is possible to determine whether or not the results of an experiment truly represent the state of the world.

Hypothesis Testing. In most cases where one is conducting a formal test to decide whether a relationship exists or not, one begins with two opposing hypotheses. One is that the relationship exists (i.e., some non-random factor is operating to produce the observed results); the alternative, or "null hypothesis," is that it does not exist (i.e., the observed distribution of scores is most likely due to random variation). When the data have been collected, a statistic is calculated that will tell the researcher the probability that the observed result would have occurred if nothing but chance were operating. For instance, suppose a graphologist selects two groups of people, one of which she claims are good leaders and the other poor leaders. If we are evaluating the claim that the graphologist can make such distinctions, we would state the alternative hypotheses as follows: "The differences between these groups on the criterion (an accepted indicator of leadership) are large enough to be unlikely to be due to chance," versus the null hypothesis that "the observed differences are due to nothing more than chance variations." If we fail to reject the null hypothesis, we are, in effect, saying that the observed differences are sufficiently likely to have occurred by chance that it is reasonable to conclude that the graphologist has failed to substantiate her claim. By convention, scientists reject the null hypothesis if the statistical test determines that the observed differences between groups would occur by chance alone only five times out of a hundred. Details of the technique and rationale for this procedure are available in any statistics text (e.g., Keppel 1991).

The Need for Control Groups. Even if a statistical test provided satisfactory evidence that the graphologist had exceeded chance in detecting some trait, that by itself would not prove that his success was due to his graphological judgment rather than some other way of gaining information about the subjects. E.g., were there useful clues in the contents of the handwriting samples or in the background data supplied? This underscores the need for something else that distinguishes a formal test from anecdotal observations—the principle of scientific control. If we wish to conclude that variable X is the cause of effect Y, we must rule out (or "control for," as a scientist would say) other possible variables that could have produced it. In the case of graphology, we would also need to demonstrate that subjects' acceptance of graphological readings is due to their accuracy and precision rather than to something else, such as the Barnum Effect, discussed below. It was this lack of such controls in a local newspaper's informal test of a graphologist that prompted us to undertake the experiments presented later in this chapter.

Procedures like the foregoing are essential before conceding the validity of any psychological measurement technique and that is why every job candidate should demand that any selection test he or she is subjected to can pass these criteria. As Geoffrey Dean's review in chapter 12 clearly shows, this is something graphology cannot do.

THE BARNUM EFFECT

When personnel managers are informed of graphology's numerous failures on well-controlled validity tests, they frequently discount such criticisms because the graphologist's character sketch seemed "amazingly correct and precise." These executives might be less impressed with this seeming accuracy if they were aware that a group of randomly selected people, given the same description, would find it equally applicable to themselves. Indeed, this has been demonstrated repeatedly with groups ranging from college students (Forer 1949) to personnel managers (Stagner 1955). The subtle psychological processes that underlie this so-called "Barnum Effect" are discussed by Dean and his co-authors in chapter 13. It is also known in the psychological literature as the "subjective validation effect" or the "personal validation effect."

The term "Barnum Effect" was popularized by Paul Meehl (1950) who reminded fellow psychologists that conventional personality measures also benefit from these spurious impressions of validity and ought not to be accepted unless they can pass tests that control for subjective validation. Meehl warned against tests that seem accurate merely because their assertions are vague enough (despite their seemingly precise language) that they invite the client to unconsciously "fill in the gaps." This is easy for them to do because such assertions are true, in some form, of most people in the population. This is the same phenomenon that contributes illusory accuracy to pronouncements of fortune tellers, astrologers, and mediums and forms the basis of a very effective form of stage magic called "Cold Reading" (Hyman 1977).[2]

One of the first demonstrations of the compelling nature of subjective validation was provided by Forer (1949) who told student volunteers that the personality description they received had been derived from a graphological analysis of a sample of their writing. Though they all received the same intentionally vague, internally contradictory sketch, there was overwhelming agreement that it was remarkably accurate. Forer cautioned that:

> The positive results obtained from personal validation can easily lull a test analyst or a therapist into a false sense of security which bolsters his conviction in the essential rightness of his philosophy or his diagnostic prowess. . . . A great danger arises when the confirmation of a prediction is extended uncritically to the instrument or conceptual system or person making the prediction. Such uncritical extension occurs too frequently in the clinical field. (p. 118)

Since Forer demonstrated the power of subjective validation, many studies have examined the factors that contribute to this willingness to accept general statements as though they were specific, revealing depictions of ourselves (see reviews by Snyder et al. 1977, Dickson and Kelly 1985; and by Dean et al., chapter 13, this volume). The effect is so robust that subjects will even concede the accuracy of a putative test whose items have no obvious connection to personality. E.g., Delprato's (1975) subjects were merely required to circle certain digits in a long list. They were then given a general character description, allegedly derived from their performance, and asked to rate the whole procedure as a means of testing personality. Sixty percent of the subjects rated it as good or excellent. This result is so easy to obtain that one of the present authors often uses this procedure as a class demonstration of the subjective validation effect.

Investigators such as Greene (1977) have noted that the uniformly high accuracy ratings in demonstrations like the foregoing could be because the statements may indeed be correct for the individuals concerned. But even if its descriptions do fit a person quite well, this does not necessarily indicate that graphology (or any other insufficiently validated technique) is an acceptable way to measure personality, select people for specific jobs, or recommend them as mates. The reason is that such tests cannot *differentiate* among individuals. As Forer (1949) reminds us, ". . . a universally valid statement is a description of a cultural group rather than a personal psychological datum."

Many studies (e.g., O'Dell 1972) have found that people consider Barnum-type generalities to be better descriptions of themselves than more realistic profiles derived from well-validated scales that *do* measure specific traits. Merrens and Richards (1970) suggested that this is so because subjects may see discrepancies between specific statements about their traits and their self-perceptions, whereas the global statements arouse no such dissonance.

The ease with which intelligent, educated people can be misled by the Barnum Effect makes it clear why personal testimonials, such as those relied upon extensively by graphologists, are worthless as scientific evidence. Along with the increasing media interest in graphology, there has been, for the most part, a deplorable lack of critical analysis of its claims. In the city of Denver alone, articles and programs have uncritically published the following claims by advocates of the school of handwriting analysis known as Graphoanalysis:[3]

- Personnel officers in major companies use graphology in hiring and promotion decisions. According to the *Wall Street Journal,* the following companies have used handwriting analysis: New England Mutual Life Insurance Co., the New York Branch of the Equitable Life Assurance Co., Sears Roebuck and Co., U.S. Steel, and the Bendix Corporation.

- The police use graphology in criminal investigations (but see Nickel's comments on this in chapter 4).

- Graphology is also used extensively elsewhere in the legal system (see chapters 4, 9, and 17, this volume). E.g., judges use it in sentencing decisions and in regard to educational and vocational matters for juvenile offenders. Lawyers use it to help select jurors and evaluate the criminal mind. Graphologists have also been consulted in parole decisions.

- The U.S. Government hired a Denver graphoanalyst to provide personality profiles in regard to the Watergate scandal.

- Graphotherapy (changing one's handwriting style) effectively corrects learning disabilities and personality disorders. One Denver judge was so impressed that he often made graphotherapy a condition of parole.

- Graphoanalysis can determine marital compatibility.

- Handwriting exercises can alleviate pain, improve marital difficulties, and treat declining sexual performance.

- Graphoanalysis is 97 percent accurate: "One page of handwriting unerringly reveals more than all the psychological tests combined."

Many of these claims that important people use graphology are undoubtedly true, but this supplies no compelling evidence for its validity. After all, President Reagan used an astrologer too! Many of the foregoing claims are so fanciful as to call the entire enterprise of handwriting analysis into question, but they serve to belie the common misconception that the dispute over graphology is only of academic interest. Obviously, it has serious consequences for those who may be unfairly denied positions or falsely accused (see also chapter 1).

TESTING GRAPHOLOGY

The authors have been intrigued by the broad public acceptance of graphology despite its poor track record in properly controlled tests. Given the research reviewed in Section Four of this book that seriously questions the validity of graphology, one must ask why the public reception has been so favorable. We think this is because graphology can be quite impressive in casual demonstrations that do not control for subjective validation effects or "leakage" of clues from sources other than the script itself. Thus we decided to explore some of the ways in which graphology could gain a spurious aura of validity.

We chose to test a graphologist who is a follower of the Graphoanalytic method. That was because this school has been responsible for some of the most immoderate assertions in the media and because it is most vocal in asserting its scientific status.[4] In addition, it was a Graphoanalyst who had received such enthusiastic endorsements in the informal tests done by the Denver newspaper. Realizing that the high praise in this uncontrolled demonstration could have been due to the Barnum Effect,[5] we decided to pursue this possibility.

We set out in Experiment One to improve on the methods used in our local newspaper's test of graphology. Therein, six prominent citizens submitted samples of their writing for blind rating by a Graphoanalyst. They then commented on the accuracy of their own personality profiles. All the comments were laudatory; e.g., "That's great," "Isn't that deep?—I think it's very accurate." Although this demonstration served to enhance public belief in graphology, it is woefully inadequate as a scientific test. It included no control for the Barnum Effect—simply asking each person to pick out his or her own profile after reading all six would have made the test more credible. So we instituted this blind selection procedure among our other controls.

Given the ease with which people are led to feel that almost any personality profile describes them accurately, the possibility arises that this is because most of us are not sufficiently aware of our own personality makeup. Thus, in addition to having each individual try to select his or her own profile out of an anonymous stack, we also tested the ability of a group of well-acquainted individuals to identify each others' profiles. This procedure was followed with profiles produced by a Graphoanalyst and by two well-validated personality tests.

In Experiment Two, we tested the hypothesis that randomly selected recipients will find a graphologist's profiles just as general, and hence as applicable to themselves, as intentionally vague Barnum-type profiles. We also predicted that profiles derived from valid psychological tests would (because they do contain more specific information) be less acceptable to randomly chosen recipients than the graphologist's descriptions if given to randomly chosen recipients. And finally, we tested a proposition, derived from the literature on the Barnum Effect, that acceptability of global personality sketches is affected by one's belief that the profile was produced specifically for them.

EXPERIMENT ONE

METHOD

Experiment One had several purposes. First, it provided needed materials for the larger-scale study, Experiment Two. Second, it also provided an opportunity to check the reliability of the Graphoanalyst's readings; i.e., to see if similarly trained graphologists would arrive at the same conclusions from the writing samples. Finally, it provided the opportunity for a small-scale pilot study, replicating earlier studies of the Barnum Effect but with two additional conditions that could be worth incorporating into future research. One of these was to have individuals very familiar with the participants try to match the descriptions to their owners as well as the more usual procedure where people try to identify their own profiles. The other was to compare participants' success in identifying their own and others' graphological profiles relative to their success with psychometrically derived profiles. We also asked participants to express their degree of confidence in their ascriptions, for later comparison with their accuracy scores. Because the sample sizes in Experiment One were small, the results were not expected to be definitive and are presented here as a recommended paradigm to pursue in future research with larger sample sizes.

Subjects. Participants in the experiment were nine college administrators who had worked closely with one another in the same unit for about ten years. Five were male and four were female. All submitted handwriting samples for Graphoanalysis and also took two standard psychometric tests of personality: the California Psychological Inventory (CPI) and the Myers-Briggs Type Indicator (MBTI).

Handwriting Samples and Analysis. The handwriting samples were one-page, two-paragraph essays containing each person's attitudes concerning legal prohibition of smoking in public.[6] The samples were evaluated blind (i.e., without names) by a prominent handwriting analyst from Denver, Colorado, who is certified by the International Graphoanalysis Society. The graphologist knew the purpose of the experiment and was paid the normal fee for preparing the personality profiles.

Reliability Checks for Handwriting Analyses. The requirement of test reliability is dealt with extensively in chapters 10 and 11 of this volume. The reliability of the Graphoanalyst's technique used in this study was evaluated in two ways. A second Graphoanalyst, who did not know the identity of the preparer, compared the handwriting samples with the personality descriptions and evaluated the overall accuracy and suitability for purposes of the experiment. The first Graphoanalyst's work was rated as excellent and no suggestions for improvement were offered. A third certified graphologist was then given the script samples and graphological profiles in unmatched sets and asked to match each sample of writing to its corresponding personality synopsis. This graphologist correctly matched seven of the nine pairs, a success rate that is highly improbable by chance alone.[7] Thus we accept that this Graphoanalytic technique demonstrates what is called inter-rater reliability. Note that this says nothing about the correctness of the ascriptions (i.e., the method's "validity" as discussed in chapters 10, 11, and 12), only that practitioners trained in the same method are consistent in their assignment of the same traits to features of handwriting.

Scoring of Psychometric Tests. The MBTI was scored by the Center for Applications of Psychological Type. A computerized narrative personality report was prepared by the Center for each participant. Before participants judged them, these narratives were retyped on standard bond paper with the usual four-letter type designation omitted from the telescript.

The CPI was scored by Behaviordyne of Palo Alto, California, and a computer generated psychodiagnostic report was prepared for each participant. Because these psychodiagnostic reports were designed for use by correctional counselors, all references of a forensic nature were omitted when the reports were retyped on standard bond paper. The retyped personality profiles from the CPI and the MBTI were stapled together and names were replaced by an identification code affixed to each one.

Evaluation Procedure. The participants evaluated the Graphoanalytic profiles first. Each participant was given all nine profiles and a scoring sheet that contained sections for the self-selection and co-worker selection tasks. In the self-selection task, the participants were allowed to choose one or more profiles as possibly their own and were asked to rate each profile chosen, according to their degree of confidence that it was theirs. The co-worker selection process involved matching the code letters for the profiles to the names of the members of the group. Participants were given one week to complete these tasks and were asked not to discuss their choices among themselves.

The psychometric profiles were evaluated by the same procedure used with the Graphoanalytic profiles. Sadly, one of the participants died prior to evaluating the psychometric personality profiles, so the self-selection and co-worker matching was completed by only eight individuals. They were given one week to complete the task. After its completion, the participants were debriefed and the correct profiles for each person were revealed.

RESULTS OF EXPERIMENT ONE

Graphoanalytic Profiles. In the self-selection process, the average number of profiles each participant selected as possibly being his or her own was 3.67. Three persons included their own profiles among those they considered to be possibly their own. Assuming that, on average, one could select one's own profile (i.e., a hit) by chance one in nine tries, the probability that three or more individuals would do so by chance alone is 0.623. In other words, if these individuals were to pull three profiles out of a hat 1,000 times in a row, this many or more hits would be expected on 623 of those attempts. Obviously, this does not suggest that the participants were able to recognize the profile the Graphoanalyst had done for them with any certitude.

Even though the ability to recognize one's own Graphoanalytic profile did not exceed chance expectancy, it could still be asked whether the confidence one has in a correctly selected profile might not be superior to that expressed when the selected profile was somebody else's. This does not seem to be the case. We compared the subjects' mean confidence ratings for their hits with those for incorrect selections (false alarms). The mean confidence rating for hits was 2.67, which is slightly below the midpoint of the range, and the mean rating for false alarms was 3.35, which indicated somewhat more than average certainty. Thus it appears that under conditions designed to reduce the Barnum Effect, people are less willing than they are under everyday conditions to accept, unequivocally, the profiles derived for them by a Graphoanalyst.

Matching Graphoanalytic profiles to co-workers was also quite difficult. Of the 72 assignments of profiles to co-workers, only five were correctly matched, a hit rate of 0.07.

Psychometric Profiles. An interesting comparison with the selection of profiles derived from Graphoanalysis is provided by those obtained from the psychometric tests. An average of only 1.75 profiles were selected by the eight persons participating in this phase of the study. This suggests that the psychometric profiles were less general than the Graphoanalytic ones. Their greater specificity gave the subjects a better chance of identifying their own profiles. Four of the eight participants correctly identified their own profile. Assuming each person selected, on average, 1.75 profiles as possibly their own, the probability of selecting his or her own by chance alone would be 0.22. Therefore the probability that four or more would be correctly identified is 0.075. This is slightly greater than the 1 in 20 probability scientists conventionally set as the borderline for considering an outcome too unlikely to have been due to chance. However, because the sample size in this pilot study was small, it would be wise to reserve judgment about the adequacy of psychometric techniques for describing personality in self-selection paradigms. Our preliminary results cast no doubts on the validity of the CPI or MBTI as personality tests because both have already passed the rigorous tests of reliability and validity that legitimate psychometricians demand before marketing a test.

Matching of psychometric profiles to other participants was also somewhat easier than matching Graphoanalytic profiles. Of the 56 possible matches that could be made, 13 were correct. The hit rate in the peer selection phase was 0.23 for the psychometric profiles as opposed to 0.07 with the Graphoanalytic profiles. Although the small sample size in this pilot study does not allow a definitive decision of the relative merits of the two approaches, there is certainly no indication of the superiority of the Graphoanalytic technique as claimed by its advertising. The trends established in this small scale study suggest that if it were replicated with an adequate sample size, the participants' superior performance with the psychometrically derived report would prove statistically significant. This would be consistent with the results of the meta-analysis of graphological versus psychometric effect sizes reported by Dean in chapter 12.

EXPERIMENT TWO

In tests of the Barnum Effect, subjects are typically asked to provide some sort of personal information and later to rate the accuracy of global personality descriptions purportedly derived from it. In most studies (see the review by Dean et al., chapter 12), everyone received the same generalized sketch, and almost everyone rated it a very good portrayal of themselves.

Experiment Two followed this time-honored procedure, but included additional groups of subjects who were given different personality descriptions of varying degrees of specificity. The Barnum Effect has been shown to depend on a number of factors. The feedback should be applicable to the general population but phrased in ways that seem more specific, and the recipient should believe that the statements were derived individually for them. Because most members of the general public are not familiar with the difficulties in establishing test validity exemplified in Table 1, the majority will not test the possibility that their descriptions would be as applicable to their friends and neighbors as to themselves. Thus they will consider the presenter (whether graphologist, palmist, astrologer, or psychologist) to be a discriminating judge of character.

As some have suggested (e.g., Forer 1949; Meehl 1956), the global personality descriptions are essentially statements about commonalities in a given culture. If so, such generalizations ought to be acceptable to most members of the culture, whereas a truly specific description would be accepted only by that subset who shared the unique cluster of attributes and experiences described. Thus it is reasonable to assume that profiles derived for particular individuals by a valid technique would be less acceptable than global descriptions when both are presented to randomly selected individuals (cf. O'Dell 1972).

METHOD

Subjects in Experiment Two were recruited from the students in lower-division psychology courses at Metropolitan State College in Denver, Colorado. A total of 276 volunteers participated in the experimental condition and 235 in the control condition.

In the experimental group, subjects submitted a short sample of their handwriting and were told that a certified graphologist would derive a personality description for them. They were told that because these would be blind evaluations the graphologist would be unaware of their gender, so all profiles would be written in the masculine gender. One week later each student received a personality description with his or her name typed at the top. The students were asked to read the profile carefully and to rate its overall accuracy on a seven-point scale, with one being the lowest and seven the highest accuracy. In fact, the descriptions they received were not based on their writing samples, but were selected randomly from one of the following four categories of profiles.

1. *Barnum Profiles (BP).* An ambiguous, general personality sketch consisting of thirteen statements that had been used in previous studies of the Barnum Effect.

2. *Graphoanalytic Profiles Done for Prominent Local People (GPP).* These were six descriptions prepared by a Denver graphologist and featured in a local newspaper article describing this informal test of graphology.

3. *Graphoanalytic Profiles of College Administrators (GCA).* The nine profiles produced by a certified Graphoanalyst for the participants in Experiment One.

4. *Psychometric Profiles (PP).* Sixteen personality profiles produced from the California Personality Inventory (CPI) and Myers-Briggs Type Indicator (MBTI) tests taken by the participants in Experiment One.

Students in the experimental condition were randomly assigned to groups that received one of the profile types described above. Those in the control condition (referred to as the "self-relevance condition" in Table 2) were also randomly assigned a profile from one of the foregoing groups. The name had been removed and the subjects were told that the profile was that of another person. Nonetheless, they were asked to rate how well they felt it described their own personalities. Both groups used a seven-point rating scale, with higher numbers representing greater accuracy.

RESULTS OF EXPERIMENT TWO

The results of Experiment Two were analyzed using the statistical technique known as Analysis of Variance (ANOVA) (Keppel 1991). This procedure compares the differences between groups receiving different treatments to the internal variability of scores among subjects within the different treatment conditions. A statistical measure of differences among cases is the variance. It is derived by squaring the differences between each pair of values in the data set and taking the mean of those squared values. It is assumed that the greater the difference among pairs of cases within groups treated alike, the higher the probability that any mean differences between the groups who received different treatments would also be due to random variation. In other words, in order to conclude that any differences among conditions are not merely due to happenstance, the variance between groups must be large relative to that within groups.

As shown in Table 2, there were a total of eight conditions in Experiment Two: four types of personality profiles and two different "relevance" conditions (Self: "this profile was done for you" vs. Other: "this profile was done for someone else").

Table 2

Mean Acceptability Ratings for Personality Profiles

Profile Type	Believed Relevance of Profile to Self or Other	
	Relevant to Self Mean	Relevant to Other Mean
Barnum (Global)—**BP**	6.17	4.88
Graphoanalytic (College Administrators)—**GCA**	5.80	5.47
Graphoanalytic (Prominent People)—**GPP**	5.94	5.25
Psycometric Profiles—**PP**	5.11	3.40

The ANOVA technique allows us to compute four subcomponents of the overall variance: (1) a component related to the individual differences in ratings among all subjects; (2) a component based on whether perceived accuracy was affected by the belief that the profile was done for themselves or someone else (its "relevance" to self); (3) a component based on which of the four profile types a subject evaluated; and (4) a component based on whether or not the perceived accuracy of the various profile types was affected differently if participants believed that the profile they were reading was their own or someone else's.

Component (4) is referred to as the "interaction" of profile type with its relevance. The statistical significance of the interaction, or lack thereof, determines whether the overall effect of one variable in an experiment can be considered in isolation or must be interpreted in light of the different values of another experimental variable. In the present instance, absence of a significant interaction would permit us to consider the different effects of the various profile types without concern for the effect of subjects' belief that the statement were relevant to themselves or someone else. Presence of an interaction would require us to examine the comparison among different profile types separately for subjects in the experimental and control conditions.

In an ANOVA, the F statistic is computed in order to determine the probability that the observed results would have occurred if only random fluctuations were affecting subjects' ratings. The average value for F if the experimental manipulations have no discernible effect (i.e., only random variation is present) is 1.0. As mean differences among groups in the various experimental conditions become large (in any direction), the value of F increases. The probability of obtaining large Fs is small,[8] so when a large F is obtained, we can be confident that the observed differences among groups in the experiment were unlikely to have been chance occurrences. Therefore we say these differences are "statistically significant" and conclude that the different experimental treatments had reliably different effects. In Experiment Two, the obtained F value (using an unweighted means ANOVA) for the interaction of relevance and profile type was less than 1.0, and therefore not statistically significant. So we proceeded to test the effects of the other variables without differentially considering them in light of the relevance factor.

The relevance factor produced an F value of 64.61. With 503 degrees of freedom,[9] for the denominator term of the F ratio, such a value is extremely improbable (< 1 in 10,000) if the difference between these two groups were accidental. Accordingly, we can conclude, as expected, that the assumption that a profile is relevant to one's self as opposed to someone else affects the degree to which it is perceived as accurately describing one's self.

The "Profile Type" factor (BP, GPP, GCA, or PP) also produced a statistically significant difference, with an F value of 28.38 (again with 503 degrees of freedom for the denominator of the F ratio). Because random variation should produce such a result only once in 10,000 times, we can reasonably conclude that the contents of the profile affected the subjects' willingness to accept it as an accurate reflection of their personalities. Thus assured that there are statistically significant differences among groups that received the different profile types, we performed additional tests to reveal exactly where those differences lay. These supplementary tests provided no reason to believe that the subjects who received the Graphoanalytic profiles (GPP or GCA) rated them any differently than did the subjects who received the Barnum profiles (BP). In all specific comparison tests, the F values were less than 1.0. This is compatible with the assumption that any differences among them were due to random fluctuations. The similarities in mean acceptability ratings for the Barnum and Graphoanalytic profiles are apparent in Table 2.

The differences in mean accuracy ratings between the group that received the psychometric profiles (PP) and each of the other groups (BP, GPP, and GCA) were statistically significant (all $Fs > 15$). The probability of this being due to chance is less than 0.001. The logical inference from these results is that when people received a randomly selected psychometric profile, they reliably rated it as a less accurate description of themselves than Barnum-type generalities or someone else's Graphoanalytic profile. In other words, psychometric data are particular to the person who took the test; with graphological profiles and Barnum sketches, "one size fits all."

DISCUSSION

No single experiment, or even a modest series of experiments, provides a definitive answer to a broad question such as whether or not handwriting analysis is a valid technique for evaluating personality. This underscores the need for large-scale meta-analyses of published results such as that conducted by Dean in chapter 12, and for studies to be replicated with ever improved methodologies. The experiments reported in the present chapter demonstrate the sorts of factors that must be controlled before it can be concluded that handwriting analysis (or any other character-reading technique) provides any unique information about people's personalities.

The present experiments indicate that when people are told that a randomly selected personality profile is their own, they will tend to see elements in the description that match their personalities. The higher mean ratings given by all groups that were led to believe the sketches were relevant to themselves (see table 2) support this conclusion. Furthermore, descriptions that contain global generalities that are common to almost everyone in our culture will be considered more accurate than those which provide more specific, concrete information. Intentionally vague Barnum-type statements and the pronouncements of a certified Graphoanalyst were equally acceptable to randomly selected recipients, but profiles derived from well-validated psychometric instruments were significantly less likely to be embraced under the same conditions.

Of particular interest with respect to the newspaper's informal "test" of graphology with the Denver celebrities was the fact that our subjects showed no significant difference in applicability to themselves between the Barnum profile and the Graphoanalyst's descriptions done for this demonstration. This suggests that, despite claims of astounding specificity, the GPP profiles were as global and non-specific as the intentionally vague Barnum statements. Furthermore, the Graphoanalytic profiles produced for the college administrators in Experiment One were rated essentially the same in applicability to self as the Barnum and GPP descriptions. This suggests that although there are enough differences among profiles produced by Graphoanalysts that fellow practitioners can determine which scripts they were derived from, there is not much in them that differentiates members of the same culture from one another. A common failing, even among those who should know better, is the tendency to mistake the occurrence of a consistent result with respect to a single variable as indicating that a relationship exists between that variable and another one we desire to predict. Unless it can be demonstrated that manipulation of one variable produces lawful differences in the other variable, we have not shown the validity of the relationship, no matter how consistent our measurement of the predictor variable.

The overall results of Experiment Two are precisely what one would expect from the assumption that the more non-specific the contents of the profile, and the more one is led to believe that it is relevant to one's self, the greater the tendency to embrace it as an accurate depiction of one's personality. Although it could be argued that the Graphoanalytic profiles for the prominent Denver citizens were not definitely shown to be that global in nature, the results of Experiment One strongly suggest that the profiles derived by the same technique for the college administrators were more universally applicable than those based on the psychometric tests. In addition, if one presumes that the more specific the profile, the less acceptable it would be to any randomly selected individual, and if the Graphoanalytic profiles were indeed uniquely descriptive of the writer, then they should have been rated as less accurate than the Barnum profile, which they were not.

We cannot rule out the possibility that here, as in any experiment that exceeds the 5 percent confidence interval conventionally required for statistical significance, the lack of a difference between the Barnum and Graphoanalytic profiles was simply an aberration due to sampling error (known to statisticians as a "Type 2 error"). However, there are several reasons to doubt this possibility. First, there is the fact that our results are consistent with those of many other published tests of graphology reviewed by the authors in Section Four of this volume. Moreover, as sample sizes become quite large, as they were in Experiment Two, sample means tend to be closer and closer approximations to the true means of the populations from which they were drawn. And finally, there were 14 Graphoanalytic profiles used in this experiment. While one or two of them might be similar to the Barnum profile, if graphologists produce highly specific descriptions there should be a sufficient number that were in fact unique to produce a statistical difference vis-a-vis the Barnum profile.

Of course, if the graphological community finds our conclusions unpalatable, the same option is open to them as to any investigator who feels the results of a study are methodologically flawed or may be due to a Type 2 statistical error: replicate the study, improving the methodology. In Experiment One, for instance, a larger sample size should be used, though this is much easier said than done. It would create practical difficulties in obtaining a sufficiently large group, all of whom knew each other intimately enough to judge the accuracy of the graphological profiles. This might necessitate, instead, getting a separate group of close acquaintances for each person the graphologists describe and have this group choose their friends' profile from an array of others. Though this could make the experiment quite unwieldy, it would partially get around another possible problem with the procedure used in Experiment One. That is a problem of "restricted range." It is conceivable that people who work together are more alike in various ways than members of a group randomly selected off the street. This would make even valid depictions of them more similar than usual, and thus more difficult to discriminate correctly. This problem, of course, applies equally to the Graphoanalytic and the psychometric profiles. The subjects in Experiment One did considerably better with the latter than the former, although the difference only approached rather than reached statistical significance. We predict that with a larger sample size, discrimination using the psychometric data would be statistically significant but the graphological results would remain statistically non-significant.

In deciding contentious issues in science, the a priori probabilities of the alternatives are also relevant. It is generally agreed that extraordinary claims demand extraordinary proof. The aforementioned objections to graphology on theoretical grounds are sufficiently daunting to demand far more than anecdotal evidence. Another reason for demanding a very high standard of proof from graphologists is that their pronouncements can have significant consequences for people's reputations, professional advancement, and general well-being. Vigorously advertising, as they do, a product that makes claims of breadth and accuracy that no reputable psychologist would make panders to a vast audience desperate for quick fixes to the hardships and uncertainties of life. People who would not think of buying a toaster without consulting *Consumer Reports* are curiously willing to put much more serious matters in the hands of advisors who cannot pass the simplest empirical tests (such as blind evaluations that control for placebo and Barnum effects). In this chapter we have shown some reasons why graphology in everyday settings, and even in poorly controlled experiments, can seem deceptively accurate. Unless a service, in conventional psychology or its numerous fringe imitators, can document its claims under conditions that prevent such spurious appearances of accuracy, it has no ethical right to sell its wares to the public. We contend that graphologists have not lived up to the required standard of proof.

NOTES

1. Another difference—emphasized by Klimoski (this volume)—is that a competent psychologist would rarely, if ever, rely on a single technique, even to measure a single attribute of a client, whereas graphologists claim they can depend entirely on one method, handwriting analysis, as a measure of everything. E.g., psychologists use different tests to assess different attributes of a client (such as intelligence, aptitudes, personality, psychopathology, etc.). Graphologists' assertions that handwriting analysis works in all of these disparate domains lowers their credibility even further.

2. Actual examples of the subjective validation effect are contained in chapter 13.

3. "Graphoanalysis" is capitalized because it is a registered trademark of the International Graphoanalysis Society (IGAS) of Chicago. IGAS advocates a global or "holistic" approach to discern traits from writing (see Crumbaugh, chapter 7). Practitioners become certified by the IGAS by completing a home study course. The basic course requires approximately 1,000 hours of study, and an additional 1,000 hours is required for the optional master's course.

4. As shown by quotations in chapter 9, officials of the International Graphoanalytic Society (IGAS) condescendingly dismiss competing graphological systems as unscientific parlor games.

5. Knowing that all participants were prominent public personalities would also supply useful clues for conscious or unconscious inferences, even if the analyst

was not aware of their names. E.g., none of these people was likely to be a shrinking wallflower.

6. Note that this procedure allows some advantages to the graphologist from the outset, because what subjects express on this controversial issue, and how they express it, could provide some clues to personality quite independently of what may or may not be revealed by their script alone. Also, if the writer admitted that he or she was a smoker, this could supply additional useful information because it is known that smokers and non-smokers tend to differ on certain personality variables (e.g., smokers, as a group, tend to be more extroverted). As an alternative, subjects could be asked to copy a set piece instead, but graphologists complain that this distorts variables of interest to them. It would be quite revealing to see if graphologists could distinguish, under blind and controlled conditions, copy from spontaneously written pieces. If the graphologists had demonstrated any appreciable success in the present study, it would have required another control experiment to rule out the possibility that their success had stemmed from inferences derived from the content, rather than from the bare features of the writing itself.

7. There are 9! (9 factorial) or 362,880 possible matches that could have been made, but only 36 ways in which seven correct matches could be made. Thus the probability that these graphologists could have achieved the observed hit rate by random matching is approximately one in 10,000.

8. What statisticians consider to be a large F value becomes smaller as the number of cases studied in the experiment increases. This is reflected in a term called "degrees of freedom" that enters into the mathematical formulas in the ANOVA (Keppel 1991).

9. This value is determined by the number of subjects and conditions in the experiment (see Keppel 1991).

REFERENCES

Delprato, D. J. 1975. "Face Validity of Test and Acceptance of Generalized Personality Interpretations." *Journal of Personality Assessment* 39 (4): pp. 345–348.

Dickson, D. H., and I. W. Kelly. 1985. "The 'Barnum Effect' in Personality Assessment: A Review of the Literature." *Psychological Reports* 57: pp. 367–382.

Forer, B. 1949. "The Fallacy of Personal Validation: A Classroom Demonstration of Gullibility." *Journal of Abnormal and Social Psychology* 44: pp. 118–123.

Greene, R. L. 1977. "Student Acceptance of Generalized Personality Interpretations." *Journal of Consulting and Clinical Psychology* 45: pp. 965–966.

Hyman, R. 1977. " 'Cold Reading': How to Convince Strangers You Know All about Them." *The Zetetic* (Spring/Summer): pp. 18–37.

Keppel, G. 1991. *Design and Analysis: A Researcher's Handbook.* 3rd ed. Englewood Cliffs, N.J.: Prentice-Hall.

Meehl, P. E. 1956. "Wanted: A Good Cookbook." *American Psychologist* 11: pp. 262–272.

Merrens, M. R., and W. S. Richards. 1970. "Acceptance of Generalized versus 'Bona Fide' Personality Interpretations." *Psychological Report* 27: pp. 691–694.

O'Dell, J. W. 1972. "P. T. Barnum Explores the Computer." *Journal of Consulting and Clinical Psychology* 38: pp. 270–273.

Richards, W. S., and M. R. Merrens. 1971. "Student Evaluation of Generalized Personality Interpretations as a Function of Method of Assessment." *Journal of Clinical Psychology* 27: pp. 457–459.

Snyder, C. R., R. J. Shenkel, and C. R. Lowery. 1977. "Acceptance of Personality Interpetations: The 'Barnum Effect' and Beyond." *Journal of Consulting and Clinical Psychology* 45: pp. 104–114.

Stagner, R. 1955. "The Gullibility of Personnel Managers." *Personnel Psychology* 11: pp. 347–352.

Section Six

Graphology and the Law

17

Legal Implications of Graphology in the United States

John D. Reagh

In this chapter, John D. Reagh reviews the most significant U.S. federal and state law, as well as the common law, for its implications for the practice of graphology. Reagh emphasizes that many of his conclusions are speculative, since there is not a large body of precedent to use to predict the courts' rulings. The relevant Canadian law is reviewed by Robert Carswell in chapter 18. In the present chapter, graphology as used in hiring is considered: the recourses open to a job applicant who alleges defamation, discrimination, or invasion of privacy, and those open to an employer who considers that he or she has been saddled with an unsuitable employee because of the recommendation of a graphologist. The same considerations apply when graphology is used to judge loan applications or suitability of a renter of an apartment. Reagh considers the trend in the courts to employ graphologists as questioned document examiners—a confusion deplored by Nickell in chapter 4—and as expert witnesses to testify to the psychological states of witnesses, and for advice on jury selection. Reagh points out that the use of graphology in the courts is by no means endorsed by the majority of the legal profession; and its justification requires a demonstration of its scientific validity. However, the jury is still out on this question.

INTRODUCTION

The expert analysis of handwriting has long played a role in the law. The interpretation and authentication of handwritten documents and the detection of alterations and forgeries are common ingredients of lawsuits, and much has been written about such applications of handwriting analysis. The law has dealt less often with the practice of analyzing handwriting to determine the mental and physical characteristics of the writer. Whether or not such analysis is accurate, the fact that graphology is sometimes relied upon in matters which profoundly affect people's lives is enough to justify legal scrutiny.

This book demonstrates that graphology is the subject of learned disagreement, and in our society most controversial practices will soon find themselves the subject of litigation. Because the use of graphology in our economic life is relatively new, there is little legal precedent. Also, each state has its own courts, statutes, and common law; so important details will vary from state to state. Therefore, this chapter will not be a comprehensive survey of the law but, rather, an attempt to predict some of the directions we might expect the law to take. I hope that it will provoke thought both by those who practice graphology and by those who may become the subject of graphological analysis, so that they will be sensitive to their legal rights and responsibilities.

I will discuss graphology as it is used (1) in the evaluation of employees for jobs, credit, or rental housing; and (2) in the courtroom, either to analyze jurors and witnesses or to serve as expert testimony. These uses of graphology will have serious implications for whether or not graphology "works."

THE USE OF GRAPHOLOGY IN EMPLOYMENT, CREDIT, AND RENTAL HOUSING

Let us start with a hypothetical example from the field of employment, but keep in mind that the legal considerations raised by our example and by the law cited are basically the same for those applying for credit or rental housing.

Hiram Fast, the personnel manager of Widgets, Inc., has seen an advertisement for Write Stuff Inc., which claims that its graphologists can determine job applicants' aptitudes, personality traits, and suitability for particular jobs merely by examining their handwriting. Mr. Fast is impressed by these claims and sends handwriting samples of several job applicants to Write Stuff for analysis.

Ms. Candi Date applies to Widgets, Inc. for a job as a bookkeeper and provides a half-page handwritten essay as part of her application. After analyzing Ms. Date's writing, Write Stuff reports that Ms. Date is unsuited for the bookkeeping job. According to Write Stuff, Ms. Date makes friends easily and is extroverted, but she is not a detail person and is bad with figures. Furthermore, she is likely to steal from her employer, and she shows a tendency toward sexual deviancy. After reading the Write Stuff report about Ms. Date, Mr. Fast hires Mr. Art Cursive, whom Write Stuff reported to be introverted, loyal, diligent, reliable, and honest. Six months later, Mr. Cursive disappears with the company payroll. Our scenario might lead to several interesting lawsuits.

CANDI DATE VS. WRITE STUFF, INC.: DEFAMATION

The disappointed job applicant might sue Write Stuff, Inc. and the individual graphologist for defamation. Defamation is any false statement, written (libel) or spoken (slander), that is made to a third person and that tends to expose a person to public hatred, contempt, or ridicule, or causes that person to be shunned or avoided, or to be injured in his or her business or occupation.

Write Stuff, Inc. and the individual graphologist who wrote Ms. Date's analysis made a written statement and communicated that statement to Mr. Fast, a third party. In our example, the report resulted in Ms. Date's failure to get the job with Widget, Inc., thereby injuring Ms. Date in her occupation. In addition, Write Stuff's statement that Ms. Date has a tendency to sexual deviancy could also be libelous because it potentially exposes her to public hatred, contempt, or ridicule.

It is important to keep in mind that, despite Ms. Date's injury, Write Stuff's report was not defamatory *unless it was false*. Write Stuff's ultimate defense would be to prove the truth of its statements. Before the court gets to the question of truth, however, it must consider whether Write Stuff was protected by a legal privilege when it reported to Widget about Ms. Date.

There are certain situations in which, as a matter of public policy, the law gives extra protection to free expression. For example, participants in judicial proceedings, in legislative proceedings, or in the conduct of their duties as executive officers of government are given absolute privileges to speak out in the conduct of their official duties, without fear of defamation suits. Such a privilege is *absolute* in the sense that it has no exceptions or loopholes.

The law also provides a variety of *qualified* or *conditional* privileges. A qualified privilege protects a statement made in good faith when it is on a subject in which the speaker or writer has an interest or a duty, if the statement is made to a person with a corresponding interest or duty. In addition, the statement must be limited in scope to the protected purpose and communicated only to the proper parties.

It is frequently held that a communication which defames the character of an employee or a job applicant may be protected by a qualified privilege. To qualify for the privilege, the person making the statement must have either a pecuniary interest or a duty to speak to the employer. The statement will be privileged even though it is false, unless the defendant acted with knowledge of its falsity or with reckless disregard of whether it is false. For example, a qualified privilege will cover a supervisor's report about the conduct or performance of a subordinate. Also, judicial precedent recognizes that outside consultants such as Write Stuff and the individual graphologist are covered by a qualified privilege to report the findings they were hired to make.

In *Thibodeaux v. S.W. Louisiana Hospital Assn.*, 488 So. 2d 743 (La. App. 3 Cir. 1986), the defendant hospital, located in Louisiana, hired Newman & Associates (a firm licensed to conduct lie detector tests in Texas) to test employees. Newman tested numerous hospital employees and reported that four were not completely truthful in their answers. The hospital fired the four employees, who then sued Newman, the hospital, and others. The plaintiffs claimed that Newman had defamed them, but the court found that Newman was protected by a qualified privilege. The court explained at page 748:

> [Newman] enjoyed a position of privilege in that regard and may not be held liable for the disclosure. There is a clear unrebutted showing that Newman did not make a defamatory statement concerning the plaintiff. Even were the opposite the case, it was made in good faith, to one having a corresponding interest, by one having a duty in that regard, and defendant would not be liable therefore even if the information should later turn out to be incorrect.

A qualified privilege may be lost if the speaker did not believe his statement, if he did not have a reasonable reason to believe in the truth of the statement, if the statement was not relevant to or went beyond the scope of the situation, or if it was excessively publicized. There may be some question about whether Ms. Date's alleged sexual deviancy was relevant to her fitness as a bookkeeper. Certainly, the graphologist must take care to limit his report to matters which are relevant to the inquiry at hand. Publication of irrelevant but damaging information might not be protected by the privilege. Even relevant statements might lose their privilege, if the publisher acted recklessly or dishonestly.

The test for overcoming a qualified privilege was explained more fully in *McDermott v. Hugly,* 561 A.2d 1038 (Md. 1989), U.S. cert. den. 1989. In this case, a candidate for a job as a mounted policeman was examined by a psychologist who had been hired as a consultant by the police department. The psychologist reported that the candidate had a fear of horses. After the candidate failed to get the job, he sued the psychologist for defamation. The court noted that communications arising out of the employer-employee relationship are protected by a qualified privilege:

> A person may lose that qualified privilege, however, if the plaintiff can demonstrate that the publication is made for a purpose other than to further the social interest entitled to protection or can prove malice on the part of the publisher. Regarding the scope of "malice", "Knowledge of falsity or reckless disregard of truth is the standard by which the malice required to defeat the conditional privilege defense is to be measured in cases of private defamation."[1]

In order to win her case, Ms. Date would have to prove that the graphologists either knew that their report was false—an unlikely event—or that they had a reckless disregard for the truth of their report. Either of these issues could place the practice of graphology on trial.

The court might then consider the scientific evidence regarding the usefulness and accuracy of graphology, the extent of training or experience of the graphologist, the graphologist's "track record," and other evidence of success or failure. Ms. Date might prevail if she could prove by a preponderance of the evidence that the graphologist could not reasonably have believed he could accurately determine Ms. Date's qualities merely by examining a sample of her handwriting. Even if Ms. Date succeeded in defeating the qualified privilege, the graphologists would still have a chance to prove the truth of their report which is, after all, the ultimate defense to a claim of defamation.

CANDI DATE VS. WIDGETS, INC.: DISCRIMINATION

Title VII of the Civil Rights Act of 1964 prohibits discrimination in employment and public accommodation based on race, color, religion, sex, or national origin. Although state and municipal statutes sometimes expand on these categories, Title VII remains the basic anti-discrimination law of the land.

It shall be an unlawful employment practice for an employer—(1) to fail or refuse to hire or to discharge any individual, or otherwise to discriminate against any individual with respect to his compensation, terms, conditions, or privileges of employment because of such individual's race, color, religion, sex, or national origin; or (2) to limit, segregate, or classify his employees or applicants for employment in any way which would deprive or tend to deprive any individual of employment opportunities or otherwise adversely affect his status as an employee, because of such individual's race, color, religion, sex, or national origin. (Sec.42 U.S.C. Sec. 2000e-2(a))

Other statutes prevent unwarranted discrimination against the handicapped.

Graphology could run afoul of these laws in a variety of ways. Most fundamentally, the use of graphology could either intentionally or innocently introduce discrimination into an employer's employment practices. Intentional discrimination is, of course, illegal but, most often, hard to prove. The Supreme Court has decided, however, that intent is not required. In *Griggs v. Duke Power Co.,* 402 U.S. 424 (1971), the employer based job assignment decisions on professionally developed general intelligence and mechanical comprehension tests. The result was that blacks were assigned predominantly to the lower paying jobs.

The U.S. Supreme Court decided that the purpose of Title VII was to eliminate the consequence of discrimination, not simply the motive. The Court held at page 432 that "good intent or the absence of discriminatory intent does not redeem employment procedures . . . that operate as 'built-in head winds' for minority groups and are unrelated to measuring job capability." The Court went on to conclude that once the adverse or discriminatory effect had been established, the employer had the burden to prove "that any given requirement [has] a manifest relationship to the employment in question." Duke Power failed to carry its burden and was found liable for the "disparate impact" its employment tests had on minority groups.

In *Albermarle Paper Co. v. Moody,* 422 U.S. 405 (1975), the Court considered what an employer must show to establish that pre-employment tests which are discriminatory in effect, but not in intent, are sufficiently job-related to survive a challenge under Title VII. To demonstrate that a test is "job-related" the employer must show "by professionally acceptable methods [that the test results are] predictive of or significantly correlated with important elements of work behavior which comprise or are relevant to the job or jobs for which candidates are being evaluated" (supra. at page 431). This standard raised the issue of professional validation of employment tests, a subject of substantial difficulty.[2]

If the use of graphology results in a statistically significant tendency to disfavor any protected minority, the employer could be required to prove the validity of the test. Indeed, the employer would be liable for any discrimination that resulted, even though an outside agent performed the tests.

The Equal Employment Opportunity Commission Office of Personnel Management, and the Departments of Justice and the Treasury have adopted "Testing Guidelines" by which personnel tests are evaluated. Generally, the Guidelines favor professionally developed ability tests which can be shown to be job-related. Courts and enforcing agencies will also favor a test which is supported by a professional job analysis. Under the Guidelines, a test will not be validated by the tester's promotional literature, frequency of the test's use, testimonials, credentials of the testers, or anecdotal accounts of successful results.

As a practical matter, when employers hire graphologists, the employers should require graphologists to provide the data which would validate the test should it ever be challenged. The graphologist should also demonstrate the ability to defend the test in court, if necessary. In particular, there should be data that show that the test measures what it claims to measure and that what it measures is in fact related to job performance.

There is reason to fear that, by its nature, graphology can inadvertently cause discrimination based on race, national origin, age, or physical handicap. All these personal attributes can directly or indirectly affect handwriting and thereby influence the results of handwriting analysis.

For example, handwriting is taught differently in different parts of the United States and throughout the world. Therefore, handwriting is to some extent a reflection of the race and national origin of the writer.

> The general character of handwriting is influenced by the system of writing studied during an individual's formative period of life, the amount and quality of family tutelage, and how handwriting is used by a person during his or her everyday endeavors. (Muehlberger 1989)

> Style characteristics may be used to determine the nationality of the writer or, more correctly, the country where he was taught to write. (Harrison 1958, 289)

It follows that to analyze a job applicant's handwriting accurately, you must know about his national origin, schooling, and family background. Questions into such areas would be offensive to many people, would appear discriminatory on their face, and would invite litigation. The alternative is to make assumptions about the cultural factors which influenced the formation of the applicant's handwriting and risk the inaccuracy which could result from mistaken assumptions.

INVASION OF PRIVACY

Even if the handwriting analysis is perfectly correct and, therefore, not defamatory, and if it has no improper discriminatory effect, an employee or candidate could still have a legal complaint that his or her privacy had been invaded.

> One who intentionally intrudes, physically or otherwise, upon the solitude or seclusion of another or his private affairs or concerns, is subject to liability to the other for invasion of his privacy, if the intrusion would be highly offensive to a reasonable man. (*Phillips v. Smalley Maintenance Serv. Inc.*, 711 F. 2d 1524 [11th Cir. 1983])

Of course, a person's handwriting is usually not considered private. After all, it is intended in most cases to be shown to others. On the other hand, graphology purports to extract from handwriting information which is not apparent to most readers, including information which most people would consider private in the extreme.

The greatest risk occurs if there is disclosure of such private information. The right of privacy protects persons from the public disclosure of private facts even if the disclosure is true. Thus, invasion of privacy could be claimed if the graphological report were widely distributed to the general public or to a narrower group of the employee's work associates, friends, and acquaintances. Generally, evaluations of employees or applicants are not distributed widely enough to raise such a privacy issue. It is also possible that the mere inquiry into areas of personal privacy would be actionable, if the inquiry is not limited to areas which are clearly related to work performance.

Finally, it could be argued that an applicant has the right to know the manner of examination to which he or she will be subjected. This putative right is not always satisfied by companies making use of graphology for personnel selection. Sometimes companies will ask in their advertisement for a handwritten cover letter without telling the job applicant what the letter is for—in fact, this request is often a signal that the letter will be sent to a graphologist. A court might well be disturbed by the surreptitious analysis of a job applicant's handwriting. Such secret analysis would either reveal details of the applicant's life, attitudes, or personality in greater depth than the applicant might expect or, at least, cause the prospective employer to form opinions of the applicant's characteristics, which may or may not be founded. Simple fairness dictates that a job applicant be told how much of his privacy he must surrender to apply for a job, so that he has a chance to choose between privacy and employment. An employer should warn the applicant if a handwriting sample will be analyzed and should inform him of the kinds of information that will be sought from the sample.

There are numerous statutes in the United States which regulate or prohibit the administration of honesty tests as conditions of employment. These statutes vary considerably, and employers and graphologists should take care to examine the local law to avoid violations.

In *State by Spannaus v. Century Camera,* 309 NW 2d 735 (Minn 1981), the state of Minnesota sued an employer and its consultant for conducting polygraph examinations of employees. Minnesota statute prohibited employers from requiring employees to take "polygraph, voice stress analysis, or any test purporting to test honesty." The employer argued that this statute denied the company its constitutional rights and that the language of the statute was too vague.

The court upheld the statute, in general, holding that the state had a substantial public interest in encouraging the maintenance of a harmonious labor climate, protecting employees' expectations of privacy, and discouraging practices that demean the dignity of employees. On the other hand, the court held that the term "any test purporting to test honesty" was overly broad and undefined, and it limited the effect of the statute to tests and procedures which purported to assess honesty by measuring physiological changes in the subject tested. This decision left open the possibility that a more clearly worded statute could prohibit graphological testing of employees or candidates.

WIDGETS, INC. VS. WRITE STUFF, INC.: MALPRACTICE

In our example, Write Stuff advertised that handwriting analysis could determine, with a high degree of reliability, job applicants' intellectual capacity, honesty, reliability, motivation, and even physical and mental health. Unfortunately, Write Stuff reported that Art Cursive, the successful applicant, was reliable and honest. Mr. Cursive got the bookkeeping job and stole the payroll. If Write Stuff promised foolproof results, they could be liable for breach of that warranty.

Even if Write Stuff were more careful with its promises, they might still be liable for the damage caused by Mr. Cursive. If the handwriting analyst promises to generate a psychological profile of the job applicant from the applicant's handwriting, then, arguably, the analyst could be expected to live up to the same standards of professional skill as would be expected of a psychologist or psychiatrist. In effect, the handwriting analyst is claiming to function as a psychologist, though by alternate means. He may well find himself judged by those standards and compelled in court to defend the scientific validity of his methods in comparison to the traditional methods of psychological analysis.

GRAPHOLOGY IN THE COURTROOM

GRAPHOLOGY AS A TOOL FOR LAWYERS

Lawyers are always eager to find tools which will give them added insight into the veracity and motivations of witnesses, the attitudes or prejudices of jurors, and the secrets an opposing party wants to conceal. Graphology claims to be able to grant all of these wishes, and lawyers have been repeatedly urged to sample its benefits.

> Graphologists are most familiar in the courtroom as questioned document examiners. They are also sometimes used to help select juries. Increasingly, they are hired as expert witnesses to testify about personality characteristics. (Moore 1988)

Ms. Moore has written several other articles in *Case & Comment* extolling the virtues of graphology for the legal profession, and similar articles appear from time to time in the legal press (see, for example, Forte 1989, 10). Even in the legal profession, however, graphology is not universally accepted.

> Barristers and solicitors, as well as other professionals, are precluded by ethics from utilizing graphology as a component of a selection or testing procedure due to its lack of validity. (Quesnel and Lawrence 1990, 248)

GRAPHOLOGISTS AS EXPERT WITNESSES

The rules of evidence permit experts to testify about their findings. Rule 702 of the *Federal Rules of Evidence* provides:

> If scientific, technical, or other specialized knowledge will assist the trier of fact to understand the evidence or to determine a fact in issue, a witness qualified as an expert by knowledge, skill, experience, training, or education, may testify thereto in the form of an opinion or otherwise.

In a proper case psychologists have testified about the mental capacities of a subject. Polygraph (lie detector) and voice stress analysis test results have also been admitted into evidence, although such evidence is very controversial. The reliability of these tests is often called into question, as would certainly be true for graphology.

Warren v. Hartnett, 561 SW 2d 860 (TX Civ App 1977, reh den 1978), was a will contest over a holographic (handwritten) will. A hand-writing expert was called upon to testify that, based upon the handwriting in the will, the decedent was an alcoholic and that her alcoholism had reduced her mental capacity so that she was unable to understand her business. The court held that the expert's opinion was without probative value because the expert had never met the decedent. The court was not impressed by the expert's experience in working with alcoholics, and it held at page 863:

> We cannot give this testimony any probative effect. The evaluation of ab-normal mental conditions is peculiarly within the field of *medical* science, particularly psychology, and also, perhaps, abnormal psychology, but we are aware of no recognized field of scientific inquiry which permits divination of mental capacity by persons whose expertise is limited to handwriting analysis. [Emphasis in the original]

Before graphology is widely accepted as a proper basis for expert testi-mony, the scientific community will have to reach a consensus that graph-ology is capable of making reliable findings.

CONCLUSION

Graphology is claimed to be a powerful tool for the analysis of aptitudes, attitudes, and personality. Such power or even the claim of such power carries a heavy burden of responsibility. To the extent that the results of handwriting analysis are accurate or at least believed to be accurate, they will have a potent effect on people's lives. Practitioners of graph-ology should understand that the legal system will hold them responsible for the consequences of their analyses and conclusions. They should take care to establish the accuracy of their methods and to apply those methods in a responsible manner.

NOTES

1. This formulation of the rule follows the *Restatement (Second) Torts* (1977), an influential treatise covering tort law.

2. See "Courts, Psychologists, and the EEOC's Uniform Guidelines: An Analysis of Recent Trends Affecting Testing as a Means of Employee Selection," *Emory Law Journal* 203 (1987): p. 36.

REFERENCES

Forte, Lowell. 1989. "Lawyers Turn to Graphologist for Expertise." *California Law Business* (Monday, November 13, 1989).

Harrison, W. R. 1958. *Suspect Documents: Their Scientific Examination.* London, U.K.: Sweet & Maxwell, Ltd.

Meuhlberger, Robert J. 1989. "Class Characteristics of Hispanic Writing in the Southeastern United States." *Journal of Forensic Sciences* 34 (March): pp. 371–376.

Moore, Maurine. 1988. "Your Witness, Counselor." *Case & Comment* (January-February).

Quesnel, Lionel J., and Wade C. Lawrence. 1990. "Graphology, Personnel Selection and Litigation." *Solicitor's Journal* 134 (March 2): p. 248.

18

Graphology: Canadian Legal Implications

Robert S. Carswell

Robert S. Carswell explores the Canadian Criminal Code and other federal and provincial statutes and legislation relevant to graphology. Since the vast majority of graphologists sincerely believe in what they are doing, even if what they believe is false, they would not be considered to be engaging in fraud under the Canadian Criminal Code. However, there may be civil proceedings that could be brought against graphologists. For example, the graphologist may be liable for damages if a graphologist recommends someone for employment who turns out to be much less competent or honest than the evaluation indicated, and the company suffers as a result. Carswell explores what would have to be proved if such a suit were to be successful.

It is possible that some graphologists could run afoul of provisions of provincial consumer protection laws. As well, graphologists who diagnose medical or psychiatric conditions from handwriting may be prosecuted under provincial statutes governing the medical profession. Employers using graphology in personnel decisions may violate discrimination provisions in the human rights codes of some provinces. Carswell explores these possibilities.

Readers may wish to compare the Canadian legal implications for the use of graphology with those in the United States, discussed by John Reagh in chapter 17.

INTRODUCTION

If, as some of the contributors to this book assert, graphology lacks scientific validity, then its practitioners may run the risk of civil liability to those who suffer damages as a result of its use. They may even find themselves in contravention of legislation intended to protect consumers or, in extreme cases, they may be charged with a criminal offense. In this chapter, I will describe in very general terms some of the Canadian laws on this subject.

CIVIL LIABILITY OF GRAPHOLOGISTS

It is easy to imagine a company losing money as the result of hiring the wrong person on the basis of his handwriting. Say, for example, an accomplished thief is hired for a sensitive executive position involving the handling of significant amounts of money, on the advice of an independent graphologist who reported that the handwriting had all the requisite indications of honesty and competence. If it happens that the executive in question bilks the company of some thousands of dollars, does the company have a good civil case to recover that money from the graphologist? Or, if the executive was bonded, will the bonding company, after payment to the employer, have that recourse? To take a less obvious example, suppose that a company, again relying on the advice of a graphologist, hires a new vice-president in charge of sales. Although his *t*'s may be perfectly crossed and his words perfectly slanted and broken, the sales of the company may suffer if he is incompetent. Will the company have a case to recover from the graphologist its losses or the decline in its revenues?

In both the common law and civil law systems in Canada, the company will be obliged to prove three principal elements: first, that the graphologist was negligent or intentionally at fault; second, that the company suffered damages; and third, that these damages were caused by that negligence or fault.

Proving damages may be easy if the employee has simply gone to Brazil with the company's funds. It will be considerably more difficult if the employee has been merely incompetent, but this is a familiar challenge for the legal and accounting professions.

To prove fault or negligence on the part of the graphologist, the company would have to show that the graphologist was not able, as he claimed, to identify or measure the intelligence, qualifications, or competence of a prospective employee, and that in fact he did not do so. Establishing the fact that the graphologist did not do what he claimed to do would, I suppose, be relatively easy, at least in the case of fraud. Merely showing that the employee defrauded the company or was incompetent may bring with it a presumption that the graphologist's advice was wrong. Normally, a consultant's fault consists in his lack of expertise or in his negligence in applying the principles of his field of expertise to the particular case. Indeed, if the graphologist has analyzed the handwriting poorly, this argument could be used. More interesting, however, would be the assertion that graphology is not a science, that it cannot substantiate its claims. In this event, the plaintiff's claim would be that the graphologist was negligent or disingenuous in thinking that graphology could produce valid information.

Against these arguments, the graphologist will raise many of his own. Most important, he will argue that he was only an advisor, that the hiring of the executive was strictly the company's doing; that if there were previous instances of fraud and defalcation or indications of incompetence, the company should have noted them and acted accordingly (even though this argument would implicitly admit the uselessness of the handwriting analysis). Just as the law does not require a psychologist or a lawyer to guarantee the results of his interventions, so too the accuracy of a graphologist's advice is not guaranteed. He will also assert that he himself has all the necessary training and knowledge (having passed all the required correspondence courses of a bona fide graphological society) to act as a qualified graphologist, and that he applied all the skills of his profession to the particular case. He may add that the employee must have undergone a change in character after his handwriting analysis, because at the time of the test his character was obviously unblemished.

In addition, the graphologist may argue that the company was itself at fault, that there was at least contributory negligence on its part. For example, he may say that the company should have noticed the employee's fraudulent or incompetent tendencies soon after his hiring, notwithstanding the graphologist's glowing report. Again, he may claim that the company created opportunities for theft and fraud by not having in place a system for determining or detecting such actions. The company will have to be prepared to counter these allegations.

Finally, the company will have to show a link between the graphologist's fault and the damages the company has suffered. Again, this will be relatively straightforward where the employee has absconded with its funds, but very much more difficult where general incompetence has given rise to a diminution of revenues. In the case of the vice-president in charge of sales, for example, the graphologist will be tempted to argue that the company's losses were due to unfair competition, or poor products, or a general economic decline, or someone else's incompetence.

In all of this, the burden of proof will, generally speaking, lie on the company. It will not be up to the graphologist to show that he gave sound advice and that the company did not suffer because of it, but rather the company will have to prove, on the balance of probabilities, that the graphologist was at fault and that the company suffered damages as a result of that fault.

Discharging this burden will be particularly difficult where the company wishes to call into question the very legitimacy of the graphologist's field of expertise. This will mean calling witnesses who are themselves sufficiently expert that they can credibly refute the principles of graphology. How does the company choose such an expert witness? Normally, an expert from the same field would be used to discredit the testimony of the defendant, but this option is not available when the profession itself is being attacked. Some philosophers, and in particular, philosophers of science, may be eminently qualified to give expert evidence on the topic, but their own expertise may not be scientific. I suspect that the Courts would rather hear from established scientists, even in unrelated fields such as physics, who are sufficiently prestigious that their judgment would be regarded as impeccable. Better, perhaps, to have the Dean of the Faculty of Science testify, or the Chairman of the Department of Psychology, than a less eminent academician.

The graphologist, for his part, will also call upon experts, doubtlessly other graphologists and—if he can find one or two to testify on his side—scientists or other academicians, to prove the legitimacy of his expertise. He will also be tempted to produce satisfied customers, but the Courts should be persuaded to disregard anecdotal evidence of this sort. Indeed, the company should object to any such testimony as inadmissible because it is neither expert nor pertinent to the particular litigation.

As everyone knows, the costs of civil litigation are high. If the company wins, it would normally be able to recover some of those costs (not all of them) from the graphologist. By the same token, if it loses, it would be obliged to pay costs to the winning side. The prospect of high costs and the uncertainty inherent in litigation undoubtedly act as strong disincentives to an employer who might otherwise wish to sue a graphologist. There is also the possibility that even if a judgment is obtained, the graphologist may not have the money to satisfy it.

Whether for these reasons, or because few companies have used the services of graphologists (notwithstanding frequent claims to the contrary), or (conceivably) because companies are satisfied with the advice they get, I am not aware of any civil litigation in Canada involving graphologists.

EMPLOYER'S LIABILITY FOR DISCRIMINATION

In Canada, as elsewhere, employers must be careful not to discriminate illegally in their hiring practices. For example, Section 15 of the *Canadian Charter of Rights* provides as follows:

> Every individual is equal before and under the law and has the right to the equal protection and equal benefit of the law, without discrimination and in particular, without discrimination based on race, national or ethnic origin, colour, religion, sex, age or mental or physical disability.

Where an employer uses a graphologist's report to choose between two prospective employees who are otherwise similarly qualified, then if it can be shown that graphology is not a legitimate science, a case can be made that the unsuccessful employee was the victim of discrimination. The other employee was, in effect, chosen over him for no reason at all.

In 1982, the Supreme Court of Canada was called upon to determine whether certain occupational qualifications or requirements were discriminatory under *The Ontario Human Rights Code* (*The Ontario Human Rights Commission v. Etobicoke* [1982] 1 S.C.R. 202.). The Court discussed criteria for determining non-discriminatory qualifications (in the context of age discrimination) in the following terms:

> A bona fide occupational qualification must be imposed honestly, in good faith, and in the sincerely held belief that it is imposed in the interests of adequate performance of the work involved with reasonable dispatch, safety and economy and not for ulterior or extraneous reasons that could defeat the Code's purpose. The qualification must be objectively related to the employment concerned, ensuring the efficient and economical performance without endangering the employee or others. Evidence as to the duties to be performed and the relationship between the aging process and the safe, efficient performance of those duties is imperative, with statistical . . . evidence being of more weight than the impressions of persons experienced in the field.

If graphology is unscientific, the imposition of a handwriting test can hardly be said to "be objectively related to the employment concerned."

CRIMINAL LIABILITY

Whereas the majority of graphologists are sincere believers in the value of graphology, there may be some who engage in fraud. Section 380.(1)

of the *Criminal Code* of Canada provides that anyone guilty of criminal fraud is guilty of an indictable offense and liable to imprisonment for up to fourteen years, where the amount in question exceeds $1,000. (The penalties are less severe if the amount is less than $1,000). Fraud, in turn, is defined in the Code in the following terms:

> **380.**(1) Every one who, by deceit, falsehood or other fraudulent means, whether or not it is a false pretense within the meaning of this Act, defrauds the public or any person . . . of any property, money or valuable security.

The key words are "deceit, falsehood or other fraudulent means." They are, of course, open to multiple interpretations, and it will be up to judges and juries to decide whether they will fit the particular case if charges are laid against a graphologist. Over the years, however, the decisions of the Canadian courts have provided some guidance.

We know, for example, that one of the essential elements of the infraction is that the victim must have been deprived of property or money. The fact that the victim is only temporarily dispossessed (because, for example, the accused pays back the amount of his fees) will not be a defense. Equally, the fact that the victim was negligent and could have prevented the fraud by being more vigilant is not a defense (and not one likely to be raised by a graphologist in any event).

In the case of a fraudulent graphologist, the deprivation of money would appear relatively easy to prove. The fraudulent advice was given and paid for. The victim is the client, and the money of which he was defrauded is the graphologist's fee for services. It could be argued too that the graphologist defrauded the *public*. Knowingly making false claims that graphology will assist employers in hiring and firing may result in losses, and the courts have held that it is not necessary to show that the accused personally profited or benefited from the fraud. It is not even required to show a loss; a *risk* of loss is sufficient.

It is not enough, of course, to prove that a graphologist has caused a loss or a risk of loss through his actions; it must also be proven that he was dishonest, that he employed "deceit, falsehood or other fraudulent means." The classic definition or description of the offense is given in *Re London & Globe Finance Corp.* [1903] 1 Ch. 728:

> To deceive is, I apprehend, to induce a man to believe that a thing is true which is false, and which the person practising the deceit knows or believes to be false. To defraud is to deprive by deceit: it is by deceit to induce a man to act to his injury.

Accordingly, the Crown would have to prove that the graphologist's claim to be able to determine a person's qualities by his handwriting is false. It is not the particular advice that constitutes the fraud, but rather the pretext that the theory on which the advice is based is of value. The fraud, in other words, would lie in the knowing use of a theory which is false.

Proving criminal intent (*mens rea*) is an essential part of most criminal offenses. The irony is, of course, that far from knowing that the tenets of graphology are false, many graphologists believe them to be true. The Crown is in the curious position of having to prove (beyond a reasonable belief, as we will see) that the accused really does *not* believe in what he preaches. It will not be enough to show that graphology cannot live up to its claims; neither will it be enough to show that the particular graphologist's claims are preposterous; rather, it will be necessary to show that the graphologist is not sincere. The ignorant believer in graphology will avoid conviction because of his ignorance; the clever non-believer will avoid conviction because it will be very difficult to prove his lack of sincerity.

A closely related issue came before the Canadian Courts in the fortunetelling case of *Labrosse* v. *The Queen*.[1] This case involved the Criminal Code provision which makes an offense of fortunetelling *when it is fraudulent*. What happened was that an investigator from the Montreal police force visited the apartment of a clairvoyant named Lucette Labrosse. After ascertaining his astrological sign and having him cut a deck of cards several times, she made some precise predictions: that he would get married and have two children, that at the age of about 50 he would have kidney problems, and that one of his work companions would have an accident. She also advised him not to accept a job offer he had received, but rather to keep his present job at the James Bay hydroelectric project. For all of this information, the policeman was charged $15.00.

At her trial before the Montreal Municipal Court, Labrosse admitted that she had foretold the future, for payment, but denied that she had done so fraudulently. Three of her satisfied clients, a journalist, a cook, and an unemployed nurse, told the Court that she had accurately predicted future events on the basis of card-reading and palmistry. Thus the defense maintained that not only did she truly believe she had powers of prediction, but also that she truly had those powers.

The chief judge of the Municipal Court, Mr. Justice Tourangeau, found her guilty from the bench and fined her $100. In an oral judgment, he said that "the accused knows full well that she has no basis for her claim to be able to predict what will happen in people's futures," and "the fact of claiming to find in cards or in the lines of a hand the unforeseen occurrence of events of which a person has no knowledge whatsoever, is absolutely without scientific foundation."[2]

Labrosse instructed her lawyer to appeal this decision. As permitted by the Criminal Code, there was a new trial before a higher Court, the Quebec Superior Court. Again, Labrosse admitted she had foretold the policeman's fortune and had charged him for it, but denied having acted fraudulently. In a very brief judgment,[3] the Superior Court judge agreed with her that no proof had been made of any fraudulent utterances. Accordingly, he reversed the verdict of the Municipal Court and acquitted her.

The prosecution then appealed this judgment to the Court of Appeal of Quebec. In a split decision the Court of Appeal reversed the decision of the Superior Court and restored the conviction imposed by the Municipal Court. Both majority judges asserted that in fortunetelling, the fraud is in the pretext, not in the prediction. As Mr. Justice Bernier put it, "fraud does not lie in the falsity of the utterances in predictions but in the acts and things done and remarks made to make one believe in the power to know and predict the future." What was necessary for a conviction, according to the other majority judge, Mr. Justice Mayrand, was proof that the accused "acted in a fashion to make others believe that she possessed the power or gift" of divination. Of this proof, there was an abundance.

Labrosse then appealed the judgment to the Supreme Court of Canada. Unfortunately for those of us in the legal profession who would have preferred a definitive statement of the law, the Supreme Court could scarcely have been more laconic: "given the finding of fact by the trial judge that (translation) 'the accused knows full well that she has no basis for her claim to be able to predict what will happen in peoples' futures,' we are agreed that the defense of honest belief is not open on the facts of this case." The door, therefore, is open to such a defense in the future, not just in fraudulent fortune-telling prosecutions, but also in those involving fraudulent graphology.

One procedural point should be made here. Under Canadian criminal law, anybody may file a criminal complaint, so long as he has reasonable and probable grounds for believing that a criminal offense has been committed, but this does not guarantee that a summons or warrant will be issued. The authority of a Justice of the Peace is required for that purpose. If the Justice considers that no case has been made out, the case will simply not proceed.

LIABILITY UNDER CONSUMER PROTECTION LAWS

If a graphologist advertises his skills, claiming that handwriting analysis reveals qualities of a person's character and that businesses worldwide rely on graphology for hiring, and if these claims are false, then members of the public may be able to take advantage of consumer protection laws which prohibit false advertising.

In Canada, there is both federal and provincial legislation on this subject. In Quebec, for example, the *Consumer Protection Act* contains the following interesting provisions:

219. No . . . advertiser may, by any means whatever, make false or misleading representations to a consumer.

220. No . . . advertiser may, falsely, by any means whatever,

(a) ascribe certain special advantages to . . . services;

(b) hold out that the . . . use of . . . services will result in pecuniary benefit . . .

222. No . . . advertiser may, falsely, by any means whatever, . . .

(c) hold out that . . . services have been furnished

239. No . . . advertiser may, by any means whatever, . . .

(d) rely upon data or analysis falsely presented as scientific.

The key words here, of course, are "false" and "falsely." As is proper, the burden is once again on the prosecutor to prove that the advertisements in question are based on falsehood. Although the facts need not be proven beyond a reasonable doubt, it will still be difficult, as noted above, to prove to the satisfaction of the Court that graphology is unscientific.

I mention this Quebec statute because I am aware of a prosecution under it based on pseudoscientific claims, *Procureur Général* v. *Centre d'Enquètes Internationales de Parapsychologie (C.D.I.P.) Ltée.* In this case, the defendants had published newspaper advertisements claiming the power to predict the winning numbers in lotteries. They were found guilty of false advertising under Section 219 and, accordingly, were ordered to publish a notice stating that the defendant was not able to predict the winning numbers.

As in the case of criminal proceedings, prosecutions under consumer protection legislation may have to be undertaken by government authorities, so the first step will be to convince these authorities that the advertising in question is false. In particular, note Section 239 of the Quebec statute, or its equivalent in other provincial legislation, which explicitly refers to pseudoscientific analysis.

The applicable federal legislation in Canada is the *Competition Act*, Section 36 of which prohibits any "representation to the public that is false or misleading in a material respect." This is a criminal offense, requiring proof of the facts beyond a reasonable doubt, but the offense is one of strict liability, not requiring proof of intent to deceive or mislead the public.

MEDICAL DIAGNOSES

If graphologists go so far as to diagnose physical or mental disorders, they may also find themselves in violation of statutes governing the medical profession. Every province has laws prohibiting the illegal practice of medicine, and there are many reported cases involving pseudoscientific medical theories, from pyramid power to diagnosis by channeling. Even if graphology is not a pseudoscience, its practitioners should not be diagnosing cases of schizophrenia or epilepsy if they wish to avoid prosecution under these laws, unless of course they are also qualified medical doctors.

CONCLUSION

If a person is seeking a remedy for damages from those who use graphology in ways that are harmful, Canadian law provides several possible routes that might be pursued. I emphasize "possible" here because I have uncovered nothing that specifically mentions graphology in the relevant case law cited above. Since the workplace is so important and affects so much of our interests, it is the source of much civil litigation and criminal prosecution. The fact that graphology has not entered the courts yet may be a sign either that proponents of graphology are overestimating its use in Canada as a tool in personnel matters, or that its use is too recent to have come to the attention of the courts. However, if graphology moves from the parlor, where it served as an innocent amusement, into the workplace where significant interests are at stake, we can expect litigation in Canadian courts along the lines of those described in this chapter.

NOTES

1. File no. 18–902 of the Montreal Municipal Court. The judgment is unreported. The transcription of the oral judgment can be found in an annex to the joint record in the Court of Appeal.
2. The quoted sentences (with the exception of the last one in this section) are unofficial translations from the French.
3. File no. 36–016–80.
4. File no. 500–10–000082–816.

5. Reported at [1987] 1, S.C.R. 310.
6. Court of Sessions of the Peace, Montreal, file no. 500-27-017076-896.

Contributors

BARRY L. BEYERSTEIN received his Ph.D. in experimental and biological psychology from the University of California at Berkeley. He teaches in the Psychology Department at Simon Fraser University in Burnaby, British Columbia, and does research in the Brain Behavior Laboratory and Drug Studies Laboratory at S.F.U. His research interests include the brain mechanisms of consciousness and the psychobiology of addiction. Dr. Beyerstein serves as a scientific consultant to the Committee for the Scientific Investigation of Claims of the Paranormal (CSICOP) and is a member of the CSICOP Executive Council. He is also chair of the Society of British Columbia Skeptics. Dr. Beyerstein has held several fellowships and has been awarded the gold medal of the British Columbia Psychological Association and the Donald K. Sampson Memorial Award of the British Columbia College of Psychologists. At present, he sits on a committee of the latter organization that will recommend guidelines for protecting the public from abuses of psychological testing, including that of being subjected to scientifically unsound tests.

DALE F. BEYERSTEIN teaches philosophy at Vancouver Community College, Langara Campus, in Vancouver, B.C., Canada. He did his M.A. at the University of Toronto. His main interests are in medical ethics and critical thinking. He is on the Boards of the Society of British Columbia Skeptics, an organization that provides scientific responses to occult and pseudoscientific claims, and the British Columbia Civil Liberties Association, which he served for several years as Chairman of the Access to Information and Privacy subcommittee.

MARILYN L. BOWMAN received her Ph.D. from McGill University. She teaches and does research at Simon Fraser University in Burnaby, British Columbia. She specializes in the areas of personality theory, psychological measurement, and clinical psychology. Dr. Bowman has served as Chair of the Psychology Department at S.F.U., Director of the Clinical Psychology Program, Associate Dean of Graduate Studies, Acting Vice-President, and as a member of the university's Board of

Governors. Dr. Bowman has also served on the Board of Directors of the Canadian Psychological Association and was elected a fellow of that association.

ROBERT S. CARSWELL is a partner in the Montreal law firm of Beyers Casgrain. He specializes in commercial law. He is a founding member of the Quebec Skeptics and has contributed to *The Skeptical Inquirer* on the legal status of fortunetelling.

JAMES C. CRUMBAUGH is a Certified Graphoanalyst and a clinical psychologist at the Veterans Administration Medical Center in Gulfport, Mississippi. He has authored many general works on Graphoanalysis and has done several research projects on Graphoanalysis. Dr. Crumbaugh practices Graphoanalysis, a school of graphology distinct from that practiced by Wellingham-Jones (chapter 15) and Lockowandt (chapters 5 and 6).

GEOFFREY A. DEAN received his Ph.D. in analytical chemistry from the University of London. After ten years as a research scientist in various countries around the world, he started another career in technical writing and editing, which he describes as "making complex things simple, not simplistic." His classic two-part examination of astrology, originally published in *The Skeptical Inquirer* and widely regarded as the best ever done, has been reprinted in *The Hundredth Monkey* anthology published by Prometheus Books.

ADRIAN FURNHAM received his D.Phil. from Oxford University and taught at Oxford until he assumed his present position as Reader in Psychology at University College, London. He has held a wide range of visiting professorships and is on the editorial board of several international journals. A fellow of the British Psychological Society and a director of the International Society for the Study of Individual Differences, he ranks among the most frequently cited psychologists in the U.K. for his over 200 articles and ten books. Among these are reports of several tests of handwriting analysis that found it inadequate as a means of measuring personality traits.

EDWARD W. KARNES received his Ph.D. in experimental psychology from Temple University. He is a professor and former Chair of the Department of Psychology at Metropolitan State College in Denver, Colorado. In addition to his teaching and research duties, Professor Karnes is a frequent consultant to industry and the courts in various areas of applied psychology.

IVAN KELLY, whose Ph.D. is from the University of Calgary, is Professor of Educational Psychology at the University of Saskatchewan, Saskatoon, Canada. Kelly specializes in statistics and research design, and is the Chairman of the Astrology Subcommittee of the Committee for the Scientific Investigation of Claims of the Paranormal (CSICOP) and has authored many critical works on astrology, alleged lunar effects on behavior, and the "Barnum Effect."

RICHARD KLIMOSKI received his Ph.D. in industrial and organizational psychology from Purdue University and is currently Professor and Vice-Chairman of the Psychology Department at the Ohio State University in Columbus, Ohio. He is the author of numerous articles and co-author, with J. Schmitt and J. Neal, of the 1991 textbook, *Research Methods in Human Resources Management* (Cincinnati: South-West Publishers). Dr. Klimoski is active in many professional societies and has served on the executive committee of the Personnel and Human Resources Division of the National Academy of Management.

S. DAVID LEONARD received his Ph.D. from the University of Iowa. He is on the faculty of the Department of Psychology of the University of Georgia in Athens, Georgia. His primary interests are in experimental psychology, particularly the area of learning.

OSKAR LOCKOWANDT is a Professor of Psychology in the Faculty of Psychology and Sports Science at the University of Bielefeld in Germany. He received his Ph.D. in psychology in 1966 from the University of Freiburg. His supervisor was Dr. Robert Heiss. In addition to his work on graphology, Dr. Lockowandt's academic research centers around the humanistic psychology of Abraham Maslow. Dr. Lockowandt has published two books, both in German and not (yet) translated into English. One book is on happiness, and the second is a personal reflection on self-actualization, which grew out of a year-long series of daily readings of Maslow's descriptions of self-actualized people and meditations on these readings.

JOE NICKELL teaches business and technical writing at the University of Kentucky. His doctoral dissertation, at that institution, focused on aspects of "literary investigation," including dating and authenticating written texts. These academic pursuits grew out of his earlier career as an investigator for a world-famous detective agency. He is a registered Questioned Document Examiner, which explains his interest in chapter 4 in distinguishing between questioned examination and graphology. Dr. Nickell employs his investigative skills on a wide range of paranormal claims, and is the author of *Inquest on the Shroud of Turin* (1987), and (with John F. Fischer) *Secrets of the Supernatural* (1988). He has also published articles in *The Skeptical Inquirer, Journal of Police Science and Administration, Identification News, Pen World*, and other periodicals. He is also a calligrapher, with an extensive collection of historical documents, books on penmanship, and antique writing materials. These interests motivated his latest book, *Pen, Ink and Evidence* (Lexington: The University Press of Kentucky, 1990).

ZHANG JING PING is a senior student in the English program of the Department of Foreign Languages and Literatures, Jilin University, Changchun, People's Republic of China.

JOHN D. REAGH has a physics degree from Stanford University and a law degree from the University of Chicago. He has practiced commercial law in Seattle, Washington, for 15 years and worked as an investment banker and as counsel for a contact lens manufacturer where he also wrote computer software for the optical design and manufacture of contact lenses. His law practice has emphasized contracts, bankruptcy, and intellectual property.

DONALD H. SAKLOFSKE received a Ph.D. from the University of Calgary and is a professor of Educational Psychology at the University of Saskatchewan in Saskatoon, Saskatchewan. He also holds associate memberships in the Psychology Department and the Department of Education of Exceptional Children at the University of Saskatchewan, and lists among his research interests the measurement of individual differences in personality, intelligence, and cognitive processes.

PATRICIA WELLINGHAM-JONES is a graphologist living in Tehema, California. She is a former psychiatric nurse and received her Ph.D. from Columbia Pacific University, where she is presently a faculty mentor. Dr. Wellingham-Jones is a practitioner of the Roman-Staempfli school of graphology.

Subject Index

advertising of graphological services, 27, 197

age, writing and
advanced, effects on, 46, 117
children, 62, 72-74
disagreement among graphologists in measurability, 191
personality tendencies in graphic movements, 11

allegory, 167-68. *See also* metaphor.

analogical thinking, 170

analysis, methods,
analytical, 25, 274
holistic, 39, 274
objective, 210, 211, 212, 273
subjective, 108, 211, 273

anecdotal evidence of handwriting analysis, 39, 383

astrology, 32, 122, 125, 166-67, 172, 191-92, 215, 295, 297, 343, 345, 380, 400, 445, 447, 452
similarity to graphology, 167, 168, 172, 186

augury. *See* divination.

"Aunt Fanny effect," 216, 363

Baldi, Camillo, 24, 107
Baldo, Camillo. *See* Baldi.
Binet, Alfred, 80, 108, 340
"Barnum Effect," 145, 192, 195, 215, 216, 277, 359, 365, 369, 379, 384, 386, 415, 436, 444-60

baselines, writing, 187

behavior,
base rates, 208, 209, 216, 376
base rates, predictions from, 208, 209, 376-77
influences on, 206, 207
learned, 109
stability, individual differences in, 205

Bildung. See Intelligence, graphologists' concept of.

biorhythms, graphology and, 126, 376

bookstores,
occult section, 14, 19
new age section, 14, 19

blind tests, 36, 137, 193, 435
double-blind, 136, 151
need for, 176, 198, 417, 423

brain,
damage and writing, 73, 412, 416
evolution of, 413-14
graphologists' interpretation of function, 171
IQ, correlation with, 383
localization of function, 194, 383, 404-406, 416
neurology, 402-412
personality, biological theories of,

Name Index